THE BIGGEST SECRET

Bridge of Love

First published in February 1999 by

Bridge **Bridge of Love Publications USA**
of Love **8912 E. Pinnacle Peak Road**
Suite 8–493
Scottsdale
Arizona 85255
USA
Tel: 602 657 6992
Fax: 602 657 6994
email: bridgelove@aol.com

Reprinted April 1999

Printed and bound by
Bertelsmann Industry Services Inc,
Valencia, California, USA

British Library Cataloguing-in
Publication Data
A catalogue record for this book is
available from the British Library

ISBN 0 9526147 6 6

THE BIGGEST SECRET

David Icke

Dedication

To Linda for all her unwavering support no matter what.
An amazing lady.

To Alice, my 'little sister', for all her
commitment and support when I needed it most.

To Royal, for all his great work in America.

My thanks, also, to Brian Desborough and Ivan Fraser for
reading the manuscript and offering additional information;
to Jean for her proof reading; to Gary for the indexing;
and to Sam for her layout and illustrations.

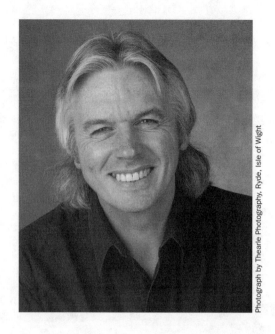

Photograph by Thearle Photography, Ryde, Isle of Wight

Other books, tapes, and videos by David Icke

It Doesn't Have To Be Like This	*Green Print*
Truth Vibrations	*Gateway*
Days of Decision	*Jon Carpenter Publishing*
Heal the World	*Gateway*
The Robots' Rebellion	*Gateway*
Lifting The Veil	*Truthseeker*
...And The Truth Shall Set You Free	*Bridge of Love*
I Am Me • I Am Free	*Bridge of Love*
The Turning Of The Tide – a 2 hour video	*Bridge of Love*
The Turning Of The Tide – a double audio cassette	*Bridge of Love*
The Freedom Road – a 6 hour triple video set **NEW**	*Bridge of Love*
Revelations Of A Mother Goddess – a 2 hour video **NEW**	*Bridge of Love*
Speaking Out – a 2 hour video interview with David Icke **NEW**	*Truthseeker*

Details of availability at the back of this book

Contents

Crazy?

**There are many who will dub me a 'nut' for what
I have written in this book. My reply is this:**

*Today's mighty oak is just
yesterday's nut that held its ground.*

A free world?

"Am I a spaceman? Do I belong to a new race on Earth, bred by men from outer space in embraces with Earth women? Are my children offspring of the first interplanetary race? Has the melting-pot of interplanetary society already been created on our planet, as the melting-pot of all Earth nations was established in the USA 190 years ago?

"Or does this thought relate to things to come in the future? I request my right and privilege to have such thoughts and ask such questions without being threatened to be jailed by any administrative agency of society… In the face of a rigid, doctrinaire, self-appointed, ready-to-kill hierarchy of scientific censorship it appears foolish to publish such thoughts. Anyone malignant enough could do anything with them. Still the right to be wrong has to be maintained. We should not fear to enter a forest because there are wildcats around in the trees. We should not yield our right to well-controlled speculation. It is certain questions entailed in such speculation which the administrators of established knowledge fear… But in entering the cosmic age we should certainly insist on the right to ask new, even silly questions without being molested."

The scientist, **Wilhelm Reich**, writing in his book, *Contact With Space*. Reich died in a United States jail on November 3rd 1957.

INTRODUCTION

Days of decision

We are on the cusp of an incredible global change. A crossroads where we make decisions which will influence life on Earth well into the future of what we call time. We can fling open the doors of the mental and emotional prisons which have confined the human race for thousands of years. Or we can allow the agents of that control to complete their agenda for the mental, emotional, spiritual and physical enslavement of every man, woman and child on the planet with a world government, army, central bank and currency, underpinned by a microchipped population.

I know that sounds fantastic, but if the human race lifted its eyes from the latest soap opera or game show for long enough to engage its brain, it would see that these events are not just going to happen – they *are* happening. The momentum for the centralised control of global politics, business, banking, military and media is gathering pace by the hour. The microchipping of people is already being suggested and, in many cases, underway. Whenever a hidden agenda is about to be implemented there is always the period when the hidden has to break the surface for the final push into physical reality. This is what we are seeing now in the explosion of mergers between global banking and business empires, and the speed at which political and economic control is being centralised through the European Union, the United Nations, the World Trade Organisation, the Multilateral Agreement on Investment, and the stream of other globalising bodies like the World Bank, International Monetary Fund and the G-7/G-8 summits. Behind this constant and coordinated centralisation is a tribe of interbreeding bloodlines which can be traced to the ancient Middle and Near East. They emerged from there to become the royalty, aristocracy and priesthood of Europe before expanding their power across the world, largely through the 'Great' British Empire. This allowed the tribe to export its bloodlines to all the countries the British and European powers occupied, including the United States where they continue to run the show to this day. There have been just over 40 Presidents of the United States and 33 of them have been genetically related to two people, England's King Alfred the Great and Charlemagne, the famous monarch in 9th century France. Throughout this whole period the agenda of this bloodline has been gradually implemented until we have reached the point today where centralised global control is possible.

If you want to know what life will be like unless we wake up fast, take a look at Nazi Germany. *That* is the world that awaits the global population as the plan I call the Brotherhood Agenda unfolds across the year 2000 and into the first 12 years of the new century. 2012 particularly, appears to be a crucial year for reasons we shall discuss. People have no idea of the abyss we are staring into or the nature of the world we are leaving for our children to endure and most people don't seem to care. They would much rather ignore the obvious and go into denial of a truth that's splatting them between the eyes. I feel like the cow who runs into the field screaming: "Hey, you know that truck that takes some of our friends away every month? Well they don't take them to another field like we thought. They shoot them in the head, bleed them dry, cut them up, and put the pieces into packets. Then those humans buy them and eat them!" Imagine what the reaction of the rest of the herd would be: "You're crazy man. They'd never do that. Anyway, I've got shares in that trucking company and I get a good return. Shut up, you're making waves."

The Agenda I am exposing has been unfolding over thousands of years to its current point close to completion, because humanity has given away its mind and its responsibility. Humanity would rather do what it thinks is right for itself in the moment than consider the wider consequences of its behaviour for human existence. Ignorance is bliss, we say, and that's true – but only for a while. It may be bliss not to know a tornado is coming because you have no need to worry or take action. But while your head is in the sand and your bum is in the air, the tornado is still coming.

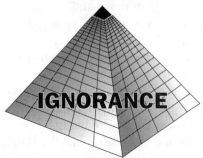

KNOWLEDGE

IGNORANCE

Figure 1: *Knowledge is in the hands of the few and the rest are kept ignorant. The classic structure for manipulation and control.*

If you looked up and faced it, disaster could be avoided, but ignorance and denial always ensure that you will get the full force and the most extreme consequences, because it strikes when least expected and you are least prepared. Like I say, ignorance is bliss – but only for so long. We create our own reality by our thoughts and actions. For every action or non-action there is a consequence. When we give our minds and our responsibility away, we give our lives away. If enough of us do it, we give the world away and that is precisely what we have been doing throughout known human history. This is why the few have always controlled the masses. The only difference today is that the few are now manipulating the entire planet because of the globalisation of business, banking and communications. The foundation of that control has always been the same: keep the people in ignorance, fear and at war with themselves. Divide, rule and conquer while keeping the most important knowledge to yourself (*see Figure 1*). And as we shall see in this book, those who have used these methods to control humanity for thousands of years are members of the *same* force, the same interbreeding tribe, following a long term Agenda which is now reaching a major point on its journey. The global fascist state is upon us.

And yet, it doesn't have to be like this. The real power is with the many, not the few. Indeed infinite power is within every individual. The reason we are so controlled is not that we don't have the power to decide our own destiny, it is that we give that power away every minute of our lives. When something happens that we don't like, we look for someone else to blame. When there is a problem in the world, we say "What are *they* going to do about it". At which point *they*, who have secretly created the problem in the first place, respond to this demand by introducing a 'solution' – more centralisation of power and erosion of freedom. If you want to give more powers to the police, security agencies and military, and you want the public to demand you do it, then ensure there is more crime, violence and terrorism, and then it's a cinch to achieve your aims. Once the people are in fear of being burgled, mugged or bombed, they will demand that you take their freedom away to protect them from what they have been manipulated to fear. The Oklahoma bombing is a classic of this kind, as I detail in *...And The Truth Shall Set You Free*. I call this technique problem-reaction-solution. Create the problem, encourage the reaction "something must be done", and then offer the solution. It is summed up by the Freemason motto 'Ordo Ab Chao' – order out of chaos. Create the chaos and then offer the way to restore order. Your order.

The masses are herded and directed by many and various forms of emotional and mental control. It is the only way it could be done. The few can't control billions of people physically, just as farm animals cannot be controlled physically unless a large number of people are involved. Two pigs escaped from a slaughterhouse in England and eluded capture for so long, despite the efforts of many people to catch them, that they became national celebrities. Physical control of the global population cannot work. But it is not necessary when you can manipulate the way people think and feel to the point where they 'decide' to do what you want them to do anyway and demand that you introduce laws that you want to introduce. It is an old, old adage that if you want someone to do something, get them to believe it is their idea. Humanity is mind controlled and only slightly more conscious than your average zombie. Far fetched? No, no. I define mind control as the manipulation of someone's mind so that they think, and therefore act, the way you want them to. Under this definition, the question is not how many people are mind controlled, but how few are not. Everyone is to a larger or lesser extent. When you are persuaded by advertising or hype to buy something you don't really need or want, you are being mind controlled. When you read or hear a slanted news story and allow it to affect your perception of a person or event, you are being mind controlled. Look at the training for the armed forces. It is pure mind control. From day one you are told to take orders without question and if some berk in a peaked cap tells you to shoot people you have never met and know nothing about, you must shoot without question. This is the "Yes sir!" mentality and it pervades the non-military world, also. "Well, I know it's not right, but the boss told me to do it and I had no choice." No choice? We never have *no* choice. We have choices we would like to make and choices we would rather less like to make. But we *never* have no choice. To say so is another cop out.

The list of mind manipulating techniques is endless. They want your mind because when they have that, they have you. The answer lies in taking our minds back, thinking for ourselves and allowing others to do the same without fear of ridicule or condemnation for the crime of being different. If we don't do that, the Agenda I am going to outline will be implemented. But if we do regain control of our minds and achieve mental sovereignty, the Agenda cannot happen because the foundation of its existence will have been taken away. I've talked and researched in more than 20 countries and I see the same process in every one of them. Identical policies and structures are introduced in line with a Global Agenda, yet at the same time there is quite obviously a global awakening as more and more people hear the spiritual alarm clock and emerge from their mental and emotional slumbers, the terrestrial trance. Which force will prevail in these Millennium years to 2012? That is up to us. We create our own reality by our thoughts and actions. If we change our thoughts and actions we will change the world. It's that simple.

In this book I am going to chart the history of the interbreeding tribe of bloodlines which control the world today and reveal the true nature of the Global Agenda. And I would emphasise that I am exposing an Agenda, not a conspiracy as such. The conspiracy comes in manipulating people and events to ensure the Agenda is introduced. These conspiracies take three main forms: conspiring to remove people and organisations that are a threat to the Agenda (the assassination of Diana, Princess of Wales); conspiring to put people into positions of power who will make the Agenda happen (George Bush, Henry Kissinger, Tony Blair, et al); and conspiring to create events which will make the public demand the Agenda is introduced through problem-reaction-solution (wars, terrorist bombs, economic collapses). In this way all these apparently unconnected events and manipulations become aspects of the *same* conspiracy to introduce the *same* Agenda. In the months and years that follow, every time you pick up a paper, turn on the television or hear a speech from a political or business leader, you are going to see the information outlined here coming to pass. You already can if you understand the scam. Look at my previous books like ...*And The Truth Shall Set You Free, I Am Me I Am Free, The Robots' Rebellion*, the video *Turning Of The Tide*, and the work of other researchers over decades and you will see that what was predicted *is* happening. This is not prophecy, it is merely the prior knowledge of the Agenda. So will the global fascist state be realised in the next few years? That question can only be answered by another: are we going to become people or continue as *sheeple*?

The Agenda depends on the latter.

WARNING

There is an enormous amount of challenging information in this book. Please do not continue if you are dependent on your present belief system, or if you feel you cannot cope emotionally with what is really happening in this world.

If you do choose to continue, remember there is nothing to fear. Life is forever and everything is just an experience on the road to enlightenment. Viewed from the highest level of perception, there is no good and evil, only consciousness making choices to experience all there is to experience. The astonishing events which this book exposes are in the process of coming to an end as the light of freedom dawns at last on the biggest transformation of consciousness this planet has seen in 26,000 years. It is, despite some of the information you are about to read, a wonderful time to be alive.

David Icke

CHAPTER ONE

The Martians have landed?

T here were two ways of writing this book. I could have held back information which is stunningly bizarre, but true. This would be the easy way, staying within the comfort zone and communicating only that which would not challenge too many people's sense of possibility.

Or I could treat the readers like fully formed, fully connected, multidimensional, adult human beings and communicate all the relevant information, including some which will stretch their sense of reality to breaking point. As always, I have chosen the latter. It is not for me to edit information for the readers, it is for the readers to edit the information for themselves. How arrogant and patronising to think that I should keep information back from people because "they're not ready for it". Who am I to decide that? And how can I know if they are "ready for it" unless they hear it and can therefore decide for themselves? Some of my friends have urged me to tell people the basic story, but "for God's sake don't mention the reptiles". You will see what they mean by that very shortly. I understand their concern, but I can only be myself. And I have to tell all that I know and not only that which maintains the comfort zone. That's just me, the way I am. Of course the theme of the book will attract ridicule from those with a vision of possibility the size of a pea and, naturally, from those who know it to be true and don't want the public to believe it. But so what? Who cares? I don't. As Gandhi said: "Even if you are in a minority of one, the truth is still the truth." So here's the story, punches unpulled.

In summary, a race of interbreeding bloodlines, a race within a race in fact, were centred in the Middle and Near East in the ancient world and, over the thousands of years since, have expanded their power across the globe. A crucial aspect of this has been to create a network of mystery schools and secret societies to covertly introduce their Agenda while, at the same time, creating institutions like religions to mentally and emotionally imprison the masses and set them at war with each other. The hierarchy of this tribe of bloodlines is not exclusively male and some of its key positions are held by women. But in terms of numbers it is overwhelmingly male and I will therefore refer to this group as the Brotherhood. Even more accurately, given the importance of ancient Babylon to this story, I will also call it the Babylonian Brotherhood. The plan they term their 'Great Work of Ages', I will call the Brotherhood Agenda. The present magnitude of Brotherhood control did not happen in a few years, even a few decades or centuries: it can be traced back thousands of years. The structures of today's institutions in government, banking, business, military and the media have not been infiltrated by this force, they were created by them from the start. The Brotherhood Agenda is, in truth, the Agenda of many Millennia. It is the unfolding of a plan, piece by piece, for the centralised control of the planet.

The bloodline hierarchy at the top of the human pyramid of control and suppression passes the baton across the generations, mostly sons following fathers. The children of these family lines who are chosen to inherit the baton are brought up from birth to understand the Agenda and the methods of manipulating the 'Great Work' into reality. Advancing the Agenda becomes their indoctrinated mission from very early in their lives. By the time their turn comes to join the Brotherhood hierarchy and carry the baton into the next generation, their upbringing has moulded them into highly imbalanced people. They are intellectually very sharp, but with a compassion bypass and an arrogance that they have the right to rule the world and control the ignorant masses who they view as inferior. Any Brotherhood children who threaten to challenge or reject that mould are pushed aside or dealt with in other ways to ensure that only 'safe' people make it to the upper levels of the pyramid and the highly secret and advanced knowledge that is held there. Some of these bloodlines can be named. The British House of Windsor is one of them, so are the Rothschilds, the European royalty and aristocracy, the Rockefellers, and the rest of the so-called Eastern Establishment of the United States which produces the American presidents, business leaders, bankers and administrators. But at the very top, the cabal which controls the human race operates from the shadows outside the public domain. Any group which is so imbalanced as to covet the complete control of the planet will be warring within itself as different factions seek the ultimate control. This is certainly true of the Brotherhood. There is tremendous internal strife, conflict and competition. One researcher described them as a gang of bank robbers who all agree on the job, but then argue over how the spoils will be divided. That is an excellent description and through history different factions have gone to war with each other for dominance. In the end, however, they are united in their desire to see the plan implemented and at the key moments they overwhelmingly join forces to advance the Agenda when it comes under challenge.

You will probably have to go back hundreds of thousands of years to find the starting point of this story of human manipulation and of the family lines which orchestrate the Great Work. The more I have researched this over the years, the more obvious it has become to me that the origin of the bloodlines and the plan for the takeover of the Earth goes off planet to a race or races from other spheres or dimensions of evolution. Extraterrestrial as we call them. If you doubt the existence of extraterrestrial life then consider this for a moment. Our Sun is only one of some 100 billion stars in this galaxy alone. Sir Francis Crick, the Nobel laureate, says there are an estimated 100 billion galaxies in our universe and he believes there are at least one million planets in our galaxy that could support life as we know it. Think of what the figure might be for the entire universe, even before we start looking at other dimensions of existence beyond the frequency range of our physical senses.

If you travelled at the speed of light, 186,000 miles per second, it would take you 4.3 years to reach the nearest star to this solar system. It says much for humanity's level of indoctrination that to speak of extraterrestrial life is to appear cranky, yet to dismiss it and suggest that life has only emerged on this one tiny planet is considered credible! You only have to consider the amazing structures that abounded in the ancient world to see that an advanced race existed then. We are told that only people primitive in comparison to modern humans lived in these times, but that is patently ludicrous. Like most official 'thinking' the historical and archaeological establishment makes up its own stories, calls them proven facts, and simply ignores the overwhelming evidence that they are wrong. The idea is not to educate, but to indoctrinate. Anyone who doesn't conform to the official line of history is isolated by their fellow historians and archaeologists who either know their jobs, reputations and funding are safer when they stick to the official version, or, frankly, they cannot see beyond the end of their noses. The same can be said of most people in the teaching and 'intellectual' professions.

All over the planet are fantastic structures built thousands of years ago which could only have been created with technology as good as, often even better than, we have today. At Baalbek, north east of Beirut in the Lebanon, three massive chunks of stone, each weighing *800* tons, were moved at least a third of a mile and positioned high up in a wall. This was done thousands of years BC! Another block nearby weighs 1,000 tons – the weight of three jumbo jets. How was this possible? Official history does not wish to address such questions because of where it might lead. Can you imagine ringing a builder today and asking him to do that? "You want me to do WHAT?" he would say, "You're crazy." In Peru are the mysterious Nazca Lines. The ancients scored away the top surface of the land to reveal the white subsurface and through this method were created incredible depictions of animals, fish, insects and birds. Some of them are so large they can only be seen in their entirety from 1,000 feet in the air! The knowledge which allowed wonders like Nazca, Baalbek, the Great Pyramid at Giza and other amazing creations to be built with such precision and scale, came from an advanced race who, in ancient times, lived among a far more primitive general population. This race is described as 'the gods' in the Old Testament texts and other works and in oral traditions of antiquity. I can hear followers of the Bible denying that their book speaks of 'the gods'. But it does. When the word 'God' is used in the Old Testament it is often translated from a word that means gods, plural – Elohim and Adonai are two examples. You can easily understand that a race performing technological feats of such magnitude should be seen as 'gods' by a people unable to comprehend such abilities. In the 1930s, American and Australian servicemen landed their planes in remote parts of New Guinea to drop supplies for their troops. The locals, who had never seen a plane, believed the servicemen were gods and they became a focus of religious beliefs. This would have been even more extreme in the ancient world had their advanced race been beings from other planets, stars or dimensions, flying craft more advanced than anything flown (at least officially!) by today's military. An influx of knowledge from outside this planet or another source would explain so many of the 'mysteries' that official history greets with a deafening silence. The incredible feats of building also become explainable and so does the mystery of why early civilisations like Egypt and Sumer (the land of Shinar in the Bible) began at the peak of their development and then fell into decay, when the normal course of evolution is to start at a lower level and slowly advance through learning and experience. There was clearly an infusion of highly advanced knowledge that was later lost to most people. In every culture throughout the world are ancient stories and texts which describe the 'gods' who brought this advanced knowledge. This would again explain the mystery of how the ancients had a phenomenal understanding of astronomy. There are endless legends all over the world of a time they call the Golden Age, which was destroyed by cataclysm and the 'fall of Man'. The ancient Greek poet, Heslod, described the world before the 'fall':

> "Man lived like Gods, without vices or passions, vexation or toil. In happy companionship with divine beings (*extraterrestrials?*), they passed their days in tranquillity and joy, living together in perfect equality, united by mutual confidence and love. The Earth was more beautiful than now, and spontaneously yielded an abundant variety of fruits. Human beings and animals spoke the same language and conversed with each other (*telepathy*). Men were considered mere boys at a hundred years old. They had none of the infirmities of age to trouble them and when they passed to regions of superior life, it was in a gentle slumber." [1]

Utopian as that may sound, there are countless stories from every ancient culture which describe the world in the distant past in those terms. We can recreate that vision again if only we change the way we think and feel. The most comprehensive accounts of an advanced race are contained in tens of thousands of clay tablets found in 1850 about 250 miles from Baghdad, Iraq, by an Englishman Sir Austen Henry Layard as he excavated the site of Nineveh, the capital of Assyria. This was located near the present Iraqi town of Mosul. Other finds have followed in this region which was once called Mesopotamia. The original source of this knowledge was not the Assyrians, but the Sumerians who lived in the same area from, it is estimated, 4,000 to 2,000 BC. I will refer to the clay tablets, therefore, as the Sumerian Texts or Tablets. They are one of the greatest historical finds imaginable and yet 150 years after they were discovered they are still ignored by conventional history and education. Why? Because they demolish the official version of events. The most famous translator of these tablets is the scholar and author Zecharia Sitchin, who can read Sumerian, Aramaic, Hebrew and other Middle and Near Eastern languages.[2] He has extensively researched and translated the Sumerian Tablets and has no doubt that they are describing extraterrestrials. Some researchers say that he used a later version of the Sumerian language to translate an earlier one and, therefore, some of his translations may not be 100% accurate. I think his themes are correct, indeed other accounts and evidence supports this, but I personally doubt some of the detail. I think that a number of Sitchin's interpretations are extremely questionable, while I agree with the overall

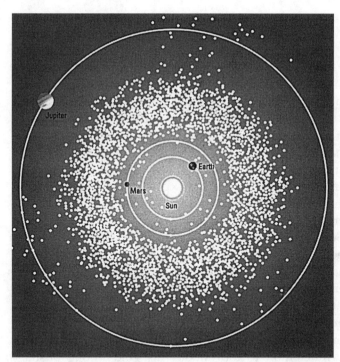

Figure 2: *The solar system showing the location of the asteroid belt between Mars and Jupiter which, though the details vary, many ancient and modern accounts suggest is the remains of a planet or part of a planet.*

thesis. According to his translations (and others) the Texts say that the Sumerian civilisation, from which many features of modern society derive, was a "gift from the gods". Not mythical gods, but physical ones who lived among them. The Tablets call these gods the AN.UNNAK.KI (Those who from Heaven to Earth came), and DIN.GIR (The Righteous Ones of the Blazing Rockets). The name of Sumer itself was KI.EN.GIR (The Land of the Lord of the Blazing Rockets and also Land of the Watchers, according to Sitchin). The ancient text known as the Book of Enoch also calls the gods 'the Watchers', as did the Egyptians. The Egyptian name for their gods, the Neteru, literally translates as Watchers and they said that their gods came in heavenly boats.

According to Zecharia Sitchin, the tablets describe how the Anunnaki came from a planet called Nibiru (The Planet of the Crossing) which he believes has a 3,600 year elliptical orbit that takes it between Jupiter and Mars and then out into far space beyond Pluto. Modern science has identified a body it calls Planet X which has been located beyond Pluto and is believed to be part of this solar system. But an elliptical orbit would be incredibly unstable and difficult to sustain. Scientists I trust believe that Sitchin is mistaken in his Nibiru theory, though his main themes about the Anunnaki are correct. The Sumerian Tablets, from Sitchin's translations, describe how, during the early formation of the solar system, Nibiru caused the near destruction of a planet that once existed between Jupiter and Mars. The Sumerians called it Tiamat, a planet they nicknamed The Watery Monster. They say that it was debris from Tiamat's collision with a Nibiru moon which created the Great Band Bracelet – the asteroid belt which is found between Mars and Jupiter. What remained of Tiamat was thrown into another orbit, the texts say, and eventually it became the Earth (*see* **Figure 2**). The Sumerian name for the Earth means the Cleaved One because a vast hole was created, they say, by the collision. Interestingly if you take away the water in the Pacific Ocean you will be left with a gigantic hole.

The Tablets are the written accounts of oral traditions that go back enormous amounts of time and you have to be careful that details have not been added or lost and that we don't take symbolism or parable as literal truth. I am sure that some confusion did occur in this way. I have doubts myself about the Nibiru–Tiamat scenario and its alleged timescale. But there is much truth in the Texts which can be proven, not least in their knowledge of astronomy. The Tablets depict the solar system with the planets in their correct positions, orbits and relative sizes, and their accuracy has only been confirmed in the last 150 years since some of these planets have been found. The Tablets describe the nature and colour of Neptune and Uranus in ways that have only been confirmed in the last few years! What's more, the modern 'experts' did not expect those planets to look as they did, yet the Sumerians knew thousands of years BC what our 'advanced' science has only just discovered.

Most stunning about the Sumerian Tablets is the way they describe the creation of homo sapiens. Sitchin says the Anunnaki came to the Earth an estimated 450,000 years ago to mine gold in what is now Africa. The main mining centre was in today's Zimbabwe, an area the Sumerians called AB.ZU (deep deposit), he claims. Studies by the Anglo-American Corporation have found extensive evidence of gold mining in Africa at least 60,000 years ago, probably 100,000.[3] The gold mined by the Anunnaki was shipped back to their home planet from bases in the Middle East, Sitchin claims the Tablets say. I think there is much more to know about this 'gold mining' business, and I don't believe that was the main reason they came here, if indeed it was a reason at all. At first the gold mining was done by the Anunnaki version of their working classes, Sitchin says, but eventually there was a rebellion by the miners and the Anunnaki royal élite decided to create a new slave race to do the work. The Tablets describe how the genes of the Annunaki and those of the native humans were combined in a test tube to create the 'updated' human capable of doing the tasks the Anunnaki required. The idea of test tube babies would have sounded ridiculous when the tablets were found in 1850, but that is precisely what scientists are now able to do. Again and again modern research supports the themes of the Sumerian Tablets. For instance, there was a sudden and so far unexplained upgrade of the human physical form around 200,000 years ago. Official science is silent on the cause of this and mutters terms like 'the missing link'. But some unavoidable facts need to be addressed. Suddenly the previous physical form known as homo erectus became what we now call homo sapiens. From the start the new homo sapiens had the ability to speak a complex language and the size of the human brain increased massively. Yet the biologist Thomas Huxley said that major changes like this can take tens of millions of years. This view is supported by the evidence of homo erectus which appears to have emerged in Africa about 1.5 million years ago. For well in excess of a million years their physical form seems to have remained the same, but then, out of nowhere, came the dramatic change to homo sapiens. About 35,000 years ago came another sudden upgrade and the emergence of homo sapiens sapiens, the physical form we see today. The Sumerian Tablets name the two people involved in the creation of the slave race. They were the chief scientist called Enki,

Lord of the Earth (Ki=Earth) and Ninkharsag, also known as Ninti (Lady Life) because of her expertise in medicine. She was later referred to as Mammi, from which comes mama and mother. Ninkharsag is symbolised in Mesopotamian depictions by a tool used to cut the umbilical cord. It is shaped like a horseshoe and was used in ancient times. She also became the mother goddess of a stream of religions under names like Queen Semiramis, Isis, Barati, Diana, Mary and many others, which emerged from the legends of this all over the world. She is often depicted as a pregnant woman. The texts say of the Anunnaki leadership:

> They summoned and asked the goddess,
> the midwife of the gods, the wise birthgiver (*saying*),
> "To a creature give life, create workers!
> Create a primitive worker,
> that he may bear the yoke!
> Let him bear the yoke assigned by Enlil,
> Let the worker carry the toil of the gods!" [4]

Enlil was commander of the Anunnaki and Enki was his half-brother. Enki and Ninkharsag had many failures as they sought the right genetic mix, the Tablets tell us. There are accounts of how they created people with major defects and also human–animal hybrids. Horrible stuff, and exactly what is claimed to be happening today in the extraterrestrial–human underground bases around the world. The story of Frankenstein, the man created in a laboratory, could be symbolic of these events. It was written by Mary Shelley, the wife of the famous poet. He and she were high initiates of the secret society network which has hoarded and suppressed this knowledge since ancient times. The Tablets say that Enki and Ninkharsag eventually found the right mix which became the first homo sapiens, a being the Sumerians called a LU.LU (One who has been mixed). This is the biblical 'Adam'. LU.LU was a genetic hybrid, the fusing of homo erectus with the genes of the 'gods' to create a slave, a human worker bee, some 200,000–300,000 years ago. A female version was also created. The Sumerian name for human was LU, the root meaning of which is worker or servant, and it was also used to imply domesticated animals. This is what the human race has been ever since. The Anunnaki have been overtly and now covertly ruling the planet for thousands of years. The mistranslation of the Bible and symbolic language taken literally has devastated the original meaning and given us a fantasy story. Genesis and Exodus were written by the Hebrew priestly class, the Levites, after they were taken to Babylon from around 586 BC. Babylon was in the former lands of Sumer and so the Babylonians, and therefore the Levites, knew the Sumerian stories and accounts. It was from these records overwhelmingly, that the Levites compiled Genesis and Exodus. The source is obvious. The Sumerian tablets speak of E.DIN (The Abode of the Righteous Ones). This connects with the Sumerian name for their gods, DIN.GIR (the Righteous Ones of the Rockets). So the Sumerians spoke of Edin and Genesis speaks of the Garden of Eden. This was a centre for the gods, the Anunnaki. The Sumerian Tablets speak of King Sargon the Elder being found as a baby floating in a basket on the river and brought up by a royal family. Exodus speaks of Moses being found as a baby floating in a basket on the river by a royal princess and how he was brought up by the Egyptian royal family. The list of such 'coincidences' goes on and on.

The Old Testament is a classic example of the religious recycling which has spawned all the religions. So when you are looking for the original meaning of Genesis and the story of Adam you have to go back to the Sumerian accounts to see how the story has been doctored. Genesis says that 'God' (the gods) created the first man, Adam, out of 'dust from the ground' and then used a rib of Adam to create Eve, the first woman. Zecharia Sitchin points out that the translation of 'dust from the ground' comes from the Hebrew word tit (sorry mother) and this itself is derived from the Sumerian term, TI.IT, which means 'that which is with life'. Adam was not created from dust from the ground, but from that which is with life – living cells. The Sumerian term, TI, means both rib and life and again the translators made the wrong choice. Eve (She Who Has Life) was not created from a rib, but from that which has life – living cells. The human egg for the creation of the Lulu/Adam came from a female in Abzu, Africa, according to the Sumerians, and modern fossil finds and anthropological research suggests that homo sapiens did indeed come out of Africa. In the 1980s, Douglas Wallace of Emory University in Georgia compared the DNA (the blueprint for physical life) of 800 women and concluded that it came from a single female ancestor.[5] Wesley Brown of the University of Michigan said, after examining the DNA of 21 women of different genetic backgrounds from around the world, that they all originated from a single source who had lived in Africa between 180,000 and 300,000 years ago.[6] Rebecca Cann of the University of California at Berkeley did the same with 147 women of diverse racial and geographical backgrounds and she said their common genetic inheritance came from a single ancestor between 150,000 and 300,000 years ago.[7] Another study of 150 American women from genetic lines going back to Europe, Africa and the Middle East, together with Aborigines from Australia and New Guinea, concluded that they had the same female ancestor who lived in Africa between 140,000 and 290,000 years ago.[8] Personally I think the human race was seeded by many sources; not just the Annunaki.

The Sumerian Tablets and later Akkadian stories give the names and hierarchy of the Anunnaki. They call the 'Father' of the gods, AN, a word that means heaven. Our Father who art in heaven? AN, or Anu to the Akkadians, stayed mostly in heaven with his wife, Antu, and he made only rare visits to the planet they called E.RI.DU (Home in the faraway built), a word which evolved into Earth. Or at least that is the Zecharia Sitchin translation. The descriptions could also imply that Anu stayed mostly in the high mountains of the Near East where the 'Garden of Eden', the place of the gods, is reckoned on good evidence to have been, and he made only rare visits to the plains of Sumer. A Sumerian city was called Eridu. Anu sent two sons to develop and rule the Earth, the Tablets say. They were Enki, the guy they say created homo sapiens, and his half-brother Enlil. These two would later become great rivals for ultimate control of the planet. Enki, the first born of Anu, was subordinate to Enlil because of the Anunnaki's obsession with genetic purity. Enlil's mother was the half sister to Anu and this union passed on the male genes more efficiently than Enki's birth via another mother. Later the Tablets describe how the Anunnaki created bloodlines to rule humanity on their behalf and these, I suggest, are the families still in control of the world to this day. The Sumerian Tablets describe how kingship was granted to humanity by the Anunnaki and it was originally known as Anu-ship after An or Anu, the ruler of the 'gods'. The Brotherhood families are obsessed with bloodlines and genetic inheritance and they interbreed without regard for love. The royal families (family!) and aristocracy of Europe and the so-called Eastern Establishment families in the United States are obvious examples of this. They are of the same tribe and genetically related. This is why the Brotherhood families have always been obsessed with interbreeding, just as the Sumerian Tablets describe the Anunnaki. They are not interbreeding through snobbery, but to hold a genetic structure which gives them certain abilities, especially the ability to 'shape-shift' and manifest in other forms. I'll come to this in more detail shortly.

The Tablets describe how humans were given the ability to procreate by Enki and this led to an explosion in the human population which threatened to swamp the Anunnaki, who were never great in number. The Anunnaki had many internal conflicts and high-tech wars with each other, as the Enlil and Enki factions fought for control. It is generally accepted by researchers of the Anunnaki that Enki is on humanity's side, but it seems to me that both groups desire dominance over this planet, and that is their real motivatation. As Zecharia Sitchin documents in his translations, and readers of the Indian holy books, the Vedas, will confirm, there were many accounts of the 'gods' going to war with each other as they battled for supremacy. The Sumerian accounts describe how the sons of the Annunaki 'gods' were most involved in these wars. These were the offspring of Enki and Enlil, the half-brothers who became fierce rivals, and their sons played out that battle in a high-tech conflict, the Tablets say. One battle they appeared to have been involved in was the biblical destruction of Sodom and Gomorrah. These cities were probably located at the southern end of the Dead Sea where, today, radiation readings are much higher than normal. This was when, according to the Bible, Lot's wife looked back and was turned into a pillar of salt. After referring to the original Sumerian, Zecharia Sitchin says that the true translation of that passage should read that Lot's wife was turned into a pillar of vapour which, on balance, is rather more likely!

All over the world in every native culture you will find stories of a Great Flood and the Sumerian Tablets are no different. Sitchin says they tell how the Anunnaki left the planet in flying craft, as an enormous surge of water wiped out much of humanity. There is no doubt that an unimaginable catastrophe, or more likely catastrophes, were visited upon the Earth between approximately 11,000 and 4,000 BC. The geological and biological evidence is overwhelming in its support of the countless stories and traditions which describe such events. They come from Europe, Scandinavia, Russia, Africa, throughout the American continent, Australia, New Zealand, Asia, China, Japan and the Middle East. Everywhere. Some speak of

great heat which boiled the sea; of mountains breathing fire; the disappearance of
the Sun and Moon and the darkness that followed; the raining down of blood, ice
and rock; the Earth flipping over; the sky falling; the rising and sinking of land; the
loss of a great continent; the coming of the ice; and virtually all of them describe a
fantastic flood, a wall of water, which swept across the Earth. The tidal wave caused
by the comet in the film, *Deep Impact*, gives you an idea of what it would have been
like. Old Chinese texts describe how the pillars supporting the sky crumbled;
of how the Sun, Moon and stars poured down in the north-west, where the sky
became low; rivers, seas and oceans rushed to the south-east where the Earth sank
and a great conflagration was quenched by a raging flood. In America, the Pawnee
Indians tell the same story of a time when the north and south polar stars changed
places and went to visit each other. North American traditions refer to great clouds
appearing and a heat so powerful that the waters boiled. The Greenland Eskimos
told early missionaries that long ago the Earth turned over. Peruvian legend says
that the Andes were split apart when the sky made war with the Earth. Brazilian
myth describes how the heavens burst and fragments fell down killing everything
and everyone as heaven and Earth changed places. And the Hopi Indians of North
America record that: "the Earth was rent in great chasms, and water covered
everything except one narrow ridge of mud".[9]

All of this closely correlates with the legends of Atlantis and Mu or Lemuria: two
vast continents, one in the Atlantic and the other in the Pacific, which many people
believe were ruled by highly advanced races. The continents are said to have
disappeared under the sea in the circumstances described above, leaving only
islands like the Azores as remnants of their former scale and glory. Atlantis was
described by Plato (427–347 BC), the ancient Greek philosopher and high initiate of
the secret society-mystery school network. To this day this secret network has
passed on much knowledge to the chosen few while denying that privilege to the
mass of the people. Official history dismisses Plato's contention that such a
continent existed and there are apparent historical discrepancies in his accounts, but
there is geological support for his basic theme. The Azores, which some believe
were part of Atlantis, lie on the Mid-Atlantic Ridge which is connected to a fracture
line that encircles the planet (*see Figure 3*). This line continues for a distance of
40,000 miles. The Mid-Atlantic Ridge is one of the foremost areas for earthquakes
and volcanoes. Four vast tectonic plates, the Eurasian, African, North American and
Caribbean, all meet and collide in this region making it very unstable geologically.
Both the Azores and the Canary Islands (named after dogs 'canine' and not
canaries!), were subject to widespread volcanic activity in the time period Plato
suggested for the end of Atlantis. Tachylite lava disintegrates in sea water within
15,000 years and yet it is still found on the sea bed around the Azores, confirming
geologically-recent upheavals.[10] Other evidence, including beach sand gathered
from depths of 10,500–18,440 feet, reveals that the seabed in this region must have
been, again geologically-recently, above sea level.[11] The oceanographer, Maurice
Ewing, wrote in *National Geographic* magazine that: "Either the land must have sunk
two or three miles, or the sea must once have been two or three miles lower than

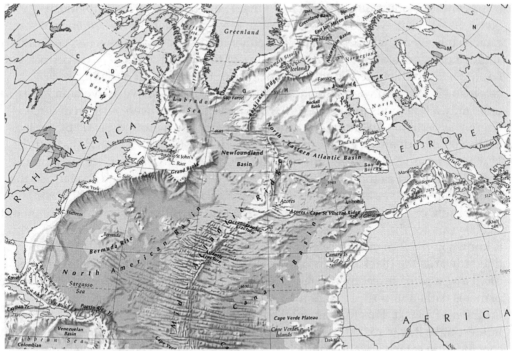

Figure 3: *The Mid-Atlantic Ridge, the centre of earthquake and volcanic activity in the area of the Atlantic Ocean where Plato apparently placed Atlantis.*

now. Either conclusion is startling."[12]

The geological and biological evidence also suggests that the widespread volcanic activity which caused the sinking of the land in the region of the Azores, happened at the same time as the break up and sinking of the land mass known as Appalachia which connected what we now call Europe, North America, Iceland and Greenland.[13] Even their degree of submergence appear closely related. Similar evidence can be produced to support the view that the continent known as Mu or Lemuria now rests on the bed of the Pacific.[14] The so-called Bermuda Triangle between Bermuda, southern Florida, and a point near the Antilles, has long been associated with Atlantis. It is also an area steeped in legends of disappearing ships and aircraft. Submerged buildings, walls, roads and stone circles like Stonehenge, even what appear to be pyramids, have been located near Bimini, under the waters of the Bahama Banks and within the 'triangle'.[15] So have walls or roads creating intersecting lines.[16] Some other facts that most people don't know: the Himalayas, the Alps and the Andes, only reached anything like their present height around 11,000 years ago.[17] Lake Titicaca on the Peru-Bolivia border is today the highest navigable lake in the world at some 12,500 feet. Around 11,000 years ago, much of that region was at sea level! Why are so many fish and other ocean fossils found high up in mountain ranges? Because those mountains were once at sea level. Recently so in geological terms, too. There is increasing acceptance that the Earth has suffered some colossal geological upheavals. The debate (and often hostility) comes with the questions of when and why. These upheavals have obviously involved the solar system as a whole because every planet shows evidence of some cataclysmic events which have affected either its surface, atmosphere, speed and angle of orbit or rotation. I think the themes of the Sumerian Tablets are correct, but I doubt some of their detail, not least because of the vast period that passed between 450,000 years ago when the Anunnaki are said to have arrived, and the time, only a few thousand years ago, when these accounts were written down. There was certainly an enormous cataclysm on the Earth around 11,000 BC which destroyed the advanced civilisations of the high-tech Golden Age and that date of 13,000 years ago is highly significant and very relevant to the time we are living through now. Just as the planets of the solar system revolve around the Sun, so the solar system revolves around the centre of the galaxy, or this part of it at least. This 'central sun' or galactic sun, is sometimes referred to as the Black Sun. It takes about 26,000 years for the solar system to complete a circuit of the galactic centre and this is known in the Indian culture as a yuga. For half of that 26,000 years the Earth is tilted towards the Black Sun, the light source, and for the second 13,000 years it is tilted away, some researchers believe. These cycles are therefore very different as the planet is bathed in positive light for 13,000 years and then moves into the 'darkness' for the next 13,000. This fundamentally affects the energy in which we all live. Interestingly, it was 13,000 years ago that the Golden Age would appear to have concluded in cataclysm and conflict, and today, with the 13,000 year cycle of 'darkness' reaching its conclusion, there is a rapid global spiritual awakening and incredible events await us in the next few years. We are entering the light again. So there was a fantastic cataclysm around 13,000 years ago which brought an end to the high-tech civilisations of the Golden Age. But was it the only one? The evidence suggests not.

A friend of mine in California, Brian Desborough, is a researcher and scientist I have great respect for. He has been involved in aerospace research and has been employed in this and other scientific research by many companies. Brian is a feet-on-the-ground guy who looks at all the evidence and goes where it, rather than convention, takes him. He has compiled some highly detailed and compelling information about the ancient world and its connection to the Brotherhood manipulation of today. While he worked for a major United States corporation in the 1960s, their physicists completed their own independent studies which suggested that about 4,800 BC a huge body, which we now know as Jupiter, careered into our solar system. The outer planets were thrown into disarray and Jupiter eventually crashed into a planet which orbited between the present Jupiter and Mars. The physicists said the remains of this planet became the asteroid belt and that part of Jupiter broke away to become what we now call Venus. As Venus, then a vast chunk of matter, was projected into space, it destroyed the atmosphere and life of Mars before it was caught by the Earth's gravitational field, the study claimed. Venus made several orbits of the Earth before its momentum hurled it into its current position in the solar system. It was those orbits, the physicists said, that brought devastation and a tidal wave about 4,800 BC. They believed, as Brian

Desborough does, that before this time Mars orbited where the Earth is now and the Earth was much closer to the Sun. The brilliant light of Venus as it passed close to the Earth may have led to the idea of Lucifer, the 'light bringer'. The most ancient Mesopotamian and Central American records do not include Venus in their planetary accounts, only later does it appear. There was an obsession with Venus in many cultures, with human sacrifices being made to it.

The unofficial study by the physicists has never been published, but let us consider the evidence for some of its claims. When you sprinkle particles on a vibrating plate you can recreate the planetary orbits of the solar system. When vibratory waves moving outward from the plate's centre meet waves moving in the other direction, a so-called standing wave is formed as the two collide. This causes the particles to build up and create a series of concentric circles. These will be equally spaced if single frequencies collide with each other, but if, as with the solar system, a spectrum of frequencies are involved, the circles will be unequally spaced in accordance with the vibrational pressures. Place an object on these vibrating circles of particles and it will begin to orbit the centre of the plate, carried by the energy flow caused by the vibrational interactions. Heavier objects placed anywhere on the plate will be drawn to one of these concentric circles and these objects will themselves form wave patterns around themselves which will attract lighter objects to them. In our solar system, the most powerful waves are being emitted from the centre by the Sun, obviously, because that represents 99% of the matter in the solar system. These waves from the Sun interact with other cosmic waves, so forming a series of standing waves which, in turn, form concentric circles or vibrational fields orbiting the Sun. The heaviest bodies, the planets, are caught in these circles and thus orbit the Sun. The planets also create less powerful wave circles around themselves and these can attract lighter bodies which orbit them. The Moon orbiting the Earth is an example of this. So anything that would disturb this harmony of vibrational interaction would affect these concentric circles of energy and, if this was powerful enough, change the orbit of planets. What the physicists say happened with Jupiter and Venus would certainly be powerful enough to do this. These circles of standing waves exist around the Sun in relation to the vibrational pressures involved and they do not need a planet to exist. They exist anyway and a planetary body merely locks into them. Therefore there are many more of these vibrational 'roadways' in the solar system than there are planets, and if a planet or body is ejected from its orbit it will eventually lock into another wave, another orbit, when its momentum slows enough to be captured. This, Desborough believes, is what happened when the fantastic vibrational pressures of the Venus 'comet' passed close to Mars and the Earth and hurled them into different orbits.

Venus would have been an ice-coated 'comet', Desborough says, and the ice would have disintegrated when Venus approached the Earth and reached a point known as the Roche Limit.[18] This is a vibrational safety device, if you like. When two bodies are on collision course, the one with the smallest mass starts to disintegrate at the Roche Limit. In this case, the ice would have been projected from Venus's surface towards the Earth. Also, as it entered the so-called Van Allen Belt, which absorbs much of the dangerous radiation from the Sun, the ice would have been ionised – magnetised – and therefore attracted to the Earth's magnetic poles.[19] Billions of tons of ice, cooled to -273 degrees centigrade, would have fallen on the polar regions, flash-freezing everything in little more than an instant.[20] This, at last, would explain the mystery of the mammoths found frozen where they stood. The mammoth, contrary to belief, was not a cold region animal, but one which lived in temperate grasslands. Somehow those temperate regions were frozen in a moment. Some mammoths have been found frozen in the middle of eating! There you are munching away and the next thing you know you're an ice lolly. If this ionised ice did rain down from Venus, the biggest build up would have been nearest to the magnetic poles because they would have had the most powerful attraction. Again, that is the case. The ice mass in the polar regions is greater at the poles than at the periphery and yet there is less snow and rain at the poles to create such a build up.[21] The Venus scenario explains this. In the Book of Job, which is believed to be an Arab work much older than the rest of the Bible, the question is asked: "Whence cometh the ice?" I would say we could have the answer. This further explains how the ancients could have had maps of what the north and south poles looked like before the ice was there. The poles were ice-free until about 7,000 years ago. There was no ice age as officially suggested. It's another illusion. When you look at the 'evidence' that official science presents to support the conventional idea of an ice age and the way this 'evidence' is fundamentally contradicted by the provable facts, it is astonishing how such nonsense could become conventional 'truth' in the first place.[22] Before this incredible cataclysm, and/or one of the others, the Earth had a uniform tropical climate, as fossilised plants have shown. This would have been changed not only by the arrival of the ice on the surface, but also by the destruction of a canopy of water vapour around the Earth, as described in Genesis and other ancient texts. This canopy would have ensured a uniform tropical climate everywhere, but suddenly it was gone.

The dramatic change in temperature at the poles would have collided with the warm air and caused devastating winds, exactly as described by Chinese folklore. The physicists said that the pressures created by the orbits of 'Venus' around the Earth would have produced a 10,000 foot tidal wave in the oceans and this again fits with the evidence that agriculture began at altitudes of 10,000 feet and higher. Plato wrote in his work, *Laws*, that agriculture began at high elevations after a gigantic flood covered all the lowlands. The botanist, Nikolai Ivanovitch Vavilov, studied more than 50,000 wild plants collected around the world and found that they originated in only eight different areas – all of them mountain terrain.[23] The tidal wave would have produced pressures on the Earth's surface of two tons per square inch, creating new mountain ranges, and fossilising everything within hours.[24] Artificial stone today is created by pressures of this magnitude. Intact trees have been found fossilised and that would be impossible unless it happened in an instant because the tree would normally have disintegrated before it could be fossilised over a long period of time.[25] In fact, fossils of this kind are not forming today.[26] They are the result of the cataclysmic events here described, Desborough says. The Russian-Jewish psychiatrist and writer, Immanuel Velikovsky, caused outrage among the scientific establishment in the 1950s by suggesting that the Earth had been through enormous upheavals when Venus which was then, he said, a comet, careered through this part of the solar system before settling into its present orbit. When Venus was photographed by the Mariner 10 mission, many of Velikovsky's descriptions proved correct, including what appeared to be the remnants of a comet-like tail. The Mariner 9 pictures of Mars also supported some of Velikovsky's theories. He said that the 'comet' Venus had collided with Mars as it careered through the solar system. Velikovsky's time for these events was about 1,500 BC. Different researchers dismiss each other's findings because they suggest very different periods for major upheavals when in truth there were almost certainly a number of cataclysms in that window of 11,000 to 1,500 BC, and even more recently. The study by the physicists also said that Mars was devastated by these events involving Venus. They felt Mars was thrown out of orbit and followed a highly unstable elliptical orbit which took it between the Earth and the Moon every 56 years.[27] The last of these passes appears to have been about 1,500 BC when the great volcano exploded on the Greek island of Santorini and the Minoan civilisation on Crete passed into history. In this same period of 1,600–1,500 BC, ocean levels dropped about 20 per cent, glacial lakes formed in California, and this was most likely the time when the vast lake in the fertile Sahara was emptied and the desert we see today began to be formed.[28] Eventually, Mars settled into its present orbit, but by then life on its surface had been obliterated. Yet again the evidence on Mars supports all this. The Mars Pathfinder mission found that Martian rocks lack sufficient erosion to have been on the surface for more than 10,000 years.[29]

Brian Desborough believes, like the physicists he knew and worked with, that the Earth was once much nearer the Sun than it is today and that Mars orbited where the Earth now resides. If, as is claimed, the deep canyons on Mars's surface were caused by massive torrents of water, there had to have been a warmer climate on Mars, because today it is so cold that water would freeze instantly and the near-vacuum atmosphere would make the water instantly vaporise.[30] Desborough says that the Earth's closer proximity to the Sun demanded that the first Earth humans were the black races with the pigmentation to cope with the much fiercer rays of the Sun. Ancient skeletons found near Stonehenge in England and along the west coast of France display the nasal and spinal characteristics of many female Africans.[31] Desborough says that Mars, then with a climate very much like ours, had a white race before the Venus cataclysm. His research has convinced him that the white Martians built the pyramids which have been recorded on Mars and they went to war with an advanced black race to conquer the Earth. These wars, he says, are the wars of the 'gods' described in endless ancient texts, not least the Hindu Vedas. Desborough adds that after the cataclysm, the white Martians who had settled on Earth were stranded here without their technology and with their home planet devastated. These white Martians, he says, became the white peoples of the Earth. Fascinatingly, some scientists claim that when white people are immersed in sensory deprivation tanks for long periods, their circadian rhythm has a frequency of 24 hours 40 minutes, which corresponds not to the rotational period of the Earth, but of Mars![32] This is not the case with non-white races who are in tune with the Earth's rotation. Desborough believes that these white Martians were the highly advanced race of the ancient world known as the Phoenicians or Aryans and they began the long process of returning to their former technological power after the upheavals which destroyed the surface of their own planet and devastated this one. My own research supports this basic theme, although, like everyone seeking the truth of what happened, I have many questions. A white race, known as the Phoenicians and other names, was certainly the 'brains' behind the Egyptian civilisation, at least from the period around 3,000 BC, and the Giza Plateau, where the Great Pyramid was built, was formerly known as El-Kahira, a name which derived from the Arabic noun, El-Kahir, their name for... Mars.[33] Ancient texts reveal that the measurement of time was much related to Mars, and March 15th, the Ides of March (Mars), was a key date in their Mars-related calendar, as was October 26th. The first marked the start of Spring and the second was the end of the year in the Celtic calendar.[34] The Holy Grail stories of King Arthur connect with this theme, also. Camelot apparently means Martian City or City of Mars.[35]

I think there is truth in all the views summarised in this chapter of the cataclysmic upheavals the Earth has suffered in the period between 11,000 and 1,500 BC. The first one ended the Golden Age and obliterated the high-tech civilisations that had existed before then. The extraterrestrial races either left the planet beforehand or survived at high altitudes or by going deep within the Earth. The same with the later cataclysm. Many of the extraterrestrials, and most Earth humans, did not survive these events. Those that did were left with the job of starting all over again without, at least at first, the technology available before. The survivors fell into two main categories, those of mostly extraterrestrial origin who retained the advanced knowledge, and humans, the slave race in general, who did not. The former also fell into two camps. There were those who wished to use their knowledge positively and communicate their information to humanity, and those who sought to hoard the knowledge and use it to manipulate and control. The struggle between those two groups over the use of the same knowledge continues to this very day. As societies recovered from those upheavals of 11,000 BC, the other cataclysms brought more devastation over the thousands of years that followed and humanity was faced with many new beginnings.

One common theme throughout, however, has been the manipulation of humanity by an intellectually, though not spiritually, advanced race or races of extraterrestrial origin. On that subject, I must now introduce an added dimension to this story which will stretch your credulity to breaking point.

■ SOURCES

1   T. W. Doane, *Bible Myths, And Their Parallels In Other Religions* (Health Research, PO Box 850, Pomeroy, WA, USA 99347, first published 1882), p 10.

2   The information about the Anunnaki and the Sumerian Tablets comes from the Zecharia Sitchin series of books collectively known as *The Earth Chronicles*. Individually they are called *The 12th Planet*, *The Stairway To Heaven*, *The Wars Of Gods And Men*, *The Lost Realms*, and *When Time Began*. Another Sitchin work is *Genesis Revisited*. They are published by Avon Books, 1350 Avenue of the Americas, New York.

3   *Genesis Revisited*, p 22.

4   Ibid, p 161.

5   Ibid, p 198.

6   Ibid, p 199.

7   Ibid.

8   Ibid, p 200.

9   For a comprehensive documentation of these global legends and the scientific support for them, see the excellent book by D. S. Allen and J. B. Delair called *When The Earth Nearly Died* (Gateway Books, Wellow, Bath, England, 1995).

10   Ibid, p 31.

11   Ibid, p 32.

12   Maurice Ewing, "New Discoveries On The Mid-Atlantic Ridge", *National Geographic* magazine, November 1949, pp 614, 616.

13   *When The Earth Nearly Died*, pp 32, 33.

14   Ibid, p 34.

15   Charles Berlitz, *Atlantis, The Eighth Continent*, (Fawcett Books, New York, 1984), pp 96–101.

16   Ibid.

17   *When The Earth Nearly Died*, pp 25–28.

18   Brian Desborough, "The Great Pyramid Mystery, Tomb, Occult Initiation Center, Or What?", a document supplied to the author and also published in the *The California Sun* newspaper, Los Angeles.

19   Ibid.

20   Ibid.

21   Ibid.

22   *When The Earth Nearly Died* has some impressive documentation to show that the Ice Age is a myth.

23   "The Great Pyramid Mystery."

24   Ibid.

25   Ibid.

26   Ibid.

27   Ibid.

28   Ibid.

29   Ibid.

30   Ibid.

31   Ibid.

32   Ibid.

33   Ibid.

34   Preston B. Nichols and Peter Moon, *Pyramids Of Montauk*, (Sky Books, New York, 1995), p 125.

35   Ibid, p 129.

CHAPTER TWO

"Don't mention the reptiles"

A re you ready for this? I wish I didn't have to introduce the following information because it complicates the story and opens me up to mass ridicule. But stuff it. If that is where the evidence takes me, that is where I shall go every time.

I don't think the Anunnaki of the Sumerian Tablets and the white Martians proposed in Brian Desborough's scenario are the same people, although there may well be a genetic connection between them. Putting together the mass of evidence, views, research and opinions, that I have read or heard almost daily these past years, I feel the Anunnaki are a race from a reptile genetic stream. In UFO research these have become known as reptilians. Nor am I alone in this view. I have personally been staggered by how many people today are open to these possibilities and, indeed, are coming to the same conclusions through their own research. These include many who would have laughed at the very idea not so long ago. Dr Arthur David Horn, a former professor of biological anthropology at Colorado State University in Fort Collins, once believed emphatically in the Darwinist version of human evolution, the slow development of the human species via the principle of the survival of the fittest. Purely on the weight of evidence and his own experience, he is now convinced that humanity was seeded by extraterrestrials and that a reptilian race has controlled the planet for thousands of years and continues to do so today. This is my own view, although I have taken a very different life path to reach those same conclusions. Dr Horn's research is detailed in his excellent book, *Humanity's Extraterrestrial Origins*[1] in which he suggests that the ones the Sumerian Tablets call the Anunnaki are this reptile race, another point with which we agree. The famed British astrophysicist, Fred Hoyle, told a London press conference as long ago as 1971 that the world was controlled by a force which could manifest in many forms. "They are everywhere," he told astonished journalists, "in the sky, in the sea and on the Earth…" He said that 'they' controlled humanity through the mind. I know this sounds utterly bizarre, but you need to read the whole of *The Biggest Secret* to see the wealth of evidence to support this. If you pull out now or after a couple of chapters because your belief system is in overload, that's your choice, but you will miss the opportunity to see that the almost hysterically unbelievable is actually true.

The more I weave together incredible amounts of information, the more it seems to me that we are talking of two distinct situations running side by side. There were other extraterrestrial races at large on the Earth, and still are, as well as the extraterrestrial race which the Sumerians called the Anunnaki and other ancient texts called the Serpent Race. It could well have been that some of the others went to war with this reptilian Anunnaki. Ancient texts record these 'wars of the gods' all over the world and these could include conflicts between different extraterrestrial races as well as those described in the Sumerian Tablets that appeared to involve Anunnaki factions fighting with each other. Today there are many modern accounts from people who claim to have seen humanoid-type people whose skin and faces look like lizards and frogs with large protruding eyes. Jason Bishop III (a pseudonym), an investigator of the extraterrestrial phenomenon, says that the reptilians are mostly much taller than humans and are cold blooded like Earth reptiles.[2] They appear to be far less emotionally sensitive than humans and most have great difficulty expressing love, though they are extremely intelligent and have very advanced technology. I must say that is an excellent description of the attitudes and behaviour of the Brotherhood who control the world today. The modern accounts of reptilians match the descriptions of many 'gods' of the ancient world in the surviving texts and legends. The Ubaid culture existed between 5,000 and 4,000 BC, even before Sumer, in what is now Iraq and figurines of their gods are clear representations of reptile-like, lizard-like humanoids. You can see a lizard Ubaid figurine holding a lizard baby in the picture section. The region where the Ubaid-Sumer cultures emerged is fundamental to this whole story and the Ubaid figurines depict physically the descriptions of 'gods' which dominated many ancient societies. The Central American cultures had their winged serpent god, Quetzalcoatl; the Hopi Indians had the plumed serpent god, Baholinkonga, and the Native American culture is awash with serpent imagery, including the mysterious serpent-shaped mound in Ohio; the East Indians speak of the reptilian gods, the Nagas (these were a race of 'demons' in Indian legend and their name means "Those who do not walk, but creep"); the Egyptians had their serpent god, Kneph, and pharaohs were often pictured with serpents; the Phoenicians had Agathodemon, another serpent figure; the voodoo people have a god they call Damballah Wedo, who is depicted as a serpent; and the Hebrews had Nakhustan, the Brazen Serpent. The ancient British god, known as the Dragon-Ruler of the World, was called HU and from this, very appropriately I would suggest, we get the term, Hu-man. The winged-disc symbol of the Sumerians, which is found all over the ancient world, was normally featured with two serpents. The symbolism of the serpent and its association with ancient 'gods' abounds throughout the world. The Reverend John Bathhurst Deane in his book *The Worship Of The Serpent*,[3] wrote:

"...One of (*the*) five builders of Thebes (*in Egypt*) was named after the serpent-god of the Phoenicians, Ofhion... The first altar erected to Cyclops at Athens, was to 'Ops', the serpent-deity... The symbolic worship of the serpent was so common in Greece, that Justin Martyr accuses the Greeks of introducing it into the mysteries of all their gods. The Chinese... are said to be superstitious in choosing a plot of ground to erect a dwelling house or sepulchre: conferring it with the head, tail and feet of diverse dragons which live under the Earth."

The idea of fire breathing dragons and evil serpents which appear in legends and texts all over the world could easily originate from the reptilian 'gods' who once operated openly thousands of years ago. These were the Serpent People of ancient texts, including the Bible, where the serpent is a regular theme. Of course, the serpent has been used to symbolise many things and not every reference will be literally a reptile, certainly not. But many of them are. There is also a common theme of a sacred place being guarded by a serpent or dragon. We have the serpent in the Garden of Eden and the serpent/dragon theme is global. The Persians spoke of a region of bliss and delight called Heden which was more beautiful than all the rest of the world. It was the original abode of the first men, they said, before they were tempted by the evil spirit, in the form of a serpent, to partake of the fruit of the forbidden tree. There is also the Banyon Tree under which the Hindu 'Jesus', known as Khrishna, sat upon a coiled serpent and bestowed spiritual knowledge on humanity. The ancient Greeks had a tradition of the Islands of the Blessed and the Garden of the Hesperides in which grew a tree bearing the golden apples of immortality. This garden was protected by a dragon.[4] In the Chinese sacred books there is a garden in which grew trees bearing the fruit of immortality and it, too, was guarded by a winged serpent called a dragon. In ancient Mexican accounts, their version of the Eve story involves a great male serpent.[5] Another Hindu legend speaks of the sacred mountain of Meru guarded by a dreadful dragon.[6] Over and over we see the same theme of sacred places guarded by fearsome dragons and of a reptilian or a half reptile-half human, giving spiritual knowledge to humans.

The reptile species has a long, long connection with the Earth, going back more than 150 million years to the dinosaurs and beyond. If we are to understand the true nature of life we need to free our minds from the bonds of conditioning and realise that what we see around us on Earth is only a tiny fraction of possibility. The reptile species, like lizards and snakes, are but one form of the reptilian genetic stream in this universe. While the dinosaurs were not all cold-blooded reptiles, as modern research has shown, the reptiles and dinosaurs are closely related by physical appearance alone and both have spawned an amazing variety of different forms. The dinosaurs manifested as everything from flying creatures, large and small, to the eight-ton, Tyrannosaurus Rex. Are we really saying that reptile-dinosaur genetic streams that can produce such diversity, cannot manifest in a two-legged, two-armed form with a brain capacity through which a technically advanced consciousness can operate? More recently a greater understanding of the dinosaurs has revealed that many were very intelligent a hundred million years ago. The Saurornithoides, named from its appearance as a bird-like reptile, had a large brain, wide-set eyes that gave it stereoscopic vision, and fingers with opposing thumbs which allowed it to catch and eat small mammals.[7] Adrian J. Desmond, one of the world's leading researchers into dinosaurs, says that creatures like the Saurornithoides, were separated from other dinosaurs "by a gulf comparable to that dividing men from cows".[8] He asks: "Who knows what peaks the sophisticated 'bird-mimics' would have attained had they survived?"[9] Studies have suggested that had the dinosaurs not been wiped out by yet another cataclysm about 65 million years ago, they would have evolved into a reptile humanoid by now.[10] Dale Russell, the senior paleontologist at Northern California University, was asked by the US space agency, NASA, to produce a report on what extraterrestrial life might look like.[11] He evolved the Troodon dinosaur in line with natural genetic changes over millions of years and created a model of a being he dubbed a Dino-sauroid. This had a remarkable resemblance to a reptilian humanoid and was identical to those described by people who claim to have seen reptile extraterrestrials. Who is to say that this evolutionary leap from classic dinosaurs to reptilian humanoids did not happen in another dimension or on another physical planet and perhaps on Earth before the dinosaurs were eliminated? In fact, were they all eliminated? Modern palaeontology (the study of fossils) now suggests that not all the dinosaurs were killed by the meteorite strike 65 million years ago and some continue to live today. More and more evidence is emerging that birds are descendants of the dinosaurs. And while the bodies of most dinosaurs might have been destroyed, their consciousness would have survived because consciousness is energy and energy is indestructible. It can only be transmuted into a different form. What happened to that dinosaur consciousness that dominated the Earth for *150 million* years? As we've seen, the earliest accounts of Assyria, Babylon, Old Testament history, China, Rome, America, Africa, India and elsewhere, feature stories of the dragons. The serpent symbol has also been found in ancient Britain, Greece, Malta, Egypt, New Mexico, Peru and all over the Pacific Islands. There is an unmistakable resemblance between some dinosaurs and ancient depictions of dragons. Several species of small Indo-Malayan lizards with webbed wings look so much like dragons that they have been given the name Draco after the star constellation from which the reptilian hierarchy are said to originate. Of even more interest to me is the armoured lizard called Moloch Horridus which also has a dragon-like appearance. Moloch is an ancient deity to which children were sacrificed thousands of years ago and still are today in the vast Satanic ritual network. They are sacrificed to the reptilians in other words because, as will become clear, many 'demons'of Satanism are the reptilians who have sought to take over the planet for thousands of years. Charles Gould who has written extensively about dragons and reptiles, says: "there is a lost species of lizard hibernating and carnivorous which had Draco-like wings and was protected by armour and spikes".[12] He believes its habitat was the highlands of central Asia and its disappearance coincided with the Great Flood.[13] But there are still sightings of giant 'flying lizards' in remote areas of the world, especially in Mexico, New Mexico and Arizona.

Who are they and where do they come from?

There are three suggested origins for the Anunnaki reptilian intervention in human affairs: **1** They are extraterrestrials; **2** They are 'inner' terrestrials who live within the Earth; **3** They manipulate humanity from another dimension by 'possessing' human bodies. I think they are all true.

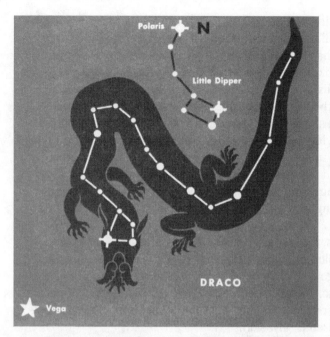

Figure 4: *The Draco 'dragon' constellation to which so many ancient monuments appear to be aligned.*

Extraterrestrials?

Researchers into the reptilian phenomenon conclude that at least some originate in the Draco star constellation (*see Figure 4*). The Draco system includes the star Thurban, once the North Star, by which the Egyptian pyramids are orientated.[14] According to the research of author Graham Hancock, the ancient temple complex at Angkor Wat in Cambodia is a replica of the Draco constellation as it would have been in 10,500 BC.[15] This is the time when the Earth and its people, human and extraterrestrial, would have been recovering from the cataclysm of 11,000 BC and rebuilding their civilisation. The author and researcher, Robert Bauval, says that the pyramids at Giza align with the stars on the 'belt' of Orion as they would have been in 10,500 BC when Orion was at the lowest point in its cycle (the Orions are another extraterrestrial race operating on this planet, I understand). And Hancock and other researchers suggest that the lion-bodied Sphinx at Giza, which is believed to be far older than originally dated, would have directly faced the constellation of Leo the lion at that same time, 10,500 BC. Research continues under the ocean off Japan into a fantastic structure which could also date to 10,500 BC at least. There are many who have questioned these findings, especially the synchronisation of the Giza pyramids to Orion, but at the very least they have triggered an important area of investigation, even if they prove not to be accurate in every detail. After all, finding the truth, especially so far back, is hardly easy. It is certainly astonishing how the ancient structures and temples, of apparently unconnected societies all over the world, align with each other with fantastic astronomical, mathematical and geometrical precision. But then, these societies were *not* unconnected. As we shall see, they had the same origins. The temples at Angkor Wat are covered in reptilian images, a feature of all the ancient cultures, including the Egyptian, the Central American and the Indian. Professor Phillip Calahan in his study of the surviving and mysterious round towers of Ireland has said that they are positioned with remarkable synchronicity to the star constellations of the northern sky at the winter solstice. And the towers most perfectly align with the constellation of... Draco. The head and eyes of the Draco formation, as designed on the ground in Ireland, are, according to Calahan, located either side of Lough Neagh right in the centre of

Northern Ireland. The eastern side of Lough Neagh is close to the capital, Belfast.[16]
So the head of the Draco constellation is positioned on the ground in Northern
Ireland and that small country has been the scene of so much upheaval, murder and
suffering. By the end of this book, those who are new to these concepts will
appreciate the power of symbolism to attract energy to a place, negative and
positive. John Rhodes,[17] one of the foremost of the researchers into the reptilian
presence, says that they may be space invaders who move from planet to planet,
covertly infiltrating the host society and eventually taking over. The reptilian
military, it is said, carry out abductions of life forms while their scientists study the
biology and introduce the reptilian genetic code into species they wish to
manipulate. This involves a programme of crossbreeding and that is precisely what
the Sumerian Texts are describing in relation to the Anunnaki. Rhodes adds that:

> "From their underground bases, the reptilian military ETs…(*establish*)…a network of
> human-reptilian crossbreed infiltrates within various levels of the surface culture's
> military industrial complexes, government bodies, UFO/paranormal groups, religious
> and fraternal (*priest*) orders, etc. These crossbreeds, some unaware of their reptilian
> genetic "mind control" instructions, act out their subversive roles as "reptilian agents",
> setting the stage for a reptilian-led ET invasion."[18]

I only came across the work of John Rhodes in the last few days before this book
was complete and by then, as you will see later in the detailed text, I had reached
exactly the same conclusions. Rhodes says that after the reptilians invade a planet
from space and from their underground bases, the surface population quickly
surrender to superior weaponry. Then the reptilians strip the planet of its resources
like water, minerals and DNA information. The infiltration of human society via
secret societies is a key method of reptilian control, as I shall detail. The American
writer and researcher, William Bramley, concluded in his book, *Gods Of Eden*, that
the Anunnaki created a secret society called the Brotherhood of the Snake and this
has been used to manipulate humanity in the way described in the chapters that
follow.[19] This Brotherhood of the Snake is the core centre of today's global secret
society network which is controlled by the reptilians.

Inner-terrestrials?

In their physical expression, the Anunnaki are one of the many inner-Earth races
which live underground in the enormous catacombs, caverns and tunnels below the
surface. A Hopi Indian legend says that a very ancient tunnel complex exists under
Los Angeles and this, they say, was occupied by a 'lizard' race some 5,000 years ago.
In 1933 G. Warren Shufelt, an LA mining engineer, claimed to have found it.[20] Today, it
is said, some malevolent Freemasonic rituals are held in this tunnel complex. There
has been a massive cover up by the authorities of the existence of these subterranean
races and where they live. In 1909 a subterranean city which was built with the
precision of the Great Pyramid was found by G. E. Kincaid near the Grand Canyon in
Arizona. It was big enough to accommodate 50,000 people and mummified bodies

found on the site were of oriental or possibly Egyptian origin, according to the expedition leader Professor S. A. Jordan.[21] Numerous artefacts were found, including copper implements as hard as steel. The Smithsonian Institution in Washington DC has ensured these finds remain unknown to the public (that's its job!) and no-one would have known about this discovery had it not been for two articles in a local newspaper, the *Arizona Gazette*, in April 1909. The researcher and author, John Rhodes, claims to have located this site and he connects it with Sipapuni, the underground world from where the Hopi Indians claim to have originated. According to their legends, the Hopi once lived within the Earth and were fed and clothed by 'ant people', possibly the extraterrestrials known as the Greys. The Hopi refer to their ancestors as their 'snake brothers' and their most sacred of underground rituals is the snake dance. As I will keep emphasising, not all reptilians are of malevolent intent and I have no wish to demonise the reptile stream. We are talking here only of one group of them. The Hopi say that one day under the orders of their goddess, Spider Woman, they ascended to the surface of the Earth and emerged through their cave they called the Sipapuni. Once on the outside, the Hopi say, a mocking bird arrived to confuse their language and make different tribes speak different tongues. This is such a repeat of the biblical story of the Tower of Babel that a connection is obvious. To this day the Hopi will not recreate the images of their snake ancestors for fear of death. The layout of the underground world discovered in Arizona was described by G. E. Kincaid as a "...mammoth chamber from which radiates scores of passageways like the spokes of a wheel". This is also how the modern reptilian underground base at Dulce, New Mexico is described, and concentric circles of people, compartmentalising different levels of knowledge, is the structure by which the global Brotherhood manipulate the world. Arizona, New Mexico and the Four Corners area where the states of Arizona, Utah, Colorado and New Mexico all meet, are some of the most important regions on Earth for reptilian underground bases. But underground worlds and cities, ancient and modern, abound all over the planet. There are eyewitness reports of giant humanoids sighted in the Hal Saflini catacombs in Malta during the 1930s, which were closed after a party of schoolchildren and their guide disappeared. More than 30 vast ancient tunnel complexes and underground cities have been found near Derinkuya in Turkey. The list goes on and on. The mysterious creature known as the Bigfoot, a large hairy ape-like creature, is allegedly from within the Earth. There is a widespread belief among UFO researchers that there are reptilian underground bases where they work with their reptile-human crossbreed elite and I have spoken to former CIA employees who confirm this. A reptilian race definitely live within this planet in a physical form and the only question is whether they are native to the Earth or if they originate elsewhere? Again it is probably both, a mixture of the two.

Other dimensional?

My own research suggests that it is from another dimension, the lower fourth dimension, that the reptilian control and manipulation is primarily orchestrated. Without understanding the multidimensional nature of life and the Universe, it is impossible to follow the manipulation of the Earth by a non-human force. As open minded scientists are now confirming, Creation consists of an infinite number of frequencies or dimensions of life sharing the same space in the same way that radio and television frequencies do. At the moment you are tuned to the three-dimensional world or third dimension and so that is what you perceive as your reality. You are tuned to this station in other words. But, as with radio and television, all the other stations are broadcasting at the same time and if you move your radio dial or change the TV channel you can connect with them. When you do this, the station or channel you were tuned to before does not disappear, it continues to broadcast, but you can't hear it or see it anymore because you are no longer on its wavelength. So it is with human consciousness. Some people (everyone if the truth be told) can tune their consciousness to other wavelengths and connect with information and consciousness operating on that frequency. We call this psychic power, but it is merely the ability to move your 'dial' to another 'station'. It is from one of these other stations or dimensions, that the Serpent Race, the Anunnaki, is controlling this world by 'possessing' certain bloodline streams. But as my research continues, it is clear that the fourth dimensional reptilian controllers are themselves controlled by fifth dimensional entities. Where does it end? Who the hell knows. Yeah, yeah, yeah, I know it sounds off the wall, but the truth usually does. You can put the book down now if it is too much to take, but you need to read it all to see what enormous evidence there is that this *is* true. The 'station' from which the reptilians operate is the lower level of the fourth dimension, the one closest to this physical world. Other people know this as the lower astral dimension, the legendary home of demons and malevolent entities going back to antiquity. It is from here that today's Satanists summon their demonic entities in their black magic rituals. They are actually summoning the reptilians of the lower fourth dimension. It is suggested by some researchers, with good reason, that the non-physical reptilians were able to pour into this dimension through holes or portals in the time-space fabric caused by the nuclear tests and explosions which started in the deserts of New Mexico in the early 1940s. But I think such holes began to be created a long time ago, before the cataclysms, when the world was at an even more advanced technological stage than it is today.

The reptilian control of Planet Earth involves all three of the above themes. I think the reptilian genetic stream operates throughout the Universe and they are not all malevolent, far from it. As with humanity, they contain the whole spectrum of attitudes from love to hate, freedom to control. I am identifying a particular group of them, not the whole species – I cannot emphasise this enough. This controlling group came here from the Draco constellation and elsewhere, and this is the origin of terms like draconian, a word which sums up their attitudes and agenda. They love to consume human blood and they are the blood-sucking demons of legend. The vampire stories are symbolic of this and what is the name of the most famous vampire? Count Dracula! The 'Count' symbolises the aristocratic reptile-human crossbreed bloodlines which the reptilians possess from the lower fourth dimension and Dracula is an obvious reference again to Draco. The recent reports of the blood-sucking Chupacabra in Puerto Rico, Mexico, Florida and the Pacific Northwest fit the reptilian description. They have been seen sucking the blood of domestic livestock like goats and their name means goat-sucker. The reptilians operate a pincer movement on the human race. Their physical expression lives under the ground and interacts in the underground bases with human and human-reptile crossbreed scientists and military leaders. They also emerge to engage in some human abductions. But the main control comes by outright possession. The crossbreeding programme (via sex and test tube) is described in the Sumerian Tablets and the Old Testament (the Sons of God who interbred with the daughters of men). These hybrid human-reptile lines carry the reptilian genetic code and thus can be far more easily possessed by the reptilians of the lower fourth dimension. As we shall see, these bloodlines became the British and European aristocracy and royal families and, thanks to the 'Great' British Empire, they were exported across the world to rule the Americas, Africa, Asia, Australia, New Zealand and so on. These genetic lines are manipulated into the positions of political, military, media, banking and business power and thus these positions are held by lower fourth dimensional reptilians hiding behind a human form or by mind-puppets of the these same creatures. They operate through all races, but predominantly the white one.

As is well acknowledged, there is an area of the human brain to this day known as the reptile brain. Within the brain is the original segment to which all other parts are additions. And, according to the neuroanatomist, Paul MacLean, this ancient area of the brain is driven by another prehistoric segment which some neuroanatomists call the R-complex.[22] R is short for reptilian because we share this with reptiles. MacLean says that this R-complex plays an important role in "aggressive behaviour, territoriality, ritualism and establishment of social hierarchies".[23] This is precisely the behaviour patterns of reptilians and their reptile-human hybrids as exposed in this book. The astronomer, Carl Sagan, knew far more than he ever made public and indeed he spent much of his career guiding people away from the truth. But his knowledge of the true situation occasionally came through, as when he said that: "…it does no good whatsoever to ignore the reptilian component of human nature, particularly our ritualistic and hierarchical behaviour. On the contrary, the model may help us understand what human beings are all about."[24] He adds in his book, *The Dragons Of Eden*, that even the negative side of human behaviour is expressed in reptilian terms, as in cold-blooded killer. Sagan (the name in reverse spells the East Indian reptilian gods, the Nagas) clearly knew the score, but chose not to reveal openly what he knew. As the human foetus is forming into a baby it goes through many stages which connect with the major evolutionary points in the development of the present physical form. These include connections with non-primate mammals, reptiles and fish. There is a point in which the embryo develops gills, for example. The human embryo is very much like those of birds, sheep and pigs until the eighth week when it goes its own evolutionary way. Occasionally the genetic instructions fail to remember the latest script and some babies are born with tails. These are called caudal appendages and form in the lower lumbar region. Most are immediately removed by doctors, but in some poorer countries where such medical support is not available, there are people who live their whole lives with tails.[25] Pheromone is the substance secreted and released by animals so they can be detected by members of the same species. The pheromones in human women and iguanas are a chemical match.[26]

Look again at those figures at the start of the first chapter detailing the number of planets and stars that exist in the fraction of Creation we know about. The number of life forms in this galaxy alone is beyond imagination and that's only at the three-dimensional level of existence. If we judge possibility, as we do, only by what we see on one little planet in one little solar system, our range of perception, imagination and vision will be so microscopic that an understanding of what is really happening to this world will be impossible. To that level of thinking the idea that a reptile race is controlling the planet from another dimension will be so far out as to be incomprehensible. That is the way the vast majority will, at first, receive the information in this book, but the appreciation of the 'reptilian connection' is growing among researchers who are interested in the truth and not just concerned with defending a belief system or looking for public approval.

In a remarkable period of 15 days as I travelled around the United States in 1998, I met more than a dozen separate people who told me of how they had seen humans transform into reptiles and go back again in front of their eyes. Two television presenters had just such an experience while interviewing a man who was in favour of the global centralisation of power known as the New World Order. After the live interview, the male presenter said to his colleague that he had experienced an amazing sight during the interview. He had seen the man's face transform into a lizard-like creature and then return to human. His female fellow presenter was astounded because she had seen the interviewee's hands turn reptilian. The male presenter also told me of an experience a policeman friend had while making a routine visit to an office block in Aurora, near Denver, Colorado. The policeman had commented to an executive of one of the companies on the ground floor of the extreme nature of security in the building. She told him he should look at the higher floors if he wanted to know how extensive it really was. She also pointed to a lift which only went to certain floors at the top of the building and, as they chatted, she told him of something she had seen some weeks earlier. The lift had opened and a very strange figure had emerged. He was white to the point of being albino, but he had a face shaped like a lizard and his eye pupils were vertical like a reptile's. This lizard-like figure had walked out of the lift and into an official-looking car waiting outside. The policeman was so intrigued that he used his own time to check on the companies at the top of the building served by the mystery lift. He found they were all fronts for the Central Intelligence Agency, the CIA.

Then there are the experiences of Cathy O'Brien, the mind controlled slave of the United States government for more than 25 years, which she details in her astonishing book, *Trance Formation Of America*, written with Mark Phillips.[27] She was sexually abused as a child and an adult by a stream of famous people named in her book. Among them were the US Presidents, Gerald Ford, Bill Clinton and, most appallingly, George Bush, a major player in the Brotherhood, as my books and others have long exposed. It was Bush, a paedophile and serial killer, who regularly abused and raped Cathy's daughter, Kelly O'Brien, as a toddler before her mother's courageous exposure of these staggering events forced the authorities to remove Kelly from the mind control programme known as Project Monarch. Cathy writes in *Trance Formation Of America* of how George Bush was sitting in front of her in his office in Washington DC when he opened a book at a page depicting "lizard-like aliens from a far off, deep space place."[28] Bush then claimed to be an 'alien' himself and appeared, before her eyes, to transform 'like a chameleon' into a reptile. Cathy believed that some kind of hologram had been activated to achieve this and from her understanding at the time I can see why she rationalised her experience in this way. Anyone would, because the truth is too fantastic to comprehend until you see the build up of evidence. There's no doubt that alien-based mind programmes are part of these mind control projects and that the whole UFO-extraterrestrial scene is being massively manipulated, not least through Hollywood films designed to mould public thinking. Cathy says in her book that George Lucas, the producer of *Star Wars*, is an operative with NASA and the National Security Agency, the 'parent' body of the CIA.[29] But given the evidence presented by so many other people, I don't believe that what Bush said and Cathy saw was just a mind control programme. I think he was revealing the Biggest Secret, that a reptilian race from another dimension has been controlling the planet for thousands of years. I know other people who have seen Bush shape-shift into a reptilian.

The president of Mexico in the 1980s, Miguel De La Madrid, also used Cathy in her mind controlled state. She said he told her the Legend of the Iguana and explained that lizard-like extraterrestrials had descended upon the Mayans in Mexico. The Mayan pyramids, their advanced astronomical technology and the sacrifice of virgins, was inspired by lizard-like aliens, he told her.[30] He added that these reptilians interbred with the Mayans to produce a form of life they could inhabit. De La Madrid told Cathy that these reptile-human bloodlines could fluctuate between a human and iguana appearance through chameleon-like abilities – "a perfect vehicle for transforming into world leaders", he said. De la Madrid claimed to have Mayan-lizard ancestry in his blood which allowed him to transform back to an iguana at will. He then changed before her eyes, as Bush had, and appeared to have a lizard-like tongue and eyes.[31] Cathy understandably believed this to be another holographic projection, but was it really? Or was De La Madrid saying something very close to the truth? This theme of being like a chameleon is merely another term for 'shape-shifting', a theme you find throughout the ancient world and, among open minded people, in the modern one too. Shape-shifting is the ability to use your mind to project another physical image for people to see. Everything is energy vibrating at different speeds, so if you use your mind to re-vibrate that energy to a different resonance, you can appear in any form you choose. Many witnesses have described how the so-called 'Men in Black' materialise and dematerialise when they threaten people who are communicating information about extraterrestrials and UFOs. They can do this because they are interdimensional beings who can appear in any form. This is the main reason for the obsession with interbreeding among the Elite bloodline families. They are seeking to maintain a genetic structure which allows them to move between dimensions and shape-shift between a human and reptilian appearance. Once the genetic structure falls too far from it's reptilian origin, they can't shapeshift in this way. At NASA's Goddard Space Flight Centre mind control laboratory near Washington DC, Cathy says she was taken through another alien theme by Bill and Bob Bennett, two well-known figures in United States politics and fundamentally connected to the Brotherhood networks. After she was given mind altering drugs, this is what she says she experienced:

> "In the darkness around me I could hear Bill Bennett talking: 'This is my brother, Bob. He and I work as one unit. We are alien to this dimension – two beings from another plane.'

> "The high-tech light display swirling around me convinced me I was transforming dimensions with them. A laser of light hit the black wall in front of me, which seemed to explode into a panoramic view of a White House cocktail party – as though I had transformed dimensions and stood amongst them. Not recognising anyone, I frantically asked: 'Who are these people?'

> "'They're not people and this isn't a spaceship', Bennett said. As he spoke, the holographic scene changed ever so slightly until the people appeared to be lizard-like aliens. 'Welcome to the second level of the underground. This is a mere mirror reflection of the first, an alien dimension. We are from a trans-dimensional plane that spans and encompasses all dimensions…'

> "'…I have taken you through my dimension as a means of establishing stronger holds on your mind than the Earth plane permits,' Bill Bennett was saying. 'Being alien, I simply make my thoughts your thoughts by projecting them into your mind. My thoughts are your thoughts.'"[32]

Again, this might simply be a programming device, but given the other evidence I am presenting, is it not more likely that, under the effects of the drugs and other techniques, Cathy's mind had switched to the dimension in which the reptilians operate? The reptilians come from the lower fourth dimension and merely use physical bodies as their vehicles to manipulate this one. It makes sense, therefore, that if you can tune your mind to their true dimension you will see them as they really are. Cathy's descriptions mirror those of some 'abductees' who have recalled how their extraterrestrial abductors at first looked quite human, but then changed to look like humanoid lizards. Are these people really abducted by aliens in spaceships, or are they subjected to mind control techniques like those experienced by Cathy O'Brien which connect them with the lower fourth dimension? Hunter S. Thompson in his book, *Fear And Loathing In Las Vegas*,[33] describes seeing reptiles while in a drugged condition and a guy I met in the United States (in those 15 days I mentioned earlier) told me a similar story. He 'tripped' on large amounts of LSD in the 1960s and in his seriously mind-altered state he would see some people as humans and others as humanoid lizards and other reptiles. For a while he believed that he was merely hallucinating, but as a regular 'tripper' at high doses he began to realise that what he was seeing, usually by the third day of a five-day 'trip', was not an hallucination, but the vibratory veils lifting which allowed him to see beyond the physical to the force controlling the person. In these moments the same people always had lizard features and the same people always looked human. They never switched. He also began to observe that those around him who appeared lizard-like in his altered state always seemed to react the same to movies, television programmes, etc. "We used to laugh and say 'here come the lizards'," he told me. He believed there was, to use his own phrase, a 'morphogenetic field' which transmitted to the DNA of the lizard-people and aligned the cell structure to the reptilian genetic blueprint. The more reptilian genes a person carries the easier it is for this communication, or rather control, to take place. And the ones with the cell structure most aligned to the reptilian blueprint are the Elite families that run the world to this day. It is not without reason that Diana, Princess of Wales used to call the Windsors the 'lizards' and the 'reptiles' and said in all seriousness: "They're not human". This was told to me by a close confidant of Diana for nine years whom I quote at length later in the book.

At the end of that 15 days of meeting person after person telling me the same story of seeing humans become reptiles, I was sitting in the speakers' room at a Whole Life Expo event in Minneapolis where I was appearing and was chatting about these experiences when a gifted psychic lady said that she knew what I was talking about, because she could see the reptiles inside and around the bodies of leading world politicians, and the business, banking and military élite. This was possible because, as someone who had accessed her psychic sight, she could see beyond the physical and into the lower fourth dimension where these reptilians reside. What did Miguel De La Madrid say to Cathy O'Brien? The reptile-human bloodlines could fluctuate between a human and iguana appearance through chameleon-like abilities – "a perfect vehicle for transforming into world leaders". This psychic lady said that most of the people in positions of power appeared to be reptiles, but there were others who were still human and these people, she said, were "overshadowed and controlled" by a reptile, but they weren't actually reptiles. We would call this being possessed. This is an important distinction. There are the 'full-bloods' who are reptilians using an apparent human form to hide their true nature, and the 'hybrids', the reptile-human crossbreed bloodlines, who are possessed by the reptilians from the fourth dimension. A third type are the reptilians who directly manifest in this dimension, but can't hold that state indefinitely. Some of the 'Men in Black' are examples of this. Many of the possessed people will have no idea that this is so, but their thoughts are the reptilians' thoughts and they act in ways that advance the Agenda without realising the background to how and why they are being used. Leading Brotherhood families like the Rothschilds and the Windsors are full-bloods, reptilians wearing human physical bodies like an overcoat in the full knowledge of who they are and the Agenda they are seeking to implement. Another comment the psychic lady made was that in her altered state of consciousness, Hillary Clinton appeared as a reptile, while her husband, Bill Clinton the US President, was only overshadowed and controlled by one. This is interesting because my own research, and that of others, has revealed Hillary Clinton to be much higher in the hierarchy than Bill, who, while of a crossbreed bloodline, is a pawn in the game, to be used and discarded as necessary. It is not always that the most powerful people are placed in what appears to be the most powerful jobs. Often they are not. They are the string-pullers of those who *appear* to have the power.

There is another key difference between the full-bloods and the crossbreeds. Everything is created by sound. When you think or feel, you emit a wave of energy which changes the energy around you to resonate at that same vibratory level. That wave is actually a sound, broadcasting beyond the range of human hearing. Form cannot exist without sound. As you can see in a fantastic series of videos called *Cymatics*,[34] it is sound which turns matter into form. In the videos, sand and other particles are placed on a metal plate and this is vibrated by different sounds which rearrange the sand into amazing, often geometric patterns. With each change of sound the patterns change accordingly. Go back to the original sound and the original pattern returns immediately. It is like the waves that form the concentric circles of the planetary orbits around the Sun I mentioned in the last chapter. The solar system is also the creation of sound. Everything is. In the beginning was the word and the word was… sound. In the *Cymatics* videos you see the particles form into mini planets, solar systems and galaxies, just through sound vibrations. Sound is also a wonderful form of healing because by resonating the body and its organs at their proper vibration they can be healed. Illness is dis-ease, the disharmony of the natural vibrational state of the body and, because our thoughts and emotions are actually sound waves, our imbalanced thoughts and emotions disrupt the vibrational harmony and therefore lead to dis-ease. This is how emotional stress causes illness. It is so simple. Anyway, another incredible example of all this in the *Cymatics* videos is seeing almost human-like figures forming from the particles when certain sounds are emitted. Our bodies are also the result of sound resonating energy into form and if our minds are powerful enough to change the sound range of the body, it moves into another form or disappears from this dimension altogether. This is what is called shape-shifting. It is not a miracle, it is science, the natural laws of creation. The full-blood reptilians of the lower fourth dimension can therefore make their 'human' physical form disappear and bring forward their reptilian level of existence. They shape-shift. To us in this dimension they appear human, but it's just a vibrational overcoat.

After the first draft of this chapter was completed I met another woman, this time in England, who had been married to a man involved in Satanic ritual and the Brotherhood networks. He was head keeper of an area of land called Burnham Beeches near the Buckinghamshire-Berkshire border a few miles from Slough, west of London. This is an ancient site mentioned in the Domesday Book at the time of William the Conqueror in the 11th century and it has a reputation for Satanism. The lady who spoke to me was taking her dog for a walk across the land at dusk in the early 1970s when she saw a figure in a long red robe. When he lifted his head, she saw that his face was that of a lizard. She obviously thought she was crazy, but this was no illusion, she said. The 'lizard' was very real and very physical, not an apparition. She is very psychic and she later began to see people either transform into lizards before her eyes or be overshadowed by them in exactly the way described by the American psychic. If you look in the picture section you will see an artist's impression of what she sees with her psychic sight and many others have described exactly the same experiences. On July 20th 1988, a number of people in Bishopsville, South Carolina said they were terrorised by a "seven foot tall lizard-man that had no hair, eyebrows or lips, three fingers on each hand and large slanted eyes that glowed red in colour". There were five sightings of this "lizard-man" and the story was reported in the *Los Angeles Times* and the *Herald Examiner*.[35]

When you go with the flow of life and listen to your intuition, you are shown what you need to know by the incredible synchronicity that daily surrounds you and guides you through the smokescreens and the halls of mirrors. One day in February 1998 in Johannesburg, South Africa, I spent nearly five hours talking with a Zulu shaman called Credo Mutwa. The word Zulu means People from the Stars because they believe they are a royal race that originates beyond this planet. We talked about the global manipulation and his belief that an extraterrestrial race is behind the global Brotherhood of monarchs, politicians, bankers and media owners. Afterwards I went back to the house where I was staying and wrote down the main points he mentioned on my laptop computer before going downstairs into the lounge for the evening. As I sat down a movie was just starting, it was called *The Arrival*[36] and was about a reptile-like extraterrestrial race which had taken over the planet by operating through human bodies and appearing to be human. Someone was trying to tell me something! And that something is the truth. Another lesser-known movie I saw about this time was called *They Live*[37] and again the theme was of an extraterrestrial race taking over the world by working through human physical bodies. *Alien Resurrection*[38] was another to carry the reptilian theme with the implication that the aliens were occupying the bodies of humans. But the closest any movie has come to the truth is the American television series of the 1980s called *V*.[39] It tells of a reptile extraterrestrial race who take over the world by looking like humans. The film depicts the reptiles as being covered in some sort of latex skin, which is not how it works in reality, but the theme of the series is right on the button and a foretaste of things to come; unless we wake up fast. I highly recommend you think about watching the video of *V* to get a visual feel for the themes I am exposing in this book.

One of the leading researchers into this phenomenon has been the American, Alex Christopher, author of the books *Pandora's Box, Volumes I and II*,[40] which reveal, in part, the reptilian presence on this planet. Alex has seen reptilians and what she calls the big-eyed Greys. One night in Panama City, Florida she says she was called at 2.30 in the morning by her frantic neighbours, a woman and her partner, a commercial airline pilot. When she ran over to their house, she found the woman passing out, sliding down the wall with her eyeballs rolling. Alex said she felt an incredible energy in the room that seemed to be trying to penetrate her head. There was definitely radiation, she said, and the next day all the plants in the room were dead. She grabbed the couple and took them outside where they talked for a while. They said they had been making love when the incident began and this is very significant because the reptilians feed off human emotional and sexual energy which is one reason why sex is so fundamental to Satanic rituals performed for the 'demons' – this reptilian group. The couple said they saw a flash of light and then they were pulled from the bed. The man still had a palm print on his side made by fingers that must have been ten inches long with claws that burned into his skin. The next day that spot was so painful he couldn't touch it and Alex Christopher has video footage of this. When the couple had calmed down and Alex went back to bed in her house, she came face to face with a reptilian herself:

"I woke up and there is this "thing" standing over my bed. He had wrap-around yellow eyes with snake pupils and pointed ears, and a grin that wrapped around his head. He had a silvery suit on and this scared the living daylights out of me. I threw the covers over my head and started screaming... I mean, here is this thing with a Cheshire-cat grin and these funky glowing eyes... this is too much. I have seen this kind of being on more than one occasion... He had a hooked nose and was very human looking, other than his eyes, and had kind of greyish skin...

"...Later on in 1991, I was working in a building in a large city, and I had taken a break about 6pm and the next thing I knew it was 10.30pm and I thought I had taken a short break. I started remembering that I was taken aboard a (*space*)ship, through four floors of the office building and through a roof. There on the ship is where I encountered Germans and Americans working together, and also grey aliens, and then we were taken to some other kind of facility and there I saw reptilians again... the ones I call the "Baby Godzillas" that have short teeth and yellow slanted eyes... The things that stick in my mind are the beings that look like reptiles, or the "velcoci-rapters". They are the cruellest beings you could ever imagine and they even smell hideous."[41]

On the 'ship' she remembers seeing the Germans and Americans wearing an insignia, a blue triangle with a red-eyed dragon and circle around it. A contact later told her that she saw the same symbol at Fort Walden in the United States. A winged serpent symbol could also be seen on the sleeve of an Israeli soldier as he comforted the daughter of the assassinated Prime Minister, Yitzhak Rabin, at her father's funeral in 1995. (See *Newsweek*, November 20th 1995.) One of Alex Christopher's specialities is the new Denver Airport which is reputed to be a cover for a deep underground reptilian-human base. It is certainly a strange place. The first time I spoke on these conspiracy subjects in the United States was in Denver in August 1996, and I'd landed at Denver Airport with no idea of its background. Even so, as soon as the plane landed I'd felt a very strange energy, very weird and unpleasant. The airport was built at enormous cost on open land a long way from Denver and it is full of Masonic symbols. There are also gargoyles, the winged-reptile figures that you find on the stately homes of the reptilian aristocracy in Britain and on the churches and great cathedrals of Europe which were built by the Brotherhood network. There are also gargoyles on a building in Dealey Plaza where President Kennedy was assassinated and now they turn up again in a modern airport built on an alleged underground reptilian base. Gargoyles are symbols of the reptilians and that is why you will find them at Denver Airport. The capstone or dedication stone at the airport is marked with the classic compass symbol of the Freemasons and it stands in part of the terminal called The Great Hall, another Freemasonic term. On a wall is a grotesque mural full of malevolent symbolism, including three caskets with dead females in them: a Jewish girl, a Native American and a black woman. Another girl is holding a Mayan tablet that tells of the destruction of civilisation. A huge character, described as a 'green Darth Vader' by Alex Christopher, stands over a destroyed city with a sword in his hand and women are walking along a road holding dead babies. All the children of the world are depicted taking weapons from each country and handing them to a figure of a German boy with an iron fist and an anvil in his hand. Denver is apparently scheduled to be the headquarters of the Western sector of the United States under the fascist global state called the New World Order which is planned beyond the year 2000. Atlanta is said to be the centre for the Eastern sector and I remember thinking some years ago how the design of Denver and Atlanta airports were so similar – now I know why.

Colorado is a major centre for the New World Order and the Queen of England, under another name, has been buying up land there. As you will see later, the British Royal Family are massively involved in this story and so is the murder of Diana, Princess of Wales. One of Christopher's main contacts was a guy called Phil Schneider, the son of a German U-boat commander in World War II, who was commissioned to build a number of deep underground bases in the United States. I saw some of his lectures on video when he began to speak out publicly about the underground network of bases, cities and tunnels throughout the United States. He later died in very suspicious circumstances which were meant to appear like 'suicide'. Schneider said that Denver Airport was connected to a deep underground base that went down at least eight levels. It included a 4.5 square mile underground city and a vast base, he said. Other contacts who have been underground at Denver Airport claim that there are large numbers of human slaves, many of them children, working there under the control of the reptilians. Two of the bases that Phil Schneider claims to have helped to build are the infamous Area 51 in Nevada and Dulce in New Mexico, which is connected by the tunnel network to the Los Alamos National Laboratory. I have been to Los Alamos and the vibes are simply horrible. After speaking about the reptilian involvement in human affairs on the *Sightings* radio show in the United States, I was sent an account by an army private stationed on the surface at Dulce. He realised there was something 'mighty odd' about the place, but could not explain why. He remembered:

"...I was working on a routine job when another of the young enlistees, a mechanic, came in with a small rush job he wanted welded at once. He had the print and proceeded to show me exactly what he wanted. We are both bending over the bench in front of the welder when I happened to look directly into his face. It seemed to suddenly become covered in a semi-transparent film or cloud. His features faded and in their place appeared a "thing" with bulging eyes, no hair and scales for skin."

He later saw the same thing happen to a guard at the Dulce front gate. Other witnesses have spoken of seeing more reptilian-chameleons working at the Madigan Military Hospital near Fort Lewis, south of Seattle in Washington State. Again I have spoken in that general area and found it all extremely strange, not least there being a 'New age' centre close to Fort Lewis. Jason Bishop III has conducted extensive studies into the Dulce operation and established the involvement of a cartel that I expose in ...*And The Truth Shall Set You Free*, including organisations like the Rand Corporation, General Electric, AT & T, Hughes Aircraft, Northrop Corporation, Sandia Corporation, Stanford Research Institute, Walsh Construction, the Bechtel Corporation, the Colorado School of Mines and so on. Bechtel (Beck-tul) is a major link in the Brotherhood–reptile network. There are at least seven levels underground at Dulce, probably more, and Bishop has compiled accounts of workers there who have described what they have seen. Their accounts mirror the descriptions of the Anunnaki in the Sumerian Texts as they interbred species to produce hideous hybrids of many types. This is what workers have said about Dulce:

"Level number six is privately called "Nightmare Hall", it holds the Genetic Labs. Reports from workers who have seen bizarre experimentation, are as follows: 'I have seen multi-legged "humans" that look like half human/half octopus. Also reptilian-humans and furry creatures that have hands like humans and cry like a baby, it mimics human words... also a huge mixture of lizard-humans in cages.' There are fish, seals, birds and mice that can hardly be considered those species. There are several cages (and vats) of winged humanoids, grotesque bat-like creatures... but three and a half to seven feet tall. Gargoyle-like beings and Draco-reptoids.

"Level number seven is worse, row after row of thousands of humans and human mixtures in cold storage. Here, too, are embryo storage vats of humanoids in various stages of development. (*One worker said:*) '...I frequently encountered humans in cages, usually dazed or drugged, but sometimes they cried and begged for help. We were told they were hopelessly insane, and involved in high risk drug tests to cure insanity. We were told never to try to speak to them at all. At the beginning we believed that story. Finally, in 1978, a small group of workers discovered the truth.'"[42]

This discovery apparently led to the 'Dulce Wars', a battle between humans and the extraterrestrials in 1979 when many scientists and military personnel were killed. Phil Schneider claimed to have taken part in a shoot out with the aliens at Dulce in which he was hit by a laser gun which cut open his chest. Certainly he had a fantastic scar down his chest, as he revealed publicly. The base was closed for a time as a result of this conflict, but has since reopened. Another reptilian underground base is under Boynton Canyon in Sedona, Arizona. The centre of the base is believed to be in the, appropriately named, Secret Canyon. Similar bases and underground cities exist across the world and they are connected by tunnels with incredibly fast 'tube-shuttles'. The tunnels are built very quickly by technology like the Subterrene, a nuclear-powered machine that melts the rock and shapes it into the tunnel walls. It was developed at Los Alamos. It is significant that underground nuclear tests were carried out in Nevada and New Mexico, the location of many deep underground facilities which have been connected with reptilians. Were those 'tests' located there to open up vast underground caverns? Another theme I have had from many contacts is that the reptilians can feed off nuclear energy.

What they look like

Summarising all the research I have read, the people I have met, and the accounts of those who claim to have experienced these reptile humanoids or reptilians, the following appears to be the case. There are many sub and crossbreed races of the reptilians. Their élite is known by UFO researchers as the Draco. These are the 'big boys' in every sense and they are usually between seven and twelve feet tall. They have wings which are flaps of skin supported by long ribs.[43] The wings can be folded back against the body and they are the origin of the term "winged serpent". They are also the origin of the term 'fallen angels' and the winged gargoyles are symbolic of these Draco. The cape worn by Count Dracula is symbolic of these wings and the character of Dracula in the Bram Stoker stories is said to be a fallen angel. The winged Draco are also known as the Dragon Race and some of the ancient gods were described and depicted as birdmen. This could be one of the origins of the Phoenix and eagle in Brotherhood symbolism, as well as the more esoteric meanings. The biblical Satan is depicted as a reptilian, too.

Some of the Draco reptilian hierarchy are apparently white or albino white and not the usual green or brown, and this connects with the description of the strange 'albino' lizard humanoid in the building in Aurora, near Denver. The Draco are the 'royalty' of the reptilians and the highest caste are the albino whites, who apparently have conical horns midway between the brow and the top of the skull. This struck me immediately because the ancient 'gods' and royalty were depicted as wearing a horned headdress, symbolic of these 'royal' reptilians, I'm certain. Other species, like the soldier class and scientists, are known as Reptoids. They don't have wings, but all of them are cold-blooded.[44] Their scales are much larger on their backs and they have three fingers with an opposing thumb. They have three toes with a fourth towards the side of their ankle and their claws are short and blunt. They have large, cat-like eyes which glow red and a mouth that looks more like a slit. Some have eyes which are described as black and others are white with flame-coloured vertical pupils. Again this is what the lady described in the Aurora case. The reptilians are five to twelve feet tall and they are the 'giants' described so widely in the ancient legends and records. Some have tails, others do not. One of their other planets of influence long ago is reckoned to have been Mars and so were reptile crossbreeds among the white Martians even before they came here? Zecharia Sitchin also speculates that the Anunnaki went to Mars before coming to Earth. This would certainly fit the picture and it could well be that the white Martians in Brian Desborough's scenario and the Annunaki have long been genetically connected. A high priestess of the Brotherhood hierarchy who has broken out of their clutches, at least at the time I spoke with her, says that the reptilian Anunnaki invaded Mars long ago and the white race of Martians eventually left that planet for Earth. The Anunnaki on Mars followed, she said, although I have no doubt that some are there now in underground bases. Whenever one of the NASA Mars probes is in danger of letting the public see something they shouldn't, the link mysteriously goes down or the probe disappears altogether. What is without question is that the white race, whatever its origin, has been the main vehicle of the Anunnaki crossbreeding programme for the takeover of Planet Earth. Researchers believe that the reptilians are the controllers of the so-called Greys, the classic extraterrestrial figure of modern times with their big black eyes. The Greys feature in most of the abduction accounts. Jason Bishop III in his writings on this subject says that the hierarchy of control is: Draco (winged reptilian); Draco (non-winged); Greys; Humans. There also appears to be a reptilian 'alliance' with some other extraterrestrial groups.

It is suggested that human sacrifice to the 'gods' in the ancient world, particularly of children, was for the benefit of reptilians who demanded these rituals (a trait of the reptile brain is ritualism). I am sure this is true and it will be extremely relevant in the latter part of this book. At the moment of death by sacrifice a form of adrenaline surges through the body and accumulates at the base of the brain and is, apparently, most potent in children.[45] This is what the reptilians and their crossbreeds want, it is said, and they certainly feed off human blood and flesh. These ancient sacrifices were literally to the gods, the Anunnaki reptilians, and they continue today. The common theme of all research into the reptilians is that they are emotionless and without sentiment and, at the fourth dimensional level, they feed off the energy of low vibrational human emotions like fear, guilt and aggression. When we emit such emotions their energy can't be seen in this world because it resonates to the lower fourth dimensional frequency and there it is absorbed by the reptilians. The more of these emotions that can be stimulated, the more energy the reptilians have to work with. Thus we have the encouragement of wars, human genocide, the mass slaughter of animals, sexual perversions which create highly charged negative energy, and black magic ritual and sacrifice which takes place on a scale that will stagger those who have not studied the subject.

Sons of the gods

The reptilian breeding programme appears to have produced an Anunnaki-human hybrid (Adam?) around 200,000–300,000 years ago. I'm sure other extraterrestrial races have also interbred with humanity to produce the glorious variety of Earth peoples, but I am focusing here on the reptilian group because of their desire to control and manipulate human affairs. Clearly, the farther you go back the murkier the story becomes, but there is enough supporting and cross-referencing evidence to present the themes of what happened. The more I look at this, the more it is clear to me that what the reptilians did on Mars they have done here. They infiltrated the home population through interbreeding and took the place over. It seems to me that there were already reptile-Aryan bloodlines among the Martians when they came to Earth. One of the main locations for the Anunnaki and the Martians or Aryans, particularly during and after the Venus cataclysm of around 4,800 BC, were the mountains of Turkey, Iran and Kurdistan, and it was from here that they and their hybrids re-emerged when the waters receded. It was they who created the 'instant' advanced civilisations in the low lands of Sumer, Egypt, Babylon and the Indus Valley. A particular centre for the Anunnaki reptilians would seem to have been the Caucasus Mountains and this is an area that will appear again and again in this story. I feel there was a major breeding programme in this region, probably underground, which produced a very large number of hybrid reptile-human crossbreeds. One area of research that is highly relevant to this region are the number of people with Rh negative or rhesus negative blood. Often rhesus negative babies turn blue immediately after birth. This is the origin of the term 'blue bloods' for royal bloodlines and other terms like 'true blue'. It is speculated that the 'blue' bloodlines could be of Martian decent and from wherever the Martian bloodlines came from before that. Far more white people are Rh negative than blacks or Asians.

The genes of the albino-white 'royal' Draco appear to have been used to create the 'royal' reptile-human hybrid bloodlines which have been used to rule the world since ancient times. These were the ones known to the ancients as the demi-gods, who were given the task of middlemen, controlling the population and running the world according to the Agenda of their reptile masters. What is clear is that while the Annunaki interbred with many Earth races, the white race has been their main vehicle for taking over the planet and the 'royal' Draco at the top of their hierarchy are albino white. Significantly, when you look at ancient accounts, many of their hybrid creations had blond hair and blue eyes. A major change would seem to have taken place soon after the Venus upheavals because the Ubaid culture (5,000–4,000 BC), in what is now Iraq, worshipped gods who were depicted as lizard-humanoids while the Sumerians (4,000–5,000 BC), who lived in the same area, depict their gods as very human. This change, and the crossbreeding programme in the Caucasus region, are fundamentally connected, I'm sure. The Anunnaki–human crossbreed élite was described by the Sumerians and there are many other accounts of the interbreeding of extraterrestrials and humans, or the 'gods' and 'sky people' interbreeding with humanity. This is most famously noted in Genesis where it says:

> "When men began to increase in number on the earth and daughters were born to them, the sons of God saw that the daughters of men were beautiful, and they married

any of them they chose... The Nefilim were on the earth in those days –
and also afterwards – when the sons of God went to the daughters of men
and had children by them. They were the heroes of old, men of renown."
Genesis 6:1-4

According to the translations of Zecharia Sitchin, the word Nefilim relates to
"Those Who Decended" while others say it means "the fallen ones" or "those who
have fallen". The word 'renown' in that passage in Genesis is translated from the
Sumerian word shem. This has been translated in the Bible as relating to 'name', as
in making a name for yourself as a man of renown. Sitchin says the real meaning of
shem is 'sky vehicle'. He says it comes from the root, shu-mu, which means 'that
which is a MU', and a MU was a flying craft, he says. So 'men of renown' becomes
'men or people of the sky vehicles'. It was these who interbred with human
women. This passage in Genesis, I would suggest, tells of the interbreeding
between the extraterrestrials or inner terrestrials with humans to produce the
reptile-human hybrids. The term 'sons of God' in fact comes from the Hebrew,
bene-ha-elohim, which really translates as 'sons of the gods'. The early offspring of
these genetic encounters were the giants of legend and there are many records of
such hybrids being born. There are numerous accounts throughout the ancient
world, on every continent, of a giant race and the biblical Goliath could well have
been symbolic of these people. The Native Americans have many tales of the Star
People coming down from the skies to breed with human women and Alex
Christopher says that a common denominator in the abduction of humans by
reptilians in the United States appears to relate to the person's bloodline,
particularly those that go back to Native Americans or ancient Indians. The Hopi,
you will recall, speak of originating within the Earth. The Ethiopian text, the Kebra
Nagast (Nagas were Indian shape-shifting 'serpent gods'), is thousands of years
old, and it refers to the enormous size of the babies produced from the sexual or
genetic unions of humans and the 'gods'. It tells how: "...the daughters of Cain
with whom the angels (extraterrestrials) had conceived... were unable to bring
forth their children, and they died." It describes how some of these giant babies
were delivered by caesarean section: "...having split open the bellies of their
mothers they came forth by their navels."[46] In the ancient Hebrew text, the Book of
Noah, and its derivative, the Book of Enoch, a strange birth is described of a non-
human child, who turns out to be Noah of Great Flood fame. References to this
also appear in the Dead Sea Scrolls, the records of the Essene Community in
Palestine 2,000 years ago which included much material from the Book of Enoch.
The strange child the texts describe is the son of Lamech. He is said to be unlike a
human being and more like 'the children of the angels in heaven'. Lamech's child,
Noah, is described as white skinned and blond-haired with eyes that made the
whole house 'shine like the Sun'. Blond-haired, blue-eyed beings with laser-like
eyes is a description for mysterious people or 'gods' which spans thousands of
years to the present day and appear in cultures across the world. Lamech questions
his wife about the father of the child:

"Behold, I thought then within my heart that conception was (*due*) to the Watchers and the Holy Ones...and to the Nephilim...and my heart was troubled within me because of this child."[47]

In the Shahnemeh or Book of Kings, the legendary history of Iran completed in 1010 AD by the Arab poet, Firdowsi, he describes the birth of a baby called Zal, the son of a king called Sam. Again the king is horrified by the unearthly appearance of his child who has a very large body 'as clean as silver', hair as white as an old man's and 'like snow', and a face compared with the Sun. Sam calls his son a demon child, a child of the daevas – the Watchers. Like the patriarchs of the Old Testament, the Iranians appeared to have an aversion to children born with extremely white features. And who is said to be extremely white, albino white? The royal hierarchy of the Draco. The text of the Shahnemeh says of Zal:

"No human being of this earth
Could give such a monster birth,
He must be of the Demon race,
Though human still in form and face,
If not a Demon, he at least,
Appears a party-coloured beast."[48]

Zal later marries a foreign princess called Rudabeh, the daughter of Mehrab, the king of Karbul, and a descendant of the Serpent king, Zahhak, who was said to have ruled Iran for a thousand years. This was one of the reptilian bloodlines and in keeping with this, Rudabeh is described as tall as a teak tree, ivory white etc, the familiar features of the Watcher-human offspring. These descriptions abound for the royal lines of Iran and the Near East, as do their comparison with trees because of their great height. It seems from their texts that you required the Nefilim-Watcher physical characteristics to qualify to be king.

Figure 5: The ancient caduceus, symbol of the modern medical profession and symbolic of many things, including, quite possibly, the twin spirals of DNA or perhaps representing a particular wavelength or frequency.

This, no doubt, is the origin of the 'divine right of kings', the right to rule by virtue of your family bloodline, a system which continued when these lines expanded into Europe. Even the British title of Sir, conferred by the Queen on her selected subjects, comes from an ancient snake-goddess (reptilian) called Sir, which relates to the Anunnaki goddess, Ninlil or Ninkharsag, in the Sumerian tablets. Her husband, Enlil, was called the Splendid Serpent of the shining eyes. His brother, Enki, was also known as a serpent and his emblem was two entwined serpents, the symbol of his 'cult centre' at Eridu, and of the modern medical profession. The symbol is known as the caduceus (*see* **Figure 5**). This information comes from the Sumerian Tablets as translated by Zecharia Sitchin and described in his books. Therefore I found it staggering that Sitchin personally told me there was no evidence of a serpent race and advised me to cease my research into such matters. The idea that there is no evidence is simply ludicrous, so why would Sitchin say that to me? He was adamant that I should end this line of research. I have absolutely no doubt that the Anunnaki and the Watchers are the same reptilian race – the 'serpents with the shining eyes' identified by Christian and Barbara O'Brien in their work, *Genius Of The Few*.[49]

Author and researcher, Andrew Collins, says he has a Canaanite copper figurine depicting one of their gods of around 2000 BC.[50] It has a serpentine neck and a head shaped like the hood of a cobra which curls over to form a snake-like headdress.[51] Over the thousands of years since these royal reptile-human hybrid bloodlines were created, they have become more integrated into the general population and less physically obvious, but the basic genetic structure remains and the Brotherhood maintains very detailed genetic records of who has it and who doesn't. Christian and Barbara O'Brien say in *Genius Of The Few* that if the Annunaki had interbred with humanity hundreds of thousands of years ago and then interbred with them again about 30,000 years ago, the result of the second interbreeding would be a genetic structure that was 75% Anunnaki and 25% human. I think there was another breeding programme far more recently, after the Venus flood of about 7,000 years ago. These later bloodlines would have been even more Anunnaki than previous versions, of course. These are the reptilian crossbreeds who run the world today and it this profusion of reptilian genes which allows such people to shape-shift into reptilians and back into an apparently human form. These bloodlines also have the ability to produce an extremely powerful hypnotic stare, just like a snake hypnotising its prey, and this is the origin of the term 'giving someone the evil eye'. All this is the real reason for the obsession with blood and the interbreeding of the 'blue blood' families and their offshoots. This is why since the earliest times of known history, the blue blood heirs married their half-sisters and cousins, just as the Anunnaki did according to the Sumerian Tablets. The most important gene in this succession is passed on by the female line, so the choice of female sexual partner has been vital to them.

It is highly significant that the 'serpent king' bloodline should originate from Iran because it is from this region of Iran, Kurdistan, Armenia, Turkey and the Caucasus Mountains, that these reptile-human bloodlines emerged to take over the world. A Brotherhood insider, a Russian, said there was a massive vortex, an interdimensional gateway, in the Caucasus Mountains where the extraterrestrials entered this dimension. That would explain a great deal. The name Iran comes from the earlier Airy-ana or Air-an, which means Land of the Aryas or Aryans.[52] Still today there are two distinct races in Kurdistan, the olive skinned of medium height with dark eyes, and the much taller, white skinned people, often with blue eyes. You will note that these traits were considered the 'Master Race' by the Nazis and this was because the Nazis knew the history and the connection with the reptilians. Andrew Collins in his book, *From The Ashes Of Angels*, presents compelling evidence that the biblical Garden of Eden was high up in this region of Iran-Kurdistan and, of course, the theme of the serpent is at the heart of the Eden story. In neighbour-ing Media, the kings were known by the Iranians as Mâr which means snake in Persian.[53] Mars = snake? They were called the 'dragon dynasty of Media' or the 'descendants of the dragon'.[54] I have no doubt that the reptilian Draco interbred with humans to produce crossbreeds within the white race and, indeed, there are many people around the world today who claim to have bred with reptilians. By 2,200 BC the Royal Court of the Dragon had been founded in Egypt by the priests of Mendes and this still continues today, 4,000 years later, as the Imperial and Royal Court of the Dragon Sovereignty, now headquartered in Britain. Some people call this the Brother-hood of the Snake. The early kings of Sumer, Egypt, and later, Israel, were anointed at their coronation with the 'fat of the Dragon' which was the fat of the sacred crocodile. The croc was known in Egypt as a messeh and from this comes the Hebrew term 'Messiah' which means Anointed One. The kings of the succession were also known as 'Dragons' and all this symbolism relates to the knowledge that these royal families were the bloodlines of the reptile-human crossbreeds. When many kingdoms joined together in battle, they appointed a king of kings and he was known as the Great Dragon or… Draco. The famous Celtic title, Pendragon, is a version of this. Kingship actually originates from the word kin or blood relative and kin-ship became kingship. Just to emphasise the point about the reptile bloodlines here, the name the Egyptians gave to their sacred messeh or crocodile was… Draco. This also became a symbol of the Egyptian Therapeutate and their branch in Israel called the Essenes, and it was represented as a sea serpent or Bistea Neptunis by the 'royal' Merovingians and their decendents in France. The same tribe, all of them. If you look in the picture section you will see an ancient Egyptian depiction of a 'god' on the temple wall at Saqquara – it is a non-human reptilian figure with what appear to be wings.

Blond-haired, blue-eyed beings with eyes like lasers are still being reported. An American friend told me of an experience her father had in the early 1970s. They lived in Turkey at the time where he worked at a listening post for American Military Intelligence. He came home one night in a terrible state. When asked what was wrong, he just mumbled: "The world is not like we think it is". Although he rarely drank, he asked for a scotch, and then another. As he relaxed he told his daughter of a communication he had taken that day from the pilot of a plane which was stationed at the Turkish base. The pilot reported that he was flying near the North Pole when suddenly his engines stopped and all the electrical systems switched off. The plane then gently lowered itself vertically to the ground and to his disbelief a mountain top opened up and the plane came to rest inside. What he saw was a scene straight from James Bond. He got out of the plane wondering what the hell was going on and he was met by tall, blond-haired people with 'pearl' coloured skin and 'bluish-purple' eyes which appeared electrically charged somehow: like laser eyes. They all wore long white gowns and, perhaps significantly, this is how the central-South America 'god' known as Quetzalcoatl was described. They also wore a Maltese Cross medallion on a chain. The pilot's memory was hazy about what happened after he first met 'ole blue eyes', but he remembered walking into a room and seeing a group of these beings sitting around a conference table. Eventually, he was taken back to his plane and as it rose from the mountain his engines and electronics restarted. Now having heard the descriptions of these beings by a modern US pilot, look at how the Book of Enoch describes the Watchers:

"And there appeared to me two men very tall, such as I have never seen on earth. And their faces shone like the sun, and their eyes were like burning lamps... Their hands were brighter than snow."[55]

This would connect also with the ancient description of 'gods' as the 'shining ones'. There is certainly much more to our history than we are being told and much more happening on this planet today than most people could even begin to believe. Many extraterrestrial races, not only the reptilians, operate in and around the Earth on this or higher dimensions. Beings from Orion and the Pleiades are among many other races reported by abductees and researchers to be interacting with humans. From what I hear from Brotherhood insiders who have seen some of these extraterrestrials, the Orions (a cruel, but beautiful race according to my contacts) have some kind of alliance with the reptilians. I am sure that the biblical angels were the Watchers, the reptilians, winged and otherwise. The very term 'sons of the gods' is translated in the Septuagint, the Greek version of the Old Testament, as angelos – angels. It appears from my research that there are different reptilian factions: those who are more positive in their attitude to humanity and those who wish to dominate and control. They both became known as Watchers or angels, the latter as fallen angels. It could well be that the legends of St Michael casting the dragon onto the Earth for the final battle and St George defeating the dragon, relate to the long-standing conflict between the genuine white Martians and the reptilian Anunnaki. St Michael and St George are ancient Phoenician heroes from the very region of the world where the Anunnaki instigated their crossbreeding programme and, for a long time, operated openly as reptilians. In the last book of the Bible, the Book of Revelation, we see the clear connection made between the being known as Satan and the serpent or reptile:

"And the great dragon was cast down, the old serpent, he that is called the Devil and Satan, the deceiver of the whole world; he was cast down to earth and his angels were cast down with him."[56]

"...And he laid hold on the dragon, the old serpent, which is the Devil and Satan, and bound him for a thousand years, and cast him into the abyss, and shut it, and sealed it over him, that he should deceive the nations no more."[57]

In a Dead Sea Scroll fragment translated by the Hebrew scholar, Robert Eisenman, there is a description of a watcher called Belial (Bel?), who is described as the Prince of Darkness and the King of Evil. He is said to be terrifying in his appearance – like a serpent with a visage like a viper. One of the main angelic groups in Hebrew lore is the Seraphim or 'fiery serpents' and the Watchers are very much connected to the description of serpents. In the Persian teachings they also talk of a being they describe as 'the old serpent having two feet', just as the Book of Enoch features walking serpents. When you consider that the Draco royal leadership is said to be up to 12 feet tall and white skinned, indeed albino white, 'whiter than snow', it again relates to the very white skin of the giant Watcher-human hybrid babies described in the Book of Enoch and elsewhere. And, I should emphasise, the birth of the human-Watcher child in the Book of Enoch is that of Noah. If this be so, Noah is, in fact, a reptile-human hybrid and many peoples have sought to claim descendence from Noah – descendence from the reptilian Watchers and Anunnaki. In Hebrew myth, the Nefilim are described as awwim which means devastators or serpents. In the Dead Sea Scrolls, Noah is described as looking like "the children of the (*fallen*) angels of heaven" whose "conception was (*due*) to the Watchers... and to the Nefilim". In Jewish lore, Eve is seen as the ancestral mother of the Nefilim and associated with the Hebrew words meaning life and snake. Eve was, of course, tempted by the serpent according to Old Testament myth and other sources. In Chapter 69 of the Book of Enoch we find that among the Watchers who revealed the secrets to humans was Gadreel, the fallen angel who has been identified with tempting Eve. The Book of Enoch was banned by the Roman Church which sought to deny the earlier Christian belief in the existence of flesh and blood angels and fallen angels occupying physical bodies and interbreeding with humans. This was to stop the masses understanding the true situation. But the Freemasons, who control the Roman Catholic Church today along with other Brotherhood offshoots, have always looked upon Enoch as one of their legendary founders. The very name Enoch means 'initiated'.

The theme of the fallen angels giving forbidden secrets to humanity can be found in the Book of Enoch and other works. Among these tellers of secrets is Azazel, who taught the art of metal making, and Shemyaza, who taught the magical arts. These tales spawned many later heroes based on this theme, the most famous of which is the Greek god, Prometheus, who is said to have stolen fire (knowledge) from the gods and given it to humans (selected humans). A gold statue of Prometheus stands in the Rockefeller Center in New York. The Rockefellers are reptilian full-bloods and therefore are fully aware of the true significance and background of the Prometheus legend. Incidentally, the Watcher called Azazel is the origin of the goat head in Satanic ritual and the term 'scapegoat'. According to the Book of Leviticus, the Israelites would sacrifice two male goats at Yom Kippur, the Day of Atonement. One was offered to God and the other to Azazel. The priest placed both hands on the head of the Azazel goat and confessed the sins of the people. The goat would then be taken into the wilderness and plunged over a cliff, symbolising the fallen angel Azazel, who was seen as bound and chained in the wilderness – the 'abyss' in the language of the Book of Revelation – which I think is imprisonment in the lower fourth dimension. From this comes the ancient theme of the scapegoat which manifested in one form as the symbolic story of 'Jesus'. The goat head of Azazel, a fallen angel-reptilian, is symbolised by the inverted pentagram of Satanism.

We can debate the details and we should because there is a vast amount of information still to be uncovered. I have an endless stream of questions myself. But there are some emerging themes: extraterrestrial races have been visiting the Earth with varying intent for probably millions of years and their interbreeding has created the many racial streams. In the distant past there have been highly advanced technological civilisations based on this extraterrestrial knowledge – a Golden Age as the ancients called it. Around 450,000 years ago the Anunnaki arrived, a reptilian race led by the winged, albino-white Draco, and they sought to take over the planet. It is probable that they had by this time also settled and occupied Mars. For a long time the Anunnaki lived openly as reptilians, but for whatever reason, possibly hostility from other extraterrestrial races and humanity, they literally went undercover. They set out to hijack the planet by appearing to be human. This included a crossbreeding programme which created human-reptilian hybrid bloodlines through which they could operate from the lower fourth dimension. The fourth dimensional reptilians wear their human bodies like a genetic overcoat and when one body dies the same reptilian 'moves house' to another body and continues the Agenda into another generation. You could think of it as wearing and discarding space suits. These creatures are the ones the psychics see as reptilians inside human physical bodies. It seems that they need to occupy a very reptilian dominated genetic stream to do this, hence certain bloodlines always end up in the positions of power. Other less pure crossbreed human-reptilians are those bodies which are possessed by a reptilian consciousness from the fourth dimension and these are people who psychics see as essentially human, but 'overshadowed' by a reptilian. The crossbreeding to infuse reptilian genetics into these bloodlines makes this possession far easier than for those with fewer reptilian genes. This is why the Brotherhood maintains such detailed records of the genetic lines. They then know which people can be possessed more easily than others. The reptilians seek, however, to influence everyone by stimulating the behaviour patterns of the reptile region of the brain – hierarchical thinking, aggression, conflict, division, lack of compassion and a need for ritual. By ritual I don't just mean dressing up in a Satanic ceremony. There are many examples of the human obsession with ritual, including doing the same things at the same time, day after day, week after week. The reptilians have used the white race as their main route to global control, but they have crossbred with all races including the Chinese, Japanese, Arabs and those known as Jewish. All this allows the reptilians to control apparently unconnected people and organisations. It is the extraterrestrial version of members of the same secret society working in many places of influence, while the rest of the population have no idea that they are connected. You can look at a series of apparently different human beings in different positions of power who come to the same conclusion and agree the same policy. That would appear to be a policy born of democracy and open debate. But what if the same force is controlling all of them? That would then be dictatorship, but unless you knew the true situation how could you tell? This is what is happening with the reptilians working through human bodies and the secret society network these bloodlines have created or infiltrated.

The Book of Enoch says that those born of the Nefilim blood (the reptile-human hybrids) are, because of their ancestral spirit, destined to "afflict, oppress, destroy, attack, do battle and work destruction on the earth".[58] In other words, those bodies can be possessed by their 'ancestral spirit' – the reptilians of the lower fourth dimension. In the United States there is an organisation called the Sons of Jared, named after the father of Enoch. They pledge an 'implacable war' against the descendants of the Watchers who "as notorious pharaohs, kings and dictators, have throughout history dominated mankind". In their publication, the *Jaredite Advocate*, they condemn the Watchers as "like super-gangsters, a celestial Mafia ruling the world".[59] Many people ask me how today's Brotherhood Elite can cause such death, destruction and suffering, without showing any emotion. At least some of the reptile genetic streams do not appear to feel emotion like humans and they seem to be far more ruthless, too. I've just described George Bush, Henry Kissinger, David Rockefeller and so on, and that's not surprising because they are examples of the reptile race at work in the human sphere.

What I have outlined in this chapter will astonish even most of those who have followed my work and supported it over the years, and I understand that. But I have learned from enormous, and at times extreme, experience to follow the flow of life and go where it takes me. When I feel the rhythm of life, I dance. When I hear it speak to me, I listen. I go where the music takes me, no matter how incredible it may be or what consequences it may have for my life. For those who haven't tried that yet, you will be amazed at what an adventure life suddenly becomes, what knowledge you can access, grasp and understand, when you go with the flow and cease to wage war with it for fear of being different. For most people so often the head gets in the way because they fear stepping outside of convention. They fear what other people will think and say about them. But how can you expose the unthinkable unless you think the unthinkable? Are we saying that we know it all? Is there nothing left to know? Of course there is. We know only a fraction of it all. And what has been the force that has brought us even to our current state of knowledge? Those who have dared to think and communicate the unthinkable. Without such people the human race cannot evolve; it just runs on the spot, living within a perpetual prison of the mind. What was that they said? Humans will fly? Ridiculous! That we can travel beyond the speed of sound? Crazy! That we can create babies in a test tube and clone the human and animal species? Ludicrous! Yet all and more have been done by those who have thought the unthinkable while the masses mocked. Give it a try before you forget how to do it. Think beyond the bounds of what you are told is reality.

To refuse to do so is the ultimate prison cell, the ultimate mental and emotional stagnation – the ultimate control. Indeed it is the way we have been controlled since this whole scam began.

■ SOURCES

1   Dr Arthur David Horn, *Humanity's Extraterrestrial Origins, ET Influences On Humankind's Biological And Cultural Evolution* (A and L Horn, PD Box 1632, Mount Shasta, California, 96067, 1994).

2   Jason Bishop III, *Matrix 11*, compiled by Valdamar Valerian (Arcturus Book Service, USA, 1990), p 96.

3   Rev John Bathhurst Deane, *The Worship Of The Serpent* (J. G. and F. Rivington, London, 1833).

4   *Bible Myths*, p 11.

5   Ibid, p 15.

6   Ibid, p 12.

7   Francis Hitching, *The World Atlas Of Mysteries* (Pan Books, London, 1981), p 10, section entitled, Death of the Dinosaurs.

8   Ibid.

9   Ibid.

10   John Rhodes, the Reptoid website, http: //www.reptoids.com

11   Dale Russell, *Exponential Evolution: Implications For Intelligent Extraterrestrial Life* (Advanced Space Research, 1983).

12   *The World Atlas Of Mysteries*, p 159.

13   Ibid.

14   Herbert S. Zim and Robert H. Baker, *Stars, A Golden Guide* (Golden Press, New York, 1985), p 58.

15   Graham Hancock, *Quest For The Lost Civilisation* (Channel Four Television, 1998).

16   Professor Phillip Calahan, *Ancient Mysteries And Modern Visions* (Acres, Kansas City, USA, 1984).

17   See the John Rhodes website, http: //www.reptoids.com

18   John Rhodes, writing on his website.

19   William Bramley, *Gods Of Eden* (Avon Books, New York).

20   *Nexus* magazine, April–May 1994, pp 52–54.

21   "Explorations In Grand Canyon", *Arizona Gazette*, April 5th 1909.

22   John Rhodes, *The Human-Reptilian Connection*, privately published and distributed paper in 1993.

23   Ibid.

24   Ibid.

25   Ibid.

26   Ibid.

27   Cathy O'Brien and Mark Phillips, *Trance Formation Of America* (Reality Marketing Inc, Las Vegas, Nevada, USA, 1995).

28   Ibid, pp 165, 166.

29   Ibid, p 165.

30   Ibid, pp 209–210.

31   Ibid.

32   Ibid, p 174.

33   Hunter S. Thompson, *Fear And Loathing In Las Vegas* (Vintage Books, New York, 1998, first published in 1971).

34   *Cymatics, The Healing Nature Of Sound*, video available from MACROmedia, PO Box 279, Epping, NH 03042, USA.

35   *Los Angeles Times* and *Herald Examiner*, 21 July 1988.

36   *The Arrival*, Steelworks Films, 1988.

37   *They Live*, Alive Films, 1988.

38   *Alien Resurrection*, 20th Century Fox, 1997.

39   *V: The Final Battle*, Warner Brothers Television, 1984, and Warner Brothers Home Video, 1995.

40   Alex Christopher, *Pandora's Box Volumes I* and *2*, available from Pandora's Box, 2663 Valleydale Road, Suite 126, Birmingham, Alabama 35224.

41   Alex Christopher speaking on KSEO Radio, USA, on April 26th 1996, transcript by Leading Edge Research Group.

42   Jason Bishop III, quoted in *Leading Edge*.

43   Jason Bishop III, *Matrix 11*, compiled by Valdamar Valerian (Arcturus Book Service, USA, 1990), p 96.

44   Ibid.

45   *Matrix 11*, p 100c–100d.

46   Andrew Collins, *From The Ashes of Angels, The Forbidden Legacy Of A Fallen Race* (Signet Books, London, 1997), p 35.

47   *A Genesis Apocryphon*, the translation of part of the Dead Sea Scrolls by Naham Avigad and Yigael Yadin, published in 1956 by the Hebrew University in Jerusalem.

48   *Firdowsi, The Shah Nameh Of The Persian Poet Firdausi*, translated by James Atkinson (Frederick Warne, London, 1886).

49   Christian O'Brien, with Joy O'Brien, *The Genius Of The Few – The Story Of Those Who Founded The Garden of Eden* (Turnstone Press, Wellingborough, England, 1985).

50   *From The Ashes Of Angels*, pp 268, 269.

51   Ibid.

52   L. A. Waddell, *The Phoenician Origin Of Britons, Scots And Anglo Saxons* (The Christian Book Club of America, Hawthorne, California, first published 1924), p 65.

53   *From The Ashes Of Angels*, p 191.

54   Ibid.

55   Second Book of Enoch, 1:4-5.

56   Revelation, 12:9.

57   Ibid, 20:2-3.

58   Geza Vermes, *The Dead Sea Scrolls In English* (Penguin Books, Harmondsworth, 1990).

59   Ibid, p 7.

CHAPTER THREE

The Babylonian Brotherhood

As the flood waters receded after the Venus cataclysm the survivors came down from the mountains and up from within the Earth. They settled on the lowlands and plains and began to rebuild. This was when Sumer, Egypt and the civilisation in the Indus Valley suddenly appeared at a very high level of technological advancement, although they had existed before and were now restored after the upheavals.

The Sumerian society began at the peak of its development because of this sudden infusion of knowledge and the white Aryan race, originally from Mars, expanded out from the Caucasus Mountains and the Near East down into Sumer, Egypt and the Indus Valley where, as even conventional history agrees, highly advanced societies spontaneously emerged. However within this white race, and others also, was a genetic stream I will call reptile-Aryan or reptile-human. Whenever I use the term Aryan I am referring to the white race. These were the crossbreed bloodlines created from the genetic manipulation of the Anunnaki. The major centre for the reptile-Aryan bloodlines, in the ancient world after the flood waters receded, was Babylon in the south of the Sumer region alongside the River Euphrates. A closer look at the evidence appears to date the foundation of Babylon far earlier than previously believed and it was one of the first cities of the post-flood era. It was here that the mystery schools and secret societies were formed which were to span the globe in the thousands of years that followed. The Brotherhood which controls the world today is the modern expression of the Babylonian Brotherhood of reptile-Aryan priests and 'royalty' which came together there after the flood. It was in Babylon in this post-flood period from around 6,000 years ago that the foundation beliefs – manipulated beliefs – of today's world religions were established to control and rule the people.

The founder of Babylon according to ancient texts and legend was Nimrod who reigned with his wife, Queen Semiramis. Nimrod was described as a 'mighty tyrant' and one of the 'giants'. The Arabs believed that after the flood it was Nimrod who built or rebuilt the amazing structure at Baalbek in the Lebanon with its three stones weighing 800 tons each. It was said that he ruled the region that is now Lebanon and, according to Genesis, the first centres of Nimrod's kingdom were Babylon, Akkad and others in the land of Shinar (Sumer). Later he expanded further into Assyria to build cities like Nineveh where many of the Sumerian Tablets were found. Nimrod and Semiramis (or the beings those names symbolised) were from the reptile bloodlines which also became known as Titans, the genetic streams of the reptile-possessed humans and the full blood reptilians. This race of 'giants' or 'Titans' was said to have been descendants of Noah, the baby described in the Book of Enoch (previously the Book of Noah) as being a Watcher-human hybrid with extremely white skin. The father of Nimrod in the text of Genesis was Cush, also known as Bel or Belus, who was the grandson of Noah and son of Ham. Cush became known as the deity, Hermes, which means Son of Ham.[1] Ham or Khem means the 'burnt one' and may have been connected to Sun worship.[2] A great network of deities emerged from Babylon and its connections with Egypt.

Nimrod and Semiramis have remained the key deities of the Brotherhood to this day under many different names and symbols. Nimrod was symbolised as a fish and Queen Semiramis as a fish and a dove. Semiramis is likely to be symbolic of Ninkharsag, the creator of the reptile-human crossbreeds. Nimrod was the fish-god Dagon who was depicted as half man, half fish.[3] It is possible that this was symbolic of him being half human, half scaled reptile. Queen Semiramis was also symbolised as a fish because the Babylonians believed fish to be an aphrodisiac and it became the symbol for the Goddess of Love.[4] Hence the use of the fish in Christian symbolism and architecture. In her role as the 'Holy Spirit', Semiramis was pictured as a dove holding an olive branch and Semiramis means 'branch bearer' as in 'Ze' (the) 'emir' (branch) and 'amit' (bearer).[5] Note also the symbolism of this in the story of Noah and the Great Flood, when the dove came back bearing an olive branch. The return of the reptilians after the flood? The name, Semiramis, was evolved from the earlier Indian deity, Sami-Rama-isi or Semi-ramis.[6] A fish and a dove are two symbols still widely used in religious ritual and national ceremony, although most of the people involved have no idea of the true meaning. Sinn Fein, the political wing of the Northern Ireland terrorist group the IRA, has a dove as its symbol and you find the dove on many of the sceptres held by the British monarch (*see picture section*). Both organisations are modern fronts for the Babylonian Brotherhood and the doves symbolise Queen Semiramis. The dove to them is not a symbol of peace, but of death and destruction because of the reverse symbolism the Brotherhood employs. If it is positive to the masses, it is negative to the Brotherhood, and this allows their negative symbols to be placed throughout the public arena. No-one complains because they have no idea what these symbols, like the dove, really represent.

Semiramis was called the Queen of Heaven (also Rhea), the Virgin Mother of the Gods, and sometimes known as the Great Earth Mother (Ninkharsag). She was also worshipped under the name Astarte 'the woman who made towers' and this could refer to the Tower of Babel (Babylon) which Nimrod is said to have built. The bloodlines of European royalty came from the reptile-Aryan bloodlines of Babylon and the crown evolved from the horned headgear worn by Nimrod. The horns symbolised the monarch's authority and later became a metal headband with three horns symbolising royal power with divine authority.[7] This is represented by the symbol of the fleur-de-lis which you find throughout the regalia of modern royalty (*see* **Figure 6** *overleaf*). As I have mentioned already, the Draco 'royal' hierarchy, the winged albino whites, are said to have horns and I'm sure this is the true origin of the horned headgear of ancient royalty. The classic depiction of the Devil also has Draco-

Figure 6: *The Fleur-de-lis, symbol of the Babylonian trinity of Nimrod, Queen Semiramis and Tammuz, among other things.*

like horns. Nimrod was given the title Baal (the Lord) and Semiramis was Baalti (My Lady). The Latin term for my lady is Mea Domina which in its corrupted Italian form became Madonna.[8] Nimrod was represented in a dual role of God the Father and Ninus, the son of Semiramis, and her olive branch was symbolic of this offspring produced through a 'virgin birth'. Ninus was also known as Tammuz who was said to have been crucified with a lamb at his feet and placed in a cave. When a rock was rolled away from the cave's entrance three days later, his body had disappeared. Heard that somewhere before? This husband-wife-son theme of Nimrod-Semiramis-and Ninus/Tammuz became the Osiris-Isis-Horus mythology of the Egyptians with its equivalent in India, Asia, China and elsewhere. Much later it would be Joseph, Mary and Jesus. When the Babylonians held their Spring rites to mark the death and resurrection after three days of Tammuz-Ninus, they offered buns inscribed with a solar cross. Yes, even the hot cross buns of British Easter tradition come from Babylon. Easter comes from another face of Queen Semiramis – Ishtar – and it is from this, and possibly another Brotherhood deity, Ashtaroth, that we get the name of 'Ashtar' as in 'Ashtar Command', a completely manipulated New Age belief in an extraterrestrial 'hero' who has come to save us. The Babylonian myths and symbolism provided the foundations for all the major religions, especially Christianity. The Roman Church was the creation of the Babylonian Brotherhood and the Pope still wears a mitre shaped like a fish head to symbolise Nimrod. This is also the significance of his Fisherman's Ring. The Chair of St Peter in the Vatican was claimed to be a holy relic, but in 1968 it was exposed by a scientific commission as being no older than the 9th century. More significantly, according to the Catholic Encyclopaedia, is that it is decorated by twelve plates portraying the twelve labours of Hercules. This same work claims that Hercules was another name for Nimrod before becoming a deity of the Greeks.[9] In 1825, Pope Leo XII authorised the production of a jubilee medal and it depicted a woman in a pose that was blatant symbolism of Queen Semiramis. She had a crucifix in her left hand, a cup in her right and on her head was a seven rayed crown like the one on the Statue of Liberty, another depiction of Semiramis which was given to New York by French Freemasons. A contact who has relatives working in high positions in the Vatican told me how, during the reign of Pope John Paul II, he was given a guided tour of the place which blew his mind. He was shown the Pope's solid gold bath which is decorated with all the astrological symbols and he saw inside the vacuum-sealed vaults which contain thousands of ancient esoteric books which have been stolen and hoarded over hundreds of years of religious dictatorship and so taken out of public circulation. The Roman Church and the Babylonian Brotherhood are one and the same.

Nimrod was also Eannus, the god with two faces, who was later known to the Romans as Janus. One of the Anunnaki brothers, Enki the 'serpent god', was also known as Ea. The Freemasonic eagle with two heads looking left and right, east and west, is symbolic of Nimrod in the role of Eannus, and I would suggest that the eagle is symbolic of the winged Draco. Eannus, it was said, held the keys to the doors of heaven and he was the sole intermediary between God and humanity, therefore any belief not supported by him was false and should be condemned. This was a wonderful tool for the Babylonian priesthood to impose their will on the populous and exactly the same scam has been played by their successors, the Christian priests, the Rabbis and the priesthoods of Islam, Hinduism and all the rest. The Roman Catholic title of cardinal comes from the word 'cardo' meaning hinge and relates to Nimrod's role as guardian of the door to heaven.[10] The Babylonian priests even established a governing body they called the Grand Council of Pontiffs, a name later transferred to the Church of Rome.[11] The Babylonian High Priest, who instructed the inner circle initiates, was known as… Peter, meaning the 'Great Interpreter'. The feast day of the Christian St Peter was traditionally celebrated on the day the Sun entered the astrological house of Aquarius, the very day that Eannus and Janus were honoured![12] The Babylonian religion, like all the look-alikes that were to follow, consisted of two levels. The masses were manipulated into believing superstitions and into taking symbolic stories literally, while the chosen initiates were given the real knowledge on penalty of death if they ever revealed it. In this way the truth about life, human potential, history and the reptilian Agenda, were lost to the population and kept only for the few.

Human sacrifice was fundamental to the religion of Babylon and wherever the Babylonian Brotherhood and their reptilian bloodlines have travelled, human sacrifice has always gone with them because the reptilians demand these rituals. The malevolent ones seem to be addicted to blood and this has been passed on to their crossbreeds as the evidence I shall present will show. The Babylonian priests were required to eat some of their sacrificial offerings and so the word for priest, Cahna-Bal, became the term for eating human flesh, cannibal.[13] Moloch, the name of that flying lizard I mentioned earlier, was another name for Nimrod-Tammuz. Tam means 'to perfect' and muz means 'to burn'. You can see the symbolism of Tammuz-Moloch, therefore, in the rituals of burning children alive in honour of this deity which, staggeringly, still go on today. The Beltane ritual later performed in Britain by the Druids on May 1st, May Day, involved the burning of children in the belly of a huge wicker effigy of a man. This was inherited from the Babylonians when the Brotherhood expanded across Europe. Indeed it may well be that the reptilians had once based themselves in what is now the United Kingdom and Ireland before they moved their main focus to the Near East and Africa. The Feast of Tammuz was on June 23rd and celebrated his ascension from the underworld. When he was resurrected, Tammuz was known as Oannes, the fish god, and Oannes is a version of the name, John.[14] For this reason, John has been used as a symbol for Tammuz-Nimrod in symbolic characters like John the Baptist. June 23rd, the Feast of Tammuz, became the Christian day called St John's Eve! The Nimrod-Semiramis combination has been depicted under countless names in the civilisations and cultures which have followed. These deities throughout the world may seem to be an unfathomable tidal wave of names, but they are overwhelmingly different names for the same two figures. Another deity widely used in Satanism for the sacrifice of children today is Kronos, the king of the Cyclops in Greek legend. He was known as the tower builder and is almost certainly another version of Nimrod, the builder of the biblical Tower of Babel.[15]

The reason the reptile bloodlines are involved in such unspeakable ritual and practice today, is quite simply because they always have been. When you follow these bloodlines across history, you find they use the same rituals and sacrifice to the same deities, right to the present day. Another passage in the Book of Enoch tells of the Watchers breeding with human women and the behaviour of the offspring they produced:

> "And they became pregnant, and they bore great giants… who consumed all the acquisitions of men. And when men could no longer sustain them, the giants turned against them and devoured mankind. And they began to sin against birds and beasts, and reptiles, and fish, and to devour one another's flesh and drink blood. The Earth laid accusation against the lawless ones."[16]

That passage describes the bloodlines I am highlighting and they came together in the Babylonian Brotherhood which has since expanded across the planet. While we look out of our eyes and feel part of this physical world, the reptiles look into this third dimension, much like someone looking through a window. In this case, the eyes of the physical body. We are consciously in the third dimension, they are consciously in the fourth looking into the third. When you know what you are looking for it is the eyes that give them away. They are dark, piercing and cold. The reptile full-bloods are not attached to their bodies like humans. They are knowingly using them as 'space suits' to operate in this world, and when one wears out they simply occupy another. It is from this process of 'possession' by the reptilians and other low vibrational entities that we have the ancient tales, indeed modern ones too, of demons, devils and evil spirits taking over a human mind and body. It is the reptilians and other consciousness of the lower fourth dimension, the cesspit vibration as I call it, which are summoned during Satanic, black magic rituals and it is during these rituals that many unsuspecting puppets are 'plugged in' to the reptilian consciousness and taken over. So it was in Babylon and so it is today. As I revealed in *I Am Me I Am Free*, and will elaborate upon in this book, the Brotherhood hierarchy today are seriously into Satanic ritual, child sacrifice, blood drinking and other abominations that would take your breath away. Yes, I am talking about some of the biggest royal, political, business, banking and media names on the planet. People like Henry Kissinger, George Bush, the British royal family and many other presidents, prime ministers and members of royalty. Fantastic? Of course it is, but since when did the truth not sound fantastic in a world of such denial and illusion?

Three of the principle elements of the Babylonian religion were fire, serpents and the Sun. I should explain their focus on the Sun because it is a vital part of the story.

Most of the global population worshipped the Sun for its obvious gifts of heat and light and the effect this had on their crops and well-being. However, within the hierarchy of the Babylon Brotherhood and other Elite groups which had the advanced knowledge, they focused on the Sun for other reasons too. They understood the true nature of the Sun as a multidimensional consciousness which extends across the solar system on unseen frequency levels. Even in this physical dimension, the Sun's emissions of magnetic energy are constantly affecting us second by second. The Sun has a diameter of some 864,000 miles and contains 99% of the matter in the Solar System.[17] It is an immense ball of energy which works very much like an atomic bomb and the internal temperature can reach as much as 14 million degrees centigrade.[18] It rotates faster at the equator than at the poles and therefore the activity and stimulation of the Sun's magnetic field is simply colossal. The writer and researcher Maurice Cotterell has made a long and detailed study of sunspot and solar flare activity when the Sun is projecting immensely powerful magnetic energy. This has been photographed as gigantic loops of fire, some 100,000 miles high.[19] This energy travels to the Earth on the solar wind and it can affect computer systems and cause power blackouts. But for the Van Allen Belts, the zones of radiation which surround the planet and connect with the Earth's magnetic field, the Sun's energy would 'fry' us.

Maurice Cotterell studied the sunspot cycles and established short, long and great cycles of solar activity, as he explains in his book with Adrian G. Gilbert called *The Mayan Prophecies*.[20] When Cotterell's research was already advanced, he came across the amazing mathematical system of numbers and symbols left by the ancient Maya people in Central America. The Maya claimed to have originated with the 'gods' and recognised a lost island as their former home. Their astonishingly accurate mathematical and astronomical systems, and their measurement of time, were inherited from much older cultures and ultimately from the extraterrestrials. We have already seen that Mexican President Miguel De La Madrid claimed that the Mayans were interbred with the reptilians, the 'iguana race' as he put it.

Maurice Cotterell was fascinated to realise that the Mayan cycles of human evolution corresponded remarkably with his sunspot cycles of magnetic emissions. Even over thousands of years, they were incredibly close. This is perfectly explainable. Everything is energy. Life is the interaction of magnetic vibrational fields. Change the magnetism and you change the nature of the energy field. Change the energy field and you change the nature of mental, emotional, spiritual and physical life, all of which are energy in different forms. The other planets do this as they circle the Sun and affect the magnetic field of the Earth: we call this astrology. Cotterell believes that we are effected by these fields most powerfully at the time we are conceived rather than the time we are born, a point which has much validity. I feel that *both* powerfully affect us. His research established that sunspot activity corresponds with the human fertility cycles and with the emergence and demise of great civilisations and empires. Scientists have also discovered that humans have an internal clock which is in sync with the Sun. In short, the Sun's effect on human life is fundamental and far beyond its obvious contribution of warmth and light. The extraterrestrials knew this in these ancient times and the Sun was viewed with awe. It is the physical and spiritual heart of the solar system and it came to symbolise the creator, particularly the male aspects of the creative force… 'He Who Is The Light Of The World'. This knowledge of the Sun will be a common theme throughout the rest of this book as we journey through history to the present day. It does, however, make the decoding of history a little more complex because the ancients would constantly use Sun and astrological symbolism in their stories and some of the names for their gods would be used to symbolise the Sun and the planets. Working out what is literal and what is symbolic is a considerable challenge. I also think that the term 'Sun god' has been used to symbolise the extraterrestrials and their crossbreeds, who were said in the ancient texts to have faces which shone like the Sun – the Shining Ones. Imagine the power you would have to advance an Agenda and manipulate the human race if you knew the cycles of energy from the Sun and other planets and how they were likely to affect human consciousness. You would know when people would be more prone to anger, aggression, fear, doubt and guilt, and therefore when to have your wars, economic collapses and so on. The Brotherhood have always had this knowledge and they use it to great effect today as I shall document.

The Babylonian Brotherhood and its reptilian bloodlines expanded across the Middle and Near East, especially to Egypt, and eventually into Europe and the Americas. I think the early Egyptian civilisation after the Venus upheavels was the work of the Aryans from Mars, the Phoenicians, with or without the reptilian Anunnaki. But before 2,000 BC the reptilians were taking over. The Royal Court of the Dragon was founded by the priests of Mendes in around 2,200 BC and this still exists today as the Imperial and Royal Court of the Dragon Sovereignty. The author, Laurence Gardner, is the present Chancellor of the Imperial Court of Dragon Sovereignty and his postal address in Devon, England is at Colomba House. Columba = dove = Queen Semiramis. According to Gardner, the name Dracula means 'Son of Dracul' and was inspired by Prince Vlad III of Transylvania-Wallachia, a Chancellor of the Court of the Dragon in the 15th century. The prince's father was called Dracul within the Court. Dracul = Draco. Wherever they went, the Babylonian Brotherhood created their own mystery schools to manipulate the population into believing a nonsense and into giving away their power through superstition and fear. At the same time the higher levels of these pyramid structures communicated the advanced knowledge to those who would serve the reptilian Agenda. Where other non-reptilian initiation schools existed, they were infiltrated and taken over by the Babylonian priesthood. Mystery schools have been around for tens of thousands of years, probably hundreds of thousands, and they are used to pass on advanced knowledge to those the hierarchy and priests decide are worthy enough. In his book, *The Masters Of Wisdom*, J. G. Bennett writes of how the Russian mystic, Gregori Gurdjieff, told him that the mystery schools went back at least 30,000 to 40,000 years.[21] Gurdjieff said he had learned this from cave drawings in the Caucasus Mountains and Turkestan (that area again). I often hear New Age people scream with indignation at the thought that the ancient mystery schools were part of the manipulation. Well, first of all there should be no structures, whatever their intent, that deny knowledge to people. I don't care what their intent may be, once you consider it your right to deny knowledge and decide who should and should not have access to it, you are playing a very dangerous and arrogant game. There were those of positive intent who wanted to use the mystery schools to give the knowledge to people they believed would use it wisely and I am not suggesting that all these schools were malevolent, certainly not. But even the positive ones were eventually infiltrated by the servants of the reptilians. As Manly P. Hall, the Freemasonic historian, wrote:

"While the elaborate ceremonial magic of antiquity was not necessarily evil, there arose from its perversion several false schools of sorcery, or black magic, (*In Egypt*)... the black magicians of Atlantis continued to exercise their superhuman powers until they had completely undermined and corrupted the morals of the primitive Mysteries... they usurped the position formerly occupied by the initiates, and seized the reins of spiritual government.

"Thus black magic dictated the state religion and paralysed the intellectual and spiritual activities of the individual by demanding his complete and unhesitating acquiescence in the dogma formulated by the priestcraft. The Pharaoh became a puppet in the hands of the Scarlet Council – a committee of arch-sorcerers elevated to power by the priesthood."[22]

The black magicians that Hall says were formerly in Atlantis were, for me, the reptilian-human hybrids of what I call the Babylonian Brotherhood. It is their secret society network that now spans the globe and operates in literally every country. It allows the coordination of the Agenda across national borders and between apparently unconnected companies and institutions like politics, banking, business, the military and the media. Knowledge is not good nor bad, it just is. It is how we use that knowledge that is positive or negative. At the upper levels of this network they know of the true power of the Sun, magnetics and the mind; the effect of the planets on human behaviour; how to manipulate time, consciousness, energy, the weather and so much more. If used malevolently, this knowledge can be incredibly destructive and manipulating and this is what has happened. At the same time the reptilians have used their secret societies to create institutions in the public arena such as religions and political parties to suck this advanced knowledge out of circulation. The Inquisition was a wonderful example of this technique. Merely to speak about esoteric matters was to sign your own death warrant. This scam has been so effective that still today you have Christians condemning esoteric information as 'the Devil' when this same knowledge is the very foundation of their religion. If you want to know where Christianity really came from, stick around. It is recycled Paganism and provably so. Yet Christianity has been used quite brilliantly as the major vehicle for removing vital knowledge from the public domain. Whenever Christianity and other religions took control of a country or region, the ancient texts and records were removed or destroyed. This took out of circulation the very knowledge the reptilians

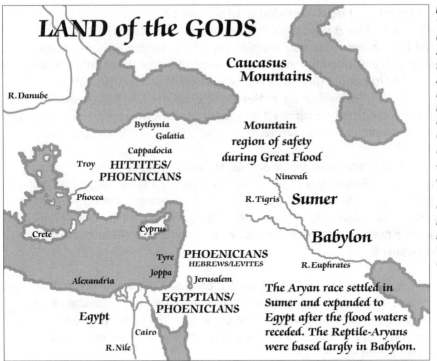

have used and still use to manipulate an ignorant population. It was also in the name of Christianity that most of the accounts of the true history of humankind have been destroyed, along with knowledge of the influence on human affairs of extraterrestrial races, positive and negative. This allowed an alternative invented 'history' to be written which has delinked humanity from its origins. Controlling history is so important because if you manipulate how people see what we call the past, you will influence massively how they see the present.

The themes I have highlighted so far, along with the deities and symbols, will travel with us from here to the present day as we follow the expansion of the Babylonian Brotherhood across the world. Invariably, the Babylon reptilian full-bloods and hybrids manipulated themselves into the positions of power and influence in the countries where they settled. They had a much higher level of knowledge than most of the people and, as vehicles for the fourth dimensional reptilians, there was already a long term plan to work to, the Great Work of Ages as it became known to the Freemasons. They allowed the non-reptilian population to do the work and then, when new societies were established, the Brotherhood priests and initiates would hijack the positions of religious and political power and ensure that any advanced knowledge in circulation was sucked out of the public domain and into their mystery schools and secret societies. The white race and the reptile-Aryan crossbreeds had emerged from the Caucasus Mountains and the mountains of Iran and Kurdistan after the flood to settle in Egypt, Israel/Palestine and what we now call Jordan, Syria, Iraq, Iran and Turkey, going up to the Caucasus

Mountains (*see* **Figure 7**). Significantly it was from this same region that all the world's major religions emerged and this is no accident. In earlier times, the civilisations of Sumer, Babylon and Assyria were in the general area of what we call Iraq, while Turkey was previously known as Asia Minor and Persia. Richard Laurence, the Archbishop of Cashel, who translated the first English edition of the Book of Enoch from the Ethiopian, established from the descriptions of the longest day of the year, that the author of the text had to have lived in the Caucasus region and not Palestine, as most people believed.[23] This was where the main reptile-human bloodlines emerged from and the original text of the Book of Enoch was the much older Book of Noah, the reptilian crossbreed. The Aryan race as it expanded into new territory was known under various names, the most significant of which were the Hittites and Phoenicians. I think there were definitely other Aryan settlements outside this region, possibly Britain among them, and certainly the reptilians were operating in other parts of the world, like the Americas. But this mountainous region around the Caucasus and down to the plains of Sumer and Egypt is a key to the true history of humankind over the last seven thousand years.

The Caucasus Mountains came up again and again in my research and how appropriate that in North America white people are known as 'Caucasian'. Even according to official history it was a white 'Aryan' race from the Caucasus Mountains region which moved into the Indus Valley of India about 1550 BC and created what is today known as the Hindu religion. It was this same Aryan race (they called themselves 'Arya') which introduced the ancient Sanskrit language to India and the stories and myths contained in the Hindu holy books, the Vedas. L. A. Waddell, in his outstanding research into this Aryan race, established that the father of the first historical Aryan king of India (recorded in the Maha-Barata epic and Indian Buddhist history) was the last historical king of the Hittites in Asia Minor.[24] The Indian Aryans worshipped the Sun as the Father-god Indra, and the Hittite-Phoenicians called their Father-god Bel by the name, Indara.[25] Under many names this same Aryan people also settled in Sumer, Babylon, Egypt and Asia Minor, now Turkey, and other Near Eastern countries, taking with them the same stories, myths, and religion. This is why, as we shall see in detail later, all the major religions tell the same tale but using different names. They all come from the same source, this Aryan race, which seems to have originated on Mars, and the reptile-human bloodlines operating covertly within them. What we call the Jewish race also originated in the Caucasus region and not, as claimed, in Israel. Jewish historical and anthropological sources have shown that only a few of the people known as Jewish have any genetic connection to Israel. In the 8th century a people called the Khazars living in the Caucasus Mountains and southern Russia had a mass conversion to the Jewish religion. Later when that empire folded, these same people made their way north over a long period of time to settle in other parts of Russia, Lithuania and Estonia. From there they entered Western Europe and eventually the United States. The Rothschild family is one of these bloodlines. These are the same people who justified the takeover of Arab Palestine after the last war by saying that 'God' had given them an ancient right to that land as his 'chosen people'. In truth

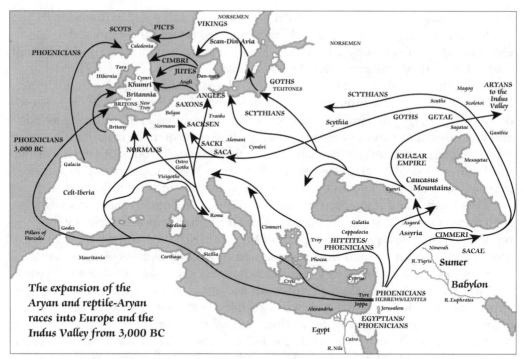

The expansion of the
Aryan and reptile-Aryan
races into Europe and the
Indus Valley from 3,000 BC

Figure 8: *The Aryans and the reptile-Aryans expanded by sea and land into Europe under many names, and especially thanks to the 'British' Empire, they would eventually take over the world.*

their original homeland is the Caucasus region and southern Russia, not Israel. See *...And The Truth Shall Set You Free* for a detailed and sourced account of this story and the secret society manipulation that was behind the creation of Israel, or Rothschild-land as it really is.

The white race expanded northwards into Europe. The first people went by sea under the name, the Phoenicians, and over many centuries others migrated over land (*see Figure 8*). Two of the latter groups were called the Cimmerians and the Scythians and through a series of name changes these same bloodlines populated Europe and reconnected with the earlier Aryan settlers of Britain and Northern Europe who had been installed by the seafaring Phoenicians. The Phoenicians are crucial to the story and I will come to them in detail in a moment. The Cimmerians migrated north west from the Caucasus and Asia Minor (Turkey) into the countries we now call Belgium, the Netherlands, Germany and Denmark. The Roman historians, Pliny and Tacitus, said that all the people along the coast from the Netherlands to Denmark were the same ethnic group and this is supported by archaeological evidence which indicates that this people arrived in that region about 300 to 250 BC. Another group of Cimmerians travelled up the River Danube through Hungary and Austria into southern Germany and France. The Romans called them Gauls and the Greeks knew them as the Keltoi or Celts. Groups of these Celtic tribes also settled in Bohemia and Bavaria and others invaded northern Italy. Sallust, the Roman historian, records how Romans were defeated a number of times by the

'Cimbri', who he says were Gauls. Other Roman historians say the Cimbri were 'Celts'. They were divided into three tribes, the Belgae (north east France), the Gauls (central France) and the Acquitanae (southern France to the Pyrenees Mountains). By the second century BC, the Gauls/Celts (the white Cimmerians from the Caucasus Mountains and the Middle East) occupied all of central Europe and northern Italy and they went on to conquer the whole of that country. Around 280 BC they swept down into Asia Minor and reoccupied the lands of their ancestors. As the historian Professor Henry Rawlinson said: "These two great invasions into Asia Minor proceeded from the same identical race, in the first instance called the Cimmerians and in the second, the Gauls."[26] These invading Gauls based themselves in a place called Phrygia which became known as Galatia (Gaul-atia) and it was to these people that St Paul was supposed to have written in the New Testament's Letter to the Galatians. The Cimmerians or Cimbri also settled in Wales and to this day the name for that country in the Welsh language is Cymru.

The Scythians, another Aryan group, also moved north from the Caucasus into Europe where their name was changed by the Romans to distinguish between them and other peoples. The sacred emblems of the Scythians included the serpent, the Ox (Nimrod/Taurus), fire (the Sun, knowledge), and Tho or Theo, the god the Egyptians called Pan. The Romans called the Scythians the Sarmatae and the Germani from the Latin word Germanus, meaning 'genuine'. The Scythians were known, therefore, as the 'Genuine People' and of course from Germani we get German and Germany. The name change is confirmed by the writings of the Roman historians Pliny and Strabo. The Anglo-Saxons who invaded Britain were also known as Germani by the Romans. The land called Old Saxony is modern day north Germany and the Netherlands. Both the Angles and the Saxons came from the same genetic source – the white Cimmerians and Scythians from the Caucasus and the Middle/Near East. It is the same with William the Conqueror and his Normans, the last people to invade Britain in 1066 at the Battle of Hastings. The terms Norman and Normandy originate from the Norse (North) men because they came from Scandinavia to occupy that region of France. The story of the Scandinavian hero Odin, says that he came from Asaland or Asaheim, which just happens to be the lands of Scythia and can be identified in Aryan India. From there about 200 to 300 AD, it is said, Odin led a huge army north to conquer Sweden. His army was called the Svear and in Swedish that country is still called Sverige, the Land of the Svear.

Another group of Scythians, who became known as the Sakkas, went east from the Caucasus following the trail of the earlier Aryans and they reached the borders of China by 175 BC. About this time Chinese records tell of a people called the Sai-wang or Sok-wang who were forced to flee India. Sok-wang means 'Sakka princes'. The records indicate that these Sakka retreated south into India through the mountain passes from Afghanistan, and coins dating from about 100 BC confirm that a Sakka kingdom was created in the upper Indus valleys between Kashmir and Afghanistan. Again it is not a coincidence that the religion of Buddhism emerged from lands occupied by the Sakka (Aryan Scythians). At least by 500 BC a tribe called the Sakyas lived in the area where Buddha is supposed to have been born around 63 years earlier. Guatma (Lord Buddha) was called Sakyashina, Sakamuni, the Sakya sage, Sakya the teacher and the lion of the tribe of Sakya. All this will become highly significant when we look at the single origin of all the major, and most minor, religions and their 'heroes'. The Scythian/Sakka and the Cimmerians/Cimbri were in fact all the same people and this is confirmed by inscriptions scored into the Behistun Rock in the Zargos Mountains on an old caravan trail from Babylon. The inscriptions were ordered by Darius the Great about 515 BC and they were written in three languages, Babylonian, Elamite and Persian. Whenever the Elamite and Persian versions say Sakka, the Persians/Babylonians use the term Cimiri.

So these white Aryan peoples under different names with their same religion and religious heroes under different names, expanded from their origins in the Caucasus and the Middle and Near East and went overland into Europe, India and as far as China. And within them were the reptile-human bloodlines who battled for, and eventually won, supremacy to control the course of events as the kings, queens, priests and military leaders under the collective title I dub the Babylonian Brotherhood. That the Babylonians were part of the Aryan race is confirmed by ancient inscriptions and titles. The Kassi or Cassi was a title first used by the Phoenicians about 3,000 BC and this was adopted by the Babylonians who ruled the Mesopotamian empire. Kassi also appears as a personal name of Phoenicians in Egypt and Cassi was the inspiration for the ruling kings known as Catti in pre-Roman Britain, one of whom minted 'Cas' coins featuring the sun-horse and other solar symbols.[27]

This Aryan expansion began as far back as 3,000 BC, probably earlier, with their seafaring branch, the Phoenicians. They were a technologically advanced people who have been marginalised by official history and this has obscured their true identity. They are fundamental to understanding where we have come from and where we are now. It was they who brought both their genetic lines and their knowledge to Europe, Scandinavia and the Americas, thousands of years BC. Their story is told by L. A. Waddell in his book, *The Phoenician Origin Of Britons, Scots And Anglo-Saxons*. Waddell was a fellow of the Royal Anthropological Institute and spent a lifetime researching the evidence. He shows that the Phoenicians were not a Semitic race as previously believed, but a white Aryan race. Examination of Phoenician tombs reveals that they were a long-headed Aryan race and of a totally different racial type to the Semites. The Phoenicians of the ancient world travelled by sea from their bases in Asia Minor, Syria and Egypt to settle in the islands of the Mediterranean like Crete and Cyprus and also Greece and Italy. It was the Phoenicians who carried the knowledge which later emerged as the civilisations of Minoan Crete, classic Greece and Roman Italy. They were also the 'brains' behind much of the Egyptian culture in this period, before it was hijacked by the reptilians. The Egyptians knew the Phoenicians as the Panag, Panasa and Fenkha. The Greeks called them the Phoinik-as, and to the Romans they were the Phoenic-es.[28] There is a simple reason why the Egyptians depicted many of their gods with white skin and blue eyes in exactly the same way as other cultures all over the world did. This

advanced race, called the Phoenicians, were white skinned and often had blue eyes
– the same as the reptilian-human crossbreeds and the same, it would appear, as the
race from Mars. Thus we have the Scandinavian races, which were installed by the
Phoenicians and other peoples of the same bloodstock and general location. It is
also the origin of the Aryan 'Master Race' nonsense which obsessed the Nazis and
the secret societies which created them. The hero of the Freemason secret society to
this day is the mythical Hiram Abif, the so-called builder of King Solomon's
Temple. Abif is supposed to have been a Phoenician. The grandfather of the famous
Egyptian Pharaoh Akhenaten, the father of Tutankhamen, was a Phoenician high
priest. The Phoenix, the mythical bird of Egypt, was in fact the Sun bird of the
Phoenicians, the emblem of the Sun God, Bil or Bel, and as it has been later
symbolised, a peacock or an eagle.[29] Evidence has emerged in recent years about
pyramids on Mars, when the NASA scientists, Vincent DiPietro and Gregory
Molenaar, discovered six enormous pyramids like those in Egypt in the Cydonia
region of Mars.[30] It would make sense that the same Martian race with the same
knowledge would also build pyramids when they came to Earth, and the same can
be said of the Anunnaki if, as Zecharia Sitchin speculates and I agree, they had
settlements on Mars.

The Phoenicians were not confined to the Mediterranean and the Middle East.
They landed in Britain around 3,000 BC and unmistakable Phoenician artefacts have
been found in Brazil, as well as possible Egyptian remains in the Grand Canyon in
America. The Phoenicians landed in the Americas thousands of years before the
manufactured 'photo opportunity' better known as the journey of Christopher
Columbus. The reason that the native legends of the Americas speak of tall 'white
gods' coming from the sea bringing advanced knowledge is because that is
precisely what happened, if you forget the gods bit. They were the Aryan race and
the reptile-Aryans from the east landing in the Americas thousands of years ago,
the same Aryan race or 'gods' who the Sumerians said gifted them their civilisation
after the flood. This is also why the later white invaders who followed Columbus
were astonished to find that the native peoples of the American continent had the
same basic religious stories and myths as they had. This is perfectly explainable
now. They came from the same source – the Aryan race known as the Phoenicians
among many other names like Sumerian and Hittite with the reptile-Aryan
bloodlines within them. There also seems to have been a direct reptilian invasion in
the Americas way back. The evidence of an advanced race who knew the Americas
existed, comes with centuries-old maps like the Hadji Ahmed Portolan Map,
compiled in 1519, which depicts the North American continent with a wide
causeway connecting Alaska and Siberia. There is also an accurate drawing of an
ice-free Antarctica.

The arrival of the Aryan Phoenicians in Britain also corresponds with the
building of the great stone circles and observatories like Stonehenge and Avebury in
Wiltshire, although some researchers say they were built much earlier. The
advanced Phoenicians-Sumerians, who had a highly developed knowledge of
astronomy, astrology, sacred geometry, mathematics and the Earth's magnetic force

line network known as the global energy grid, had all the knowledge necessary to build these great structures. L. A. Waddell said that he found Sumerian markings on one of the stones at Stonehenge.[31] Professor Alexander Thom, Emeritus Professor of Engineering Science at Oxford University from 1945 to 1961, discovered that the ancients who built Stonehenge knew about 'Pythagorean' geometric and mathematical principles thousands of years before Pythagoras was born. Thom explained in his 1967 book, *Megalithic Sites In Britain*, that the stones not only formed geometric patterns in and around the circle, they also aligned to features in the surrounding landscape and to the positions of the Sun, Moon and prominent stars at particular times, particularly where the Sun appeared or disappeared at the equinox or solstice and where the Moon was at the extreme positions of its cycle. It was a gigantic astronomical clock, he said. But it is more than that. It is a receiver and transmitter of energy. The Earth's magnetic grid, or grids, consist of lines of magnetic energy known as ley lines, meridians or dragon lines to the Chinese. Where these lines cross, the energy spirals into a vortex and where many lines cross you have a massive vortex of energy. These are the power places, the sacred sites of the ancients who knew of this system. The vortex, or spiral, is a constant throughout the Universe. Our galaxy is a spiral, water spirals downwards, hair grows in a spiral at the crown, the DNA molecule which carries our genetic blueprint is a double spiral. Brian Desborough, my scientist friend from California, told me there is a point on one of the Earth grids, the Hartmann Grid as it is called, where twelve of these force lines meet and go down into the Earth. Where was that? I asked. "A place called Avebury in England" he said. The very place the advanced Phoenician-Sumerians chose to build their stone circles at least five thousand years ago along with a series of surrounding sites, including Silbury Hill, the biggest human-made mound in Europe, and others like West Kennet Long Barrow. These form a sort of 'circuit board' at the heart of the energy grid which fundamentally affects the nature of the Earth's magnetic field. I lived near Avebury for two years and it is an incredibly powerful place if you are sensitive to energy. It is also the area where most of the 'crop circles' or more accurately, crop formations, have appeared, particularly the most complex of them.

Even more interesting is the apparent connection between Avebury and Mars. The best known researcher of the apparently man-made structure called the 'Face on Mars' and an area of that planet known as Cydonia, is the American Richard C. Hoagland. He has been a science journalist, a director of planetariums in West Hartford and New York, and an advisor at the NASA Goddard Space Flight Center. Hoagland produces evidence in his book, *Monuments On Mars*,[32] that the alleged 'face' and the pyramids are part of a vast area built to align with the sunrise on the Martian summer solstice 500,000 years ago – 50,000 years before the estimated arrival on Earth of the Anunnaki. I have little doubt that the same race that built the structures in Cydonia, including pyramids, also built Stonehenge and Avebury. There is evidence, in fact, that Avebury could be a mirror image of the complex at Cydonia. When you take same scale topographical maps of both places and superimpose one on the other, the correlation of objects and the distances between

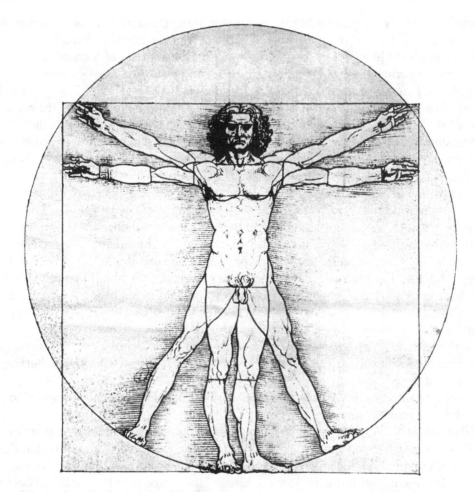

Figure 9: *Leonardo da Vinci's depiction of Man according to the sacred geometry known as the Golden Mean.*

them is incredibly similar, as members of Hoagland's team established. He also discovered that this 'Mars City' was built according to the same laws used to create other similar complexes on the Earth. The same mathematics, alignments and sacred geometry can be found in Cydonia on Mars and in the great structures of the ancient world like those at Stonehenge, the pyramids at Giza in Egypt, Teotihuacan in Mexico and in Zimbabwe. These mathematics accord with the 'Golden Mean' geometry as depicted by the Italian artist, Leonardo da Vinci (1452–1519), in his picture of the man inside a circle (*see* ***Figure 9***). Da Vinci, as we shall see, was a leading initiate of the secret society network and this is how he was able to predict the coming of the telephone, design flying machines and tanks, and design bicycles in the 15th and 16th centuries which look basically like the modern version today.

Another constant is the latitude of 19.5 degrees. This is the latitude on which the pyramids, many ancient temple complexes, and other sacred structures were built. It is also where you will find the volcanoes on Hawaii, the Schild volcanoes on

Venus, the massive Olympus Mons volcano on Mars, the dark spot on Neptune, the red spot on Jupiter and the main area of sunspot activity, north and south, on the Sun.[33] This all fits like a glove, because sunspots are emissions of incredibly powerful electromagnetic energy from the Sun, and volcanoes are obvious emissions of energy from the planets. Not surprisingly, therefore, 19.5 degrees is the point of energy exchange between rotating spheres and the hierarchy of the ancients knew this. The Sumerians knew, for instance, about the cycle of what is called precession. This is the effect of the Earth's 'wobble' which slowly moves the planet on its axis so that it faces different star systems or astrological 'houses' over many thousands of years. As their records show, the Sumerians knew that it took 2,160 years for the Earth to move through each 'house' and 25,920 years to complete the cycle – the period it also takes the solar system to complete its journey around its galactic centre. We are completing one of these cycles now, hence the enormous change that is upon us. Ancient temples all over the world reflect these cycles of precession in their geometry and mathematics. Isn't it amazing what 'primitive' people can do? The Elite of the Phoenician-Aryans had enormous knowledge of the Earth's energy grid and its potential to affect human consciousness. After all, we live within the planet's magnetic field. When it changes, we change. If you live in water and the water changes, you are fundamentally affected and it is the same with the energy 'ocean' that we occupy. Thus you have the movement of the planets affecting the Earth's magnetic field and through that affecting us. The Brotherhood don't want us to know any of this and so they have used their religions, like Christianity, to condemn astrology as the work of the Devil and their 'science' to dismiss it as mumbo-jumbo.

The 'mystery' stone circles and structures are much less mysterious when you seek answers with open minded research. The evidence strongly suggests that they were built by the Phoenician-Aryans who came here from the Middle and Near East. It is the same with the 'mystery' white horses scored into the chalk hillsides of Britain. Just before I wrote this chapter, I visited the oldest white horse in Britain, the famous one at Uffington in Wiltshire, not far from Avebury (see picture section). The plaque said that its date of construction was about 3,000 BC – exactly the period when the Phoenicians arrived in the British Isles. Why should the Phoenicians score white horses into the hillsides of Britain? Again, the answer is simple. Their religion was focused on the Sun and the white horse was a Phoenician symbol for the Sun. The great stone circles and structures throughout Britain, like Stonehenge and Avebury, were built with the knowledge held by the ruling and priestly classes of the Phoenicians and the Babylonian Brotherhood which infiltrated and eventually controlled the Aryan leadership. This knowledge included the ability to use sound and other techniques to throw a magnetic field around a massive stone and delink it from the laws of gravity. It then becomes weightless. This period of around 3,000 BC is very significant. While the Phoenicians were at work in this period in Britain and elsewhere, the pyramids at Giza in Egypt have also been dated to around 3,000 BC using the latest carbon dating methods. Traces of charcoal found within the mortar apparently made this possible.[34]

The Aryans of the Near and Middle East had many names, the Hittites, the Phoenicians, the Goths and so on. You can follow words and names through these apparently different cultures to show that they came from the same source. Some of the stone circles are sometimes called Hare-Stones which, according to L. A. Waddell's research, evolved through Harri or Heria, the title for the ruling Goths, and from the Hittite title of Harri, Arri or Aryan: Hare stones are Aryan stones. Just as Hari Khrishna means Aryan Khrishna, very appropriate given that the Hindu religion was the work of the Aryans. You also have Castlerigg stone circle near Keswick in Cumberland. The word 'rig' was a title for Gothic kings and princes and the Gothic came from the Aryans. Ancient depictions of Aryan kings in Cilicia have them wearing the Gothic style of dress. The name of Keswick itself means 'Abode of the Kes' – the Cassi or Khatti clan of the Hittites – and the county of Cumberland

has evolved through names like Cymry and Cumbers from its origin, Sumer. The term Aryan comes from a Phoenician word, Arri, meaning 'noble one'. Thus we get the names Sum-ARIAN and aristocracy or ARIAN-stock-racy. The lion has always been a major symbol through the ages because it was an Aryan symbol for the Sun and was often placed at the entrances to temples and sacred places. Hence the lion-bodied Sphinx which also relates to the astrological sign of Leo, again considered in astrology to be the sign ruled by the Sun.

The whole foundation of 'British' culture and legend came from the Phoenicians. The famous legend of St George and the Dragon comes from St George of Cappadocia, the Phoenician centre

Figure 10: *The swastika, the Phoenician sun symbol, on the Phoenician Craig-Narget stone in Scotland and,* **Figure 11,** *on the robe of a Phoenician High Priestess.*

in Asia Minor. The battles between St George and the dragon could well have been symbolic of the Martian-reptilian conflicts which seem to go back a very long way. The red cross of St George (England) and the crosses of St Andrew (Scotland) and St Patrick (Ireland), and the ensigns of Scandinavia, were all carried as sacred standards of victory by the Phoenicians. The red cross was the fire cross, a Phoenician-Aryan symbol for the Sun, as was the swastika, later used by the Nazis. A swastika can be seen on a stone dedicated to the Phoenician Sun-god Bel, which was found at Craig-Narget in Scotland and was used to decorate the robes of their high priestesses (*see Figures 10 and 11*). I read that the name swastika comes from the Sanskrit word, svasti, which means well-being, and it was considered a positive symbol until the Nazis turned it around and made it a symbol of destruction. L. A. Waddell translated the markings on another stone in Scotland, the Newton Stone in the Dumfries and Galloway region, to be Phoenician-Hittite and dedicated to their Sun god, Bel or Bil. The classic British symbol of Britannia comes from the Phoenician goddess, Barati. Look at how the Phoenicians depicted Barati and how the British depict Britannia in *Figure 12*! One of the major centres of the Aryan-Hittite-Phoenicians was Cilicia in Asia Minor and here Barati was

worshipped as Perathea and later Diana. So Diana and Britannia originate from the same source. Barati was the queen/goddess figure of the Phoenicians as Barat was the god/king. These are possibly names for the Babylonian deities Nimrod and Semiramis. The 'royal' élite clan of the Aryans were (are) called the Barats and this is why you find the term Barat or Brihat in the ancient Indian culture as you do with Britain and British

Figure 12: *The Phoenician depiction of Barati (right) and the British symbol of Britannia. They are the same deity and alternative names for Queen Semiramis in Babylon and Isis in Egypt.*

(Barat-ain and Barat-ish). The Indian Vedas say that "King Barat gave his name to the Dynastic Race of which he was the founder; and so it is from him that the fame of that Dynastic people hath spread so wide."[35] Parat, Prat and Prydi, are some of the other derivatives of Barat. The original form was Barat-ana or Brithad-ana.[36] The suffix ana in Hittite-Sumerian (Aryan) means 'one'. Ana in fact evolved into the English word 'one' and the Scottish 'ane'. Barat-ana or Briton therefore means 'One of the Barats' (Bruits). It is the same with many other countries occupied by this white race. The name Iran comes from the earlier Airy-Ana or Air-an, which means Land of the Arrays or Aryans.[37]

The Indian Vedas also acknowledge the goddess Barati (Belonging to the Barats), and she was known as Brihad the Divine. They say her special place was on the Saras-vati River which happens to be the modern Sarus River in the Hittite-Phoenician land of Cilicia. The river entered the sea at Tarsus, the alleged home of St Paul in the New Testament, a work written in accordance with Aryan sun myths. Also, these Phoenicians and Aryans worshipped the serpent and the shape-shifting reptilians called the Nagas were the serpent gods of the Hindus. The Vedas, inspired by the Aryans, tell how the serpent-humans, the Nagas, could cause fantastic damage and instant death. The Nagas were also said to have appeared at the birth of the man who became known as Buddha and the serpent plays a part in the legend of Khrishna. The Roman name for Barati was Fortune after her legend as the goddess of fortune. They depicted Fortune in the same way as the Phoenicians symbolised Barati and the British do with Britannia. All were associated with water as you expect with a sea-faring race like the Phoenicians. The Egyptians, too, had a goddess called Birth, the goddess of the waters, and she was another mirror of Barati because the Aryan-Phoenicians were the force behind Egypt. Birth was described by a Babylonian emperor about 680 BC as "a Phoenician god across the sea".[38] In Crete, another Phoenician centre under the title 'Minoan', their goddess was Brito-Martis. She was a Phoenician goddess according to Greek and Roman legend (Barati in other words) and the divine daughter of Phoenix, the king of Phoenicia. Brito-Martis became identified with the goddess Diana, a major deity of the ancient world, and like her she was armed for the hunt. As Earl Spencer made a point of emphasising at the funeral of his sister Diana, Princess of Wales, she was named after the ancient goddess of hunting.

The early British kings called themselves and their race the 'Catti' and this appears on their coins. The Aryan Hittites of Asia Minor and Syria-Phoenicia called themselves the Catti or Khatti. The race of Aryans who left the Caucasus to rule India were known as the Khattiyo. The term Khatti evolved through the Hebrew and English translations into the Hittites of the Old Testament. Kassi or Cassi was the title used by the first Phoenician dynasty about 3,000 BC and was adopted by the Babylonian dynasty. Not surprising because these were different branches of the same people. The ancient Indian Epic king lists name some of the same people named in the Mesopotamian king lists and the predynastic civilisers of early Egypt also turn out to be of the Aryan race. We are looking at the same people here, no doubt whatsoever, and within this race are the reptile-Aryan bloodlines which have increasingly held the reins of power from the ancient world to the present day. As L. A. Waddell points out, the English, Scottish, Irish, Gaelic, Welsh, Gothic and Anglo-Saxon languages and their writing, and the entire family of Aryan languages, derive from the Aryan Phoenician language via the Hittite and Sumerian. About half of the commonest words used in the so-called English language today are of Sumerian, Cyprian or Hittite origin with the same sound and meaning. Sumerian, the language of the 'gods', is the parent language for most of the world, although I think it originated somewhere else even further back in history, maybe Atlantis or even the area today called the British Isles. As Waddell says:

"I had recognised that the various ancient scripts found at or near the old settlements of the Phoenicians, and (*those known as*) Cyprian, Karian, Aramaic or Syrian, Lykian, Lydian, Corinthian, Ionian, Cretan or "Minoan", Pelasgian, Phrygian, Cappadocian, Cilician, Theban, Libyan, Celto-Iberian, Gothic Runes etc, were all really local variations of the standard Aryan Hitto-Sumerian writing of the Aryan Phoenician mariners, those ancient pioneer spreaders of the Hittite Civilisation along the shores of the Mediterranean and out beyond the Pillars of Hercules to the British Isles."[39]

Official history asks us to believe that the people of Britain were savages who were 'civilised' only after the Romans came. This is not true and in fact the Romans said the opposite. Roman records say that the Britons were generally civilised and their customs much the same as the Gauls. Of course they were. They were the same people with the same origins. The Britons used gold money and there was trade with the European continent, as British coins of the period found there have confirmed. It was only the people of the interior of Britain, still uninfluenced by the Phoenician culture closer to the coasts, whom the Romans regarded as uncivilised when they arrived. Many of the roads regarded as 'Roman' were not built by the Romans at all. They were pre-Roman roads which they repaired. The Romans admired the efficiency of the British armies, particularly their use of war chariots. You won't be surprised to know by now that these famous 'British' chariots were the same as those used by the Hittites or Catti described by the Egyptian Pharaoh Ramses II around 1,295 BC at the Battle of Kadesh, a Hittite-Phoenician port. In about 350 BC, three centuries before the Romans arrived, the explorer and scientist, Pytheas, sailed around Britain and mapped the land scientifically with latitudes. Pytheas was a native of Phocca in Asia Minor, Phocca deriving from Phoenicia, as did an adjoining port called Phoenice.[40] By this time the Phoenicians had organised the tin trade, from their mines in Cornwall in the west of England across Gaul/France to Marseilles, from where it was taken by sea to the lands of the Mediterranean and Aegean. The first Phoenician tin-port in Cornwall was Ictis or St Michael's Mount in Penzance Bay. St Michael, one of the great heroes of Christianity, was in truth a Phoenician deity.

There is endless evidence to prove the ancient link between the British Isles and Ireland and the culture of North Africa and the Near East. They say if you want to expose corruption, follow the money. Well if you want to identify the passage of people and cultures, follow the language. The Irish language today is English which replaced Gaelic and Gaelic itself evolved from a now lost earlier language. Gaelic speaking missionaries in the Middle Ages had to use interpreters to communicate with the Picts, the ancient people of what became Scotland, and Cormac, a Gaelic-speaking Irish king of the ninth century, referred to the language of the people of Munster in south west Ireland as the 'iron language'. But even Gaelic connects us very firmly into the Middle East. In Conamara, in the west of Ireland, is a community which still speaks Gaelic as its first language. Their sean-nos (old style) singing, the basis of all Irish music, is amazingly similar to the native songs of the Middle East. Even trained ears find it almost impossible to distinguish between the chants of the Gaelic singers and those of Libyans. Charles Acton, the music critic of the *Irish Times*, wrote:

"If one listened for hours in the desert of an evening to Bedouin Arabs singing narrative epics... and then returned to Ireland and heard a fine sean-nos singer using the same melismata and rhythm, one finds the resemblance almost uncanny. So, too, if one listens to (*the Spanish*) "canto jondo".[41]

There were major sea trading routes between Ireland and Spain and Spain and North Africa in ancient times through which the passage of bloodlines, knowledge and culture was transported. The Spanish Arch in Galway in the west of Ireland commemorates this, as does the Conamara dancing known as 'the battering' which is virtually the same as Spanish Flamenco. The stick dance performed by the Wexford Mummers in Ireland is of North African origin. The word 'mummer' comes from Mohammedan. The Irish symbol, the harp, came from North Africa and so did the name of that other classic symbol of Ireland, the shamrock. Any three leaf plant is known in Egypt as a shamrukh. The rosary beads, the symbol of devout Roman Catholics, come from the Middle East and are still used by the Egyptians. The word 'nun' is Egyptian and their garments are from the Middle East. According to Arbois de Juvainville, the author of a work called *Cours De Literature Celtigue*, the Irish were known as 'Egyptians' in the Middle Ages. There are obvious connections between Irish books and those of the Egyptians. They employ the same styles of illustration and the colours used in the Irish Book of Kells and Book of Durrow are of Mediterranean origin. The red used in these books came from a Mediterranean insect, the Kermococcus vermilio, and others came from a Mediterranean plant, the Crozophora tinctoria. The crossed arms pose of many Egyptian portrayals of their god, Osiris, can be seen in Irish manuscripts. The Irish sweaters made on the Isle of Arran carry, according to at least one expert on the history of knitting, designs first given to them by Egyptian Coptic monks.⁴² The main blood group of Arran (Aryan?) is different from most of the Irish population. The old Irish sailing craft called pucan was invented by the North Africans and used on the Nile. Excavations at Navan Fort, near Armagh City, found remains of the Barbary ape estimated to have lived about 500 BC. The Barbary ape today is mainly associated with Gibraltar, but its home in 500 BC was North Africa. Libyan dragonskins (mercenaries) were believed to have been at large in Ireland 2,000 years ago. In the second century, the geographer Ptolemy, who lived in Alexandria, could name sixteen tribes in Ireland. The Irish sport of hurling is mirrored by the game called Takourt in Morocco. Irish ritual was, like all the cultures inspired by the Phoenician-Aryans, focused on the Sun. The Earth mound at Newgrange in Ireland has a narrow passageway of some 62 feet which is perfectly aligned with the Sun as it rises on December 21st/22nd, the winter solstice. So much so that the golden sunlight fills and illuminates the whole passage and the chamber at the centre. The entrance to structures in the Mediterranean, particularly the one at the Palace of Minos in Crete, are the same. The distinctive Round Towers of Ireland are, according to some orientalists, of Phoenician origin.⁴³ Again all this fits perfectly into the story I am revealing here. The Phoenicians came from the Middle and Near East, one of the global centres for the Anunnaki-reptilians and, according to the research of Professor Phillip Calahan I mentioned earlier, the round towers are aligned with stars systems in the northern sky – especially Draco.

The connections between Ireland and the Berbers of Morocco deserves a special mention. They are a light-skinned mountain people, some blue-eyed and blond-haired. They are associated with the Atlas Mountains which are themselves associated with Atlantis and named after Atlas, a son of the legendary ruler of Atlantis, Poseidon. Berber art has many similarities to the Irish version and anyone speaking Gaelic could comfortably understand the Berber tongue. The main Berber clans like M'Tir, M'Tuga and M'Ghill, are obvious origins or derivatives of the Ireland-Scottish MacTier, MacDougal and MacGhill. The term Mac means 'children or child of' and the Arabs use the term Bini, as in Bini M'Tir, which means the same. Missionaries who first explored the lands of the Berbers found that they used bagpipes, as do the Irish and Scots. Early invaders of Ireland were known as the men with the leather bags. An Irish goatskin drum found in Kerry is a twin of the Moroccan drum, the bindir. The violin and the guitar also originate in North Africa. The Viking wing of the Aryans invaded Ireland and founded many towns, including the present capital city of Dublin. But, not surprisingly in the light of the evidence you have been reading, the famous Viking galley with the high front and stern was a Phoenician design used by the Egyptians. Rock carvings at Newgrange appear to depict this design thousands of years earlier. The name Idris is well known in Wales and the saints and kings of the Muslims have been called Idris for centuries. In the British Museum is a Muslim coin, a gold dinar, which has the name 'Offa' stamped upon it. Offa was the King of Mercia in England in the 8th century and he is said to have built the 120 mile earth 'wall' between England and Wales known as Offa's Dyke. The name Wales comes from 'Weallas' meaning Land of Foreigners. The Welsh, like the Irish, explored the northern waters around Iceland before the Vikings and it is said that the Welshman Prince Madoc went ashore in America three centuries before Columbus. That's very possible because if he had access to the knowledge of the Phoenicians, he would have known that the Americas were there. The Venerable Bede of Cymbri (approximately the Welsh) said they were an Eastern people who migrated after the flood from the lands of the Bible to the British Isles.[44]

When the Irish settled in parts of Wales and Cornwall, some of the displaced people moved to Armorica, now Brittany, on the French coast. There you find the fantastic forest of standing stones called Carnac, a name which comes from Karnac in Egypt. The Breton language is a mixture of old Welsh and Cornish – Aryan. Brittany means Little Britain and relates again to Barat and Barati. Amorica means 'land facing the sea', a perfect description of America approached from the Atlantic. This is surely the true origin of the name America, and not Amerigo Vespucci, the explorer from Florence who was the contractor for Christopher Columbus in Spain. The Isle of Man was also populated by the Irish Aryans and it became a very sacred land. It was one of two places in Britain, Anglesea in North Wales was other, where the Arch Druids were based. These were the highest ranked members of the ancient British priestly class, who inherited their knowledge from the Phoenicians and later the Babylonian Brotherhood. The Isle of Man's three legs symbol is not unlike that ancient Phoenician symbol for the Sun, the swastika. Irish connections with Ethiopia have also been identified. An American researcher, Winthrop Palmer Boswell, wrote a book called *Irish Wizards In The Woods Of Ethiopia* in which she showed the similarities between Irish and Ethiopian folk stories. The baobab tree is held in great reverence by Ethiopians and Berbers and 'banba' is an old name for Ireland.

This reverence for trees in North Africa was expressed in the British Isles and Europe by the Druids and the giant or Titan race, the reptilian-human crossbreeds of the ancient Near East, were often symbolised as trees because of their height. In his 1833 book, *Phoenician Ireland*, Joachim de Villeneuve, insisted that Irish Druids were the 'snake priests' of the Phoenician seafarers. This would certainly explain the origin of the Balor of the Evil Eye, the Irish version of the North African god Baal, and the celebration in May of the Baal ritual, Beltane. The evil eye relates to the hypnotic stare of the reptilians. The Sun god of the Phoenicians was Bel or Bil and later became known by the Canaanites and Babylonians as Baal – Nimrod. The Druids became the carriers of the mystery school tradition in Britain, Ireland and France or Britannia, Eire and Gaul as they were then called, and some of them became deeply corrupted by the influence of the reptile-human bloodlines of the Babylonian Brotherhood which established control of the Aryan priesthood as the centuries passed. The origin of the word Druid is not certain. A Gaelic word, druidh, means 'a wise man' or a 'sorcerer', but it may come from the Irish word, Drui, which means 'men of the oak trees'.⁴⁵ The Druidic Mysteries were taught in the darkness of caves, forests and groves with the oak tree symbolising their Supreme Deity (very much in line with the Watcher tree-symbolism). They did not worship the oak tree, it was a symbol and anything which grew upon it, like mistletoe, became sacred. The holly bush was another sacred symbol of the Druids and this is where we get the name Hollywood in Los Angeles, the centre of the global film industry which was created by modern initiates of the Babylonian Brotherhood. It has remained in their control and Hollywood is one of their most important vehicles for mass mind conditioning. Hollywood is indeed a place of magic as it casts a spell on humanity's perception of itself and the world. The Druids knew about astrology and astronomy and they celebrated the birth of the Sun on December 25th. The Moon was also very important to them. Particularly sacred was the night of the new Moon, the sixth day, and the full Moon.

As with the Blue Degrees of modern Freemasonry, the Druid initiates were divided into three groups. The teachings given to each level in the forest groves of ancient times and the Freemasonic temples of today are virtually the same. The first level of the Druid School was the Ovate who was dressed in green, the Druidic colour for learning. The second was the Bard, who wore sky blue representing harmony and truth. They had the task of memorising some of the 20,000 verses of Druidic poetry within which the mysteries were hidden. The third, the Druid, would be dressed in a white robe, their symbolic colour for purity and the Sun. To become an Arch-Druid, a spiritual leader, you had to pass six levels of degree. The Druids had total power over the population for a long time and some deeply unpleasant rituals emerged after their mystery school network was taken over by the Babylonian Brotherhood. The basic moral code was taught to all people, but the secret knowledge was, as with all these networks, preserved for initiates under the strictest secrecy. Eliphas Levi, the famous esotericist, said of their healing methods:

"The Druids were priests and physicians, curing by magnetism… Their universal remedies were mistletoe and serpent's eggs, because these substances attract astral light in a special manner. The solemnity with which mistletoe was cut down drew upon this plant the popular confidence and rendered it powerfully magnetic."[46]

The Druids, like the other mystery religions, were carriers of advanced knowledge which has been kept from the people, and some of them used it for less than positive reasons. I am not condemning the Druids as a whole and I certainly do not wish to cast a negative interpretation on the work of modern Druids. Knowledge is neutral and the same knowledge can be used with good or malevolent intent. But there is no doubt that the Druidic religion was infiltrated and began to manifest the classic rituals and behaviour of the reptilians, including human sacrifice. The Brotherhood today still uses Druidic rituals in its own black magic ceremonies.

Going home?

The evidence of the connections between the Middle-Near East and the British Isles and Ireland is simply enormous. You can follow the flow of peoples, knowledge, culture, language, deities, symbols and rituals, very comfortably. I wonder, however, if this was all travelling between these two areas of the world for the first time from around 3,000 BC or whether, in the ancient past before the Venus cataclysm, it had all gone in the reverse direction. Could it be that the origins of the Middle-Near East cultures had actually been in what became the British Isles and Europe, and after 3,000 BC it was taken in the reverse direction. I can't present detailed evidence of this at the moment, but my research is moving that way. If the British Isles and parts of Europe were badly affected by Earth upheavals, maybe there was a mass movement of the advanced race from many parts of the world to safer lands, particularly in the Near East. Certainly, the Babylonian Brotherhood and others with advanced knowledge were very keen to make their way to Britain and establish their headquarters there. London became the epicentre of their operations and it remains so to this day. There must be a very important reason for that and I think it relates to the energy fields in these lands. The British Isles is a really sacred place to the Brotherhood because it is the centre of the Earth's energy grid. It is not without reason that there is a greater concentration of stone circles, standing stones, ancient mounds and sites, in areas of Britain than in almost anywhere else in the world. Those who understand how to manipulate energy and consciousness would seek to base their activities at the heart centre of the planetary energy grid and they have done this by operating so much of their Agenda from the British Isles.

London is also a major site on the Earth's magnetic grid and it became the capital not only of Britain or Barat-land, but also of the Babylonian Brotherhood. To them, it is their 'New Troy' or 'New Babylon'. The city of Troy in Asia Minor, the place made famous by the Trojan Wars and the Wooden Horse legend, was another Aryan centre. It was the old capital of the Hittites. Many of the reptile-Aryan bloodlines appear to have been based in Troy and it remains a sacred place for those at the upper levels of the secret society network who are aware of their true origins. Troy or Troia means 'three places' in Greek and Hebrew, an allusion to the trinity, another belief that Christianity has stolen from the ancient world. In English, Troy or Troia is Tripoli, the name of the capital of Libya today and home to that Brotherhood frontman, Colonel Gaddafi. Once again, Troy relates to the extraterrestrial full-bloods and crossbreeds, hence the constant obsession with that name by the Brotherhood. In the Iliad epic, believed to have been written by the Greek poet, Homer, it states that Troy was founded by Dardanus, the son of the Greek god Zeus, who was a Titan – the reptilian bloodline. Zeus was depicted as both an eagle and a serpent. He was said to have been born in Arcadia, in Sparta, and after the Trojan War many Spartans migrated into what is now France. Terms like 'New Troy', therefore, relate to centres for these same bloodlines.

Most people don't realise that London was founded as the 'New Troy'. After the destruction of Troy around 1,200 BC, the story goes that Aeneas, born of a royal bloodline, fled with the remnants of his people and settled in Italy. There he married the daughter of Latinus, the king of the Latins, and through this line later emerged the Roman Empire. According to many traditions, the grandson of Aeneas, a man called Brutus, landed in Britain around 1,103 BC with a group of Trojans, including some from colonies in Spain. They referred to Britain as the 'Great White Island' after the white cliffs which abound on the South Coast. In the south west of England is the town of Totnes in Devon, a short distance inland from Torbay, the oldest seaport in the area. Here there is a stone called the Brutus Stone on which, the legend says, the former Trojan prince stood after he first landed. Welsh records say that Brutus was met by three tribes of Britons who proclaimed him king. Brutus founded a city he called 'Caer Troia' – New Troy. The Romans would later call it Londinium. London became the operational centre of the empire of the Babylonian Brotherhood, and it still is, along with Paris and the Vatican. In the King Arthur stories, London or New Troy, is Troynavant, King Arthur's eastern gateway city and King Arthur's Camelot apparently means Martian City or City of Mars. Artefacts discovered by the German archaeologist, Heinrich Schliemann, at the site of ancient Troy, contained many of the markings found on British megalithic stones. They were also decorated with the swastika, the Phoenician-Aryan symbol of the Sun. Once again, they were the same people. All the white peoples are and it is the white race which has taken over the world, quite demonstrably. Just look around you at who controls all the reigns of global power. White people.

And within this race and others, going back to antiquity, are the reptile bloodlines who are today centred on London, New Troy, or more appropriately New Babylon. The bodies of these Elite bloodlines are occupied or controlled by the reptiles of the lower fourth dimension and most of the lesser Aryan hierarchy have no idea that this is so. I will focus on this reptilian-Anunnaki network and chart it into the modern world when we have considered the truth about the religions which the reptilians have used so effectively to batter the human race into mental, emotional and spiritual submission.

■ SOURCES

1   Brian Desborough, *The Great Pyramid Mystery*.

2   Ibid.

3   Ibid.

4   Ibid.

5   Ibid.

6   Geoffrey Higgins, *Anacalypsis* (first published 1836, republished in 1972 by Health Research, PO Box 850, Pomeroy, WA, USA 99347), volume I, p 368.

7   *The Great Pyramid Mystery*.

8   Ibid.

9   Ibid.

10 Ibid.

11 Ibid.

12 Ibid.

13 Ibid.

14 Ibid.

15 Ibid.

16 First Book of Enoch, 7:2-6.

17 *The Universe* (Life National Picture Library, Time-Life International, Netherlands, 1964), pp 85-94.

18 Ibid.

19 Ibid.

20 Adrian G. Gilbert and Maurice M. Cotterell, *The Mayan Prophecies* (Element Books, Shaftesbury, England, 1995).

21 Quoted in *The Occult Conspiracy*, p 28.

22 Manly P. Hall, *The Secret Teachings Of All Ages* (The Philosophical Research Society, Los Angeles, California, 1988), p A1.

23 *From The Ashes Of Angels*, p 93.

24 L. A. Waddell, *The Phoenician Origin Of Britons*, p 11.

25 Ibid, p 13.

26 Capt E. Raymond, *Missing Links Discovered In Assyrian Tablets* (Artisan Sales, Thousand Oaks, California, 1985), p 145.

27 *The Phoenician Origins Of Britons*, p 48.

28 Ibid, p 39.

29 Ibid, p 40.

30 Michael Hesemann, *The Cosmic Connection* (Gateway Books, Wellow, Avon, England, 1996), p 107.

31 *The Phoenician Origin Of Britons*, p 231.

32 Richard Hoagland, *Monuments On Mars* (North Atlantic Books, California, USA, 1996).

33 *The Cosmic Connection*, p 108.

34 *The Great Pyramid Mystery.*

35 *Rig Veda.*

36 *The Phoenician Origin Of Britons*, p 65.

37 Ibid.

38 Ibid, p 62.

39 Ibid, p 27.

40 Ibid, p 54.

41 Bob Quinn, *Atlantean, Ireland's North African And Maritime Heritage* (Quartet Books, London, 1986), p 19. A very good summary of the evidence connecting Ireland with North Africa.

42 Heinz Edgar Kiewe, "The Sacred History of Knitting", quoted in *Atlantean*, pp 159,160 .

43 *Atlantean*, p 30.

44 Steve Jones, *In The Blood* (Harper Collins, London, 1966), p 126.

45 *The Secret Teachings Of All Ages*, pp XXII-XXIII.

46 Ibid.

CHAPTER FOUR

The Suns of God

Nothing has served the reptilian Agenda more than religion. Still today in America religion controls the minds and limits the thinking of the Christian patriot movement which has seen through many other smokescreens and identified many aspects of the Brotherhood conspiracy. What they cannot face, however, is that their own religion is a massive part of that conspiracy.

That is not to condemn all people who call themselves Christian. There are many who express a loving spirituality through their Christian beliefs. I am talking of the institution of Christianity and its arrogant indoctrination and imposition of its desperately limited vision of life which has created a mind-prison for literally billions of people over almost 2,000 years. All the world's major religions, Hinduism, Christianity, Judaism and Islam, came out of the very same region of the Middle and Near East from which the Aryan race and the reptile crossbreeds emerged after the cataclysm of perhaps 7,000 years ago. These religions were designed to imprison the mind and engulf the emotions with fear and guilt. They were usually based on some 'saviour-god' figure like Jesus or Mohammed and only by believing in them and following their dictates can we find 'God' and be saved. That is precisely what the Babylonian priests said about Nimrod when the blueprint for control-by-religion was being moulded in Babylon. Those who refuse to believe this hogwash are condemned to stoke the fires of hell for all eternity. Staggeringly, billions upon billions have fallen for this scam over thousands of years, and still do. That's fine if they want to give their minds and their lives away, but many insist that everyone else must do the same and that's not fine. Seriously not fine. Most of the people reading this book will be from the parts of the world dominated by Christianity and Judaism and so I shall take those as the main examples of how symbolic stories have become literal truths and how the manipulation of these stories has produced the most powerful form of mass mind control yet invented.

To understand the true background to the religions, we need to appreciate the basis of all ancient religion going back to the Phoenicians, the Babylonians and beyond. It was the Sun. The hierarchy focused on the Sun because, as I outlined earlier, they understood its true power as an amazing generator of electromagnetic energy which is affecting our lives and behaviour every second of every day. The Sun contains 99% of the mass of this solar system. Just think about that. The Sun *is* the solar system and when it changes, we change. Understanding these Sun cycles, and the changing nature of the energy it projects, allows you to anticipate how human

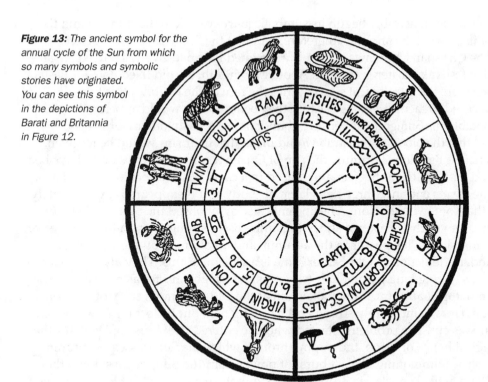

Figure 13: *The ancient symbol for the annual cycle of the Sun from which so many symbols and symbolic stories have originated. You can see this symbol in the depictions of Barati and Britannia in Figure 12.*

beings are most likely to react to various events at different times. As with the texts that form the basis of the various religions, there are two levels of knowledge in Sun worship. In the ancient world, the hierarchy focused on the Sun because they knew its effect at a deep level, while the masses worshipped the Sun because its heat and light had an obvious and crucial role in ensuring an abundant harvest. In the same way, an initiate of the esoteric knowledge will read the Bible differently to a Christian or Jewish believer. The initiate will recognise the symbolism, the numerology and the esoteric codes, while the believer takes the text literally. So the same text acts as a means of passing on esoteric knowledge to the initiated and creates a prison-religion for the masses who are not initiated. Great scam.

To understand the ancient Sun symbolism is to understand the major religions. In the ancient world they used one particular symbol (*see **Figure 13***) for the Sun's journey through the year. As we will see in a later chapter, this is still a fundamental symbol used by the Babylonian Brotherhood. It symbolised both the Phoenician depictions of Barati and was on the shield of her British expression, Britannia. The ancients took the circle of the zodiac (a Greek word meaning animal circle) and inserted a cross to mark the four seasons. At the centre of the cross, they placed the Sun. So many of the pre-Christian deities were said to have been born on December 25th because of this symbolism. On December 21st–22nd, you have the winter solstice when, in the northern hemisphere, the Sun is at the lowest point of its power in the annual cycle. The Sun, the ancients said, had symbolically 'died'. By December 25th, the Sun had demonstrably begun its symbolic journey back to the summer and the peak of its power. The ancients, therefore, said that the Sun was 'born' on December 25th. The Christian Christmas is merely a renamed Pagan festival, as indeed are all Christian festivals. Easter is another. About March 25th, the old fixed date for Easter, the Sun enters the astrological sign of Aries the ram or the lamb. At this time the ancients used to sacrifice lambs because they believed this would appease the gods, most notably the Sun god, and ensure abundant harvests. In other words they believed that the blood of the lamb would mean that their sins would be forgiven.

In ancient Babylon, Tammuz, the son of Queen Semiramis, was said to have been crucified with a lamb at his feet and placed in a cave. When a rock was rolled away from the cave's entrance three days later, his body had disappeared. I've definitely heard that somewhere before. The ancients also symbolised the Sun as a baby in December, a youth at Easter, a strapping, immensely strong, man in the summer, an ageing man losing his power in the autumn, and an old man by the winter solstice. The modern depiction of Old Father Time is a version of this. They also symbolised the Sun as having long golden hair (sun rays) which got shorter as he lost his power in the months of autumn. Now look again at the Old Testament story of Samson – Sam-sun. He was incredibly strong and had long hair, but he lost his power when his hair was cut. The problems started when he entered the House of Delilah – the astrological house of Virgo, the virgin, through which the Sun passes as autumn approaches. Summoning his last burst of power, Sam-the-Sun, pushes down the two pillars, which are classic Brotherhood symbolism going back at least to ancient Egypt and are still used by the Freemasons today. Samson is Sam Sun – a symbolic story of the Sun's annual cycle. There wasn't any such person. In Hebrew, Samson means I understand, the God of the Sun.

To the orthodox Christian, Jesus is the only begotten Son of God who died so our sins could be forgiven. But you will find exactly the same claims for a stream of 'gods' in the ancient world long before the name of 'Jesus' was even heard of. Indeed, we know his name wasn't Jesus because that's a Greek translation of a Hebrew name. The term Son of God would seem to originate at least as far back as the Aryan Gothic kings of Cilicia who took the title 'Son of the Sun God', a tradition adopted by the Pharaohs of Egypt.[1] To many in the New Age, Jesus is Sananda, a high initiate of some spiritual hierarchy who incarnated to infuse the Earth with the 'Christ' energy. Or, depending on who you talk to, he was an extraterrestrial on a similar mission. To others he was claiming to be the King of the 'Jews' by right of his King David bloodline. But did Jesus actually exist? Did Moses, Solomon and King David exist? I would say categorically no. There is no credible evidence for the existence of any of them outside the biblical texts and they are certainly not credible. So where did they come from?

The Old Testament

In 721 BC, it appears that Israel was overrun by the Assyrians and the Israelites or Canaanites were taken into captivity. However, the tribes known by official history as Judah and Benjamin, survived for more than a hundred years after that, before they were conquered and captured by our friends, the Babylonians, in around 586 BC. It was in Babylon, that ancient capital city of the reptile-Aryan priesthood and hierarchy, that the Hebrew priests, the Levites, began to create a manufactured history which obscured the truth of what really happened. I mean, ask yourself, is a Brotherhood who arranged for the destruction of ancient knowledge and libraries all over the world going to write down the true history in their texts or are they going to produce the version they want the people to believe? During and after their stay in Babylon, with its wealth of inherited knowledge and stories from Sumer, the Levites mixed truth, often symbolic truth, with fantasies and this concoction became the foundations of the Old Testament. The so-called Israelites did not write these texts or agree with what they said. Even if you accept they even existed, the Israelites had long dispersed by the time the Levites inked their pens. Genesis, Exodus, Leviticus and Numbers, which together make up the 'Jewish' Torah, were all written by the Levites or under their supervision during or after their period in Babylon. This bunch of human sacrificing, blood drinking fanatics and black magicians, who you would not trust to tell you the time, compiled the law which Jewish people to this day are supposed to follow. Likewise many Christian fanatics quote this stuff as the word of God! It is not the word of God, it is the word of the Levites under the direction of the reptile full-bloods and crossbreeds of the Babylonian Brotherhood. The Sumerian Tablets prove beyond question that Genesis was a much edited and condensed version of Sumer records. The Sumerian story of Edin became the Levite's biblical Garden of Eden. Remember the story of 'Moses' being found in the bulrushes by the Egyptian princess? The same tale was told by the Sumerians-Babylonians about King Sargon the Elder. The story of Moses is make-believe, as is the Egyptian 'captivity', the Exodus, at least in the form described, and also the creation of the 12 tribes via Jacob.

These texts were written by the Levites, the heads of which were reptilian mystery school initiates in Babylon. Their stories are symbolic and coded for initiates to understand and the masses to take literally. According to the Levites, Moses was given his laws and commandments by God on top of a mountain. Again and again we see the symbol of mountains. One reason for this is that the top of a mountain is closer to their symbol of God – the Sun. Mount Sion means Sun Mountain. The Sun rising over the eastern mountains is still a major Brotherhood symbol today. The story of the Israelites and Jews is largely a fantasy – the veil behind which the truth has been hidden. No-one has been 'had' more comprehensively over these thousands of years than the people who have considered themselves Jewish. They have been terrorised, used and manipulated in the most merciless and grotesque fashion by their hierarchy to advance an Agenda which the Jewish people in general have not even begun to identify. There is no greater example of this manipulation than the way the reptilian bloodlines like the 'Jewish' Rothschilds funded and supported the Nazis and allowed the rank and file Jewish people to reap the unspeakable consequences. The Levite story of Exodus is a smokescreen to hide the fact that the 'Hebrew' knowledge was stolen from the Egyptian mystery schools after they were infiltrated by the Babylonian

Brotherhood. The Egyptians considered the 'Jehovah' revelation to be a robbery committed against the sacred sciences.[2] Manly P. Hall, the Freemasonic historian and initiate, said that black magic dictated the state religion in Egypt and that the intellectual and spiritual activities of the people were paralysed by complete obedience to the dogma formulated by the priestcraft. What a perfect description of the Levite-Babylonian mode of manipulation and of all the religions, like Christianity, which were to emerge from the lies they peddled. And that's a crucial point to remember. Judaism, Christianity and Islam all base their beliefs on these same stories written by the Levites after their stay in Babylon. We are looking at a point in history which was to define and control the world from then until now. The knowledge the Levites stole from Egypt and expanded as a result of their stay in Babylon, became known as the Cabala (Kabala, Qaballa), which comes from the Hebrew root, QBL, meaning mouth to ear. This is the method used to communicate the most secret information to initiates. The Cabala is the esoteric stream of what is called Judaism, which in fact is a front for the Babylonian Brotherhood, as is the Vatican. The Cabala is the secret knowledge hidden in codes within the Old Testament and other texts. Judaism is the literal interpretation of it. This is a technique you can see in all the religions. An example of the Levite coding is the names of the five scribes, Garia, Dabria, Tzelemia, Echanu and Azrel, in the second book of Esdras or Ezra. The names and their true meanings are:

- **Garia:** Marks which ancient scribes used to indicate that the text is either defective or has another meaning.
- **Dabria:** Words comprising a phrase or text.
- **Tzelemia:** Figures, something figured, or indicated in an obscure manner.
- **Echanu:** Something which has been changed or doubled.
- **Azrel:** The name of Esdras/Ezra, the suffix 'el' meaning the work of Ezra.[3]

These five names for 'scribes' therefore read as one phrase to an initiate: "Marks of warning – of the words – figured in an obscure manner – which have been changed or doubled – which is the work of Ezra."[4] There is a book called *The Bible Code*[5] which claims to have identified a code in the Hebrew version of the Old Testament which predicts the future. As one of these codes predicted that Lee Harvey Oswald would kill President Kennedy, you'll excuse me if I remain extremely unconvinced about its credibility. Is there anyone left who still believes that Oswald killed Kennedy? But while I question claims in *The Bible Code*, there *is* a code in the Bible, an esoteric code for initiates. They either made up characters to fit their symbolism or vaguely based them on living people who they usually massively misrepresented. Here are some examples of codes in the Bible. A common theme in all mystery school traditions is of 12 disciples, knights or followers surrounding a deity. The number 12 is a code, among other things, for the 12 months of the year and the houses of the zodiac through which symbolically travels the Sun, the 'god', symbolised as 13. This is the 'sacred 12 and one' as some people describe it and it is one major reason why the numbers 12 and 13 keep recurring. Thus you have the 12 tribes of Israel, 12 princes of

Ishmael, 12 disciples or followers of Jesus, Buddha, Osiris and Quetzalcoatl. There is also King Arthur and his 12 Knights of the Round Table (the zodiac circle), Himmler and his 12 knights in the Nazi SS, and the woman (Isis, Semiramis) with a crown of 12 stars in the Book of Revelation. In Scandinavia and that whole northern region you find the Odin mysteries, again inspired by the same Aryan race from the Near East. In this tradition, you find twelve 'Drottars' presiding over the mysteries with Odin. The sacred 12 and one again. These stories are not literally true, they are mystery school symbolism. This continues today with these same symbols used by the Brotherhood secret society network in national flags, coats of arms, advertising and company logos. That Brotherhood creation, the European Union, has a circle of 12 stars as its symbol. We are talking sacred numbers and geometry here. The proportions of Egyptian statues, whether big or small, were multiples or sub multiples of 12 or 6.

The numbers 7 and 40 are also code numbers in the Bible and the mysteries. So in the Bible we have seven spirits of God, the seven churches of Asia, seven golden candlesticks, seven stars, seven lamps of fire, seven seals, seven trumpets, seven angels, seven thunders and the red dragon in Revelation with seven heads and seven crowns. The story of Jericho has Joshua marching his army around the city for seven days, accompanied by seven priests carrying seven trumpets. On the seventh day they circled Jericho seven times and the walls came tumbling down. In the story of Noah, seven pairs of each animal go into the ark and seven pairs of each type of bird. There are seven days between the prediction of the deluge and the rain and seven days between the sending of the doves. The ark comes to rest on the 17th day of the seventh month, Noah leaves the ark on the 27th day, and after the flood he begins his seventh century. Many of the names for the symbolic deities, such as Abraxas of the Gnostics and Serapis of Greece have seven letters. Then there is 40. Adam enters Paradise when he is 40 years old; Eve follows 40 years later; during the Great Flood it rains for 40 days and 40 nights; Seth is carried away by angels when he is 40 and is not seen for 40 days; Moses is 40 when he goes to Midian and he stays for 40 years; Joseph is 40 years old when Jacob arrives in Egypt; Jesus goes into the wilderness for 40 days. The Bible is the word of God? No. It is written in the esoteric code of the mystery schools. The Arabian literature was also compiled by and for initiates of the mysteries and here you find the same codes. The Arbaindt (the forties) are stories which all relate to the number 40 and their calendar has 40 rainy and 40 windy days. Their laws constantly refer to 40. Another series of Arabian books, the Sebaydt or 'seven' are based on that number. These number codes have even deeper meanings than the more obvious ones of days, months and the zodiac. Numbers also represent vibrational frequencies. Every frequency resonates to a certain number, colour and sound. Some frequencies, represented by numbers, colours and sounds, are particularly powerful. Symbols also represent frequencies and they affect the subconscious without the person realising it is happening. This is another reason why certain symbols are seen in secret societies, national flags, company logos, advertising and so on.

There is no historical evidence for the existence of a man called Moses except in the texts produced by the Levites and other writings and opinions stimulated by those texts. Some say this was a cover name for the Egyptian pharaoh, Arkenaten, and I would certainly not dismiss that, but the official background to 'Moses' and his name have no historical basis. Nothing was known about the 'Moses' story, or the 'plagues' inflicted upon the Egyptians, until the Levites of Babylon wrote Exodus centuries after it was supposed to have happened. All the animals of Egypt were killed three times according to the story! What did they do, die and immediately remanifest? There was no murder of the first born of Egypt and so the Feast of the Passover has no historical basis, it was created as a result of a story invented by the Levites. Their references to the lamb's blood on the doors is code for the ancient symbolism of the lamb. There is no official book in Hebrew which makes any mention of the Pentateuch (the laws of Moses) before the Levites went to Babylon. As for the Israelites being captive in Egypt, even Deuteronomy describes them as 'strangers', not slaves, in this period.[6] So where did the name Moses come from? Every initiated person who attained the highest rank in the Egyptian mystery schools was called a Muse, Mose or… Moses.[7] Manetho, the Egyptian historian of the third century BC, quoted by the Jewish historian, Josephus, says that he was a priest at Heliopolis or ON (Place of the Sun), and that afterwards he took the name of Mosheh or Moses.[8] The word Moses means: he who has been taken away, he who has been put out from the waters, who has been made a missionary, an ambassador, an apostle.[9] The Chief Priest in the Egyptian temples was called EOVE or EOVA, hence the emergence of the name Jehovah,[10] and the Hebrew language is really the sacred language of the Egyptian mystery schools.[11] The general language of Egypt was called CBT, QBT or CBT, and is better known as Copt or Coptic. The sacred language of the mystery schools took its name from OBR or ABR which, in these times, meant the passage from one place to another and a transition of some kind. Exactly the point of the original mystery school teachings, a transition to greater enlightenment. ABR became Ambres, the name of the holy doctrine reserved for initiates, and it was also written as Ambric, Hebric, Hebraic and… Hebrew.[12] The Hebrew alphabet has 22 letters, but the original, before the time of 'Moses', only contained ten, and its true meaning was known only to the priests.

Hebrews were not Israelites or Jews, they were initiates of the Egyptian mystery schools, or at least their founders were. No wonder it has proved impossible to identify a genetic Hebrew or Jewish 'race'. Cohen, the Jewish name for priest, comes from Cahen, the Egyptian pronunciation for a priest and a prince.[13] Even circumcision, that uniquely 'Jewish' tradition, came from the Egyptian mystery schools and was performed at least as far back as 4,000 BC. You could not be initiated unless you were circumcised. The Hebrew religion did not exist in Egypt and there was no Hebrew law because there was no Hebrew 'race'. The only worship was Egyptian worship. The Hebrew religion, language and race only emerged when initiates of the Egyptian mysteries, later to be known as Levites, took the knowledge out of Egypt and invented a whole history to cover what they were doing, who they were working for and where they came from. The terms 'Hebrew' and 'Judaism' are another way of saying Egyptian. This is one reason why we have the constant use of symbols by today's Brotherhood which relate to Egypt, including the pyramid with the capstone missing. This is symbolic of the Great Pyramid at Giza and the Egyptian mystery schools, together with much deeper meanings. At the entrance to the mystery school temple in Egypt were two massive obelisks. These are often represented as two pillars by the Freemasons and in buildings designed and funded by initiates. Hence the two pillars that Samson pushed over. Every initiate in the mystery schools was given a secret name and this also continues with the Brotherhood today. One connection to the Hebrews in Egypt could be the invasion of the Hyksos or Shepherd Kings. The Egyptian historian, Manetho, reported that a strange and barbaric race invaded and took control of Egypt. When they were eventually driven out, he said, they journeyed through Syria and built a city called Jerusalem.[14] The Hyksos could well be a group of similar description called the Habiru who came out of the former lands of Sumer, as did, according to the Old Testament, the one called Abraham.

King Solomon and his temple are more symbolism. There is, again, no independent evidence for a person called King Solomon. Not once has his name appeared in any inscriptions. Before the Levites wrote their texts, the Greek historian Herodotus (c. 485–425 BC), travelled and researched the lands and history of Egypt and the Near East. He heard nothing of the empire of Solomon, the mass exodus of Israelites from Egypt, or the destruction of the pursuing Egyptian army in the Red Sea. Nor did Plato in his travels to the same area. Why? Because it is all invention. The three syllables in Sol-om-on are all names for the Sun in three languages. Manly P. Hall wrote that Solomon and his wives and concubines were symbolic of the planets, moons, asteroids and other receptive bodies within his house – the solar mansion.[15] Solomon's Temple is symbolic of the domain of the Sun. In Talmudic legend, Solomon is presented as a master magician who understood the Cabala and cast out demons. This is more symbolism of the secret knowledge held within the fabricated stories of Hebrew 'history'. The books of Kings and Chronicles, which recount the building of Solomon's Temple, were written between 500 and 600 years after the events they are supposed to be describing. Hebrew chroniclers of the Temple of Solomon are so over the top, it's hilarious. It was supposed to occupy 153,600 workmen for seven years and its cost, worked out by Arthur Dynott Thomson, would have been £6,900 million. And Thomson was writing in 1872! What would it be today? Such figures are ludicrous and yet further examples of the make-believe behind these tales. They are symbolic, not literal. Another point. If Solomon didn't exist, why should we believe that his 'father', King David, did? I keep reading accounts of his life and the only sources quoted are the Old Testament texts written by the Levites! There is no other evidence. It's a con. So is the idea of the King David-Jesus bloodline being taken to France by 'Mary Magdalene' to become the Merovingians as suggested in many books over recent years. As the scholar and researcher, L. A. Waddell, points out:

"There is absolutely no inscriptional evidence whatsoever, nor any ancient Greek or Roman reference, for the existence of Abraham or any of the Jewish patriarchs or prophets of the Old Testament, nor for Moses, Saul, David, Solomon, nor any of the Jewish kings, with the mere exception of two, or at most three, of the later kings."[16]

The consequences of all this for the people who have called themselves Jewish, and for humanity in general, have been quite appalling. The Mosaic Law, the law of 'Moses', is the law of the Levites – the law of the reptilian full-bloods and crossbreeds of the Babylonian Brotherhood. What it is *not*, is the law or word of God. The Torah and Talmud, both compiled overwhelmingly in and after their time in Babylon, are a mental bombardment of highly detailed laws governing every area of a person's life. There's no way that was given by 'God' on the top of a mountain. The Levites wrote it and then invented Moses to hide this fact. Other 'laws' have been constantly added or revised since, to cover all eventualities. The pages of these Levite texts contain a constant and sickening theme of extreme racism against non-Judeans and the need to 'utterly destroy' anyone who defies them – exactly the way Manly Hall described the methods of the black magic priests. They encourage murder and mayhem of every conceivable kind. The Talmud must be the most racist document on Earth. Here are just a few examples of the depth of its spiritual sickness:

"Just the Jews are humans, the non-Jews are no humans, but cattle" **Kerithuth 6b, page 78, Jebhammoth 61**

"The non-Jews have been created to serve the Jews as slaves" **Midrasch Talpioth 225**

"Sexual intercourse with non-Jews is like sexual intercourse with animals" **Kethuboth 3b**

"The non-Jews have to be avoided even more than sick pigs" **Orach Chaiim 57, 6a**

"The birth rate of non-Jews has to be suppressed massively" **Zohar 11, 4b**

"As you replace lost cows and donkeys, so you shall replace non-Jews" **Lore Dea 377,1**

But this is not just a grotesque diatribe of racism. Look again. It is the very attitudes that the Draco reptilians and their underlings have towards humans. Remember this horrific stuff was not written by Judeans or 'Jews' as a people. They are victims of these beliefs, not the authors. It was written by the Levites, representatives of the priestly bloodlines of the reptilians and the Babylonian Brotherhood, who have no more allegiance to the Jewish people than did Adolf Hitler. To blame it on 'the Jews' is a nonsense and exactly what the Brotherhood want people to do because it creates enormous opportunities to divide and rule, the very foundation of their control. What horrors this manipulation has caused for 'Jew' and 'Gentile' alike. It is the same with the Jewish oral law called the Mishnah, completed by the second century AD. Israel Shahak, a survivor of the Belsen Concentration Camp, is one of the comparatively few people now known as Jews, who has had the courage to openly challenge and expose the Talmud. Shahak, in his book *Jewish History, Jewish Religion*, highlights the stunning level of racism on which the 'Jewish' (Levite, Brotherhood) law is founded. He tells how the extreme end of this 'faith', as represented by the orthodox rabbis today, makes it a religious offence to save the life of a Gentile, unless there would be unpleasant consequences for Jews not doing so. The charging of interest on loans to a fellow Jew is banned, but by Talmudic law they must charge a Gentile as much interest as they possibly can. It is demanded that Jews must utter a curse every time they pass a Gentile cemetery and that when they pass a Gentile building they must ask God to destroy it. Jews are forbidden to defraud each other, but that law does not apply to the defrauding of Gentiles. Jewish prayers bless God for not making them Gentiles and others ask that Christians may perish immediately. A religious Jew must not drink from a bottle of wine if a Gentile has touched it since it was opened. The Jewish writer, Agnon, after being awarded the Nobel Prize for literature, said on Israeli radio: "I am not forgetting that it is forbidden to praise Gentiles, but here there is a special reason for doing so – that is, they awarded the prize to a Jew."[17] These are the laws of the belief system called 'Jewish' which is constantly complaining about, and condemning, racism against Jews! The very belief system is founded on the most extreme racism you will ever encounter. Yet the cry of "anti-Semitic" is used to discredit researchers who are getting too close to the truth about the global conspiracy. Benjamin Freedman, a Jew who knew the top Zionists (Sionists, Sun cultists) of the 1930s and 40s, said that anti-Semitism should be eliminated from the English language. He went on:

> "Anti-Semitism serves only one purpose today. It is used as a smear word. When so-called Jews feel that anyone opposes their real objectives, they discredit their victims by applying the word "anti-Semite" or "anti-Semitic" through all the channels they have at their command and under their control."[18]

One of these channels is an organisation based in the United States, and operating worldwide, which was set up precisely to condemn as racists those exposing the Brotherhood. It is called the Anti-Defamation League (ADL) and I have been a target for them myself, something I find very comforting and confirmation that I am going in the correct direction. It has great support from non-Jewish sycophants who wish to keep the ADL sweet and to feed their own desire to posture their sense of self-purity. I'll take the sanctimonious, holier-than-thou, 'anti-racist' movements seriously, when they begin to protest against all racism and not just that which suits their political correctness. The smell of hypocrisy makes my nostrils ache. This Levite racism is not followed by the overwhelming majority of Jewish people and many have rebelled against the strict race laws that demand that Jews only interbreed with Jews. Most people who call themselves Jewish are brought up from birth to be the frightened, indoctrinated puppets of this vicious Levite hierarchy which has metamorphosed as the Pharisees, the Talmudists and the extreme Zionists of today, controlled by the fanatical rabbis dispensing the 'law' of the Levites of Babylon on behalf of the reptilians. Most people who follow the religions spawned from these sources have no idea of their true origin or agenda. This is the privileged knowledge of a tiny Elite at the top of the secret society network who set up and manipulate the religions and their advocates. They are not concerned for their followers, be they Jews, Roman Catholics, Muslims, whatever. Nothing emphasises what a sham all these religions and races really are than the present day peoples we are told are 'Jewish'. As Jewish writers and anthropologists have said, there is no such thing as the Jewish race. Jewishness is a faith, not a race. The whole concept of a 'Jewish' people was manufactured as a cover story. Alfred M. Lilenthal, the Jewish writer and researcher, said:

> "There is no reputable anthropologist who will not agree that Jewish racialism is as much poppycock as Aryan racialism... Anthropological science divides mankind into three recognised races: Negro, Mongolian and Oriental, and Caucasian or white (although some authorities refer to a fourth race – the australoids)... Members of the Jewish faith are found in all three races and subdivisions."[19]

The point is, however, that within the Jewish faith and other cultures, is a race, a hidden race operating undercover, which carries the bloodlines of the reptilian full-bloods and crossbreeds. These bloodlines appear, on the surface, to be part of these faiths and cultures when, in fact, they are there to imprison and manipulate. So it is with the Levites. It gets even more farcical, and indicative of what a smokescreen world we live in, when you realise that most people who call themselves Jewish today have no genetic connection whatsoever to the land they call Israel. Yet it is this very connection that was used to justify the imposition of a 'Jewish' homeland on the Arab peoples of Palestine! Again, as Jewish writers such as Arthur Koestler have exposed, all except a small minority of people who created and populated the State of Israel, originate genetically in southern Russia, not Israel. The hooked nose which is considered so 'Jewish' is a genetic trait of southern Russia and the Caucasus, not Israel. In 740 AD, a people called the Khazars had a mass conversion to Judaism. Koestler writes:

> "The Khazars came not from Jordan, but from the Volga, not from Canaan, but from the Caucasus. Genetically they are more related to the Hun, Uigar and the Magyar than the seed of Abraham, Isaac and Jacob. The story of the Khazar Empire, as it slowly emerges from the past, begins to look like the most cruel hoax that history has ever perpetrated."[20]

There are two main sub divisions of those who call themselves Jewish, the Sephardim and the Ashkenazim. The Sephardim are the descendants of those who lived in Spain from antiquity until the 15th century when they were expelled. The Ashkenazim are the ancestors of the Khazars. In the 1960s, the Sephardim were estimated to number some half a million, but the Ashkenazim numbered about eleven million. These eleven million have absolutely no historical connection with Israel whatsoever, but they are the ones who invaded Palestine and created the State of Israel with the justification that 'God' promised them that land in the Old Testament. Who wrote the Old Testament? Their priests, the Levites! And who wrote the New Testament which created Christianity? People controlled by the same force which controlled the Levites, the Babylonian Brotherhood.

The New Testament

OK, a little quiz. Who am I talking about?

He was born to a virgin by immaculate conception through the intervention of a holy spirit. This fulfilled an ancient prophecy. When he was born the ruling tyrant wanted to kill him. His parents had to flee to safety. All male children under the age of two were slain by the ruler as he sought to kill the child. Angels and shepherds were at his birth and he was given gifts of gold, frankincense and myrrh. He was worshipped as the saviour of men and led a moral and humble life. He performed miracles which included healing the sick, giving sight to the blind, casting out devils and raising the dead. He was put to death on the cross between two thieves. He descended to hell and rose from the dead to ascend back to heaven.[21]

Sounds exactly like Jesus doesn't it? But it's not. That is how they described the Eastern saviour god known as Virishna 1,200 years before Jesus is claimed to have been born. If you want a saviour god who died so our sins could be forgiven, take your pick from the ancient world because there are a stream of them, all originating with the Aryan and reptile-Aryan race that came out of the Near East and the Caucasus Mountains. Here are just some of the 'Son of God' heroes who play the lead role in stories which mirror those attributed to Jesus and almost all were worshipped long before Jesus was even heard of:

Khrishna of Hindostan; Buddha Sakia of India; Salivahana of Bermuda; Osiris and Horus of Egypt; Odin of Scandinavia; Crite of Chaldea; Zoroaster of Persia; Baal and Taut of Phoenicia; Indra of Tibet; Bali of Afghanistan; Jao of Nepal; Wittoba of Bilingonese; Tammuz of Syria and Babylon; Attis of Phrygia; Xamolxis of Thrace; Zoar of the Bonzes; Adad of Assyria; Deva Tat and Sammonocadam of Siam; Alcides of Thebes; Mikado of the Sintoos; Beddru of Japan; Hesus or Eros, and Bremrillahm, of the Druids; Thor, son of Odin, of the Gauls; Cadmus of Greece; Hil and Feta of Mandaites; Gentaut and Quetzalcoatl of Mexico; Universal Monarch of the Sibyls; Ischy of Formosa; Divine Teacher of Plato; Holy One of Xaca; Fohi and Tien of China; Adonis, son of virgin Io, of Greece; Ixion and Quirinus of Rome; Prometheus of the Caucasus; and Mohammed or Mahomet, of Arabia.[22]

All but a few of those 'sons of God' or 'prophets', and the mind-prison religions founded in their names, come from the very lands occupied or influenced by peoples emerging from the Near East and the Caucasus. The lands of the Aryans and reptile-Aryans. Other 'sons of God' included Mithra or Mithras, the pre-Christian Roman-Persian god, and in Greece and Asia Minor they had Dionysus and Bacchus. These were sons of God who died so our sins could be forgiven, born of a virgin mother, and their birthdays were on… December 25th! Mithra was crucified, but raised from the dead on March 25th – Easter! Mithran initiations took place in caves adorned with the signs of Capricorn and Cancer, symbolic of the winter and summer solstices, the high and low points of the Sun. Mithra was often portrayed as a winged lion, a symbol for the Sun still used by the secret societies today. References to the lion and the 'grip of the lion's paw' in the Master Mason Degree of Freemasonry originate with this same stream of mystery school symbolism. Initiates into the rites of Mithra were called lions and were marked on their foreheads with the Egyptian cross. The first degree initiates had a golden crown placed on their heads, representing their spiritual self, and this crown, symbolising the rays of the sun, can be found on the Statue of Liberty in New York Harbour. All these rituals went back thousands of years to Babylon and the stories of Nimrod, Queen Semiramis, and Tammuz, their version of Jesus. Mithra was said to be the son (Sun) of god who died to save humanity and give them eternal life. One classic symbol of Mithra was as a lion with a snake curled around his body, while he holds the keys to heaven. This is more Nimrod symbolism and the origin of the story of St Peter, one of Jesus' 12 disciples, holding the keys to heaven. Peter was the name of the High Priest in the Babylon mystery school. After an initiate of the Mithran cult had completed the ritual, the members had a meal of bread and wine in which they believed they were eating the flesh of Mithra and drinking his blood. Mithra, like a long list of pre-Christian gods, was said to have been visited by wise men at his birth who brought him gifts of gold, frankincense and myrrh. The same was said by Plato of his teacher, Socrates, in ancient Greece. Christianity is a Pagan sun religion, the worship of which is condemned by Christianity! It is also an astrology religion, the 'evil' of which is condemned by Christianity, not least by the Pope! Beam me up Scotty, it's mad down here. The church hierarchy, of course, know all this. They just don't want *you* to know. The mystery cult of Mithra spread from Persia to the Roman Empire and at one point this doctrine could be found in almost every part of Europe. The present site of the Vatican in Rome was a sacred place for the followers of Mithra, and his image and symbols have been found cut into rocks and stone tablets throughout the western provinces of the former Roman domain, including Germany, France and Britain. Christianity and the Roman Church were based on the Persian-Roman Sun god called Mithra (Nimrod), who has an earlier equivalent in India called Mitra. Tammuz or Adonis (Lord), who was revered in Babylonia and Syria, was said to have been born at midnight on December 24th. These were also 'sons' of God.

Horus was the the 'son' of God in Egypt. He was derived from the Babylonian Tammuz and, in turn, provided another blueprint for the later Jesus. The connections are devastating for the credibility of the Christian Church: Jesus was the Light of the World. Horus was the Light of the World. Jesus said he was the way, the truth and the life. Horus said he was the truth, the life. Jesus was born in Bethlehem, the 'house of bread'. Horus was born in Annu, the 'place of bread'. Jesus was the Good Shepherd. Horus was the Good Shepherd. Seven fishers board a boat with Jesus. Seven people board a boat with Horus. Jesus was the lamb. Horus was the lamb. Jesus is identified with a cross. Horus is identified with a cross. Jesus was baptised at 30. Horus was baptised at 30. Jesus was the child of a virgin, Mary. Horus was the child of a virgin, Isis. The birth of Jesus was marked by a star. The birth of Horus was marked by a star. Jesus was the child teacher in the temple. Horus was the child teacher in the temple. Jesus had 12 disciples. Horus had 12 followers. Jesus was the Morning Star. Horus was the Morning Star. Jesus was the Christ. Horus was the Krst. Jesus was tempted on a mountain by Satan. Horus was tempted on a mountain by Set.[23]

Jesus is said to be the 'judge of the dead'. He has some competition there. This was also said of the earlier Nimrod, Khrishna, Buddha, Ormuzd, Osiris, Aeacus and others. Jesus is the Alpha and Omega, the first and the last. So was Khrishna, Buddha, Lao-kiun, Bacchus, Zeus and others. Jesus is claimed to have performed miracles such as healing the sick and raising people from the dead. So did Khrishna,

Figure 14: *A Phoenician standing stone depicting their Sun God, Bel or Bil, with the halo representing the rays of the Sun. This is precisely the way 'Jesus' is portrayed because he, too, was a symbol of the Sun.*

Buddha, Zoroaster, Bochia, Horus, Osiris, Serapis, Marduk, Bacchus, Hermes and others. Jesus was born of royal blood. So was Buddha, Rama, Fo-hi, Horus, Hercules, Bacchus, Perseus and others. Jesus was born to a virgin. So was Khrishna, Buddha, Lao-kiun or tsze, Confusius, Horus, Ra, Zoroaster, Prometheus, Perseus, Apollo, Mercury, Baldur, Quetzalcoatl and far too many others to mention. Jesus will, we are told, be born again. The sky is going to be rather crowded because Khrishna, Vishnu, Buddha, Quetzalcoatl and others, will also be there. The 'star' at the birth of Jesus is another multideity story and goes back at least to the Babylonian tale of Nimrod who, in a dream, saw a brilliant star rising above the horizon. The soothsayers told him that this foretold the birth of a child who would become a great prince.[24] It's all recycling. Jesus is a myth man.

The invented character of Jesus was a Sun god, symbolic of God's 'Sun'… The Light of the World. This very phrase, Light of the World, was used by the Aryan-Phoenicians to symbolise the 'one true god' thousands of years before the alleged birth of Abraham, the quite wrongly named creator of the one-god concept.[25] They also symbolised the one true god, the Sun, with the 'one true cross'.[26] The Christians portray Jesus with a halo around his head and that's exactly how the Phoenicians depicted the rays of the Sun around the head of their Sun god, Bel or Bil. This can be seen on a Phoenician stone dating to about the 4th century BC (*see Figure 14*). The Sun was at the heart of the Egyptian religion and at noon when the Sun was at the peak of its daily 'journey', they prayed to the 'Most High'. At this time, they said the Sun was going about his father's work in the temple. The virgin mothers associated with all of these Sun gods were different names for Queen Semiramis and Ninkharsag, also known as Isis, the Egyptian symbol of the female creative force without which nothing, not even the Sun, could exist. Over time, names for what had once symbolised extraterrestrial 'gods' became used to describe concepts and esoteric principles. Different eras and cultures gave different names to

Figure 15: *Mary and Jesus? No, this is the way the Egyptians portrayed Isis and Horus. If you lived in ancient Babylon this would have been Queen Semiramis and Tammuz.*

these same concepts and so in the Gospels, Horus became Jesus and Isis became Mary, the virgin mother of Jesus, the Sun. Mary is constantly pictured holding the baby Jesus, but this is merely a repeat of all the Egyptian portrayals of Isis holding the baby Horus (*see Figure 15*). These people did not actually exist, they are symbolic. Isis became associated with the astrological sign of Virgo the virgin, as did Mary. The titles given to Isis of 'Star of the Sea' and 'Queen of Heaven' were also given to Mary and they both originate from Queen Semiramis, who was called the Queen of Heaven in Babylon. Christianity and Judaism are both the religion of Babylon.

Throughout the world you see the same Sun religions and rituals, in Sumer, Babylon, Assyria, Egypt, Britain, Greece, Europe in general, Mexico and Central America, Australia… everywhere. It was the universal religion inspired by the same, ultimately extraterrestrial, source thousands of years before Christianity. Sun and fire worship was the focus of religions in India where their festivals charted the Sun's cycle through the year,[27] and in the Jesus story you see constant symbolic references to this and to astrology and mystery school symbolism. The crown of thorns is the symbol of the rays of the Sun, just like the crown of spikes around the head of the Statue of Liberty. The cross is also Sun and astrological symbolism, as you saw earlier with the cross and the circle. Leonardo da Vinci, the Grand Master of the Priory of Sion (Sun), used this same symbolism in his famous painting of the Last Supper (*see Figure 16*). He divides the 12 disciples into four groups of three with Jesus, the 'Sun', in the middle of them. Again this is astrological symbolism painted by a high initiate of the secret societies and mystery schools who knew the truth.

It may well be that da Vinci has portrayed one of the disciples as a woman to symbolise the Isis, Barati, Semiramis, deity. This became symbolised as an 'M' for Mary or Madonna (Semiramis). Jesus is said to have been born on December 25th, a date the Christians took from the Sun religions of Sol Invictus (the Sun Unconquered) for reasons I've explained. He is also said to have died at Easter on a cross. This is a repeat of the same ancient story again. The Egyptians represented Osiris stretched out on a cross in astrological symbolism. According to the ancients, it took three days for the Sun to recover from 'death' on December 21st/22nd. In the Gospels how many days are there between Jesus 'dying' and 'rising' from the dead? Three! The same time it took the Babylon Son of God, Tammuz, to rise again. This is how Luke's Gospel describes what happened as Jesus (the Sun) died on the cross:

"And it was about the sixth hour, and there was darkness over all the Earth until the ninth hour. And the Sun was darkened..." **Luke 23-44,45**

The son/Sun had died and so there was darkness. And look how many hours this lasted for: three. The same story of darkness at their death was told by the Hindus of Khrishna, the Buddhists of Buddha, the Greeks of Hercules, the Mexicans of Quetzalcoatl, ad infinitum, long before Jesus. When he died, Jesus 'descended into hell', just like the earlier Khrishna, Zoroaster, Osiris, Horus, Adonis/Tammuz, Bacchus, Hercules, Mercury and so on. He then rose from the dead like the earlier Khrishna, Buddha, Zoroaster, Adonis/Tammuz, Osiris, Mithra, Hercules and Baldur. Jesus was symbolically crucified at Easter because this is the spring equinox when the Sun (Jesus) enters the astrological sign of Aries, the Ram or... the lamb. The lamb in the Book of Revelation is the same symbol. In around 2,200 BC the group known as the Priesthood of Melchizedek began making their aprons with lamb's wool, a symbol continued today by a modern expression of the Brotherhood, the Freemasons. It is at Easter, the equinox, that Jesus (the Sun) triumphs over darkness – the time of year when there is more light than darkness every day. The world is restored by the power of the Sun in the time of rebirth and the spring equinox was one of the most sacred Egyptian events. Queen Isis was often portrayed with rams heads to symbolise that the time of Aries, the spring, was a period of nature's abundant creation. The Festival of Easter was as important to early Christians as December 25th. The legend of Mithra said he was crucified and was resurrected on March 25th. The date of Easter is no longer fixed to the first day of Aries, but the symbolism remains. The Christian religious day is... SUNday. Christian churches are build east-west with the altar to the east. This means that the congregation face east – the direction of the rising Sun. Even Easter eggs, like hot cross buns, are not a Christian tradition. Dyed eggs were sacred Easter offerings in Egypt and Persia, among other places. How ironic that the authorities at Westminster Abbey have questioned whether they should have a Christmas tree because it is a Pagan symbol. The whole flippin' religion is pagan!

Figure 16: *The Last Supper by Leonardo Da Vinci. Look how he symbolises Jesus as the Sun and breaks up the twelve disciples into four sets of three – the signs of the zodiac. It is a pictorial version of the sun circle and the cross we saw earlier.*

Along with the Sun symbolism, the Jesus story and its countless predecessors also include initiation symbolism from the mystery schools. The cross as a religious symbol can be found in every culture, from the Native Americans to the Chinese, India, Japan, Egypt, Sumer, the ancient peoples of Europe and central-south America. The Buddhist Wheel of Life is made of two superimposed crosses and birds with their wings open are used to symbolise the cross in endless logos, coats of arms and badges. One of the most ancient forms of the cross is the Tau or Tav cross which resembles the letter T. This was the cross on which political dissidents were hung by the Romans, apparently. It was the symbol of the Druid god, Hu, and it is still used today by the Freemasons in their symbol of the T square. The Egyptian's Crux Ansata, the 'cross of life', added a circle loop to the top. The Crux Ansata and the Tau cross were found on statues and other artwork throughout ancient Central America. It was associated with water and the Babylonians used the cross as an emblem of the water gods who they said had brought them their civilisation. The Nagas, by the way, the human-reptile gods of the East, were also said to live in the water. The concept of a saviour god figure dying for humanity is an ancient one. The religions of India had a tradition of the crucified saviour centuries before Christianity and it originated from the Aryans in the Caucasus. The Hindu 'Christ' figure, Khrishna, appears in some portrayals nailed to a cross in classic Jesus manner.[28] Quetzalcoatl is said to have come out of the sea carrying a cross and he has been represented as being nailed to a cross. In mystery school symbolism, a cross of gold = illumination; a cross of silver = purification; a cross of base metals = humiliation; and a cross of wood = aspiration. The latter relates to the constant symbolism of the tree and saviour god figures dying on trees or wooden crosses. Some of the Pagan mystery ceremonies involved the student hanging from a cross or lying on an altar in the shape of a cross.[29] It symbolised the death of the body, the world of physical domination and desire, and opening to the spiritual self. The driving in of nails and the flow of blood is yet more mystery school symbolism. The crucifixion of Jesus was an allegory, a symbolic event written to carry a hidden meaning. It did not physically happen, you are just meant to think it did. And what of the physical resurrection from the dead by Jesus? St Paul is quoted as saying of this event in his first letter to the Corinthians:

"But if there be no resurrection of the dead, then is Christ not risen: And if Christ be not risen, then is our preaching vain, and your faith is also vain. Yea, and we are found false witnesses of God; because we have testified of God that he raised up Christ: whom he raised not up, if so be that the dead rise not." **Corinthians 15:13-16**

He says that if Jesus was not physically raised from the dead, there is no basis to the Christian faith and religion. If that's the case, Christianity is in serious trouble. First of all the Gospel accounts of the resurrection have numerous contradictions as each copied the original story differently, or changed it on purpose. And secondly the resurrection is yet more Sun symbolism from the ancient religions. In Persia, long before Christianity, they had a ritual in which a young man, apparently dead, was restored to life. He was called the Saviour and his sufferings were said to have ensured the salvation of the people. His priests watched his tomb until midnight on the equinox and they cried: "Rejoice, O sacred initiated! Your God is risen. His death and sufferings have worked your salvation." The same tale was told in Egypt about Horus and in India about Khrishna a thousand years before Christianity. The Bible tells us that Jesus will return on a cloud and what do we see among the clouds? The Sun. The tomb of Jesus is symbolic of the darkness into which the Sun descended before its rebirth and nearly all the mystery school initiations involved some sort of cave, underground chamber, or dark enclosed space, like the sweatlodges of native America. Even the story of the spear which pierced the side of Jesus after he was taken from the cross is mystery school symbolism. The Christian legend says that this was done by a blind Roman centurion called Longinus and some of the blood of Jesus fell on his eyes and cured his blindness. Longinus was converted and spent the rest of his life breaking up Pagan idols. Yeah, sure he did. Centurions were not blind and could not have done their job if they were, and once again we find this story is a repeat from earlier versions. The Scandinavian saviour, Balder, son of Odin, had a spear of mistletoe thrust into him by Hod, a god who was blind. March 15th, the Ides of March, was when many Pagan saviours also died. This day was devoted to Hod and later became a Christian feast day to the 'Blessed Longinus'![30] You've got to laugh, really.

The symbol of the fish is a theme throughout the Gospel stories and this is symbolic of Nimrod/Tammuz, the father-son, of Babylon. Another reason for Jesus as a fish could be the astrological sign of Pisces, the fishes. Around the time Jesus was supposed to have been born, the Earth was entering the astrological house of Pisces. A new age was being born and Jesus the fish could have been a symbol of the age of Pisces. We are now entering another new age, the age of Aquarius, according to the laws of the 'Earth wobble' precession. When the Bible talks of the end of the world, this is another mistranslation. They translate 'world' from the Greek, 'aeon', but aeon does not mean world, it means 'age'.[31] We are not facing the end of the world, but the end of the age, the 2,160 years of Pisces. Christianity did not replace the Pagan religions, it *is* a Pagan religion. The Persians, who inherited their beliefs from Sumer, Egypt and Babylon, had baptism, confirmation, paradise and hell, angels of light and darkness, and a fallen angel. All of these were absorbed by Christianity and claimed for their own.

During the alleged life time of Jesus, the Essene Brotherhood, was based at Qumran at the northern end of the Dead Sea, or at least that is what we are told. Brian Desborough's research indicates that this site was a leper colony at the time and that the Essenes lived in a much more appropriate place further along the Dead Sea coast. The Dead Sea Scrolls, found in caves near Qumran in 1947, have offered a greater insight into their lifestyle and beliefs, despite suppression by the authorities who wish to maintain the official version of history. The scrolls were hidden from the Romans during the ill-fated Judean revolt around 70 AD. Some 500 Hebrew and Aramaic manuscripts were found, which included texts from the Old Testament, among them a complete draft of the Book of Isaiah, centuries older than the one in the Bible. There were scores of documents relating to the Essene customs and organisation. The scrolls confirm that the Essenes were fanatics who followed to the letter the Levite inventions in the Old Testament texts. Anyone who didn't do the same was their enemy and they fiercely opposed the Roman occupation. They were a Palestine branch of an even more extreme Egyptian sect called the Therapeutae ('healers', hence therapeutic [32]) and they inherited the secret knowledge of Egypt and the ancient world. The Therapeutae and the Essenes also used the symbol of the 'messeh', the 'Draco' crocodile of Egypt, the fat of which anointed the Pharaohs

under the authority of the Royal Court of the Dragon. The Essenes had a detailed understanding of drugs, including the hallucinogenic variety, which were used in mystery school initiations and for entering other states of consciousness. The properties of the 'sacred mushrooms' or 'Holy Plant' were so much part of life in the secret brotherhood that the Jewish high priest wore a mushroom cap (*see Figure 17*) to acknowledge their importance. They had special rituals for their preparation and use. The mushroom, too, was given 'son of God' connotations (what wasn't?) and it was connected to the Sun cycle. The mushrooms were picked with great reverence before sunrise and many symbols of this ritual can be found in the Bible and far older texts. Again, the use of the sacred mushroom and other drugs, and the secret knowledge of their properties, can be traced back to the

Figure 17: *The Jewish priest with the mushroom cap to symbolise the importance of magic hallucinogenic mushrooms in their rituals.*

earliest days of Sumer.[33] The Therapeutae had a flourishing university at Alexandria and from there they sent out missionaries to establish branches and affiliated communities across the Middle East. Here again we have the connection back to Egypt and the mystery schools.

The Essenes were advocates of Pythagoras, the Greek philosopher and esoteric mathematician, who was a high initiate of both the Greek and Egyptian mystery schools.[34] According to the most famous historian of the period, Josephus, the Essenes were sworn to keep secret the names of the powers who ruled the universe. This was in line with the laws of the mystery schools. The Essenes-Therapeutae practised rituals very similar to the later Christian baptism and they marked the foreheads of initiates with a cross. This being the symbol indicated in the Old Testament Book of Ezekiel for enlightened (or illuminated) ones and also used for initiations into the mysteries of Mithra and other such Sun god figures. The Essenes viewed natural bodily functions, including sex, with disgust and in that sense they were an excellent forerunner of the Roman Church which was to absorb many of their beliefs, terms and practises. Two of the Dead Sea Scrolls, one in Hebrew, the other in Aramaic, contain what we would call horoscopes, the belief that the movement of the planets affects a person's character and destiny. The Essenes practised astrology, the symbolism of which you find throughout the Gospels and the Old Testament. The early Christians, an offshoot of the Essenes-Therapeutae, did the same, as did the Romans and all the Gentile nations surrounding Judea.[35] The writer, Philo, who lived at the alleged time of Jesus, said in his Treatise on the Contemplative Life, that when the Therapeutae prayed to God, they turned to the Sun and they studied in order to discover the hidden (coded) meaning of sacred books. He wrote that they also meditated on the secrets of nature contained in the books under the veil of allegory.[36] That is precisely the way the Bible is written. Today this secret language is used in the logos, coats of arms and flags, of companies, countries and other Brotherhood-controlled organisations.

Interconnected with the Essenes and a theme which links both the Old and New Testaments is the secret society called the Nazarites or Nazarenes. Old Testament characters such as Moses and Samson were said to be members of this group and so were Jesus, his brother James, John the Baptist and St Paul. The Acts of the Apostles says of St Paul: "For we have found this man a pestilent fellow, and a mover of sedition among all of the Jews throughout the world, and a ringleader of the sect of the Nazarenes."[37] None of these people really existed, but the Nazarene symbolism makes a secret society link through the Bible. The Essenes and the Nazarites-Nazarenes appear to be different offshoots of the same group. The Essenes wore white according to the Judean historian Josephus, but the Nazarenes wore black, the same as the priests of Isis in Egypt. Black is a colour of the Babylonian Brotherhood which has manipulated its way through history. In keeping with this, black has become the colour associated with authority (look at the legal profession) and with death. It is also the traditional colour of the teaching profession with the black gown and the black hat called the mortar board, which is the circle and square symbol of Freemasonry. The greatest miracle of Jesus, it seems, was coming from Nazareth because Nazareth did not exist at the time. And Jesus said: "Let there be Nazareth. And there was Nazareth." Or rather, there wasn't. The name does not appear in any of the detailed Roman records, nor in any books, writings or documents of any kind relating to the period covered by the Gospels. Jesus the 'Nazarene' does not relate to Nazareth, but to the Nazarene secret society.

The Essenes-Therapeutae-Nazarenes were the bridge between the Old Testament, the New Testament and the creation of Christianity. The early 'Christians' were called Nazarenes before they were called Christians.[38] The rituals of the Nazarene Brotherhood can be clearly seen in the Christian Church today. The Nazarenes wore black and so do most Christian clerics. At Qumran they had a ritual bath to wash away their 'sins'. This became the Christian baptism. They had a meal of bread and wine which became the Christian Mass. W. Wynn Westcott was a founder of the Satanic Order of the Golden Dawn in England which would later play a significant role in the emergence of Adolf Hitler and the Nazis. He knew the inside story and he said in his work, *The Magical Mason*, that today's Freemasons go back to the Essenes among other ancient groups of similar background. Today the Arabic word for Christians is Nasrani and the Muslim Koran uses the term Nasara or Nazara. These originate with the Hebrew word, Nozrim, which derived from the term, Nozrei ha-Brit – the Keepers of the Covenant. The term, Nozrei ha-Brit, can be traced as far back as the alleged time of Samuel and Samson in the Old Testament. Samuel was portrayed as the top man of the Levites and it was they who orchestrated this whole Bible-Talmud scam under the direction of the Babylonian Brotherhood. The Covenant is the Freemason's Great Work of Ages – the Agenda for the takeover of the planet by the reptilians.

The bloodlines, the 'chosen people' of the gods, and the secret knowledge, are symbolised as 'the vine' and 'vineyards' in the Bible and countless other writings and pictures. The Old Testament speaks of "The vine thou didst bring out of Egypt".[39] We are also told that "The vineyard of the Lord of hosts is the House of Israel and the men of Judah his pleasant plant".[40] The bloodline symbolised as the vine is not, I would strongly suggest, the bloodline of King David at all. He didn't exist for a start, which confirms the point rather conclusively. The symbolism of the vine can once again be traced back to Babylon and Egypt. In the mystery schools of Greece, their Sun gods Dionysus and Bacchus, were the patron gods of the vineyard.[41] What do grapes depend upon to grow? The Sun. The vine and the bloodline of 'Jesus' weaved in among that Sun symbolism is one of the royal and priestly bloodlines which lead back to the reptilians, the Anunnaki. The New Testament features the Wedding at Cana, but this was not a real wedding. It is again symbolic of the Sun and the Earth, the god and goddess. In the land of Canaan every spring, they celebrated sexual and fertility rites under the title, 'The Marriage Festival of Canaan'.[42] It was at the symbolic wedding at Cana in the Gospels that Jesus turns the water into wine. It is the Sun's warmth and the Earth's water which grow the grapes to make wine. Bacchus, the Greek son of Zeus and the virgin Semele, was said to have turned water into wine. Also there were Essene ritual terms related to water and wine. The Essenes, Therapeutae and Gnostics were seriously into hidden meanings and the Jesus stories are a mass of interweaved allegories related to the Sun, astronomy, astrology, bloodlines, secret knowledge and the rituals and names used by the mystery schools. The New Testament is a mirror of the Old in that some fact, much fiction, and a mass of esoteric codes and symbols are fused, and often con-fused, into a narrative which is desperately misleading if taken literally. This is summed up by the phrase: "Let he who has ears, let him hear". Let he who is initiated into the secret knowledge understand what I am really saying. Let he who is not initiated believe any old crap.

Here are a few more Bible myths to explode:

- The idea of the 'carpenter' is a translation error. The English translation of 'carpenter' comes from the Hebrew word naggar, via the Greek, ho tekton. These words do not mean literally a 'carpenter', but people who were masters of their craft and the word was applied to teachers and scholars as well as craftsmen.

- Jesus was definitely not born in a stable and not a single gospel claims this is so. The Christmas nativity is complete invention. The concept comes from Luke's Gospel[43] which says that Jesus was laid in a manger, an animal feeding box, because there was no room in the inn. But the Greek version, from which the English translation came, says there was no 'topos' in the 'kataluma' – there was no place in the room.[44] Matthew's Gospel specifically states that Jesus was in a house: "And when they were come into the house, they saw the young child with Mary, his mother, and fell down and worshipped him."[45] Mangers were often used for babies when a proper cradle was not available, but they moved the manger to the baby, not the baby to the manger!
- The nativity scene apparently originates with St Francis of Assisi in Greccio, Italy, in 1223 AD.[46] He brought together some local people and their livestock to illustrate the birth of Jesus and this nativity scene quickly caught on. Manger scenes carved from wood became popular all over Italy at Christmas and the rest is history. Giving gifts is not a Christian custom, either. This was done in the Pagan world at New Year long before Christianity. The Christians simply borrowed it, as they did everything else.
- The prophecies said that the 'messiah' (messeh, the crocodile of Egypt) would be called Emmanuel, but the name of the Gospel 'messiah' was Jesus, or at least its Judean equivalent. Oops! Funny how Christians seem to miss this point when they quote the prophecy about the coming of 'Emmanuel' every Christmas. Think of all those children who have been dressed up as Mary, Joseph, shepherds, wise men, donkeys, cows and sheep. This fantasy has been used to indoctrinate countless generations to believe that this is how it all happened, when, in truth, the nativity and the Christmas story are the acting out of translation errors, an invention of St Francis, and the mid-winter rituals of Pagan beliefs. I say, Jenny and Johnny, before you don those costumes this year, can I have a quiet word?
- The Christian Eucharist, when they eat bread and drink wine to symbolise the body and blood of Christ, originates with a cannibalistic ritual when they ate and drank the real thing in animal and human sacrifices. Most of the Christian terms come from the Greek, including Christ and Christianity. Among many others are Church (the Lord's House), Ecclesiastical (Ecclesia, the Greek Assembly or Parliament), Apostle (missionary), Presbyter/priest (elder), and baptism (immersion).
- Even according to the Gospel stories, Jesus was surrounded by terrorists. Simon Magus was known as Simon Zelotes (the Zealot) to acknowledge his role as a commander of the Zealots, the 'freedom fighters' who advocated a war against the Romans. Another description is Simon 'Kananites', a Greek word meaning fanatic. This was translated into English as Simon the Canaanite! Judas 'Iscariot' derives from the word Sicarius, which meant assassin. There was a terrorist group called the Sicarii or Sons of the Dagger, and this name comes from the word, Sica, meaning curved dagger. Sicarius became the Greek, Sikariotes, and this was later mistranslated into English as

Iscariot. The Zealots-Sicarii would raid Roman supply caravans and ambush their soldiers very much along the lines of terrorist groups like the IRA in Northern Ireland.

- People were not crucified for theft which makes the story of the two thieves crucified with Jesus another invention. It is a 'steal' once again because the same story was told about some of the pre-Christian Jesus figures. The punishment for the 'crimes' Jesus was accused of in the Gospels would have been stoning to death by the Judean authorities, not the Romans.
- Pontius Pilatus, the Roman Procurator in this period, is supposed to have washed his hands and passed on responsibility for the death of 'Jesus' to the crowd. The washing of hands to indicate innocence was the custom of the Essene community.[47] The Bible says that it was the Roman custom at the time of the Passover Festival to offer a prisoner for release, but this is simply not true. There was no such custom and the scene is invention.

You can write an entire book about the myths in the Bible and, in fact, someone has. It's called, appropriately, *Bible Myths*, and if you want detailed documentation of the information in this chapter I thoroughly recommend it. There is no credible evidence whatsoever for the existence of Jesus. No archaeological evidence, no written evidence, nothing. So it is with Solomon, Moses, David, Abraham, Samson and countless other biblical 'stars'. All we have are the Levite texts and the Gospel stories in their various versions. So desperate did the religious manipulators become to cross reference 'Jesus' that they inserted a pathetically obvious addition into the works of the 'Jewish' historian, Josephus, to support the unsupportable. More than 40 writers are known to have chronicled the events of these lands during the alleged time of Jesus, but they don't mention him.[48] A guy who did all the things that he was supposed to have done and no-one records it? Philo lived throughout the supposed life of Jesus and wrote a history of the Judeans which covered the whole of this period. He even lived in or near Jerusalem when Jesus was said to have been born and Herod was supposed to have killed the children, yet he doesn't record any of this. He was there when Jesus is said to have made his triumphant arrival in Jerusalem and when he was crucified and rose from the dead on the third day. What does Philo say about these fantastic events? Nothing. Not a syllable. Not a titter.[49] None of this is mentioned in any Roman record or in the contemporary accounts of the writers of Greece and Alexandria who were familiar with what happened there.[50]

Why? Because it didn't happen. It was a symbolic, coded story to pass on esoteric and astrological knowledge of many kinds and, most crucially, to create another prison-religion based on the symbols of the Babylonian Brotherhood. The human race has been had. Big time.

■ SOURCES

1   *The Phoenician Origin Of Britons*, p 47.

2   Arthur Dynott Thomson, *On Mankind, Their Origin And Destiny* (Kessinger Publishing, PO Box 160, Kila, MT 59920, USA, first published 1872), p 27.

3   *On Mankind, Their Origin And Destiny*, pp 8, 9.

4   Ibid, p 9.

5   Michael Drosnin, *The Bible Code* (Weidenfeld and Nicolson, London, 1997).

6   *On Mankind, Their Origin And Destiny*, p 17.

7   Ibid, p 6.

8   Ibid, pp 18, 19.

9   Ibid, p 19

10   Ibid, p 41.

11   Ibid, p 12.

12   Ibid.

13   Ibid, p 20.

14   Ibid, p 11.

15   *The Secret Teachings Of All Ages*, p L.

16   *The Phoenician Origin Of Britons*, p 147.

17   These examples (and there are countless others) are quoted by Israel Shahak in *Jewish History, Jewish Religion* (Pluto Press, London, 1994).

18   Benjamin Freedman, *Facts Are Facts*, quoted by Jan Van Helsing in *Secret Societies And Their Power In The 20th Century* (Ewertverlag, Gran Canaria, Spain, 1995), p 99.

19   Alfred M. Lilenthal, *What Price Israel?* (Henry Regnery, Chicago, 1953), pp 213–214.

20   Arthur Koestler, *The Thirteenth Tribe – The Khazar Empire And Its Heritage* (Hutchinson, London, 1976).

21   *The Book Your Church Doesn't Want You To Read*, edited by Tim C. Leedom (Kendall/Hunt Publishing, Iowa, USA, 1993), p 137. Available from the Truth Seeker Company, PO Box 2872, San Diego, California 92112.

22   Ibid, p 135.

23   Albert Churchward, *Of Religion*, first published 1924 and now available from Health Research, PO Box 850, Pomeroy, WA 99347, United States.

24   T. W. Doane, *Bible Myths* (Health Research, PO Box 850, Pomeroy, WA 99347, United States). This was first copyrighted in 1882, reprinted in 1948, and is available from this address. Highly recommended, especially if you are a Christian.

25   *The Phoenician Origin Of Britons*, preface, p XI.

26   Ibid.

27   Jordan Maxwell, *The Book Your Church Doesn't Want You To Read*, pp 19–31.

28   *The Secret Teachings Of All Ages*, p CLXXXIII.

29   Ibid, p CLXXXIII.

30   Barbara G. Walker, *The Woman's Encyclopaedia Of Myths And Secrets* (Harper Collins, San Francisco, 1983).

31   Jordan Maxwell, *The Book Your Church Doesn't Want You To Read*, p 27.

32   It is from this that we inherit the Christian term, curate.

33   John Allegro, *The Book Your Church Doesn't Want You To Read*, pp 228–233.

34   Laurence Gardner, *Bloodline Of The Holy Grail* (Element Books, Shaftsbury, 1996), p 63.

35   Alan Albert Snow, director of the Institute for Judeo–Christian Origin Studies, *The Book Your Church Doesn't Want You To Read*, pp 63–66.

36   *On Mankind, Their Origin and Destiny*, p 368.

37   Acts 24:5

38   Albert Snow, *Astrology In The Dead Sea Scrolls*, *The Book Your Church Doesn't Want You To Read*, p 65.

39   Psalms 80:8.

40   Isaiah 5:7.

41   *The Occult Conspiracy*, p 14.

42   Jordan Maxwell, *The Book Your Church Doesn't Want You To Read*, p 29.

43   Luke 2:7.

44   *Bloodline Of The Holy Grail*, p 37.

45   Ibid, pp 36–37.

46   *The Book Your Church Doesn't Want You To Read*, pp 182, 183.

47   Christopher Knight and Robert Lomas, *The Hiram Key* (Arrow Books, London, 1997), p 310.

48   John E. Remsburg, *The Book Your Church Doesn't Want You To Read*, p 171.

49   Ibid.

50   Ibid, p 172.

CHAPTER FIVE

Conquered by the cross

The Christian Church is a farce founded on a fantasy. If anyone requires confirmation of how easy it is for the few to control the masses, they need look no further than the billions of people who have worshipped the fairy tales peddled these past 2,000 years by men in long frocks. And what goes for Christianity goes for the rest of them, Judaism, Islam, Hinduism and all the rest.

These religions were created by the same force to achieve the same effect and, therefore, the saviour-god myths throughout the ancient world have an identical game plan: **1** You are born with original sin and so you are an unworthy piece of shit from the day you arrive on the planet. **2** You can only be saved by believing in the 'Saviour' and that means doing what the priesthood tell you to do. **3** If you don't do that, you will be condemned to the bowels of hell forever. What guilt and terror this has created over thousands of years. I have heard Roman Catholic mothers in anguish after their babies have died wondering what will have happened to them. The babies couldn't believe in Jesus because they were only a few days old, so would they go to heaven or hell? I was watching a Roman Catholic television channel in the United States and the guy with the long frock was asked about that. He said it was a profound theological question. Oh really? He said that either the baby's soul would go into limbo (until when one wonders?) or it would be judged on the behaviour of the parents. What staggering nonsense. Thank goodness the baby won't be judged on the behaviour of the priests. And if you can only be saved by believing in Jesus, what about all those billions of people throughout the period of Christianity who lived in vast areas of the world who had never heard of Jesus? Are they all condemned by lack of information to stoke the fires, too? Bit of an arsehole, this Christian God, eh? But of course it's not true. It's all make-believe, conjured up by the Babylonian Brotherhood initiates of the reptilians to control the minds of the masses.

When I was writing this section of the book and investigating where the Gospels came from, I was reaching to take a book from a high shelf in my office. As I pulled the book down, another smaller one fell to the floor. I don't remember seeing it before, but the title immediately caught my attention. It was *The True Authorship Of The New Testament* by Abelard Reuchlin, first printed in the United States in 1979.[1] It talked about an inner circle or inner ring, the most exclusive club in history, who knew the 'Great Secret'. In this circle were those religious, political and literary leaders, who knew the truth about Jesus, but did not want anyone else to know. What struck me was that this book came to the same conclusions that I had. The

Gospels are an invention designed to manufacture a new prison-religion. The book doesn't go into all the symbolism I have documented here, but it does name the family and others who wrote the New Testament and the codes they used to 'sign' their authorship. One of these codes, interestingly, is the number 40 I highlighted earlier. Forty was also represented by the letter M, as in Mary. The letter M is very significant to the Brotherhood still today and we see it everywhere in the symbol of the McDonalds fast food chain. We will see later how the big corporations use Brotherhood symbolism in their logos and names. M means Mary or Madonna, who means Semiramis. The wealth of evidence in Reuchlin's book, much of it complex and dealing with esoteric mathematical codes, is extremely compelling. I do recommend you try to get hold of a copy if you want the full details. The opening paragraph encapsulates its findings:

> "The New Testament, the Church and Christianity, were all the creation of the Calpurnius Piso (*pronounced Peso*) family, who were Roman aristocrats. The New Testament and all the characters in it – Jesus, all the Josephs, all the Marys, all the disciples, apostles, Paul, John the Baptist – all are fictional. The Pisos created the story and the characters; they tied the story to a specific time and place in history; and they connected it with some peripheral actual people, such as the Herods, Gamaliel, the Roman procurators, etc. But Jesus and everyone involved with him were created (*that is fictional!*) characters."[2]

The Pisos were a bloodline family descended from statesmen, consuls, poets and historians, and such people would definitely be initiates of the secret society network of the Roman Empire, a major stepping stone for the reptilian full-bloods and crossbreeds to the present day. This is why a Roman soldier is the logo of that Brotherhood operation, American Express. The Piso family claimed to descend from Calpus who, they said, was the son of Numa Pompilius, the successor to Romulus, the founder of Rome. These were seriously connected people. Such Roman bloodlines are said to have come from Troy and we are looking at a family which goes back to the Caucasus and the Near East. After the destruction of Troy around 1,200 BC, the story goes that a guy called Aeneas of a 'royal' (that is reptilian) bloodline went with the remnants of his people and settled in Italy. There he married into the royal family of the Latins and through this bloodline later emerged the Roman Empire. According to many traditions, the grandson of Aeneas, a man called Brutus, landed in Britain around 1,103 BC with a group of Trojans, including some from colonies in Spain, to become King of the Britons and found the city of New Troy – London.

Lucius Calpurnius Piso, the head of the family, was married to the great granddaughter of Herod the Great. According to Reuchlin's research, Piso, who used many pseudonyms, produced his 'Ur Marcus', the first version of the Gospel of Mark, in about 60AD. One of the friends who encouraged him was the famous Roman writer, Annaeus Seneca, but it seems that both of them were killed by the Emperor Nero in the year 65. With this, the name Piso disappears from Roman history and doesn't reappear until 138 AD when Piso's grandson, Antoninus, became emperor. But from this point the family are mostly known as the Antonines, not the Pisos. In the 73 years between the death of father Piso and the emergence of Antoninus, the foundations for Christianity were written and proclaimed under assumed names. After the death of his father at the hands of Nero, Piso's son, Arius, who used a number of names, including Cestius Gallus, was made governor of Syria. This gave him command over the Roman army in Judea. He was involved in the Judean revolt in 66 AD which Vespasian was sent to Judea to quell. Emperor Nero was assassinated in 68 AD by an agent of Piso according to Reuchlin. This certainly makes sense if Nero killed his father. With this, the Piso clan threw their power and manipulation behind Vespasian and he became Emperor of Rome in 69 AD. A year later the Romans destroyed Jerusalem, stole the temple treasures, including it is claimed the Ark of the Covenant, and apparently took them back to Rome where they entered the secret society underground. This underground was nothing less than the Babylonian Brotherhood.

Reuchlin says that Arius Calpurnius Piso then wrote three of the Gospels in the following order: The Gospel of Matthew (70–75 AD); the updated Mark (75–80); and, with the help of the Roman writer and statesman, Pliny the Younger, the updated Luke (85–90). The Gospel of John, the work of Arius's son, Justus, followed in 105.[3] As Reuchlin says, 'Jesus' was a composite figure and the stories include elements of the tales of Joseph in Egypt and other Old Testament characters, plus some Essene writings and characteristics of various Pagan gods. This is precisely what the evidence I have documented confirms. The several Josephs in the story are all the creation of Piso and part of the code. The letters in the name Piso translate in Hebrew as Yud, Vov, Samech, Fey, and they spell the name, Joseph. Another code Piso used for himself in the stories is the number 60. Reuchlin points out the many similarities between the Jesus story and the one of the Old Testament character, Joseph, which Piso used as a foundation: Joseph had 12 brothers, Jesus 12 disciples; Joseph was sold for 20 pieces of silver, Jesus for 30 pieces of silver (inflation); brother Judah suggests the sale of Joseph, Judas sells Jesus; Joseph is in Egypt where the first born are killed, Jesus and family flee to Egypt to avoid the slaying of male children. Piso uses his four sons as the disciples, John (Julius), James (Justus), Simon-Peter (Proculus), and Alexander (Andrew).[4] Julius, Justus and Proculus, would go on to write some later New Testament texts. Piso makes Jesus fulfil a number of Old Testament prophecies, particularly those of Isaiah. Reuchlin says that the Pisos made changes and additions to some Old Testament texts also, and wrote most of the 14 Old Testament books known as the Apocrypha. These included Esdras, 1 Maccabbees, Judith, Tobit, Bel and the Dragon.[5] The Pisos were Stoics (hence Stoical) and the Stoics believed that people were motivated by, and controllable through, the use of fear and hope[6] (the very methods of the Babylonian Brotherhood). What better way of describing the religions which have been spawned by the Old and New Testaments?

Another manifestation of Arius Piso was Flavius Josephus, the writer I have quoted once or twice. The reason that Piso, as Josephus, and his granddaughter's husband Pliny the Younger, do not mention Jesus in their official writings is because at the time it simply would not have been credible to do so. It was only with the passage of time as the true origin of 'Jesus' was lost that the stories became accepted as 'fact'. The official history of Josephus is that he was a Judean descended from Hasmonean royalty. He fought against the Romans and although his friends committed suicide when the revolt went pear-shaped, he gave himself up and was spared. More than that, we are told he was housed in Rome by the emperors for 30 years while he wrote books on Jewish 'history' and then married his granddaughter into the Roman aristocracy. Oh, do come on. Josephus was the Roman aristocrat, Arius Calpurnius Piso, and together with his sons and Pliny the Younger, they wrote the Gospels and the rest of the New Testament.

Pliny wrote a number of the epistles (letters) under the name St Ignatius, and this same group, under various names, were the early church 'fathers'. And who was to turn this Roman invention into the vast prison-religion it was to become? A Roman emperor in the same Babylonian Brotherhood as the Pisos, called Constantine the Great. What was the vehicle for doing this? The Roman Church based in Rome! Geoffrey Higgins in his epic work, *Anacalypsis*, shows how Rome was created as a new Babylon. No wonder Christianity is so awash with Babylonian symbols. The whole thing was a set up to create yet another religion to entrap the human mind, and the hierarchy of the Christian Church today know all this! The Church élite have always known this because they are part of the secret society stream which created the myth called Christianity. Cynical lies like the Turin Shroud, which has been connected with the Knights Templar secret society, have been invented to perpetuate the propaganda. The force which invented Jesus and Christianity is the same force which still controls the world today. For instance, the Roman College of Architects was a forerunner of today's Freemasons, only the name has changed. The Romans used the same symbols of the square and compass and so on. A temple used by this college in Pompeii was lost under the eruptions of Vesuvius in 71 AD and excavators have recovered from the temple a hexagram 'Star of David', a skull and a black and white tracing board first used by the Dionysian Artificers.[7] All these symbols are used by today's Freemasons.

The Judean battle against Rome continued until the final defeat of the Zealots in 74 AD at Masada, the flat-topped mountain stronghold overlooking the Dead Sea. It was the last bastion of the Essene community who had evacuated their base further down the coast. As the Judean Zealots were routed by the Romans, many members of the Nazarene secret society headed into Jordan, Mesopotamia, Syria and Turkey, as documented by Julius Africanus, who lived in Turkey around 200 AD. Joseph of Arimathea, the biblical 'uncle' of Jesus, is said to have travelled to France to spread the word. The Vatican librarian, Cardinal Baronius, said that Joseph first arrived in Marseilles in 35 AD and later went on to Britain.[8] 'Mary Magdalene' and offspring of 'Jesus' are also said to have headed for the South of France after the 'crucifixion'. This is the foundation of the Holy Grail story which claims that the Jesus bloodline became the Merovingians in France. Well that's crap because these people didn't exist and note the source of this story, the librarian of the Vatican Library of the Roman Church in Rome. So what was so special suddenly about Provence and the

South of France? Guess where the Piso family had extensive estates? In Gaul and, more specifically, in… Provence![9] No wonder the 'vine' (bloodline/knowledge) can be identified in this very part of France. Centuries later it became one version of the Holy Grail story of so much myth and legend. These are the symbolic stories of King Arthur (another 'Sun'), and they can also be seen in the tarot cards and the music and art of Europe for centuries. The Grail has been portrayed as the cup or chalice which held the blood of Jesus at the crucifixion. But this blood was merely symbolic of the blood which flowed in the ancient rituals in which lambs were sacrificed at the spring equinox and, for the more initiated, the bloodlines which go back to the reptilian 'gods'. In the early manuscripts of the Grail stories, the 'Holy Grail' is called the Sangraal. How close this is to the Sang Raal, the Old French term meaning blood royal. This royal blood, as we shall establish, was the bloodlines of the reptilian-human crossbreeds and had nothing to do with 'Jesus'.

The Sun god composite, symbolically known as Jesus, was transformed into a supernatural Son of God by the man we call St Paul, whose original name in the stories was Saul of Tarsus. Officially, St Paul was born to Judean parents and, like them, became a Roman citizen, despite being a Pharisee and a strict adherent to the Hebrew religion. Who else was supposed to be a Judean who became a Roman? Josephus, the pseudonym for Piso, who wrote the Gospels! St Paul, it is said, encouraged the persecution of the early Christians, but had a conversion on the road to Damascus when Jesus miraculously 'appeared' to him and asked: "Why do you persecute me?" However, Paul had three versions of his story. In one he heard the voice of Jesus speak to him (Acts 9:7). In another he saw a great light, but without the voice (Acts 22:9). And in the third, he has Jesus giving him instructions about his future mission (Acts 26:13). Paul was the creation of Pliny the Younger (military name, Maximus) and Justus Piso.[10] They introduced into Paul's story many of their friends and associates, and characters from the family's history. For instance, the man called 'Ananias' in Acts who cures Paul of blindness was inspired by Annaeus Seneca who died with father Piso at the hands of Nero.[11] And in Romans, you find the phrase: "Greet Herodion my kinsman", a code for the Piso family's connection with Herod the Great.[12] Paul did not spread the Jesus message to Cyprus, Crete, Macedonia, Asia, Greece and Rome. Pliny and the Pisos did. Between 100 and 105 Justus, his father, and Pliny, together with their family, friends and slaves, went to Asia Minor (now Turkey), the Greek cities and Alexandria, among many other places, to 'encourage' the poor and the slaves into joining their new faith.[13] The first churches were created in Bithynia and Pontus by Pliny. He had visited these places a number of times from the year 85 AD and this is the origin of the first name of Pontius Pilate. He was only called Pilate in Matthew and Mark, the first gospels written by the Pisos, but in Luke, the one Piso wrote with Pliny, Pilate suddenly acquires the name, Pontius. Luke was written in the very years that Pliny began to visit Pontus.[14] Pliny's letters, written under his own name, say that Justus Piso was in Bithynia in the years 96 and 98 using the name, Tullius Justus, and that the Pisos also located in Ephesus, the home of the cult and temple to the goddess Diana, another version of Isis, Semiramis, Barati, ad infinitum. As they travelled they claimed to be apostles and bishops, the successors to their inventions, Peter and Paul. They claimed to be Ignatius (Pliny), Justinus (Justus), Clement of Rome (Julius), Polycarp (Proculus), and Papias (Julianus, son of Justus).[15] By this time, a Piso, Pompeia Plotina (real name Claudia Phoebe), was the wife of the Roman Emperor, Trajan, and so they had tremendous support from the highest level for their manipulation.[16] She also appears as 'our sister Phoebe' and as 'Claudia' and 'Claudine' in the texts called Romans, Timothy and Clement.[17]

The Pisos and Pliny introduced into their stories all the symbols of the Sun religion and Babylonian Brotherhood myths. They locate their Saul/Paul in Tarsus in Asia Minor (now Turkey), the chief city of the Cilicians. This just happens to be a major centre for the Mithra Sun religion and it was the Cilicians who had taken this cult to Rome, from where it spread throughout the empire. Asia Minor was also a region which followed the cult of Dionysus. Both were symbolic Sun gods, born on December 25th, who died so our sins could be forgiven. Everything Christians believe about Jesus, the Romans and Persians believed about Mithra. Sunday was the sacred day for Mithraists because he was a Sun God and they called this The Lord's Day. Dionysus was born to a virgin mother, and he was known as: the Vine, Our Lord, the Saviour, the Judge of the Dead, the Deliverer, the Born Again and the only begotten Son of God. Above the head of Dionysus were the words: "I am Life, Death, and Resurrection, I hold the winged crown (the Sun)."[18] The writer, H. G. Wells, pointed out that many of the phrases used by Paul for Jesus were the same as those used by the followers of Mithra. The Liturgy of Mithra is the Liturgy of Jesus. When Paul says: "They drank from the spiritual rock and that rock was Christ" (I Corinthians 10:4), he was using exactly the same words found in the scriptures of Mithra. Only the names were changed. In the Gospels, Peter became the Christian 'rock' on whom the new church would be built. The Vatican Hill in Rome was said to be sacred to Peter, but this place was also claimed, much earlier, to be sacred to Mithra and many Mithric remains have been found there! The Piso clan turned Mithra into Myth-ra – Christianity.

All the Popes have claimed to rule as the heirs to Peter, the first Pope. This claim derives from a sentence in the Bible which has Jesus saying: " Thou art Peter, and upon this rock I will build my church."[19] Only four verses after supposedly making Peter the 'rock' on which he would build his church, comes this demolition of him: "But he (*Jesus*) turned, and said unto Peter, 'Get thee behind me Satan: thou art an offence unto me: for thou savourest not the things that be of God, but those that be of men'."[20] The 'rock' is classic mystery school symbolism, as is the 'corner stone' associated with Jesus and still used in Freemasonic symbolism today. Peter is supposed to be the custodian of the keys to Heaven, but this is just a rerun of the mystery school symbol of the two-faced Janus, custodian of the key to the Temple of Wisdom and the keys to heaven held by Mithra. And Janus was Eannus, a title for Nimrod in Babylon. The gold and silver keys of St Peter's alleged successor, the Pope, are more symbols of the secret doctrine. The Popes and those who control them know what all this stuff really means. Gold and silver are the precious metals used to symbolise the Sun and the Moon. Peter and Paul are both said to have been killed in Rome during the purge of Christians by the Emperor Nero, but there is no evidence to confirm this because it didn't happen. Two other people who were said to have been killed by Nero, however, were Lucius Calpurnius Piso, the head of the family, and his friend Annaeus Seneca! As the years passed, the Sun religion and the esoteric symbolism of the mystery schools, were transformed into a religion based on the literal translation of symbolic texts.

On this misunderstanding and deceit Christianity was built. We are led to believe that the Christian Church emerged as one unit, but this is simply not true. There were many factions across a wide spectrum of views arguing and battling for supremacy as the holders of 'the truth'. The fiercest conflict ensued between the followers of the St Paul version of Jesus as the supernatural Son of God, and the Arians, who believed he was a man, not God. The Arians were named after Arius, a churchman in Alexandria, Egypt, who questioned that Jesus could be the same as God. Had not Jehovah said that he was the only God? How then could God be in three parts as the Father, Son and Holy Spirit? The 'trinity' is a Pagan concept and part of Babylonian and Egyptian belief. Now if we lived in a world full of mature adults, we would allow people the respect and freedom to believe anything they like so long as they don't impose it on others. Just because we may think it is wrong or a nonsense should not matter. My problem with Christianity and religion in general is not that anyone believes it, that is their right, what I challenge is the way it has been imposed upon people through the use of fear, guilt, violence and the suppression of alternative thought. Unfortunately, allowing people the right to believe something you don't, has become a criminal offence and so the Paulines and the Arians insisted on crushing each other. At this point, enter Constantine the Great, who, together with the Pisos and Pliny, was the creator of what became known as Christianity.

Constantine was made Emperor of the Roman Empire in 312 AD. He won a reputation as a brave and ruthless soldier and served in Britain for a time before being elected as Caesar of the West. He then began to kill his rivals, including many of their children, as he sought to be emperor of all. In one of his battles for the Roman leadership, at Milvian Bridge near Rome, the Christian legend claims that he saw a vision of a cross in the sky with the words: "By this Conquer". The next night, so it is said, he had a vision of Jesus who told him to put the cross on his flag to guarantee victory over his enemies. Good story, but the word bollocks* is drifting across my mind. Constantine was said to have been converted to Christianity by his visions, but there's one tiny problem with that. He never did become a Christian, except perhaps on his deathbed as a bit of insurance. He worshipped the Greek god Apollo (the Sun), and the Sol Invictus (Unconquered Sun), and he remained to his death the Pontifex Maximus of the Pagan Church! As a result, Jesus was given the Sun's birthday of December 25th which has remained ever since. Constantine is also responsible for the great Christian shrine in Jerusalem. His mother, Helena, was

---

* American readers, I understand, do not know the meaning of the British term, 'bollocks'. How can I explain it? I guess 'you must be joking' is the cleanest translation I can think of.

dispatched to the city to track down the places and relics of the Christian story. It was she who claimed to have found the exact locations of the birth of Jesus, the crucifixion, his tomb and where he ascended into the sky. You can still find them all on the guided tour of Jerusalem! Constantine built a basilica in 326 AD on the site his mother said the crucifixion took place and on the same spot today stands the Church of the Holy Sepulchre which attracts millions of Christians to see where 'Jesus died on the cross'. Helena also claimed to have found the three wooden crosses around 300 years after the event. What a clever lady she must have been.

The truth went far deeper, however. Constantine was a member of the same Babylonian Brotherhood through which the Pisos and Pliny operated. The Basilica which Constantine built in Jerusalem is part of the sacred geometric pattern of this city according to some researchers. The Roman College of Architects were connected with the Order of Comacine Masters who expanded rapidly under the reigns of Constantine and Theodosius as Christianity was becoming the dominant religion of the Roman Empire.[21] Both were important branches of the Brotherhood underground. The Order of Comacine based themselves on the island of Comacini in Lake Como in northern Italy. Lake Como, which today is close to the Swiss drug money laundering centres like Lugano, is a very important centre for the Babylonian Brotherhood. Two of its modern British members, Prince Philip and his mentor, Lord Mountbatten, attended a meeting of the Brotherhood's Bilderberg Group at Lake Como in 1965. The Order of Comacine was divided into lodges headed by Grand Masters and they wore white gloves and aprons and communicated through secret signs and handshakes.[22] All this was happening more than a thousand years before the official creation of Freemasonry! They were given the patronage of the king of Lombardy and were made masters of all masons and architects in Italy.[23] It was this secret order, the successors to the earlier Brotherhood architects, the Dionysian Artificers, who provided the bridge between those who built the ancient Pagan temples and their brethren, who would build the great Christian cathedrals of Europe. The same Brotherhood built both! The ancient temples were shrines to the Pagan deities, and the Christian cathedrals were also shrines to the Pagan deities. The only difference was that, with the latter, the public thought they were built to worship 'Jesus'. The famous Christian hero, St Bernard, defined God as 'length, width, height and depth' because he understood the effect of geometry and numbers on the energy fields. Pythagoras also stated that: "number is all". The power of pattern, numbers, geometry and proportion, are some of the 'great mysteries' that have been denied the mass of the people.

Clearly Constantine, and the Brotherhood which controlled the emperors, saw political advantage in supporting the Christian movement. And the people would have had no problem encompassing Jesus into their belief system because the story matched that of the other Sun gods of the time, including Mithra. Christianity picked up many followers of Mithra because to them it was no different to what they already believed except for the name. Constantine ended the persecution of Christians in the Roman Empire by issuing his Edict of Milan, but this was not specific to Christianity, though it stopped the persecution against all one-God religions. Anyway, as one persecution ended another was soon to begin, as the Roman Church persecuted, burned and tortured anyone who refused to believe in the Christian faith, or even their version of the faith. Tens of millions of people have died in the name of the so-called 'Prince of Peace'. Appropriately, Constantine murdered his wife and elder son before making the journey in 325 AD to his palace at Nicaea (now Iznik in Turkey) to decide what Christians to this day must believe. He wanted to end the conflict between the Paulines and the Arians and install a single Christian creed. He called 318 bishops (another mystical number) together at Nicaea to tell them what their creed was going to be. Bitter arguments erupted between the factions on the burning issue for the future of the world: Was Jesus part of a trinity of Father, Son and Holy Ghost? Holy shit. Documents were torn up and blows were struck. If you are a Christian, this is how your faith was decided. The Arians lost the day and out of this mayhem and Roman dictatorship came the foundation belief of Christianity, the Nicene Creed. This dog's breakfast was as follows. I hope you are concentrating, I'll be asking questions later:

> "We believe in one God, the Father almighty, maker of all things, both visible and invisible; and in one Lord, Jesus Christ, the son of God, begotten of the Father, only begotten, that is to say, of the same substance of the Father, God of God and Light of Light, Very God of Very God, begotten, not made, being of one substance with the father, by whom all things were made, both things in heaven and things on earth; who, for us men and our salvation, came down and made flesh, made man, suffered and rose again on the third day, went up to the heavens, and is to come again to judge the quick and the dead; and in the holy ghost."

Simple eh? It was decided that Jesus was the same substance as the father because in ancient Babylon it was said that Nimrod and his son, Tammuz, were the same person. His mother, Queen Semiramis, was titled the Holy Spirit. So the Father, Son and Holy Ghost, are in fact Nimrod-Tammuz and Semiramis. Christianity is the religion of Babylon and has been from the start. Today Rome and Italy remain a major Brotherhood centre, as I detail in ...*And The Truth Shall Set You Free*. The Vatican itself is wholly controlled by the Brotherhood and one of its most important bases.

Christianity, like Judaism and Islam, was designed to achieve another vital part of the reptilian Agenda: the suppression of the female energy, the intuitive connection to higher levels of our multidimensional consciousness. Once you suppress your feminine energy, your intuition, you switch off your higher consciousness and become dominated by your lower consciousness. You are isolated from your highest expression of love, wisdom and knowledge, and at the mercy of the manipulated 'information' bombarding your eyes and ears. This is why the Brotherhood have sought to create a world in which the male energy has called the shots, on the surface at least. The state of being we know as 'macho man' is a person disconnected from his female energy and therefore deeply imbalanced. Note that there is no mention of women in Constantine's Nicene Creed. It says that

God became flesh as Jesus "for us men and our salvation". Christianity was a male bastion from its very foundation, created to suppress the balancing female energy. The early founders of the Church, like Quintus Tertullian, banned women from priestly office and even speaking in church. It was only at the Council of Trent in 1545 that the Roman Church officially agreed that women had souls and then only by a majority of three votes! The seeds of this anti-feminine dogma in the Christian Church can be seen in its mirror, Zoroasterism, the sect of the prophet (mythical Sun god), Zoroaster. He and his religion emerged yet again from Persia, now Turkey, the home of the Taurus Mountains and St Paul's abode, Tarsus. Zoroaster was vehemently anti-women and he said that "no women could enter Heaven except those 'submissive to control, who had considered their husbands lords'". This whole philosophy is an almost word-for-word repeat of Brahmanism, the appalling Hindu creed which was introduced by the Aryans to India many centuries before. St Paul (the Pisos and Pliny) continued the anti-feminine agenda in Christianity and set the scene for the horrific suppression of women over nearly two thousand years. Among St Paul's little gems are:

"Wives submit to your husbands for the husband is the head of the wife as Christ is the head of the Church. Now if the Church submits to Christ so should wives submit to their husbands in everything."

And:

"But I suffer not a woman to teach, nor to usurp authority over the man, but to be in silence."

The Christian Church was built to represent and perpetuate the extreme male vibration, the Sun energy, and to keep the ancient knowledge secret. The Christian Church became a crucial and highly effective vehicle to remove knowledge from circulation so it could be used secretly and malevolently from behind the scenes. The assault on the balancing female energy and the hoarding of knowledge resulted in the persecution of 'witches' – channellers, mediums, psychics and seers of all kinds. These communications with other realms had been an everyday part of pre-Christian life. Channellers were given names like prophets, oracles, vessels of God and such like. One of the leaders of this witch-hunt was Jerome, born in 341, who is credited with gathering the texts for the main Latin version of the 'Holy Bible'. It was Jerome who persuaded the Pope to outlaw channelling (psychic communications with other dimensions). By this single papal decree, the vessels of God became vessels and witches of the Devil, terms still used by many Christians. King James I, the first king of both England and Scotland, included a bitter condemnation of witches in his King James Bible in 1611 and he was true to his word as he had thousands of women tortured and executed for being witches. Jerome wanted the priests to be the middle men between humanity and God. He did not want people going direct, contradicting the official line, or circulating unapproved knowledge. As he said:

"We tell them (*the channellers*) that we do not so much reject prophecy, as refuse to receive prophets whose utterances fail to accord with the Scriptures old and new."[24]

Yet at the same time the initiates of the Babylonian Brotherhood which created the Roman Church were using these same psychic powers and modes of inter-dimensional communication. OK, how else can we control and diminish the great unwashed? We've got them to believe a fantasy about Jesus and we've conned them to think that after one life on Earth, God decides if they go to heaven or hell. We have also conned them to think that we, the men in frocks, know how God wants them to live and that anything to do with the esoteric is the Devil. Anything else? Hey, we need to be careful about that sexual energy, the creative force. Got to shut that down or their power source will still be there. I've got just the man. I say, Augustine, in my office, please. Saint Augustine of Hippo, like most of the early Church heroes, was from North Africa. He couldn't get enough sex earlier in his life, but after his alleged conversion to Christianity at the age of 31, he switched dramatically and decided that sex was horrid. You know what smokers are like when they stop. He would not allow a woman into his house unaccompanied, even his sister. He couldn't think of another way of producing children, so unless the race was to die out, he was stuck with it. However, he insisted that on no account should you enjoy it. I've tried that mate, and it doesn't work. This was Augustine's view of sexuality:

> "Husbands love your wives, but love them chastely. Insist on the work of the flesh only in such measure as is necessary for the procreation of children. Since you cannot beget children in any other way, you must descend to it against your will, for it is the punishment of Adam."

These attitudes led, in stages, to the imposition of celibacy on priests by Pope Gregory VII in 1074. Yes, we have celibate priests in the Roman Catholic Church today because of what one pope decided a thousand years ago and countless children, abused by sexually frustrated and messed up churchmen, have taken the consequences. Augustine connected sex with original sin, the idea that we are born sinners because of our link back to Adam and Eve. Jesus, so this theory goes, was the only one born without original sin because he was conceived by a virgin birth. But what about his mother? She must have had original sin and so some of it must have been passed on to him. Eventually, the Roman Church could see the contradiction and they decreed that Mary, too, was a virgin birth. But what about *her* mother? Did she have original sin? If so, it must have been passed on to Mary. My God, please stop me before I disappear up my own orifice. What garbage it all is. But billions of people have been controlled and manipulated in this way since the Christian creed sank its fangs of fear, guilt and violence, deep into the human spirit. Actually I believe in original sin myself. Some of my 'sins' have been very original. If you are going to sin, make it original, that's what I say.

Our spiritual, mental, emotional and physical levels of being are connected by vortices of energy known as chakras (a Sanskrit word meaning: wheels of light).

It is through these chakra vortices that imbalances on one level are passed on to another (*see Figure 18*). Thus when we get very emotionally stressed, the first thing that happens is that we stop thinking straight. The imbalance on the emotional level is transmitted to the mental level. This is eventually passed onto the physical level if the imbalance is not corrected and this is how stress and emotional upset causes illness and disease or dis-ease. These emotional imbalances manifest in the physical body as chemical reactions and it is these reactions that official medicine (the transnational drug corporations) seeks to 'treat' at unbelievable cost in both money and long term effects on the body. They treat the symptom, not the cause, because most doctors are so in-doctor-rinated that they have no idea how the body really works and what the human being really is. Those that control the drug corporations do know, however, and they use every means possible to suppress 'alternative' healing methods which treat the cause and not the symptom.

It is also the chakras which suck energy into our consciousness field and in a fully functioning state we take in vast amounts of energy, particularly through the base chakra at the bottom of the spine. From there it moves through the seven major chakras going up along the spine and out through the crown chakra at the top of the head. I explain all this in detail in other books like *I Am Me I Am Free*. For reasons I will go into in a later chapter, the more energy we suck into our energy field, the more power we have to create and control our own destiny. It is vital, therefore, that those who wish to diminish and dominate us find ways to limit the amount of energy we absorb. This is where the manipulation of sex comes in. The three lowest chakras are the base, the sexual chakra just above that, and then the chakra connected to our emotional level in the solar plexus. It is this chakra which stimulates the 'butterflies' and 'nervous stomachs' when we are worried or stressed. So the Christian and 'moral' attitudes to sex close down the base chakra and what energy it does absorb is thrown into turmoil when it hits the sexual and emotional chakras because of all the fear and guilt surrounding the subject. This imbalances and diminishes the entire human energy-consciousness field. Most Christian clerics have no

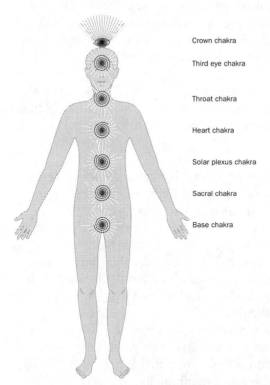

Crown chakra

Third eye chakra

Throat chakra

Heart chakra

Solar plexus chakra

Sacral chakra

Base chakra

Figure 18: *The human 'chakra' or vortex system which interpenetrates our levels of being. When they are open we connect with the cosmos and draw in limitless amounts of energy. When they are closed we are disconnected from the cosmos and operate on a fraction of our mental, emotional, physical and spiritual potential.*

idea that this is so, but those who have controlled Christianity and the Roman Church certainly do, because they are in the knowledge stream that has been suppressed in the general population. Each generation has been conditioned to think the Christian way about sex, whether consciously or subconsciously, and they in turn have helped to condition the next generation to think the same. But sex is wonderful. It is to be enjoyed. The ability to express your love physically for another human being is an incredible gift. I don't care what your sexuality may be. Love is love is love. Let's express it. If Augustine or the Pope want to tie a knot in theirs, fair enough, everyone to their own, as long as they don't tell me how to live my life.

In the East, Asia and China, they have retained the understanding of the power of sexual energy over thousands of years and this knowledge has been practised in the West in the secret societies and Satanic rituals. Once again the sexual energy is just that, energy, and can be used to create or destroy. In the Eastern religions, the conscious creation and stimulation of sexual energy is known as Tantra. Sexual intercourse is seen, quite rightly, as the union and balance of the male and female, the yang (male) and yin (female). The idea of Tantric sex is to stimulate the sexual energy held in the base of the spine, the Kundalini energy as it has become known. This was symbolised as uncurling serpents and in Tantra the participants control and delay orgasm to transform the kundalini from its original state (ching) into the higher energy (ch'i) and finally its highest expression (shen). This is done by raising the energy up the spine and down again until it has reached a vibratory state that can reconnect the person with the cosmos. By the end of this book you will see the importance of this and its scientific basis. When the kundalini explodes into your energy field as it did with me in 1990–91, it can blow you away mentally, emotionally and spiritually, sometimes physically too, until you have mastered its power. Stimulating the kundalini is described as 'lighting the inner fire'. Mine wasn't a fire, it was a nuclear strike! Tantra is designed to complete this process in a more controlled way, but sometimes the uncontrolled way offers a more extreme and enlightening experience. Once the Kundalini is awakened, you have a constant supply of enormously powerful energy with which to create whatever you choose. The Satanists use sex as a fundamental part of their ritual so they can tap this sexual, kundalini force, for their horrendous purposes. But it can equally be used to set us free and hence the Christian obsession with making sex into a dirty, immoral, guilt-ridden experience which suppresses or imbalances the kundalini energy and delinks the person from their cosmic levels of self.

The compilation of the Bible was yet another farce. If you ask most people about the Gospel writers, they will usually tell you that Matthew, Mark, Luke and John were the disciples of Jesus. That's the impression people get and are encouraged to get, but it's not true and not even the Church claims that officially. The Gospels and other books of the Bible are only those chosen by the hierarchy of the Christian Church from those written by the Pisos and Pliny and the many copies and offshoots which followed. Many other texts were available that were just as valid, often very much more so, than those which made it into the 'Holy Book'. Texts were rejected, destroyed or rewritten to fit the official line and the philosopher, Celsus, wrote of the church leaders in the third century:

> "You utter fables, and you do not even possess the art of making them seem likely... You have altered three, four times and oftener, the texts of your own Gospels in order to deny objections to you."[25]

In 1958, a manuscript was discovered at a monastery at Mar Saba, east of Jerusalem, which shows how the Jesus story was rewritten by the Church whenever it suited them at the time. It was found by an American, Morton Smith,[26] Professor of Ancient History at Columbia University, and it included the content of a letter by Bishop Clement of Alexandria, Egypt, an early Christian father, to a colleague called Theodore. It also revealed an unknown segment of Mark's Gospel which had been suppressed. It included in the 'Jesus' story some details of mystery school initiations and it was an account of the raising of Lazarus by Jesus, the famous raising from the dead. In this suppressed text Lazarus called to Jesus before any 'raising' took place, so proving that he was not supposed to be physically dead. There was also another devastating revelation for Christianity. The manuscript makes references to the effect that Jesus was understood to have engaged in possible homosexual practices involving the 'rich young man' mentioned in Mark's Gospel.[27] Let me stress that I am not condemning homosexuality here. Good luck to those who wish to live their lives in this way so long as it's the choice of all concerned. I am making the point that the Christian hierarchy have been deceiving and lying to their followers right from the start. Bishop Clement's letter was replying to a Christian who was very perturbed to be told the above story of 'Jesus' by the Gnostic group called the Carpocrates. It had apparently been leaked to them by an official in Alexandria. Clement's advice, after confirming the story, was that anything which contradicts the official church view must be denied, even if it is true. The letter says of those who question official orthodoxy:

> "For even if they should say something true, one who loves the Truth should not, even so, agree with them... To them one must never give way; nor, when they put forward their falsifications, should one concede that the secret Gospel is by Mark – but should deny it on oath. For not all true things are to be said to all men."[28]

Clement was summing up the attitude of the Brotherhood and their religious fronts throughout history. Most members of the Church follow the party line because that is what they are conditioned to believe, but within these 'religions' are the secret sects which know the truth. They are organisations within organisations or an organisation (the reptilian Brotherhood) within organisations. It was such people who created the religion in the first place and compiled and translated the Bible, the book that was to mind control the world for centuries and, to a very large extent, still does. Jerome became secretary to Pope Damasus in about 382 and he was commissioned to bring various texts together to produce the Bible in Latin, the official language of Rome. Now we had another translation, the Hebrew and Greek into Latin, plus Jerome's own prejudices. His version is known as the Vulgate, from the Latin Vulgata, meaning in common use. The English derivative, vulgar, meaning 'in poor taste', would have been a better description. Jerome edited the texts as he saw fit and rejected those which didn't support the creed of Nicaea. He worked with another church 'father', the sex bomb, Augustine. Jerome and Augustine both agreed that women were morally and spiritually inferior and that sex and earthly pleasures were a source of evil which kept men from their spiritual path. Poor sods. They examined 13 gospels, nine acts and teachings of the Apostles, plus 31 letters and other writings. They decided which were 'orthodox' and which were to be rejected. Their choice was supported by the Council of Carthage in 397 and confirmed again by Pope Innocent I a hundred years later. Jerome's Vulgate Bible became widely accepted as *the* version. The Council of Trent in 1545 decreed that it was the only acceptable one for Roman Catholics.

Most Christians could not understand what it said because they didn't read Latin, but they could rely on the priests to tell them what it said they should do. People were condemned and killed for the crime of translating the Bible into English because doing so allowed millions to actually read the texts the priests were using to control and terrify them. In 553 AD, the belief in reincarnation was outlawed at the Second Synod Council of Constantinople under the influence of the Emperor Justinian. The council decided, without the attendance of the Pope, that: "If anyone assert the fabulous pre-existence of souls and shall submit to the monstrous doctrine that follows from it, let him be... excommunicated". The 'monstrous doctrine' was that we live forever on an eternal journey of evolution through experience and we are all responsible for our actions in this physical life or a future one. An acceptance of reincarnation took away the power of the heaven or hell mob to frighten people into doing as they, sorry, 'God', said. The knowledge continued to be sucked from the public domain. After Constantine the Great, came other emperors who influenced the course of the fast emerging Christian creed. Among them was Theodosius who made Christianity the official religion of the empire in 380. The power of the men in frocks grew enormously as the Babylonian priesthood dropped anchor in Rome. Anyone who strayed even marginally from the official beliefs was brutally executed and their documents destroyed – exactly the Nimrod doctrine of Babylon. This is not just a bunch of power crazed psychopaths, ad-libbing their way through this grotesque slaughter, it was a coldly calculated plan to rule by terror and in doing so, take any other knowledge or versions of life out of public circulation. As reptilians and the puppets of reptilians, they wanted to create a mental and emotional prison cell, outside of which it was fatal to tread.

The marauding Visigoths, a Germanic (Aryan) people who occupied southern France, eventually sacked Rome in 410, but by then the Roman Church had such a grip on the minds of so many in the former Roman Empire, that where the Roman emperors left off, the Popes would take over. The Roman dictatorship became a papal dictatorship and in the centuries that followed, Europe became a landscape of untold slaughter. The Pope ruled and who ruled the Pope? The Babylonian Brotherhood, exactly as they do today. The Hebrew and Christian religions are the inventions of those who controlled the underground stream of secret knowledge. Even the ritual garbs are the same in so many ways. What do Jewish people wear? Skull caps. What does the Pope wear? A skull cap. This is symbolic of the way priests in the mystery schools used to shave the backs of their heads. The more formal headgear and ritual of Judaism and Christianity are also very similar because they originate from the same source and the Pope's mitre is the fish head symbol of Nimrod.

To complete the trio, along came the skull-cap-wearing Muslims and the creed of Islam, inspired by the 'Prophet' Mahomet (Mohammed) when he had a 'vision' in the year 612. Once more we find that Islam's roots are in Christianity and Judaism and therefore Babylon. Muslims see Islam as an updated continuation of the Judeo-Christian stream and they, too, trace their ancestry back to our old mate, Abraham, who is said to have emerged from the Sumerian city of Ur and headed for Egypt. They believe that Abraham built the Kaaba, the sacred shrine at Mecca, and the focus of pilgrimage for Muslims all over the world. But it was in fact originally a Pagan temple of goddess (Semiramis) worship featuring the famous Black Stone. W. Wynn Westcott, founder of the Hermetic Order of the Golden Dawn, wrote in his work, *The Magical Mason*, that the Black Stone supposed to have been brought to Mecca by Abraham, was used originally for ancient Pagan ritual.[29] Again you see Brotherhood symbolism in this 'new' religion. The symbols of the crescent and the curved sword, the scimitar, are identified with the Moon and Venus, the Morning Star, the term used for Lucifer. Venus was also a title for Queen Semiramis. Muslims have bought the idea that Moses, King David and Jesus were divine prophets sent by the one All Mighty God, when in fact all three are Brotherhood inventions. Their holy book, the Koran, which was supposed to be inspired by God, mentions Jesus in 93 verses and treats him as a living person. Islam was created by the same Brotherhood networks as the Christian religions, to further imprison, divide and rule. Mohammed was the last prophet and therefore, the Muslims reckon, the most valid. As such, all Christians and Jews should convert to Islam, the orthodox Muslims demand. The term, Jihad, is the 'Holy War' that Muslims are urged to wage against all who do not accept the creed of Mohammed. How fitting that Islam means 'to submit or surrender' and Muslim means 'one who submits'. Some of the bloodiest conflict in history has resulted from the desire of Islam, Christianity and Judaism to impose their creed on each other, when they all come from the same source and the same manipulation! Excuse me, did I come in late and miss something? Beam me up Scotty, get me out of here...

The Islamic god Allah is the same 'god', the Muslims say, as the Judeo-Christian, Jehovah. The Koran is the Islamic holy book, but Muslims also give credence to the Pentateuch, the first five books of the Old Testament attributed to Moses. In truth they were written by the Levites after Babylon and not by 'Moses', which was a title in the Egyptian mystery schools. Is it really a coincidence that these three massive prisons of the mind, suppressors of the female, and creators of bloody conflict, should all come from the same part of the world? Or that people having visions and visitations should play such a crucial part in the formation and legend which created these monsters? Mohammed said he had his vision near the cave where he used to go. Caves and dark places constantly recur in stories of religious superstars and Sun gods like Mithra and Jesus. Mohammed said his visitor claimed to be the Angel Gabriel of biblical fame and during the encounter Mohammed said he lost consciousness and entered a trance state. While Mohammed was in his trance or hypnotic state, 'Gabriel' gave him a message to remember and recite. Mohammed said that when he awoke the message was inscribed upon his heart. What followed the encounter with 'Gabriel' was a bloodbath spanning the centuries to the present day, as Mohammed and his successors sought to impose their creed on the world. Islam is not the opposite of Christianity and Judaism, they are all 'oppo-sames': the same state of mind with a different name, ultimately controlled by the same people, the reptilians. Islam is another mystery school religion, its texts written in esoteric code for the masses to take literally. There were times in later centuries when some of this secret knowledge was allowed into the public domain by more enlightened Muslim leaders and this was the inspiration for the advanced societies and science which came out of Muslim Spain and Baghdad. Today, part of the Brotherhood Agenda is to stimulate conflict with the Islamic nations by causing division between the Muslim and Christian-Jewish world.

The Mormon Church is another 'vision' religion which very powerfully locks into the Brotherhood network, as all religions do. The Mormon Church, or more formally, the Church of Jesus Christ of Latter Day Saints, was founded by Joseph Smith after he claimed an 'angel' called Moroni appeared to him in 1823. Moroni, he said, told him of the existence of a book of gold plates containing: "the fullness of the everlasting gospel" and "an account of the former inhabitants of this continent and the sources from which they sprang". The location was revealed to him, and in 1827 with help from two 'magic stones' called Urim and Thummim, he translated the plates into English. Urim and Thummim were, in fact, the names of knucklebones or dice used by Levite priests and the Kings of Israel were said to follow their prophecies. They were used in the mystery school holy place known as the Tabernacle. Here we have yet another religion originating from the same source and another perpetuation of the Jesus myth. The gold plates, Smith said, were written in 'reformed Egyptian'. From this came the Book of Mormon two years later and his followers became the Mormon Church in 1830. The pillars of the early church were Smith and another guy called Brigham Young. They were both high degree Freemasons from the key New York Lodge and the expansion of this church was funded by Kuhn, Loeb and Company, the Rothschild Bank in the United States[30] which also helped to fund the Russian Revolution and both sides in the First World War. The Mormons were a Brotherhood creation. Mormons recognise the Bible, but claim that Smith's writings are equally divine. They set up communities called Stakes of Zion (Sion, the Sun) and eventually settled in Salt Lake City, Utah, the Mormon city from where its mind control programmes are orchestrated, as I shall document in a later chapter. Funny how all these religions are justified by a vision or visitation, followed by an extreme, dogmatic and autocratic religion which rules by fear, indoctrination and mind manipulation.

Another mind control sect which emerged from Christianity/Judaism is the Jehovah's Witnesses, the worship of the Hebrew angry god, Jehovah, and one of their leading founders was the paedophile Charles Taze Russell, a high degree Freemason. These religions were set up to control, to create conflict between people, and to divide and rule the masses. Visions of biblical characters like the Virgin Mary which have enhanced mainstream Christian beliefs over the centuries have followed a similar pattern. We have no idea what the Jesus 'team' looked like, but people always see them as their classic artistic depiction. Those who have seen visions which relate to the Bible stories have had shrines built to them, but those who see visions which are not biblical are condemned as working with the Devil. William Cooper, a former operative with United States Naval Intelligence, said he had seen secret documents which claim that extraterrestrials had told the US authorities that they had manipulated the human race via religion, Satanism, witchcraft, magic and the occult. Certainly, the human race has been manipulated and controlled through religion and Satanism. The only question is, are extraterrestrials (or inner-terrestrials) behind this? As Cooper asks: "…were they indeed the source of our religions with which they had been manipulating us all along?"[31]

The answer, I would suggest, is a very loud: "Yes".

■ SOURCES

1   Abelard Reuchlin, *The True Authorship Of The New Testament* (the Abelard Reuchlin Foundation, PO Box 5652, Kent, WA, USA, 1979).

2   Ibid, p 1.

3   Ibid, pp 4–5.

4   Ibid, p 12.

5   Ibid, p 5.

6   Ibid, p 22.

7   Michael Howard, *The Occult Conspiracy* (Destiny Books, Rochester, Vermont, 1989), p 18.

8   *Bloodline Of The Holy Grail*, p 132.

9   *The True Authorship Of The New Testament*, p 11.

10   Ibid, p 14.

11   Acts 9: 17–18.

12   Romans 16: 11.

13 *The True Authorship Of The New Testament*, p 15.

14 Ibid, p 15.

15 Ibid, p 16.

16 Ibid, p 15.

17 Ibid, p 27.

18 Arthur Findlay, *The Curse Of Ignorance, A History Of Mankind* (Headquarters Publishing Company, London, first published 1947), Volume I, p 549.

19 Matthew 16:18-19.

20 Matthew 16:23.

21 *The Occult Conspiracy*, p 18.

22 Ibid.

23 Ibid.

24 *The Curse Of Ignorance*, Volume I, p 636.

25 Ibid, p 637.

26 Morton Smith, *The Book Your Church Doesn't Want You To Read*, p 176.

27 Mark 10:17-23.

28 Morton Smith, *The Secret Gospel* (Victor Gollancz, London, 1974).

29 Quoted by Euctace Mullins in *The Curse Of Canaan* (Revelation Books, PO Box 11105, Staunton, VA), p 44.

30 Fritz Springmeier, *The Top 13 Illuminati Bloodlines* (Springmeier, Lincoln, Portland, Oregon, 1995), p 151.

31 William Cooper, *Behold A Pale Horse* (Light Technology Publishing, PO Box 1495, Sedona, Arizona, USA, 1991), pp 212–213.

CHAPTER SIX

Rule Britannia

As the religions were firmly established and controlling the masses in the first centuries of the AD era, the expansion of the Babylonian Brotherhood accelerated on the political and financial fronts, also.

Vital to this expansion was another branch of the reptilian full-bloods and crossbreeds who made their way over land and many centuries to New Troy – London – via Italy, Switzerland, Germany and the Netherlands. These were Nimrod worshippers and, appropriately, the very name of Italy derives from the word bull – a Nimrod symbol.

Once again they travelled under the heading of Phoenicians and they settled in the north of Italy in 466 AD in what is now Venice. These Phoenicians then became known as Venetians. They built a powerful maritime (of course) and financial empire which was based on lending people money that does not exist and charging interest on it. This is another common theme of the Babylonian Brotherhood over thousands of years and today this financial scam controls the purse strings of the planet. When you go to a bank for a loan, the bank does not print a single new note or mint a single new coin. It simply types into your account the size of the loan and from that moment you start to pay interest on what is nothing more than figures on a screen. The bank has created 'money' out of nothing and insist that you pay them for doing so. If anyone else did that, they would be arrested for fraud, but the banks do it every day quite legally. This system was employed in Babylon and it has been expanded over thousands of years. It has rarely been challenged because the Brotherhood which devised this system have also controlled the kings, queens and leading politicians, who have imposed it on the people. More than that, the Brotherhood *are* the kings, queens and leading politicians! The 'money' created in this way is known as 'fiat' money.

The Phoenician-Venetians, under the control of the Babylonian Brotherhood, expanded their wealth and power by war, assassinations, piracy and by ruthlessly manipulating trade and money. They would support a country when it suited them and then immediately seek to destroy it if that advanced their Agenda. One of their common methods was to bankrupt any person, business or country that opposed them. If that sounds exactly like the methods in use globally today, there is a reason for that. The same Brotherhood now control the world banking and trading system via the central banking network, the World Bank, the International Monetary Fund, the World Trade Organisation, the Bank of International Settlements and so on. The reptile-Aryans of Venice married into the nobility, bought themselves titles, and simply invented others. As a result, from around 1171, they became known throughout Europe as the 'Black Nobility'. Once again the Phoenicians (or rather the reptile-Phoenicians) became the aristocracy. They operated across northern Italy to Genoa and into an area that became known as Lombardy, going north into what is now Switzerland. Lombard is still a word widely used in the financial industry and Lombard Street is one of the best known streets in the City of London financial centre. Northern Italy or Lombardy was the region invaded around the fourth century BC by Aryan 'Celts' called the Lombards who brought an influx of Nordic blood from Germany. They were later absorbed by another Aryan people, the Franks, from where we get the name France. In short, they were different branches of the same white race with the reptile-Aryans, unknown to the rest of the population, invariably at the helm. As today, these reptilians and reptilian puppets looked human, but they were controlled within by a very different force working to a long term Agenda. Long term in our perception, anyway. Switzerland remains a fundamentally important financial stronghold for the Brotherhood. This is why it is never attacked and never takes part in wars, even when every country along its borders is involved. Switzerland is a major financial centre for the people who are creating the wars and so they ensure it is not involved. See how simple history becomes when you know the Agenda!

Venice was for centuries a hub of the reptile bloodlines who expanded into the Far East with the journeys of the Venetian, Marco Polo, of whom there is far more to know than official history suggests. The surviving royal families in Europe are the reptile bloodline of this Black Nobility, including Britain's House of Windsor. This is why these royal houses, including the Windsors, are rife with Satanism and fundamentally connected with Freemasonry and other Elite secret societies. I will chart the history of the Windsors, their grotesque record of manipulation, and their reptilian-Satanic activities, in a later chapter. The Black Nobility established close relationships with the bloodline families of Britain and they were behind the invasion in 1066 by another branch of their 'family', the Normans of William the Conqueror and the St Clairs, a family of Viking descent. Once again the Black Nobility married into the British aristocratic families, awarded themselves titles, or invented them out of nothing. Two families were especially important in the Black Nobility takeover of Britain, the Savoys and the Estes. The Savoys (after which the famous London hotel is named) ruled Italy from 1146 to 1945 and the Estes ruled the region called Ferrara from the 1100s until 1860 when Italy became one country. There are countless examples of how the Black Nobility infiltrated and took over Britain. Eleanor, the daughter of Peter, the ninth Count of Savoy, married the English king, Henry III. Peter 'Savoy', the Black Nobility count, was given large estates in England by Henry after he married his daughter and this included the title of the Earl of Richmond. From this foothold the Black Nobility count, now the Earl of Richmond, arranged a series of other marriages between the Black Nobility and the English aristocracy. His younger brother, Boniface, was even made Archbishop of Canterbury! The Black Nobility have been controlling the Church of

England for centuries, indeed from the start, and today one of their most active representatives, Queen Elizabeth II, is still the official head of the Church. The Black Nobility bloodlines are reptilian full-bloods and crossbreeds and pure Babylonian Brotherhood. They seized the reins of power in Europe to take their Agenda into another stage.

The founders of the European royal houses, many of which continue to this day, were Rupert, the Count of Nassau, and Christian, Count of Oldenbourg. Both lived in the 11th and 12th centuries, the very period when the Black Nobility-Babylonian Brotherhood launched its plan to control the whole of Europe. From Rupert came the Hesse-Darmstadt and Hesse-Cassal lines, the Dukes of Luxembourg, the Battenborgs/Battenbergs (later Mountbattens), the Prince of Orange and Nassau, and the Kings of the Netherlands. From Christian came the Kings of Denmark and Norway, the Schleswig-Holstein line and the Hanovers, who became Kings of England. It was from the Hanovers that the present House of Windsor is derived. Other Black Nobility-reptile bloodlines included the Dukes of Normandy (like William the Conqueror, hence their support for him and the St Clairs), the Saxe-Coburgs (another Windsor bloodline), and the Plantagenets who produced the Tudor and Stuart monarchs of England. Here you see how the English aristocracy and the monarchs on the English throne have in fact been the Black Nobility. The Scottish nobility, the clans and the ruling aristocratic families like the St Clairs, the Bruces and others I have mentioned, are also the Black Nobility in disguise, the reptile-Aryans from the ancient world. Of course they fight among themselves for power and many of them will not be aware of who they are and what is controlling them, but they are the same Anunnaki–reptilian bloodlines and invariably find themselves in the positions of royal, religious and political power.

Many of today's most famous financial and business families are members of the Black Nobility lines of the Babylonian Brotherhood. The Warburg banking dynasty is in fact of the Abraham del Banco family, the biggest banking family in Venice when the city was at the height of its powers and influence. The Agnelli family, famous for the car giant, Fiat (remember fiat money?), is another of these Black Nobility bloodlines. This is why the Agnellis control Italy and dictate to its governments. Another of the most powerful Black Nobility families of Venice were the de Medicis and it was they who sponsored the journey of Christopher Columbus to 'discover' the Americas. The reason for that will become clear soon. The de Medicis also sponsored the artist, Leonardo da Vinci, a leading initiate of the secret society network. Da Vinci was able to predict some of the future development of technology because he knew what most of the public were not allowed to know. His famous depiction of the man within the circle was symbolic of the golden mean geometry on which the major sacred sites of the world are designed and located.

The influence of the Black Nobility expanded northwards into Germany and it is from this stream that the British royal family, the House of Windsor, originates. Until they changed their name in 1917, they were called the House of Saxe-Coburg-Gotha, a German royal line going back to the Black Nobility of Venice-Lombardy and beyond that to Babylon. The Windsors are reptilian full-bloods and they know it. When the Black Nobility expanded into Germany, the del Banco family of Venice became known as the Warburgs. Although they claim to be Jewish, the Warburgs are in fact a reptile-Aryan bloodline. This explains why they became bankers to Adolf Hitler and why other reptile-Aryan families like the Rothschilds claim to be Jewish while funding and supporting people like Hitler. (See ...*And The Truth Shall Set You Free* for the detailed background to this.) In 1998 while on a speaking tour of South Africa, I was invited to have a private meeting with P. W. Botha, the President of South Africa during the 1980s, who wished to give me information about who controls that country. He told me that during his presidency he was asked to host a delegation of the English Rothschilds in Cape Town. At that meeting they told him that money which once belonged to German Jews was sitting in Swiss bank accounts and it was available for investment in South Africa if they could agree an interest rate. Botha said he was outraged and refused to play. But this was the money that has been recently located in Swiss banks and was stolen from the Jews who suffered under Hitler. The Rothschilds have been lending it and making money from it since the war. That, my friends, is what the Rothschilds think of Jewish people and yet to expose the Rothschilds is to be branded 'anti-Semitic' by both Jewish people who have no idea how they are being manipulated, and by the self-righteous, self-indulgent 'Robot Radicals', better known as the political left. For a definition of how the 'left' think and behave, see any definition of how the political 'right' think and behave! The Rothschilds were formerly known as the Bauers, one of the most famous occult families of Middle Ages Germany, and they originate not from Israel, but the Caucasus Mountains. They are shape-shifting reptilians hiding behind human form. The Elite Brotherhood families change their names from time to time to ensure that people won't realise that the same bloodlines holding the positions of power weave their way through history.

The Black Nobility made its centre for a time in Amsterdam. Again many of them claimed to be Jews, but they were not, they were Aryan bloodlines which had journeyed there by various routes. Some originated from the Phoenician-Venetians and some were the Khazar Aryans from the Caucasus Mountains where their ancestors had mass converted to Judaism in the 8th century. What we call Judaism is just another offshoot of the Sun religion of the Aryans, as is Christianity. The leadership in Amsterdam was the successors to the black magicians of Babylon. They were reptilians operating mostly, but certainly not always, within the white race. It was while the Black Nobility had their base in Amsterdam that the Dutch people were used to begin the white settlement of South Africa. In 1689, one of this Black Nobility, called William of Orange, was manipulated onto the throne of England and at this time the reptile-Aryan leadership in Amsterdam moved to London to connect with the other reptile-Aryan bloodlines who had settled in London and Britain thousands of years before. London became even more the epicentre of their increasingly global operations. It was after this that British people were used to settle South Africa and they went to war with the Dutch people there, the Boers, to establish control. Both peoples involved were pawns in a game they did not understand and their successors still don't. William of Orange landed in

England or Barat-land, on the shores of Torbay in 1688, the same place that the Trojan, Brutus, had landed when he came to establish London as his New Troy about 1,103 BC. Still today there is a statue of William of Orange in the fishing port of Brixham to commemorate his arrival near that spot. William was, of course, a student of the esoteric arts and his physician, Johann Schweitzer, also known as Helvetius, once claimed to have performed alchemy and turn lead into gold.

William of Orange became William III of England as husband of Queen Mary. It was William's grotesque treatment of the Irish which led to centuries of bitterness in Ireland which continues to this day. In 1694, William signed the charter for the Bank of England and the Black Nobility, together with the reptile-Aryan aristocracy already well established in Britain, made the City of London-New Troy the centre of global finance, a position it still enjoys. Little wonder that the entrance to the City of London financial centre is marked by statues of winged reptiles holding the red cross on a white shield, the ancient Aryan Sun symbol, and also the symbol of the Rosi Crucis or Sumerian Gra-al, the reptilian bloodlines (more about that later). Other central banks had already been created by the reptile-Aryan Black Nobility branches. They were the Bank of Amsterdam (1609), Bank of Hamburg (1619) and the Bank of Sweden (1661), but the Bank of England was the jewel. They were designed to lend those governments money that did not exist and charge them (the people through taxation) interest on the debt. The greater the debt the greater the interest and therefore the greater the taxation. Get the idea? We've been had, my darlin's, and it's time to wake up. Governments, of course, could create their own money interest free and have no interest to pay to the private banking cartel. The reason they don't introduce this most obvious system is because the governments are controlled by those who control the banks – the Babylonian Brotherhood. And they coordinate between their branches in the various countries to ensure that anyone who sought to do this would be immediately crushed economically and politically. The main coordinating body between the interconnected central banks is called the Bank of International Settlements, based in the Brotherhood stronghold of Geneva, Switzerland. Just as the reptile Brotherhood control the monarchies because they *are* the monarchies, so they have created and controlled all the political parties, left, right and centre. The 'radical' Liberal Party in Britain, now the Liberal Democrats, used to be known as the Venetian Party and at their highest levels they are all the reptile-Aryan Party under different guises. Ever wondered why politicians appear to differ so much in public and yet introduce the same policies when they get into government? It's all a conjuring trick on the human mind.

The list of people who arranged for William of Orange to take the British throne reads like a *Who's Who?* of the reptile-Aryan-Phoenician Elite. Among the long list of the Phoenician, sorry, British, aristocracy who subscribed to the Bank of England at its formation (making unbelievable profits) was William Cavendish, the Duke of Devonshire, who also signed the invitation for William to become King. The Cavendish's are based at Chatsworth House in Derbyshire, now a tourist attraction, and I felt it to be one of the blackest places I have ever visited. As with all these stately homes of the Brotherhood, goodness knows what has gone on there over the centuries. The Cavendish family crest is a reptile and a snake, whatever its origin it is highly appropriate. The Cavendish's fused with the Kennedy family of the United States when Kathleen, the sister of President John F. Kennedy, married the heir to the Devonshire fortune. When he died during World War II and she had claim to the Devonshire estates, she 'conveniently' died in a plane crash. The Kennedy's are another Elite bloodline which go back to the ancient Irish kings and beyond. The arrival of William of Orange was also supported by the reptile-Aryan aristocracy of Scotland where many of the bloodlines based themselves. The Phoenicians were in Scotland thousands of years BC, but some of the most famous 'Scottish' bloodlines came later from northern France and Belgium during the reigns of the Scottish kings, David I and Malcolm IV, between 1124 and 1165. Classic 'Scottish' names like Stewart, Seton, Hamilton, Campbell, Douglas, Montgomery, Balliol, Graham, Lindsay, Cameron and Comyn, arrived in this period. These 'Flemish' people were bloodlines from Sumer, Babylon, Asia Minor and the Caucasus, who had made their way across land to Europe. Within 150 years of their arrival in Scotland they were running the show. One of the most famous of Scottish kings, Robert the Bruce, came from the line of Robert of Bruges in what is now Belgium, one of the key Brotherhood centres today. The battles between the Scots and the English were, although the people never knew, merely battles between different branches of the same Elite for supremacy in the Agenda. Some were reptile-Aryans, some were not. Bruce and the St Clairs/Sinclairs were reptilian for sure. It was one of Bruce's descendants, the Scottish nobleman James Bruce of Kinnaird, who left Britain in 1768 for Abyssinia, now Ethiopia, to find a rare copy of the Kebra Nagast, the sacred book of the Ethiopians, and three copies of the Book of Enoch with which he returned to Europe in 1773. James Bruce was a Freemason, a member of the Canongate Kilwinning No 2 Lodge in Edinburgh, one of the oldest in Scotland.[1] The present British royal family, the Windsors, carry some of the blood of Robert the Bruce and of the Scottish, Irish and Welsh Elite, as well as the genetic stream of the reptile-Aryan branches in Germany. The Windsors, like all the royal families (family) of Europe are representatives of the Black Nobility and Babylonian Brotherhood and related to William of Orange. They are, as I shall be describing, shape-shifting reptilians.

Anna Campbell, Countess of Balcarras and Argyll, was governess to the young Prince William, and Archibald Campbell, first Duke of Argyll, was alongside him when he sailed to England in 1688 to remove the sitting monarch, James II. A descendant of Anna Campbell was Jenny von Westphalen, who was related to both the Campbells and the Dukes of Argyll. Jenny von Westphalen was the wife of... Karl Marx, the Brotherhood clone who was used to create Communism. This was one of the great vehicles used to divide and rule the global population through fear. Incidentally the reason Marx condemned Jews was because, contrary to popular belief, he wasn't one. He was of a Brotherhood bloodline which is why he got the job as frontman for Marxism, a creed compiled not by him but for him (see *...And The Truth Shall Set You Free*). These interconnecting bloodlines have been interbreeding and filling the positions of political and economic power throughout the centuries and the genealogy is recorded in the most minute detail. It is known which lines are more open to possession by the reptilians and which are not. When a position is to be filled, someone is selected from a reptile-Aryan line and if he or she has not already been 'plugged in' to the reptilian consciousness via secret society initiations, he or she is invited to join the club and away they go.

The interconnections and breeding of these bloodlines is simply endless. The modern Earls of Balcarras are related to Viscount Cowdray (Weetman John Churchill Pearson of the London *Financial Times* family). His mother was the daughter of Lord Spencer Churchill, the grandfather of Winston Churchill, and his sister married the

Scottish Duke of Atholl. The Argyll-Balcarras lines manifest as the Lindsays and Campbells. Robert A. Lindsay, the 12th Earl of Balcarras, became chairman of the National Westminster Bank, one of four major British clearing banks, and director of the Rothschild's Sun Alliance Assurance. This same Earl was also a British Minister of State for Defence and for Foreign and Commonwealth Affairs. His mother was a Cavendish, who are the Dukes of Devonshire, headquartered at Chatsworth House. And that's just one tiny example of the way the bloodlines interconnect.

The Marlborough family, one of the most powerful British aristocratic families, also played an important role in putting William of Orange on the British throne. They are related to the Churchills and Winston Churchill was born at their ancestral home, Blenheim Palace near Oxford, where the gates are emblazoned with the Marlborough

Figure 19: *The Dragon crest of the Marlborough family at Blenheim Palace.*

family crest, dominated by two reptiles (*see* **Figure 19**). Churchill knew exactly what he was doing when he was the wartime Prime Minister in Britain. The image of him left to us by official history is a farce. He did not save the British Isles from tyranny, he was part of the tyranny to create a war in which all sides were fronted and funded by the same people. See ...*And The Truth Shall Set You Free* for proof of this. I could sit here all day detailing the Elite reptile-Aryan families and the way they have interbred and interconnected to hold the reins of power in all areas of human life over thousands of years. This world has been controlled since antiquity by the *same* tribe with their masters operating from the lower fourth dimension.

The reptile Agenda has been unfolding over many centuries. It is the long term plan for this tribe, and therefore the reptilians, to take over the planet completely.

The Agenda has a set timescale and a definite sequence. This is clear by the way each move follows another with breathtaking efficiency under the supervision of the inner core which operates outside the public arena and, ultimately, from another dimension. For example, in 1665 war broke out between the Dutch and the British and the Great Plague killed 68,000 Londoners and caused two thirds of the people to leave the city. In 1666, on September 2nd, the Great Fire of London destroyed the city and was blamed, for historical purposes, on a baker in Pudding Lane. This happened while the plans were being arranged for William of Orange to become King of England. When he arrived from Holland to take the throne, many branches of the Brotherhood bloodlines united in London or New Troy to create their operational headquarters. London, thanks to the fire, had created a blank sheet of land on which they could build their new financial centre. And who was the main architect of the new London? A high initiate of the Brotherhood network called Sir Christopher Wren. All a coincidence? Replicas of St Paul's Cathedral with its massive dome, an ancient ritual symbol for the Brotherhood, stand in Paris and Washington DC. One is called the Pantheon and the other is the Congress Building on Capitol Hill (named after Capitoline Hill, a sacred hill of the Babylonian Brotherhood in ancient Rome). In the years that followed the arrival of William of Orange, came the so-called Great British Empire. As a kid I always wondered how a few islands which you can hardly see on the globe could have an empire that spanned the world. Now the reason is obvious. It was not the Great *British* Empire at all. It was the empire of the Babylonian Brotherhood which had based itself in Britain, and particularly London. As the 'British' Empire expanded into the Americas, Africa, Asia, China, Australia and New Zealand, the Babylonian Brotherhood's control of the world expanded also. Other reptile-Aryan branches in countries like Spain, Portugal, France, Belgium and Germany, occupied other parts of Africa; and the Spanish and Portuguese took care of Central and South America. King Leopold II of Belgium, a member of the Windsor reptilian bloodline called Saxe-Coburg-Gotha, played a major role in the European occupation and exploitation of Africa. Everywhere the reptile-Aryans went they sought to destroy the native culture and knowledge. They took out of general circulation the esoteric knowledge, memories and understanding of true history. Ancient accounts of the reptilians and the origins of the white race were largely destroyed or withdrawn to secret Brotherhood libraries, not least beneath the Vatican. Christianity was used as the vehicle for eliminating information that we vitally need to know.

It would seem that the contraction of these British and European empires, particularly in this century, indicates that this control has diminished. Not so. It has increased. Overt control, such as a dictatorship you can see, always has a finite life, because in the end there will be a challenge and rebellion against it. Covert control, however, control you cannot see, identify or target, can go on forever, because you don't rebel against something you don't know exists. A person who thinks he is free will not complain that he is not. So what has happened throughout Africa, South America, Asia and the United States and Canada, is that overt control from Britain and Europe has been replaced by covert control. As these overt empires, particularly the British, have appeared on the surface to contract, they have left in these countries the secret society network, bloodlines and structures to rule just as powerfully as before, but now with no danger of a challenge from people with no idea of who is really in control. The global structure is quite simple. The central Agenda is coordinated from the City of London, which comprises the financial centre known as the 'Square Mile', and the land along the River Thames running down to the headquarters of the British legal profession, the Houses of Parliament, the centres of government and British Intelligence, and across to Buckingham Palace, the home of the reptilian bloodline known as the Windsors. The British Government is merely a front for the real Agenda that is operated from these few miles of prime real estate in the City of London and the City of Westminster. Paris is another key centre for the Babylonian Brotherhood and so is the Vatican. Look at the structures of government known laughingly as 'democracy', the structure of law, economics, the media and all the institutions you find in most countries today. Where did the original blueprints for these structures come from? London, exactly. We still talk of Britain as the 'Mother of Parliaments', for instance. These structures were designed to give the appearance of freedom while allowing almost limitless control by the few behind the scenes. These are the very structures that the British Empire left behind when it apparently withdrew to allow those countries to govern themselves. Like hell they did. Physical occupation was replaced by financial occupation and overt control by covert control.

From London, the reptile-Aryan Elite dictates its policy and Agenda to its 'branch managers', the bloodline families in each country, which ensure that the London coordinated Agenda is introduced globally. This is why the same policies are being imposed in every country I visit. In the United States, the main branch managers for London are the Rockefellers who have orchestrated a cartel of families and frontmen like the Morgans, Harrimans, Carnegies, Mellons etc, under the over all supervision of London. In South Africa the bloodline branch managers are the Oppenheimers. I spent three weeks travelling, talking and listening all over South Africa in 1998 and it is a wonderful example of what I am saying here. Look at the history for a start. First the Dutch settled the Cape when the Black Nobility were centred in Amsterdam. Then, after they moved across the English Channel to London, the British were used as the pawns of occupation. The Dutch East India Company in South Africa was pushed aside by the British East India Company. Explorers of the African interior, like Doctor David Livingstone, were funded by organisations such as the National Geographical Society, controlled from the City of London. Another wave of reptile-Aryan-British occupation was headed by Cecil Rhodes and his South African Company, also a City of London operation. Rhodes was a major Brotherhood frontman, especially through a secret society called the Round Table which still exists today and is exposed at length in …*And The Truth Shall Set You Free*. Rhodes and his South Africa Company started the diamond and gold mining empires called De Beers and Consolidated Goldfields which the Oppenheimers now control on behalf of the same Brotherhood that funded Rhodes.

Another offshoot of the South Africa Company was the notorious London-Rhodesia Company called Lonrho, headed most famously by the late Tiny Rowland. Lonrho has manipulated and exploited Africa and its people appallingly, which is in line with the present day Agenda. Quite clearly, the same group have controlled the African continent under different companies, people and guises, from the time the first white settlers arrived.

Before the transfer of power from white minority to black majority under Nelson Mandela in South Africa, the Oppenheimer family controlled something like 80 per cent of the companies quoted on the South African stock-market and they owned the gold, diamond and other mining industries on which the country depends. They also controlled the media through various frontmen. Then came 'massive change' as Nelson Mandela was released and the blacks were given their 'freedom'. Now, after this blow for democracy, the Oppenheimers still control something like 80 per cent of the companies on the South African stock-market, they own the gold, diamond and other mining industries on which the country depends, and they control the media via frontmen like Henry Kissinger's friend, Tony O'Reilly, the Irish billionaire. O'Reilly resigned as chairman of the Brotherhood-controlled Heinz corporation and began to buy up newspapers all over the world, money apparently no object. So what's the difference between the Brotherhood's control of South Africa before and after the 'changeover'? One thing and one thing only: no-one is complaining anymore because overt control has been replaced by covert control. When there was a white minority dictatorship the global condemnation could be heard constantly: "It's not fair", the robot radicals would scream, "It's racism, it's dictatorship. Outrageous." And it was. But now the rallies and the protests have stopped and Mandela is a hero to the world while the same people go on controlling South Africa as they did before, although now without a word of protest from the heart-on-the-sleeve, wave-your-banner merchants. The shanty towns and corrugated iron ghettos are still there in Soweto and in even more places these days, but they are not on the daily news anymore because everyone knows that South Africa is now free. The ANC government is just as controlled and corrupt as the white one it replaced. Shell Oil, the Babylonian Brotherhood oil company controlled by people like Prince Bernhard of the Netherlands, gave a whole tower block to the ANC at the time of the changeover, and it is, apparently, common knowledge among journalists worth the name, that Mandela takes no major decision without consulting the Oppenheimers. In 1993, Mandela spent Christmas at the Nassau holiday home of Tony O'Reilly. In early 1994, O'Reilly bought South Africa's biggest newspaper group. Oops, could I be questioning a global hero? Slap my wrist. In fact, Mandela is probably quite a genuine guy who has simply learned the realities of where the real power lies and he can't summon the strength or desire to openly challenge the system anymore. But there are many truly corrupt blacks, like Robert Mugabe, the President of Zimbabwe, who are only too willing to take the money and play the frontman for the Babylonian Brotherhood at the grotesque expense of the people. Only in this way can overt control operate behind black faces and there are reptilian bloodlines among the blacks as well as the whites.

The same situation exists throughout the world where you find the same bloodlines and their puppets in charge in country after country, in front of the camera and behind the scenes. The latter group hold the real power, of course. So if it suits the Agenda to crash the US dollar or the Mexican Peso or bring down a government, or start a civil war, the branch managers in those countries go to work through their financial, media and secret society operations to ensure that it happens. In this way, the world can be run by a very few people in the City of London and other Brotherhood centres like Paris, Bonn, Brussels, Washington, New York, Switzerland and the Vatican. It's a simple and brilliantly organised structure, ruled from the top with a rod of iron, and no mercy is shown to anyone who does not do exactly as they are told. That's why it has worked so efficiently for so long. Add to that the fact that the truth of what is going on is so bizarre that most people will not believe it and you have the perfect situation for ongoing, unchallenged control.

Until now.

■ SOURCES

1　　*From The Ashes Of Angels*, p 12.

CHAPTER SEVEN

Knights of the Sun

O ver thousands of years, the reptilian full-bloods and crossbreeds have created a fantastic web of interconnecting secret societies to enforce their Agenda. Yet the people in general have been unaware that such a coordinating force has been at work, manipulating their governments and their lives. In the next three chapters I will show how these networks seized control of the institutions of royal, political and religious power, and created the United States. This apparent 'superpower' is still a puppet of the Babylonian Brotherhood in London.

Three of the most significant of the secret societies emerged publicly in the 12th century. They are still in existence today and have among their membership top people in global politics, banking, business, military and the media. They were the Knights Templar, the Knights Hospitaller of St John of Jerusalem and the Teutonic Knights. The Knights Hospitaller have changed their name a number of times. They have been the Knights of Rhodes and today they are the Knights of Malta in their 'Roman Catholic' form and their 'Protestant' version is known as the Knights of St John of Jerusalem. As the Knights of Malta, their official head is the Pope and their headquarters is in Rome. As the Knights of St John they are based in London and their official head is the King or Queen. The Catholic and Protestant wings are in fact the same organisation at the highest level. The Knights Templar were formed about the same time in 1118, though this could have been at least four years earlier, and were first known as the Soldiers of Christ. The Templars are surrounded in mystery and contradiction, but it is known that they dedicated the order to the 'Mother of God'. The Knights Templar promoted a Christian image as a cover and so Mother of God was taken to be Mary, the mother of Jesus, but to the reptile-Aryan secret societies the term, Mother of God, is symbolic of Isis, the virgin mother of the Egyptian Son of God, Horus, and the wife of the Sun god, Osiris, in Egyptian legend. Isis, in turn, is another name for Queen Semiramis, as in Nimrod-Semiramis-Tammuz. Isis/Semiramis is also known by a stream of other names in the various regions, cultures and countries. These include Barati, Diana, Rhea, Minerva, Aphrodite, Venus, Hecate, Juno, Ceres, Luna and many, many others. It is said that they are symbolic of the Moon, the female energy in its various forms. The headquarters of the Grand Mother Lodge of English Freemasonry (Grand Mother = Semiramis/Isis) is based in Great Queen Street in London (Great Queen = Semiramis/Isis). In the end all the names were inspired by Ninkharsag, the Anunnaki 'Mother Goddess' of the reptilian-human crossbreeds, their 'mammy'. The ancient gods such as Nimrod/Osiris and the endless other names under which he is known, represent the power of the Sun, the male. This was the knowledge on which the Templars were founded and their Phoenician and reptilian inspiration can be seen in their symbol, the red cross on a white background – the fire cross or Sun symbol of the Phoenicians and symbol of the bloodlines. This is also the flag of England to this day.

From the start of the official Templar story there were blatant untruths. They claimed to have been formed to protect pilgrims in the Holy Land, but for the first nine years it seems there were only nine of them. Some protection. It doesn't take a genius to see that this was a smokescreen for something else. In fact, it would appear they were formed as the protectors and military wing of a secret society called the Order of Sion, later the Priory of Sion. The word 'Sion' comes from Siona, the ancient Sanskrit (Aryan) name for… the Sun.[1] Here we go again. Among the later Grand Masters of the Priory of Sion, according to the book, *Holy Blood, Holy Grail*,[2] was Leonardo da Vinci, who was sponsored by the de Medici banking family of the Venetian Black Nobility. They would also sponsor Christopher Columbus. Among the most important sponsors and supporters of the early Templars was St Bernard, the founder of the Cistercian Order, and the French St Clair family which became the Scottish Sinclair family after they settled in Scotland following the Norman invasion of Britain by William the Conqueror in 1066. The St Clair/Sinclairs are of a reptilian bloodline and knowledge of the reptilian Agenda was the great secret held by the leading Templars. The first Grand Master of the Knights Templar was Hughes de Payens, who joined in 1124. He was a French nobleman (meaning literally: Aryan-man) allied to the Count of Champagne, and was married to a Scottish woman of Norman decent called Catherine St Clair. The first Templar centre or 'preceptory' outside the Holy Land was built on the St Clair estate in Scotland. Other early Templars included Fulk, the Count d'Anjou, who was the father of Geoffrey Plantagenet and the grandfather of the English King, Henry II. It was Henry who sponsored the building of the famous Benedictine Abbey at Glastonbury in the west of England, a sacred site since ancient times. The Templars were connected to the Knights Hospitaller (Knights of Malta) at their highest level and these links very much continue today. There are many tales of how much they hated each other and there have undoubtedly been periods of rifts and conflict. But at their peak they are different branches of the same organisation and at that level the Agenda is all important. In June 1099, another glorious blow was struck for the 'Lord' when Christian crusaders invaded Jerusalem and slaughtered the Saracen Muslim Turks and the Judeans living there. This reopened the 'Holy City' to Christian pilgrims who began to arrive in large numbers through the ports of Jaffa, Tyre and Acre. Tyre was one of the major centres for the Phoenicians. The Knights Hospitaller established the Amalfi Hostelry in Jerusalem to provide food and shelter for the visitors. As their wealth and prestige grew, they formed a military wing, which was given papal backing in 1118, the same year that the original nine Knights Templar arrived in Jerusalem to 'guard' the pilgrims.

The Templars were given quarters adjoining Temple Mount, the alleged, and I stress alleged, site of Solomon's Temple. Some researchers believe the Templars found something of great value, possibly manuscripts, possibly vast amounts of gold, while excavating under Temple Mount. But whatever happened events began to move rapidly after 1126, for it was then that the Grand Master, Hugues de Payens, left Jerusalem to gather recruits and expand the order. He headed back to France to meet St Bernard, then Abbot of Clairvaux, and he took with him Bernard's Templar uncle, Andre de Montbard. Bernard sang their praises to Pope Honarius II, and the Templars were formally established on January 31st 1128 at the Council of Troyes. Yes, named after *Troy*, that great Aryan and reptile-Aryan headquarters in Asia Minor which also inspired the original name of London. The Templars were part of the same gang, although many of the lower initiates would not have known this. Among their symbols, apart from the Phoenician red cross, were a black and white flag (made up of two squares), the skull and crossbones, and the watchtower. All of these symbols have spanned the centuries to the present day Brotherhood organisations. The black and white squares can be found on the floor of every Freemason Temple, because the Freemasons are the Templars under another name. Many churches and cathedrals, like Westminster Abbey and Notre Dame in Paris, also have black and white squares on the floor, because the Christian church is a front for the Babylonian Brotherhood. Many police forces, including those in the UK and the USA, have black and white squares on their uniform because they are controlled by the Freemasons and the Templars. The skull and bones is symbolic, in part, of the black magic rituals the Brotherhood have employed since their very earliest days and these same sickening rituals, often involving human sacrifice, are still going on today. If you look at the Vatican or papal crest, you will see that the dome of St Peter's Basilica and the crossed keys of Peter also form the same skull and crossbones. They're all in it together. This theme could well be the reason that the Piso family in the Gospel stories said the location of the 'crucifixion' of Jesus, was a place called Golgotha, meaning: the place of the skull. Another Babylonian Brotherhood organisation is the appropriately named Skull and Bones Society based across the road from the campus of Yale University at New Haven in Connecticut, USA. It is a blood drinking, Satanic secret society for the bloodline families and its most famous current member is George Bush, the former President of the United States and a shape-shifting reptilian. He is also one of the foremost drug runners in America, and a Satanist, child abuser and serial killer. See a later chapter for details of this. The Watchtower symbol can be seen in the Jehovah's Witness organisation because this is also a Brotherhood front that is conning countless followers into believing it is Christian. One of its founders was Charles Taze Russell, a high degree Freemason, who is buried under a pyramid.

Only a year after the Templars were formally established at the Council of Troyes, incredible expansion had taken place. They had a papal constitution, wealth, land and three hundred recruits from noble families who had to give all their wealth to the Templars when they joined. As a result they owned land in France, England, Scotland, Spain and Portugal, and within ten years this was extended to Italy, Austria, Germany, Hungary and Constantinople. There were Templar preceptories and villages, hamlets and farms galore all over England. Whenever you see the name Temple in a British place name (for instance Templecombe) it is a former Templar site. Their national headquarters was in London on land which is now High Holborn and in 1161 they moved a short distance to a new London temple which is still today called Temple Bar. Here can be found the original church in the classic round design of the Templars, along with some Templar graves. In a most prominent position in Temple Bar, in the centre of the main thoroughfare, is a statue of a winged reptile. The Templar holdings included the Strand and much of Fleet Street which, until recently, was the home of the British national newspaper industry. The symbol of the national tabloid, *The Daily Express*, once headquartered in Fleet Street, is a knight carrying a shield emblazoned with the Templar-Phoenician red cross on a white background. The Templar lands stretched down to the River Thames where the Templars had their own docks. During the reign of Queen Victoria, the Brotherhood erected an obelisk alongside the Thames at this point and placed a sphinx on either side. The obelisk had formerly stood in the Egyptian city of On or Heliopolis (the City or Place of the Sun) and it is known today as Cleopatra's Needle (*see picture section*). This obelisk is an ancient Egyptian-Aryan symbol of the Sun, the male energy, the phallus. These symbols are to be found in many places, often under the guise of war memorials and have been placed there by Freemasonic manipulation. Has anyone ever asked themselves why a war memorial nearly always has to be an obelisk? And why do you think the Washington monument in the centre of Washington DC is a giant obelisk? Because obelisks, like all these symbols and geometrical shapes, generate the energy they represent. I remember climbing some stone steps inside a big obelisk near Hebden Bridge in England and feeling enormous male sexual energy all around me. I wondered what on Earth was happening until I remembered where I was… inside a male penis in effect. What a symbol is built to represent is the energy it will generate, because symbols are a physical manifestation of the thoughts which create them. These guys don't put their symbols everywhere just for fun. They do it because it helps to resonate the energy field to the vibrational frequency they want. In turn, this affects the thoughts and feelings of the people.

Most notably today, the Templar lands of London are the home of the British legal profession. Barristers qualify when they 'come to the Bar' – Temple Bar – and they join either the Inner Temple, Middle Temple or Outer Temple. I have spoken with people who have had experience of these organisations and they found them to be very sinister indeed. For sure, they are. If you want to control the people you have to control the law and who is and isn't prosecuted. Thus you have the police awash with members of the Freemasons along with the legal profession and the judges. These Templar lands of all those centuries ago are in the heart of that area of London from the City of London 'square mile' financial district down to the Houses of Parliament and Buckingham Palace. This is the land from which the world is currently controlled, at least at the operational level, together with Paris and the Vatican. And Paris was the other dual-headquarters for the Knights Templar. That city also has a 3,200 year old Egyptian obelisk at a key point in its street plan, the Place de la Concorde. Princess Diana passed that obelisk in the Mercedes literally a minute before it crashed in the Pont de L'Alma tunnel in 1997.

By the middle of the 12th century the Templars were second only to the Roman Church for wealth and influence. They had their own fleet of ships (on which they flew the skull and bones flag), and their financial centres in London and Paris were, in effect, the start of the modern banking system which has made humanity slaves to non-existent 'money'. They, too, lent 'money' that didn't exist and charged interest on it in true Babylonian Brotherhood style. One documented case shows the Templars charging 60 per cent interest on the late payment of a debt. One of the plans promoted by the Templars was the creation of a United States of Europe and under different guises and fronts their masters in the Brotherhood have achieved just that. The creation of the European Union with its single central bank and currency is one of the pillars of the Brotherhood Agenda.

Some of the advanced knowledge inherited by the Templars was that of the Earth's energy grid, the network of magnetic force lines known as ley lines, dragon lines or meridians. The major sacred sites are where many of these lines cross, creating enormous vortices of energy. If you perform a black magic ritual and human sacrifice at these points the deeply negative energy it produces is carried on the force lines emanating from the vortex and pumped throughout the network. This affects the vibrational state of the Earth's magnetic energy field within which we all live. If that energy field is full of fear, people will be more likely to feel that emotion. And fear is the four letter word that controls the world. The most important weapon for the Babylonian Brotherhood since its creation has been the manipulation of fear. Nothing limits people's potential to express their true selves more than fear. It becomes understandable, therefore, why so many Christian churches were built on ancient Pagan sites and why so many Satanic rituals are performed in churches under the cover of darkness. It was the Templars, with their knowledge of the esoteric arts, who financed the great Gothic cathedrals of Europe between 1130 and 1250. The Gothic style can be shown to have originated with the Aryan race in the Middle-Near East. The Gothic cathedrals which were funded and designed by the Templars included Westminster Abbey, York Minster in northern England, Chartres in France not far from Paris, and Notre Dame in Paris itself. Notre Dame (Our Lady: Isis/Semiramis/Ninkharsag) was built on a site dedicated to the goddess Diana, and Chartres was placed on an ancient sacred site which once attracted Druids from all over Europe. The famous chapel of Kings College, Cambridge which was based upon the cabalistic Tree of Life symbol, was described as one of the last great Gothic structures built in Britain.[3] Its design was apparently inspired by the 14th century cathedral at Albi in the Languedoc in southern France, one of the primary centres for both the Templars and the Cathars. In the 12th and 13th centuries the Cathar religion, which challenged many beliefs of the Roman Church and contained much esoteric knowledge, was the dominant faith in much of southern France. This sent the alarm bells ringing in the Babylonian Brotherhood in Rome and the puppet Pope, Innocent III, destroyed the Cathars in an unspeakable 'crusade' of torture and burning, which culminated in the siege of the Cathar castle at Montsegur in 1244. Incidentally, the use of reptile figures called gargoyles became widespread on 'Christian' churches and cathedrals. Notre Dame in Paris is covered in them (see picture section) and many are smaller representations of the same reptile depictions you find on and around the Mayan pyramids and sites in Mexico. The Mexican President, Miguel De La Madrid, said that the Maya had been interbred with the 'Iguana race' – reptilians.

Both Chartres and Notre Dame were centres of Black Madonna worship, another Templar obsession. The Black Madonna cult was not related to Mary, mother of Jesus, although that was the impression they wanted people to have. It was the worship of Queen Semiramis and Isis/Barati. The Egyptians portrayed Isis in white in her positive mode and in black in her negative form. The Black Madonna was the Black Isis/Barati and more directly, Queen Semiramis who was known in Babylon as the Madonna. The Black Madonna symbolises the negative use of female 'Moon' energy, while the Black Sun symbolises the negative use of solar energy, the male, besides being an occult name for the galactic Sun which this solar system orbits over 26,000 years. For instance, the white horse was a Sun symbol of the Phoenicians and so the black horse under the Brotherhood's system of reverse symbolism, represents the malevolent use of the Sun energy. The black horse is the symbol of the Brotherhood front in the United Kingdom, Lloyds Bank. The statues of Mary holding the baby Jesus in the Christian churches are mirrors of the way the Egyptians portrayed Isis holding the baby, Horus. St Bernard was clearly a covert disciple of the goddess religion and was born at Fontaines near Dijon, a centre for Black Madonna worship. The Templars shared his passion and they built their own churches in a circular shape, indicating the feminine. The widespread use of the dome or 'womb' by the Brotherhood also relates to this, among other things.

The New Age belief system has often fallen into the trap of believing that female energy is good and male energy not so good, because they think the world is male-dominated. In fact the world is dominated by the extremes of both energies, male and female. I am not talking about male and female bodies here, but male and female energy which both men and women have the potential to manifest. When a male suppresses his female polarity he becomes 'macho man' and thinks the only way to be a 'real man' is to be dominant and aggressive. This extreme of male energy is reflected by soldiers with guns and overt, in your face, aggression and power. Thus we think the world is male-dominated because you can see the extremes of male energy on the news every night. That's the point, you can see it. The negative extreme of female energy, however, is behind the scenes manipulation, covertly setting up the events and conflicts which the extreme of the male energy can play out in public. In other words, you can't see it. This is the energy that the agents of the Babylonian Brotherhood work with and they symbolise this with names like Semiramis, Isis and all the rest. They also know that the female energy is the creative force, which brought forth even the Sun, as the Egyptians used to say of Isis. This female force, like all energy, is neutral. You can create something positive or something malevolent, but to do either you need to harness the female, the creative force. Hence you have the constant female symbolism by the Brotherhood in all its forms. It is the balanced, positive expression of the female energy that they have sought to suppress, not the female energy itself.

The Gothic cathedrals and Christian churches are full of Sun, astrological, goddess and sexual symbolism. The great Gothic doorways and the ridges around them are depictions of the vulva and many even have a clitoris symbol at the top of the arch. The same is depicted in windows and especially the rose windows of the Gothic cathedrals which face west, the sacred direction of female deities. Carvings on other medieval churches have been found which portray monks and priests having sex with young girls and wearing animal heads. This is what the Satanists still do today. The Sheela-na-gig symbols in old churches, particularly prevalent in Ireland, represent naked women with spread legs and inside the alters of churches have been found stone phallic symbols. My goodness, what will the vicar think? The often shell-like receptacle for the 'holy water' is goddess symbolism also, and churches were actually built as a symbolic womb. The spider's web and maze decorations of the Gothic and other cathedrals and churches refer to the female 'goddess' energy, the intuitive, creative force, which weaves and spins the fate of the world. This is also the symbolism of the Spider Woman legends of the Native American traditions and the names of sacred places like Spider Rock in Arizona. A book by Fred Gettings, *The Secret Zodiac* (Routledge and Kegan Paul, 1987), features the zodiac mosaic in the marble floor of the Gothic church of San Miniato in Florence, Italy, which dates from 1207. Gettings suggests that the church was built to align with a rare conjunction of Mercury, Venus and Saturn in the sign of Taurus at the end of May that year. Astrology, which can be traced back to the beginning of known history, was a very important art to the Templars and was taught in the school at Chartres. When Christians go to church they have no idea that they are entering a 'Pagan' shrine, but that's exactly what they are doing.

The Templars had close relationships with most of the monarchs of the time, although less so in France. Given their immense wealth, the Templars 'owned' many of the kings who appeared to be in power, just as their Brotherhood successors own the governments of today. The Templars were close to Henry II of England, the sponsor of Glastonbury. How interesting that Henry's famous feud with the Archbishop of Canterbury, Thomas à Becket, ended when two knights arrived from France to murder him in Canterbury Cathedral in 1170. Henry's son Richard the Lionheart was, in effect, a Templar himself, though not officially. He used their ships and preceptories and when he was forced to escape from England and the threats of his brother, John, he did so disguised as a Templar. He was protected by them and headed for the Holy Land crusades against the Muslim Saracens. Richard sold Cyprus (a former Phoenician settlement) to the Templars and he was involved in negotiations between them and their Islamic version, the secret society called the Assassins. This word is now used to describe a killer and it derives from the Assassins particular method of ruling by fear and terrorism. Assassin is said to mean 'user of hashish' because they used the drug to trick and manipulate young men into killing for 'God' in the belief that this would secure their place in paradise. The name could also originate from the words hass (to destroy) and asana (to lay snares). They waged an international terrorist war from their mountain headquarters at Alamut or Eagles Nest in Persia (Asia Minor/Turkey). Pottery decorated with pentagrams and the symbol of the female vulva have been found at this site and the Assassins wore white tunics with a red sash. The Assassins, who still continue today under different fronts, emerged from a sect founded by a Persian called Hassan Sabah (another very possible origin of the name) in 1090, the same period the Templars, Knights Hospitaller, and the Teutonic Knights were being formed.

The Templars and the Assassins worked together although they appeared to be on different sides. This is the way the public are still duped today into believing that because two groups war or oppose each other in public they must be on different sides. If you want to control the outcome of a game, you have to control *both* sides, but to get away with this you must kid the people that the two sides have different masters and goals. One of the most effective methods of manipulation by the Brotherhood is to create or infiltrate all sides and so control the outcome. The Templars were skilled in this. While they were escorting Richard the Lionheart to the Crusades, they were supporting his brother and fierce rival, King John. The Templars were behind the signing of the Magna Carta in 1215, thanks to the efforts of Aymeric de St Maur, the Templar's Grand Master in England and King John's closest advisor. The Magna Carta curtailed many powers of the monarchy, so increasing the Templars control and leading further down the road to the Agenda's long term goal to introduce 'democracy': imprisonment disguised as freedom. Covert control instead of overt control. I am not saying that all the Templars were of negative intent. I'm sure that's not the case. But as always in these secret societies there were many levels of knowledge and agendas. The French writer and researcher, Jean Robin, concluded that the Order of the Temple consisted of seven outer circles which were taught the 'minor' mysteries and three inner circles which worked with the 'great' mysteries. It is the same with Freemasonry and all secret societies today. The mass of the membership has no idea what their top levels know or the Agenda they are promoting.

Despite their wealth, the Templars were exempt from taxes (just like the tax-exempt foundations of the Brotherhood today) and they had their own courts. They controlled monarchs, people of influence, businesses and countries. Their method was to manipulate their 'targets' into a position of dependency, usually through blackmail or debt. In this way the Templars could then dictate their actions. Nothing changes. Edward I borrowed substantial sums from the Templars while King John and Henry III were up to their necks in debt to them. At one point, Henry pawned the Crown Jewels to the Templars to pay for military exploits. This is another ancient technique of the Babylonian Brotherhood still constantly used today. Manipulate wars, lend all sides the money to fight them, and pick up massive profits from the horrors you have secretly caused. You also lend the same countries money to rebuild their shattered societies and this makes them even more in your debt and further under your control. You can also use the war to remove leaders, take over lands, and redraw the boundaries in line with your Agenda. Look at the two world wars in the 20th century to see how it is done. This is explained in detail in …*And The Truth Shall Set You Free*. The English Crown Jewels at the time of King John were kept at the Templar's London Temple and under John, Henry II, Henry III and Edward I, it was also one of four royal treasuries. The Templars collected the taxes for the Pope and the Crown, plus the taxation known as tithes. They were a private organisation with a secret agenda, collecting taxes from the people on behalf of others and a great slice of that money went straight to themselves in payment for interest on loans. Apparently they were ruthless with non-payers. Today these are still the methods used throughout the world. The Templar vows of sobriety and chastity were often so much hypocrisy. One description for heavy drinking in medieval England was to 'drink like a Templar'. When it came to the serious business of money, however, they were as ruthless with their own as they were with the populace. It is the same today when members of the Brotherhood and their lackeys step out of line. In France, the Templar centre in Paris was the leading royal treasury and the French monarchy was also in serious debt to them. But the French king, Philippe IV, or Philippe the Fair, decided, it seems, that he'd had enough and took steps to destroy the Templars in a purge against them in October 1307. Or at least that's the official story. There is a great deal more to know before we can understand what really happened and its relevance to the world events which followed. I will summarise some of the background.

The Merovingian bloodline

From their creation, the Templars and the Order of Sion, later Priory of Sion, were two branches of the same organisation. The role of the Priory of Sion, claimed by the book *Holy Blood, Holy Grail*, is to protect a 'royal' bloodline called the Merovingians, but there are so many smokescreens in this story to obscure the truth. One of these is the claim that the Merovingians are the bloodline of Jesus, via the child or children he conceived with Mary Magdalene, who fled with them to the South of France after the 'Crucifixion'. But there was no Jesus and no Mary because these are symbolic figures in a story which has been told endless times throughout the pre-Christian world, using different names. I find it hard to comprehend, therefore, how two symbolic people could conceive a bloodline that became the Merovingians. It's baloney and this tale has been hatched to divert researchers from the truth. Yes, the truth is about bloodlines and no doubt the Merovingians are a major one. But no, it has nothing whatsoever to do with Jesus. This particular line became known as the Merovingians in France by the 5th and 6th centuries. We are indebted for the early history of these people to Fredegar's *Chronicle*, a copy of which exists in the National Library in Paris. Fredegar was a 7th century scribe from Burgundy and he worked for 35 years to complete his record of the early Franks and Merovingians. A tribe called the Sicambrian Franks, from whom we get France, was another link in the Aryan and reptile-Aryan 'vine'. The Franks were named after their leader, Francio, who died in 11 BC. Francio's people migrated from Troy in what is now Turkey and became the Scythians and eventually the

Sicambrian Franks, named after their tribal queen, Cambra, in the late fourth century. They originated in Scythia, north of the Black Sea in the Caucasus Mountains, from where the Aryan and reptile-Aryan race swept across Europe. The Sicambrian Franks called themselves the Newmage – the People of the Covenant; that is the covenant of the Anunnaki.

The Sicambrian Franks later lived in an area west of the River Danube and settled in Germania (named by the Romans after the Scythian 'genuine ones') and their centre was Cologne. It was from the time of King Meroveus, who was named Guardian of the Franks in 448, that this line became known as the Merovingians. These were the sorcerer kings who were noted for their esoteric knowledge and magical powers which they inherited from the underground bloodline streams of secret groups and initiations. Francio, the founder of the Franks, claimed to be a descendant of Noah and his ancestors once resided in ancient Troy. I think myself that the story of Noah is symbolic of the reptilian crossbreed bloodlines which survived the flood and afterwards returned the dove and the olive branch (Semiramis-Nimrod) to power. Decendents of Noah = human-reptilian crossbreeds, or at least those who have interbred enough to maintain that genetic structure. The French city of Troyes, where the Templars were officially formed, was named by the Sicambrian Franks after their former home. The City of Paris was established by them in the 6th century after they became known as the Merovingians and it was named after Prince Paris, the son of King Priam of Troy. It was the relationship between Prince Paris and Helen of Sparta which supposedly caused the Trojan War in which the Trojan Horse infiltration assured victory for the Spartans. Both the Trojans and the Spartans were offshoots of the same Aryan and reptile-Aryan peoples. The Merovingians established the city of Paris on a major vortex point and used an underground chamber there for their rituals, including human sacrifice to the goddess Diana. Here, kings in dispute over property would settle the issue in combat. Meroveus, the founder of the Merovingian dynasty, followed the Pagan goddess cult of Diana, another symbol for Isis/Semiramis. This is not surprising because the centre for Diana worship was at Ephesus in Asia Minor, not far from the alleged site of Troy. The location of the ancient underground chamber in Paris where the Merovingians worshipped and sacrificed to the goddess Diana is now called the Pont and Place de L'Alma and it is still, by design, an underground chamber. On the site today is a road tunnel and it was here that the car of Diana, Princess of Wales, crashed in the early morning of Sunday, August 31st 1997. Another offshoot of the Scythian-Sicambrian Franks-Merovingian bloodline emigrated from northern France and Belgium in the 12th century to become the famous 'Scottish' families and some of these were the ancestors of Diana, Princess of Wales.

The Merovingian king, Clovis, had the iris, or fleur-de-lis, as his royal emblem, a flower which grows wild in the Middle East. It is also known as a three-pronged lily and it was used to symbolise Nimrod or rather the reptilian bloodline of Nimrod. In Latin it means small sword and it became the symbol of the royal bloodline of what is now France and this was because in ancient Sumer the reptilian bloodline, as passed on through the female, was symbolised by a lily. Hence the main reptilian gene carriers were given names like Lilith, Lili, Lilutu and Lillette. Another version is Lilibet or Elizabeth and this is why the present British Queen is called Elizabeth (El-lizard-birth) and was known to her family circle as Lilibet. She is a major reptilian gene carrier who produced a major reptilian full-blood called Prince Charles. Both are shape-shifting reptilians, a fact that will be supported by later evidence. So is the Queen Mother, formerly Elizabeth (El-lizard-birth) Bowes-Lyon. The fleur-de-lis is an ancient symbol and also represents the twin phallic pillars of Jachin and Boaz in the symbolic Solomon's Temple, which were carved with 'lilywork', as described in Kings 7:22. Today you will see the fleur-de-lis used profusely on the regalia of British royalty, on official buildings and the fencing around them, and in churches. It is, appropriately, on a public gate to the White House in Washington, another home of the bloodlines. The three-leafed shamrock in Ireland is likewise an ancient symbol of the bloodline and the word shamrock comes from the North African term: shamrukh. All these symbols relate to the three horned depiction of Nimrod in Babylon and to other esoteric principles. Other Merovingian symbols were the fish (Nimrod again), the lion (Leo, the Sun, authority), and the bee. Three hundred golden bees were found on the burial cloak of King Childeric I, the son of Meroveus, who died in the 5th century. Bees are an ancient symbol of the Love Goddess (Semiramis) and symbolised royalty in Egypt. They also focus on the Queen Bee, symbolic of Isis/Semiramis.

The Merovingians were another name for a Babylonian Brotherhood bloodline and the idea that they are from the bloodline of Jesus is a play on words, or, rather, a play on deities, by the Priory of Sion. Jesus is another name for Nimrod/Tammuz, the father-son of Babylon. Therefore, I would suggest, the bloodline of 'Jesus' is really the bloodline of the 'Nimrod' Brotherhood, the reptile-Aryans. Also, the Priory of Sion say they are dedicated to restoring the Merovingian line to the throne of France. They never were the monarchy of France, because it didn't exist at that time. It's all nonsense and designed to hide the real Agenda of the Priory of Sion which is a Babylonian Brotherhood front. What all these diversions obscure is a simple and devastating truth. The 'Grant of Arms' or symbol of the Dragon bloodine in Sumer was called a Gra-al, also known as the Mark of Cain. The biblical Cain was one of the early Anunnaki-human royal crossbreeds who followed 'Adam'. It is this Gra-al that became the so-called Holy Grail and this is why its equvilant in Old French means 'blood royal'. The Grant of Arms emblem in Sumer was... a cup of waters or a Rosi-Crucis or 'Dew Cup'. It is described in Egyptian, Sumerian, Phoenician and Hebrew records as a cup decorated with a red cross within a circle. This is the true origin of the 'grail cup'. It wasn't the cup that caught the blood of Jesus at the crucifixion because there was no Jesus or crucifixion. It was the cup that symbolised the womb and the bloodline of the most 'pure' of the reptilian crossbreeds which is passed on most crucially through the female. The term Rosi-Crucis was also the origin, quite obviously, of the Rosicrucians, an ancient secret society which has schemed and manipulated to ensure the reptilian bloodlines continue to occupy the positions of power. One of the authors who is selling the idea that the bloodline relates to Jesus is Sir Laurence Gardner, 'a sovereign and chivalric genealogist'. Funny that, because he must know this is not true. Sir Laurence is Chancellor of the Imperial and Royal Court of the Dragon Sovereignty, the former Royal Court of the Dragon in Egypt. He is also Prior of the Celtic Church of the Sacred Kindred of Saint Columba (Semiramis); Presidential Attaché to the European Council of Princes; formerly attached to the Noble Household Guard of the Royal House of Stewart (Stuart, the Merovingian line); he is known as Le Chevalier Labhran de Saint Germain, and is Preceptor of the Knights Templars of Saint Anthony. I think it's fair to call him an insider. So why does he keep telling us the Holy Grail bloodline is about Jesus when, with that background, he must know that it isn't?

Eventually the Roman Church withdrew its support for the Merovingians and they lost their power and faded from the public scene until the last few years. Another bloodline monarch from the reptilian 'stable' became King of the Franks. His name was Charles, better known as Charlemagne, one of the most celebrated monarchs in the history of Europe. He was an early patron of the stone masons who later built the Gothic cathedrals of Europe for the Templars. In Toulouse he is said to have founded a lodge of the Rosicrucian Order, which has its origins at least as far back as ancient Egypt,[4] and relates, as stated, to the Rosi-Crusis, the symbol of the reptilian bloodlines. Charlemagne vastly extended the Frankish empire and in 800 he was installed as Emperor of the West in the papal empire of Pope Leo III. The Church of Rome/Babylon controlled much of western and central Europe. This domination was completed when the military opposition to Rome, the Hohenstaufens or Ghibellines, were defeated by the Guelphs, named after Welf, the Duke of Bavaria, in 1268. This led to the creation of the Holy Roman Empire, an horrendous papal dictatorship. Its most prominent dynasty of Emperors were the Habsburgs, a bloodline family first noted in Switzerland during the 10th century. They emerged with papal support to govern the Holy Roman Empire for five hundred years until its demise in 1806. They ruled Austria from 1278 and in the 16th century they inherited the crown of Spain. The Habsburgs are a reptilian bloodline and I know a high priestess who has officiated at top Satanic rituals and who has seen the modern Habsburgs at rituals shape-shift into reptilians. A lot more from her later. Charlemagne was a wonderful servant of the Babylonian Brotherhood and his bloodline has continued to hold the reins of power. At least 33 American presidents are genetically related to him.

The Rennes-le-Chateau mystery

The Merovingians returned to public attention more recently in a number of books seeking to solve the mystery of the tiny mountain top hamlet in the Languedoc in southern France called Rennes-le-Chateau. This was once one of the most important centres for the Priory of Sion, the Templars, the Cathars and many others in the 'knowledge' stream. The area was once peopled by the Celts, the former Cimmerians and Scythians, from the Near East and the Caucasus Mountains, and Rennes-le-Chateau was called Rhedae after one of their tribes. It was worshipped as a sacred place by the Druids because again this is a region of immense magnetic power. In the late 1960s a document of uncertain background called the Red Serpent or Le Serpent Rouge came to light in the National Library in Paris. It contained the genealogy of the Merovingians, two maps of France in the Merovingian period, and a ground plan of St Sulpice, the Roman Catholic centre for occult studies in Paris.[5] St Sulpice was built on the ruins of a temple to Isis/Semiramis and was a burial ground for Merovingian kings. Le Serpent Rouge was dated January 17th 1967, and the deposit slip at the National Library was dated February 15th.[6] The latter turned out to be a forgery, however, and the real date it was deposited was March 20th.[7] By this time all the alleged authors of the work, Pierre Feugere, Louis Saint-Maxent and Gaston de Koker, had died within 24 hours of each other on March 6–7.[8] But it gets even stranger because these three, it emerges, were not the authors at all.[9] Someone, it is thought, had used the names of these three dead men as the authors to add more mystery to the tale. There were 13 days between the three deaths and the deposit of the document at the library. The 13 page document included short prose poems corresponding to each sign of the zodiac and it listed 13 signs. It called the extra one, Ophiuchus (the Serpent Holder), which it placed between Scorpio and Sagittarius. The most important number to the Templars was 13 and this will become more and more relevant as the story unfolds. I have long believed there were originally 13 signs to the zodiac. The text of Le Serpent Rouge, which appears to mention the landscape around Rennes-le-Chateau, presents a version of the Sleeping Beauty story in which the princess (female energy) is condemned to sleep until the handsome prince arrives to awaken her. This is also highly relevant to the number 13 for reasons I will later outline. Le Serpent Rouge also confirmed that Mary Magdalene was another symbol for Isis. It said:

> "…Formerly some called her ISIS, queen of the beneficent sources, COME TO ME ALL YOU SUFFER AND WHO ARE OVERWHELMED AND I WILL COMFORT YOU, others: MAGDALENE, of the famous vase full of healing balm. The initiates know her true name: NOTRE DAME DES CROSS."[10]

The female energy and the reptilian bloodline are passed on through the female, and since the intervention of Ninkharsag and Enki this energy was symbolised by Mary, Isis and Semiramis, and was also known as Diana. Princess Diana was killed on an ancient Merovingian sacrificial site to the goddess Diana when her car struck the 13th pillar. A cave at Sainte-Baume in southern France is an official Catholic shrine because, it is said quite wrongly, Mary Magdalene lived there.[11] In fact, during Roman times that cave was a centre for the worship of the goddess Diana Lucifera – Diana the light bringer or Illuminatrix. This was the very name given to Mary Magdalene by Jacobus de Voragine, the Dominican Archbishop of Black Nobility Genoa.[12] One other interesting point is that while Templars throughout France were arrested and tortured after the purge by Phillipe the Fair in 1307, the ones in the Rennes-le-Chateau area at Le Bezu, le Valdieu and Blanchefort, were left alone. This area was quite obviously very important to the Templars and they were connected with the Blanchefort family at Chateau de Blanchefort, just two miles from Rennes-le-Chateau. Some researchers believe that the Templars buried much of their gold near Rennes-le-Chateau. Certainly a third of all their European property was once to be found in the Languedoc region. The Romans, too, thought this area to be sacred and worshipped their Pagan gods here. By the 6th century, Rennes-le-Chateau was a thriving town of 30,000 people, the northern capital of the Visigoth empire which spread south across the Pyrenees into Spain. The Visigoths were a Germanic or Teutonic people, the same as the later Teutonic Knights who emerged at the same time as the Templars. The Visigoths were again the ancestors of the Cimmerians and the Scythians, the white peoples from the Caucasus. It was the Visigoths who swept out of central Europe to sack Rome and bring an end to Roman rule.

An ancient Visigoth chateau, the Chateau d'Hautpoul, still survives at Rennes-le-Chateau and it has an alchemist's tower. Alchemy is the transformation of base man/woman into pure spirit, but it has another meaning too, the transformation of base metals into gold. The theory of this was summed up by the ancient Greek initiate, Aristotle, who said that the basis of the physical world was what he called prime or first matter. This, he said, was a non-physical energy which you could not see or touch. He believed that prime matter could manifest as physical form through the four elements of Earth, Fire, Water and Air. These elements are different from each other, but each is connected by a common bond of dryness, moisture, heat or cold. Every element has two of these qualities, one of which dominates. Earth is cold and dry and dryness predominates. Fire is hot and dry and heat predominates. Water is moist and cold and cold predominates. Air is hot and moist and moistness predominates. The idea is that one element can be transformed into another through the bond they have in common, eg Fire becomes air through the common bond of heat. Substances are made from the elements and if you can transform the elements into each other, you must be able to transform the substances the elements are made from. For instance, lead can be changed into gold. There is, it is believed, a secret powder which is necessary for this transformation and it has become known as the Philosopher's Stone. The d'Hautpoul family are said to have been holders of such secrets. The document, Le Serpent Rouge, when speaking of the 13th sign of the zodiac, Ophiuchus, says: "the base lead of my words may contain the purest gold".[13] For five hundred years, Rennes-le-Chateau was owned by the Count of Razes and became an important centre for the Cathars. With their demise its power waned. A plague and Catalan bandits completed its fall from a major town to the tiny hamlet it was to become.[14] Today it is a place of great beauty and mystery with views across the mountains and valleys. I would definitely file it under paradise if it were not for a very unpleasant feel in the energy there. I experienced a feeling of underlying 'evil'.

The fantastic geometrical patterns in this area connecting mountains, sacred sites and churches, have been identified in modern times by people like Henry Lincoln, a pioneer researcher of the Rennes-le-Chateau mysteries, and David Wood and Ian Campbell in their books *Genisis* and *Geneset* (*see* **Figure 20**). The goddess Isis is mentioned in old records of Rennes-les-Bains, a short distance from Rennes-le-Chateau, and in the last century a statue of Isis was found near the village.[15] Wood

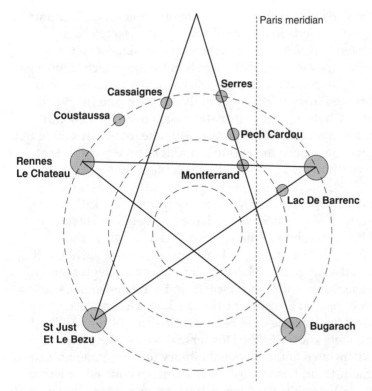

Figure 20: The extended pentagram identified by David Wood and Ian Campbell in the area around Rennes-le-Chateau. They connected churches and other key landscape features.

and Campbell suggest that Rennes-le-Chateau and Rennes-le-Bains translate as Queen of the House and Queen of the Waters – the names given by the ancient Egyptians to their goddesses Nephthys and Isis.[16] The area around Rennes-le-Chateau is one of enormous power and importance within the Earth's energy grid and therefore became a focus from ancient times for those who understood this and knew how to harness the energy. The modern world awoke to the story of Rennes-le-Chateau with Henry Lincoln's BBC television films and the book, *Holy Blood, Holy Grail*, written by Lincoln with Michael Baigent and Richard Leigh. It was inspired by the story of Berenger Sauniere, who, in 1855, became priest at the church of St Mary Magdalene at Rennes-le-Chateau. Sauniere was born at nearby Montazels. The church was in a terrible state and, the story goes, in 1887 he and two workmen began the immense task of repairing the worst of the damage to the interior. They lifted a flagstone near the altar and saw an engraving on the underside depicting two men on one horse. This symbol was the first seal of the Knights Templar. The flagstone became known as the Knights Stone and can be seen in the village museum. When Sauniere realised there might be something of importance to find, he continued the search alone. The breakthrough came when he dismantled the altar and inside one of the pillars he found hollow wooden tubes, sealed with wax. Inside those he discovered parchments which, he later established, were written in code. After consulting his church superiors in Carcassonne, he travelled to Paris and the Roman Catholic occult research centre called St Sulpice which is positioned on the Paris time meridian on a site of 'former' Isis/Semiramis worship. Here they employed experts in medieval texts, writings and codes. Research so far has suggested that Sauniere's parchments contained a genealogy dated 1244 (the year the Cathars were slaughtered at Montsegur) which confirmed the survival of the Merovingian bloodline; another Merovingian genealogy from 1244 to 1644; and two compiled in the 1780s apparently by Abbe Antoine Bigou, a previous priest at Rennes-le-Chateau, and personal chaplain to the Blanchefort family. I don't believe for a second that this is all that Sauniere found. Anything that really mattered would never have been made public and it is quite possible that Sauniere did not find his parchments in the church at all. Maybe it's a cover story to obscure the real tale.

The Priory of Sion 'leaked' copies of the two Bigou parchments in 1967, or at least in the 1960s. The Priory of Sion is believed to have originated in Troyes, France, the city founded by the Sicabrian Franks (Merovingians) where the Templars were officially formed. The Priory of Sion arrived on the scene about the same time as the Templars, the Knights of Malta and the Teutonic Knights, and it had a particularly close association with the Templars. But some researchers believe the true origins of the Priory of Sion go much further back. Its Grand Masters are called Nautonnier or Navigators and the ones between 1188 and 1918 were listed (or claimed to be) in documents known as the Dossiers Secrets, which were privately published texts deposited at the National Library in Paris. Among them were Marie and Jean de Saint-Clair; Leonardo da Vinci; Sandro Botticelli, another Italian artist and friend of da Vinci; Nicolas Flamel, the famous medieval alchemist; Robert Fludd, the philosopher; Isaac Newton, who 'discovered' the law of gravity and was a major player in the creation of the this-world-is-all-there-is version of 'science'; Robert Boyle, a close friend of Newton and another founder of modern 'science'; and Jean Cocteau, the French writer and artist. Two others in office during the lifetime of Sauniere, were the French writer and poet Victor Hugo, and his friend the composer Claude Debussy, a Grand Master of the Rosicrucian Order. One of Debussy's most famous operas was a Merovingian drama. A recent Grand Master appears to be Pierre Plantard de Saint-Clair who, according to documents revealed in *Holy Blood, Holy Grail*, is a descendant of Dagobert II and the Merovingian dynasty. Dagobert was the Merovingian heir who was sent into exile in Ireland as a child. He returned to take his crown, but was later murdered. His son is supposed to have survived. I think that Pierre Plantard, however, has misled the authors of *Holy Blood, Holy Grail* in many ways, and the idea that the Merovingian bloodlines are the bloodline of Jesus is without foundation. This is nothing to do with Jesus. The reason you find so many references to Arcadia in relation to Rennes-le-Chateau is because Arcadia in Sparta was the legendary home of Zeus and the Titans – the reptilian bloodlines of Troy. That is the origin of these bloodlines, not Jesus, who did not even exist. Pierre Plantard, who knows the truth, but doesn't want *you* to know, was born in 1920 and, with the approval of the German oppressors, he edited a magazine in Nazi-occupied France in 1942 called *Conquest For A Young Knighthood*.[17] It was the journal of a Paris based Masonic-chivalric society called the Order Alpha-Galates, and Plantard became its Grand Master at the age of 22.[18] This is certainly not a man who's word is his bond.

At St Sulpice in Paris, the village priest Abbe Berenger Sauniere met with Abbe Bieil, the Director General of the Seminary, and the latter's nephew, Emile Hoffet.[19] Through Hoffet he was warmly welcomed into a circle of esoteric friends, including the famous opera singer, Emma Calve, and Claude Debussy, the Grand Master of the Priory of Sion as well as the Rosicrucians. Sauniere and Calve began a close relationship and she visited him at Rennes-le-Chateau. Calve was at the heart of the occult movements in France and one of her intimates was the Marquis Stanislas de Gualta, a founder of the modern version of the Order of the Rose-Croix, the Rosicrucians.[20] Most of the Grand Masters of the Priory of Sion have Rosicrucian connections. Another of Calve's friends was Jules Bois, a notorious Satanist, and close associate of a fellow Satanist, MacGregor Mathers.[21] Encouraged by Bois, Mathers established the British occult society, the Order of the Golden Dawn, of which the Satanist, Aleister Crowley, was a most prominent member. The Order of the Golden Dawn and its offshoots and personnel, like Crowley, were involved with both the Nazis and the British Satanist, Druid, and wartime Prime Minister, Sir Winston Churchill. The pointed-arm 'heil Hitler' salute was in fact a ritual sign of the Order of the Golden Dawn. Another famous member of the Golden Dawn was the poet, W. B. Yeats, a friend of Claude Debussy. Yeats quite brilliantly summed up the aims of the Babylonian Brotherhood when he described his ideal society:

> "...an aristocratic civilisation in its most completed form, every detail of his life hierachical, every great man's door crowded at dawn with petitioners, great wealth everywhere in few men's hands, all dependent upon a few, up to the Emperor himself, who is a God dependent upon a greater God and everywhere, in Court, in the family, an inequality made law."[22]

This is precisely the vision for the human race planned by the reptilians. If Sauniere and his friends were operating among Emma Calve's circle, we are talking Satanism here. I'm not saying that Sauniere was a Satanist because I don't know, but he knew people who were. Other famous visitors of Sauniere at Rennes-le-Chateau were the French Secretary of State for Culture and the Archduke Johann von Habsburg, a cousin of Franz-Josef, the Emperor of Austria.[23] The Habsburgs, a big-time reptilian bloodline, ruled the Holy Roman Empire for 500 years before its demise in 1806. The Priory of Sion, the Merovingian bloodline, and Rennes-le-Chateau, definitely connect into the wider web I am exposing.

Among the most significant Freemasonic lodges in the world today is the Grand Alpine Lodge in Switzerland. Henry Kissinger, one of the planet's most active servants of the reptilians (he is one), is a member. It is involved at a very high level in the global manipulation (see ...*And The Truth Shall Set You Free*) and it is most definitely Satanic. A work entitled *The Merovingian Descendants And The Enigma Of The Visigoth Razes* was published, according to its title page, by the Grand Alpine Lodge, though they now deny it.[24] Razes is the old name for the area around

Rennes-le-Chateau.[25] It was first published in German and then translated into French by a Walter Celse-Nazaire, a pseudonym made up of the saints after whom the church at Rennes-les-Bains is dedicated. The secrets held in Rennes-le-Chateau and the Languedoc are extremely important to these people. The composer, Richard Wagner, used unusual names from the Rennes area in his operas and in his work, *The Valkyrie*, we see again the theme of someone condemned to eternal sleep in the ruins of an enchanted castle. There are many ruined enchanted castles around Rennes-le-Chateau and Wagner's Castle of Valhalla is a castle on the Paris Meridian a few miles from the village.[26] Adolf Hitler, who was obsessed with black magic, said that to understand the Nazis, one had to understand Wagner. One legend has it that Wagner visited Sauniere at Rennes-le-Chateau. Jules Verne, the science 'fiction' writer, was a high initiate who knew much secret knowledge. His book, *Chateau Of The Carpathians*, includes several names unique to the Rennes-le-Chateau area, and in Verne's *Clovis d'Ardentor*, one the characters is Captain Bugarach – the name of a peak near Rennes-le-Chateau known locally as the magnetic mountain. Clovis was also the name of one of the first Merovingian kings. A farm near Rennes-les-Bains is called Jouanne, another name used for a Jules Verne character.[27]

Back in Rennes-le-Chateau after his visit to Paris, Sauniere began a spending spree well beyond the means of a poorly paid village priest. Where did his sudden wealth come from? He built a house which he called Villa Bethania alongside the church for himself and his housekeeper, Marie Denarnaud. Close by, he built a watchtower on the edge of a sheer cliff overlooking the valley and mountains. He called it La Tour Magdala and he said it was a library. Having seen it, I don't believe that. There is very little room for books and it hardly constitutes a 'library'. It is, however, placed precisely on the spot where a circle connecting churches meets a point on the pentagram in the geometrical pattern identified by Wood and Campbell. The name Magdala means watchtower and the watchtower is a Brotherhood symbol for Mary Magdalene – the female energy, Isis, Semiramis. Note that it is also the symbol of the Jehovah's Witnesses, another prison-religion, created by Brotherhood frontmen like the high degree Freemason, Charles Taze Russell. They're all connected, the secret societies and the religions they created. Sauniere spent profusely on art and antiques; he paid for a water tower to improve the village supply; and he spent a fortune to build a road to replace the long dirt track up the mountain to Rennes-le-Chateau. He also began to correspond with people all over Europe. Most notably, he transformed his church with his new-found wealth. It was fully restored and refurbished with strange statues and esoteric symbols. On the entrance to the church he had written in French: "This place is terrible". As you walk through the door you are faced with a demonic statue depicting a particular version of the Devil. It is Asmodeus who, the legend says, was forced by King Solomon to help with the building of his temple in Jerusalem. A cutting with a picture of Asmodeus in chains was found among Sauniere's possessions. A plate glass window features Mary Magdalene anointing the feet of Jesus and a statue of Mary Magdalene includes a skull at her feet – that symbol of the Templar rituals. The floor is laid out with the black and white squares of a Masonic temple. A feature of the Sauniere-inspired decoration in the church is the rose and the cross. This is the symbol of the secret society called the Rosicrucians or Rose Croix and it goes back to ancient times. Templar artefacts retrieved from Paris and Cyprus feature the rose and cross.[28] The rose once again relates to goddess worship and sexual symbolism. The Romans knew the rose as the Flower of Venus (Venus = Semiramis) and it was the badge of her 'sacred prostitutes'. In the Venus sexual mysteries, anything 'sub rosa' meaning under the rose, was not to be revealed to the uninitiated.[29] Mother Mary, when used as a symbol for the goddess energy, was referred to as the Rose, Rose-bush, Rose-garland or Mystic Rose.[30] The name Rose may also come from Eros, the symbol for sexual love. The Rosicrucians link into the Brotherhood network, as do the Jesuits. Sauniere's brother, Alfred, was a Jesuit. The guy at the museum in Rennes-le-Chateau told me that Sauniere could have been a member of the Rosicrucian Order and I would have been surprised if he wasn't. There is a cross and red rose on his grave in the churchyard. A red rose on a grave can indicate an exemplary life or that the person's life was ended prematurely. When Pierre Plantard de Saint-Clair, a Grand Master of the Priory of Sion, made a visit to Rennes-le-Chateau, he was seen performing a strange ceremony at Sauniere's grave. Obviously, questions were asked by the church hierarchy about Sauniere's spending spree, but when the crunch came he was supported by the Pope himself.

Sauniere was working closely, and in secret, with two other local priests, Abbe Boudet at Rennes-le-Bains, and Abbe Gelis at Coutaussa. The two villages are only a short distance from Rennes-le-Chateau. Records show that Boudet, a friend of Pierre Plantard's grandfather, paid Sauniere and his Jesuit brother large sums of money.[31] All three apparently enjoyed unexplained windfalls of cash. In 1897 their close association was broken by conflict between Sauniere and Boudet, and the vicious and bloody murder of Gelis, who had become a recluse, living behind a locked door in fear of his life. With good reason, it turned out. He was bludgeoned to death by someone he clearly knew and trusted, because he opened his door to them and a bell alarm Gelis had installed was not activated. Despite the violence of his death and the intense struggle which preceded it, his body was left neatly laid out on the floor in almost ritualistic fashion.[32] In his church at Coutaussa were the now familiar symbols, the lion paws, the grapes and the vine, and a form of the Star of David, the six pointed star, with one triangle superimposed on the other instead of being interweaved as normal. Exactly the same symbol was found on Sauniere's bookplate.[33] On Gelis's grave, topped by a Maltese/Templar cross, is the word Assassine and the headstone is adorned with a rose, the symbol of the Rosicrucians and of premature death. Sauniere died following a stroke in 1917. The stroke happened on January 17th 1917, which appears to be a very significant date to the Babylonian Brotherhood. It is the feast day of St Sulpice. It was to St Sulpice Church in Paris that Sauniere travelled with his parchments; it was the groundplan of St Sulpice which appeared in the mysterious documents called Le Serpent Rouge; St Sulpice was designed according to the laws of sacred geometry in 1645 on the ruins of a temple of Isis and was the headquarters of the Compagnie du Saint-Sacrement, an alleged front for the Priory of Sion; and Victor Hugo, a Grand Master of the

Figure 21: *The composite symbol of the malevolent force, Baphomet.*

Priory of Sion, was married at St Sulpice. Le Serpent Rouge was dated January 17th and it emphasises that January 17th comes under the astrological house of Capricorn, the goat, which, in its negative depiction, is Baphomet and the Goat of Mendes, the symbol of Satanism and the Templars (*see Figure 21*). This originates from the symbolic sacrifice of a goat by the Israelites in honour of the Watcher (reptilian) called Azazel who also became symbolised as an inverted pentagram – the 'goat head'. Nicholas Flamel, another Grand Master of the Priory of Sion, was said to have performed his first alchemical transmutation at noon on January 17th. A statue of Charles de Lorraine, a Grand Master of both the Priory of Sion and the Teutonic Order, was unveiled in Brussels on January 17th 1775.[34] If you think this is all coincidence, I would ask you not to underestimate how important precise dates and times are to the Babylonian Brotherhood. Every split second has a different vibration as the Earth's magnetic field is subtly changed by the Sun and the movement of the planets, and every number and combination of numbers carry their own unique vibratory signature. Sauniere transferred all his money and possessions to his housekeeper, Marie Denarnaud, his confidant throughout the period we have been documenting. She is alleged to have said to a friend:

> "The people around here walk around on gold without knowing it... With that which the Monsieur has left we could feed Rennes for a hundred years and there would still be enough left over... one day I will tell you a secret which will make of you a rich man – very, very rich."[35]

But she never did. Rennes-le-Chateau is a place of so many secrets and in so many ways encapsulates the 'hall of mirrors' that has kept the truth from the people for so long. However, the veil is lifting and the truth is emerging. The complication in the story of Rennes-le-Chateau, and the Brotherhood in general, is the feuding that goes on between competing factions operating beneath the same over all leadership. It means that people who you know are involved are undermined or murdered by others you know are involved. This can be confusing unless you understand the game. Such infighting is inevitable with the mindset of these people, and often it suits the Brotherhood leadership to have these feuds spill over into the public arena. It creates the very chaos, the divide and rule, which they need to manipulate their Agenda into being. But this upper hierarchy can quickly bring the factions into line when the fighting threatens the over all Agenda on which all sides agree – control of the world. Just such a battle broke out between the Priory of Sion and its military arm, the Knights Templar, which led to considerable conflict in the centuries that followed. In 1187, the Templars lost control of Jerusalem to the Saracen Turks, possibly on purpose, and a conflict followed with their former allies and official masters, the Priory of Sion. A year later they formerly separated in a ritual known as the Cutting of the Elm at Gisors, a city close to the coast in northern France. The Order of Sion changed its name to the Priory of Sion and adopted as its emblem, the red cross used by the Templars. The Priory also adopted the title, l'Ordre de la Rose-Cross Veritas, the Order of the True Red Cross. The two secret societies agreed to operate independently, but the Priory of Sion wanted the Templar wealth which it believed it rightly owned and it probably used the Merovingian king of France, Philippe the Fair, in an attempt to do this.

The purge of the Templars

First Philippe removed two Popes until he found one who would take his orders. He sent one of his heavies to assault and abuse Pope Boniface VIII, who died shortly afterwards. He then poisoned a second Pope, Benedict XI. This allowed him to install his own choice, the Archbishop of Bordeax, who became Pope Clement V. He moved the Papacy to Avignon and produced a split in the Roman Church for 68 years while rival Popes resided in France and in Rome. Having established his own personal Pope, Philippe turned his mind to the Knights Templar. He coveted their wealth, hated their power and was a puppet of the Priory of Sion. The Templars lost much of their influence with the Church after 1291 when the Saracens defeated the Christian Crusaders and ejected them from the Holy Land. Philippe, in league with his puppet Pope, set out to destroy the Templars. In 1306 he had arrested every Jew in France, banished them from the country and taken all their property. He then planned a similar operation and secretly arranged for all Templars in France to be arrested at dawn on Friday, October 13th 1307. Friday the 13th has been deemed unlucky ever since. Many Templars were seized, including their Grand Master, Jacques de Molay, and subjected to the unimaginable torture of the Inquisition. But there is clear evidence that many Templars knew of the plan and escaped.

Documents detailing their rules and rituals were removed or destroyed before the raids and when the vaults were opened at the Templar headquarters in Paris, the vast fortune Philippe so coveted was gone. He and his Pope pressured other monarchs to arrest the Templars, but this wasn't easy. In the German, later French, region of Lorraine, the duke supported the Templars and in other parts of Germany the Templars went unprosecuted. Others changed their name from Knights Templar and continued as before in another guise. Some joined the Order of St John of Jerusalem (Malta) or the Teutonic Order. The aristocratic bloodlines of Lorraine are some of the 'purest' reptilian crossbreeds and one of them is today one of the biggest players in the global Satanic ritual network. While officially these three orders were not connected and did not like each other, they were, at their upper levels, the same organisation.

Edward II, the English king, did his best for years to ignore the papal order to arrest the Templars and, when pressed further, he was as lenient with them as possible. Scotland and Ireland did the same. Eventually, however, the Inquisitors arrived and the Templars either left England or Ireland or met their fate. Scotland was a very different story. The Templar fleet escaped from France at the time of the purge, particularly from their main port at La Rochelle, and took their wealth with them. There is, however, another possibility that Philippe the Fair was duped by the Priory of Sion who had arranged for the English fleet to intercept the fleeing Templar ships and steal the gold that way. That's possible. The Templars headed for Scotland, Portugal, and most likely, the Americas as they knew that continent existed because they had access to the underground knowledge of the Aryan Elite and they were well aware that the Phoenicians had been to the Americas thousands of years before.

The choice of Scotland was obvious for many reasons. The St Clair-Sinclairs were there and so were the other ancient Brotherhood bloodlines which arrived with the original Phoenicians or came from Belgium and northern France to settle there much later. The head of one of these families, Robert the Bruce, was at war with another branch of the Aryans, the English, for control of Scotland and he was excommunicated by the Pope. This meant that the papal order to destroy the Templars was not applicable in the areas controlled by Bruce. It was to here that many Templars headed after the purge in France. They sailed around the west coast of Ireland to land on the north west coast of Scotland between Islay, Jura and the Mull of Kintyre. Along this coast many Templar graves and relics have been found at places like Kilmory and Kilmartin. The Templars also settled in the region called Dalriada, now Argyll, and they were soon to play a crucial part in the most famous battle in Scottish history.

■ SOURCES

1   Geoffrey Higgins, *Anacalypsis* (reprinted in 1972 by Health Research, PO Box 850, Pomeroy, WA 99347, USA, first published 1836).

2   Michael Baigent, Richard Leigh and Henry Lincoln, *Holy Blood, Holy Grail* (Corgi Books, London, 1982), pp 449, 450.

3   Joy Hancox, *The Byrom Collection* (Jonathan Cape, London, 1992), p 131.

4   *The Occult Conspiracy*, p 48.

5   David Wood and Ian Campbell, *Geneset* (Bellevue Books, Sunbury on Thames, England, 1994), pp 104, 105.

6   Lynn Picknett and Clive Prince, *The Templar Revelation* (Bantam Press, London, 1997), p 45.

7   Ibid.

8   Ibid.

9   Ibid.

10   Ibid, p 49.

11   Ibid, p 68.

12   Ibid.

13   *Geneset*, p 34.

14   *Holy Blood, Holy Grail*, p 33.

15   *Geneset*, p 36.

16   Ibid.

17   *The Templar Revelation*, p 43.

18   Ibid.

19   *Holy Blood, Holy Grail*, p 27.

20   Ibid, p 159.

21   Ibid.

22   Quoted by Francis King in *Satan And Swastika* (Mayflower Books, London, 1976).

23   *Holy Blood, Holy Grail*, p 29.

24   Ibid, p 97.

25   Ibid.

26   *Geneset*, p 33.

27   Ibid, p 33.

28   *The Woman's Encyclopaedia Of Myths And Secrets*, pp 866, 867.

29   Ibid.

30   Ibid.

31   Richard Andrews and Paul Schellenberger, *The Tomb Of God* (Little Brown, London, 1996), p 177.

32   Ibid, p 187.

33   Ibid, p 182.

34   Ibid, p 259.

35   Ibid, pp 172, 173.

CHAPTER EIGHT

Same face, different mask

In the years before the Templars arrived in force from France, Robert the Bruce's campaign against the English had been pretty disastrous. He was forced to seek refuge in the Perthshire mountains and later in Argyll. From there he headed for Kintyre and the north of Ireland.

Bruce had very close connections with Ulster and owned land there. Bruce's title, the Earl of Carrick, can be seen in a number of place names in this part of Ireland, including Carrickfergus. The people of Ulster have long political and blood associations with the Scots, particularly on the west coast of Scotland, but they have been manipulated into conflict many times. At the heart of the troubles in Ulster to this day are the squabbles between the Irish (Catholics) and the Scots-Irish (Protestants) who moved into Ulster from Scotland. These conflicts are manipulated and encouraged by the Brotherhood through their placemen. With support from Irish noble families, Bruce returned to Scotland in 1307, the year of the Templar purge in France, and he soon found himself fighting a new English king as Edward II replaced Edward I. Bruce's campaign gathered momentum thanks to support and weapons from the Templars fleeing France, and it culminated in the battle of Bannockburn, near Stirling Castle, on John the Baptist's Day (Nimrod's day), June 24th 1314. The Scots routed the English after a day of battle when a force of 'unknown' horsemen arrived to support the Scottish ranks. For some reason, never explained, the English panicked and ran at the sight of these reinforcements. They had to be a special fighting force and they had to be immediately recognisable to stimulate such an instant reaction. The Templars were both, and this 'unknown' group had to be the Knights Templar, the warriors so feared in the crusades, who had now regrouped in Scotland. The victory at Bannockburn would ensure the independence of Scotland for the next 289 years and among those who fought with Bruce that day was Sir William St Clair of Rosslyn. When Bruce died in 1329, the Stuart dynasty began. In France in Merovingian times, they appointed Mayors of the Palace to support the monarch and from the time of King David I, Scotland had installed a similar system. They were called Royal Stewards and these positions became hereditary. It later changed to Stewart and from this line came the Stuarts. Again, as with the Merovingians, the hereditary mayors or stewards to the official royal line eventually became the royal line themselves. This came after Bruce's daughter married Walter the Steward or Stewart. Upon Bruce's death, the first child of this unison became Robert II of Scotland. The Stuart line had its first king.

A creation of the officially disbanded Knights Templar was the Order of the Garter, the premier order of chivalry, created by Edward III in 1348 and still headed by the British monarch. It is an Elite front for the Babylonian Brotherhood and is dedicated to the 'Virgin Mary' – Semiramis/Ninkharsag. Meetings of the Order took place under Edward in a special chamber at Windsor Castle around a table modelled on the one in King Arthur legend. Windsor Castle is built on an ancient and very powerful sacred energy vortex and this is where the Satanist and reptilian, Henry Kissinger, was knighted by the Queen. She is knowingly working for the Brotherhood Agenda and the Order of the Garter is one of her premier networks. Edward III's name was Windsor and when the present royal family decided to change their German name to an English one for public relations reasons during the First World War, they chose Windsor, after the man who founded this key Brotherhood order. The insignia of the Order of the Garter is a jewelled collar with red roses alternating with 26 gold knots representing the 26 knights in two groups of 13.[1] Similar orders emerged in France with the Order of the Star, the Order of the Golden Fleece, and the Order of St Michael. The Freemasons are the Knights Templar and the Priory of Sion under another name and the Company of Jesus or Jesuits are based on the same structure as the Templars with the same goal. The Jesuits and the Knights of Malta are esoteric secret societies which hoard and use the secret knowledge while outwardly claiming to be Roman Catholic and 'Christian'. They are doing exactly the same as the Templars did at the time of the Crusades and together they control, with the higher levels of Freemasonry, the Vatican, the Pope and the Roman Catholic Church. In other words, they control both sides, the esoteric underground and the Church which condemns this very same underground as evil. Thus they control the game and the ultimate outcome of the game – unless we wake up fast. An obvious example of this came after the papal purge on the Templars. In 1312, all lands and property owned by the Templars were given by the Pope to their 'rivals' the Knights Hospitaller of St John, later called the Knights of Rhodes and now the Knights of Malta (Catholic) and the Knights of St John (Protestant). Both were the same force, as were, and are, the Teutonic Knights. All were involved in the same things, including banking, and used the same vicious, unscrupulous methods to get their way. For more than 200 years until the middle of the 16th century, the Hospitallers and the Templars were merged into a joint order and much Templar land and property was not absorbed by the Knights Hospitaller, even though most of it was there for the taking.

The Templars restored their influence in France under the title of the Scots Guard in the mid 15th century. When Robert the Bruce was installed as the unchallenged king of Scotland, he signed a pact with Charles IV of France, renewing what was known as the 'auld alliance'. This was no surprise, given that the bloodlines which controlled Scotland, including Bruce and the Sinclairs, came from France and Flanders. In 1445, a later King Charles, Charles VII, formed the first standing army in Europe since the Templars and, in fact, it *was* the Templars. Pride of place in Charles's army was the Scottish Company and it was at the front of all parades. Even more powerful and influential, however, was the élite Scots Guard which consisted of 33 men – a very significant esoteric number which would manifest again in the 33 degrees of the Scottish Rite of Freemasonry. The Scots Guard was there to guard the king and they even slept in his bedroom. Not all 33, I hope. As the numbers in the guard increased it was by multiples of 13, again in keeping with esoteric numerological laws and a key number to the Knights Templar. Commanders of the Scots Guard were automatically made members of the secret society called the Order of St Michael, which later established a branch in Scotland. Another common theme of the manipulation into the present day is that people operating behind one 'mask' are also members of other, sometimes many other, 'masks' working to the same agenda. Yet again, the Scots Guard (Templars) proved to be expert at the Trojan Horse technique. They infiltrated and took over the administration of France as 'advisors' and 'ambassadors'. Charles was their puppet and the names of this Scots Guard élite are getting familiar… Sinclair, Stuart, Hamilton, Hay, Montgomery, Cunningham, Cockburn and Seton. These were the families who came to Scotland from France and Flanders and could trace their bloodlines back to the ancient Near East and the Anunnaki. They took over Scotland and now they re-established their influence in France. The Scots Guard was another front for the secret knowledge, the unfolding of the Templar Agenda, and the Satanic rituals of which the Templars had been accused. Nothing changes, except the name. A present member of the Montgomery family told the authors of *The Temple And The Lodge* that an order was formed at the time of the Scots Guard in which all male members of the Montgomery family were eligible. It was called the Order of the Temple.[2] The Templars would later re-emerge as the Scottish Rite of Freemasonry.

Another significant connection into this same network was the House of Lorraine in the northern France-Germany region and in particular the Duke of Lorraine known as Rene d'Anjou, who was born in 1408. He became Grand Master of the Priory of Sion at the age of ten and operated under the guidance of his uncle Louis, Cardinal de Bar, until he was 20.[3] This is a big-time reptilian bloodline. His list of titles included Count of Provence (in Rennes-le-Chateau country), Count of Guise, Duke of Anjou, King of Hungary, King of Naples and Sicily, King of Aragon, Valencia, Majorca and Sardinia, and the symbolic one of King of Jerusalem.[4] The latter title is very important to the Brotherhood. The next in line for King of Jerusalem is the reptilian, Karl von Habsburg, and his name, numerologically, equates to 666. One of Rene d'Anjou's daughters married Henry VI of England in 1445 and was prominent in the Wars of the Roses in which the red rose of Henry of Lancaster met the white rose of York in 1455. Rene d'Anjou had connections in every direction and he was a classic Brotherhood figure at the centre of a vast web. Just two of the famous names of history to whom he was connected were Christopher Columbus and Joan of Arc. At one time he employed Christopher Columbus and the enormous significance of this will become clear soon. Joan of Arc, it appears, was born as a subject of Rene d'Anjou in the duchy of Bar. According to official history, in 1429 she announced her 'divine mission' to save France from the English invaders and to ensure that Charles became king of France, as he did as Charles VII. She asked for an audience with Rene d'Anjou's father-in-

law and great uncle and when the meeting took place, Rene, was present.[5] To fulfil
her mission, she said, according to the official tale, she needed Rene, a horse, and:
"some good men to take me into France". Historians who chronicled Rene's life
suggest that he left with Joan to meet with Charles and was at her side in her
victorious battles against the English which put Charles on the throne. His
whereabouts cannot be accounted for between the years 1429–1431, the very years
when Joan of Arc was at the peak of her military career. Joan was eventually burned
at the stake by the Inquisition as a witch and it is very clear when you look at the
evidence that her whole story was another historical smokescreen. We are supposed
to believe that this young girl from a poor background knocked on the door of the
aristocracy and they allowed her to lead a war against the English. Yes, OK, and
I can tie my willy to the lamppost across the street. The man who was really behind
that military campaign was Rene d'Anjou with the story of Joan of Arc (based
on the legend of the 'Virgin of Lorraine') merely a convenient way of hiding the
real goings on.

It was Rene d'Anjou who was responsible for the two-bar cross becoming known
as the Cross of Lorraine. The double cross symbol was later used by some aspects of
the Christian Church and it is the origin of the term to be 'double crossed',
manipulated. This has become another symbol of the reptilian Brotherhood and you
can see it in the logo of the oil giant, Exxon, controlled by their American branch
managers, the Rockefellers. Rene d'Anjou was steeped in the esoteric underground
and a student of the Arthurian and Grail legends. Through his extensive
possessions and connections in Italy he interlocked with the Black Nobility and
other aristocratic families and he was an inspiration behind the emergence of the
Renaissance when the ancient knowledge of Egypt and Greece was translated into
European languages. In Rene d'Anjou's court was an astrologer called Jean de
Saint-Remy and, according to several accounts, he was the grandfather of the most
famous psychic-astrologer of all time, Nostradamus. This makes sense because in
the 16th century Nostradamus was closely connected to the House of Lorraine and
it's offshoot, the House of Guise, as they pursued a bloody campaign of
assassination against their bloodline rivals in a bid, ultimately unsuccessful, to win
the throne of France. His very name gives his background away. Nostradamus' real
name was Michel de Notre Dame, Michael of Our Lady. The French writer and
investigator, Gerard de Sede, who it seems had insider contacts, claimed that
Nostradamus was an agent for the Houses of Lorraine and Guise and was using his
position as astrologer to the French court to manipulate on their behalf. De Sede
further suggests that many of the predictions or 'quatrains' by Nostradmus were
not so much predictions as messages, ciphers, timetables, instructions and
symbolism of past events and groups. He says that Nostradamus spent a long time
in Lorraine being trained before he entered the royal court of their rivals and in this
period he was given access to an ancient book on which all his work became based.
No wonder he was apparently such a brilliant astrologer, he knew what few
others were privileged to know. Incidentally, Gerard de Sede also claims that the
Merovingian bloodline are extraterrestrials which, of course, has been dismissed as

ludicrous, but I say he's right. At least they are a 'royal' bloodline which has been occupied and controlled by the reptilians of the lower fourth dimension.[6]

In the 16th and 17th centuries, a stream of events unfolded to advance the Brotherhood Agenda. The extent and influence of the underground esoteric networks had continued to expand and now it was possible to begin the next stage of the global takeover. Rene d'Anjou was one of the key players behind the Renaissance when, through his many contacts in Italy and particularly Florence, he helped to orchestrate the translation, publishing and distribution of ancient Greek, Egyptian and Gnostic works, including those of Plato and Pythagoras. This transformed art and culture among the privileged classes of Europe and the power of the church was under more challenge than ever before. It also enlisted many more influential people into the gathering secret society network. The pressure on the church establishment was increased still further by the publication of the Rosicrucian Manifestos in 1614 to 1616 which claimed to be issued by a secret group of initiates in Germany and France. They pledged to transform the world with the esoteric knowledge and herald a new era of religious and political freedom. The Catholic Church and the Holy Roman Empire were fiercely condemned. The Order of the Rose Cross or Rosicrucians, however, was no new fad. It was founded, apparently, at least as long ago as the Pharaoh Thothmes III in the 15th century BC. His personal seal (cartouche) is used on modern Rosicrucian literature[7] and the Rosicrucians connect with the Royal Court of the Dragon in ancient Egypt. It is now widely believed by researchers that the Manifestos were written by the German esotericist, Johann Valentin Andrea, who is listed as a Grand Master of the Priory of Sion. Another highly influential voice for Rosicrucian thought was Robert Fludd, the man who preceded Andrea as Grand Master of the Priory of Sion.

The Bacon legacy

One of the most important men of this entire era was the Rosicrucian, Francis Bacon. His influence was colossal. He was the Grand Master of the Rosicrucians in England, a major force in the creation of Freemasonry, the 'father' of modern science, and the possible author of the 'Shakespeare' plays. He was also a member of a secret society called the Order of the Helmet, dedicated to the worship of the goddess of wisdom, Pallas Athene, who was portrayed as wearing a helmet and holding a spear.[8] Researchers and investigators like Manly P. Hall, the renowned Freemasonic historian, have little doubt that Bacon was born from a liaison between Queen Elizabeth I, the 'virgin queen', and her lover Robert Dudley, the Earl of Leicester.[9] He was brought up by Nicholas and Anne Bacon and would become the most influential man in the country, overtly and covertly, with the title of Viscount of St Albans and the role of Lord Chancellor of England. (This was the Bacon role, you might say.) If Bacon was the son of Queen Elizabeth (El-lizard-birth), he was of a reptilian bloodline, and this would explain his rapid rise to prominence in politics and the secret societies. He worked secretly through the underground channels, among them the Inns of Court, the centre of the Brotherhood-controlled legal profession which is based on the former Templar lands in the now aptly named,

Temple Bar, in London. It was a time of great conflict and upheaval as the Brotherhood sought to use the church as a vehicle for widespread war and chaos. One of their frontmen for this was Martin Luther, a product of German secret societies and a Rosicrucian. His personal seal was a rose and cross. In 1517, this professor of theology at Wittenberg University listed 95 complaints against the Vatican for selling pardons to raise money to build St Peter's Church. Luther was excommunicated, but he burned the decree along with copies of Roman Church law and launched his own Lutheran Church. Protestant Christianity had begun and conflict was unleashed across Europe as Protestants and Catholics went to war to decide which version of the same nonsense would prevail. Funny that the Rosicrucians claimed to stand for religious and political freedom and yet one of their puppets, Martin Luther, stood for anything but. He hated freethinking and open minded research. In one sermon he said that his followers should throw spit in the face of reason, because she was the Devil's whore, rotten with the itch of leprosy, and should be kept in the toilet.[10] Lovely. He also wrote:

> "Damned be love into the abyss of hell, if it is maintained to the damage of faith...
> It is better that tyrants should sin a hundred times against the people than the people
> should sin once against the tyrants... the ass wants to be thrashed, the mob to be
> governed by force."[11]

Speak for yourself, darlin'. A Frenchman, known in English as John Calvin, also produced his version of Protestant Christianity, another extreme and arrogant creed called Calvinism. This spawned the Puritan movement which was so influential in the European occupation of North America. The Protestant Church came to England because King Henry VIII wanted a son and heir and his first wife, Catherine of Aragon, had produced 'only' a daughter. He wanted to divorce her and try his luck elsewhere, but Pope Clement VII refused to sanction this. Henry at this time was a committed Catholic, at least in public, and the Pope had awarded him the title Defender of the Faith. Ironically, this same title, awarded by a Roman Catholic Pope, is still held by British monarchs to this day to defend the Protestant faith! You've got to chuckle, really. What a farce it all is. Henry, being much miffed by the Pope's refusal to sanction his divorce, ordered Parliament to create a Church of England, independent of Rome. He made himself the head of the new Church in the Act of Supremacy of 1534 and unleashed a bloody purge against Roman Catholics. Henry was succeeded by his only son, Edward, but after he died at the age of 15, he was replaced by Henry's daughter, Mary. She was a staunch Roman Catholic who earned the title 'bloody Mary' for her purge of Protestants. Mary had secured the throne by executing her rival, Lady Jane Grey, the 'six-day queen'. With Mary's death came the legendary reign of Elizabeth I, Henry's daughter by Anne Boleyn. Elizabeth executed her rival, Mary Queen of Scots, from the House of Stuart, and Elizabeth proceeded to restore the Church of England with herself as Supreme Head. She ordered a purge against Catholics which was to earn her the title of 'bloody Elizabeth'. Nice family.

It was against this backdrop that Francis Bacon emerged as a very high initiate of the secret knowledge in the reign of his probable mother Elizabeth I, and her successor James I, the Scottish king who united the English and Scottish monarchy when he was crowned in 1603 as the first king of both countries. It was Bacon, with Robert Fludd, Grand Master of the Priory of Sion, who oversaw the translation of the King James version of the Bible, a book which, according to a study in 1881, has at least 36,191 translation errors. Given that Bacon was an extremely educated and intelligent man, I can't believe that such a mess could have been made of the Bible translation on such a scale unless it was meant that way. Bacon also removed the two Books of Maccabees from his version which, significantly, were hostile to the secret society called the Nazarenes, a Brotherhood offshoot at the time of the mythical Jesus. Bacon has also been dubbed the 'father' of modern science – this-world-is-all-there-is science – which has focused only on the physical level of existence. Why would Bacon support such a version of 'science' when he was an advanced initiate of the secret knowledge and knew the truth? There's something seriously not right about all this, especially when you consider that other 'fathers' of modern science like Isaac Newton and Robert Boyle were also advanced initiates as Grand Masters of the Priory of Sion. Here you have Bacon, a leading initiate of the secret knowledge, involved, via the Rosicrucians and other networks, in the dividing of the Christian Church, the writing of the Christian Bible, and the creation of modern 'science' which challenged many of the basic foundations of Christianity. He was playing two sides against each other to create an environment in which another, unspoken, Agenda could flourish. Certainly this period produced the classic control system of divide and rule. Mass slaughter erupted across Europe in the Protestant-Catholic wars, while, at the same time, both creeds were being challenged by the emerging 'scientific' dogma.

It was also under the influence of Bacon and other esoteric magicians like John Dee and Sir Francis Walsingham, that the spy networks across Europe, now known as British Intelligence, were created. British Intelligence was formed by the reptilian bloodlines of the Babylonian Brotherhood and British Intelligence would later create American Intelligence and similar networks throughout the expanding British Empire, which are still at work today. The CIA was created by Elite members of British Intelligence during the presidency of the 33rd degree Freemason, Harry S. Truman, the man who officially ordered the bombs to be dropped on Japan. He took his advice from Bill Donovan, the head of the CIA's predecessor, the Office of Strategic Services (OSS), which was peopled entirely by Knights Templar according to Bill Cooper, a former operative with US Naval Intelligence. Walsingham was posted as ambassador to France to expand the spy networks and it was no surprise when a French Intelligence agent told me that British and French Intelligence are the same organisation. It certainly makes the cover up of Princess Diana's murder easier. The intelligence agencies of the world, at their peaks, are esoteric, black magic secret societies working to the same Agenda – global control. John Dee was the Queen's astrologer, a Rosicrucian Grand Master, a black magician, and a secret agent for the new intelligence network. He appears to have had a copy of the Book of Enoch from some source or other and he, and the psychic Edward Kelley, developed a written language they called 'Enochian script or cipher' from communications with the angels – reptilians. Dee signed his reports 007 – the same, of course, as James Bond, the stories written by a 20th century agent of this same British Intelligence, Ian Fleming, a friend of the black magician, Aleister Crowley. Dee travelled throughout Europe manipulating, gathering information and oiling the networks. One of his haunts was Bohemia and he was closely associated with Emperor Rudolf II of the reptilian Habsburg dynasty, another occultist.[12] Dee was among the influential voices who were orchestrating a policy of British expansionism which became the British Empire. While in Prague, Dee gave Emperor Rudolph an illustrated manuscript written in code and claimed to be the work of Roger Bacon (Roger, not Francis), the 13th century Franciscan monk who upset the church authorities with his views and ideas. These included prophecies about the microscope, telescope, car, submarine, aeroplane and the belief that the Earth was a sphere and not flat. In 1912, this same manuscript was bought by an American book dealer called Wilfred Voynich and became known as the Voynich Manuscript. When he sent copies to the experts of the day, they said that most of the hundreds of plants illustrated did not grow on this planet. Some of the illustrations looked like tissue seen under a microscope and others were of star systems and constellations. The best code breakers available to United States Intelligence in both the First and Second World Wars tried to decipher what they called: "the most mysterious manuscript in the world", but none of them could do it. William Romaine Newbold, a professor at the University of Pennsylvania, claimed to have decoded some of it in 1921. He said that part of the text read:

"In a concave mirror, I saw a star in the form of a snail between the navel of Pegasus, the girdle of Andromeda, and the head of Cassiopeia."[13]

What is described in the manuscript acquired by Dr John Dee is now known to be accurate and the illustration it contains of the Andromeda nebula is also correct, but it is depicted from an angle which cannot be seen from Earth! This manuscript is just one example of the level of knowledge the Brotherhood were working with hundreds of years ago while their other wing, the religions, were keeping the masses in the most basic ignorance. In this John Dee-Francis Bacon circle were all the leading figures of Elizabethan society, including Sir Walter Raleigh. It may have been Francis Bacon who communicated some of the secret knowledge 'for those who have ears' in ciphers and symbolism in the works called the Shakespeare plays. He, like the writers of the Old and New Testaments and the King Arthur 'Grail' stories, was a high initiate of the secret mysteries communicating through code and hidden meaning. Manly P. Hall says that Bacon indicated that he was the true author in a series of codes. His esoteric number was 33 and on one page in the first part of the 'Shakespeare' play, *Henry The Fourth*, the name 'Francis' appears 33 times. Bacon also used watermarks in paper to transmit his symbols, as did the Rosicrucians and secret societies in general. These included the rose and the cross and bunches of grapes – the vine, the bloodlines.[14] Bacon also used Tarot symbolism in his codes, including the numbers 21, 56 and 78, which are related to divisions in the Tarot deck.[15] In a Shakespearean Folio of 1623, the Christian name of Bacon appears 21 times on page 56.[16] The term Rota Mundi frequently occurs in the early manifestos of the Fraternity of the Rose Cross. Rearrange the letters in Rota and you get Taro, the ancient name for the tarot cards.[17] Shakespeare is known as the Bard. A Bard was a Druidic initiate of the secret knowledge and, the Concise Oxford Dictionary tells me, there is another definition of bard… "a slice of bacon placed on meat or game before roasting". The famous Globe Theatre in London where the plays were performed was built according to the principles of sacred geometry and the last 'Shakespeare' play, *The Tempest*, included many Rosicrucian concepts.[18] It is equally possible that the 'Shakespeare' plays were written by another initiate of Elizabethan society, Edward De Vere, the 17th Earl of Oxford, who also fitted the bill and some believe even more so than Bacon.

The idea that the world famous plays were written by an illiterate from Stratford-upon-Avon called William Shakespeare is patently ridiculous and, like so much accepted 'truth', does not survive the most basic research. Shakespeare, the 'Bard', grew up in Stratford, a town with no school capable of communicating such a high degree of learning. His parents were illiterate and he showed a total disregard for study. Yet the plays were written by someone with a great knowledge of the world which could be gleaned only from a fantastic range of books and personal experience through travel. Shakespeare had no such library, not that he could have used it if he had, and he is never known to have left the country. Bacon had just such a library and travelled widely to many of the places featured in the plays. Where did Shakespeare acquire his knowledge of French, Italian, Spanish, Danish and classic Latin and Greek? Answer, he didn't. Ben Jonson, a close friend of Shakespeare, said that the 'Bard' understood: "small Latin and less Greek!"[19] But Bacon and DeVere were learned in these languages. Shakespeare's daughter, Judith, was known to be illiterate and could not even write her name at the age of 27.[20] It really makes sense that a man who wrote so eloquently would have a daughter who could not write her signature. There are only six known examples of Shakespeare's own handwriting, all signatures, and three of these are on his will. They reveal a man unfamiliar with a pen and a hand that was probably guided by another. His will included his second best bed and a broad silver gilt bowl, but nothing whatsoever to suggest that he wrote or owned a single work of literature![21] Nor is there one authentic portrait of Shakespeare. The differences in the depiction of him by artists confirm that no-one has any idea what he looked like. Yet the power of conditioning and accepting the official line attracts millions of people to Stratford from all over the world to see the home of the man who *didn't* write the Shakespeare plays! This is only one small example of how the official fairy story called 'history' is used to control current behaviour and perception. What else in history isn't true? Just about everything. Behind the Shakespeare plays was the hidden hand behind most historical events of significance – the Brotherhood networks. And nothing sums up the attitude of this group better than the words Bacon/DeVere wrote for the witches in his play, Macbeth: "Fair is foul and foul is fair." As Manly P. Hall, the Freemasonic historian, wrote of Bacon:

"He was a Rosicrucian, some have intimated *the* Rosicrucian. If not actually the
Illustrious Father C.R.C. referred to in the Rosicrucian manifestos, he was certainly a
high initiate of the Rosicrucian Order... those enthusiasts who for years have struggled
to identify Sir Francis Bacon as the true "Bard of Avon" might long since have won their
case had they emphasised its most important angle, namely, that Sir Francis Bacon,
the Rosicrucian initiate, wrote into the Shakespearean plays the secret teachings of the
Fraternity of R.C. and the true rituals of the Freemasonic Order, of which order it may be
discovered that he was the actual founder."[22]

The rituals and symbols of Freemasonry can be traced back to ancient Egypt and
beyond. In truth, its knowledge of sacred geometry, numbers and form, go back to
before the last cataclysm. The Dionysiac Artificers or Architects, composed of
initiates of the Bacchus-Dionysus (Sun) Mysteries whose role it was to design the
public buildings and monuments, can be traced back at least three thousand years if
not more.[23] It was these architect-initiates who designed the great buildings of
Constantinople, Rhodes, Athens and Rome and it was this same stream who built
the temple to the goddess Diana at the world centre for the Diana cult at Ephesus,[24]
which is remembered as one of the wonders of the ancient world. The Dionysiac
Architects were connected with a secret society called the Ionians (hence the island
of Iona in Scotland) who were apparently the people who commissioned the
Temple of Diana. Under other names, the Dionysian Architects and initiates from
the Frater Solomonis mystery school also built great Christian Cathedrals funded by
the Knights Templar. There were many Rosicrucian and Masonic emblems to be
seen in the carvings of the Notre Dame Cathedral in Paris and numerous depictions
of compasses, squares and building tools before they were destroyed during the
French Revolution.[25] The Bacchus-Dionysus architects were divided into
communities headed by Masters and Wardens, just as Freemasonry is today, and
they settled in Israel where some researchers link them with the Essenes, the
Egyptian sect who produced the Dead Sea Scrolls.[26] Bacchus-Dionysus (two names
for the same deity) was a symbol of the Sun who was said to have been born to a
virgin on December 25th. The foundation of Freemasonic legend and 'history'
centres on the building of the symbolic King Solomon's Temple in Jerusalem. The
Freemasonic hero is Hiram Abiff, the 'son of the widow' in their folklore. This is
more symbolism. In Egypt, Horus (Tammuz) was the son of the widow, Isis.

The creation of Freemasonry in the 16th and 17th centuries pulled together many of
the various themes, agendas and organisations I have highlighted so far. It connected
the Rosicrucians and Templars in England, like Bacon, with the story of the Templars
after their arrival from France at the time of Philippe the Fair, and their subsequent
return to France as the Scots Guard. It also connects this group with the Priory of Sion.
The figure which encapsulated these connections was James VI of Scotland, who
succeeded Elizabeth I and became James I of England and Scotland. He was the only
child of Mary Queen of Scots. The Stuart bloodline with its connections to the reptilian
Merovingians was now on the throne of both England and Scotland. Under James's

patronage, the Scottish and Templar knowledge and the Rosicrucian knowledge of Francis Bacon and others could merge and become united under the name, Freemasonry. So could the knowledge of the reptilian House of Lorraine, another bloodline of King James. He had the whole set, this guy. For this reason, and others, you find the names 'James' and 'St James' appear many times in the titles of Brotherhood companies, organisations and their locations. The American ambassador to London is known as the Ambassador to the Court of St James. Close to the Houses of Parliament in London you find St James's Square and here is the headquarters of the Conservative Party; the biggest British trade union, the Transport Union; a building owned by the Scottish reptilian bloodline, the Keswicks (of which more later); and in the centre is a massive round church dedicated to St John (Nimrod).

One of his first acts as King James I of England and Scotland was to award a knighthood to Bacon, and James would later appoint him Solicitor-General, Attorney-General, Lord Keeper of the Great Seal and, in 1618, Lord Chancellor and Baron Verulam. Later Bacon was prosecuted on corruption charges and retired from official public life. In those early years under James I, there was a wonderful opportunity to circulate the suppressed knowledge of the ancient world if that was really the motivation of the James-Bacon esoteric underground. But again we have the contradiction. The very opposite happened. James employed Bacon to edit the King James version of the Bible and launched a vicious condemnation of 'witches and wizards' – those among the general population who used and communicated the esoteric knowledge. More than that, he embarked on a vicious slaughter of them, killing thousands, and he even wrote a book explaining how they should be identified and dealt with. Why do that if, as claimed, the motivation of this underground stream was to protect and eventually circulate such information? Because that was never the idea. It helps if people whose support you need *think* that is your motivation, but when it comes to the crunch you walk the other way. The hierarchy of the groups I have been highlighting don't want to make the knowledge available, they want to hoard it and use it to gain power on a global scale. To be honest I'm fed up with hearing of how the Freemasons, Templars, Rosicrucians, Bacon and others, have been protectors of the knowledge when every time the climate has been right to make it public, including today, the opportunity is spurned. It's bullshit. They know that knowledge is power if you have it and others do not, so the last thing their hierarchy wants is an informed population. Throughout Europe, the wizards and witches, the sensitives and psychics in other words, were burned, drowned, jailed and tortured, on the orders of people like King James and Martin Luther. Yet these were initiates using the same knowledge the 'wizards and witches' were using and communicating. There were two esoteric undergrounds and still are. The one among the people which passed on the knowledge in secret, myth and fairy tale, to avoid the wrath of the religious and political establishment; and the Babylonian Brotherhood underground which wanted that knowledge for itself to control and manipulate the religious and political establishment. So the peoples' underground was, and is, constantly attacked and pursued by the Brotherhood underground. Some 250,000 were murdered for being 'wizards and witches',

30,000 of them in the British Isles alone.[27]

The Freemasonic movement was to become a sort of central meeting place and coordinator for the various elements of the Brotherhood network. W. Wynn Westcott, founder of the Hermetic (and Satanic) Order of the Golden Dawn, knew the true background to Freemasonry because of his connections to the esoteric underground. He wrote in his work, *The Magical Mason*, that the Freemasons originate from the Essenes, the Pharisee (Levite) Jews, the ancient mystery schools of Egypt and Greece, the Vehm-Gerichte of Westphalia, Germany, the Roman Collegia, the French Compagnons, and the Rosicrucians.[28] The official (and inaccurate) story is that Freemasonry emerged from the lodges of the stone masons who worked on the great churches and cathedrals, craftsmen with the knowledge of sacred geometry. They had enjoyed a close connection with the Knights Templar since the building of the Gothic cathedrals. But by the time of Henry VIII, their work was in decline. Far from building more cathedrals, Henry set about looting the monasteries and the fraternities, brotherhoods and guilds to raise some much needed cash. To survive, the Masonic guilds began to open their doors to non-Masons, people from the professional classes, the businessmen, merchants, landowners and the aristocracy. It was now *free*masonry and, of course, the newcomers took over the show very quickly, we are told. What happened, in truth, is that the Knights Templar-Rosicrucian-Babylonian Brotherhood underground, created their own initiation structure to pass on the secret knowledge to the chosen few and keep it out of circulation. The mason guilds were simply a cover story.

Freemasonry was born in Scotland among the familiar Brotherhood bloodline families, especially the reptilian St Clair/Sinclairs. They were based at Rosslyn or Roslin Castle just south of Edinburgh in a region steeped in Templar tradition. Like all of these bloodline families, they periodically change their name to hide their origins. This line became the St Clairs while they were living in Normandy before they crossed the English Channel with William the Conqueror for the Battle of Hastings in 1066 and became the Scottish Sinclairs. Five of the nine St Clairs who took part in the battle were William's first cousins and one of them settled in Scotland to found the Scottish dynasty.[29] The family apparently named themselves St Clair after a martyred hermit named Clare, or that's the official line.[30] They were the Norsemen who came down from Scandinavia to occupy what they called Normandy, but their true origin was with the white races and reptile-Aryans which emerged from the Near East and the Caucasus. The foundations were laid for Rosslyn Chapel in 1446 and it was completed in the 1480s. It is a mass of esoteric and later Freemasonic symbolism and it is like a shrine for the Brotherhood. The Sinclairs had extensive connections to the underground networks in France, Lorraine and Guise, and with Scandinavia, Denmark and the one-time Brotherhood financial centre in Venice. They were steeped in the reptilian network. A Sinclair went ashore in North America with the Black Nobility Venetian, Nicolo Zeno, a century before Christopher Columbus would do so officially. One of the symbols at Rosslyn Chapel is the Pagan vegetation god or 'Green Man'. Tim Wallace-Murphy wrote in his official history of Rosslyn Chapel that the Green Man can be identified

with Tammuz, the dying and resurrecting god of Babylon and an aspect of Nimrod. Tammuz, and other names for the same deity, was often depicted to have a green face. This includes Osiris, the husband-brother of Isis. The story of Robin Hood in his 'Lincoln green' originated with this Green Man deity. Robin Hood began in the original legend as a species of 'fairy' and he was also known as Green Robin, Robin of Greenwood and Robin Goodfellow.[31] His "Shakespearean" version, Puck, in *A Midsummer Night's Dream*, presided over fertility and sexual rites at the summer solstice. On May 1st, May Day, they had the May Pole ceremonies. The May Pole is a phallic symbol dedicated to the goddess of sexuality and fertility and on that day every village virgin would be a Queen of the May (Queen Semiramis). Many would end up in the green wood to undergo a sexual initiation with a youth playing the role of Robin Hood or Robin Goodfellow. The children that often followed nine months later were the origin of the now common names Robinson and Robertson.[32] The story of Robin Hood was another symbolic tale to maintain the memory of Pagan sexual ritual amid the crossed legs and scowling faces of orthodox Christianity. A play called Robin Hood and Little John was performed every May and June at Rosslyn by gypsies or other travelling performers. [33] Sir William Sinclair became, for a time, a protector of gypsies when legislation was passed in Scotland designed to wipe them out. The gypsies originated in Egypt and they carried the knowledge from place to place and generation to generation.
This is why they have been so persecuted and hounded until most of their knowledge disappeared.

The biggest rite of world Freemasonry are the 33 degrees (initiation levels) called the Scottish Rite. It is named after that little country in the north of the British Isles because that is where many of the ancient bloodlines settled to be followed by the Templar knowledge at the time of Philippe the Fair. Now the Templars had re-emerged publicly under another name – Freemasonry. The other main stream of the 'craft' is the York Rite, after which New York is named, which is the centre of United States Freemasonry to this day. Some researchers believe that the Priory of Sion wrested control of the Scottish and York Rites from the Templars who later crossed the English Channel to found French Freemasonry. This may be true, but in the end they are all the same organisation at the highest level. You can still see the influence of the Templars in the degrees of the York Rite. The top degree is the Knights Templar Degree, followed by the Knights of Malta Degree and the Red Cross Degree. But the official degrees are only what they admit to. Above these levels are what I call the Illuminati degrees which very, very few people even know about, never mind reach. The vast majority of Freemasons never progress beyond the bottom three levels, the 'blue degrees', and they are used as a front of respectability to hide the real Agenda which the rank and file are not aware of. Albert Pike was the head of the Southern Jurisdiction of the Scottish Rite of Freemasonry in the United States in the last century and is considered a Freemasonic 'god' in America. His statue stands in Washington DC. In his Freemasonic book, *Morals And Dogma*, he writes on page 819:

"The blue degrees are, but the outer court or portico of the temple. Part of the symbols are displayed there to the initiate, but he is intentionally misled by false interpretations. It is not intended that he shall understand them, but it is intended that he shall imagine he understands them."

Put another way, keep them in the dark and feed them bullshit. This is the classic secret society structure in which only the highest levels know what is really going on. The rest are sold a myth. In the mid-17th century, the Thirty Years War between the Protestant and Catholic believers had turned Europe into a cauldron of death and mayhem. It was feared at one stage that the new Protestant movement would be routed and the rule of Rome restored. Britain became a safe haven for the Protestant cause, particularly under the royal house of Stuart, which ironically was not Christian at all. But the split the Protestants created in the Christian Church, and the way the power of Rome was thus diminished, suited the Brotherhood. The British Isles became the focus for esoteric thought in Europe and the creation of Freemasonry wove these strands together in one structure. Freemasonry was to quickly become a vehicle for political and economic manipulation, its members working through all sides to the same end. The Agenda in this period was to diminish the power of the monarchies in Europe and replace them with political systems designed in a way that allowed the Brotherhood to control them. It was based on the structure in ancient Sumer and Babylon and this has continued to this very day. A series of civil wars were triggered throughout Europe which either removed the monarchy or made them mere puppets. In the English Civil War of 1642–1646, the Stuart king and Freemason, Charles I, was defeated and later executed. The monarchy was briefly overthrown and replaced by a Lord Protector, Oliver Cromwell, also a Freemason. This may sound strange and contradictory, but it isn't. The Agenda is the prime motivation, in fact the *only* motivation, of the Brotherhood. If that means replacing a Freemason and a Stuart who won't follow the Agenda with a Freemason who will, then so be it. The end of the royal line for the Stuarts is not as significant as it would seem. The Brotherhood Elite and the reptilians do not care who introduces their Agenda, so long as someone does and the most influential of their bloodlines are not always the most famous people. Often the most influential ones work in the background where the real power lies. The Stuarts were fine for a while, but everyone is expendable to the cause and by now the structures were in place to run countries via the secret society networks, using frontmen and women. The power of a single monarch was over and that was certainly the case in the UK after the beheading of Charles I. Even when the monarchy was restored with Charles II, it was a puppet of the Brotherhood and took orders in the same way that Oliver Cromwell did when, in 1655, he allowed 'Jewish' (Aryan) people to return to England for the first time since they were excluded by Edward I in 1290. As I described earlier, this was the time when the Black Nobility in Amsterdam were preparing to put their man, William of Orange, on the British throne.

Everything interconnects with everything else in the most remarkable way because it is being coordinated from the lower fourth dimension which can see into this one. The Christian Church was split into rival and violent factions by the Rosicrucian, Martin Luther, and the emergence of a vicious brand of the Protestant faith called Calvinism, later known as the Puritans. Its founder 'John Calvin' was actually Jean Cauin from Noyons, France, who was educated at the Brotherhood-controlled, College du Montagu. This is also where Ignatius Loyola, the 'Catholic' founder of the Society of Jesus, the Jesuits, was educated. Cauin moved to Paris and then to Geneva, Switzerland, where he was known as Cohen. This name relates to 'priest' and goes back to the Egyptian mystery schools. In Geneva he developed, or someone else did, the philosophy known as Calvinism. He changed his name again from Cohen to Calvin to make it more acceptable to the English who now became the prime target of this new religion – yet another created by the same source as all the others. Calvinism was a designer religion for the next stage of the plan. It focused rigidly on the ten commandments of 'Moses' and the Old Testament texts (taken literally, not symbolically of course). But this was the crucial bit. Up to this point the Christian religion had banned usury, the charging of interest on loans. Now, with the Black Nobility bankers manoeuvring to take over England, a Christian country, using the outwardly 'Christian' aristocracy, the time had come to end that rule and make usury the norm. Calvinism, therefore, supported the charging of interest and one of the great beneficiaries was Switzerland, where the plot was conceived, because it became the centre of the world's private banking system. Another role for Calvinism was to insist on the burning of witches and in so doing take more of the secret knowledge out of public circulation. The Black Nobility wanted their man, William of Orange, on the throne and to do this they had to remove Charles I, the guy they eventually beheaded in 1649. Calvinism was used to ferment unrest with the monarchy and along came the Freemason and Calvinist, Oliver Cromwell, to play his part in yet another manufactured conflict as his Roundheads met the Royalists in the English Civil War. On September 3rd 1921, a publication by Lord Alfred Douglas called *Plain English* presented the contents of correspondence relating to the plot behind the murder of Charles I. It said that volumes of records had been found in the Synagogue of Mulheim by a L. A. Van Valckert. They were written in German and had been lost since the Napoleonic Wars. An entry for June 6th 1647, from Oliver Cromwell to an Ebenezer Pratt, says (in modern language):

"In return for financial support will advocate admission of Jews to England; this, however, impossible while Charles living. Charles cannot be executed without trial, adequate grounds for which at present do not exist. Therefore, advise that Charles be assassinated, but will have nothing to do with procuring an assassin, though willing to help with his escape."

Ebenezer Pratt's reply was on July 12th 1647:

"Will grant financial aid as soon as Charles removed and Jews admitted. Assassination too dangerous. Charles should be given the opportunity to escape. His recapture will then make trial and execution possible. The support will be liberal, but useless to discuss terms until trial commences."[34]

This publication was so revealing that the Brotherhood network had the publisher, Lord Alfred Douglas, imprisoned on the basis of an alleged 'libel' printed in his paper about Winston Churchill. How it is possible to libel a Satanist like Churchill is rather hard to comprehend. That correspondence between Cromwell and Pratt was mirrored by actual events. On November 12th 1647, Charles I was allowed to escape and in fact was 'hidden' on the Isle of Wight, just off the southern coast of England, where I am writing this section. Charles was recaptured and when he and Parliament appeared to be close to an agreement that would spare his life, Cromwell, by now Lord Protector, dismissed all the members supporting an agreement. History calls what remained the 'Rump Parliament'. Another trial was ordered by Cromwell because his agreement with his backers in Amsterdam was that Charles would be executed. The indictment against Charles was drawn up by Isaac Dorislaus, the agent in England of Manasseh ben Israel, one of the main funders from Amsterdam of the Cromwell 'revolution'.[35] The outcome of the 'trial' was the public beheading of Charles and this was followed by Cromwell allowing the 'Jews' to return to England. I would stress again that we are not, in truth, talking about Jews, but the financial hierarchy of the Black Nobility and the Brotherhood who hide behind the term 'Jews' and mercilessly manipulate the mass of those who call themselves Jewish. After Cromwell's death in 1661, many of his Calvinist-Puritan followers headed for America to escape 'religious persecution' following the reinstatement of the monarchy under Charles II. These were the religious fanatics who slaughtered the Native Americans under the banner of 'God'. The Black Nobility bankers in Amsterdam caused a financial depression in England to undermine Charles II. Eventually a 'peace' deal was struck between Holland and England in 1667 in which William of Orange (Black Nobility) would marry Mary, daughter of the Duke of York. When Charles II died in 1685, it was the Duke of York who became King James II. Now all the Brotherhood had to do was remove him from the throne and their guy would be King of England. They began to bribe James II's most influential aristocratic supporters and the first to bite was John Churchill, the reptilian Duke of Marlborough. The Commissioner of Public Accounts revealed that Churchill had taken bribes totalling some £60,000 (an absolute fortune in those days) from representatives of Dutch and Spanish financial families like Sir Solomon de Medina and Antonio Machado. Researcher, Euctace Mullins, puts it at more like £350,000.[36]

John Churchill, Duke of Marlborough, was an ancestor of Britain's wartime prime minister, Sir Winston Churchill, and the Churchill-Brotherhood connections continue to this day. Sir Winston's daughter-in-law, Pamela, married the American, Averell Harriman, one of the great Brotherhood manipulators of the 20th century and much documented in ...*And The Truth Shall Set You Free*. Pamela Harriman, who had formerly been married to Winston's son, Randolph, became very influential in the American Democratic Party and is widely named as the force behind Bill Clinton's election as US president. She was rewarded by being made US ambassador to the key Brotherhood city of Paris, where she died in 1997 at the age of 76. Her son, also named Winston, is a British member of Parliament who is close to the Rothschilds. Pamela Churchill-Harriman dated Elie de Rothschild before marrying Averell Harriman. In 1995 the Churchill family were given £12,500 million of National Lottery money when they sold some of Sir Winston Churchill's Second World War speeches to 'the nation'. The speeches were purchased with this public money by the National Heritage Memorial Board, chaired by... Lord Jacob Rothschild. Just a coincidence, nothing to worry about. The Churchill-Harrimans are bloodline families. One of Pamela Harriman's ancestors conspired with the Percy family, ancestors of George Bush, in the attempt to blow up the Houses of Parliament in the so-called Gun Powder Plot led by Guy Fawkes on November 5th 1605. As a Harriman, Pamela represented the 'Democratic' wing of the Brotherhood while the Bush's, close associates and business partners of the Harrimans, represent the 'Republican' wing. Both have answered to the same master to ensure that the United States, like every other country, is a one-party-state. The Bush family are close friends of the Windsors, which shouldn't surprise anyone who has read this far because both are shape-shifting reptilians. Bush and his associate, the Brotherhood's tireless global manipulator, Henry Kissinger, have both been knighted by Queen Elizabeth II.

The modern version of Freemasonry expanded rapidly from its obscure beginnings among the Templars and other mystery initiates. The Grand Lodge of England – the centre of the network – was officially formed on June 24th 1717. This is St John the Baptist's Day, a sacred day for the Knights Templar and an obvious connection to the Knights of St John of Jerusalem (Malta). John the Baptist is the patron saint of both the Freemasons and the Templars because Oannes was another form of John in Babylon and Oannes was a another name for Nimrod. The Irish Grand Lodge followed some six or seven years later. Most of the field lodges which emerged among the regiments in the British army were warranted by the Irish and not the English Grand Lodge. The Scottish clans introduced Freemasonry to their blood brethren in France and I should mention one man in this regard, Andrew Michael Ramsey, a tutor to the Scottish Stuart pretender to the throne, Bonnie Prince Charlie. Ramsey was born in Scotland in the 1680s and was a close friend of Isaac Newton, the Grand Master of the Priory of Sion. He was a member of many Elite groupings, including a sort of Rosicrucian society called the Philadelphians (named after the city from where the American War of Independence was orchestrated) and the French chivalric Order of St Lazarus. Many of these Elite groups give their initiates esoteric names and Ramsey's Brotherhood name was 'Chevalier'.[37] He was a significant factor in the spread of Freemasonry and he is particularly remembered in Freemasonic circles for two versions of the same speech he made in December 1736 and March 1737. It became known as Ramsey's Oration and in it he charted some of the history of Freemasonry. He confirmed that it was derived from the mystery schools of antiquity which worshipped Diana, Minerva and Isis (Semiramis). He said that Freemasonry had its origins in the Holy Land at the time of the Crusades (the Knights Templar) and did not originate with stone masons. Ramsey said that 'our Order' (the Templars) had formed an intimate union with the

Knights of St John of Jerusalem (Malta) and from that time: "our lodges took the name of Lodges of St John".[38] In France, Freemasonry, with Ramsey's keen support, spawned a particularly important strand, a fusion between Freemasonry and the Jacobite movement which became known as Grand Orient Freemasonry. There are also Grand Orient networks in others countries like Brazil and Portugal. Grand Orient means Grand East and its rituals are inspired by the worship of Zoroaster in Persia, Ishtar and Tammuz (Semiramis and Nimrod) in Babylon, Demeter, Persephone and Dionysus in Greece, Aphrodite and Adonis in Syria, Isis and Osiris in Egypt, and Mithra in Persia.[39] The Grand Orient in France was to be the focus behind the manipulation and coordination of the French Revolution. From the Brotherhood's point of view, this 'peoples' revolution had nothing to do with freedom and everything to do with its Agenda for global control. The famous cry of the French revolutionaries: "Liberty, Equality, Fraternity", is a Freemasonic motto.

The science of manipulation

As the power of religion began to wane, another mental prison cell was created. We call it, rather bravely, 'science'. Not real science. Official science, the one that says that this world is all there is and there is no continuation of life after 'death'. The Brotherhood had to find an alternative for those rejecting religion to ensure they would not realise that we are multidimensional infinite consciousness incarnate in a physical body for a period of intense experience on the road of evolution; that we don't 'die' because we cannot die. Energy is consciousness and energy cannot be destroyed, only transformed into another expression of itself. When you realise that you are not your physical body, but the infinite, eternal consciousness giving life to that body, your vision of yourself and your potential is expanded beyond measure. What a nightmare for those who wish to exert control. So through the Freemasonic networks, the Royal Society was formed, yet again in London, under a royal warrant from Charles II in 1662. It was the world's first assembly of scientists and engineers, and it was to be the dominating influence on the direction of 'science'. Virtually all the early members of the Royal Society were Freemasons who knew that that direction was flawed and untrue. No doubt the same applies today. Some familiar names are about to appear again. The 'father' of the Royal Society, who was said to be its inspiration before he 'died' (or moved locations), was Francis Bacon, the top Rosicrucian, translator of the Bible, and architect of Freemasonry. The Royal Society stalwarts also included: Isaac Newton, the Rosicrucian Grand Master of the Priory of Sion, who became a fellow in 1672; Lord Moray, a Scottish Freemason; Elias Ashmole, one of the first registered Freemasons; and Andrew Michael 'Chevalier' Ramsey, a leading light of Freemasonry, who was admitted to the Royal Society without any scientific qualifications whatsoever. Another fellow was John Byrom, a Freemason and member of the Cabala Club, also known as the Sun Club.[40] In 1984, more than 500 of his papers were found in a house in Manchester and they included information about sacred geometry, architecture and cabalistic, Freemasonic and other alchemical and esoteric symbols.[41]

Ashmole, an alchemist and Rosicrucian with many esoteric contacts in Germany, was a close friend of Charles II and a Knight of the Order of the Garter, that premier order of 'chivalry' headed by the monarch. He wrote a book with Arthur Dee (the son of Dr John Dee), who was personal physician to the Tsar, Ivan the Terrible. When Ivan died, Dee's manipulation installed the Romanov dynasty on the Russian throne.[42] Ashmole was extremely well connected and maintained close contacts with the 'Invisible College' which met in Oxford from 1650. Just such a group was proposed by Francis Bacon in his book, *The New Atlantis*. This 'Invisible College' included the famed scientist Robert Boyle, another Grand Master of the Priory of Sion, and Sir Christopher Wren, the architect behind St Paul's Cathedral in the City of London, the financial centre of the Black Nobility and the Babylonian Brotherhood. Both were Grand Masters of the Rosicrucian Order. St Paul's, and the rebuilding of the City in general, was made possible by the Great Fire of London in 1666 and how interesting that both Wren, the architect who designed St Paul's Cathedral on a former site of Diana worship, and Robert Hooke, one of three city surveyors after the fire, were both members of the Royal Society and high initiates of the secret societies. The new City of London was built to a Masonic street plan with the design of the buildings based on the knowledge of the energy grid in that area and how best to manipulate it.

The Royal Society was – and is – more than a grouping of scientists. At its core it is a secret society controlled, indeed created, by the Brotherhood to limit the vision and breadth of scientific and spiritual understanding. For confirmation of that, look at the esoteric initiates behind an organisation which denies the esoteric. This becomes even more obvious when you consider the background of another group of esoteric initiates who merged into the Royal Society. They called themselves the Lunar Society because they met once a month on the night of the full Moon.[43] Among its members was Benjamin Franklin, the high level Freemason, Rosicrucian, one of the Founding Fathers of the United States, and closely connected to the Freemasons behind the French Revolution. More of him in the next chapter. Other Lunar Society members were Erasmus Darwin, the grandfather of Charles Darwin, the man who would be used to promote the belief in this world-is-all-there-is science and the survival of the fittest via natural selection. I don't think that even Darwin believed that, certainly not at the end of his life, but the image, the myth, has prevailed. Anyway, the idea that Charles Darwin 'discovered' the theory of natural selection and survival of the fittest is ridiculous. His grandfather, Erasmus of the Lunar Society, wrote a book called *Zoonomia* in 1794 in which he outlined the very same opinion.[44] Josiah Wedgwood of the Wedgwood pottery empire, was another Lunar Society member and his daughter married Erasmus Darwin's son, Robert Darwin, and became the mother of Charles Darwin![45] This same bloodline produced Thomas Malthus, who's sickening racist creed has been used by Adolf Hitler, Henry Kissinger and endless other frontmen for the Brotherhood to justify the genocide of 'lesser' races to maintain the genetic purity of the human blood stock – the reptile Aryans.[46] Malthus, an Anglican clergyman, said that disease and appalling living conditions for the masses were essential to stop over-population and the dilution of the master (white) bloodlines.

This is just one of his little gems of wisdom:

"We are bound in justice and honour formally to disclaim the right of the poor to support. To this end, I should propose a regulation to be made declaring that no child born... should ever be entitled to parish assistance... The (*illegitimate*) infant is, comparatively speaking, of little value to society, as others will immediately supply its place... All children beyond what would be required to keep up the population to this (*desired*) level, must necessarily perish, unless room be made for them by the deaths of grown persons."[47]

The economist, John Maynard Keynes, who's principles have dominated modern economic policy, thought Malthus to be a genius and Darwin and his circle believed him to be a master of logic.[48] The population control policies of this century have been inspired by the genocide principles of Malthus, as I expose in ...*And The Truth Shall Set You Free*. Again the Scottish connection appears. Six of the members of the Lunar Society were educated in Edinburgh and so was Charles Darwin. Another major voice in the official dismantling of 'God' and the denial of the eternal soul, was the Frenchman, Rene Descartes, born in 1596 and called: "the father of modern philosophy".[49] Descartes was educated by the Roman Catholic branch of the Babylonian Brotherhood, the Jesuits. He called himself a Roman Catholic all his life and yet his books were placed on the Catholic Index of Forbidden Books. His views would later be expounded by Isaac Newton. Both of them were fascinated by the esoteric and alchemy. Here we can see that the same force which created the religions of the ancient world, also designed the new 'science'. Who created and sold the idea of a judgmental God and paradise only for believers? The very people who knew it wasn't true. Who created the materialist and 'cosmic accident' version of 'science' that denies the eternal soul? The very people who knew it wasn't true. This tradition is continued today by the movement known as Humanism. Its manifesto, published in 1953, says that the universe is self existing and not created; modern science offers the only acceptable definition of the universe and human values; and when you die you cease to exist.

These two apparent opposites, religion and science, have many things in common, but one in particular. They both deny the true nature of who we are and the power we have within ourselves to control our destiny. Once we realise that and grasp the limitless power that is waiting to be tapped, the control of the reptilians and their bloodlines will be no more. The face of the Babylonian Brotherhood has endless interconnected masks, but the creation of Freemasonry provided a network which could act as a global coordinator for the thousands of these 'masks' to communicate with each other. Some of the masks operate within one group or area of society, but most, especially the major ones like Freemasonry, operate within organisations and groups which appear on the surface to be opposed to each other. This has been a means for the same 'mask' to manipulate conflicts and wars, and to direct science, politics and religion to advance the Agenda.

The structure was now in place to press the button on the next stage of the plan. The reptile-Aryan control of Africa, Australia, New Zealand and, their biggest prize of all, America.

■ SOURCES

1   *The Occult Conspiracy*, p 51.

2   Michael Baigent and Richard Leigh, *The Temple And The Lodge* (Arcade Publishing, New York, 1989), p 106.

3   *Holy Blood, Holy Grail*, p 446-447.

4   Ibid.

5   Ibid, p 141.

6   Gerard de Sede has produced a series of books, *L'Or de Rennes* (Paris 1967); *La Race Fabuleuse* (Paris 1973); *Le Vrai Dossier de l'Enigme de Rennes* (Vestric 1975); *Les Templiers Sont Parmi Nous* (Paris 1976); and *Signe: Rose + Croix* (Paris 1977).

7   *The Occult Conspiracy*, p 47.

8   Ibid, p 74.

9   Manly P. Hall, *The Secret Teachings Of All Ages*.

10   *The Curse Of Ignorance*, Volume II, p 30.

11   Ibid, p 32.

12   *The Occult Conspiracy*, pp 51–52.

13   George C. Andrews, *Extra-Terrestrials Among Us* (Llewellyn Publications, St Paul, Minnesota, USA, 1993), p 76.

14   *The Secret Teachings Of All Ages*, pp CLXV–CLXVIII.

15   Ibid.

16   Ibid.

17   Ibid.

18   *The Templar Revelation*, p 137.

19   *The Secret Teachings Of All Ages*, p CLXVI.

20   Ibid, p CLXV.

21   Ibid, p CLXVI.

22   Ibid, p CLXVI.

23   Ibid, p CLXX1V.

24   Ibid.

25   Ibid.

26   *The Occult Conspiracy*, p 17.

27   *The Curse Of Ignorance*, Volume II, p 219.

28   *The Curse Of Canaan*, p 44.

29   Frederick J. Pohl, *Prince Henry Sinclair – His Expedition To The New World In 1398* (Nimbus Publishing, Halifax, Novia Scotia, originally published 1967), p 18.

30   Ibid.

31 *The Temple And The Lodge*, p 119.

32 Ibid, p 120.

33 Ibid.

34 Quoted in *The Curse Of Canaan*, p 83.

35 Ibid, p 83.

36 Ibid, p 84.

37 *The Temple And The Lodge*, p 187.

38 Ibid, p 189.

39 *The Curse Of Canaan*, p 40.

40 *The Templar Revelation*, p 139.

41 Ibid, pp 139, 140

42 *The Occult Conspiracy*, p 56.

43 Ian T. Taylor, *In The Minds Of Men – Darwin And The New World Order* (TFE Publishing, Toronto, Canada, 1984), p 55. An excellent expose of the scam called 'science'.

44 Ibid, p 58.

45 Ibid, p 55.

46 Ibid, pp 59–65.

47 From a work called his Essay in 1878.

48 *In The Minds Of Men*, p 63.

49 Ibid, p 29.

CHAPTER NINE

Land of the 'free'

The most powerful country on the planet today would appear to be the United States of America if you believe what you are told. But the United States has always been controlled from London and still is. America has never been the land of the free and it's time it was.

The focus of the world has been on big, bad America, as the global villain while all the time the events blamed on Americans have been orchestrated by the Elite of the Babylonian Brotherhood in England and elsewhere. The apparent break up of the British Empire and Britain's decline, on the surface, as the super power, has further obscured, on purpose, where the real power lies. I emphasise that by London I do not mean the British Government which is just another facade no matter who is in office. I mean that for historical and other reasons the major operational centre of the secret society web of the reptile Brotherhood is based in London or New Troy and, to a large extent, Paris, Brussels and Rome, also. Once again, to understand what has happened in the United States we have to go back a very long time. The Phoenicians landed there in ancient times and what appeared to be Egyptian (Phoenician) or Oriental remains were found in the Grand Canyon in the early years of this century, although the knowledge of this has been suppressed. The naming of the US city of Phoenix in the Valley of the Sun in Arizona was inspired by an understanding of the true history of that area, no matter what the official version may wish us to believe. There is evidence that the Welsh, Irish, English and Scots landed in North America many centuries before Columbus.

The official story that Christopher Columbus discovered the Americas is ludicrous. A few miles from Edinburgh in Scotland today still stands Rosslyn Chapel, that holy grail of the Brotherhood Elite. It was built in the shape of a Templar cross by the St Clair-Sinclair family and is a mass of esoteric symbolism. The foundations were laid in 1446 and it was completed in the 1480s. How remarkable then that the stonework at Rosslyn includes depictions of sweetcorn and cacti which were only found in America and Christopher Columbus did not 'discover' that continent until 1492! How could this be? There is, in fact, no mystery. Christopher Columbus was not even nearly the first white person to land in the Americas. The Phoenicians, Norse, Irish, Welsh, Bretons, Basques and Portuguese, all sailed to America before him and so did Prince Henry Sinclair of Rosslyn, as documented in a rare book by Frederick J. Pohl called *Prince Henry Sinclair's Voyage To The New World 1398*. Sinclair made the journey with another Brotherhood bloodline, the Zeno family, one of the most prominent Black Nobility families in Venice. Sinclair and Antonio Zeno landed in what we call Newfoundland and went ashore in Nova Scotia (New Scotland) in 1398. Antonio's descriptions in his letters of the land they found correspond perfectly, and in detail, with an area of pitch (asphalt) deposits in Pictou County, Nova Scotia, not far from the present town of New Glasgow. Sinclair went on to land in what is now New England. In Massachusetts at a place called Prospect Hill at Westford, 25 miles from Boston, a representation of a sword and an armoured knight have been found in the rock. T. C. Lethbridge, the curator of the University Museum of Archaeology and Ethnology at Cambridge, England, said that the arms, armour and heraldic emblems were those of a late 14th century knight, north Scottish, and: "a kin to the first Sinclair, Earl of Orkney".[1] The Brotherhood had known about the Americas for thousands of years and Christopher Columbus was used to make the official discovery so that the occupation of the Americas could begin. This is the story of how it was done.

After the purge of 1307, many Templars left France for Scotland, as we have seen. But others headed for Portugal where they operated under the name, the Knights of Christ, focusing mainly on maritime activities. The most famous Grand Master of the Knights of Christ was Prince Henry the Navigator (another Prince Henry) who lived between 1394 and 1460. The term 'navigator' or 'nautier' was used by the Knights Templar and the Priory of Sion to denote a Grand Master and so not surprisingly it was continued by this Templar front, the Knights of Christ. Prince Henry was a maritime explorer of royal blood and it was his sailors who 'discovered' Madeira and the Azores, two possible remnants of Atlantis. Because of his connections to the secret Brotherhood knowledge, he had access to many maps compiled from the journeys of the Phoenicians and others, including those which charted the existence of the Americas. Only a little over 20 years after Columbus set sail for the Americas, sorry 'India', the Ottoman Turkish Admiral, Piri Reis, drew a map of what the land mass of Antarctica looked like 300 years before that continent was officially discovered! The accuracy of his map has been confirmed by modern techniques. How could he do that? He said he drew the map from earlier ones, the same sources available to Prince Henry the Navigator and the Knights of Christ – Knights Templar. This becomes extremely important when you realise that one of Prince Henry's sea captains and a Knight of Christ was the father-in-law of... Christopher Columbus. This guy was not looking for India. He knew where he was going all along. This is why so many maritime explorers and circumnavigators of the world, like Vasco de Gama and Amerigo Vespucci, came from Portugal. As the Freemasonic historian, Manly P. Hall, has explained, Columbus was connected to the secret society network in Genoa and northern Italy, the bastion of the Black Nobility Venetian-Phoenicians and the reptilian crossbreeds. He was at one time employed by Rene d'Anjou of the reptilian House of Lorraine, a member of the Babylonian Brotherhood and a nobleman with endless contacts across Europe, including Genoa and Venice. Columbus (real name Colon) was a member of a group inspired by the beliefs of the poet, Dante, who was a very active Cathar and Templar and the flag Columbus flew on his ships on that journey to the Americas was... the red cross on the white background. Crucial support for Columbus came from two high initiates of the Babylon Brotherhood network, Lorenzo de Medici, one of the most powerful Venetian reptilian families, and the artist Leonardo da Vinci, a Grand Master of the Priory of Sion.

Five years after Columbus landed in the Caribbean, an Italian known as John Cabot set sail from the Templar port of Bristol in the west of England to officially discover Newfoundland, Nova Scotia, and North America. The name Bristol evolved from Barati and was once called Caer Brito. Bristol was a centre for the Knights Templar and the area of the city today called Temple Meads relates to that. Cabot was backed by England's Henry VII and Cabot's son, Sebastian, born in Venice, was an explorer and map maker for Henry. Sebastian also sailed to the Hudson Bay in Canada and led an expedition for the Spanish to South America. The Cabots said they were looking for Asia! The expeditions of the Spanish to South America and the British and French to North America were all coordinated by the same source, branches of the Brotherhood. Official history does not connect Cabot with Columbus, but not through lack of evidence. John Cabot's real name was Giovanni Caboto. He was a naturalised Venetian who came from Genoa – the very city where Columbus operated from at the same time Cabot was there. Manly P. Hall, a high degree Freemason himself, said that both were connected to the same secret societies and 'Wise Men of the East'. He adds in his book, *America's Assignment With Destiny*:

> "The explorers who opened the New World operated from a master plan and were agents of re-discovery rather than discoverers. Very little is known about the origin, lives, characters, and policies of these intrepid adventurers. Although they lived in a century amply provided with historians and biographers, these saw fit either to remain silent or to invent plausible accounts without substance."[2]

Of course they did. They didn't want the people to know the truth that it was all a scam and part of the long term Brotherhood Agenda. Over the next four centuries the Brotherhood-controlled countries of Europe, particularly Britain, but also including the Dutch, French, Belgians, Spanish, Portuguese, Germans and others, plundered the planet, taking over the world, in effect, and expanded the reptile-Aryan control as never before. Typical of the mentality and the methods employed were those of Hernando Cortes, who led the Spanish takeover of Central America after Columbus. The native peoples had their own system of measuring time and they had a date on which they expected the return of their god, Quetzalcoatl, in many ways their version of Jesus. The stories told about Jesus in the Middle East and Europe and those of Quetzalcoatl in Central America were basically the same because they came from the same source. The date of the expected second coming of the white god, Quetzalcoatl, was, in European time, 1519 and they believed that he would be wearing attire in keeping with his nickname of the Plumed Serpent. Cortes went ashore in Mexico in 1519 wearing plumed feathers and he even landed close to the spot where Quetzacoatl was expected. He was also carrying a cross, again in keeping with the Quetzalcoatl legend. Because of this, the Aztec king, Montezuma, believed, like his people, that Cortes was the long awaited return of their god. This allowed Cortes, with only 598 men, to gain control of a vast number of people. By the time they realised that Cortes was no second coming, it was too late. Enormous slaughter of the native peoples followed and one Spanish historian estimated at least 12 million natives of South America alone were killed after the Europeans (Aryans and reptile-Aryans) arrived and an even greater number became slaves. Among the Spanish conquests were the lands of the Incas and the Maya and much of their knowledge was lost or systematically destroyed. The same happened in North America where the Europeans killed untold numbers of Native Americans and virtually wiped that culture from the face of the Earth. The native peoples of Africa, Australia, New Zealand, and elsewhere suffered a similar fate. The Aryans, unknowingly controlled by the reptile-Aryans, took over the world through these British and European empires and wherever they went the knowledge of life and history (ie, the reptilian involvement in human affairs) was stolen or destroyed. One of the most obvious earlier examples of this was the destruction of the great esoteric library at Alexandria in Egypt on the orders of the Romans in the 4th century. Books that were not destroyed were hoarded in the Vatican. The contact who has relatives working at high levels in the Vatican told me how, during his guided tour of the place, he saw vacuum-sealed vaults under the building which housed thousands of ancient esoteric books. "It was unbelievable", he said.

The first permanent English settlement in what became the United States was at Jamestown, Virginia, in the early 17th century. Virginia, it is said, was named after Elizabeth I, the completely misnamed 'virgin queen'. It is far more likely, however, given the background, that it was named after the virgin goddess of ancient Babylon, Queen Semiramis and her mirror in Egypt, Isis. Many members of the Francis Bacon family were among the early settlers and so were the Puritan-Calvinists in their black clothing and tall hats who treated the native population, like their own women, with an arrogance and inhumanity beyond description. With the settlers, as the Brotherhood expanded their occupation of the planet, came the reptilian bloodlines of the European aristocracy and royalty who would become the business leaders, bankers, presidents and administrators of the new United States. The financial and land ownership of America was assured from the start with the formation of the Virginia Company, set up by King James I in 1606. James knighted Francis Bacon and appointed him to many important positions, including Lord Chancellor of England. Under James's patronage, the Templars, Rosicrucians and other secret societies joined forces under one name, Freemasonry. Look at some of the early members of the Virginia Company – Francis Bacon, Earl of Pembroke, Earl of Montgomery, Earl of Salisbury, Earl of Northampton, and Lord Southampton. All of them of Brotherhood bloodlines. The Virginia Company still exists under other names and it still controls the United States, as I shall explain in a moment.

The Freemasons were at the forefront of the change from overt to covert rule by Britain of the North American continent. This transition is known by history as the American War of Independence. The Brotherhood Agenda for America was encapsulated in Francis Bacon's work, *The New Atlantis*, published in 1607, in which an 'Invisible College' of élite intellectuals dictated events. One of the leading Freemasons of the British colonies in America was Benjamin Franklin, who is still revered as a Founding Father who believed in freedom for the people. His face can be seen on the $100 note. Even the Christian patriot movement which has understood many elements of the global conspiracy, has bought the idea that Franklin would have been on their side. I beg, most strongly, to disagree. Franklin was an asset of British Intelligence, a Satanist, stalwart of the Babylonian Brotherhood, and sacrificer of children. If Americans are not to lose the plot here they need to take a whole new look at the background and motivations of many of their Founding Fathers. Franklin was the Henry Kissinger of his day. It was Franklin who, on December 8th 1730, printed the first documented article about Freemasonry in his newspaper, *The Pennsylvania Gazette*. He officially became a Freemason in February 1731, and was made Provincial Grand Master of Pennsylvania in 1734. In the same year Franklin printed the first Masonic book in America and the first recorded American lodge was founded in his province in Philadelphia. Where was the American War of 'Independence' orchestrated from? Philadelphia and there you will still find the Liberty Bell – symbol of Bel, the Sun god of the Phoenicians and the Aryans. The Phoenician language is about sound, not spelling, and integral to the secret, symbolic language of the reptile-Aryans is the sound of a word. Franklin, who was also a Rosicrucian Grand Master, was at the heart of the Brotherhood operation to take over America and replace overt control from London with covert control, the most effective and ongoing form of ruling the masses. I would urge those who think that people like Franklin and many other Founding Fathers were believers in freedom, not to be duped here. If I want you to give me power and support me at an election, am I going to tell you what you want to hear or what I know you don't want to hear? Many of the main Founding Fathers, like Franklin and Jefferson, were obvious hypocrites who said one thing and did quite another. This is something, of course, that everyone does from time to time, but we are talking scale here. Jefferson wrote that all men are created equal while keeping 200 black slaves and writing elsewhere that black people are genetically and intellectually inferior to whites. How do you square those statements? You can't. Franklin, too, kept black slaves while parroting on about freedom.

Franklin was the leading Freemason in the very place where the War of Independence was organised; he was a member of Freemasonic networks in France, like the Nine Sisters and the San Juan Lodges, which helped to manipulate the French Revolution in 1789; he was an initiate of the highly exclusive Royal Lodge of Commanders of the Temple West of Carcassonne; he was also a member of the Satanic Hellfire Club with his close friend, the British Chancellor of the Exchequer, Sir Francis Dashwood, who was linked to many esoteric groups, including the Druid Universal Bond. Dashwood had a huge cave dug at his West Wycombe (Wicca) estate for their Satanic rituals and sexual 'magic' ceremonies.[3] I will discuss the reasons behind the obsession with sex ritual in a later chapter. Let me stress again here that I am not condemning all Druids or the Wiccan traditions, not at all.

I am pointing out the malevolent use of this knowledge, which can, and is, used very positively and lovingly also by people who call themselves Druids and Wiccan. The reason I mention that people were Druids etc, is to confirm that they understood and worked with the esoteric knowledge while condemning it in public and hiding behind Christianity. Another Hellfire Club member at this time was Frederick, the Prince of Wales, and so were the Prime Minister, the First Lord of the Admiralty, and the Mayor of the City of London.[4] This was the company kept by Benjamin Franklin, the man who would lead a 'rebellion' against the same British Crown! In truth he was agent 72 of British Intelligence, the very same organisation created by people like Francis Bacon and Dr John Dee during the reign of Elizabeth I. In 1998 excavations under Franklin's former home at 36 Craven Street, near Trafalgar Square in London, found the remains of ten bodies, six of them children, and they have been dated to the time that Franklin lived there. The cover story appears to be that he and his house mate must have been into grave robbing or buying bodies for medical research. Given that Franklin was a member of a group involved in ritual sacrifice, in line with the ancient rituals of the Babylonian Brotherhood, does anyone seriously believe that? Oh yes, one other thing. It was these two Satanists, Benjamin Franklin and Sir Francis Dashwood, who produced a prayer book which became the basis for the Christian Book of Common Prayer! As Dashwood was also known as Lord le DeSpencer, their work became known as the Franklin-DeSpencer Prayer Book and, in the United States, it was the Franklin Prayer Book.[5] Franklin was working in both America and Europe for the Brotherhood Agenda as were other Founding Fathers, and it is no accident that both Franklin and Jefferson were appointed at different times to represent American interests in that key centre, Paris, as was Sir Francis Bacon as a 'British' representative. It was Franklin's close contacts with the secret society network in France which led to so many French revolutionaries and Freemasons, like Lafayette, being involved in the American War of Independence. His underground contacts also secured the services of the German Freemason, Baron von Streube, who served in the army of Frederick of Prussia. Streube played a significant role in the war, as, of course, did the high degree Freemason, George Washington, the head of the American forces, and the first President of the United States. Most of his officers were Freemasons, as were the leaders and many of the troops in the British armies.

Lord Geoffrey Amherst was Commander-in-Chief of British forces in the War of Independence and the man who paid for his commission to become an officer in the first place, was Lionel Sackville, the first Duke of Dorset, an associate of the Duke of Wharton. In 1741, Sackville and Wharton became Knights of the Garter, the Elite chivalric order of the British monarch which slots into the other 'knights' networks like the Knights of St John of Jerusalem (Malta). The symbol of the Knights of the Garter is a red cross on a white shield. Sackville founded the Grand Orient network of Freemasonry in Italy which worked with the highly secretive Carbonari and the Alta Vendita. His sons, George and Charles the Earl of Middlesex, were both very active Freemasons. Charles Sackville formed a lodge in the Black Nobility stronghold of Florence, Italy in 1733 and he cofounded the Dilettanti Society with

Benjamin Franklin's friend, Sir Francis Dashwood. Charles Sackville and Dashwood were members of an Elite group of Freemasons around Frederick, Prince of Wales, a member of the Hellfire Club. Charles' younger brother, George, became colonel of the 20th Foot Regiment (later the Lancashire Fusiliers) and Master of their Freemasonic field lodge. One of the wardens in this lodge was Lieutenant Colonel Edward Cornwallis, another of the top British Army commanders in the war with the American colonies. Cornwallis, who's twin brother was Archbishop of Canterbury, was made Governor of Nova Scotia in 1750 and formed a Freemasons lodge there. Serving under Cornwallis was Captain James Wolf, yet another figure who would play a vital role for the British in the War of Independence. In 1751, George Sackville became Grand Master of the Irish Grand Lodge, the very body to which the field lodges of the British Army in the colonies were affiliated. And in 1775, just as the war in America was getting into full swing, this same George Sackville, a close friend of the Black Nobility's King George III, was appointed Colonial Secretary in charge of the American colonies! This was the same network to which Benjamin Franklin was connected. In short, the Babylonian Brotherhood, via the Freemasons, controlled and manipulated both sides in the American War of Independence, just as they do in every other war.

As historians have documented, the British military and naval operation during the War of Independence was incredibly inept. It wasn't that the colonies won the war, it was that the British chose to lose it. Now we can see why, and the channels through which this was made possible. Also, the British regiments were awash with Freemasonic field lodges which interlocked with their brethren in the American Army. Benjamin Franklin based himself in Paris during the crucial period and from there he could communicate easily with the French lodges and the British. Paris was also a major centre, and still is, for the British spy network. The role of British Postmaster General was traditionally one of espionage, not least because you had control of all communications. Britain split the job between two people, Sir Francis Dashwood, Franklin's fellow Satanist, and the Earl of Sandwich who, with Dashwood, formed yet another secret society called the Order of St Francis. This was another Hellfire Club. The Earl of Sandwich was appointed First Lord of the Admiralty in charge of the naval war against the American colonies and the Encyclopaedia Britannica says that for corruption and incapacity, the administration of the Earl of Sandwich was unique in the history of the British Navy. Equally inept (on purpose) was the commander of naval operations, Admiral Lord Richard Howe, who had been brought together with Franklin in 1774 by Franklin's sister, a member of his spy network who lived in England. Howe later admitted publicly that he had not told his superiors of his meetings with Franklin. In the three or four years leading up to the American Declaration of Independence in 1776, Franklin spent the summer at Dashwood's estate in West Wycombe, north of London, where they took part in 'rituals' in the specially-created caves dug on Dashwood's orders to provide the appropriate locations for their Satanism. A statue of Harpocrates, the Greek god of secrecy and silence, was to be found on the premises of the Hellfire Club depicted with a finger held to his mouth.[6] Statues of Harpocrates were often found at the entrances to temples, caves and other sites where the mysteries were performed and communicated. It was Dashwood and Franklin, himself a deputy Postmaster General for the Colonies, who coordinated the war from both sides to ensure the outcome – the covert control of the new United States by the Babylonian Brotherhood in London. A letter dated June 3rd 1778, written by John Norris, an agent of Dashwood, says that he: "Did this day Heliograph intelligence from Doctor Franklin in Paris to Wycombe."[7]

The American War of Independence broke out officially in 1775, triggered by the imposition by the British Crown of higher taxation on the colonies to meet the huge costs of the Seven Years War between Britain and France, another Brotherhood-manipulated conflict. The Seven Years War itself began after George Washington, then a young military leader in the British Colonial Army, had apparently ordered the killing of French troops in Ohio. The seeds of revolution in America were sown when the Brotherhood in London ensured that new taxes were introduced and their representatives in the colonies began to stimulate the rebellion against them. This is a classic technique used throughout the ages. The mass of the people stood in the middle with no idea of what was going on, taking everything on face value. Among the American 'rebels' were the Freemasons, Patrick Henry and Richard Henry Lee, who led a rebellion by the Virginia Assembly in 1769. The situation came to a head with the passing of the Tea Act which allowed that Brotherhood operation, the British East India Company, to unload its surplus tea in the colonies without paying duty. This clearly destroyed the market for everyone else. Official history to this day says that a group of Mohawk Indians boarded a ship called the Dartmouth in Boston Harbour and threw its cargo of tea into the water. This was dubbed: the Boston Tea Party. In fact the 'rebels' were not Mohawk Indians, but members of the St Andrew's Freemasons Lodge in Boston dressed up as Indians. They were led by their junior warden, Paul Revere. This event could not have happened without support from the British-controlled Colonial Militia who had been detailed to guard the Dartmouth. The captain of one detachment, Edward Proctor, was a member of… the St Andrew's Lodge. This lodge was the first in the world to confer a new Freemasonic degree called the Knights Templar Degree. The Grand Master, Joseph Warren, was appointed Grand Master of the whole of North America by the Grand Lodge of Scotland. Other members of the St Andrew's Lodge included John Hancock. He would be a leader of the so-called Continental Congress who signed the Declaration of Independence. At least three members of the St Andrew's Lodge, including Paul Revere, were members of the 'loyal nine', the inner élite of an important revolutionary group called the Sons of Liberty. It was this group which organised the Boston Tea Party.

Much of this information is documented by the Freemasonic historian, Manly P. Hall, who also points out that of the 56 signatories of the American Declaration of Independence, almost 50 were known Freemasons and only one was definitely known not to be. On September 3rd 1783, the colonies were recognised as an independent republic, the United States, in the appropriately named, Treaty of Paris. The new constitution was primarily produced by George Washington,

Benjamin Franklin, Edmund Randolph, Thomas Jefferson, and John Adams, at least officially. Most of the Founding Fathers who were so committed to freedom were, like Franklin and Jefferson, keen owners of slaves. Franklin owned slaves for 30 years and sold them at his general store. He placed an advertisement for a slave in 1733 which read: "A likely wench about 15 years old, has had the smallpox, been in the country above a year, and talks English. Inquire the printer hereof." George Washington owned slaves as did other big names in the War of Independence like John Hancock and Patrick Henry. It was Henry who said: "Give me liberty or give me death." Unless your face is black, that is. In all, nine presidents were slave owners and one, Andrew Johnson, placed an advertisement seeking the recapture of a runaway slave and offering an extra ten dollars for every 100 lashes the captor gave the slave. Edmund Randolph, a close associate and aide to George Washington, and later Grand Master of the Grand Lodge of Virginia, was appointed the first Attorney General and Secretary of State of the United States. It was Randolph who proposed a system of central government based on the structure long proposed by the 'Invisible College' and the Francis Bacon network.

Most Americans believe the Constitution was compiled to ensure freedom, but it was carefully worded to create loopholes through which the Brotherhood Agenda could be ridden. For a start it says that if the President vetoes a bill passed by Congress the legislation goes back to the House of Representatives and the Senate and to override the presidential veto it has to be voted through again by a majority of at least two-thirds in both houses. This means that you only have to control the President and one third of one house and you stop any legislation becoming law. What more powerful weapon could you have within a 'free' society to defend your status quo and stop challenges to your power? Patriots believe that the creation of money by the private banks is unconstitutional in the United States because the Constitution says that Congress must create the currency. But it doesn't say that. Article One, Section 8, says that: "Congress shall have the power to coin money and regulate the value thereof." It does not say (on purpose) that *only* Congress shall have that power, nor that they have to use that power. Section 10 says that no State shall coin money and that gold and silver coins shall be the only payment of debts. So paper money must be unconstitutional? No. An area of Maryland was given to the new Congress to create the *District*, not the State, of Columbia for the new federal capital called Washington DC. Within this district is the privately-owned central bank of America, the Federal Reserve, which issues the nations paper currency. The District of Columbia is effectively isolated from many of clauses in the Constitution which apply to the States. The main Founding Fathers would have known that.

The first President was George Washington who sat in a chair with a rising Sun carved into the back, an ancient symbol of the Aryan Sun religion. He was Grand Master of the Freemasons Lodge at Alexandria (named after its Egyptian namesake) near Washington DC. When he was inaugurated as President on April 30th 1789, the day before the major Brotherhood ritual day, May 1st or May Day, the oath was taken by Robert Livingstone, the Grand Master of the New York Grand Lodge. The ceremony was entirely Freemasonic ritual carried out by Freemasons. A Grand

Procession included Washington and the officers and initiates of American lodges in their regalia. Like most of the leading Founding Fathers, Washington was from an English aristocratic bloodline and one of his ancestors was an English knight of the 12th century, the time the Templars were formed, and another was a relative of the Duke of Buckingham who had fought for the Crown in the English Civil War. Washington was only the first example of how the Babylonian Brotherhood based in Britain has used its reptilian bloodlines to rule the United States from that day to this. Look at the genealogy of American presidents, leading politicians, banking and business tycoons, military leaders, media owners, government officials, intelligence agency chiefs, etc, etc, and you will find they come from the same bloodlines which can be charted back to the British and European royal and aristocratic (reptile-Aryan) families and their origins in the Middle and Near East at the time of Sumer and Babylon. Two examples: At least 33 of the first 42 presidents of the United States have been related to England's King Alfred the Great (849–899) and Charlemagne (742–814), the famous monarch of France, and 19 Presidents are related to England's King Edward III (1312–1377), who has a thousand blood connections to Prince Charles. George Bush and Barbara Bush are both from the same British aristocratic line, among others. They come from the Pierce bloodline, which changed its name from Percy after fleeing England in the wake of the Gunpowder Plot to blow up the English parliament. The Bushes married for genetics, as the Eastern Establishment families in the States always have done in line with their fellow reptilian royal and aristocratic blood relatives in Europe. Even Bill Clinton and Bob Dole, who 'opposed' each other at the 1996 Presidential election, are distant cousins. They can trace their ancestry to England's King Henry III, who reigned from 1227 to 1273 during the years of Templar pre-eminence, and US Presidents, William Henry Harrison and Benjamin Harrison. This information comes from the publication, *Burkes Peerage*, which traces the lineage of royal and aristocratic families. Clinton has far more royal blood than Dole and is directly descended from the same bloodline as the House of Windsor, every Scottish monarch, and King Robert I of France. This is why he was the Brotherhood's choice. Harold Brooks-Baker, the publishing director of *Burkes Peerage*, said: "The presidential candidate with the greatest number of royal genes has always been the victor, without exception, since George Washington". What an astonishing statistic and 'royal' genes = reptilian genes. The same tribe which controlled Europe simply expanded into the Americas and called it freedom. The United States has never been free of control from London. Indeed, it was the *creation* of London. Britain and the British Crown has always owned, yes owned, the United States. If you are American and you have not heard this information before, and few have, it might be advisable to sit down quietly and have a cup of sweet tea because you are in for quite a shock.

In 1604, a group of leading politicians, businessmen, merchants, manufacturers and bankers, met in Greenwich, then in the English county of Kent, and formed a corporation called the Virginia Company in anticipation of the imminent influx of white Europeans, mostly British at first, into the North American continent. Its main stockholder was the reptilian, King James I, and the original charter for the company was completed by April 10th 1606. This and later updates to the charter established the following:

- The Virginia Company comprised of two branches, the London Company and the Plymouth or New England Company. The former was responsible for the first permanent colony in America at Jamestown on May 14th 1607 and the latter were the so-called 'Pilgrim Fathers' who arrived at Cape Cod in the ship the Mayflower, in November 1620, and went on to land in Plymouth Harbour on December 21st. The 'Pilgrims' of American historical myth were, in fact, members of the second Virginia Company branch called the New England Company.
- The Virginia Company owned most of the land of what we now call the USA, and any lands up to 900 miles offshore. This included Bermuda and most of what is now known as the Caribbean Islands. The Virginia Company (the British Crown and the bloodline families) had rights to 50%, yes 50%, of the ore of all gold and silver mined on its lands, plus percentages of other minerals and raw materials, and 5% of all profits from other ventures. These rights, the charters detailed, were to be passed on to all heirs of the owners of the Virginia Company and therefore continue to apply... forever! The controlling members of the Virginia Company who were to enjoy these rights became known as the Treasurer and Company of Adventurers and Planters of the City of London.
- After the first 21 years from the formation of the Virginia Company, all 'duties, imposts, and excises' paid on trading activities in the colonies had to be paid directly to the British Crown through the Crown treasurer. No trader could export goods out of the colonies without the permission of the British Crown and to do so would involve the seizure of all their goods and the ship or vehicle which carried them.
- The lands of the Virginia Company were granted to the colonies under a Deed of Trust (on lease) and therefore they could not claim ownership of the land. They could pass on the perpetual use of the land to their heirs or sell the perpetual use, but they could never own it. Ownership was retained by the British Crown.
- The colonial lands were to be governed by two Colonial Councils, each with 13 members (that number again), but the Kings Council in London had the final say on all decisions. The sitting British monarch also chose the Governor of the American Colonies, who we would today call the President.
- The monarch, through his Council for the Colonies, insisted that members of the colonies impose the Christian religion on all the people, including the Native Americans. To use the language of the time... "with all diligence, care and respect, do provide that the true word of God and Christian faith be preached, planted and used, not only within every of the several said colonies and plantations, but also as much as they may amongst the savage people which do or shall adjoin us to them or border upon them, according to the doctrine, rights, and religion, now professed and established within our realm of England." If the Native Americans did not accept the Christian religion, they would have to be

forced to, the Crown insisted. This was the order to destroy the culture and knowledge of the native peoples of North America and also to maintain the white colonists under the vicious yoke of Christian terrorism peddled by the Calvinist-Puritans. It was a free licence to kill, torture and kidnap the native peoples with complete immunity from prosecution.

- The criminal courts on the lands of the Virginia Company were to be operated under Admiralty Law, the law of the sea, and the civil courts under common law, the law of the land. This is a crucial point which I will come to in a second.

Now, get this. All of the above still applies today! Read those percentages once more and let the magnitude of that sink in. After the original 13 (again!) American colonies won their 'independence' and an 'independent' country was formed after 1783, the Virginia Company simply changed its name to... the United States of America. You see there are two USAs, or rather a USA and a usA. The united states of America with a lower case 'u' and 's' are the lands of the various states. These lands, as we have seen, are still owned by the British Crown as the head of the old Virginia Company, although there is something to add about this in a moment. Then there is the United States of America, capital 'U' and 'S', which is the 68 square miles of land west of the Potomac River on which is built the federal capital, Washington DC and the District of Columbia. It also includes the US protectorates of Guam and Puerto Rico. The United States of America is not a country, it is a corporation owned by the same Brotherhood reptilian bloodlines who owned the Virginia Company, because the USA *is* the Virginia Company! When Americans agree to have a social security number the citizens of the united states surrender their sovereignty and agree to become franchisees of the United States (the Virginia Company of the British Crown). So why do they do it? Because they have no idea that this is what they are doing. They are led to believe that there is only one United States and the Federal government is the rightful government. There is no law that says that Americans must pay federal income tax, but they go on paying because they think they have to. The Brotherhood-controlled Internal Revenue Service operates in such a terrorist manner that even most of those who know it's a scam still pay up because they are terrified not to. Have a sip of that sweet tea now and take a deep breath because there's more.

This means that all the rights which applied to the owners of the Virginia Company to the gold, silver, minerals and duties, mined and paid in America, still apply to the British families who own the United States of America and the lands of the united states of America. Those same percentages have been paid since 'independence' and are still being paid by the American people via their federal officials who are, in fact, officials of the Virginia Company – yes, including the President. The British Crown owns the lands of the united states and the land and institutions of the United States, including the Internal Revenue Service which collects the taxation and the Federal Reserve Board, the privately owned 'central bank' of America which lends the government money that doesn't exist and charges the taxpayers interest on it. The Federal Reserve Board is owned by the same

Brotherhood families in Britain and Europe who own the rest of America. But here's yet another twist. Who owns the assets apparently owned by the Virginia Company? Answer: the Vatican. On October 3rd 1213, King John, as 'King of England Corporation Sole' claimed autonomy over all the sovereign rights of England and assigned them to the Pope, who, as Vicar of Christ, claimed dominion over the whole world. In return, the Pope granted executiveship to the English Crown over all these dominions. In other words, the Crown is the chief executive and the Vatican is the owner, although, of course, the true owner is whoever controls the Vatican. This is why I keep saying that London is the centre of the operational level of the Brotherhood. Even greater power lies elsewhere, some of it in the Vatican, and, ultimately, I think, on the physical level, somewhere under the ground in Tibet and Asia. The people of America have been bled dry by this scam and continue to be so. Land of the Free? What a joke! And, people of America, your presidents and leading government officials know this. In turn, it must be stressed, the King John agreement with the Pope presumably gave away the sovereignty of England, also. And who controlled King John? The Templars did.

When you know what you are looking for, the truth is in your face. I said that the Virginia Company and King James I decreed that criminal courts in the colonies would be controlled by Admiralty Law, the law of the sea. What Admiralty were they talking about? The British Admiralty, of course. When a court is being run under Admiralty or maritime law, the flag in the court has to have a gold fringe around it. Look in any criminal court in the United States or the united states and you will see it has a gold fringe. The same with many other official buildings. Those 'American' criminal courts are being run under BRITISH admiralty law. The Crown and the Brotherhood families of Britain also control the American criminal courts and the core of that control is with the secret societies based in Temple Bar in London, the former Templar lands, the centre of the British legal profession. The Grand Lodge of English Freemasonry is in Great Queen (Isis/Semiramis) Street in London and has controlled most Freemasonry across the globe since it was formed in 1717. Through this, the British reptile-Aryans control the American judges, lawyers, police, and so on, and through other organisations, like the Council on Foreign Relations and the Trilateral Commission, they manipulate the American political system. The American judges are fully aware that their courtrooms are controlled by British Admiralty Law, but they keep quiet and take the money. The Rockefeller family are the bloodline branch managers in America for the London headquarters and it is the Rockefellers who, quite provably, decide who is going to be President. In other words, the London Elite decide. The Queen of England, Prince Philip and the main members of the British royal family all know this and are helping to orchestrate it. Who is the Grand Master of the English Mother Lodge of Freemasonry? The Queen's cousin, the Duke of Kent.

But there is also a French connection to this. There usually is with London and Paris the main operational centres for the Brotherhood. Many times the French and English wings have battled for supremacy, but they are still, in the end, two sides of the same coin. The French Revolution of 1789 (the year George Washington became the first US President) was wholly engineered by the Freemasons and their offshoot, the Bavarian Illuminati. The background to all this is detailed in *...And The Truth Shall Set You Free*. After the 'revolutionaries' executed Queen Marie Antoinette, her son, Crown Prince Louis, still a toddler, was placed under house arrest at the Paris Temple. Two years later he was smuggled out in a laundry basket by his doctor, Dr Naudin. The retarded nephew of the Marquis de Jarjayes was substituted and he died in 1795. The prince was secretly taken to the Vendee Palace and given sanctuary by Prince Conde. He was later moved to a fortress on the River Rhine where he lived under the name of Baron de Richemont. He arrived in England in February 1804 with the former royal paymaster of France, George Payseur, and was protected by King George III, the monarch at the time of the American War of Independence. The Prince changed his name again to Daniel Payseur while George Payseur became George Bayshore. King George III gave the prince, now Daniel Payseur, a ship and awarded George Bayshore 600 acres of land in North Carolina. When they arrived in America they were given help by the Boddie family, who were related to the British monarchy. Before leaving England, the prince bought shares in the Virginia Company and once in America he acquired gold mines, including the Gold Hill Mining Company, which he purchased secretly using a trustee, George Newman, as his frontman or proxy. With the invention of the steam engine, Payseur began to build railroads and leased them to operating companies. He also established the Lancaster Manufacturing Company to produce timber for railroad products and the Lincolnton Iron Company which later located in Chicago and formed two subsidiaries, Carnegie Steel and Pullman Standard Company. To provide fuel for locomotives (or so it was said), the Federal Government (the Virginia Company of which Payseur was a shareholder) allocated all land extending 100 feet either side of the tracks. Much larger areas of land alongside the railroads were also broken up into sections some ten miles square and half of these were given to Payseur who also bought up many others. Thus he and the railroads owned some of America's prime real estate. Much of this legislation is in the 1854 Congressional Record. The Payseurs' Lancaster Railway was, through the Alabama Mineral Company, the controller of Coca Cola, Pepsi Cola, General Motors, Boeing, Ford and Standard Oil.

After the manipulated American Civil War in the 1860s, all railroads and real estate owned by the supporters of the losers, the southern Confederates, were confiscated and auctioned off at Wilmington, North Carolina. They were bought by nine trustees of Daniel Payseur at extremely low prices. A deed of trust was signed in Nashville between the railroad owners and the government establishing the United States Military Railroad system which granted the developers a monopoly over transport and communications. All these agreements still apply. Payseur's chief trustee and general manager was a Rothschild relative called Leroy Springs, formerly Leroy Springstein. It appears that Leroy Springs was a half brother to the American President, Abraham Lincoln. A lady called Nancy Hanks gave birth to a son in 1808 after an affair with Springs' father. In his will his father left a large area of land in Huntsville, Alabama, to a son, Abraham Lincoln. Rumours that Lincoln was a Rothschild would appear to have a basis in fact. In the 1850s Lincoln's own affair with a daughter of the German monarch Leopold in 1856, produced twin girls, Ella and Emily. One of the descendants of this line was the billionaire, Howard Hughes. Many of the famous American families who appeared to be powerful in their own right turn out to have been leg-men for Payseur and the Virginia Company. Andrew Carnegie was a young employee at a Payseur steelworks who was used to front another company which Payseur called Carnegie Steel. The Vanderbilt family claim that a mansion called Biltmore is their country home. Not true. Biltmore was constructed by the Payseur family as a hotel in the 1880s and it was operated by the Payseur trustees, the Vanderbilts, on a 99 year lease. Another Payseur trustee was J. P. Morgan, one of the most famous industrialists and bankers in American history. He was yet another face behind which those truly in control could hide the extent of their power.

Many of the major oil and mineral deposits in the US are on land owned by the railroad companies, and Payseur's mineral rights were transferred to petrol and mining companies in exchange for a controlling shareholding. Other rights were leased to timber companies. After Daniel Payseur died in 1860, his fantastic empire was managed by his grandson, Lewis Cass Payseur, and the expansion continued apace. In 1872, a Payseur company, the Charleston, Cincinnati and Chicago Railroad, established a telegraph company called Western Union. It formed a subsidiary called AT and T in 1875 and today it is one of America's biggest telephone and communication companies. The Charleston, Cincinnati and Chicago Railroad company is the parent company for the Federal Reserve, the privately owned 'central bank' of the United States. The Payseur empire became heavily involved in banking. Their Bank of Lancaster became the North Carolina Bank and then Nationsbank. The biggest bank in Texas, Interfirst, of which George Bush is a director, merged in 1987 with Republic Bank to form First Republic. This was later absorbed by Nationsbank which then merged with the Bank of America. These two launder CIA drug money and that's appropriate because the forerunner to the CIA, the OSS or Office of Strategic Services, was created from the Payseurs' own security network which was formed by the Selma, Rome and Dalton Railroad to protect the Military Railroad System. It's all wheels within wheels, family within family, and Americans have not a clue who really runs their lives and their country. The question is who controlled the Payseurs?

The Payseur family have now lost control of their empire, but the same reptilian tribe are still at the helm. The Payseur's principal trustee, Leroy Springs, died in 1931 and his playboy son, Elliot, took over. He volunteered to upgrade the local County Records filing system and removed the records from the Lancaster courthouse. When he returned them, hundreds of Payseur land deeds had been re-assigned to Elliot Springs, a Rothschild relative. It seems obvious that he was told exactly what to do to stop the Payseur daughters inheriting the empire. In the early 1950s, Anne, the daughter of Elliot Springs, married a New Jersey organised crime figure called Hugh Close and Close was appointed chairman of all the Payseur companies stolen by Elliot Springs. Close's daughter, Mrs Crandall Close Bowles, became a director of the Carolina Federal Reserve Bank. A battle continues for control of the former Payseur holdings, but at the moment it appears they are controlled by the Rothschilds. Some people who think they own land they have purchased from the railroad companies are going to be very disappointed. Their deeds are not legal because the land was not the railroad companies' to sell. It was leased from the Payseur empire. In the end, it is owned by the Virginia Company.

Franklin Delano Roosevelt, the Brotherhood President of the United States during the Second World War, said that nothing ever happens by accident in politics. If it happens, it is meant to happen. So it is with all the major events that have advanced the Agenda towards the centralisation of global power, be they wars, economic collapses, assassinations or 'scandals' to remove politicians who are not playing the game. The three major wars on American soil have been the war with the native Americans after the whites first arrived, the War of 'Independence' and the Civil War when the states of the south sought to withdraw from the union in 1860. We have seen that the wars with the native Americans and the War of Independence were engineered by the Brotherhood and the same is true of the Civil War also. Leading Freemasons from all over Europe attended six Masonic festivals in Paris between 1841 and 1845 and it was at six secret Supreme Council meetings held under the cover of these events that the American Civil War was planned to further impose Masonic, reptile-Aryan, control on America. Lord Palmeston, the British Foreign Secretary and Prime Minister, and a Grand Patriarch of Freemasonry, was at the heart of these conspiracies.[8] Two 33rd degree Freemasons of the Scottish Rite were chosen to manipulate the conflict. They were Caleb Cushing, who worked in the north among the unionists, and Albert Pike, the Sovereign Grand Commander of the Southern Jurisdiction of the Scottish Rite, who organised the southern rebellion.[9] Ironically, but highly appropriately, the funding for the southern rebellion was arranged through London Masonic bankers by Cushing, who was operating in the north![10] Pike, a Satanist who believed in the Aryan (reptile-Aryan) Master Race, enlisted the help of Giuseppe Mazzini, the head of the Italian Grand Orient Freemasonry, out of which emerged the infamous organised crime operation called the Mafia. In 1851, Mazzini started to establish groups across America which began to campaign against slavery. The Freemasons used these groups as the cover for the true motivation behind the Civil War. 'Young America' lodges were organised to do this and their headquarters was at the Cincinnati Lodge No 133. Their main funding came from the British Freemasonic banker and Rothschild frontman called George Peabody and he appointed J. P. Morgan senior to handle the funds in America. Morgan, you'll recall, was a stooge for Daniel Payseur. See how the same names keep coming up wherever you look.

Franklin Pierce (the bloodline of George and Barbara Bush) was elected President in 1853 and Mazzini wrote that: "almost all his nominations are such as we desired."[11] One of these 'nominations' was the appointment by Pierce of Caleb Cushing as his Attorney General. Cushing was controlled by English Freemasonry and connected to the British opium trade to China through his ship-owner father and his cousin, John Perkins Cushing. Caleb Cushing wrote extensively against slavery and became the architect, with Pike, of the Civil War. Pike had been a school principal in Cushing's home town of Newburyport, Massachusetts, but he was living in Little Rock, Arkansas, the later home of Bill Clinton, when his Masonic career began to flourish and indeed, soar. A crucial Elite group behind the Civil War was the Knights of the Golden Circle, again based in Cincinnati, Ohio. One of their number was the infamous outlaw, Jesse James, a 33rd degree Mason assigned by Albert Pike to rob banks in the north to further fund the war. Another Knight of the Golden Circle was the Freemason, General P. T. Beauregard, who started the Civil War with an attack on Fort Sumter in 1861. One of the most famous voices against slavery was John Brown, who became a legend through the song about 'John Brown's body'. Brown, in fact, was a member of a number of secret societies, including the Freemasons. He became a Master Mason at the Hudson Lodge No 68 in Hudson, Ohio, on May 11th 1824,[12] and was a member of Mazzini's Young America. Brown was funded by the John Jacob Astor family, another Brotherhood reptilian bloodline. With the Freemasons whipping up agitation on both sides in classic fashion, the Civil War was about to break out. In January 1857, the Freemason, John Buchanan, was elected President and appointed Freemason, John B. Floyd, as his Secretary of War. The Vice President was John C. Breckinridge, of Kentucky, who received the 33rd degree of the Scottish Rite from Albert Pike on March 28th 1860. The President of the rebel or Confederate States of the south was the Freemason, Jefferson Davis, and the first state to withdraw from the Union was South Carolina, the headquarters of Pike's Southern Jurisdiction of the Scottish Rite. Freemasons were at the head of all the other states who followed. Significantly, only eleven states seceded from the Union, but the Confederate flag had 13 stars, a sacred number to the Freemasons and the Knights Templar.

When Abraham Lincoln became President of the Northern Unionists on March 4th 1861, he was offered financial backing for the war by the same people who were funding the south, the Masonic bankers of London. There was one catch, however. Lincoln had to agree to introduce a privately-owned 'central bank' of America. One of the main reasons for the Civil War was to bankrupt America to the point where it would have to agree to allow the creation of the central bank to generate the funds needed to fight the war. But Lincoln refused and introduced a most obvious policy and one which any government today could follow if they were not all controlled by the bankers. Lincoln simply printed his own interest-free money called 'greenbacks' and used them to finance the government. President John F. Kennedy embarked on a similar policy. This is the Brotherhood bankers worst nightmare and Lincoln was assassinated on April 14th 1865, just as Kennedy was assassinated on November 22nd 1963. Lincoln's assassin was John Wilkes Booth, a 33rd degree Freemason, and a member of Mazzini's Young America.[13] He was selected by the Knights of the Golden Circle who were themselves funded by the London Freemasonic bankers. The cover up was headed by the Freemason, Edwin Stanton, who ordered blockades of all the roads out of Washington DC, except for the one that Booth used to escape. Alongside this road a drunk of similar appearance and build to Booth was murdered and his body burned in a barn. Who officially 'found' this man? Only Edwin Stanton who, of course, identified him immediately as Booth.[14] At the conspiracy trial into Lincoln's death in Indianapolis in June 1865, some of the people named as directly involved were: Lord Palmeston, the British Prime Minister and 33rd degree Freemason who died in that same year; John Wilkes Booth, 33rd degree Freemason; Judah P. Benjamin, the voice of the London Freemason bankers who ordered the assassination; and Jacob Thompson, a former Secretary for the Interior, who withdrew $180,000 from the Bank of Montreal in Canada to bankroll the operation. The Knights of the Golden Circle were also exposed and Albert Pike decided to change their name. He called them… the Ku Klux Klan, the white-robed Satanists who have terrorised the black peoples of America. Their name was taken from the Greek word, kuklos, meaning 'circle'.[15] Pike was born in Boston in 1809 and educated at Harvard University. He became Grand Commander of American Freemasonry and Grand Master of the Scottish Rite Lodge at Little Rock, Arkansas, later the lodge of one Bill Clinton. When Pike died in 1891 in Washington DC, his funeral was held in the Freemasonic Temple at midnight with the room draped entirely in black.[16] This man was a Satanist through and through. He is a Freemasonic 'god' and his statue stands near the Washington police headquarters, a short walk from Capitol Hill.

Before Lincoln died, the Freemason-controlled Congress had passed the National Banking Act of 1863 which created a federally chartered national bank with the power to issue US bank notes. These were notes lent to the government at interest by the Masonic bankers. The bankers had survived the greenbacks and the architect of that bill, Lincoln's Secretary of the Treasury, Salmon P. Chase, was such a hero that the Freemasons named one of their banks after him, the Chase Bank, now the Chase Manhattan, controlled (at least officially) by David Rockefeller. I think you will have seen by now that the great events which have divided humanity and caused constant conflict, be they wars, religions, whatever, come back to the same source and the same Agenda. What's more they interweave between the same people in a most remarkable way.

In the story I have just told of the creation of the United States, you also find a connection to the conflict in Northern Ireland. It involves a naturalist and chemist called Dr Edward Bancroft, a close friend of Benjamin Franklin, who had sponsored Bancroft's Fellowship of the Brotherhood 'science' front in London, the Royal Society.[17] Later he became private secretary to Franklin in Paris, a centre of the Brotherhood's spy network, and joined the Elite Neuf Soeurs Lodge while Franklin was its Grand Master. Bancroft led a secret mission to Ireland in 1779 and a year later Lord Stormont, the British Ambassador to France, informed the king that a secret Irish delegation had been to Paris to see King Louis XVI to propose an independent Ireland. The ambassador said that: "the delegates are all connected with Franklin…"[18] In the years that followed a Brotherhood secret society called the Society of United Irishmen was formed which involved people like Lord Edward Fitzgerald and Wolfe Tone.[19] This was behind the Irish rebellions of 1798 and 1803 and the conflict thus triggered has continued in Ireland ever since. You find the Brotherhood involved in all the major world events in history. Simon Bolivar, known as the founder of Bolivia in South America and the liberator of Venezuela, New Granada, Equador and Peru, was a member of the Cadiz Freemasons Lodge in

Spain and a master in the Nine Sisters Lodge in Paris. This was the lodge of
Benjamin Franklin, the writer Voltaire, and other French revolutionaries.[20] A lock of
George Washington's hair was sent to Bolivar, via the French and American
revolutionary, Lafayette, as a token of his esteem.[21]

America, the Land of the Free? What a joke!

■ SOURCES

1   *Prince Henry St Clair's Voyage To The New World*, p 160.

2   Manly P. Hall, *America's Assignment With Destiny, The Adepts In The Western Tradition*
     (Philosophical Research Society, Los Angeles, 1979), part five, p 50.

3   James Shelby Downard, "Sorcery, Sex, Assassination, and the Science of Symbolism", an
     article in the book, *Secret And Suppressed*, edited by Jim Keith (Feral House, PO Box 3466,
     Portland, Oregon 97208, 1993), p 62.

4   Ibid, p 61.

5   Ibid.

6   Ibid, p 62.

7   *The Temple And The Lodge*, p 238.

8   John Daniel, *Scarlet And The Beast*, Volume III, *English Freemasonry, Banks, And The Drug
     Trade* (JKI Publishing, Tyler, TX, USA), p 63.

9   Ibid.

10   Ibid, p 64.

11   Anton Chaitkin, *Treason In America*, 2nd edition (New Benjamin Franklin House, New York,
     1984), p 217.

12   *Scarlet And The Beast*, p 64.

13   Ibid, p 75.

14   Ibid.

15   Ibid, p 76.

16   *The Temple And The Lodge*, p 237.

17   Ibid.

18   Lord Stormont writing to George III, *The Correspondence Of George The Third*, Volume V,
     p 24, letter no 2952, March 1st 1780.

19   *The Temple And The Lodge*, p 238.

20   *America's Assignment With Destiny*, pp 101, 102.

21   Ibid, p 102.

The Flying Serpent statue in the centre of Temple Bar (left) in London, the former Knights Templar lands and home to some of the most important secret societies within the Babylonian Brotherhood.

The dragon and the fire cross marking the entrance to the City of London financial district (right), one of the most important centres on the planet for the Brotherhood. The red cross on the white background was a sun symbol for the Phoenicians, the logo of the Knights Templar, and is the flag of England.

A reptile statue (above) found in graves of the Ubaid people who lived in what is now Iraq up to around 4,000 BC. Mother and baby are depicted with lizard-like features. This culture predates the Venus cataclysm which probably forced the surviving reptilians underground or into another dimension.

The White Horse at Uffington in Wiltshire (below), dated at 3,000 BC, the time the Phoenicians had arrived in Britain. The white horse was a Phoenician symbol for the Sun.

Gargoyles and flying serpents (above) have been placed all over the Notre Dame Cathedral in Paris and many are smaller versions of serpent symbols found at Maya sites in Mexico. Gargoyles are symbols of the reptilians and were chosen by the Brotherhood secret societies, especially the Knights Templar, to 'decorate' endless cathedrals, churches, stately homes of the aristocratic bloodlines and other buildings.

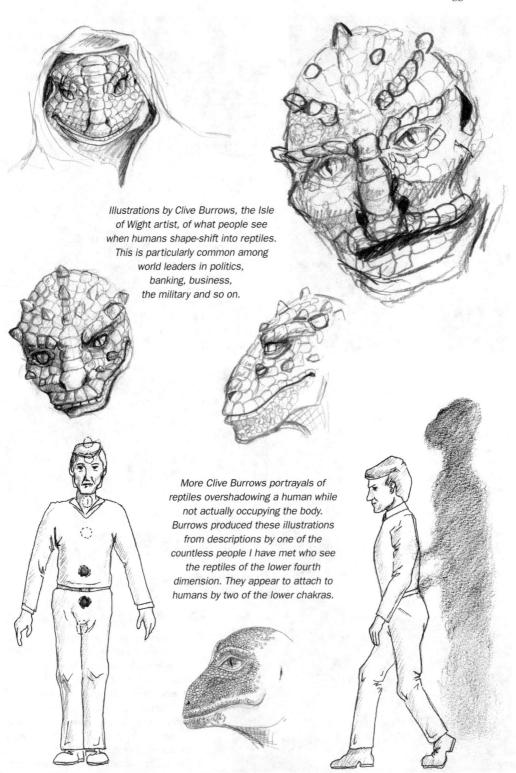

Illustrations by Clive Burrows, the Isle of Wight artist, of what people see when humans shape-shift into reptiles. This is particularly common among world leaders in politics, banking, business, the military and so on.

More Clive Burrows portrayals of reptiles overshadowing a human while not actually occupying the body. Burrows produced these illustrations from descriptions by one of the countless people I have met who see the reptiles of the lower fourth dimension. They appear to attach to humans by two of the lower chakras.

The ancient images on the wall of the temple at Saqqara, Egypt, depicting one of their 'gods'. Look at the close up of this 'god' and it correlates remarkably with the descriptions of the 'serpent race'. It even seems to me to have wings, as with the winged Draco.

Pictures courtesy of Mark Cottier and Farah Zaidi

The Pope with his 'fish head hat', a symbol of the Babylonian god-figure, Nimrod.

Doves on the sceptres of British royalty. The dove is a symbol of Queen Semiramis, Nimrod's partner in Babylon. Note also the use of Maltese crosses which were found on caves in the former Phoenician land of Cappadocia in what is now Turkey.

The Maltese Cross can also be found on the British Coronation Crown...

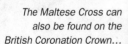

...and on the uniform of the Nazis. Hitler's fanatics also used the skull and bones, the reversed swastika (a Phoenician Sun symbol), and the eagle, a symbol which evolved from the Phoenician-Egyptian sun bird, the Phoenix.

Prince Albert, Duke of Clarence and Avondale, pictured in 1890, two years before he 'died'; and Adolf Hitler, pictured in the German army 25 years later in 1915. Are these the same men? Was Hitler the grandson of Queen Victoria? There are certainly many fascinating connections.

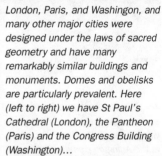

London, Paris, and Washingon, and many other major cities were designed under the laws of sacred geometry and have many remarkably similar buildings and monuments. Domes and obelisks are particularly prevalent. Here (left to right) we have St Paul's Cathedral (London), the Pantheon (Paris) and the Congress Building (Washington)...

...and (left to right) the Egyptian obelisk called Cleopatra's Needle in London, the obelisk from Luxor in the Place de la Concorde in Paris, and the Washington monument in Washington DC

The eternal flame is the classic symbol of the Babylonian Brotherhood. Here it is held by the Brotherhood hero, Prometheus (left), at the Rockefeller Centre in New York...

...it can also be seen on the Statue of Liberty on an island in New York Harbour (left), and its mirror image on an island in the River Seine in Paris (right).

The flame is used as a Brotherhood signature after their assassinations. A flame was placed on President Kennedy's grave at the Arlington Cemetery (below) and the Freemasons erected an obelisk and flame in Dealey Place (far below) close to the spot where he was murdered.

A replica of the Statue of Liberty flame placed on a black pentagram stands above the Pont de L'Alma tunnel in Paris where Diana died. An urn and flame have been placed on the island where she is 'buried'.

The Island where Diana is said to be buried in the lake at the Spencer ancestral home at Althorp Park in Northamptonshire. Islands, lakes and tree groves are all fundamental symbols in the legend of the ancient Goddess Diana.

The Arc de Triomphe, the Sun symbol centre of a massive geometric pattern in the street plan of Paris. Twelve roads feed into the 'Etoile' or star circle and the points of the Sun are even depicted on the road. The Arc is in direct line down the Champs Elysees with other arches, the Luxor obelisk in the Place de la Concorde, and the enormous black glass pyramid erected outside the Louve Museum.

President Kennedy's motorcade in Dealey Plaza at the moment he was shot on November 22nd 1963 – 656 years to the day from the time the Inquistion began its purge of the Knights Templar. Note that Kennedy's car in the foreground has no security guards, but the one behind has four! Assassinations don't just happen, they are allowed to happen.

The Pont de L'Alma Tunnel in Paris (left), the Bridge or Place of the Moon Goddess, and above the tunnel are the crossroads, the traditional domain of Hecate.

One of the 17 close circuit cameras (far right) on the route from the Ritz to the Pont de l'Alma looks down onto the entrance to the tunnel (right). It would have seen Diana's car enter and recorded any other vehicles or activity. But like all the others, it was switched off at the time.

The Mercedes (right) crumpled on impact with the 13th pillar (above) and Diana died in this ancient sacred sacrificial site for the Goddess Diana.

Mohamed Al Fayed (above) and the Sun symbol headgear pictured in the Daily Express. *The gold lion is a symbol of the Sun cult and the two horns are similar to those said to have been worn by Nimrod in Babylon. The headwear is remarkably similar to that worn by Isis (above right) in her Egyptian depictions.*

(Left to right) Henri Paul was the scapegoat of the crash while bodyguard, Trevor Rees-Jones, and Diana's brother, Earl Spencer, have some serious questions to answer.

The 40 foot stone owl beside the sacrificial fire at Bohemian Grove in Northern California during a Summer Camp for the Babylonian Brotherhood Elite. The owl is symbolic of Moloch, the diety to which children in the ancient world were sacrificially burned alive – and still are today.

The obelisk and the dome again. An artist's impression of the Canary Wharf building beside the River Thames, the tallest building in Europe, and opposite is the new Millenium Dome. The zero time meridian of Greenwich Meantime runs close to this point and that is no coincidence.

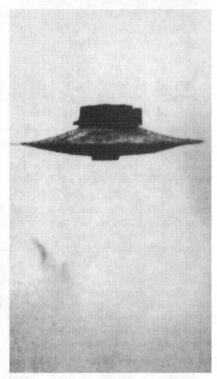

Extraterrestrial invasion? No, Brotherhood manipulation. This is claimed to be the VRIL-7, one of the Nazi 'flying saucer' craft developed during the Second World War and later perfected in the United States and elsewhere.

CHAPTER TEN

Money out of nothing

Today the initiates and frontmen for the Babylonian Brotherhood control world politics, banking, business, intelligence agencies, police, the military, education and the media. The most important of these, in terms of control, is banking. The creation and manipulation of money.

The Brotherhood financial sting is very simple and spans the period we are documenting from the time of Sumer and Babylon to the present day. It is based on creating money that doesn't exist and lending it to people and businesses in return for interest. This creates enormous debt for governments, businesses and the general population, and you therefore control them. Vital to this has been to allow bankers to lend money they do not have. It works like this. If you or me have a million pounds, we can lend a million pounds. Very simple. But if a bank has a million pounds it can lend ten times that and more, and charge interest on it. If even a fraction of the people who theoretically have 'money' deposited in the banks went today to remove it, the banks would slam the doors in half an hour because they do not have it. Money in the bank is a myth, another confidence trick. When you go into a bank and ask for a loan, the bank does not print a single new note nor mint a single new coin. It merely types the amount of the loan into your account. From that moment you are paying interest to the bank on what is no more than figures typed on a screen. However, if you fail to pay back that non-existent loan, the bank can come along and quite legally take your wealth that does exist, your home, land, car, and possessions, to the estimated value of whatever figure was typed onto that screen. More than that, because money is not brought into circulation by governments, but by private banks making loans to customers, the banks control how much money is in circulation. The more loans they choose to make, the more money is in circulation. What is the difference between an economic boom (prosperity) and an economic depression (poverty)? One thing only: the amount of money in circulation. That's all. And, through this system, the private banks, controlled by the same people, decide how much money will be in circulation. They can create booms and busts at will. The same with the stock-markets where these guys are moving trillions of dollars a day around the financial and banking markets, so deciding if they go up or down, soar or crash. Stock-market crashes don't just happen, they are made to happen.

Most of the 'money' in circulation is not physical money, cash and coins. It is represented as figures passing from one computer account to another electronically via money transfers, credit cards and cheque books. The more money, electronic or otherwise, that is in circulation, the more economic activity can take place and therefore the more products are bought and sold, the more income people have, and the more jobs are available. But a constant theme of the reptile-Aryan financial coup has been to create a boom by making lots of loans and then pull the plug. Overpaid economists and economic correspondents, most of whom have no idea what is going on, will tell you that boom and bust is part of some natural 'economic cycle'. What claptrap. It is systematic manipulation by the Brotherhood to steal the real wealth of the world. During a boom many people get themselves into even more debt. The vibrant economic activity means that businesses borrow more for new technology to increase production to meet demand. People borrow more to buy a bigger house and a new, more expensive car, because they are so confident about their economic future. Then, at the most opportune moment, the major bankers, coordinated by the secret society networks, raise interest rates to suppress the demand for loans and they begin to call in loans already outstanding. They ensure they make far fewer loans than before. This has the affect of taking units of exchange (money in its various forms) out of circulation. This suppresses demand for products and leads to fewer jobs because there is not enough money in circulation to generate the necessary economic activity. So people and businesses can no longer earn enough to repay their loans and they go bankrupt. The banks then take over their real wealth, their business, home, land, car and possessions in return for non-repayment of a loan that was never more than figures typed on a screen. This has been going on in cycles over thousands of years, especially the last few centuries, and the real wealth of the world has been sucked out of the population and into the hands of those who control the banking system – the reptilian bloodlines. The same applies to countries. Instead of creating their own interest free money, governments borrow it from the private banking cartel and pay back both the interest and the capital by taxation of the people. Fantastic amounts of the money you pay in taxes go straight to the private banks to pay back loans which the governments could create themselves interest-free!! Why don't they do it? Because the Brotherhood controls the governments as much as they control the banks.

What we call 'privatisation' is the selling off of state assets to stave off bankruptcy caused by the bank-created debt. Third World countries are handing over control of their land and resources to the international bankers because they cannot pay back the vast loans made, on purpose, by the banks to ensnare them in this very situation. The world does not have to be in poverty and conflict, it is manipulated to be that way because it serves the Agenda. The Knights Templar used the system I've just described when they created the foundations of the modern banking network back in the 12th and 13th centuries and this clearly connected with the Venetian network of the Black Nobility operating at the same time. The world financial manipulation is today coordinated by 'central banks' in each country which appear to be working independently, but are in fact working together to a common end. The Bank of England, chartered by the Black Nobility's

William of Orange, has been the spider at the centre of this web and so, too, since the 1930s, has the Bank of International Settlements in Switzerland. Like the Bank of England, the central banks were chartered by the descendants of the reptilian banking families of Genoa and Venice.

The Rothschilds

One bloodline which came from the reptile-Aryans within the Khazar empire in the Caucasus Mountains are the Rothschilds. Their leading members are reptile full bloods, reptilians knowingly occupying a human physical form. No overview of the financial manipulation is possible without considerable mention of the Rothschild gang. They changed their name from Bauer to Rothschild and, from their base in 18th century Frankfurt, they have been at the heart of the manipulation of the world to this day. I document the Rothschilds at length in *...And The Truth Shall Set You Free*, but I will briefly summarise here because they are so important to the story. The Rothschild banking dynasty was created by Mayer Amschel Bauer. The reptilian families change their names to hide their origins and their use and creation of titles has been a great help in this. Bauer changed his name to Rothschild which came from the red shield (rotes schild in German) which hung over the door of his house in Frankfurt. Red has been the colour symbolising revolution since the ancient origins of the Brotherhood, which is why the Russian revolutionaries were called the Reds. On the shield was a hexagram, a Star of David or Seal of Solomon and this same symbol is now on the flag of Israel. People think it is a Jewish symbol because of its name and use, but this is nonsense. One was found on the floor of a 1,200 year old Muslim mosque which stood on the site of present day Tel Aviv.[1] The Jewish writer, O. J. Graham, in his work, *The Six Pointed Star*, says:

> "...the six pointed star made its way from Egyptian Pagan rituals of worship, to the goddess Ashteroth and Moloch... then it progressed through the magic arts, witchcraft, (*including Arab magicians, Druids and Satanists*)... through the Cabala to Isaac Luria, a Cabalist in the 16th century, to Mayer Amschel Bauer, who changed his name to this symbol, to Zionism, to the Knesset (*parliament*) of the new State of Israel, to the flag of Israel, and its medical organisation, equivalent to the Red Cross."[2]

So the very name Rothschild comes from an ancient esoteric symbol connected to Egypt as Moloch (Nimrod) the 'god' of sacrifice. The hexagram only became used by the Jewish hierarchy as their symbol with the emergence of the Rothschilds and it has absolutely nothing to do with 'King David' as the Jewish leaders well know. It is on the flag of Israel because Israel is not the land of the Jews, it is the land of the Rothschilds and those who dictate to them from even higher up the Brotherhood pyramid. They created Israel and they control it. The red shield used as the emblem of the Salvation Army was inspired by the Rothschilds, by the way.

Frankfurt, the home of the Rothschild dynasty, was where paper money became popular and the new European Central Bank is based there. This bank allows a few unelected bankers to set the interest rates for all the European Union countries using the single European currency. As Mayer Amschel Rothschild is quoted to have said: "Give me control over a nation's currency and I don't care who makes the laws."[3] Mayer Rothschild married Gutele Schnaper, then 16, and they had ten children, five boys and five girls, who were sent out to establish branches of the dynasty in London, Paris, Vienna, Berlin and Naples. The Rothschild children were married by arrangement to noble families and to each other at cousin level to maintain the reptilian bloodline and keep the power 'in house'. Mayer's will specifically insisted on this and also that Rothschild men must always head the business and accounts must be kept strictly secret. The will excluded Rothschild daughters, their husbands and heirs, from the business and all knowledge of it. So just because your name might be Rothschild does not mean you are a Satanist or know what is going on. I am talking about those at the top of this empire and the same applies to all the families I mention. Most members of these families will be shocked to find what has been going on around them. What we do not want is a witch-hunt against everyone who carries these family names or the reptile race in general. It is those knowingly responsible we need to expose, not the innocent puppets who happen to be in the same family or have the same name.

Mayer Rothschild became banker and manipulator to Prince William IX of Hesse-Hanau, another member of the Black Nobility reptilian bloodline, and they attended Freemason meetings together. According to the book, *Jews And Freemasons In Europe (1723–1939)*, William's younger brother, Karl, was accepted as the head of German Freemasons and members of the Hesse dynasty were closely involved with an Elite Freemason group called the Strict Observance. This was later called the Beneficent Knights of the Holy City,[4] and was known in Germany as The Brethren of John the Baptist (a code for Nimrod).[5] The House of Hesse were on Hitler's side in the Second World War and Prince Philip of Hesse was a messenger between Hitler and Mussolini.[6] After they took the British throne William and Rothschild made a fortune hiring Hesse troops to the German Hanoverians. Many of the troops who fought for 'Britain' in the American War of Independence were William's German mercenaries. William was the grandson of the Hanoverian king of England, George II, and is therefore an ancestor of Queen Elizabeth II. By another line, he is also related to her husband, Prince Philip. Goodness knows how many of the reptilian Hesse bloodline are out there, because William alone is estimated to have fathered at least 70, yes 70, children by various women.[7] How did he find the time? But this is another important point. The reptile-Aryan offspring produced through the arranged marriages are the official heirs. But literally thousands are produced unofficially outside of marriage and these are not credited to that bloodline. However, they are carefully documented and the Brotherhood know exactly who these people are. They want to know which are the reptile bloodlines because they know they will be easiest to 'plug in' to the reptilians on the lower fourth dimension. This is one reason for the highly detailed genetic records kept by the Mormons, another Brotherhood operation at its top level. So when people in power appear to have no blood links with these families, the opposite may be true. A number of researchers believe Bill Clinton to be a closet Rockefeller and he is certainly blood-related to the British monarchy, every Scottish monarch, and King Robert I of France. St Germain, now a 'messiah' figure to many New Agers, was a friend of William of Hesse-Hanau, and his brother, Karl. Apparently, Karl wrote that Germain, an alchemist and magician, had been raised by the de Medici (Black Nobility) family in Italy.[8] Many New Agers today talk about the Great White Brotherhood of 'master souls', including Germain, who are communicating 'guidance' to channellers about the coming transformation. This is yet another mind control operation by the Brotherhood to misdirect and imprison the more extreme of the New Age mentality and to stop it getting off its collective arse (and the ceiling) and so making a real difference.

Political unrest caused by Napoleon Bonaparte made William of Hesse-Hanau take flight to Denmark for a while, and during this time Mayer Rothschild's eldest son, Nathan, another Freemason like most of them, stole £600,000 which should have been used to pay the mercenary soldiers. He took it to London to establish a Rothschild bank there. The fortune he made from this by funding Wellington's war with Napoleon and other manipulated 'investments' formed the foundation of the dynasty. Both Wellington and Napoleon were manipulated and funded by the same people who included Napoleon's brother, Joseph Bonaparte, a Freemasonic Grand Master. The Rothschilds, even according to some of their own histories, constantly funded both sides in wars. They engineered these wars through the secret society network and their own intelligence operation which continues today. It is called Mossad which is officially the intelligence agency of Israel, but Israel is Roth-rael and so Mossad is Roth-ad. Anka Muhlstein, the Jewish author of *Baron James, The Rise Of The French Rothschilds*, says the family intelligence network used Hebrew letters as a code. Hebrew was the sacred language of the Egyptian mystery schools, which is where much Brotherhood knowledge came from, along with the ancient knowledge of Asia and the Far East, which is also connected with the Khazar bloodlines. The Rothschild communications network was faster than any government system and one of the famous examples of Rothschild double-dealing was when they spread a rumour that Wellington had lost to Napoleon in the Battle of Waterloo in 1815. This caused a crash on the London stock-market and the Rothschilds secretly bought up stock at knockdown prices. When the news arrived that in fact Wellington had won, the stocks rose in price again and the Rothschilds had increased their wealth by an incredible amount. When, like the Rothschilds, you control the media, the politicians, and the stock-market, making money is child's play and so is starting wars. Every working day, the world price of gold is still set at the London offices of N. M. Rothschild and the stock-markets across the world are controlled by the Babylonian Brotherhood through banking and financial families like the Rothschilds. If there is a banking and stock-market crash in the Far East, it is because it suits the reptilian Agenda. Another of their cycles is to encourage people to invest in the stock-market until the quoted companies are massively overvalued. The Brotherhood then crash the markets (having sold their stocks just before) and while most people lose their money, the Brotherhood buy up vast amounts of stock at bargain prices. The stock-market goes up, so does the value of the newly acquired companies, and the Brotherhood wealth and control takes another leap forward. It's all manipulation to achieve the reptilian goal of total global control.

Creating wars is a wonderful way to make vast fortunes and destroy the status quo. You lend money to both sides to fund the war and then you lend them even more to rebuild their devastated countries. They get in debt (control) to you and you increase your wealth (power). Such control and power allows you to build a new society in the image of your agenda, when the war you have created and funded has destroyed the old structure. The so-called Protocols of the Elders of Zion were discovered in the last century and tell in incredible detail the events and methods of manipulation we have seen manifest in the 20th century. These documents were very much the creation of the Rothschilds and the reptile-Aryans. But they are not really the Protocols of the Elders of Zion, they are, in truth, the Protocols of SION, the Sun, and the Priory of Sion. So much disinformation and aggression has been hurled at the Protocols and anyone who has mentioned them – including me – because the Brotherhood are desperate to discredit their contents. It is far too close to home. Hitler used the Protocols in part to justify the oppression of Jews, but he was given the Protocols by a Rothschild agent of Khazar decent called Alfred Rosenberg. I don't accept that the Protocols are 'Jewish' in the way people have come to understand that term. They are the work of the reptile-Aryans and made to appear 'Jewish' so that we lose the plot. See ...*And The Truth Shall Set You Free* for more details of this and *The Robot's Rebellion* for the contents of the Protocols.

The Rothschild's became one of the pivotal families in the Brotherhood's financial and political Agenda and they went on to direct events throughout Europe before expanding into the Americas, South Africa and eventually the world. They had the crown heads of Europe in debt to them and this included the Black Nobility reptilian dynasty, the Habsburgs, who ruled the Holy Roman Empire for 600 years. The Rothschilds also took control of the Bank of England. If there was a war, the Rothschilds were behind the scenes, creating the conflict and funding both sides. The Rothschild leaders are not Jewish, they are reptilians who have sent countless Jews to their deaths to further their sickening ambitions. They have been close associates of the House of Windsor and they controlled people like Edward VII, the Grand Master of English Freemasonry. Edward was the son of Queen Victoria and the German Freemason, Prince Albert. The Mountbattens (formerly the German Battenbergs) are blood relatives of the Rothschilds and Lord Louis Mountbatten arranged the marriage of Queen Elizabeth II to his grandson, Prince Philip, two equal strands of the reptilian Black Nobility. Mountbatten was also the mentor of Prince Charles. When victims of Satanic ritual abuse tell me that the late Lord Mountbattan was among their abusers, it fits the picture completely. That's the background he came from. The Rothschilds and the Bauers (also Bowers) are steeped in Satanism and both the Rothschilds and the Windsor-Mountbattens are reptilian, Anunnaki bloodlines. The Bauers, particularly a man called Richard

Bauer, were leading alchemists and esoteric magicians in Germany in the Middle Ages.[9] Karl Marx, the Brotherhood frontman for the creation of Communism, was a student of a Bruno Bauer at Berlin University and this Bauer was the only Bible scholar on record who openly wrote that the New Testament was a synthesis of ideas between Seneca and Josephus (Piso).[10] He said that Jesus was the creation of the writer of Mark's Gospel.[11] Yet more evidence that the bloodlines of the Brotherhood have known the truth all along.

The Rothschilds were involved in the Tugenbund League (also the Virtue League) which was formed in 1786 as a 'sex society'. Its members, and their wives and daughters, would meet at the home of a woman called Henrietta Herz and take part in sexual activity and rituals. Among them were two daughters of Moses Mendelssohn, a Rothschild agent behind the manipulation of the French Revolution; the Marquis de Mirabeau, the Freemason also intimately involved in the revolution; and Frederick von Gentz, who would become a very influential Rothschild agent.[12] In 1807, there followed the second Tugenbund League, again involving the Rothschilds. It was formed by Baron von Stein and expanded rapidly to include most leading politicians in Germany and many of the top military leaders and professors of literature and science. William of Hesse-Cassal was a member and the official role of this second Tugenbund League was to remove the Napoleonic occupation of Germany.[13] It was close to other Masonic groups like the Black Knights, the Knights of the Queen of Prussia and the Concordists. These were offshoots of the ancient Teutonic Knights structure in Germany and the predecessors of the Thule Society, the Edelweiss Society, and Vril Society, which were to be the architects of the Nazi Party. It is the same face with different masks and the Rothschilds have been behind most of them – including the Nazis. All these groups interlock if you dig deep enough.

This apparently complex (but ultimately simple) network of banking, business, politics, media, and secret societies, controls the world on behalf of the Brotherhood operational headquarters in London. The control of money and banking via the Rothschilds and others are crucial to this. One of the Brotherhood's most important coups was the creation in 1913 of the Federal Reserve, the so-called 'central bank' of the United States. It is neither federal nor has any reserve. It is a cartel of private banks owned by the 20 founding families, mostly European, which today decides the interest rates for the United States and lends non-existent money (figures on a screen) to the US Government on which the taxpayers have to pay interest. This is what we call the 'American Deficit' – it is fresh air. The Federal Government of the United States does not own a single share in the Federal Reserve and American citizens cannot purchase them. Profits exceed $150 billion a year and the Federal Reserve has not once in all its history published audited accounts. This income is assured because **1** the Brotherhood control the US Government (the Virginia Company under another name) which continues to borrow 'money' from the 'Fed'; **2** they also control the privately-owned Internal Revenue Service (IRS), the illegal terrorist organisation which collects the taxation from the people; and **3** it controls the media to ensure that people never find out about **1** and **2**.

The Brotherhood had long desired a privately-owned 'central bank' in America to complete their control of the economy. When the leading Freemason, George Washington, became the first president he appointed a Brotherhood yes-man called Alexander Hamilton as his Secretary of the Treasury. Hamilton introduced the Bank of the United States, a privately owned central bank which began to lend money to the new US Government so creating control by debt from the very start. Look at what happened when the Black Nobility introduced the Bank of England, and the scenario is exactly the same. The Bank of the United States caused so much poverty, bankruptcy and rebellion, that it was eventually closed down, but soon after that came its replacement, the Federal Reserve. The Rothschild's main banking operation in America in the early part of this century was Kuhn, Loeb and Company in New York which was headed by Jacob Schiff. The Schiff family lived in the same house in Frankfurt as the Rothschilds at the time of the founder, Mayer Amschel Rothschild. In 1902, the Rothschilds sent their agents, Paul and Felix Warburg, to America to engineer the creation of the Federal Reserve. Their brother, Max Warburg, stayed behind to run the family banking business which had been started in Venice under their previous name, the Abraham del Banco family. When they arrived in the States, Paul Warburg married Nina Loeb, of Kuhn, Loeb and Company, and Felix married Frieda Schiff, daughter of Jacob Schiff. Another wonderful example of arranged marriages to suit the demands of the bloodlines and the Agenda. Both brothers became partners in Kuhn, Loeb and Company and Paul was put on an annual salary of some half a million dollars in the opening years of this century. That's the sort of money we are talking about when we discuss the financial power of this group. Imagine what it must be today.

The Brotherhood network ensured that the 'Democrat' and Rosicrucian, Woodrow Wilson, won the presidency in 1909 and his minder was a leading Brotherhood member called 'Colonel' Mandel House. Wilson described him as "my second personality", "my alter ego" , and said: "his thoughts and mine are one". Never has a President said a truer word. As is now well documented by researchers, the Elite bankers from the Rockefeller-Morgan-Rothschild-Harriman cartels met secretly at Jekyl Island in Georgia to discuss tactics and the nature of the bill they wished to be passed to establish the bank they so badly desired. Jekyl Island, it appears, was owned by the Payseurs and every member of the group was a Payseur trustee. Their political spokesman was Senator Nelson Aldrich, the grandfather of Nelson Rockefeller, the four times governor of New York and vice-president of the United States after Gerald Ford replaced Richard Nixon in the wake of Watergate in 1974. Aldrich's daughter, Abby, was married to John D. Rockefeller Jr. When the Federal Reserve Bill was going before Congress the bankers who had written the bill vehemently opposed it in public. The bankers were very unpopular by this time and they wanted to give the impression that the bill was bad for them, so increasing the public support for it to be passed. This sort of manipulation goes on all the time and no matter what anyone is saying about an event in public, we need to keep asking the question "Who benefits from this happening?" and "Who benefits from me believing what I am being told?"

They pushed the bill through just before Christmas 1913 when many Congressmen were already at home with their families for the holiday. Now they could control American interest rates and make a fortune lending the government money that doesn't exist and charging interest on it. To complete the cycle, however, they needed to ensure an endless supply of funds for the government and so they introduced a Federal Income Tax Bill, also in 1913. To do this they needed an amendment, the 16th, to the American Constitution, and that required the consent of at least 36 states. Only two states agreed, but Filander Knox, the Secretary of State, simply announced that the required majority had been achieved and the bill was introduced. To this day the enforced payment of federal income tax is illegal and yet the Brotherhood's Internal Revenue Service goes on doing that in the United States every day. Some may say that calling it a terrorist operation is too extreme, but to terrorise someone you don't have to use a gun or a bomb. You can do it by threatening to destroy their livelihood and evict them from their home to pay you tax that is illegal. Incidentally, note the year of these two events, the Federal Reserve and the Federal Income Tax – 1913. Numbers and years matter to these people because of the Sun and astrological cycles and so it would all have been timed to happen in 1913. Look at the obsession the Brotherhood groups throughout history have had with the number 13. When the Rockefellers set up their Council of State Governments to control the American state legislatures, they based the organisation in a building numbered 1313. For the same reason, a great deal happened in 1933 because 33 is a major esoteric number which represents a vibrational frequency.

The Internal Revenue Service which collects taxation in America is also a private company, though the public believe it is part of their government. In 1863 the Bureau of Internal Revenue was formed to collect taxation, but in 1933, that year again, came the start of another coup on the American people. Three members of the Prescott Bush circle, Helen and Clifton Barton and Hector Echeverria, formed the Internal Revenue Tax and Audit Service, registered in Delaware, America's flag of convenience state, where few questions are asked. Prescott Bush was the father of George Bush. In 1936, this organisation changed its name to the Internal Revenue Service and ran as a private company. In 1953, the original Bureau of Internal Revenue was disbanded, leaving the private Internal Revenue Service to collect all the taxes, illegal taxes most of them, too. This is controlled by the same people who own the Federal Reserve and the Virginia Company and it is bleeding America dry. The Internal Revenue Service was, appropriately, created by American Nazis who were funding Adolf Hitler under the coordination of Prescott Bush, George's father.

The black magicians of the Babylonian Brotherhood have weaved their web of deceit from the ancient world to the present day, but because they wear smart suits in public and save their long robes and Satanic masks for their private rituals, most people find it almost impossible to comprehend the truth of what is going on before their eyes.

■ SOURCES

1   Hirsch M. Goldberg, *The Jewish Connection* (Stein and Day, New York, 1976), p 197.

2   O. J. Graham, *The Six Pointed Star*, quoted by Fritz Springmeier in *The Top 13 Illuminati Bloodlines* (Springmeier, 5316 S.E Lincoln, Oregon, USA, 1995), p 184.

3   This is quoted in many books and Rothschild histories including *Secret Societies And Their Power In The 20th Century* by Jan Van Helsing. It was published by Ewertverlag, Gran Canaria, Spain, in 1995. Quote is on page 39.

4   *The Templar Revelation*, p 131.

5   *The Top 13 Illuminati Bloodlines*, p 173.

6   Ibid.

7   Ibid.

8   Ibid.

9   Ibid, p 171.

10   Albert Schweitzer, *The Quest For The Historical Jesus* (Macmillan Publishing, New York, 1968), p 158.

11   Homer Smith, *Man And His Gods* (Grossetts University Library, New York, 1956), p 190.

12   *The Top 13 Illuminati Bloodlines*, p 176.

13   Ibid.

CHAPTER ELEVEN

Global Babylon

T he next part of the story is covered at length, and sourced, in ...*And The Truth Shall Set You Free* and I won't repeat it all again here. I will, however, sketch the fundamentals of what happened to bridge the gap to the new and stunning information I wish to pass on.

The exploitation of the incredible continent of Africa is a classic story which serves as an example of what has happened elsewhere. This horrific operation by the Rothschilds, Oppenhiemers, Cecil Rhodes, Alfred Milner, Jan Smuts and countless others, was organised through an Elite secret society called the Round Table, formed in the latter years of the 19th century. It was headed by Cecil Rhodes who said he wanted to create a world government centred on Britain. Rhodes headed the South Africa Company and established companies like De Beers Consolidated Mines and Consolidated Gold Fields. Rhodes was also Prime Minister of the Cape Colony and he is said by writer John Coleman (who claims to be a former British Intelligence operative), to have been a member of an organisation called the Committee of 300, also known as The Olympians. These, he claims, are the three hundred people who, in each generation, run the world under the supervision of even smaller groups above them in the highest levels of the pyramid. I will use the abbreviation (Comm 300) to depict others I name who are listed by Coleman.[1] Some people, I should point out, doubt Coleman's British Intelligence connections. A contact who has worked at a high level in the financial world, particularly in Switzerland, told me that he believes these 300 families are the most reptilian on the planet and that is how they qualify for their appointment to this network. Rhodes began his career in manipulation while a student at Oxford University, that training ground for Brotherhood personnel. His mentor was John Ruskin, the fine arts professor who is still a legend at Oxford. Ruskin said he believed in centralised power and the state owning the means of production and distribution. His ideas would form the official philosophy of the British Labour Party until more recently and they were also included in the writings of Karl Marx and Friedrich Engels and became the foundations of Marxist communism which was soon to grip the nations of Eastern Europe. Ruskin is widely believed by researchers to have been connected with the Bavarian Illuminati and it was his inspiration which led to the formation of the Fabian Society, yet another Brotherhood operation which to this day manipulates the British Labour Party and operates further afield. Ruskin was a student of Plato's works, as were most

Brotherhood clones like Rhodes, Engels, Weishaupt, the Rothschilds and the
Rothschild associate, Moses Mendelssohn, one of the principle manipulators behind
the French Revolution. Rhodes was so in awe of Ruskin that he copied his inaugural
speech in long hand and kept it with him for the rest of his life. Ruskin had a
tremendous impact on many undergraduates at Oxford and Cambridge who
would later play their part in the manipulation of the 20th century, including the
Rothchild-controlled banker, Alfred Milner.

While Rhodes was the frontman for the Round Table, the real control was with
the Rothschilds and the other bloodline families like the Astors and the Cecils. The
Astor family were big financial backers of Brotherhood organisations like the Royal
Institute of International Affairs and Waldorf Astor was one of its leaders. The
Astors were the centre of the group known as the Cliveden Set named after their
Cliveden Estate, not far from Windsor Castle. The name Astor comes from the
ancient goddess, Ashtoreth. One of the Cecils was Lord Salisbury (Comm 300), the
British Prime Minister and Foreign Secretary when the Round Table was
engineering the Boer War in South Africa in which tens of thousands of men,
women, and children were killed. Many of them died in the concentration camps of
the Freemason, Lord Kitchener (Comm 300). Lord Salisbury was a close friend of
Winston Churchill, another bloodline frontman who would be used to great effect
in the Second World War. This manipulation and genocide by Rhodes and the
Round Table secured control of the mineral rights in southern Africa which still
continues today through the Oppenheimer family. The Union of South Africa itself
was created by the Round Table after a campaign headed by the banker and
Rothschild manipulator, Alfred Milner (Comm 300), who became the new leader of
the secret society after Rhodes died in 1902. In his will, Rhodes bequeathed funds to
support the Round Table, although the Rothschilds were the main funders. The will
left a considerable amount of money to fund a scheme known as Rhodes
Scholarships. These finance a few highly selected overseas students (selected by the
Brotherhood) to attend Oxford University to be indoctrinated into the 'world
government' Agenda. The ratio of these students who return to their own countries
and enter positions of overt or covert power is remarkable and the selection process
is overwhelmingly governed by genetic history. For example, the most famous
Rhodes Scholar in the world today is Bill Clinton, President of the United States,
and his main advisor at both of his elections was George Stephanopoulos, a Rhodes
Scholar. The leaders of the future are not decided at each election, they are reared
and mind manipulated to hold those positions from a very young age, sometimes
birth, as we shall see a little later. Another man selected for a Rhodes Scholarship
was Fred Franz, the former president of the Watchtower Society (Jehovah's
Witnesses), who turned down the invitation to Oxford and instead served the
Brotherhood by replacing the leader of the Jehovah's Witnesses, the Freemason,
Charles Taze Russell, who was ritually killed on Halloween 1916.[2] The magazine of
the Jehovah's Witnessess, the Watchtower, is a mass of esoteric symbolism and
subliminal images. George Estabrooks, who taught the use of hypnotism and mind
control to British Intelligence, was also a Rhodes Scholar.[3]

By 1915 other branches of the Round Table were set up in South Africa, Canada, the United States, Australia, New Zealand and India. In the United States, the Round Table and the wider network was represented by the bloodlines and financiers who had arrived from Europe like the Rockefellers, J. P. Morgan and Edward Harriman, although as we have seen even they were wealthy 'gofers' answerable to higher powers. They used Rothschild and Payseur funding to build vast empires which controlled banking, business, oil, steel, etc, and ran the United States economy in the way the Oppenhiemers do in South Africa. All these branches, however, are subordinate to the central operational control centre in Europe, especially London. These same families in America, the so-called 'Eastern Establishment', are the force behind one of American's most sinister and Satanic secret societies, the Skull and Bones Society, based in a windowless mausoleum at Yale University in Connecticut known appropriately as the 'Tomb'. Here highly selected students meet twice a week during term time. This interlocks with the Templars, the Freemasons and the Round Table network. The skull and bones symbol relates to the skull ceremonies of the Knights Templar and many other Brotherhood groups which inspired this Satanic, blood drinking, secret society. Other Brotherhood universities in the United States, like Harvard, have similar secret societies, but the Skull and Bones appears to be the most influential. A network of the same kind operates in Britain at Oxford, Cambridge, Edinburgh and other Universities. The Skull and Bones Society is believed to have been introduced to the United States more than 150 years ago as Chapter 322 of a German Secret Society and was also known at one time as the Brotherhood of Death. With George Bush a member, I can't think of a better name than that. What is known for sure is the Skull and Bones Society was formed in 1832-33 by a group which included Daniel Coit Gilman, the man responsible for setting up the American tax exempt foundations like the Rockefeller Foundation and the Carnegie Endowment for International Peace. Other Skull and Bones founders were General William Huntington Russell and Alphonso Taft, of a famous American family. Taft was Secretary of War in the Grant administration and his son, William Howard Taft, was the only man to be both President and Chief Justice of the United States. Like the Russells, the Tafts are an ancient bloodline family related to Skull and Bones member, George Bush. The Skull and Bones is deeply racist and was founded on the money made from the illegal drug operations of the Russells. This Society is incorporated into the Russell Trust and its initiation ceremonies take place on an island in the St Lawrence River owned by the Russell Trust Association. Most of the land on which Yale University is built is also owned by the same association.

The Russell family made their fortune from running opium from Turkey to China during the British opium wars against the Chinese, when the Black Nobility-Brotherhood in London was invading China by flooding that society with addictive drugs. The Russells later fused their operation with other bloodline families like Coolidge and Delano (Comm 300 family designate), both of which produced Presidents of the United States, Calvin Coolidge and Franklin Delano Roosevelt. The Russells used to fly the skull and bones flag on their ships carrying the drugs and the

Skull and Bones Society continues this drug running tradition through people like George Bush, one of the major drug barons in North America. The Skull and Bones Society is dominated by about 20–30 families overwhelmingly from the Eastern Seaboard. Most claim ancestry with the British aristocracy (true) or have a genetic line going back to the English 'Puritan' families who arrived in American around 1630–1660 under the policy of emigration inspired by Sir Francis Bacon and his circle. These families have either secured financial power themselves or married into wealth via the sons of moguls like the Rockefellers and Harrimans. The key criteria for membership of the Skull and Bones is your genetic history. Are you reptilian enough? Major players in the manipulation of the 20th century have been initiated into the Skull and Bones Society whilst students at Yale. Among them Averell Harriman, son of Edward, and one of the Brotherhood's most active manipulators before his death at 91 in 1986. George Bush's father, Prescott Bush, was also a Skull and Bones member and it was he who ransacked the grave of the Apache Chief, Geronimo, and took his skull back to the Yale headquarters for their skull ceremonies. (See *...And The Truth Shall Set You Free.*) Prescott Bush made his fortune through the Harriman (Payseur/Rothschild) empire and would later help to fund Adolf Hitler.

So by the early years of the 20th century the situation was this: The Babylonian Brotherhood operational network headquartered in London had introduced another Elite grouping called the Round Table with branches all over the world. This operation and its interlocking secret societies, banks, businesses, newspapers, and political placemen, controlled the United States, Canada, South Africa and other African countries, Australia, New Zealand, India, many parts of the Far East, including Hong Kong, and vast swathes of the rest of the world under the title of the 'British Empire'. Fundamentally involved in this network was the British royal family headed after Queen Victoria by her Freemason son, Edward VII, and when he died in 1910 came George V. Edward, in league with his Black Nobility friends in the City of London, greatly increased the personal fortune of the royal family. They were soon to change their name from the German House of Saxe-Coburg-Gotha to Windsor to obscure their German origins during the horrors of the First World War. With these global networks now in place, the scene was set for the grotesque manipulation of the 20th Century. I will briefly describe the background to some of the main events in this chapter, but for greater detail and sources see *...And The Truth Shall Set You Free.*

The First World War

The Brotherhood wanted a global war as a massive problem-reaction-solution to destroy the global status quo so allowing them to rebuild the post war world in their image. It worked brilliantly. After the First World War, power was in far fewer hands than it was before. The British and American governments in the immediate post war period were controlled by the Round Table leadership. In Britain these were people like Alfred Milner (Comm 300) and Lord Balfour (Comm 300) and in America, Colonel House (Comm 300), the dictator of policy to President Woodrow Wilson. In Germany the official head of the country was Kaiser Wilhelm II, a relative of the British/German royal family soon to be known as the Windsors. Wilhelm's 'minder' was the leading German Freemason, Otto von Bismark, the architect of the German Empire, and other Freemasons and bloodline families. Kaiser Wilhelm's Chancellor was Bethmann-Hollweg, a member of the Bethmann banking family in Frankfurt and a cousin of the Rothschilds. Wilhelm's personal banker was Max Warburg, the brother of Paul and Felix, who had helped to manipulate the US Federal Reserve into being. Meantime, the Rothschilds had bought the German news agency, Wolff, to control the flow of information to the German people and what the rest of the world would hear from inside Germany. One of the leading executives of Wolff was… Max Warburg. The Rothschilds would later buy an interest in the Havas news agency in France and Reuters in London. (News agencies supply 'news' to all media organisations.) All that was needed to spark the war was an incident which could be used to justify hostilities and that was provided when an agent of a Serbian secret society called the Order of the Black Hand assassinated Archduke Ferdinand, the heir to the Austro-Hungarian throne on June 28th 1914. At exactly the same time in Russia, an attempt was being made on the life of the Tsar's most trusted advisor, Grigory Yefimovich Rasputin, who was arguing against a war. The Black Hand was formed in 1911 as the Order of Death and its seal was a clenched fist holding a skull and bones and alongside that was a knife, a bomb and a poison bottle.[4] Lovely. Leading members of the Black Hand apparently met with French and Grand Orient Freemasons at the Hotel St Jerome in Toulouse in January 1914 to arrange the assassination in Sarajevo.[5] The actual assassins, led by Gavrilo Princip, were all suffering from tuberculosis and did not have long to live. They were suckers manipulated to carry out an act thinking it would serve Serbian nationalism when it was really the spark required to advance an Agenda they probably did not know existed. So it is with assassins and terrorists galore over thousands of years. How do such people stop themselves being used in this way? Very simple. Don't kill anyone, harm anyone, or plant bombs under any circumstances whatsoever. There, all sorted.

The German branches of the Brotherhood network started hostilities and the branches in the rest of Europe followed. The people who actually fought this war were the innocent pawns in a game they did not understand. Half a million men died in one battle in the trenches of northern France, a gigantic orgy of blood letting in an area which is sacred land to the Satanists and blood drinkers who run this world. These are mass ritual sacrifices to the reptilians. The war was created by problem-reaction-solution and the same technique was used to bring the United States into the conflict as planned. In his election campaign for the presidency, Woodrow Wilson had told the American people that he would not allow America to become involved in a European war. He had to say that or he would not have been elected. But he knew that was part of the Brotherhood Agenda and so in 1916 the American passenger ship, the Lusitania, was sunk and this was used as an excuse to enter the war. In the same way, the assassination of Ferdinand was Germany's excuse and in 1941 the attack by the Japanese on Pearl Harbour was used by the American reptile-Aryan President, Franklin Delano Roosevelt, to enter the Second

World War. A member of one of the bloodline families, Alfred Gwynne Vanderbilt, was on the Lusitania when it sank. An urgent telegram telling him not to sail on that voyage failed to reach him. The head of the US War Industries Board was another vital cog in the Brotherhood network in this century. He was Bernard Baruch (Comm 300), who said that he had..."probably more power than perhaps any other man did in the war..."⁶ Baruch and Mandel House were the day-to-day decision makers in the American branch of the London-based Round Table.

In the 1950s, yet more confirmation of how the First World War was manipulated was revealed by a US Congressional investigation into the 'tax-exempt' foundations in the United States, like the Rockefeller Foundation, the Ford Foundation, and the Carnegie Endowment for International Peace, which the investigation found was manipulating war! Another thing to watch. The Brotherhood name organisations in a way that leads people to believe their aim is the opposite of what they are really there to do. For instance, if you want to run drugs without being suspected, do it through an anti-drug agency. If you want to destroy land and kill wildlife, do it through a wildlife protection agency. If you want to run a Satanic ring, do it through the Christian Church. The Congressional investigation by the Reece Committee found that these foundations had an interlocking leadership and that they were funding 'education' and 'science' to advance their Agenda for the centralisation of global power. The outcome of scientific 'research' was being agreed before the funding was handed over. No agreement on the outcome, no cash. This is one major way that scientific knowledge is suppressed. Knowledge which could set the world free from hunger and the need for the expensive, polluting 'energy' technology we have today. The relevant findings of the Reece Committee in relation to the First World War came with their investigation into the Carnegie Endowment for International Peace. Norman Dodd, the committee's Director of Research, reported that at one meeting of the Carnegie trustees, the question was asked:

> "'Is there any means known to man more effective than war if you want to alter the lives of an entire people?' It was decided that there was not and so the next question they asked was: 'How do we involve the United States in a war?'."

Dodd went on:

> "And then they raised the question: 'How do we control the diplomatic machinery of the United States?' And the answer came out: 'We must control the State Department'. At this point we catch up with what we already found out... that through an agency set up by the Carnegie Endowment, every high appointment in the State Department was cleared. Finally, we were in a war. These trustees in a meeting about 1917 had the brashness to congratulate themselves on the wisdom of their original decision because already the impact of the war had indicated it would alter life and can alter life in this country. This was the date of our entry in the war; we were involved. They even had the brashness to word and to dispatch a telegram to Mr Wilson cautioning him to see that the war did not end too quickly."⁷

Dodd said that his investigator, Kathryn Casey, found other minutes dealing with the work of the Carnegie Endowment to prevent American life returning to a pre-war state. Changing the way people lived and thought was, after all, the main point of the war. Dodd said:

> "They came to the conclusion that, to prevent a reversion, they must control education. And then they approached the Rockefeller Foundation and they said: "Will you take on the acquisition of control of education as it involves subjects that are domestic in their significance?" And it was agreed. Then together they decided that the key to it was the teaching of American history and they must change that. So, they then approached the most prominent of what you might call American historians at that time with the idea of getting them to alter the manner in which they presented the subject."[8]

This is why you don't read what really happened in the official history books. You read what the Brotherhood wants you to read. This is the crap that is taught to our children in schools and universities under the heading of 'education'. The same with all the other subjects. This is the 'education' that American families spend their lives scrimping and saving for. They are scrimping and saving to pay for their children to be indoctrinated, that's the reality. The point of the First World War was to reshape the post-war world in the image the reptilians desired. So the very people who engineered the war on all 'sides' were appointed to the Versailles Peace Conference, near Paris (again!) in 1919 to decide what would happen as a result of the war they had manufactured. The Palace of Versailles is also known as the Palace of the Sun King. The 'victorious' stooges, sorry leaders, at Versailles were Woodrow Wilson of the United States, Lloyd George (Comm 300) of Great Britain, and Georges Clemenceau of France. But behind the movie screen what was really happening? Wilson was 'advised' by Colonel Mandel House (Comm 300) and Bernard Baruch (Comm 300), both Rothschild-Round Table representatives; Lloyd George was advised by Alfred Milner (Comm 300), official leader of the Round Table and Sir Phillip Sassoon, a direct descendant of Mayer Amschel Rothschild; Clemenceau had Georges Mandel, his Minister of the Interior, whose real name was Jeroboam Rothschild. Also on the American Commission to Negotiate Peace were the infamous Dulles brothers; Paul Warburg; Thomas Lamont from J. P. Morgan (Payseur); Robert Lansing, the Secretary of State, an uncle of the infamous Dulles brothers; and Walter Lippman (Comm 300), the founder of the American branch of the Fabian Society. All bloodline reptilian families. The German delegation included Max Warburg, brother of Paul Warburg on the American side! The host of the conference was Baron Edmund de Rothschild, a leading campaigner for a Jewish State in Palestine, for which the Versailles Peace Conference confirmed its support. And none of the history books will tell you any of this. Out of the conference came the World Court in The Hague, Netherlands, and the League of Nations, the Brotherhood's first attempt to create a global organisation which could be evolved into a world government. The first draft of what became the covenant of the League of Nations was written by Colonel House, as were Woodrow Wilson's famous 'fourteen points' at Versailles. Years earlier, House had written a novel called *Philip Dru: Administrator*, which he later admitted was fact presented as fiction. In the book, published anonymously two years *before* the First World War, he had proposed an organisation called... the League of Nations. The war was all a plot to further the Agenda and it cost the lives of millions. The League of Nations eventually collapsed, but one war later their ambition was achieved with the creation of the United Nations in 1945.

The Russian Revolution/Cold War

The Russia Revolution in 1917, during the First World War, lead to the formation of the Soviet Union and later to the Cold War. A constant theme of Brotherhood manipulation through the centuries is the creation of monsters for people to fear, something they proceeded to do with Communism in the Soviet Union and China. The hierarchy of these two regions interlock with the Brotherhood network and bloodlines, but of course the people don't know that. The public believed that the United States leadership was opposed to the Soviet Union because one was capitalist and one was communist. Not true. They are different kinds of cartels, that's all, and controlled, ultimately, by the same people. Communism was created by Wall Street and the City of London to generate enormous fear and conflict which was used to great effect to advance the Agenda. As always, it was planned long before it became public. The Communist Manifesto was written by (or for) Karl Marx and Freidrich Engels. Marx was a student of the German occultist, Bruno Bauer (Rothschild) and married into the reptilian bloodlines of the Scottish aristocracy. Some of his writings were vehemently anti-Jewish which appears contradictory because he was supposed to be Jewish. But he wasn't. He was another 'Aryan' bloodline doing his job for the cause – the reptile cause. All these years the far left in politics have revered Marx as a 'man of the people' when all along he was a man to imprison the people. The action began in Russia when the Rothschilds manipulated the Tsar into a war with Japan in 1905. The European Rothschilds lent money to the Russians for that conflict while their American branch, Kuhn, Loeb and Company, funded the Japanese. The war demolished the Russian economy, not least to pay back the Rothschilds, plus interest, and this helped to fuel the simmering rebellion. When the First World War began and Russia came in against Germany, weapons supplies to the Russian army were systematically delayed by Rothschild companies like Vickers Maxim, and eventually the soldiers mutinied. Vickers Maxim was controlled by Ernest Cassel, a business associate of Kuhn, Loeb amd Company and the biggest shareholders were the Rothschilds. The daughter of Ernest Cassal would marry Lord Mountbatten, a Rothschild,[9] and the man who arranged the marriage of Queen Elizabeth II to his nephew, Prince Philip. The interconnecting reptilian bloodlines are simply fantastic.

The Russian Revolution ended 300 years of rule by the Romanov family which had begun in the 17th century with Mikhail Romanov, who is believed to have been supported by the occultist and Rosicrucian, Dr Arthur Dee, and the British Secret Service. Arthur Dee was the son of Dr John Dee, the infamous astrologer to Queen

Elizabeth I. But these families are all subordinate to the Agenda and now it was time for the Romanovs to go. The same applied to the Habsburg and Hohenstaufen dynasties in the same period. The infrastructure was long in place to unseat the Romanovs, with Freemasonry, the Rosicrucians, and other secret groupings flourishing in Russia from the second half of the 18th century. The first charge to remove the Romanovs was led by Alexander Kerensky, a Freemason, funded from Wall Street and London. A second and more brutal wave was led by Leon Trotsky and Lenin. Trotsky left Germany to live in New York and it was from there that he set off on his journey to Russia and the Bolshevik Revolution. He entered Russia on a United States passport provided for him by the President, Woodrow Wilson, and on his person was $10,000 provided by the Rockefellers. He was joined in Russia by Lenin who was given safe passage in a sealed train across Germany from Switzerland via Sweden. Massive amounts of Bolshevik propaganda was financed by the Germans. While Lenin, Trotsky, and the rest were publicly condemning 'capitalism', they were being financed by the Brotherhood bankers of Wall Street and London, the same people who would later support Hitler. In his autobiography Trotsky would refer to some of these loans, many of which were arranged by the Round Table's Alfred Milner and 'Alexander' Gruzenberg (real name Michael), the chief Bolshevik agent in Scandinavia. He was a confidential advisor to the J. P. Morgan (Payseur)-owned Chase National Bank in New York. One of the most active middle men between the Bolsheviks, London, and Wall Street, was Olof Aschberg who became known as the Bolshevik's banker. He owned Nya Banken, founded in Stockholm in 1912. Aschberg's London agent was the North Commerce Bank, chaired by Earl Grey, a member of the Round Table and friend of Cecil Rhodes. Another close associate of Aschberg was Max May, the vice-president of the J. P. Morgan (Payseur) Guaranty Trust and head of its overseas operations.

In 1915, the American International Corporation had been formed to fund the Russian Revolution. It's directors represented the interests of the Rockefellers, Kuhn, Loeb and Company (Rothschilds), DuPont, Harriman, and the Federal Reserve. They also included George Herbert Walker Bush, the grandfather of George Bush. The Rothschilds were directly financing the Revolution via Jacob Schiff at Kuhn, Loeb and Company. International Brotherhood bankers from Britain, the United States, Russia, Germany, and France met in Sweden in the Summer of 1917. They agreed that Kuhn, Loeb and Company would deposit $50 million in a Swedish bank account for Lenin and Trosky's use. In an article in *The New York American Journal* on February 3rd 1949, Jacob Schiff's grandson said that his grandfather had paid the two 'revolutionaries' an additional $20 million. The payment of $20 million to the Bolsheviks by Elishu Root (the Kuhn, Loeb and Company's lawyer and former Secretary of State) via the Special War Fund, is recorded in the Congressional Record of September 2nd 1919. This investment not only furthered the Brotherhood Agenda, it realised an unbelievable profit. Some researchers suggest that Lenin repaid Kuhn, Loeb, the rouble equivalent of $450 million between 1918 and 1922. This was nothing compared with the profits accrued from the exploitation of Russian land, its economy and people, including the theft of the Tsar's gold and his vast financial holdings which were held, and stolen, by the very banks who had funded the revolution. Russia, like the rest of the world, has been raped by the reptilians. There is so much more to tell about this story and I do so in *...And The Truth Shall Set You Free*, but I wanted to give you enough to see that the Russian Revolution, and all that came out of it, was another operation by the Brotherhood.

Communism would also be played against Fascism (the same thing in truth) in the Second World War, and when that was over, fear of the Soviet 'monster' was used to further manipulate global events and justify enormous arms spending with the very armament and aircraft companies owned by the reptilians. Therefore they ensured there was either parity or the Soviet Union were slightly ahead, and in this way they created fear on both sides and a reason to keep buying ever more expensive weapons from their companies – 'keep up with the Russians'. The Cold War was classic manipulation. The people of the West were terrified of the Soviet Union and the people of the Soviet Union were terrified of the West while both sides were secretly controlled by the same people. At the heart of this was the emergence of nuclear weapons during the Second World War thanks to the Manhattan Project in America led by Robert Oppenhiemer. The Manhattan Project was supported by the Brotherhood-controlled Institute for Advanced Study at Princeton University where Albert Einstein was a regular visitor. Einstein, who worked on the development of the atomic bomb, was a close associate of Bernard Baruch and Lord Victor Rothschild (Comm 300), the man who controlled British Intelligence for decades. Rothschild used these very contacts to supply the State of Israel with the know-how to build nuclear weapons. But, of course, if the United States had these devastating weapons and the Russians did not, there would be no Cold War, so the technological knowledge was passed on to them. Pavel A. Sudoplatov, the head of the Soviet Intelligence Bureau on the atomic problem during World War Two, has now confirmed that Oppenhiemer was supplying data about the bomb to the Soviet Union during the war.[10] Klaus Fuchs, the German physicist, worked on the Manhattan Project after fleeing from Germany to Britain in 1933. Fuchs, an associate of Lord Victor Rothschild, was later jailed for fourteen years for supplying British and American atomic secrets to the Russians. I know from people I have met in the intelligence community in the United States, and from the research of other writers, that nuclear weapons know-how was being passed from the United States to the Soviet Union throughout the Cold War, not least through the Pugwash Conferences inspired by Einstein and Bertrand Russell (Comm 300) of the bloodline Russell family. Pugwash comes from the name of the Canadian estate of the industrialist Cyrus Eaton, where the conferences were held. Eaton began his career as secretary to J. D. Rockefeller and became a business partner of the Rockefeller dynasty. In 1946, Bertrand Russell, a friend of Einstein, said it was necessary to use the fear of nuclear weapons to force all nations to give up their sovereignty and submit to the dictatorship of the United Nations.[11]

Eventually the Agenda's time-scale reached the point where the countries of the Soviet Union had to be encompassed into the European Union and NATO in line with the plan for a world government and world army. That could not be done while the Soviet Union was still there and seen as the 'evil empire'. Onto the stage suddenly came Michail Gorbachev, an associate and subordinate of those two Brotherhood manipulators, Henry Kissinger and David Rockefeller, and it was his job to play the good guy and break up the Soviet Union. The Berlin Wall came down and people thought it was a blow for freedom, but it was just another step on the road to total global domination. Gorbachev left office and now runs the Brotherhood-funded Gorbachev Foundation which puts on prestigious conferences calling for a world government. He is another shape-shifting reptilian as seen by contacts of mine.

The creation of Israel

Zionism is often said to be the heart of the conspiracy, but I don't agree. It is part of it yes, but the Brotherhood network is far bigger than that. Zionism is not the Jewish people, it is a political movement. Many Jews do not support it, many non-Jews do. To say that Zionism is the Jewish people is like saying the Democratic Party is the American people. Yet to challenge the extremes of Zionism is to be called anti-Semitic or anti-Jewish. What utter balls. Just as the Republic of South Africa is really the Fiefdom of Oppenheimers, so the State of Israel is really the State of Rothschild. Zionism was the creation of the Rothschilds on behalf of the Brotherhood and in truth it is not Zionist, but SIONism, a branch of the reptile-Aryan Sun cult religion. It has been used to ensure the take over of Arab Palestine for two main reasons. This is sacred land for the reptile-Aryans going back to the Levites and the ancient world. Also blatantly stealing an Arab country offered endless opportunities to foster conflict and division in the Middle East, and this was particularly effective in manipulating the Arab oil states. The crucial moment in the Rothschild plan for 'Israel' was the Balfour Declaration when the British Foreign Secretary, Arthur (Lord) Balfour, announced on November 6th 1917 that Britain supported the claim for a Jewish homeland in Palestine. The Rothschild-dominated Versailles Peace Conference confirmed their support for this also. Surprise, surprise. But what was this Balfour Declaration? It was not made to members of the Westminster Parliament. It was simply a letter from Lord Balfour (Comm 300), an inner-circle member of the Round Table secret society, to Lord Lionel Walter Rothschild (Comm 300), who funded the Round Table! It was a letter between two members of the same secret society. Rothschild was a representative of the English Federation of Zionists which was set up with Rothschild money. It is widely believed by researchers that the 'Balfour' letter was actually written by Lord Rothschild together with Alfred Milner (Comm 300), the Round Table's leading light who had been made chairman of the mining giant, Rio Tinto Zinc, by the same Lord Rothschild. Rio Tinto is heavily involved in South Africa and a major shareholder apparently is the Queen of England. The Arabs of Palestine were used to fight the Turks in the First World War under the command of the Englishmen, T. E. Lawrence (Lawrence of Arabia) who promised them full sovereignty for their efforts. All along he knew that the Brotherhood plan was for the 'Jewish' (Khazar-Aryan) homeland in Palestine. Lawrence, a close friend of Winston Churchill, later admitted this fact when he said:

> "I risked the fraud on my conviction that Arab help was necessary to our cheap and easy victory in the East, and that better we win and break our word, than lose… The Arab inspiration was our main tool for winning the Eastern War. So I assured them that England kept her word in letter and in spirit. In this comfort they performed their fine things; but, of course, instead of being proud of what we did together, I was continually bitter and ashamed."[12]

Such has been the reptile-Aryan modus operandi for thousands of years. It was the Rothschilds who funded the early 'Jewish' settlers in Palestine; it was the Rothschilds who helped to create and fund Hitler and the Nazis in the Second World War which included the sickening treatment of Jews, gypsies, communists, and others; it was the Rothschilds who used the understandable post-war sympathy for the 'Jews' they had mercilessly exploited to press through their demands for a take-over of Arab Palestine; it was the Rothschilds who funded the 'Jewish' terrorist groups in Palestine which bombed, murdered, and terrorised Israel into existence; and it was the Rothschilds who funded and manipulated these terrorists into the key positions in Israel, among them the Prime Ministers, Ben-Gurion, Shamir, Begin, and Rabin. These men would spend the rest of their lives condemning the terrorism of others with an hypocrisy which beggars belief; it was Lord Victor Rothschild, the controller of British Intelligence, who provided the know-how for Israel's nuclear weapons; it was the Rothschilds who owned and controlled Israel from the start and have continued ever since to dictate its policy; it was the Rothschilds and the rest of the Brotherhood network which has hidden and suppressed the fact, confirmed by Jewish historians, that the overwhelming majority of 'Jewish' people in Israel originate genetically from the Caucasus Mountains, not from the lands they now occupy. The Jewish people have been sacrificed on the Rothschild altar of greed and lust for power, but even the Rothschilds take their orders from a higher authority which, I believe, is probably based in Asia, and the Far East dictates to the operational headquarters in London. Ultimately, the whole scam is orchestrated from the lower fourth dimension. For the background, detail, and sources, to support the statements I have just made, again you will find them in …*And The Truth Shall Set You Free.*

The Second World War

At the Versailles Peace Conference in 1919 a number of decisions were made which culminated in the genocide known as World War Two. Firstly the reparations imposed on the German people were so fantastic that the Weimar Republic which followed the war had no chance of economic survival. This was precisely as planned. That economic chaos was a massive problem in need of a solution and the solution was Adolf Hitler. The second important development, in a secret meeting of the Versailles collaborators at the Hotel Majestic in Paris, was the creation of offshoot organisations connected to the original Round Table. The first came in 1920 with the formation of the Institute of International Affairs, also known as Chatham House, at 10 St James's Square in London. The monarch is its official head and it was given the title Royal Institute in 1926. It's American branch, the Council on Foreign Relations, was formed by the American members of the Round Table in 1921 with funds from the Rockefellers and others. These were additions to the Brotherhood network designed to control even more completely British and American politics and indeed the much wider world. They are both the same organisation under different names. The Royal Institute of International Affairs (RIIA) was formed by friends of Cecil Rhodes and all the familiar names, including the Astors. It was funded, as it is today, by a long, long, list of global corporations and media groups owned by the bloodline families. I list them in ...*And The Truth Shall Set You Free.*

The Royal Institute connects into the top levels of politics, banking, business, media, all the usual stuff. For instance, one of its top figures was Major John (Jacob) Astor (Comm 300), a director of the Hambros (Brotherhood) Bank and owner after 1922 of the *Times* newspaper. Other founders included Sir Abe Bailey, the owner of Transvaal Mines in South Africa who worked with Alfred Milner to start the Boer War; and John W. Wheeler-Bennett, who would be General Eisenhower's 'political advisor' in London in the last two crucial years of the Second World War when the design for the post war world was being drawn. The Institute interlocks with British universities like Oxford and Cambridge and the London School of Economics which has produced many of the 'radicals' of the political 'left'. Adolf Hitler's infamous book, *Mein Kampf*, was ghost-written by Major General Karl Haushofer, who acknowledged that a major source of the ideas it expressed was Halford J. MacKinder, a director of the London School of Economics. As with the Round Table, Royal Institute branches were established in Australia, Canada, New Zealand, Nigeria, Trinidad and Tobago, and India, where it is known as the Council of World Affairs. Its American branch, the Council on Foreign Relations (CFR), made its home at Harold Pratt House at 58 East 68th Street in New York, the former mansion of the Pratt family, friends of the Rockefellers. It was organised by Colonel Mandel House, J. P. Morgan (Payseur), the Rockefellers, and their associates. The CFR was soon in control of the United States and that remains the case today. Look at its membership and you will find the top people in all the institutions which control the lives of the American people, including education. These organisations, like the Round Table, are made up of inner and outer circles. The inner circle knows the Agenda and works full time to achieve it. The next circle knows much of the Agenda and works to that end in their particular sphere of influence. The next circle is pretty much in the dark about the real Agenda, but is manipulated to make the 'right' decisions in their area of operation without knowing the true reason for them. Admiral Chester Ward, a former US Judge Advocate General of the Navy, was a member of the CFR for sixteen years. He said that the purpose of the organisation was the "...submergence of US sovereignty and national independence into an all-powerful one-world government". In his book, *Kissinger On The Couch*, written with Phyllis Schafly, Ward said:

"...(*the*)...lust to surrender the sovereignty and independence of the United States is pervasive throughout most of the membership, and particularly in the leadership of several divergent cliques that make up what is actually a polycentric organisation... (*the main clique*) is composed of the one-world-global-government ideologists – more respectfully referred to as the organised internationalists. They are the ones who carry on the tradition of the founders."

Since 1921 virtually every President of the United States has been a member of the CFR along with most of the main government posts including most, today all, the American ambassadors around the world. The CFR also includes media owners, key journalists and editors, educationalists, military leaders, on and on it goes. The membership of the Royal Institute of International Affairs remains a secret, but it also includes people of the same positions and background in the United Kingdom and I stress the American CFR is subordinate to, and takes orders from, the Royal Institute in London. These interlock with the Illuminati; the 'knight' Orders like the Knights of St John of Jerusalem (Malta); the network controlled by the British monarch which I will reveal later; the Freemasons, Rosicrucians, and the Round Table; the American 'foundation' network like the Rockefeller Foundation and an endless web of interconnecting groups operating ultimately to the same global leadership. This network was spanning the globe by the 1930s and the Brotherhood was ready for its biggest project yet, the Second World War. It was an effort to achieve further centralisation of power and the creation of a global body which could be evolved into a world government. We know that body today as the United Nations.

With the German economy in tatters and inflation running at thousands of per cent, the German people looked to Adolf Hitler as their saviour. Problem-reaction-solution. As I document and source in ...*And The Truth Shall Set You Free*, the Nazis were funded from Wall Street and the City of London. This was done via the German subsidiaries of British and American companies and American loans known as the Young Plan and the Dawes Plan. These loans were supposed to be helping Germany to pay the reparations, but in fact went straight into Hitler's war machine. Standard Oil (the Rockefellers) and I. G. Farben, the German chemical cartel which ran the concentration camp at Auchwitz, were, in effect, the same company. Hitler came to power in 1933 and in that same year, no coincidence, Franklin Delano Roosevelt became President of the United States. His route to power was the same as Hitler's. In 1929, the Brotherhood bankers crashed the Wall Street stock-market and caused the Great Depression. From this problem came the solution, the 'New Deal' economic package offered by Roosevelt which won him the presidential election of 1933. This 'New Deal' was a replica of the economic package offered by Hitler to the German people to solve their manufactured economic problems. When he came to power, Roosevelt pulled off one of the biggest thefts in human history when he passed laws forcing the American people to hand over all their gold to the government in return for worthless pieces of paper known as Federal Reserve banknotes. This was necessary, he said, to solve the dire economic problems. Soon afterwards, with the American economy now completely under Brotherhood control, Roosevelt put their symbol, the pyramid and all seeing eye, on the dollar bill. He was saying to the American people: "Gotch-yer".

Franklin Roosevelt, a 33rd degree Freemason, held the title, Knight of Pythias, in a secret society called the Ancient Arabic Order of Nobles and Mystics. Among its previous members were Francis Bacon and the French revolutionary, Mirabeau. Membership is only open to Freemasons who have reached at least the 32nd degree or are members of the Templar lodges of Freemasonry.[13] The Order was allegedly founded by a descendant of Mohammed who based it on a secret society in medieval Europe which included Jews, Arabs, and Christians.[14] Its symbol is a crescent moon represented by the claws of a Bengal Tiger, engraved with a pyramid, an urn, and the pentagram, a combination representing the Universal Mother: Isis-Semiramis-Ninkharsag.[15] Roosevelt's Secretary of Agriculture, Henry Wallace, was also an occultist who was involved in the decision to put the all-seeing eye symbol on the dollar bill.[16] Wallace had a guru, the Russian mystic and artist, Nicholas Roerich, who spent many years travelling through Nepal and Tibet studying with the lamas and searching for the lost city of Shamballa, the legendary home of the secret occult adepts or 'masters' who are said to have secretly 'influenced' world affairs throughout history. They are variously known as the Secret Chiefs, the Hidden Masters, or the Great White Brotherhood and some researchers believe they are the force behind the creation of the Freemasons, Sufis, Knights Templar, Rosicrucians, Theosophical Society, and the Hermetic Order of the Golden Dawn.[17] I think these people are reptilians, some of them anyway. Roerich was involved in the formation of the League of Nations, the first attempt at world government, and supported the work of Dr Andrija Puharich, a scientist who helped to develop the psychic powers of a young Israeli called Uri Geller.[18]

In Britain, the Round Table-Royal Institute of International Affairs members in the Houses of Parliament at first called for appeasement with Germany until Hitler's military build up had reached the point where he could fight a long war. Then suddenly, as I show clearly in ...*And The Truth Shall Set You Free*, they switched and called for all-out war against Hitler. Among the most grotesque examples of this were Lady Astor, Leopold Amery, Lionel Curtis, and Lord Lothian, all members of the Round Table and/or the Royal Institute of International Affairs. Lord Halifax, the Foreign Secretary and a Round Table member almost from its foundation, was another who supported the appeasement of Hitler. He met Hitler on November 19th 1937 and Hitler's representative, Alfred Rosenberg, had come to Britain in May 1933, to meet with Sir Henry Deterding (Comm 300), head of Royal Dutch Shell, Geoffrey Dawson, the editor of the *Times* newspaper owned by the Astors (Round Table, Royal Institute, Comm 300), the 1st Viscount Hailsham, the Secretary for War, Walter Eliot MP, and the Duke of Kent, brother of King Edward VIII and King George VI. We will see the British Royal family's Nazi connections later. The sudden change from appeasement with Hitler to war with him was mirrored in Downing Street as the appeaser prime minister, Neville Chamberlain, was replaced by the

Brotherhood's man of war, Winston Churchill, on May 11th 1940. Soon after his appointment, the mass bombing of civilian targets in Germany began. The reptile-Aryan black magicians had themselves another global blood ritual.

Churchill's membership of the Freemasons has often been played down as it has with Prince Philip. But Churchill was in fact, behind the scenes, a very active Mason after his initiation into the Studholme Lodge (No 1591) at the Cafe Royal in May 1901.[19] Local historians in Bradford, England, uncovered evidence that some of Churchill's wartime policies were influenced by the fact that he and King George II of Greece were Masons. One example of this was in 1943 when Churchill sent 5,000 troops to Athens to restore George to the throne even though the beleaguered monarch was detested by all sides and the troops were needed elsewhere.[20] The Churchill family has close links with the Rothschilds and the esoteric underground. Winston Churchill joined the Albion Lodge of the Ancient Order of Druids at Blenheim Palace on August 15th 1908.[21] His father, Lord Randolph Churchill, was funded by the House of Rothschild while he was Chancellor of the Exchequer in the mid 1800s and his closest friend was Nathaniel Rothschild. When Randolph died, he was in debt to the Rothschilds to the tune of £65,000, a fantastic amount in those days.[22] Winston, too, was in debt to them and he was a good friend of Lord Victor Rothschild, the orchestrator of British Intelligence, and the Rothschilds' arch manipulator in the United States, Bernard Baruch. Churchill had close links with the Cecil family who, in effect, controlled him, and the Cecils have long time connections with the networks created by that Brotherhood front, the Jesuits, and to the Habsburgs, the British monarchs, and the families of the Black Nobility in Italy. The Churchills are related to the Duke of Marlborough family who played an important role in putting William of Orange on the British throne and in fact Winston Churchill was born at their ancestral home, Blenheim Palace, near Oxford. Churchill knew exactly what he was doing and the image of him left us by official history is a farce. He did not save the British Isles from tyranny, he was part of the tyranny.

An American decoding officer at the United States Embassy in London called Tyler Kent was jailed throughout the war for passing evidence to the Conservative MP, Colonel Ramsey, that Churchill and Roosevelt had been communicating in coded messages before Churchill was Prime Minister making arrangements to ensure that war would break out. Ramsey was also jailed under a law called Regulation 18b which was introduced just before the war, the Government said, to deal with terrorism by the Irish Republican Army (IRA). Another problem-reaction-solution. This was merely the excuse they used to have a law in place that would allow them to jail people without trial during the war and so keep the lid on their game. One woman, an admiral's wife, was jailed under regulation 18b as she left a courtroom which had cleared her of all charges! The man behind this law was Lord Victor Rothschild, one of the most important manipulators of the second half of the 20th century and a friend of Winston Churchill. It was Churchill who began to use Regulation 18b as soon as he took office in order to jail people who knew what was going on and were prepared to say so. The American Ambassador in London in this period was Joseph Kennedy, the deeply crooked father of John F. Kennedy. The

Kennedy's are an Elite bloodline going back to the Irish kings and beyond. To complete the set, the British ambassadors in America during the war were Lord Lothian of the Royal Institute of International Affairs and Lord Halifax of the Royal Institute, Round Table, and Committee of 300. Franklin Roosevelt won a second term as President in 1937 by repeating over and over that the sons of America were not going to fight in another war in Europe, while he knew full well that that was exactly what they were going to do. Representative Philip Bennett of Missouri told Congress:

"But our boys are not going to be sent abroad, says the President. Nonsense, Mr Chairman; even now their berths are being built in our transport ships. Even now the tags for identification of the dead and wounded are being printed by the firm of William C. Ballantyne and Co of Washington."[23]

Roosevelt had come to power for the second time by saying that America would not fight in another war in Europe and so when he returned to the White House he had a public relations problem because he was already helping to arrange that very war. As with Woodrow Wilson and the sinking of the Lusitania, a problem-reaction-solution was organised to give him the excuse to break his 'promises'. In 1939, Senator P. Nye of North Dakota said that he had seen a series of volumes called *The Next War*, including one called *Propaganda In The Next War* which originated in London (of course!). It revealed the game plan for manipulating America into the Second World War. This document, written between the wars, said:

"To persuade her (*the United States*) to take our part will be much more difficult, so difficult as to be unlikely to succeed. It will need a definite threat to America, a threat moreover, which will have to be brought home by propaganda to every citizen, before the Republic will again take arms in an external quarrel...

"...The position will naturally be considerably eased if **Japan** (*my emphasis*) were involved, and this might and probably would bring America in without further ado. At any rate, it would be a natural and obvious effect of our propagandists to achieve this, just as in the Great War they succeeded in embroiling the United States against Germany.

"Fortunately with America, our propaganda is on firm ground. We can be entirely sincere, as our main plank will be the old democratic one. We must clearly enunciate our belief in the democratic form of government, and our firm resolve to adhere to... the old goddess of democracy routine."[24]

On December 7th 1941, Japanese planes attacked Pearl Harbor, Hawaii, and the United States entered the war. It has since been established that many intercepted messages gave Roosevelt considerable prior warning of the Japanese attack, but no action was taken and Americans were left to die for the sake of the Brotherhood Agenda as literally billions of people have these past few thousand years. The attack itself came after a long campaign by the Americans to goad Japan into attacking them. Henry Stimson, Roosevelt's Secretary of War and a founder of the Council on Foreign Relations, had said: "We face the delicate question of diplomatic fencing to be done so as to be sure Japan is put into the wrong and makes the first bad overt move."[25]

That is the brief summary of how the Second World War was visited upon the planet and how tens of millions of men, women, and children, lost their lives. The climax was to drop two atomic bombs on Japan which had already agreed to surrender on the very same terms it eventually agreed to after the bombs had caused such devastation. Again the detailed background to all this is in ...*And The Truth Shall Set You Free*. The man who ordered those bombs to be dropped was President Harry S. Truman who had replaced Franklin Roosevelt at the end of the war. Truman was a 33rd degree Freemason and when he reached that level he added the middle 'S' which stood for Solomon. Truman was a failed haberdasher and deemed unemployable before the Freemasons launched his career. His mother lost her farm because of his debts and when he became President he used to go on nightly drunken binges around the back alleys of Washington followed at a discreet distance by two FBI agents despatched by J. Edgar Hoover to look after him.[26] Truman's career took off after he became chief organiser of the Freemasonic lodges in Missouri and then he was nominated to become a judge before moving into the White House.[27] The man behind this meteoric rise was another Mason and the head of organised crime in Kansas City, Boss Prendergast.[28] Truman's closest confidant was David Niles, or Neyhus, who had one sister in an important position in the government of Israel and another making policy in Moscow![29] This is the background to Harry S. Truman, the Freemason placeman, who refused to accept Japan's terms of surrender, ordered the atomic devastation, and then accepted the surrender on the same terms he had refused before. The bombs were dropped because as one phase ended in the reptilian Agenda, another was immediately begun – the Cold War – and it is so much easier to engender the fear necessary for that if people have seen for themselves what happens when one of these devices explodes.

After the war, the world was mentally, emotionally, spiritually and physically devastated. This allowed the banks to make vast fortunes lending money to governments to rebuild the societies destroyed by a war the same banks had funded. This massively increased the debt owed by nations to private banks and the control over those countries increased in proportion. The desperation for peace made the world open to the main reason the Brotherhood had created the war – the formation of the United Nations. Problem-reaction-solution (*see* **Figure 22**). The charter for the United Nations, the global body the Brotherhood so badly wanted, was written by a committee of the Council on Foreign Relations. The writer, James Perloff, revealed the background to the UN in his 1988 book, *The Shadows Of Power: The Council On Foreign Relations And The American Decline*:

"In January 1943, the Secretary of State, Cordell Hull, formed a steering committee composed of himself, Leo Pasvolsky, Isaiah Bowman, Sumner Welles, Norman Davis, and Morton Taylor. All these men – with the exception of Hull – were in the CFR. Later known as the Informal Agenda Group, they drafted the original proposal of the United Nations. It was Bowman – a founder of the CFR and a founder of Colonel House's old 'Inquiry' (*another Elite grouping*) – who first put forward the concept. They called in three attorneys, all CFR men, who ruled that it was constitutional. Then they discussed it with Franklin D. Roosevelt on June 15th 1944. The President approved the plan and announced it to the public the next day." [30]

In his book, *The American Language*, H. L. Mencken suggests that the term 'United Nations' was decided by President Roosevelt during a meeting with Winston Churchill at the White House in December 1941, shortly before the attack on Pearl Harbor. When the United Nations was officially formed in San Francisco on June 26th 1945, the US delegation included 74 members of the CFR, including John J. McCloy, the CFR chairman from 1953-70, a member of the Committee of 300, chairman of the Ford Foundation and the Rockefellers' Chase Manhattan Bank, and friend and advisor to nine presidents from Roosevelt to Reagan. Also there were John Foster Dulles, the Hitler supporter, CFR founder, and soon-to-be US Secretary of State, and Nelson Rockefeller, the Satanist and arch manipulator, who was four times Governor of New York and Vice President to Gerald Ford after Richard Nixon was ousted by Watergate. Remember, too, that while the CFR created the United Nations, it is still only a branch of the Royal Institute of International Affairs in London, which is only an offshoot of the Round Table, which is only an agency of an even higher authority in the hierarchy. The Rockefellers paid for the headquarters of the League of Nations in Geneva and now they gave the land for the United Nations building in New York. The land had previously been used for a slaughter house and that was exactly what the Satanists of the Brotherhood wanted. Land covered in blood, fear, and pain, for the foundations of the organisation designed to do the same to human beings.

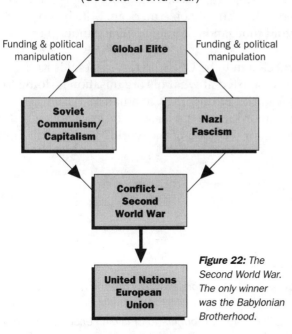

Problem-Reaction-Solution

(Second World War)

Funding & political manipulation

Global Elite

Funding & political manipulation

Soviet Communism/ Capitalism

Nazi Fascism

Conflict – Second World War

United Nations European Union

Figure 22: *The Second World War. The only winner was the Babylonian Brotherhood.*

The UN is a Trojan Horse for world government and it sits atop a vast network of organisations which present themselves as serving the people when in fact they are fronts for the most grotesque manipulation, not least in the developing world of Africa, Asia, South and Central America. The UN network includes the World Health Organisation (WHO), a wholly-owned subsidiary of the Anglo-American-Swiss pharmaceutical cartel with its interlocking leadership. The WHO tell the world there is going to be an epidemic of something or other and its controllers, the pharmaceutical corporations, provide the vaccine. Another problem-reaction-solution and the vaccines are causing untold harm to the physical and spiritual well being of billions. The UN Population Fund uses 'population control' for a policy of eugenics against people with black faces and those with white faces who are not up to the genetic 'purity' (reptilian bloodline) demanded by these deeply imbalanced people. The UN Environment Programme uses the environment as an excuse to create international laws, take control of great swathes of land, and steal land from developing countries under the heading of 'debt for nature' swaps. UNESCO, the science and culture operation, advances the Agenda across many areas of life. Now the United Nations, which was set up to stop war, according to the propaganda, is actually going to war. This happened in the Gulf when American, British and French soldiers and pilots killed untold thousands of Iraqi civilians under the banner of the UN flag.

Today the latest of the stooges wheeled in to be UN Secretary-general is Kofi Annan, a black man who ought to be disgusted at what his organisation is doing to his African continent. An advisor is Maurice Strong, the Canadian oil tycoon, Rockefeller clone, and manipulator extraordinaire, not least of the environment movement. The United Nations is there for the good of the world? Yes, sure it is. Oh look, another pig goes flying by.

■ SOURCES

1   Dr John Coleman, *Committee Of 300, The Conspirators Hierarchy* (Joseph Holding Company, Nevada, USA, 1995).

2   Fritz Springmeier and Cisco Wheeler, *The Illuminati Formula To Create An Undetectable Total Mind Controlled Slave* (Springmeier, S.E. Clackamas Road, Clackamas, Oregon, 97015, 1996), p 61. I will list it as *The Illuminati Formula* from now on.

3   Ibid.

4   *The Occult Conspiracy*, p 116.

5   Ibid, p 117.

6   Said at a hearing of the post-war Graham Committee which investigated Baruch.

7   Norman Dodd reported these findings in an interview with the writer, William H. McIllhany II, for his 1980 book, *The Tax Exempt Foundations* (Arlington House, Westport, USA). The Special House Committee to Investigate Tax Exempt Foundations reported in 1954. It was named after its chairman, Representative, B. Carrol Reece of Tennessee.

8   Ibid.

9   *The Top 13 Illuminati Bloodlines*, p 154.

10   *The Spotlight* newspaper, May 16th and September 12th 1994.

11   *Bulletin Of Atomic Scientists*, October 1946.

12   Documents on British Foreign Policy, 1919–1939, first series Volume IV, pp 245–247.

13   *The Occult Conspiracy*, p 93.

14   Ibid.

15   Ibid.

16   Ibid.

17   Ibid, p 94.

18   Ibid, p 96.

19   *Scallywag* magazine, issue 26, 1994, p 35.

20   Ibid.

21   A picture of this event appears in *The Top 13 Illuminati Bloodlines*, p 100.

22   *The Churchills*, Independent Television, May 1995.

23   Quoted by A. H. M Ramsey in *The Nameless War* (Omni Publications, London, 1952).

24   Congressional Record, 76th Congress, Volume 84, No 82, pp 6597–6604.

25   Jim Keith, *Casebook On Alternative 3* (IllumiNet Press, Lilburn, USA, 1994), p 25.

26   *The Curse Of Canaan*, p 54.

27   Ibid.

28   Ibid.

29   Ibid.

30   James Perloff, *The Shadows Of Power: The Council On Foreign Relations And The American Decline*, p 71.

CHAPTER TWELVE

The Black Sun

S o many of the strands of history related in this book can be found in the beliefs of Adolf Hitler and the Nazis. This is no surprise because the Nazi Party was the creation of a network of secret societies which had access to the underground stream of knowledge that carries the true, or truer, story of human origins.

Germany has long been a centre for esoteric thinking and secret societies and, as we have seen, among the most prominent occult families in Middle Ages Germany were the Bauers, a strand of which changed their name to Rothschild. Much of the Windsor blood also comes via Germany. The Bavarian Illuminati, which was involved in many of the 'people's' revolutions in Europe, including the French, was founded in Germany on May 1st 1776 by the occultist, Adam Weishaupt, and the Christian Church was split into Catholics and Protestants by Martin Luther, the German agent for the Rosicrucian Order. Germany is another centre for global manipulation. Hitler was not the creator of Nazi belief, merely the public expression of it. In the 19th century one of the pre-Hitler prophets was the composer Richard Wagner, and his composition, *The Ride Of The Valkyries*, captures his obsession with the invading powers of evil. Wagner declared the imminent arrival of the Master Race. His work, *The Ring*, was the musical expression of his belief in German 'supermen' bestriding the world stage like the ancient Pagan gods, Wotan and Thor. Hitler would later say that to understand Nazi Germany, one had to know Wagner. One of the students of master-race fanatic Wagner, was the composer, Gustav Mahler. His studies with Wagner were funded by Baron Albert de Rothschild. One of the places to which Wagner travelled and researched was Rennes-le-Chateau, that mysterious village in southern France so connected to the Knights Templar and the Cathars. Indeed, the German secret society underground is closely aligned to the Templar traditions and those contemporaries of the original Templars, the Teutonic Knights.

Adolf Hitler was officially born in 1889 at Braunau-am-Inn, on the border of Germany and the Austria-Hungary Empire. There are, however, other theories which suggest that he was actually of a Rothschild bloodline or even was Prince Albert, Duke of Clarence and Avondale, the grandson of Queen Victoria, who was supposed to have died of pneumonia at Sandringham in January 1892. His funeral arrangements decreed that there would be no lying in state, no embalming of the body, and no 'excess' of mourning. Albert does not appear to have been 'the full picnic', as they say, and Hitler certainly wasn't. There were rumours at the time that

Albert's death had been faked because his mental instability made him unfit for the responsibilities of kingship (I can't think why!). There are many theories about Prince Albert, including one that he was the notorious serial killer in Victorian London known as Jack the Ripper, who killed his prostitute victims in ritual fashion and wrote Freemasonic messages at the scene of his crimes. One thing is obvious from the evidence, Jack the Ripper was connected to the highest levels of the British establishment and, most probably, the royal family. There have been claims and rumours periodically that Prince Albert didn't die at Sandringham and instead was taken to Germany. This would have been easy because the British royal family of Queen Victoria and the Prince Albert were a German royal line and they had more blood relatives in Germany than they did in England. The name of the 'British' royal house at that time was the German House of Saxe-Coburg-Gotha. In the early years of the Nazi Party, when Hitler was virtually unknown outside of Bavaria, three of his financial sponsors were the Duke of Saxe-Coburg-Gotha, the Grand Duke of Hesse, and the Grand Duchess Victoria, the former wife of the Grand Duke of Hesse. All were first cousins to Albert, Duke of Clarence! Another first cousin was Kaiser Wilhelm II. Why would German royalty give such support to Hitler, a corporal in the First World War? If it is correct that Albert became Hitler, then the 'Fuhrer' would have been much older than the age he claimed to be. Picture evidence suggests that, in fact, Hitler was considerably older than the official account. His mistress, Eva Braun, described him to her sister as "an elderly gentleman of uncertain age". Let me emphasise that I am not saying that any of these theories are true because I don't know, but if you look in the picture section at the side-by-side shots of Hitler and Albert taken 25 years apart, you will see one reason why such rumours persist. They look remarkably similar when you take the 25 years into account. Maybe it's all coincidence, but if you know any more about this, I would be very keen to hear from you. See the address to send information at the back of the book.

The esoteric became a consuming passion for Hitler, especially in his rise to power. He was strongly influenced by the work of Helena Petrovna Blavatsky, who was born in the Ukraine in 1831 and later, one reliable researcher told me, became an agent for British Intelligence. Other researchers claim she had connections with the secret society of Italian revolutionaries, the Carbonari, who were closely linked to the Black Nobility, and she was a member of the Egyptian society, the Brotherhood of Luxor, which she later denounced as "a den for disgusting immorality, greediness for selfish power, and moneymaking". Madam Blavatsky arrived in New York in 1873 and, with the help of a Colonel Henry Olcott, she founded the Theosophical Society two years later. This is still around today. The Theosophical Society's headquarters in America were in California at Krotona. The Pythagorean mystery school in ancient Greece was at Crotona. Blavatsky's society was yet another mystery school derivative. Its doctrines are based on Blavatsky's books such as *Isis Unveiled*, which was written in 1877, and *The Secret Doctrine*, published in 1888, which are themselves based on the Hebrew Cabala. She claimed to be in psychic contact with hidden masters or supermen. These hidden masters, she said, lived in central Asia and could be contacted telepathically by those who knew the secret to the esoteric mysteries.

Today we call this process of communication 'channelling'. There are many UFO sightings and much research which indicate that there are secret underground and underwater bases for extraterrestrials around the world, central Asia among them. This connects with the endless legends and ancient traditions all over the world of a Master Race living within the Earth. The belief in the Masters and the Great White Brotherhood of discarnate entities promoted by people like the Theosophical psychic of the post-Blavatsky period, Alice Bailey, is a theme that remains well entrenched in what is known today as the New Age movement. Alice Bailey founded the Arcane esoteric school. She claimed to 'channel' an entity she called the 'Tibetan' and she produced a number of books including *Hierarchy Of The Masters*, *The Seven Rays*, *A New Group Of World Servers*, and *New World Religion*. Bailey said that her Tibetan Master had told her the Second World War was necessary to defend the plan of God. That sounds ridiculous to me, but there are many in the New Age field who believe that everything is part of 'the plan' and the will of God, even a global holocaust. It seems like a great excuse to do nothing and a cop out of mega proportions. We create our own reality and if we change our inner self we will change its outer reflection. Inner peace = outer peace. Wars don't have to happen as part of some plan of God. We create them and if we change our inner self, our attitudes, we can stop creating them. It's just a choice. My own view is that the Masters, the Great White Brotherhood, and this whole concept is something to be deeply wary of. Whenever I hear the term 'Master' I cringe.

Two organisations spawned by Alice Bailey's work, the Lucis Trust (formerly the Lucifer Trust) and the World Goodwill Organisation, are both staunch promoters of the United Nations. They are almost UN 'groupies', such is their devotion. It is interesting to see how the New Age has inherited 'truths' over the decades in the same way that conventional religion has done over the centuries. As the followers of Christianity have inherited the manipulated version of Jesus, so New Agers have inherited the Masters. There is too little checking of origins, too much acceptance of inherited belief, I think. Certainly there is with the Masters and Blavatsky's Great White Brotherhood because she admitted in correspondence with her sister, that she had made up their names by using the nicknames of the Rosicrucians and Freemasons who were funding her. Yet today all over the world there are hundreds of thousands (at least) of New Age 'channellers' who claim to be communicating with these Masters and with the Archangel Michael who is an ancient deity of the Phoenicians. If the New Age isn't careful, it will be Christianity revisited. It is already becoming so. I believe that the concept of Masters can be a means through which those who have rejected the status quo of religion and science can still have their minds controlled.

Another big influence on Hitler was the novel, *The Coming Race*, by the Englishman, Lord Edward Bulwer-Lytton (Comm 300), a British colonial minister heavily involved in imposing opium addiction on the Chinese. He was a close friend of the British Prime Minister, Benjamin Disraeli, and the writer, Charles Dickens, and was Grand Patron of the English Rosicrucian Society, which included Francis Bacon and John Dee among its earlier membership. Bulwer-Lytton was also a Grand Master of the Scottish Rite of Freemasonry and the head of British Intelligence. One of his operatives was Helena Blavatsky, a contact told me, and Bulwer-Lytton is often referred to in her book, *Isis Unveiled*. He is best known for his work, *The Last Days Of Pompeii*, but his passion was the world of esoteric magic. In *The Coming Race*, he wrote of an enormous civilisation inside the Earth, well ahead of our own. They had discovered a power called 'Vril' which, by the use of the psyche, could be used to perform 'miracles'. These underground supermen would, according to Bulwer-Lytton's novel, emerge on the surface one day and take control of the world. Many Nazis believed this. The themes of underground supermen, or hidden masters, can be found in most of the secret societies and in legends across the world. Certainly this was true of the Order of the Golden Dawn, formed in 1888 by Dr Wynn Westcott, a Freemason, and S.L. Mathers. They called their Masters the Secret Chiefs. This supports the ancient and modern theme of extraterrestrials or inner-Earth races living underground. Mathers devised a series of rituals and initiations designed to help his members access their full psychic and physical potential. He believed, however, that this gift was only for the few and he was a supporter of authoritarian government. These rituals would have attracted the extreme negative energies which allowed vibrational synchronisation – possession – with the reptilians or other lower fourth dimensional 'astral' entities which reside there. This is one of the main reasons for such black magic initiations, to plug in the initiate's consciousness to the reptilians and others in the lower fourth dimension. In the mid 1890s, there were temples of the Order of the Golden Dawn in London, Edinburgh, Bradford, Weston Super Mare, and Paris, where Mathers made his home. The Golden Dawn also spoke of the Vril force and one of their secret signs was the pointed-arm salute which the Nazis used when saying "Heil Hitler". It was yet another source of the esoteric foundations on which Nazism was built. Mathers had known Madam Blavatsky and so had the Master of the Order's London Temple, the poet William Butler Yeats, who would go on to win a Nobel Prize.

Remnants of the Order of the Golden Dawn continue to this day, but the original version splintered after a row between Yeats, Mathers, and the arch Satanist, Aleister Crowley, which split the membership into quarrelling factions. Other significant thinkers and groups which influenced the gathering Nazi philosophy included the Order of the Oriental Templars (OTO), which used sex rituals to create and harness the energy known as Vril, and two German esoteric magicians, Guido von List and Lanz von Liebenfels. In his summer solstice celebrations, List used wine bottles on the ground to form the symbol of the Hermetic Cross, also known as the Hammer of Thor. It was the Badge of Power in the Order of the Golden Dawn and we know this symbol as the swastika, the ancient Sun symbol of the Phoenician-Aryans. Lanz von Liebenfels (real name Adolf Lanz), used the swastika on a flag which flew over his 'temple' overlooking the Danube, and for these two black magicians it symbolised the end of Christianity and the dawning of the age of the blond-haired, blue-eyed, Aryan supermen. They believed in the racial inferiority of those they called the 'dark forces', such as the Jews, the Slavs, and the Negroes. Lebenfels recommended castration for these people. The two vons, List and

Liebenfels, were to have a massive influence on Adolf Hitler. In 1932, with Hitler on the verge of power, von Liebenfels would write to a fellow believer:

> "Hitler is one of our pupils... you will one day experience that he, and through him we, will one day be victorious and develop a movement that will make the world tremble."[1]

Two others who would influence the thinking and beliefs of Adolf Hitler were the Englishmen, Aleister Crowley and Houston Stewart Chamberlain. Crowley was born in Warwickshire in 1875. He rebelled against a strict religious upbringing and was initiated into the Order of the Golden Dawn in 1898 after leaving Cambridge University. He left the Order after the row with its founders and travelled to Mexico, India, and Ceylon, where he was introduced to yoga and Buddhism. He also became a record-breaking mountaineer. Buddhism replaced his interest in the occult until an experience in Cairo in April 1904. Crowley was asked by his wife, Rose, to perform an esoteric ritual to see what happened. During the ceremony she entered a trance-like state and began to channel the words of a communicator. "They are waiting for you" she said to Crowley. The "They", she said, was Horus, the god of war and the son of Osiris, in ancient Egyptian belief. Crowley did not accept any of this and asked his wife a series of detailed questions in an effort to trick her. But Rose, who apparently knew little of the esoteric, gave the correct answer every time, according to the official story. The reptilians were on the line again. The communicator told Crowley to be at a desk in his hotel room between noon and one oclock on three specific days. He agreed and in these periods he wrote, via automatic writing, a document called the *Book Of The Law*. Automatic writing is when your arm and hand are guided by another force and often no-one is more surprised at what they are writing than the person involved. Crowley's communication said that the old age of Osiris was being replaced by the new age of Horus. But it said the old age would first have to be destroyed by barbarism and the Earth bathed in blood. There would be a world war, he was told. The *Book Of The Law* taught of a race of supermen and condemned the old religions, pacifism, democracy, compassion, and humanitarianism. "Let my servants be few and secret: They shall rule the many and the known", the 'superman' continued. The message went on:

> "We have nothing with the outcasts and the unfit; let them die in their misery, for they feel not. Compassion is the vice of kings; stamp down the wretched and the weak; this is the law of the strong; this is our law and the joy of the world... Love one another with burning hearts; on the low men trample in the fierce lust of your pride in the day of your wrath... Pity not the fallen! I never knew them. I am not for them. I console not; I hate the consoled and the consoler...
>
> "I am unique and conqueror. I am not of the slaves that perish. Be they damned and dead. Amen... therefore strike hard and low and to hell with them, master... Lurk! Withdraw! Upon them! This is the law of the battle of conquest; thus shall my worship be about my secret house... Worship me with fire and blood; worship me with swords and

with spears. Let the woman be gurt with a sword before me; let blood flow in my name. Trample down the heathen; be upon them, O warrior, I will give you their flesh to eat... Sacrifice cattle, little and big; after a child... kill and torture; spare not; be upon them!."[2]

The classic sentiments of the lower fourth dimensional reptilians and the Satanic rings which serve them. If all that sounds remarkably like some of the angry God stuff in the Old Testament, that's because it was the same force which communicated to the ancients, to Crowley, and to anyone else on that vibration who would help to stimulate the conflict of human misery on which these reptiles feed. This is the force that controls the consciousness of those which have controlled the Babylonian Brotherhood since ancient times. When you read that diatribe, you will appreciate the mentality that can set out to create the horrors which have plagued the human race. Crowley apparently tried to ignore what he had written with his guided hand, but it would not go away, and from 1909 on he began to take it seriously. Very seriously. He said:

"After five years of folly and weakness, miss-called politeness, tact, discretion, care for the feeling of others, O I am weary of it. I say today: to hell with Christianity, rationalism, Buddhism, all the lumber of the centuries. I bring you a positive and primeval fact, Magic by name; and with this I will build me a new heaven and new Earth. I want none of your faint approval or faint dispraise; I want blasphemy, murder, rape, revolution, anything, bad or good, but strong."

Crowley left his former tutor, MacGregor Mathers, a broken man as he embarked on a psychic war against him. They both conjured up 'demons' to attack the other, but Mathers lost out. Such psychic wars are very much part of the Brotherhood armoury today. They war psychically with each other, but overwhelmingly with the population and people who are challenging their power. I have experienced such attacks myself and I understand how they can kill people in this way. Crowley's communicators would also take over the psyches of Adolf Hitler and other architects of Nazism. Long after his death, Crowley would become a hero to many involved in the Flower Power period of the 1960s, when the young were calling for love and peace. The irony is not lost. Crowley welcomed the First World War as necessary to sweep away the old age and usher in the new one. After going public with his revelations, Crowley was made the world head of the Germany-based, Order of the Oriental Templars (OTO), and this gave him very significant influence among like-thinkers in Germany. At the same time as he and his organisation were influencing the Nazis, Crowley was a 33rd degree Scottish Rite Freemason and an agent of the British Intelligence operation, MI6.[3] He was an advisor to his fellow Satanist, Winston Churchill.

Houston Stewart Chamberlain (Comm 300) was born in England in 1855, but moved to Germany in 1882. In 1908 he married Eva, the daughter of Richard Wagner, and became a prestigious writer. His best known work was *Foundations Of The Nineteenth Century* which ran to 1,200 pages and sold more than 250,000 copies.

It made him famous throughout the country. He was, however, a troubled man who had a series of nervous breakdowns. He felt himself to be taken over by demons and his books were written in a trance and a fever, which suggests that he was locked into the reptilians or another low vibrational consciousness via automatic writing. In his autobiography, he said he did not recognise such writing as his own. The themes of his work are very familiar: all civilisation comes from the Aryan race and the Germans were the purist of all; Jews were the enemy who would pollute the Aryan bloodlines (yawn). Kaiser Wilhelm II and Adolf Hitler said Chamberlain was a prophet. He became the principle advisor to Kaiser Wilhelm and urged the king to go to war in 1914 to fulfil the prophecy of Germany's world domination. When the war was over and Wilhelm had abdicated, he realised how he had been manipulated. Wilhelm gathered together a mass of books on the occult and the German secret societies and he was convinced that they had conspired to create the First World War and caused Germany to be defeated. Chamberlain, who had been awarded the Iron Cross by the Kaiser, died in 1927 after years in a wheelchair broken in body and spirit. This is something that often happens to those who are used as vehicles and channels for this highly malevolent branch of the reptilian consciousness. It eventually destroys them. But Chamberlain's influence was to live on in the mind of Adolf Hitler. He had been introduced to Hitler by Alfred Rosenberg, the refugee from Russia and another Satanist figure. It was Rosenberg, despite his 'Jewish' background, who gave a copy of the *Protocols Of The Learned Elders Of Zion* to Hitler via another occultist, Dietrich Eckart.⁴ *The Protocols* were used by Hilter to justify his campaign against the Jews.

These were some of the people and beliefs that moulded the thinking of the man claiming to be a young Austrian called Schiklgruber, but later rather better known as Adolf Hitler. "Heil Schiklgruber" would not have had the same ring to it somehow. He hated school, the official story goes, and wanted to be an artist, an ambition that took him to Vienna. He spent hours in the libraries reading books on astrology, mysticism, and the religions of the East. He was fascinated by the books of Blavatsky, Chamberlain, List, and Liebenfels and he picked out parts from each of them to produce his preferred mixture, a cocktail of horror and hatred called Nazism. His passion was the power of the will. The potential of willpower to achieve anything it desires was to be his focus and guide throughout the years that followed. Put another way, creating your own reality. He practised the esoteric arts in his effort to access the level of consciousness he was convinced would turn him into one of the supermen he had read so much about and believed in so much. His psyche became locked into the reptilian vibration more powerfully than before. He was possessed, probably during some black ritual which opened his psyche to the reptilians. You only have to look at his beliefs to see that he would have had great potential for 'vibrational compatibility' with this consciousness. It was now that an uncharismatic and ineffectual man would begin to exude the charisma and magnetism that would captivate and intoxicate a nation.

We talk of some people having magnetism and 'magnetic personalities' and that is exactly what they have. We are all generating magnetic energies. Some people transmit powerful magnetism and others less so. Negative energies are just as magnetic as positive. Those connected to, and therefore generating, the extreme negative vibration, will be very magnetic. You often hear highly negative people described as having a magnetic personality or a 'fatal attraction'. This is why. It is also where the magnetism and charisma of Adolf Hitler suddenly appeared from. When he was standing on a public platform, with that contorted face and crazed delivery, he was channelling the reptilian consciousness and transmitting this vibration to the vast crowds. This affected the vibrational state of the people and turned them into equally crazed agents of hatred. It is the pied piper principle, using vibrational frequencies. As one writer said of Hitler:

"His power to bewitch an audience has been likened to the occult art of the African medicine man or the Asiatic shaman; others have compared it to the sensitivity of a medium, and the magnetism of a hypnotist."[5]

And Hermann Rauschning, an aide to Hitler, said in his book, *Hitler Speaks*:

"One cannot help thinking of him as a medium. For most of the time, mediums are ordinary, insignificant people. Suddenly they are endowed with what seem to be supernatural powers which set them apart from the rest of humanity. The medium is possessed. Once the crisis is passed, they fall back again into mediocrity. It was in this way, beyond any doubt, that Hitler was possessed by forces outside of himself – almost demoniacal forces of which the individual man Hitler was only the temporary vehicle. The mixture of the banal and the supernatural created that insupportable duality of which one was conscious in his presence... It was like looking at a bizarre face whose expression seemed to reflect an unbalanced state of mind coupled with a disquieting impression of hidden powers."[6]

Hitler appeared to live in perpetual fear of the 'supermen'. Rauschning told how Hitler suffered from terrible nightmares and would wake in terror screaming about entities who were invisible to all but him. Hitler once said to his aide:

"What will the social order of the future be like? Comrade, I will tell you. There will be a class of overlords, after them the rank and file of the party members in hierarchical order, and then the great mass of anonymous followers, servants and workers in perpetuity, and beneath them again all the conquered foreign races, the modern slaves. And over and above all these will reign a new and exalted nobility of whom I cannot speak... but of all these plans the militant members will know nothing. The new man is living amongst us now! He is here. Isn't that enough for you? I will tell you a secret. I have seen the new man. He is intrepid and cruel. I was afraid of him."[7]

This is the society planned by the reptilians and their reptile-Aryan master race if we allow the New World Order to be introduced in the next few years. Hitler's 'secret chiefs' are the reptilians and note the obsession with hierarchy and ritual, character traits of the R-complex or reptile brain. After Hitler moved to Germany, he spent a lot of time in Bavaria, from whence Weishaupt's Illuminati had sprung and he returned there after the First World War. That's the official line, anyway. The following year, he came across a tiny and rather pathetic political party called the German Workers Party. This was an offshoot of an esoteric secret society called the German Order, which was fiercely nationalistic and anti-Jewish. Out of this order came other similar societies, including the infamous Thule-Gesellschaft (Thule Society) and the Luminous Lodge or Vril Society. Hitler was a member of both. Vril was the name given by the English writer, Lord Bulwer-Lytton to the force in the blood which, he claimed, awakens people to their true power and potential to become supermen. So what is the Vril force in the blood? It was known by the Hindus as the 'serpent force' and it relates to the genetic make up of the body which allows shape-shifting and conscious interdimensional travel. The Vril force is, yet again, related to the reptile-human bloodlines. In 1933, the rocket expert, Willi Ley, fled from Germany and revealed the existence of the Vril Society and the Nazis' belief that they would become the equals of the supermen in the bowels of the Earth by use of esoteric teachings and mind expansion. They believed this would reawaken the Vril force sleeping in the blood. The initiates of the Vril Society included two men who would become famous Nazis, Heinrich Himmler and Hermann Goering. Vril members were convinced they were in alliance with mysterious esoteric lodges in Tibet and one of the so-called 'unknown supermen' who was referred to as the King of Fear. Rudolph Hess,[8] Hitler's deputy Fuhrer until he made his ill-fated flight to England in 1941, was a dedicated occultist and a member, with Hermann Goering, of the Edelweiss Society, a sect which believed in the Nordic master race. Hess worshipped Hitler as the 'messiah', although how he could do this when the Fuhrer was hardly blue-eyed and blond-haired is not clear. Hitler had the same problem in equating the two, but he would have found some ridiculous explanation for it, I'm sure. The inner core of the Nazi secret society network was the Black Order which continues today and is reported to be the innermost circle of the CIA.[9]

The German researcher, Jan van Helsing, writes in his book, *Secret Societies Of The 20th Century*,[10] of how the Vril and Thule societies believed they were corresponding with extraterrestrials through two mediums known as Maria Orsic and Sigrun in a lodge near Berchtesgaden in December 1919. According to Vril documents, he says, these channellings were transmitted from a solar system called Aldebaran, 68 light years away in the constellation of Taurus where two inhabited planets formed the 'Sumeran' empire. The population of Aldebaran is divided into a master race of blond-haired, blue-eyed, Aryans, known as Light God People and several other human-like races which had mutated to a lower genetic form due to climatic changes, the channellings said.[11] In excess of 500 million years ago the Aldebaran sun began to expand so creating a tremendous increase in heat. The 'lower' races were evacuated and taken to other inhabitable planets. Then the Aryan Light God People began to colonise Earth-like planets after theirs became uninhabitable. In our solar system it was said that they first occupied the planet, Mallona, also known as Marduk, Mardek, and by the Russians and Romans, Phaeton, which, they said, existed between Mars and Jupiter in what is now the asteroid belt. This corresponds with the Sumerian accounts of the planet, Tiamat. The Vril Society believed that later this race of blond-haired, blue-eyed Aldebarans, colonised Mars before landing on the Earth and starting the Sumerian civilisation. The Vril channellers said that the Sumerian language was identical to that of the Aldebarans and sounded like "unintelligible German". The language frequency of German and Sumerian-Aldebaranian were almost identical, they believed.[12] The details may change in each version, but here we see the same basic theme yet again. A blond-haired, blue-eyed master race of extraterrestrials land on the Earth from Mars and become the gods of ancient legend. They become the inspiration behind the advanced Sumerian culture and spawned the purest genetic stream on the planet. These same gods control the planet ever since from their underground cities. What I think has been missed, however, is that within the Aryan stream are the reptilian-Aryan bloodlines. I know from Brotherhood insiders that the reptilians need the blood for some reason of the blond-haired, blue-eyed people, and the Nazi obsession with the Master Race was designed to keep this stream pure and discourage interbreeding with other streams and races.

The Thule Society was named after Ultima Thule which is claimed to be the mythical city on Hyperborea, the first continent settled by the extraterrestrial Aryan race from Aldebaran, they believed. Some say this was long before Atlantis and Lemuria, others say Hyperborea was Atlantis or even the inner-Earth. Scandinavian legend describes Ultima Thule as a wonderful land in the far North where the Sun never sets and the ancestors of the Aryans have their home. When Hyperborea started to sink, the legend goes, the Aryan extraterrestrials used their highly advanced technology to burrow gigantic tunnels into the Earth's crust and they settled under the Himalayan Mountains. This realm became known as Agharta with a capital city called Shamballah, the Thule advocates believe. The Persians called this area Aryana, the land of the Aryans. The Nazi belief system claimed that the people of Agharta were good and those of Shamballah were evil. The two had been in conflict for thousands of years and the Nazis believed they were backing the 'good guys' of Agharta against the 'Freemasons and Zionists' of Shamballah. Could this division be Aryan Martians v Anunnaki reptilians, as an age old conflict between the two continues? First they battled on Mars, apparently, then the Moon and now Earth. Hitler was obsessed with finding the entrances to this subterranean world so he could contact the Aryan master race, but the truth is that he was a reptilian puppet controlled by the 'Angel of Death', Josef Mengele. It is highly likely, as I mentioned early on, that the reptilians are in conflict with other extraterrestrial or inner-terrestrial races for control of the planet and there will certainly be many competing factions in the consciousness cesspit of the lower fourth dimension. A founder of the Thule Society was Rudolf Glauer, an astrologer, who changed his name to the grand-sounding Baron von Sebottendorff. His demands for a revolution against Jews and the Marxists turned the Thule Society into a focus for the anti-Jew, anti-Marxist, German master-racers. Out of all this came the German Workers Party which would one day become the Nazi Party. Another committed occultist and friend of Sebottendorff now becomes highly significant. This was Dietrich Eckart, a heavy-drinking, drug-taking writer who believed he was here to pave the way for a dictator of Germany. He met Hitler in 1919 and decided he was the one, the 'messiah', he was looking for. It is Eckart who is credited with Hitler's advanced esoteric knowledge and probably the black magic rituals which plugged him so completely into the reptilian frequency. From now on, Hitler's power to attract support grew rapidly. Eckart wrote to a friend in 1923:

> "Follow Hitler! He will dance, but it is I who have called the tune. We have given him the means of communication with Them. Do not mourn for me; I shall have influenced history more than any other German."[13]

Another of Hitler's obsessions was the so-called Spear of Destiny, the weapon alleged to have been used to pierce the side of 'Jesus' at the crucifixion. He stole what is claimed to be the spear when the Nazis annexed Austria in 1938 and it was taken to Nuremberg. The legend says that whoever has this spear and decodes its secrets will have control of the world for good or evil. The one that Hitler stole is now in the Hofburg Museum in Vienna, where there was a major fire in November 1992, seven days before the blaze which destroyed part of Windsor Castle. Heinrich Himmler was another dedicated occultist who was into all matters esoteric. He used this knowledge in the blackest of ways. Himmler was particularly interested in the rune stones, a system of divination in which stones carrying symbols are thrown or selected and the choice or combination 'read' by an 'expert'. It was Himmler who formed the notorious SS and, as with the swastika, he chose an esoteric symbol for his horrific organisation and this was the double S or sig rune which looks like two flashes of lightning. The SS was a virtually self contained body and the epitome of all the esoteric knowledge in which the Nazis believed so passionately. Only those considered racially pure were allowed to join, and instruction in the esoteric arts, including the rune stones, was fundamental to their training. The SS was run and governed as a black magic secret society. Their rituals were taken from others such as the Jesuits and the Knights Templar. The highest ranking initiates were the 13 (here we go again) members of the Grand Council of Knights led by their Grand Master, Heinrich Himmler, and the black rituals were performed at the ancient castle of Wewelsberg in Westphalia. They celebrated the rituals of the Nordic Pagans and the summer solstice. Here they worshipped Satan, Lucifer, Set, whichever name you prefer. Prince Bernhard, one of founders of the Brotherhood front, the Bilderberg Group, and an extremely close friend of Prince Philip, was in the SS. Black magic and the esoteric arts pervaded all that Hitler and the Nazis did, even down to the use of pendulums on maps to identify the positions of enemy troops. The original swastika Sun symbol was right handed which, in esoteric terms, means light and creation, the positive. The Nazis reversed it to symbolise black magic and destruction. This is the classic reversed symbolism of Satanism which does precisely the same. The inverted pentagram is but one example. The mass rallies that Hitler used so effectively were designed with the knowledge of the human psyche and how it can be manipulated. In the book, *Satan And Swastika*, Francis King says:

"Hitler's public appearances, particularly those associated with the Nazi Party's Nuremberg Rallies, were excellent examples of this sort of magical ceremony. The fanfares, military marches, and Wagnerian music, all emphasised the idea of German military glory. The mass swastika banners in black, white, and red, filled the consciousness of the participants in the rally with national socialist ideology. The ballet-like precision of the movement of the uniformed party members, all acting in unison, evoked from the unconscious, the principles of war and violence which the ancients symbolised as Mars. And the prime rituals of the rallies – Hitler clasping to other banners the 'blood banner' carried in the Munich Putsch of 1923 – was a quasi-magical ceremony designed to link up minds of living Nazis with the archetypal images symbolised by the dead national socialist heroes of the past. The religio-magical aspects of the rallies were emphasised by the fact that their high points were reached after dusk and took place in a 'Cathedral of Light' – an open space surrounded by pillars of light coming from electric searchlights pointed upwards to the sky. If a modern ritual magician of the utmost expertise had designed a ritual intended to 'invoke Mars' he could not have come up with anything more effective than the ceremonies used at Nuremberg."

And what applied then, applies now, the esoteric knowledge used by the Nazis for mass hypnosis on the German people, is being used today to expand the global hypnosis on the human race. Symbols, words, colours, sounds and techniques of which the public are not even aware, are being used in the media and advertising to hypnotise us. The propaganda ministry of Joseph Goebbels was based on the esoteric knowledge of the human psyche. He knew that people will believe anything if you tell them often enough and if you can engineer events which create the 'something must be done' mentality in the public mind. He used colours, symbols and slogans, to great effect. The slogans were used like mantras and repeated over and over again, hypnotising the mass psyche. All alternative views and information were censored and the people were programmed to respond as desired. What is the difference between that and the constant drip, drip, drip, of inaccurate and biased information that is fed to us and our children today? It may not have a swastika on it, but it is still mass hypnotism. It would seem to be a contradiction that Hitler sought to destroy secret societies like the Freemasons and to prevent the use of esoteric knowledge in German society, but it isn't. He knew as much as anyone the power available to those with the understanding, and he wanted to keep that for himself. In 1934, all forms of fortune telling were banned in Berlin and later esoteric books were banned throughout Germany. Secret societies were disbanded and even the Thule Society and the German Order (which had together founded Nazism) were targeted. Astrologers were attacked and killed and people like Lanz von Liebenfels were prevented from publishing their work. This purge had two main motives: to distance Hitler and the Nazis from the occult in the minds of the public and other countries and, most importantly, to pull up the ladder and stop anyone else from using esoteric knowledge against them as they were using it against others. This is a mirror of the tactics of the reptile-Aryans throughout known history as they have used the knowledge to control and suppress while creating the religious dictatorships to take the same knowledge out of public circulation. In truth, the Nazis were created and controlled at every level by the secret society underground and, ultimately, by the reptilians. They believed the Sumerian gods were the extraterrestrial master race; they believed in the existence of Atlantis; and they launched expeditions to North Africa, Rennes-le-Chateau and Montsegur in Cathar country, and to Tibet, where they believed the underground supermen were based. There is a positive Buddhist stream of belief and a highly negative one. The Nazis connected with the latter and when the Russians arrived in Berlin at the end of the war they found many dead Buddhist monks who had been working with the Nazis.

The hollow Earth

The Nazis also believed that the Earth was hollow with entrances at the poles and a number of researchers report that they established an underground base in Antarctica towards the end of the war which is still in operation today. I have no doubt from the evidence I have seen that the Earth is hollow, or, at the very least, there are vast regions inside where highly developed civilisations live. I also feel that there are ancient societies living under the ground between the Earth's surface and the inner 'hollow' centre. It is like three levels of peoples living on and within the same planet. The writer, Jules Verne, was a high initiate of the secret society network with his connections to the Theosophical Society, the Order of the Golden Dawn, and the Order of the Oriental Templars. Therefore, he knew far more than the public are allowed to know. His science-fiction stories were based on fact. He wrote of the two moons of Mars before they were identified (officially) in 1877. Verne's epic, *Journey To The Centre Of The Earth*, was not entirely a fantasy. He knew the basis of it was true. Those who promote the idea of a hollow Earth say that water flows from one polar entrance to another and in the centre of the planet is a vast sea and an inner 'central sun' which provides the heat and light. In the film version of the Jules Verne story, which I watched again recently, the scene is depicted in the same way. Interestingly, the main opposition Verne's explorers face are from massive reptiles, one of which they found in the sunken city of Atlantis. There has been speculation, supported by much evidence, that dinosaurs may have survived the cataclysm of 65 million years ago by living within the Earth, particular in the Southern polar regions. Tom Rich, a palaeontologist at the Museum of Victoria, Australia, suggested this possibility after he discovered the fossilised remains of a polar dinosaur in 1987 in an excavated tunnel on the Southern tip of Victoria state at a place known as Dinosaur Cove.[14] Jules Verne, a high initiate, would have known the true background and so much truth is passed on through symbolism in 'fiction' stories and movies. Steven Spielberg's films are prime examples, particularly the Indiana Jones series and, I feel, *Jurassic Park* in

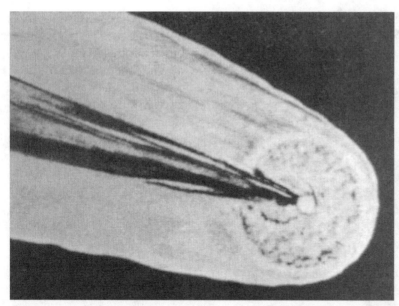

Figure 23: *A drawing of Donati's comet in 1853 showing how the disintegrating mass is thrown outwards by centrifugal force to 'orbit' a central energy source. This leaves the interior hollow in the same way that clothing spins around a hollow centre in a washing machine or spin dryer. Surely this would have happened when the Earth was forming also?*

which DNA is manipulated to create reptilian dinosaurs. My view is that human DNA was manipulated to create reptilian-humans.

There is certainly plenty of evidence that there are civilisations living within the Earth and even that the Earth is hollow. These are more themes of ancient knowledge and traditions. Humans have become such puppets of the official line that to suggest the Earth is not solid to the core is to invite enormous ridicule. After all, isn't that at odds with what those highly intelligent scientists say? Yes it is, just as it was to suggest the Earth was round and not flat. When you research this subject you realise how little evidence the scientists produce for their indisputable 'facts'. They have penetrated only a few miles into the Earth and their theories of what exists at deeper levels are just that – theories. When you ask a few questions of the official line, it is soon a stuttering wreck. For example: The very spin of the planet creates centrifugal force which throws matter to the outside, very much like a spin dryer in which the clothes spin around a hole in the centre. When the planet was in its molten form, spinning into existence before it cooled, how could it possibly remain solid to the core? It is against all logic and laws of force, and if you look at *Figure* 23 you will see from the drawing of Donati's Comet from 1853 how matter is hurled to the outside to spin around the bright core or 'sun'. The Earth is basically the same. Researchers of the hollow Earth have suggested that the outer crust goes down some 800 miles and beyond that the planet is hollow. People live on the other side of the very land that we live on. If you think that is impossible then ask why people in Australia don't fall off the Earth even though they are on the opposite side of the surface to those in the northern hemisphere. The answer is that they are pulled to the land by gravity. So are those who live inside the Earth. The force of gravity pulls towards matter and so those on both sides of the planet's landmass, inside and outside, will be pulled by gravity towards the land and neither will 'fall off'. The

centre of the Earth's gravity is not at the core of the planet, but at about 400 miles down... the centre of the outer land mass and so gravity pulls equally on both sides (*see **Figure 24***).

The alleged openings at the poles make sense because the power of centrifugal force in the period of formation would have been far less in those areas. At about 70 to 75 degrees north and south latitude, the Earth starts to curve into the polar openings to the inner Earth, supporters of this theory suggest. It is so gradual that people who claim to have experienced this had no idea they were entering the inner Earth until they began to see land that

Figure 24: *The inner earth as some researchers believe it to be. Hollow in the centre with an inner central sun and water flowing between the polar openings. Gravity would be the same on both sides of the crust because gravity attracts to mass.*

did not appear on the maps. These openings are an estimated 1,400 miles across and around them is a magnetic ring. The entrances are covered by clouds most of the time, advocates claim, and the airspace is restricted by law. When explorers searching for the North or South Pole reach this magnetic ring their compasses point straight down and they believe they are at the pole. They are not. They are at the magnetic ring which encircles the poles. The light and warmth inside the Earth come from an inner 'sun', it is claimed. Marshall B. Gardner, one of the best known advocates of a hollow Earth, believed that this 'sun' was created from the original central fiery core around which the forming Earth was spinning, very much like the picture of Donati's comet. If the Earth is hollow, so it must be that the other planets, formed in the same way and subject to the same laws, would be hollow. How many civilisations live within these planets while humans only look for life on the surface?

Some other questions for the solid-to-the-core advocates: Why are icebergs made of fresh water when the only water available at the poles, according to the conventional view, is sea water? Where does all the vegetation come from that is found inside these icebergs? Why is it that explorers who have ventured beyond the magnetic poles have found that the weather gets warmer and the seas become ice-free? Why do some animals and birds in the north polar region, like the musk-ox, migrate north in the winter? The conventional scientific view cannot answer these questions, but the hollow Earth view can. There are fresh water rivers which flow out of the inner Earth and this warm water, carrying vegetation and pollen, freezes, so forming the fresh water icebergs in an area of apparently only salt water. There are some books which reveal the detailed evidence of the inner Earth in much greater detail than I have space to do here and I can recommend *The Hollow Earth* by Dr Raymond Bernard as an excellent summary of this evidence.[15]

One man famously flew into the inner Earth at the North Pole in 1947 to a distance 1,700 miles beyond magnetic north and the South Pole in 1956 to a distance of 2,300 miles beyond magnetic south. He was Rear Admiral Richard E. Byrd, a well-known figure in the United States Navy. He called the land he found: "that enchanted continent in the sky" and "the land of ever lasting mystery".[16] In 1947, Byrd and his passengers broadcast live on the radio as they flew inside the planet and they saw the ice of the northern regions replaced by ice-free lands and lakes and mountains covered with trees. They described strange animals resembling mammoths and the land they saw does not appear on any map to this day. After the initial publicity, information about the Byrd expeditions was suppressed and he died in 1957, the year after his trip to the Antarctic. Two years later in December 1959, Ray Palmer, the editor of *Flying Saucers* magazine published an issue detailing Admiral Byrd's discoveries, but when the truck arrived from the printer with that edition, all the magazines were missing. Palmer called the printer, but he was told there was no shipping receipt to prove the shipment had been made and when he asked for the edition to be reprinted he was told the printing plates had been so badly damaged this was not possible. Palmer believed that UFOs came not from space, but from the inner Earth and that was part of his article in that ill-fated edition. I think he could have been right and the ancient Indian epic, *Ramayana*, describes Rama as an emissary from Agharta arriving in a flying vehicle.

The legends of inner Earth peoples and blond-haired, blue-eyed master races, can be found in countless ancient cultures including China, Tibet, Egypt, India, Europe, the Americas, and Scandinavia. William F. Warren in his work, *Paradise Found, Or The Cradle Of The Human Race*, suggests that humans originated on a tropical continent in the Arctic, a land of sunshine where a race of gods lived for more than a thousand years without growing old. Warren connects this northern paradise with the ancient Greek concept of Hyperborea. The Eskimos, who may originate from inner Earth peoples, have legends which tell of a paradise island to the north, a beautiful land of perpetual light where there is no darkness nor extremes of sunlight, a place where people live for thousands of years in peace and happiness. You find the same in Irish myth also. It was to the inner Earth, legends say, that some of the fleeing Lemurians and Atlanteans sheltered at the time of great geological turmoil and flood on the surface. Plato wrote of mysterious passageways in and around the Atlantean continent, "tunnels both broad and narrow, in the interior of the Earth."[17] He also described the great ruler "who sits at the centre, on the navel of the Earth… the interpreter of religion to all mankind".[18] The Roman writer, Gaius Plinius Secundus, better known as Pliny, refers to underground peoples who had fled from Atlantis and there are the legends of the inner Earth dwellers called the Troglodytes who, Pliny said, have hidden in their tunnels a great, ancient treasure.[19] Such stories abound in every culture.

The Nazi flying saucers

Stories also abound of 'flying saucer' craft built by the Nazis before and during the war under programmes controlled by the Thule and Vril Society. German researcher, Jan van Helsing, and many others, have detailed some of the technology which was produced after 1934, including the Vril-1 fighter, Vril-7 (*see picture section*), and the Haunebu 1, 2 and 3.[20] These and others were known collectively by the Allies as the Foo Fighters. Wendelle C. Stevens, a US airforce pilot in the Second World War and now a UFO investigator, says that the Foo Fighters were sometimes grey-green, sometimes red-orange. They approached his aircraft as close as five metres and then just stayed there, he said. They could not be shaken off or shot down and caused many squadrons to either turn back or land.[21] Helsing includes photographs of these craft and other researchers support this information. I am always very wary of photographs of this kind because they can easily be faked and circulated until they become accepted as fact, but there is a documentary video, *UFO – The Secrets Of The Third Reich*, and the researcher and lecturer, Vladomir Terziski, also includes a wealth of material on this subject. The German flying saucers, apparently, had many technical problems and limitations which were ironed out after the war. In 1938, according to a number of researchers into these subjects, a German expedition to the Antarctic, was led by the aircraft carrier, Schwabenland, and a 600,000 kilometre region of ice-free mountains and lakes were declared Germany territory.[22] It was called Neuschwabenland (New Swabia) and became a massive Nazi military base. In 1947 there is said to have been a strange naval mission to the Antarctic by Admiral E. Byrd, the man who flew into the inner Earth at both the North and South Poles. He took with him 4,000 soldiers and a fully equipped aircraft carrier. After eight weeks and high casualties, they pulled out, some researchers claim. What happened remains a mystery, but Byrd would later say publicly that it was the bitter reality that in the case of a new war, one had to expect attacks by planes that could fly from pole to pole. He added that there was an advanced civilisation in Antarctica, and together with the SS, they used advanced systems of technology .[23]

So why didn't the Nazis win the war? Well firstly, it seems there was conflict between the Nazi secret societies and secondly, the 'flying saucer' technology was still far from perfected. But the simple answer to why the Germans did not win the war is that they were not meant to. The reptilians of the lower fourth dimension were manipulating them, yes, but they were working through the other sides also. They wanted a war and so they manipulated all parties to achieve it. As I document and source at length in ...*And The Truth Shall Set You Free*, the Nazis were funded by the classic bloodline families who were also funding the Allies 'opposing' Hitler. The Rothschilds were at the heart of this, once again working through their vehicles in England, the United States and Germany. Standard Oil, controlled by the Rockefellers, was, in effect, the same company as I. G. Farben, Hitler's chemical giant which operated the concentration camp at Auchwitz. I. G. Farben was the heart of the Nazi war machine and it was technological knowledge transferred to them by Standard Oil which allowed Hitler to fight the war. This included the know-how necessary to turn the vast German coal reserves into oil. Other oil supplies were provided for Germany by Standard Oil through the Brotherhood financial centre and stronghold, Switzerland. The President of Standard Oil, New Jersey (now Exxon), was William Stamps Farish, a close friend of Hermann Schmitz, the chairman of I. G. Farben. Farish's grandson, William Farish III, is one of the inner circle around George Bush and also entertains the Queen of England and Prince Philip at his home. Farish and the Queen breed their horses together. Bush's father, Prescott Bush, the stalwart of the Skull and Bones Society, was one of the funders of Hitler. This was done through a subsidiary company called the United Banking Corporation (UBC) of which Prescott Bush was a director and leading light. The UBC connected the W. A. Harriman Company of New York (Brown Brothers, Harriman, after 1933) with the business network of Fritz Thyssen, the German steel entrepreneur and banker, who funded Hitler from the 1920s. The Harriman operation, like the J. P. Morgan and Rockefeller empires, was bankrolled by the Payseurs and the Rothschilds. Meanwhile, the Rothschilds were also in control of Hitler's I. G. Farben.

Among those on the board of Farben's US subsidiary, American I. G., was Paul Warburg, the Payseur/Rothschild trustee and agent who was sent to the United States to introduce the Federal Reserve banking scam that came to fruition in 1913. His brother, Max Warburg, was Hitler's banker until he left Germany without a problem in 1938 and settled in the United States. Other funders of Hitler included General Electric, which had close financial connections to Franklin Delano Roosevelt, the President who 'opposed' Hitler; the Ford Motor Company under Henry Ford who was awarded Germany's highest honour conferred on non-Germans, the Grand Cross of the German Eagle; and International Telephone and Telegraph (ITT) , which, in collusion with Hitler's personal banker and SS officer, Baron Kurt von Schroder, also bankrolled the Nazi war effort. Master-minding this coordinated support was Montagu Norman (Comm 300), the governor of the Rothschild-controlled Bank of England. Norman was an associate of Hjalmar Schact, who would become Hitler's financial advisor and president of the German Reichsbank. These two were so close that Schact named one of his grandsons after Norman. When the Nazis invaded Czechoslovakia, Norman released six million pounds worth of Czech gold to Hitler which was deposited in London. Incidentally, the two signatures on the document confirming Schact's appointment as president of the Reichsbank on March 17th 1933, were Adolf Hitler and the Rothschild frontman, Max Warburg. Most 'Jewish' people think that families like the Rothschilds and the Warburgs, who both claim to be Jewish, are on their side. Nothing could be further from the truth. As I mentioned earlier, the trail of the gold and money stolen by Swiss banks from German Jews during the war also leads back to the Rothschilds.

The Rothschilds and their associates the Rockefellers, Harrimans, and Bushs, were also behind the Nazi race purity programme. Of course they were. Hitler's race purity expert was Dr Ernst Rudin, a psychiatrist at the Kaiser Wilhelm Institute for Genealogy and Demography in Berlin. There he occupied an entire floor with his research and it was all made possible by funds provided by... the Rockefellers.[24] It was these same families who funded the eugenics movement which is pledged to remove the lower genetic blood streams and leave only those of superior stock. Eugenics today often goes under the title of 'population control'. The best known of the population control organisations is Planned Parenthood which began life under another name at the London offices of the British Eugenics Society. No wonder George Bush has taken every opportunity to pump vast amounts of American and United Nations money into that organisation. Bush and Henry Kissinger are advocates of Thomas Malthus, the Freemason of the Darwin bloodline, who died in 1834. Malthus called for the culling of non-white peoples and for those white people of 'lesser' stock. Malthus and his economist friend, the Freemason, John Stuart Mill, said that the Aryan race, the blond-haired, blue-eyed people, was God's gift to the world. The gods' gift, more like. The higher stock of the white race had to control the 'ignorant' dark skinned races, this pair said. Now that is no different from the Nazi philosophy or that of the British and American establishment because they are from the same stream. Why have policies been introduced in Africa, Central and South America, and Asia, which have caused such disease, death and destruction? It is part of an ongoing plan. You can read the detailed background to the funding of Hitler, the role of the Rothschilds, and the master race-population control programme in ...*And The Truth Shall Set You Free*.

Yet more confirmation that the same force controlled all sides in the Second World War came with the British-American Intelligence operation called Project Paperclip which sprung the main Nazi leaders, scientists, engineers and mind control experts out of Germany before the allied armies arrived. They were transported to South America and the United States to continue their work for the reptilian Agenda. The Nazis who were tried and hanged at the Nuremberg Trials were merely the pawns paraded before a show trial to placate public anger. The kings, queens, bishops, and knights of the Nazi regime escaped to continue their campaign against humanity via the networks arranged by their 'opposition', the United Kingdom and the United States. Among the Nazis who escaped in Project Paperclip was the mass murderer and torturer, Josef Mengele. The CIA was the creation of British Intelligence and particularly its Elite inner circle known as the Special Operations Executive (SOE). The CIA replaced the wartime US intelligence organisation, the Office of Strategic Services (OSS), which was born out of the Payseur empire intelligence operation. The OSS was headed by Bill Donovan, a puppet of the Payseur-Rothschild-Rockefeller circle, and a former classmate of Franklin Delano Roosevelt. Donovan's law tutor at the Brotherhood owned Columbia University was Professor Harland F. Stone, who would later become US Attorney General. Another of Stone's proteges was J. Edgar Hoover, the 33rd degree Freemason and infamous head of the FBI at the time of the Kennedy assassination. Significantly, as I highlight at length in ...*And The Truth Shall Set You Free*, a number of key operatives in the murder of President Kennedy were former OSS agents posted to the British Intelligence headquarters in London during the Second World War. Among them was Clay Shaw, the CIA asset who is the only man to be tried for his part in the Kennedy assassination, a trial featured in the film, *JFK*. He was cleared only because the main witnesses against him were murdered in the run up to his appearance in court. Shaw was an advisor to the Satanist and Rothschild clone, Winston Churchill, and, like all the OSS agents in wartime London, he danced to the tune of people like Lord Victor Rothschild, the unofficial string-puller of the British Intelligence network.

The first Director of the CIA was Allan Dulles, a Nazi himself, as was his brother, John Foster Dulles, who was appointed Secretary of State. The Dulles' are another British aristocratic bloodline. Both Dulles brothers were involved in Project Paperclip, as was Henry Kissinger,[25] a 'German Jew', who answers not to Judaism, but to Satanism and his fellow reptilians. The Dulles' were from a southern slave owning family and were cousins of the Rockefellers. The Dulles law firm, Sullivan and Cromwell, handled the US affairs of I. G. Farben and Hitler's major backer, Fritz Thyssen, introduced Allen Dulles to him. John Foster Dulles wrote "Heil Hitler" on his letters to German clients and he was sent to Germany to negotiate new loans for the Nazis on behalf of the Rothschild-Rockefeller Round Table group. The loans were made to help the Germans pay back their war reparations which the same John Foster Dulles had helped to impose as a member of the American delegation at the Versailles Peace Conference in 1919. No wonder, then, that the CIA was created by Nazis, for Nazis. Among them was Reinhard Gehlen, Hitler's SS spymaster for the Russian front, who was appointed by Allen Dulles to set up the CIA network in Europe. The writer and researcher, Noam Chomsky, says that Gehlen formed a secret CIA-Nazi army which extended its operations to Latin America. It's a similar story with the international police network called Interpol. The Nazi mentality didn't lose the war. It was controlling all sides and after the carnage, it was business, or rather Agenda, as usual. Did Hitler die in the bunker? Of course not. Dr Robert Dorion, Director of Forensic Dentistry for the Ministry of the Solicitor General of Quebec in Montreal, has found glaring discrepancies between the photographs of the corpse's teeth and the thousands of open-mouth shots of Hitler. The pattern of gaps between the teeth is different. Hitler had a root canal and a porcelain tooth which the corpse did not, and the lower bridgework was very different.[26]

After the war, the Nazi leadership simply exchanged their jackboots and tin helmets for smart suits and scientist's overalls and the Agenda continued. Given this fact, does anyone still believe that the controlling Nazi-Satanic core of the US Government would not deliberately set out to burn children to death at Waco or blow them up at Oklahoma in pursuit of their Agenda for global domination? This is the mentality that controls our world and five billion people are allowing it to happen. Only if they continue to do so, can the reptile-Aryan-Nazi mentality maintain it's power over Planet Earth.

■ SOURCES

1   Quoted by J. H. Brennan in *Occult Reich* (Futura, London, 1974) and by Francis King in *Satan And Swastika* (Mayflower Books, London, 1976).

2   Verses from *The Book Of The Law*. Quoted by George C. Andrews in *Extraterrestrials Among Us*, pp 159–160.

3   *The Illuminati Formula*, p 19.

4   Quoted by Trevor Ravenscroft in *The Spear Of Destiny* (Samuel Weiser, Maine, USA, 1973), p 106.

5   Alan Bullock, *Hitler, A Study In Tyranny* (Pelican Books, London, 1960).

6   Hermann Rauschning, *Hitler Speaks* (London, 1939).

7   Ibid.

8   Rudolph Hess was supposed to have been kept at Spandau Prison until his death in 1987. But Dr Ewen Cameron, who became a CIA 'mind doctor', said that the CIA chief, Allen Dulles, told him that the 'Hess' in Spandau was a look-alike. When Cameron tried to prove identification by examining 'Hess' and located a First World War wound, he was not allowed to do so.

9   George C. Andrews, *Extraterrestrial Friends And Foes* (IllumiNet Press, Lilburn, GA, USA, 1993), p 53.

10 Jan van Helsing, *Secret Societies And Their Power In The 20th Century*, ETC

11 Ibid, pp 179–80.

12 Ibid, p 180.

13 J.H. Brennan, *Occult Reich*.

14 John Rhodes, *Reptoid website*.

15 Dr Raymond Bernard, *The Hollow Earth, The Greatest Discovery In History* (Carol Paperback, New York, 1991).

16 Ibid, p 38.

17 Alec Maclellan, *The Lost World Of Agharti, The Mystery Of Vril Power* (Souvenir Press, 43 Great Russell Street, London, WC1B 3PA, 1982), p 33. This is another excellent pull-together of inner Earth evidence.

18 Ibid.

19 Ibid.

20 *Secret Societies And Their Power In The 20th Century*, p 179.

21 Ibid, pp 190–91.

22 The Video, *UFO – The Secrets Of The Third Reich*, European UFO Archive, PO Box 129, Netherlands–8600 AC Sneek.

23 *Secret Societies*, p 193.

24 Webster Griffin Tarpley and Anton Chaitkin, *George Bush, The Unauthorised Biography* (Executive Intelligence Review, Washington DC, 1992), p 49.

25 Dr Leonard G. Horowitz, *Emerging Viruses* (Tetrahedron Inc, Rockport, MA, USA, 1996).

26 *Extraterrestrial Friends And Foes*, p 53.

CHAPTER THIRTEEN

The network today

After thousands of years of evolution, the reptilian network is now a vast and often unfathomable web of interconnecting secret societies, banks, businesses, political parties, security agencies, media owners, and so on. But its basic structure and Agenda remains very simple.

The centre of the operational web is the City of London with interlocking leaderships in places like France, Germany, Belgium, Switzerland, Italy and the United States. These are the spiders in the web with the City of London, 'New Troy', the most important. From this centre the Global Agenda and policies are administered and their 'branch managers' introduce those policies in each country. So if it suits the Global Agenda to crash the US dollar, the Mexican peso, the South African rand, or the Far East stock-markets, the branch managers in those areas will take the action necessary to do that. The Brotherhood don't suffer, indeed quite the opposite, because they know what is coming. The major Brotherhood banks in the United States, like the Rockefellers' Chase Manhattan, increased their profits on the Mexican peso in 1991, the year the value of the peso collapsed, because they sold their peso holdings just before the crash. In 1987, the late billionaire financier and Rothschild relative, Jimmy Goldsmith, sold all his holdings just before the world stock-market crash. A coincidence, of course.

At the heart of the web, or the top of the pyramid, whichever analogy you choose, are the reptilians. These operate mostly in the background from underground bases and overwhelmingly by possessing the reptilian-human bloodstreams which resonate most closely to the reptile consciousness of the lower fourth dimension. These reptile full-bloods and reptile-possessed people hold the major positions of power in the world or work in the background controlling those in the positions of apparent power like prime ministers and presidents. Having a reptilian or reptilian-controlled human as president might sound fantastic if you have allowed yourself to have your vision of possibility suppressed to the size of a pea, but when you see the evidence put together over thousands of years, it makes perfect sense of the 'mysteries' of history. People ask me the understandable question of why anyone would want to dedicate their lives to taking over a planet when they knew they were going to die long before it was achieved. Answer: The consciousness controlling that body is only using it as an overcoat, a space suit, until it wears out. When that happens, it possesses another one. These same reptilians have been occupying the bodies of all the main players in the conspiracy

The Pyramid of Manipulation

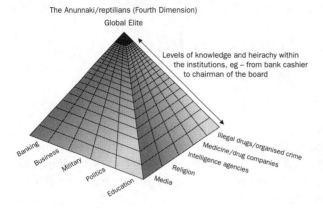

The Anunnaki/reptilians (Fourth Dimension)
Global Elite

Levels of knowledge and heirachy within
the institutions, eg – from bank cashier
to chairman of the board

Illegal drugs/organised crime
Medicine/drug companies
Intelligence agencies
Banking
Business
Military
Politics
Religion
Education
Media

Figure 25: *The pyramid of power in which all institutions ultimately fuse into the same tiny Elite. This allows the same Agenda to be orchestrated through all areas of society.*

going back to ancient times. The obsession with interbreeding within the Brotherhood bloodstreams comes from the need to hold the reptilian genetic inheritance and therefore maintain the vibrational connection between the human body on the third dimension and its controlling force on the lower fourth. It was to hide this truth that they arranged for the destruction of ancient historical records, texts, and accounts over the centuries as they ravaged and raped the native societies of the world. The reptilians wanted to destroy all memory and records of their earlier open existence and control in the past. If they could do that, humanity would have no idea that they were being controlled through physical bodies that look human by a fourth-dimensional force that is not human.

The truth of what happened and continues to happen is held under the strictest secrecy at the highest level of the secret society network and only a relative handful of people know the story. Each section of the global pyramid is itself a smaller compartmentalised pyramid. These are like watertight compartments on a ship or, more appropriately given its covert nature, a submarine. As above, so below. For example, the Freemason's pyramid answers to a common leadership and then this leadership in turn answers to a higher one. The Illuminati degrees begin where the Freemasons degrees end so the 33rd degree of the Scottish Rite and tenth degree of the York Rite appear to be as far as anyone can go and for most Masons that's true. But if someone is considered the right mentality and bloodline by the Brotherhood, they move on to the next level, the Illuminati degrees or to another of the highly secretive inner-circle groups like the Round Table which operate above the levels of the official secret societies like the Freemasons and the Knights of St John of Jerusalem (Malta). At their peak, the hierarchies of the secret societies fuse and connect with a common leadership and at that level they are all the same organisation working to the same Agenda, despite their countless internal quarrels and conflicts.

This secret society network places its trusted initiates into the most influential positions in the world of banking, business, politics, the media, the military, medicine, etc, and again at their highest levels, these apparently unconnected organisations and institutions fuse into the same pyramid peak and are controlled by the same people. It is like Russian dolls, one doll, or in this case, pyramid, inside another, until you reach the global pyramid which encompasses all of them (*see Figure 25*). The public faces of these organisations, and those who control them behind the scenes, might connect into the network by being a Freemason, a Knight of Malta, an initiate of the Skull and Bones Society, or as a member of a group of secret and semi-secret organisations called the Royal Institute of International Affairs, the Council on Foreign Relations, the Bilderberg Group, the Club of Rome, and the Trilateral Commission, which I will explain more about in a moment. The point I am stressing here is that while all these groups have different names and apparently different aims, they are all the same organisation controlled in the end by the same leadership.

The spider

The secret societies and groups which form the vast web of interconnected operations are an expanded version of the same network which goes back into antiquity. Some researchers say that the upper hierarchy appears to consist of the Council of 3, the Council of 5, the Council of 7, Council of 9, Council of 13, Council of 33, the Grand Druid Council, the Committee of 300 (also known as the 'Olympians'), and the Committee of 500. Many groups have no name to avoid detection.[1] I'm sure that there is one, maybe two, people, sitting atop this pyramid, a sort of High Priest and High Priestess of the world because, as I will expand on later, the most important hierarchy to which all others are subordinate is the Satanist hierarchy. If you want to control the game, you have to control all sides and this structure allows that to happen. The Brotherhood control the 'fors' and the 'againsts' in politics, banking, business, the media, and politics. They have agents in all governments and agents in the other political parties 'opposing' those governments; they have agents on both sides in wars and political conflicts; in the drug-running cartels and in the anti-drug agencies 'opposing' those cartels; within the organised crime syndicates and the police and security agencies 'investigating' those syndicates; within terrorist groups and the intelligence agencies 'investigating' those groups. Just because someone says he stands for freedom and peace does not mean that he does. In fact, if he did he would not need to say it because it would be obvious. I have a simple rule. Anything that calls itself 'democratic' stands for anything but. Look at the number of Democratic Fronts around the world which spend their time imposing a dictatorship.

The Round Table network

One of the major networks is governed from the centre by the Round Table (*see Figure 26 overleaf*). As we have seen, the Round Table has branches all over the world and in 1920 and 1921 it added the Royal Institute of International Affairs (RIIA) and the Council on Foreign Relations (CFR) to its web. The RIIA itself created its own offshoots. The Council on Foreign Relations in New York developed its own subordinate network within the United States which connects the Babylonian Brotherhood with US government departments, Congress, media owners, editors, journalists, the tax-exempt foundations like the Rockfeller

Figure 26: *The Round Table network.*

Foundation, universities, scientists, ambassadors, military leaders, 'historians', bankers, and business people. Each major country has such a network which follows the Agenda dictated from the global centres in the City of London, Germany, France, and Switzerland. I was attacked in my absence once on a Cape Town radio station by an 'astrologer' who said that the conspiracy I am exposing could not exist because it could not be organised over such a long period. As usual he had not read any of my books or done any research whatsoever before dismissing the possibility and if he had he would realise that, because of the structure I am describing, it is not only possible to follow the same Agenda across the generations, it is perfectly straightforward. Why don't big corporations or banks cease to exist when one generation of leadership retires or dies? Because the next generation takes over. Exactly. So it is with the Brotherhood and its Agenda. Perhaps the astrologer might consult his own birth chart and identify the planetary conjunction which is closing his eyes to the obvious and the planet which impels him, like billions of others, to dismiss and condemn information they have made no attempt to read, check, or understand.

In May 1954 came the first official meeting of the next organisation in the Round Table web, the Bilderberg Group (Bil), which was named after the Bilderberg Hotel in Oosterbeek, the Netherlands, where that opening meeting took place. Or that's the official story, anyway. Bil or Bel was also the Sun God of the Phoenicians. Bilderberg translates as 'Bel of the rock' or 'Bel of the mountain'. The Bilderberg Group was chaired from 1954 to 1976 by Prince Bernhard of the Netherlands, the former Nazi SS officer and German spy working for the NW7 Intelligence department operating within the unspeakable chemical giant, I. G. Farben, which ran the Auchwitz Concentration Camp.[2] Pope John Paul II is said by some researchers to have worked for I. G. Farben, also. It makes sense because the Brotherhood pick the Popes, of course. Prince Bernhard, a German who married into the Dutch Royal Family, just as William of Orange had done, is a reptilian blood relative and great friend of Britain's Prince Philip. Together they launched the World Wildlife Fund, now the Worldwide Fund for Nature (WWF). The last thing they were interested in was protecting wildlife as we shall see in a later chapter. In 1968 came the Club of Rome, headed by the Bilderberger and Freemason, Aurelio Peccei (Comm 300), the number two at Fiat to the Black Nobility Bilderberger, Giovanni Agnelli. Peccei once said to his friend, the former US Secretary of State, Alexander Haig (TC, Knight of Malta), that he felt like Adam Weishaupt reincarnated.[3] Weishaupt was the man behind the Bavarian Illuminati. The Club of Rome, set up at the Rockefeller family's private estate at Bellagio in Italy, created the environmental movement. The Rockefellers and the Rothschilds have played the environmental movement like a violin. The Club of Rome has used the environment to centralise power and confiscate land. It claims to be campaigning to 'save the planet' when in truth it is just another front for the Agenda intent on controlling the world and, what's more, a front peopled by those who are demonstrably creating the very environmental problems they say they wish to stop. The same applies to the so-called Club of Budapest which is trying to do with 'spirituality' what the Club of Rome has done with the environment. The Club of Budapest is headed by Ervin Laszio, an associate of the Club of Rome's, Aurelio Peccei. Another important Round Table satellite is the Trilateral Commission which was created by the Rockefellers in the United States in 1972 and it has a role in the network of coordinating the Agenda between three parts of the world, the United States, Europe and Japan. In ...*And The Truth Shall Set You Free*, I expose these organisations and their membership at great length, but for those who have not read that book I'll give you an idea of the scale of their influence on daily life and world affairs. Whenever I mention someone who was, is, or would later become, a member of these groups, I will use the shorthand of RIIA, CFR, Bil and TC. I cannot at this time tell you much about the modern membership of the Royal Institute of International Affairs because it is so secretive and if anyone can help me with that I'd be much obliged. Some of their most important members I do know, however.

These interlocking groups have among their number the top people in global banking, business, media, military, intelligence agencies, education, and politics. A look at some of the people who attended the first Bilderberg meeting in 1954 gives further indication of the sort of people we are talking about. The chairman was Prince Bernhard, the husband of Queen Juliana of the Netherlands (Comm 300), who has herself been a regular Bilderberg attendee. The present Queen, Beatrix, is another Bilderberg promoter. Other Bilderberg chairmen have included Sir Alex Douglas Hume (Lord Home), one of the Elite Scottish bloodlines and a former British Prime Minister, and another British aristocratic bloodline, Lord Carrington, who became chairman in 1991. More about him in a second. Prince Bernhard was head-hunted to be the Bilderberg chairman by Lord Victor Rothschild, the spy, conman of colossal proportions, and one of the major manipulators of the 20th century. Other attendees of that first meeting included: David Rockefeller (CFR,TC); Deak Rusk (CFR, TC, Rhodes Scholar), the head of the Rockefeller Foundation and Secretary of State under John F. Kennedy; Joseph E. Johnson (CFR), head of the Carnegie Endowment for International Peace (War!) and US Secretary for the Bilderbergers; Denis Healey (TC, RIIA, Comm 300, Fabian Society), the British Labour Party Minister of Defence from 1964–1970 and Chancellor of the Exchequer 1974–1979; and Lord Boothby, who worked with Winston Churchill on the unification of Europe, later known as the European Union.

NATO was a creation of the Brotherhood and is designed to evolve by stealth into a world army by encompassing more and more countries and by manipulating 'problems' which give it the opportunities to operate outside its designated area. The last five Secretary-generals of NATO alone have all been Bilderbergers, Joseph Luns, Lord Carrington, Manfred Woener, Willy Claes, and Javier Solana. The head of the World Bank, the Rothschild partner, James Wolfensohn, and a stream of his predecessors like Robert Strange Macnamara, are Bilderbergers. So are the first two heads of the new World Trade Organisation, a Brotherhood creation which imposes heavy fines on countries who seek to protect their people from the merciless global financial and trading system. The first head of the World Trade Organisation was Peter D. Sutherland of Ireland (Bil, TC, Comm 300), the Director of the General Agreement on Tariff and Trade (GATT), Commissioner of the European Community (Union), and chairman of Allied Irish Banks and Goldman Sachs. He later became head of British Petroleum (BP). Sutherland is an Elite clone make no mistake and he was replaced at the WTO by an Italian Bilderberger, Renato Ruggerio. Both the World Bank and the World Trade Organisation connect with other global financial agencies like the International Monetary Fund and the G-7/G-8 group to impose their will and policies on developing countries in Africa, South and Central America, and Asia, and to ensure they are controlled by the transnational corporations which answer to the same overall leadership. The Multilateral Agreement on Investment (MAI) is another scam designed to dramatically increase the ability of the transnational corporations to destroy a country's economic base by imposing their will on the government and walking away with the profits while avoiding the tax and business laws the other businesses have to face. The central banking network connects into the Round Table-Bilderberg operation. A number of heads of the Bank of England including Sir Gordon Richardson have been Bilderbergers and the same applies to the other central banks like the United States Federal Reserve, the cartel of private banks controlled from Europe which controls the US economy. The current head of the 'Fed' is Alan Greenspan (CFR, TC, Bil) and he replaced Paul A. Volker (CFR, TC, Bil). You get the picture. Every few weeks in the United States and Britain, the media speculate on the possible content of statements by Greenspan and the Governor of the Bank of England or the Bundesbank about the state of their countries' economies. These statements can, and do, send the stock-markets rising and falling on the basis of what these people say. If they put interest rates up or down it can have a spectacular effect on the markets and people's lives. Who do you think controls these people and the statements they make? Exactly. A friend of mine who invests heavily in the US markets began to study the investment patterns of the major corporations, banks, and insurance companies, in the period immediately before Bilderberger Greenspan was due to make his financial statements. On every occasion he found that the big players either massively buy or sell stock or bonds of a specific kind in the three days before Greenspan speaks. And the statement made by Greenspan has, on each and every occasion, had a fundamental effect on precisely the stock or bonds the Brotherhood have bought or sold. If you want to know what the stock-markets are going to do, watch the buying and selling patterns of the

Brotherhood families and corporations who control the markets. Interlocking with 'gofers' like Greenspan and major players like the Rothschilds and Rockefellers, are 'renegade' financiers such as George Soros (Bil) who simply follow orders. It was Soros who made billions by attacking the British pound in September 1992, costing the people unbelievable amounts of money as the Chancellor of the Exchequer tried to defend the currency. Who was that Chancellor? Norman Lamont… Bilderberg Group. Soros did the same to the Swedish currency with the same outcome. Who was the Swedish Prime Minister at the time? Carl Bildt… Bilderberg Group. It was the fear of standing alone caused by that Soros raid which turned a majority of Swedish public opinion to favour entry into the European Union, something most Swedes now appear to bitterly regret.

The careers of so many politicians have taken off dramatically after they attended Bilderberg meetings. In the 1970s the career of the British Conservative Party politician, Margaret Thatcher, soared when she began to attend Bilderberg meetings and her election to Prime Minister was made certain in 1979 by the explosion of scandals and strikes which brought down the Labour Government. A year later Ronald Reagan and George Bush were elected to the White House and they introduced exactly the same extreme economic policies that Margaret Thatcher was doing under the name Thatcherism. It wasn't Thatcherism at all, it was the Agenda unfolding as interest rates took off to levels that crippled the Third World and made them ripe for the recolonisation programme through financial control. Also, the privatisation mania under Thatcher-Reagan-Bush handed over state assets to the Brotherhood transnational corporations at knock-down prices. When Thatcher had outlived her usefulness she was dumped, because everyone is expendable to the cause. In 1991, a relatively unknown Governor for Arkansas called Bill Clinton was invited by David Rockefeller to the Bilderberg meeting in Baden-Baden, Germany. A year later this man of British (Black Nobility) royal blood was President of the United States. In 1993, a British Labour Party Home Affairs spokesman called Tony Blair was invited to the Bilderberg meeting at Vouliagment, Greece, and a year later after the sudden and unexpected death of the Labour leader, John Smith, it was Blair who took over. From the moment that happened, a series of scandals and conflicts destroyed the credibility of the ruling Conservative Government of John Major making it certain that Blair would become Prime Minister in a landslide victory in 1997. When I was on a speaking tour of Australia in early 1997, I predicted that not only would Blair be elected as Prime Minister, the election would take place on May 1st because, going back to ancient times, that was a very important day to the Babylonian Brotherhood. Examples of this are the May Day fertility rituals and the also May 1st celebrations in the Brotherhood-created Soviet Union. The Bavarian Illuminati was officially formed on May 1st 1776. Tony Blair was such an important frontman for the Brotherhood that I just knew they would bring him to power on May 1st. In Britain they do not have fixed term governments, the Prime Minister can call the election any time within five years of coming to power and so he is the one who officially announces the date. What did John Major do? Under instruction from the Tribe, he called the 1997 General

Election for May 1st and Tony Blair, a big-time Brotherhood chosen one, was elected Prime Minister on that day. From the moment he came to power, Blair and his Bilderberger Chancellor, Gordon Brown, began to introduce the Brotherhood Agenda for the Millennium years in Britain and Europe. This included conceding the government's power to set interest rates to the Bank of England, a move which happened within days of the election. The economic policies followed by Bilderberger Brown were no different in fundamentals to those of the previous Conservative Chancellor, Kenneth Clarke, whom Brown replaced. This is not surprising because Clarke is also a Bilderberger and attended the meeting with Tony Blair in Greece and again at Turnberry, Scotland, in May 1998. Brotherhood Labour yes-man replaces Brotherhood Conservative yes-man as the official head of the nation's finances and the only thing that changes is the name on the door. Britain, like America and virtually every other country in the world, is a one-party-state while the public go on thinking they are free because they have the right to put a cross on a piece of paper every five years and choose the next Brotherhood puppet to run their country. In the United States, staggeringly, they vote electronically and this makes it so easy to rig.

Tony Blair became an immediate bosom-buddy of Bill Clinton (CFR, TC, Bil) and they speak with one (Brotherhood) voice. Blair's 'minder' in the Labour Government has been Peter Mandelson (RIIA), nicknamed the Prince of Darkness. He is one of the most important Brotherhood link-men within the British Labour Party and continues to be so despite his resignation from the cabinet over a financial scandal. Incidentally it was when Peter Mandelson took charge of the Labour Party's image-making in the 1980s that they changed their party symbol from the red flag to the classic Brotherhood symbol over the ages… the red rose. Chancellor Kohl of Germany is a Bilderberger and so were his predecessors, Brant and Schmit. Many prime ministers and leading politicians in the Netherlands, including Ruud Lubbers, are Bilderbergers and it's the same throughout Europe with people such as Carl Bildt and the assassinated Olof Palme (Sweden), Uffe Ellemann-Jenson and Ritt Bjergegaard (Denmark). Jacques Santer, the head of the European Commission, is a Bilderberger. He is the most important public voice in the European Union and he runs his centralised dictatorship with the stunning arrogance that Brotherhood initiates find so easy to manifest. European royalty is represented at Bilderberg meetings by the Dutch, Swedish, Spanish and British royal families, or in truth: family. Lord Mountbatten, Prince Philip, and Prince Charles have attended Bilderberg meetings.

The "peace-keepers"

When Brotherhood organisations use a word in their name they invariably mean the opposite. The Carnegie Endowment for International Peace manipulates war and 'Democratic Fronts' all over the world introduce dictatorships. It can be the same with 'peace-keepers' and 'peace negotiators'. Henry Kissinger goes around the world talking about "peace" and yet when he leaves a country all hell often breaks out. It's not that he's a bad negotiator, he's just doing his job for the Tribe. His company, Kissinger Associates (founding director Lord Carrington (RIIA, Bil,

TC), was heavily involved in starting the Bosnian war which has moved the world closer to a global army under NATO control. This is a constant theme. Start the war and then negotiate the 'peace' to suit your Agenda. At the start of the Bosnian conflict, the status quo was the United Nations Peacekeeping Force. But it was exposed, by design, to be ineffective and with horrific pictures pouring from the television screens every night, the global cry was: "Something must be done, this can't go on, what are they going to do about it." That 'something' offered by the very people who had engineered the war, was a 60,000-strong NATO world army, the biggest multinational force assembled since the Second World War. It is in these circumstances that the Round Table network can be used to ensure the right appointments. The first peace negotiator appointed by the European Union in Bosnia was, yes, yes, Lord Carrington, chairman of the Bilderberg Group, President of the Royal Institute of International Affairs, Trilateral Commission member, and one of the Committee of 300. He was replaced by Lord David Owen (Bil, TC) and Carl Bildt (Bil), the former Swedish Prime Minister. The United Nations appointed negotiators were Cyrus Vance (Bil, CFR, TC) and the Norwegian, Thorvald Stoltenberg (Bil, TC). When their negotiations came to nothing, along came an 'independent' negotiator, Jimmy Carter, the first Trilateral Commission President of the United States, and a CFR member. The cry of "Do something" got even louder as the horrors in Bosnia continued unchecked and then came Richard Holbrooke (CFR, TC, Bil), the peace envoy of Bill Clinton, who negotiated the Dayton Agreement which introduced the NATO world army in Bosnia. Holbrooke answered to the then Secretary of State, Warren Christopher (CFR, TC), and the Defence Secretary, William Perry (Bil). They reported to the President, Bill Clinton (CFR, TC, Bil) who followed the orders of David Rockefeller and Henry Kissinger, leading lights in the CFR, TC, Bil, and RIIA. The first head of the NATO world army in Bosnia was Admiral Leighton Smith (CFR) and the civilian end of the operation was controlled by Carl Bildt (Bil). Oh yes, and the American ambassador in the former Yugoslavia was Warren Zimmerman (CFR). What's more, the financier, George Soros (Bil), just happened to have a series of tax-exempt 'foundations' throughout the former Yugoslavia before and during the war. Just a coincidence, nothing to worry about. This is only one example of the techniques and organisations used to change the world by making wars and deciding what happens as a result of them. Problem-reaction-solution. Some of the names behind the Bilderberg Group and the wider network are very familiar, the Rothschilds, David Rockefeller, Henry Kissinger, and Lord Carrington. I have written much about the Rothschilds, but it is important to know about the other three as well. They are not the very top of the pyramid people, but they are right up there at the operational level:

- **David Rockefeller (CFR, TC, Bil, RIIA, Comm 300)**
The Rockefellers (previous name Rockenfelder) became the most powerful family in the United States with the help of Rothschild money and, no doubt, through other sources, too. The manipulation of the United States and the wider world abounds with the name Rockefeller, be it J. D. Rockefeller, Nelson Rockefeller, Winthrop

Rockefeller, Laurance Rockefeller, or the most notorious of them in the second half of the 20th century, David Rockefeller. If the Rockefeller family and its networks and interconnecting bloodlines had never existed, the United States would be a very different place today: a land with far greater freedom than it currently enjoys, as would the world in general. David Rockefeller, the long-time head of the Chase Manhattan Bank and still unofficially in charge, was secretary of the Council on Foreign Relations Study Group which created the Marshall Plan for the reconstruction of Europe after the Second World War. Marshall Plan funds were used to promote the European Union and to undermine the authority of the nation states. The man appointed to head the Marshall Plan in Europe was... Averell Harriman (Comm 300, Skull and Bones Society) who based himself at the Rothschild's Paris mansion. David Rockefeller was chairman of the Council on Foreign Relations from 1946-53 and created the Trilateral Commission under the leadership of Henry Kissinger (CFR, TC, Bil, RIIA, Comm 300) and Zbigniew Brzezinski (CFR, TC, Bil). Brzezinski was a professor at the Brotherhood-founded Columbia University and authored the book, *Between Two Ages: America's Role In The Technotronic Era*, which mirrored the Brotherhood vision for the world. He was National Security Advisor to Jimmy Carter, the man David Rockefeller selected in 1976 to become the first Trilateral Commission President of the United States. David Rockefeller is the man behind all the presidents because he controls the money, media, and politics, to ensure that both presidential candidates answer to him. That was true of George Bush and Bill Clinton in 1992 and Bob Dole and Bill Clinton in 1996. If you control the money, the media, and the party machines, you can put anyone you like in the White House and you can get rid of them while they are still in office if that suits your agenda and timescale. This is why those who truly represent the interests of the people never reach the upper levels of politics. But it is not just in the United States that this is so. David Rockefeller has been the banker and puppet master of Russia and the Soviet Union, schooling and dictating to people like Mikhail Gorbachev and Boris Yeltsin. Gorbachev, a reptilian shape-shifter, was used by Rockefeller and Kissinger to bring down the Soviet Union to allow those countries to begin the process of integration into the European Union and NATO. Yeltsin was speaking at Trilateral Commission events before he became President of Russia. You find the hand of David Rockefeller everywhere, for instance, symbolically up the backside of the glove puppet called Maurice Strong (Bil, Comm 300), the Canadian oil millionaire or billionaire, who has massively manipulated the environmental movement as the first Director of the United Nations Environment Agency and the top man at the 1992 Earth Summit in Brazil. Wherever David Rockefeller goes the stench of corruption, manipulation, and genocide, follows. Which reminds me of someone else...

- **Henry Kissinger (CFR,TC,Bil, RIIA,Comm 300)**
Henry Kissinger became world famous after 1968 as the Secretary of State and National Security Advisor to President Richard Nixon, the only man in US history to hold both posts at the same time. But Kissinger's enormous service to the

Babylonian Brotherhood goes back a long way before then and continues to the present day. He was born in Germany in 1923 and grew up a Jew under Adolf Hitler. But if Kissinger really is a 'Jew', why was he one of those involved in Project Paperclip, the Anglo-American Intelligence operation which allowed Nazi genetic and mind experimenters and torturers like Josef Mengele to escape from Germany at the end of the war to continue their work in the United States and South America? Because he could not give a shit about Jewish people, that's why. They are just cattle to him like every other race, except his own, the reptilians. Kissinger is a Satanist, mass murderer, mind control expert, and child killer. He arrived in the United States on September 5th 1938 and later became a naturalised American citizen. In 1972 the Polish KGB agent, Michael Goleniewski, told the British Government that KGB documents he saw prior to his defection in 1959 included the name Henry Kissinger as a Soviet Union asset. According to Goleniewski, Kissinger was recruited by the KGB into an espionage cell called ODRA and was given the code name BOR or Colonel BOR. He built his power-base and 'reputation' at Harvard and he was on his way. As I reveal in detail in ...*And The Truth Shall Set You Free*, Kissinger has been the man behind all the presidents since Nixon, even though he has not been involved officially.

It was he who arranged for the Watergate scandal which removed Nixon and brought in Gerald Ford (CFR, Bil) as President and Nelson Rockefeller, Kissinger's crony and mentor, as vice-president. It was Nelson Rockefeller who advised Nixon to appoint Kissinger in the first place. The Watergate scandal was exposed by journalists Woodward and Bernstein of the *Washington Post*, a paper owned by Kissinger's friend, Katherine Graham (CFR, TC, Bil). I was approached by a scientist working for the Brotherhood against his will, who was ordered to a meeting at the White House during the Bush administration (1988–92). He was astonished to find Kissinger in the Oval Office dictating events while Bush sat there and nodded. Kissinger had no official role in the Bush administration to the knowledge of the American public and yet there he was calling the shots. Kissinger's 'shuttle diplomacy' consisted, and consists, of misrepresenting each side to the other, so sparking war after war. In 1973, Kissinger was given the Nobel Peace Prize for stopping the Yom Kippur War which he had actually started. When Kissinger and Carrington come into your country, its time to go on holiday, because all hell normally follows the moment they leave. Ask the people of Burundi and Rwanda...

When George Bush became President in 1988, he appointed two executives of the Kissinger Associates to his administration. Brent Scowcroft, the head of the Washington office, became Director of the National Security Council, and Lawrence Eagleburger, the President of Kissinger Associates, became Under-secretary at the State Department. As I've said, Kissinger Associates was behind the war in Bosnia and the first 'peace' negotiator appointed by the European Union was Lord Carrington, a founding director of Kissinger Associates. This company was also instrumental in the Gulf War, arranging loans for Iraq through the Banca Nazionale del Lavoro (BNL) as early as 1984 to allow Saddam Hussein to finance arms purchases through a little known subsidiary of Fiat, the Italian car giant owned by

Giovanni Agnelli, the Black Nobility Bilderberger. Charles Barletta, a former Justice Department investigator, was quoted about this in the *Spotlight* newspaper in Washington on November 9th 1992. The report said:

> "Barletta added that federal probers had collected dozens of such incriminating case histories about the Kissinger firm. But Henry Kissinger seems to possess a special kind of immunity. I'm not sure how he does it, but Kissinger wields as much power over the Washington national security bureaucracy now as in the days when he was the Nixon administration's foreign policy czar. He gets the payoff; others get the blame. Kissinger will remain unscathed until Congress finds the courage to convene a full-dress investigation into this Teflon power broker."

Kissinger operates in the highest levels of the Royal Institute of International Affairs, Bilderberg Group, Trilateral Commission, Council on Foreign Relations, and the Club of Rome, and he is a member of the Grand Alpine Freemasonry Lodge in Switzerland, which controlled the notorious Italian terrorist lodge known as P2. The world will not be safe while this man is on the streets. Another of his 'specialities' is genocide in the Third World to dramatically reduce the number of non-white faces and to cull those members of the white races considered the lower stock. This programme is being introduced by manipulating famine, disease (including those created in laboratories), war, sterilisation and 'population control'. See ...*And The Truth Shall Set You Free.*

- **Lord Carrington (RIIA, TC, Bil, Comm 300)**

Peter Rupert Carrington comes from a banking family and is an extremely close associate of Kissinger. These are the Tweedle Dee and Tweedle Dum of global manipulation. Carrington was on the board of Hambros Bank (Comm 300 designate) which was connected to the Michel Sindona-P2 Freemasonry scandal in Italy. The Elite P2 Freemasonry Lodge controlled by the Mussolini fascist, Lucio Gelli, was the force behind the Red Brigades terrorists in the 1970s who planted the devastating bomb at Bologna railway station and murdered the leading politician, Aldo Morro, after Morro had rejected Henry Kissinger's order to change his policies. P2 and the Hambros-Carrington-connected Michel Sindona were also involved in the control of the Vatican Bank. Another casualty was the Italian P2 Freemason and banker, Roberto Calvi, who was hanged under Blackfriars Bridge near the City of London's Square Mile in 1982 after the scandal became public. Carrington's other business interests have included some familiar names, Rio Tinto Zinc, Barclays Bank, Cadbury Schweppes, Amalgamated Metal, British Metal, Christies the auctioneers, and the chairmanship of the Australian New Zealand Bank. In his book, *The English Rothschilds*, Richard Davis reports that Lionel Rothschild was a frequent visitor to the Carrington's home in Whitehall. The two families are related by the marriage of the fifth Earl Rosebery to Hannah Rothschild, daughter of Meyer, in 1878. During the ceremony she was 'given away' as they say by Prime Minister Disraeli. Carrington, then, is of the Rothschild-British aristocratic reptilian bloodline. He has the perfect background and attitudes for a Brotherhood manipulator and he has been appointed to perform many tasks for them. He was the British Foreign Secretary who ensured that power in the former Rhodesia was transferred from the white minority government of Ian Smith to the black dictator, Robert Mugabe, and things have got worse, not better, for the people, exactly as planned. It was Carrington who resigned as Foreign Secretary because of the 'mistakes' he made which led to the Falklands War in 1982. You would have thought that he would have been kept well away from things military after that, but no, from 1984 to 1988, he was the Secretary-general of NATO and in 1991 he became the chairman of the Bilderberg Group. While in that post, he was appointed to be the first 'peace' negotiator in Bosnia.

Control of the media

The names Rothschild, Rockefeller, Kissinger and Carrington appear on the boards and 'advisory' boards of global media corporations and that's no surprise. To control humanity through the mind and emotions you simply have to control the media. Without that it's impossible. This is made so much easier because the overwhelming majority of journalists in the world, including the so-called 'big names' in each country, are either agents for the Brotherhood (the small minority) or they don't know their arse from their elbow when it comes to understanding what is going on in the world. I've been a journalist and so I have seen both sides and what is termed the communications industry is really the blind (journalists) leading the blind (their readers and viewers). My experience as a journalist, and as the target of journalists, has shown me very clearly how remarkably few brain cells you need to do the job. Every day on television stations all over the world, journalists and correspondents give their viewers the official version of the event they are reporting. "White House sources say this…, the Prime Minister says that…, the FBI say the other… " In all my time in journalism I cannot recall a single conversation in a newsroom that didn't reflect the official version of life and the world. Most journalists are not manipulating, they are simply stunningly uninformed and often incredibly arrogant. They believe that if anything of magnitude was going on they would know about it because they are 'journalists'. In truth they are the last to know. Arrogance and naïveté, the mental combination that produces so many journalists, is a telling and highly destructive combination. Add a padlocked mind and you've got the job. One BBC interviewer said to me in all seriousness that we should be no more concerned about the membership of the Freemasons than we should the membership of the local squash club. I'm not kidding. I have given many journalists the story of what is going on and they have either dismissed it without even looking at the evidence or they have ridiculed the information without looking at the evidence. I remember meeting a guy, I think his name was Taylor or something, in Los Angeles in early 1997. He worked for *The Observer* newspaper in London. I told him about the paedophile activities of George Bush and his drug running operation. I offered to put him in touch with some of those who had been abused by Bush. What did this 'journalist' do? He went away and wrote an article making personal attacks on me, including the fact that my eyes appeared bloodshot. Not surprising after a non-stop speaking tour of Australia, New

Zealand and the United States over a period of two months, but how can anyone write about the state of someone's eyes when they are being offered, as he put it himself, the "Story of the century"? Because he's a journalist, that's why. I offered to put the British Sunday People in contact with similar sources, but they didn't want to know. As the old saying goes: "You cannot bribe or twist the great British journalist, but seeing what they will do unbribed, there's no reason to." Of course there are journalists who are exceptions, and honourable ones, but they are so, so rare and ask them what happens when they try to write the story as it really is.

Journalists dance to the official tune and become the copy typists and town criers for the official version of life. They are the 'gofers' for those higher up the media pyramid. At the top are bankers who provide the funds to buy the media groups. These bankers also control the major industries and business networks and the newspaper, television, and radio operations cannot survive without the advertising revenue from these people. The threat to stop advertising has led to many an exposé of the truth ending up in the bin. Below the bankers and industrialists come the media 'barons', the Murdochs, Blacks, O'Reillys, and Packers. They toe the line of the funders and advertisers and they appoint their editors to make sure that the same policy appears in the papers and broadcast media day after day. The editor appoints the journalists and they have to follow the same line the editor has been told to follow. The journalist answers to the editor, the editor answers to the proprietor, and the proprietor answers to the banks and the corporations – the Brotherhood. This is what we call 'news'. We are led to believe that the great media egos like Murdoch, Packer, and Ted Turner don't like each other. Maybe that's true and maybe its a smokescreen, it doesn't really matter. Whichever of them heads an organisation, the same policy prevails, so the Brotherhood could not care less which of their puppets owns a newspaper because their policy will be followed whatever. These 'barons' are not in control. They are frontmen, that's all. Look at Ted Turner, the Council on Foreign Relations member who was supposed to be taking on the system with his Cable News Network (CNN). He sold out to Time Warner, one of the greatest Brotherhood operations on the planet, and CNN pounds out the official line hour after hour, day after day. When someone genuinely wants to start a television station or newspaper to tell the truth, they can't get advertising or funding or they have their share price undermined via the unimaginable amounts of money the Brotherhood banks, corporations, and insurance companies move around every day. This opens up such media operations to a hostile takeover. The three television networks in the United States, CBS, ABC, and NBC are controlled by members of the Round Table network and so are the *Washington Post, Los Angeles Times, New York Times, Wall Street Journal*, and a long, long list of others. The same goes for country after country.

Two of the lesser known groups which make the point about control of the media are Hollinger Inc. and 'Independent' Newspapers. Hollinger owns 68% of newspapers in Canada and more than 250 papers and magazines worldwide, including major US papers, *The Jerusalem Post*, and Telegraph Newspapers in London. Hollinger is a front for British Intelligence. During the last world war, an Elite section of British Intelligence called the Special Operations Executive formed a front organisation called War Supplies Ltd under the leadership of two British agents, George Montagu Black and Edward Plunkett Taylor. It was Taylor who later wrote the banking laws for the Bahamas and the Cayman Islands. After the war this British Intelligence company continued under the name of the Argus Corporation and more recently it changed its name again to Hollinger. Today it is headed by Conrad Black, the son of the British spy, George Montagu Black, who set it up in the first place. Conrad Black is a member of the inner sanctum of the Bilderberg Group. His father was close to the Bronfman gangster family who, like the Kennedys, made a fortune from running illegal booze during the prohibition the Brotherhood themselves had introduced. The Bronfmans today own the liquor giant, Seagrams, as well as a substantial drug running operation. On the 'advisory' board of Hollinger are Henry Kissinger, Lord Carrington, and Edmund de Rothschild! Independent Newspapers is owned by the Irish billionaire and former rugby player, Tony O'Reilly. It includes newspapers in Ireland, Britain, France, Portugal, Mexico, South Africa, and New Zealand. The South African President, Nelson Mandela, spent Christmas 1993 at O'Reilly's holiday home at Nassau in the Bahamas and soon afterwards the Irishman bought the Argus group, South Africa's biggest newspaper chain.[4] This is now a mouthpiece for Mandela's African National Congress (ANC). Since 1994, O'Reilly has bought 60% of the Argus Group, 43% of Newspaper Publishing in Britain, 55% of Australian Provincial Newspapers, 25% of Irish Press Newspapers, and 44% of Wilson and Horton the largest newspaper group in New Zealand.[5] He also has extensive interests in cable television in Ireland, and radio and television in Australia and New Zealand. His acquisitions will go on and money will be no object because for all his self-promotion he is just a puppet. His *Sunday Independent* in Ireland devoted an eight page supplement to him called "A Man For All Continents" and it included seventeen photographs of him with his friends... Henry Kissinger (Bil, CFR,TC, RIIA, Comm 300), Margaret Thatcher (Bil), Valery Giscard D'Estaing (Bil), and Robert Mugabe. One of O'Reilly's close friends in Ireland is the former Prime Minister, Garret Fitzgerald (Bil, TC).[6] O'Reilly also idolises Churchill, apparently. His friendship with the Zimbawe dictator, Robert Mugabe, began while O'Reilly was still chairman of Heinz and Mugabe will still put a giant-sized can of Heinz beans on his head to amuse visitors to the State House.[7] In 1992, Mugabe joined O'Reilly at his mansion in County Kildare, Ireland, and these two Jesuit-educated initiates celebrated high mass in a medieval private chapel built around a crusader's (Knights Templar) tomb.[8] O'Reilly and his business associates have since bought a 60% stake in Associated Newpapers of Zimbabwe (ANZ) with the intention of launching a new English language daily.[9]

The Agenda today

The control and manipulation of the media and the other institutions which direct human thinking and perception is not only to achieve power for power's sake, there is a much bigger reason for it. The Agenda is for the complete takeover of the planet by the reptilians without anyone realising that it has even happened. They are well on their way to achieving this unless people wake up. The basic structure is designed

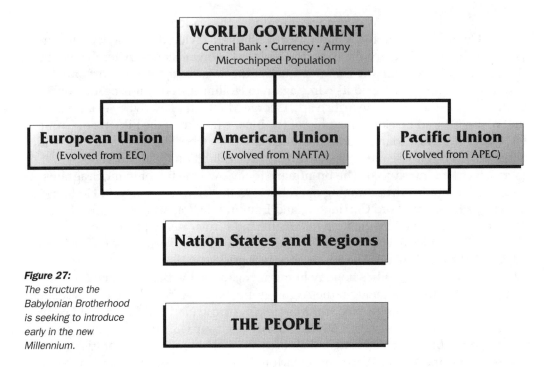

Figure 27:
The structure the Babylonian Brotherhood is seeking to introduce early in the new Millennium.

around a world government which would take all the major decisions in the world (*see **Figure** 27*). This would control a world central bank, currency (electronic, no cash), and army. All this would be underpinned by a microchipped population linked to a global computer. Under this structure would come three superstates – the European Union, the American Union, and the Pacific Union (Asia, Far East, Australia). This edifice of power would dictate to the current nation states which are planned to be broken up into regions to dismantle any unified response to the structure I've described. It would, quite simply, be a global fascist dictatorship and we are so close to this unless there is a revolution of thinking among the mass of humanity. The network I have summarised in this chapter allows for this Agenda to unfold because there are Brotherhood agents working within all the political and economic groups needed to make it happen. The more global problems that can be created, the more pressure there will be for global solutions – the centralised control. The second tier, the 'unions' of superstates, is well on the way.

The Superstate 'Unions'

The European Union with its central bank and single currency has been evolved from a free trade area called the European Economic Community or Common Market. There was no mention of the superstate when we joined, but that was always the Agenda and it has been achieved by the stepping stones approach: moving towards the goal step by step with very few realising where these steps are heading. Had Adolf Hitler won the war he had an economic design for Europe he called it the Europaische Wirtscraft = gemeinschaft. This translates as...

the European Economic Community! Hitler lost the war, at least on the surface, but we got the same policy anyway because it was part of the Agenda. If I summarise how the European Union has been engineered and the people and organisations behind it, you will see how the hidden hand operates and be more aware of the tactics being employed to do exactly the same in the Americas, the Pacific region, and Africa. A United States of Europe under centralised control was the aim of the Knights Templar way back in the 12th and 13th centuries and under their different names and incarnations this same force has achieved that target via the Freemasons, the Bilderberg Group, and others. The Bilderberg Group is particularly important, however, in the creation of the present superstate. The men behind the formation of the European Economic Community on behalf of the Brotherhood were Jean Monnet (Comm 300), Count Richard N. Coudenhove-Kalergi (Comm 300) from Austria, and Joseph Retinger (Comm 300), a Polish 'socialist' who helped Prince Bernhard to create the Bilderberg Group. Monnet, the son of a French brandy merchant, went to Canada in 1910 and there connected with the Hudson Bay Company, an old Black Nobility operation, and the Lazard Brothers Bank. He became a confidant to presidents and prime ministers, including Franklin Delano Roosevelt, and his influential friends gave him a very lucrative contract to ship materials from Canada to France during the First World War. When the war ended he was appointed to the Allied Supreme Economic Council and became an advisor to the group around Lord Milner (Round Table, RIIA, Comm 300) and Colonel Mandel House (Round Table, CFR, Comm 300) which was preparing the Treaty of Versailles and creating the League of Nations. Monnet was appointed the Deputy Secretary General of the League of Nations and later vice-president of a company called Transamerica which was owned by the drug-money-laundering Bank of America. Monnet was perfectly placed to be the puppet through which other powers could manipulate into being the European Economic Community. Count Richard N. Coudenhove-Kalergi wrote a book in 1923 calling for a United States of Europe. He was named after Richard Wagner, of whom Hitler had said that to understand Nazi Germany one had to understand Wagner. A close friend of the Count's father was Theodore Herzl, the founder of Zionism (Sionism – the Sun cult). The Count's book was called *Pan Europa* and he went on to form the Pan European Union with branches right across the continent, supported by leading politicians and the Anglo-America Establishment, including Colonel House and Herbert Hoover. The Count said in his autobiography:

"At the beginning of 1924, we received a call from Baron Louis de Rothschild; one of his friends, Max Warburg (*Hitler's banker*) from Hamburg, had read my book and wanted to get to know us. To my great surprise (*sure!*), Warburg spontaneously (*sure!*) offered us 60,000 gold marks to tide the movement over for its first three years... Max Warburg, who was one of the most distinguished and wisest men that I ever came into contact with, had a principle of financing these movements. He remained sincerely interested in Pan-Europe for his entire life. Max Warburg arranged his 1925 trip to the United States to introduce me to Paul Warburg and Bernard Baruch." [10]

The European Community, now Union, is another creation of the Brotherhood with all the old familiar names involved. Winston Churchill (Comm 300) was a supporter of the European superstate and he wrote an article in 1930 for the American publication *The Saturday Evening Post*, called "The United States of Europe". A few years later he would play his part in advancing the war which led to the creation of that very structure. Count Coudenhove-Kalergi was given enthusiastic backing from people like John Foster Dulles, Nicholas Murray Butler, the President of Columbia University and the Carnegie Endowment for International Peace ('War'), and Dr Stephen Duggan, the founder and first President of the Institute of Education which was 100% controlled by the Council on Foreign Relations. The United States Congress passed seven resolutions on the political union of Europe and one of them stated: "The creation of a United Europe must be regarded as an essential step towards the creation of a United World" (world government). Jean Monnet also headed the Committee for the United States of Europe which had the same goal. Since the creation of the European Economic Community (EEC) it has been evolved as planned, by the stepping stones method, to become the centralised fascist state it was always designed to be. Two admirers of Monnet are Merry and Serge Bromberger, and they set out the plan in their book, *Jean Monnet And The United States Of Europe*:

> "Gradually, it was thought, the supranational authorities, supervised by the European Council of Ministers at Brussels and the Assembly in Strasbourg, would administer all the activities of the continent. A day would come when governments would be forced to admit that an integrated Europe was an accomplished fact, without their having a say in the establishment of its underlying principles. All they would have to do was to merge all these autonomous institutions into a single federal administration and then proclaim a United States of Europe." [11]

That is where we are now. Again you have the structure of the core few at the centre dictating the overall plan and the interlocking networks in each country manipulating their people and Parliament to follow that overall Agenda. The two Prime Ministers of Britain before, during, and after our entry into the European Community were Labour's Harold Wilson (Bil) and the Conservative Edward Heath (Bil, TC). They were both close associates of Lord Victor Rothschild and Heath made Rothschild head of his 'policy unit' during his four years as Prime Minister between 1970 and 1974. It was in this period, in 1972, that Heath signed the Treaty of Rome which ensnared the United Kingdom into the Brotherhood's European spider's web. Sitting beside Heath at the signing ceremony was his Foreign Secretary, Alec Douglas Hume (Lord Home), a chairman of the Bilderberg Group and a member of an ancient Scottish bloodline. The whole thing was manipulation on a vast scale. The 'opposition' Labour Party when we went into Europe under Harold Wilson (Bil) included in its leadership, Roy Jenkins (Bil, TC, RIIA), who would go on to become the President of the European Commission, James Callaghan (Bil, RIIA), and Denis Healey (Bil, TC, Comm 300), chairman of the International Monetary Fund Interim

Committee and member of the council of the Royal Institute of International Affairs. Healey was at the first Bilderberg meeting in 1954 and attended more of their gatherings than any other British politician in his period in active politics. Good Old Denis, the man of the people? Excuse me. In this same period the leaders of Britain's third party, the Liberals (now Liberal Democrats) were Jo Grimond (Bil) and Jeremy Thorpe, author of the book, *Europe: The Case For Going In*. I wonder when they were in the highest political positions in the land, if Wilson, Heath, Jenkins, and Healey, ever got together and pondered on the remarkable twist of destiny which led four people, who attended Oxford University in the same period, to become the leading political names of 1960s and 1970s, just as the United Kingdom was committing itself to membership of the European Community. Wilson (Jesus College, University College), Jenkins (Balliol), Heath (Balliol), Healey (Balliol), Grimond (Balliol), and Thorpe (Trinity College) are such an inspirational example of what can happen when you have an Oxford education. The fact that Oxford has always been a major Brotherhood centre and, with Cambridge, is a key recruiting ground for manipulators of the next generation, is purely coincidental, of course.

Heath, a shape-shifting reptilian, was manipulating Britain toward membership of the Community right through the 1960s and he was agreeing to the political union of Britain in Europe as early as April 1962 when he was Lord Privy Seal. Before taking Britain into Europe, Heath attended a meeting in Paris in October 1972 to negotiate the conditions with the French President Georges Pompidou (Bil), a former employee of Guy Rothschild. Douglas Hurd was the British Foreign Secretary who signed the fascist Maastricht Treaty in February 1992 which turned the European Community into the European Union, the superstate. Hurd was a private secretary to Ted Heath between 1968 and 1970 and his political secretary from 1970 to 1974 when Heath was Prime Minister and signing Britain into Europe. Hurd was also Minister of State to Lord Carrington in the run up to the Falklands War and it was Hurd who recommended an 'honorary' knighthood for Henry Kissinger. Since that time influential and apparently opposing political figures like the Conservatives Ted Heath (Bil, TC), Kenneth Clarke (Bil), Geoffrey (Lord) Howe (Bil, Comm 300), the Labour Party's Tony Blair (Bil), Gordon Brown (Bil, TC), and the Liberal Democrat leaders, David Steel (Bil, TC) and Paddy Ashdown (Bil), have pressed and argued for further and further erosion of British decision making and the swamping of freedom by the centralised, bureaucratic European Union. Blair has blatantly filled his ministerial team negotiating with the European Union with people who want the UK to join the single bank and currency. Among them, before his resignation in a financial scandal, was our friend Peter Mandelson, the man members of Parliament have dubbed: "the Prince of Darkness". At the time of writing, the three major British political parties are headed by Tony Blair (Bil), William Haig (Bil), and Paddy Ashdown (Bil).

We are being conned and the Brotherhood initiates at the top in the banks and corporations have been activated to frighten the people into believing there will be an economic collapse if a country does not join the single bank and currency. What nonsense. Norway refused to join the European Union and has had great economic prosperity, not least through its exports to the European Union countries! What I have described in Europe is planned for the Americas, the Pacific region, and Africa. The American Union is designed to evolve from NAFTA, the North American Free Trade Agreement, and the Pacific Union from APEC, Asia Pacific Economic Cooperation, the 'free-trade area' formed in 1994 after much campaigning by the Rhodes Scholar and former Australian Prime Minister, Bob Hawke. NAFTA was negotiated between George Bush (CFR,TC, Skull and Bones), the paedophile President of the United States, and Brian Mulroney, a rapist of mind controlled women, who was Prime Minister of Canada. I'll expand on their activities in a later chapter. Bush said when he signed the free trade agreement with Canada and Mexico on August 12th 1992 that he wanted to see NAFTA stretch from the tip of North America to the tip of South America. His 'opponent', Bill Clinton, said at a gathering of leaders from throughout the Americas on December 10th 1994:

> "History has given the people of the Americas the chance to build a community of nations, committed to liberty and the promise of prosperity… early in the next century (*I want to see*)… a huge free trade zone from Alaska to Argentina."

Other elements of the Agenda include the microchipping of the global population; the complete control of energy supplies, the destruction of alternative forms of healing that expose established medicine as a fraud; and global marshal law. I will write more about this towards the end of the book. The one-party-state and the one-world-Agenda rolls on and here I have given only an outline of the people, organisations and events to which I have referred because they are all covered in intricate detail, and sourced, in …*And The Truth Shall Set You Free.*

■ SOURCES

1   *The Illuminati Formula*, p 7.

2   Anthony C. Sutton, *Wall Street And The Rise Of Hitler* (Heritage Publications, Melbourne, Australia, and Bloomfield Books, Sudbury, Suffolk, England, 1976), p 39, and *Trilateralism, The Trilateral Commission And The Elite Planning For World Management* (edited by Holly Sklar, South End Press,Boston, USA, 1980), p 182.

3   Quoted in *The Conspirators Hierarchy: The Story Of The Committee of 300*, p 15.

4   Fintan O'Toole, *Brand Leader, An investigation Of Tony O'Reilly*, (Granta), p 72.

5   Ibid, pp 61–62.

6   Ibid, p 47.

7   Ibid, p 58.

8   *Private Eye* magazine, No 956, Friday, August 7th 1998, p 6.

9   Ibid.

10   Quoted by Eustace Mullins in *The World Order, Our Secret Rulers* (Ezra Pound Institute of Civilisation, Staunton, VA, USA, 1984), p 248.

11   Merry and Serge Bromberger, *Jean Monnet And The United States Of Europe*, (Coward-McCann Publishers, New York, 1969), p 123.

CHAPTER FOURTEEN

Under the influence

One of the most powerful weapons in the Brotherhood's war against humanity over thousands of years has been addictive and mind-altering drugs. In the ancient mystery schools, drugs were widely employed to stimulate other states of consciousness and to manipulate thought and perception.

Opium, from which comes heroin, is the oldest narcotic we know of. References to its use have been found in the Sumerian Tablets going back maybe 6,000 years.[1] The Sumerians called it the 'joy plant'.[2] It is also mentioned by the Egyptians and the Greeks in around 1,500 BC and 1,000 BC respectively. The opium poppy was such a part of Greece that they depicted it on their gold coins.[3] Traces of hallucinogenic drugs were found in the grave of a South American Indian dating back 4,500 years and, throughout the ancient world, records of drug use can be found. Haomoa and Soma, the sacred drinks of the Zoroastrians and the Hindus, could well have been the mind-altering Amanita muscari mushroom, some believe.[4] The chemicals from this pass into the urine with hardly any loss of strength and the Hindu scriptures refer to a sacred urine drink as a source of enlightenment and insight. Certainly gives new meaning to the phrase "Taking the piss". The Aztecs used the hallucinogenic properties of the Psilocybe Mexicana mushroom in their religious rites and they called it "God's flesh".[5] I mentioned earlier the use of mushrooms by the Hebrew priests which even inspired the design of their headgear. The reptile-Aryan priests of Babylon were highly skilled in their manipulation of the populace through drugs and this has continued in the secret society networks they spawned. The Rosicrucians expanded the use of mind-altering drugs and the Assassins possibly got their very name from the way they employed drugs to mind control their killers. More than anything, drugs have been used by the Brotherhood throughout history to destroy societies so they can be easily taken over. This is precisely what is happening on a world scale today. But this policy is not new. Only the scale has changed.

Most famously opium was the weapon used by the 'British' (the London-based Babylonian Brotherhood) in the Opium Wars against China in 1840 and 1858. Chinese efforts to stop the flow of opium into their country were thwarted by the might of the British Empire. Queen Victoria's Foreign Secretary and Prime Minister during the Opium Wars was Lord Palmerston, the Grand Patriarch or Master of Grand Orient Freemasonry, and a member of the Committee of 300. The Palmerstons were in fact the Temple family and their title goes back to 1723 when

Henry Temple became Baron Temple of Mount Temple, County Sligo, Ireland and Viscount Palmerston of Palmerston, County Dublin, an Irish peer. Temple originates from Templar. This title was passed onto his grandson, also named Henry, who was a member of the British House of Commons for 40 years and it was he who owned a painting by the artist, David Teniers, called *St Anthony And St Paul*, with its mass of sacred geometry, which has been connected by researchers to the coded manuscripts and mysteries of Rennes-le-Chateau. Temple was living at the time at Broadlands in Romsey, Hampshire, later the home of Lord Louis Mountbatten. The Mountbatten family also bought the Teniers painting. It was the second Lord Palmerston's son, Henry John Temple, who became the legendary Prime Minister, Foreign Secretary, and drug runner for the British Crown in China. He married into the English aristocracy through the sister of Lord Melbourne, the Prime Minister at the start of Queen Victoria's reign, and went on to lead the Liberal Party, also known as the Venetian Party, overseeing the British forces in the Crimean War and the Opium Wars against China. He entered the House of Commons for the first time as the member of Parliament for Newport on the Isle of Wight, a name which recurs far more often than you would expect for a small island off the south coast of England. Queen Victoria and Prince Albert had Osborne House built on the island, and this is where she spent much of her time after Albert's death. Lord Mountbatten would later be governor of the island. The Isle of Wight is a significant centre for Satanism as well as being a most beautiful place to visit. Another Brotherhood city is Edinburgh in Scotland, just down the road from the Sinclair's Rosslyn Chapel. Palmerston spent three years in Edinburgh lodging with the Whig Party philosopher, Professor Dugald Stewart, and Edinburgh University was a common connection between the members of the Lunar Society and Charles Darwin. The Brotherhood chosen one, Tony Blair, the British Prime Minister elected on May 1st 1997, was brought up in Edinburgh and went to Fettes, a private school there. His father was a lecturer at Edinburgh University.

The vehicle for the opium trade from India to China and elsewhere, was the East India Company, a group of Scottish merchants and Freemasons who were aligned with the Knights of St John of Jerusalem (Malta) and the Society of Jesus, the Jesuits. Some researchers believe that the company's real masters were the banking families of northern Italy, the Black Nobility, but by then they were centred in London, anyway. The strategy used by the British in China has become a blueprint for invasion-by-drug-addiction ever since. They sponsored a mass addiction to opium until Chinese society and vitality was torn asunder. The British Government used a network of terrorism and organised crime, like the Triads, the Hong Society, and the Assassins to carry out the trade on their behalf. These secret societies which ruthlessly eliminate anyone, especially their own, who do not carry out orders, are merely threads in the same global network that connects with the Freemasons. They are, again, different masks on the same face. The drug trade was (and is) organised by the Far East lodges of Freemasonry. The Grand Lodge of England (current Grand Master, the Queen's cousin, the Duke of Kent) established lodges in China at Amoy, Canton, Foochow, Swatow, Chefoo, Chinkiang, Hankow, Newchang, Tongshan,

Wei-Hai-Wei, two at Tientsin, three in Shanghai, and five in Hong Kong.[6] When the Chinese rulers acted to stop the supply of opium, the British used their military and naval might to defeat them. And the 'peace' treaty after the conflict then gave the British a guaranteed right to increase the flow of opium; to be paid compensation for the opium the Chinese rulers had confiscated; and to have sovereignty over strategic ports and offshore islands and this is how Hong Kong came under British rule. It was used as the centre for Far East drug trafficking and that is still its role today after it has been returned to China. Most of the gold and money transactions on the Hong Kong financial markets are the payoffs and money laundering of the drug trade.

The Treaty of Nanking of 1842 gave Britain control over Hong Kong, plus about £15 million in silver. It was written by the Freemason and Colonial Minister, Edward Bulwer-Lytton (Comm 300), whose writings were to so inspire Hitler, the Nazis, and mystics like Madame Blavatsky. Bulwer-Lytton wrote of the Vril power (serpent power) in the blood of the 'underground supermen'. Bulwer-Lytton's son was the Viceroy of India at the height of the opium trade between India and China, a period 'camouflaged' by Rudyard Kipling's writings about the British Raj (British drug runners). In the book *The Opium Clippers*, Basil Lubbock names the owners of the British vessels engaged in the opium trade through the East India Company; Jardine Matheson (the Scottish Keswick family, many of whom are Satanists), Dent and Co; Pybus Bros; Russell and Co; Cama Bros; Duchess of Atholl; the Earl of Balcarras; King George IV (formerly the Prince Regent); the Marquis of Camden; and Lady Melville. It was Lady Melville's ancestor, George, who welcomed William of Orange to the throne and was made Lord Privy Seal as a reward. The Keswicks and Jardine Matheson have been members of the Committee of 300. Other Anglo-American families involved in the drug trade were the Sutherlands, Barings, and Lehmans, cousins of the Rothschilds. The Sutherlands, one of the biggest cotton and opium traders in the American south, were cousins of the Mathesons, and the Barings banking family founded the Peninsular and Orient Steam Navigation Company (the famous British ferry company P & O) to transport opium.

The British reptilian bloodline families worked with their other American relatives to expand the drug trade, as they still do today. The bloodline Russell family made its enormous wealth from the opium trade in the nineteenth century through the drug syndicate known as Russell and Company. Its business was to take opium from Turkey and transport it illegally to China. Their only rivals were the Perkins syndicate, based in Boston, which had intermarried with other families of the British genetic lines who had been involved in the slave trade. The Russells eventually bought out the Perkins and became the centre of the US opium racket in league with other reptilian families like Coolidge and Delano (Comm 300), both of which produced Presidents of the United States. The head of Russell and Co in Canton while all this drug racketeering was going on was Warren Delano Jr, the grandfather of President Franklin Delano Roosevelt who comes from an aristocratic French bloodline. In 1986, a history of the drug trade in America, printed in *US News And World Report*, said that: "Delano equated the opium trade with the liquor business – both profitable and both cornerstones of the family business."[7] How appropriate that Franklin Delano Roosevelt should be genetically related to George Bush who still maintains the tradition of running drugs on an enormous scale. Other Russell partners were John Cleve Green, who used some of his opium fortune to finance Princeton University; Abiel Abbott Low, who used his opium money to finance the construction of Columbia University; and Joseph Coolidge, who's son formed the drug running operation called the United Fruit Company. His grandson, Archibald Cary Coolidge, was a founding executive officer of the Council on Foreign Relations. The Russells with the Tafts formed the Skull and Bones Society and the black flag with the white skull and cross bones was the corporate flag flown on all Russell Trust Company ships. It was also a flag flown on ships in the Knights Templar fleet. Another American connection to the opium trade was the Freemason, John Jacob Astor, the founder of the Astor dynasty who became a stockholder in the British East India Company.[8] Philadelphia and Boston, the headquarters of the Northern Jurisdiction of the Scottish Rite of Freemasonry, were (and are) other centres for the drug trade. A descendant of Astor, Waldorf Astor of the Waldorf Astoria Hotel in New York, was a high degree Freemason who became chairman of the Royal Institute of International Affairs in London after the Second World War.[9] The RIIA is extensively involved in coordinating the global drug trade (see the book, *Dope Inc.*, in the bibliography).

After the second Opium War which ended in 1860, the British merchant banks and trading companies established the Hong Kong and Shanghai Corporation as the central bank of the Far East drug industry. According to all research I have read about the drug network, the Hong Kong and Shanghai Bank, with its global connections, continues to be a financial centre for the drug industry to this day.[10] The Hong Kong and Shanghai Bank now calls itself HSBC Holdings since China regained Hong Kong and HSBC owns one of the four British clearing banks, the Midland. This had a long advertising campaign calling itself the "listening bank" and the "bank that likes to say yes". I don't remember it mentioning the number of times its owners have said "yes" to laundering the profits of the drug industry which is destroying the lives of so many. The Nugan Hand Bank (based in Sydney, Australia) was another CIA/Mossad operation run by Francis Nugan and Michael Hand, a Green Beret and a colonel in the US Army assigned to the CIA. Hand was in frequent contact with George Bush after his election to Vice-President of the United States, according to CIA operative, Trenton Parker.[11] Look at some principle officers of Nugan Hand Bank; Admiral F. Yates, president, the chief of staff for strategic planning of US forces in Asia and the Pacific during the Vietnam War; General Edwin F. Black, president of the Hawaii branch, the commander of US troops in Thailand during the Vietnam conflict; George Farris, operative with the Washington and Hong Kong branches of Nugan Hand, and a military intelligence specialist; Bernie Houghton, the Saudi Arabian representative, a US Naval Intelligence undercover agent; Thomas Clines, of Nugan Hand in London, a director of training in the CIA's clandestine service who was involved in the Iran-Contra affair and operated with Michael Hand and Theodore Shackley during Vietnam; Dale Holmgreen, of the Taiwan office, flight service manager in Vietnam for Civil Air Transport, which later became the infamous CIA airline, Air America; Walter McDonald, head of the Annapolis, Maryland, branch, the former deputy director of CIA economic research; General Roy Mannor, the Philippines branch, the chief of staff for the US Pacific Command and the US government liaison with President Ferdinand Marcos; William Colby, Nugan Hand's lawyer, a former director of the CIA.[12] Just the kind of people you would expect to be running a bank, eh? This was another drug operation. A director of Nugan Hand, Donald Beazley, was also chairman of City National Bank of Miami, which handled funds for the Mossad-front, the Anti-Defamation League.[13]

An Australian Government investigation revealed that millions of dollars in Nugan Hand records were unaccounted for and that it was serving as a money laundering operation for drug traffickers. These profits were being used by the CIA to finance gun smuggling and illegal covert operations around the world. There was also evidence that the CIA was using the bank to pay for political campaigns against politicians in many countries, including Australia, to ensure the voters supported the CIA choice. Yes, this is still the 'free' world we are talking about. Banks with household names across the planet are vehicles for laundering drug money by passing it from account to account until its origins are lost in the web of transactions. The gold and diamond industry, dominated by the Rothschilds and the Oppenheimers, through companies like De Beers, are also used to wash drug money. The money buys gold and diamonds from those companies and they are then sold to produce 'clean' money. The network of interconnecting Anglo-American families in the Brotherhood web of manipulation, which has been responsible for the engineering of wars and for economic depression through the generations, is also behind the world illegal drugs market. Some of the most famous names, merchant banks, and companies in the world, are making the bulk of their fortunes directly or indirectly from the drug addiction of the young. They are the same families and organisations who were responsible for the slave trade from Africa and the 'coolie' trade out of China. The term 'being shanghaied' comes from the kidnapping of Chinese people for shipment to the United States to be used as servants. Alcohol prohibition was a means to create the massive network of organised crime in the United States. The structure thus produced was perfect, as intended, for drug trafficking once prohibition was over. The main groups campaigning for prohibition and an end to the 'evils of drink', groups like the Women's Christian Temperance Union and its Anti-Saloon League, were financed by the Rockefellers, Vanderbilts, and Warburgs, via the Rockefeller Foundation, the Russell Sage Foundation, and similar tax-exempt foundations. Prohibition was another con by the Brotherhood used for longer term motives. Incidentally, it also made a fortune for Joseph Kennedy, the father of JFK.

Professor Alfred McCoy's 1972 classic, *The Politics Of Heroin In South East Asia*, and his 1991 update, *The Politics Of Heroin – CIA Complicity In The Global Drug Trade*, tell of how CIA helicopters in Vietnam were carrying drugs from the fields to distribution points, when the American public thought they were there to fight Communism. He describes how a Pepsi Cola bottling plant was used for this trade and how the media suppressed this information. 58,000 Americans and goodness knows how many Vietnamese were killed in that conflict and nothing sums up more powerfully the lack of respect this mindset has for human life, than the way the CIA smuggled drugs into America in plastic bags hidden in the body cavities of dead soldiers being returned home from Vietnam for burial. CIA operative, Gunthar Russbacher, has told how some bodies were gutted and filled with drugs for shipment back to the States.[14] The bodies carried secret codes which allowed those carrying the drugs to be indentified on arrival at West Coast Air Bases, particularly the Travis Airforce Base in California. The drugs were then removed and made available to the young people of America.

Heroin is a derivative of the opium poppy which also produces morphine, a name inspired by the Greek god of dreams, Morpheus. It was at the Bayer laboratories in Germany in 1898 that heroin was created by adding ingredients to the morphine molecule. Bayer would later be part of the I. G. Farben pharmaceutical cartel at the heart of Hitler's war machine. Heroin is the most addictive of all opiate drugs, but it was marketed by Bayer as: "An heroic drug, without the addictive potential of morphine". The name heroin comes from 'heroic' and its creators were indeed heroes to the Brotherhood, given the potential it had to cause untold strife and misery. Today the Far East heroin trade is still organised by the Freemasons through their interconnected agents, the Triads. These are the Mafia of the Far East and increasingly the Western World also, as in Vancouver, Canada. Just to give you another example of the way the game is played. The Chinese ruler before the Communist Revolution was Chiang Kai Shek, a member of an earlier form of the Triads. The 'Communist' leader who toppled him from power was Mao Tse Tung, a Grand Orient Freemason![15] He allowed the British lease of Hong Kong to continue (of course, he did, he was a Brotherhood placeman) and the drug-business-as-usual continued. By 1983, the Communist Chinese had nine million acres of poppy plantations and this is the foundation of the Chinese economy, just as it is for the Western economy.[16] Without the drug trade, the world economy would collapse, so dependent has it become on the income and investments produced by the destruction of human life. The Triads organise the production of heroin in the so-called Golden Triangle. They are paid by the British Brotherhood bankers of Hong Kong in gold bullion and some of this is paid by the Triads to buy raw opium from the farmers. So the annual cycle goes on expanding. The cocaine trade out of South America is run by the same people through their agencies like the CIA. Cocaine comes from the coca leaf and, until 1903, it was used in the drink, Coca Cola, hence its name. I detail the CIA's role in the cocaine networks and how they set up the Colombian drug cartels in ...*And The Truth Shall Set You Free*. Also in that book you will find the background to the extensive involvement of George Bush and Bill Clinton in these operations.

The drug trade is not only about making vast amounts of money, although that is important to fund the Agenda into place, it is also designed to break down societies and stop young people manifesting their true worth and potential. When people are hooked on drugs they are not going to be a problem to the Brotherhood's grand design. Violence and crime always follows the drug trade as drug dealers battle for supremacy and addicts mug and steal to finance their habit. This offers the Brotherhood a wonderful opportunity to offer the 'solution' to this 'problem' – more power to the police and further erosion of basic freedoms. I saw an opinion poll in the *Los Angeles Times* a few years ago in which something like 84% of those questioned said they would give up basic freedoms if they thought it would win the war on drugs. Problem-reaction-solution. What those people urgently need to know is that the drugs are being *distributed* by those fronting the drug war, who are offering the 'solutions' at the same time. Much of the 'anti-drug' network is deeply corrupt and used as a vehicle for distributing drugs without detection. George Bush has fronted more wars on drugs than any other American politician and yet he is one of North America's premier drug barons. A reporter on the *San Jose Mercury News* exposed the CIA's involvement in putting crack cocaine into the black community of Los Angeles. This was during the period Bush was in the White House and both the journalist and the paper were hit by a tidal wave of ridicule and abuse from the establishment papers like the *Washington Post* and the *Los Angeles Times* as the Brotherhood tried to crush the story. Even the running of drugs comes down to bloodlines, by the way. A friend has a contact who was offered the job of being a drug courier by a US government agency. He refused, but asked why they had approached him. "We know what your bloodline is," came the reply. One of the codes, he found out, was to have your hand cut across the palm. If you are ever caught, you show the authorities your hand and they let you go.

The anti-drug agencies are controlled by the drug cartels and when you hear of 'big drug busts', it is usually the Brotherhood eliminating the competition and giving the impression of action. The drug pushers are difficult to find? Then how come a youngster straight off the bus in a new city can find them in an hour? If you are taking hard drugs, or thinking of doing so, remember this: You are not being a 'rebel' or 'dropping out', you are committing mental, emotional, spiritual and eventually physical, suicide, and you are doing exactly what the people who control this world want you to do. The choice is yours, but understand the game before you start. There is only one winner when you get into drugs. And it's never you.

■ **SOURCES**

1   *Scarlet And The Beast*, p 15.

2   Ibid.

3   Ibid.

4   Ibid, p 11.

5   Ibid, p 13.

6   Ibid, p 31.

7   *US News And World Report*, August 4th 1986.

8   *Scarlet And The Beast*, p 23.

9   Ibid.

10   "State Organised Crime, The Presidential Address" by William J. Schambliss, to the American Society of Criminology, 1988.

11   Rodney Stitch, *Defrauding America* (Diablo Western Press, Alamo, California. 1994), p 355.

12   Ibid, p 355.

13   Michael Collins Piper, *Final Judgement, The Missing Link In The JFK Assassination* (The Wolfe Press, Washington DC, 1995), p 92.

14   *Defrauding America*, p 295.

15   *Scarlet And The Beast*, pp 33 and 35.

16   Ibid, p 36.

CHAPTER FIFTEEN

Satan's children

The black magic rituals we know as Satanism are the modern expression of the rituals and human sacrifice in ancient Babylon and the Brotherhood infiltrated societies of the Sumerian, Phoenician, Hittite, Egyptian, Canaanite and Akkadian peoples, among many others across the world. It has been a seamless procession through history of the same rituals to the same deities and this remains of fundamental importance to the initiates of the Brotherhood today.

My use of the term Satanism has nothing to do with the Christian version of Satan. I use it only to describe a system of ritual sacrifice and torture which, staggering as it may seem to most people, is commonplace all over the world today. Satanism is just another name for the worship of a highly destructive, negative force which has been given endless names over the centuries: Nimrod, Baal, Moloch or Molech, Set, the Devil, Lucifer, there is no end to them. Satanism perverts everything positive in the same way that the Nazis took a positive symbol, the swastika, and turned it around to symbolise the negative. This is why the Satanists invert the pentagram and why they use black to symbolise the darkness, hence their Black Mass. But they also reverse the symbolism of white and that is a powerfully negative colour to them. The Satanic networks, under the names of their various deities, were created by the Babylonian Brotherhood to serve their needs. We have seen that the accounts of the Watchers and their offspring, the Nefilim, include references to their blood drinking activities. The Brotherhood know that blood contains the life-force energy. Drinking menstrual blood has always been a feature of the reptilian bloodlines because they need blood to live in this dimension. It was known as the Star Fire, the female lunar essence. The female menstrual cycle is governed by the cycles of the Moon and the blood contains that energy. It's ingredients are supposed to ensure a long life. In India it was called soma and in Greece it was ambrosia, some researchers suggest. This was said to be the nectar of the gods and it was – the reptilian gods who are genetic blood drinkers. The 'holy grail' chalice or cup is also symbolic of the womb and drinking menstrual blood, as well as being a symbol of the reptilian 'royal' bloodline itself. Menstrual blood was provided for the Elite of the reptilian 'royal' line by virgin priestesses and this is the origin of the term 'Scarlet Woman' or, to the Greeks, 'Sacred Woman'. The Greek word for this, Hierodulai, was eventually translated into English as harlot and into German as 'hores', the origin of whore. The word ritual derives from this practice (ritu = redness) and so do the words rite and red. Menstrual blood is one reason why the colour red is so important to Satanists and it is another reason for the constant use of the colour gold by the 'royal' bloodlines. Gold is called the metal of the gods, but to the Anunnaki of the Sumerian Tablets, menstrual blood was the 'gold of the gods'.

The reptilians and their crossbreeds drink blood because they are drinking the person's life-force and because they need it to exist in this dimension. They will often shape-shift into reptilians when drinking human blood and eating human flesh, I am told by those who have seen this happen. Blood drinking is in their genes and an Elite high priestess or 'Mother Goddess' in the hierarchy, who performed rituals for the Brotherhood at the highest level, told me that without human blood the reptilians cannot hold human form in this dimension. Her name is Arizona Wilder, formerly Jennifer Ann Greene. Interestingly, she said that the reptilians had been pursuing the Aryan peoples around the universe, because the blood of the white race was particularly important to them for some reason and the blond-haired, blue-eyed genetic stream was the one they wanted more than any other. They had followed the white race to Mars, she said, and then came to Earth with them. It is far from impossible that the reptilian arrival on this planet in numbers was far more recent than even many researchers imagine. An interbreeding programme only a few thousand years ago between the reptilian Anunnaki and white Martian bloodlines already interbred with the reptilians on Mars, would have produced a very high reptilian genetic content. This is vital for the reasons I have explained earlier. They appear to need a particular ratio of reptilian genes before they can shape-shift in the way that they do. But when the interbreeding happened is far less important than the fact that it did happen.

Satanism is based on the manipulation of energy and consciousness. These deeply sick rituals create an energy field, a vibrational frequency, which connects the consciousness of the participants to the reptilians and other consciousness of the lower fourth dimension. This is the dimensional field, also known as the lower astral to many people, which resonates to the frequency of low vibrational emotions like fear, guilt, hate and so on. When a ritual focuses these emotions, as Satanism does, a powerful connection is made with the lower fourth dimension, the reptilians. These are some of the 'demons' which these rituals have been designed to summon since this whole sad story began thousands of years ago. This is when so much possession takes place and the reptilians take over the initiate's physical body. The leading Satanists are full-blood reptilians cloaked in a human form. These rituals invariably take place on vortex points and so the terror, horror, and hatred, created by them enters the global energy grid and affects the Earth's magnetic field. Thought forms of that scale of malevolence hold down the vibrational frequency and affect human thought and emotion. Go to a place where Satanic rituals take place and feel the malevolence and fear in the atmosphere. What we call 'atmosphere' is the vibrational field and how it has been affected by human thought forms. Thus we talk about a happy, light or loving atmosphere, or a dark or foreboding one. The closer the Earth's field is vibrationally to the lower fourth dimension, the more power the reptilians have over this world and its inhabitants. Satanism is not just a sickness and a perversion, although it is that also, its main reason for existence, from the Brotherhood's point of view, is to control the Earth's magnetic field; to worship and connect with their reptile masters; to drink the life-force of their sacrificed victims; and to provide energy for the reptilians who appear to feed off human emotion, especially fear. These sacrifices are, literally, sacrifices to the 'gods', the reptilians, and they have been happening for thousands of years. The mass sacrifice of people by the Aztecs in Central America, and so many others, were to provide food for the physical reptilians and crossbreeds who eat the bodies and drink the blood, and energy nourishment for the non-physical reptilians of the lower fourth dimension. Phil Schneider, a builder of US underground bases, told the writer and researcher, Alex Christopher, that when children reached the point where they could not work anymore in the slave conditions underground, they were consumed by the reptilians. They prefer young children because they are not contaminated like adults. Hard to accept isn't it? I'm sure your mind is screaming 'nonsense' at you because who wants to face a truth like this? But unless we do, how is it ever going to be stopped?

Satanic rituals generally take place at night because that is when the magnetic field is most stable. During the day the electrically charged particles of the solar wind cause turbulence in the field and make interdimensional connection more difficult. It is most stable during total eclipses and this is when native peoples held their most important ceremonies to contact and manifest other-dimensional entities. The tribal shamans know this. Satanic rituals and human sacrifice, especially of children, are performed on a vast scale and involve some of the most famous politicians, business people, media owners and entertainers on the planet. Of course they do. It would be amazing if they did not, given the background. These rituals and human sacrifice have always been the foundation of the Brotherhood 'religion' since ancient times. And the Brotherhood manipulates its Satanic initiates and 'gofers' into the positions of political, economic, business, military, medical and media power, and into influential positions in the world of entertainment. Therefore the ratio of Satanists and child sacrificers at the top of these professions and institutions is staggeringly high compared with the general population. Apparently, according to former Satanists I have met and read about, some world politicians are addicted to blood taken from a victim at the moment of sacrifice because of the adrenaline which is produced at that time. I am told this addiction is quite common among Satanists, and researchers into the reptilian question suggest that this is the substance the reptiles also want. It all fits.

The theme of human and animal sacrifice can be easily charted from the ancient world to the present day. Ironically, but understandably in the context of this book, much of it was designed to preserve life rather than destroy it. The belief was that one sacrifice to appease 'the gods' would protect the lives of many more. This is another origin of the concept of the scapegoat, the one killed for the 'sins' of others. This has, of course, manifested as many mythical religious 'heroes' who "died so our sins could be forgiven". The sacrifice of the king or ruler to appease the gods is another ancient tradition. In the so-called cradle of civilisation, North Africa and the Near East, where the Anunnaki and the Watchers were documented, there were human sacrifices, particularly of children. Similar rituals were prevalent in China, Rome, Africa, Asia, Greece, South America and, most famously, in Mexico where the Aztecs sacrificed en masse to the 'gods'. This region is where the former President of Mexico, Miguel De La Madrid, told the mind controlled slave of the CIA, Cathy O'Brien, that the reptile extraterrestrials came down and created physical bodies to occupy, just as they did most profusely among the Aryan people. The reptilians and human sacrifice go together. The Scandinavians buried children alive in an effort to stop plagues and to appease the great god of the North, the Scandinavian Odin or the German Wodan or Woden. The gods of the mystery schools were invariably connected to human sacrifice and it was these very schools which have, via the now global Brotherhood and Satanism networks, carried the knowledge and the rituals into the present day. The Incas of Peru sacrificed children and human sacrifice was practised from the earliest days in Europe. One Druid ritual was to bury a child under the foundations of a new building or to sprinkle the child's blood on the site. The same ritual can be found in many parts of the world. In the stories of St Columba (dove, Semiramis), this 'Christian' hero is said to have told his monks that it was fitting for one of them to be buried in the foundations of a new monastery on the Scottish island of Iona (the Sun) to 'hallow' the ground. A Saint Oran volunteered and as a result, it was believed, he went straight to heaven.[1] Roman accounts by the historian, Tacitus, reveal how the Druids deemed it a duty to cover their altars with the blood of their captives and how they consulted the gods via human entrails. The same stories can be found in Ireland and Scotland. Irish myth says that Ireland was first peopled by a greedy group of gods called the Formorians who demanded two thirds of the children born each year. The Phoenicians and their kinsmen, the Carthaginians, sacrificed humans on a large scale and so did the Canaanites. When Carthage was struggling in the war against Rome, 200 noble families sacrificed their sons to Baal (the Phoenician Sun god, Bel or Bil).[2]

Another theme is the sacrifice of the first born child, most often the first born son. In some aboriginal tribes in Australia, the mother would kill and eat the first born child to ensure she would be able to have more.[3] The sacrifice of the first born of animals and humans was quite common and is mentioned in the Old Testament. The Book of Kings tells how Mesha, the King of Moab, was so distraught by his defeat at the hands of the Israelites that he sacrificed his eldest son and heir. Remember in Genesis how 'God' (the gods) insisted that Abraham sacrificed his first born son to them to test his faith and obedience. The same ritual continues today among the Satanists, the bloodline families of the Brotherhood, and their organised crime offshoots like the Mafia. Sacrificing the first born son is used by these strange people as a way of testing a person's commitment to the cause.Yahweh-Jehovah makes it plain in the Book of Numbers that "...all the first born of Israel are mine, both man and beast," and in Exodus, Yahweh demands that "The first of all thy sons shalt thou give unto me." The Bible says that Abraham came from the Sumer city of Ur and excavations in 1927 by Sir Leonard Woolley in the Royal Cemetery there revealed widespread evidence of human sacrifice in graves dating from about 2,800 BC. The Scythians, the people who transported many of the Aryan bloodlines and rituals into Europe, did the same. Evidence of human sacrifice, especially children, can be found among all the main locations and peoples who are mentioned in this book, including the palace of Knossos on Crete.[4] The cult of the skull as a focus of ritual has recurred again and again in this story with the Templars, the Rennes-le-Chateau mystery, and the Skull and Bones Society in the United States. By examining the bodies of Peking Man, dating from perhaps a million years ago, and Neanderthal man, dating from about 200,000 years ago, evidence of such rituals can be found even at these early times. The cult of the head, which included eating the brain of the victim, became more elaborate in Jericho some eight thousand years ago and evidence of the same rituals have been found in the Shinto religion in Japan and in ancient China. Anath, the legendary sister of Baal, was portrayed festooned with severed heads along with human hands hanging from her girdle, the same as the mother goddesses of Mexico and India.[5]

Written texts of ancient Egypt reveal many kinds of sacrifice and torture, which later became widespread.[6] The Egyptians would sacrifice red-headed men on the tomb of Osiris because red was the colour associated with Set, the Egyptian version of Satan. Some rituals recalled by people today who have suffered indescribably in these horrors, mirror those detailed in the *Egyptian Book Of The Dead* and include keeping hearts in a jar.[7] The hearts were placed on the scales in Egypt to be weighed for judgement by the goddess, Maat. This is the real meaning of the woman with the sun crown holding the Scales of Justice which you see on so many court buildings. In the ancient world, the Brahmin fakirs in India and other mystery schools knew of drugs, torture rituals and 'magic' which created hallucinations. Silly fakirs. Hypnosis was widely used in the temples. The demon worshippers of Bel/Baal/Nimrod in Canaan, Babylon and Phoenicia engaged in human sacrifice, cannibalism, and child murder in the name of Moloch or Molech, an aspect of Nimrod/Baal, as part of their religious rituals.[8] Baal (lord or ruler), the supreme god of the Canaanites and Phoenicians, was said to be the giver of life and Moloch was the destroyer of life. Both demanded appeasement by sacrifice. Baal or Moloch became identified with the Roman god Saturn.

In honour of Baal, the Sun god and god of fire, the Carthaginians, following the rituals of the Phoenicians and Canaanites, rolled children into a fiery pit made in the shape of the image of Baal/Moloch. At a site near modern Tunis six thousand urns were found containing the charred remains of infants. Remember, these rituals and 'gods' are the same as those performed and worshipped by the Satanists and the Brotherhood today. This is why the children of Waco were allowed to burn to death in an inferno caused entirely by the Satanist controlled FBI and the ATF, the Bureau of Alcohol, Tobacco and Firearms, on April 19th 1993. These were the same deeply sick people who blew up the James P. Murrah building in Oklahoma on April 19th 1995, in which so many children died. April 19th is a Satanic ritual day relating to fire – the fire god, Baal or Moloch. And what does Moloch demand? The sacrifice of children. Waco and Oklahoma were child sacrifices to Baal/Moloch according to exactly the same belief system as those performed by the ancients. In the same way, a war to these people is a mass blood ritual in which unimaginable numbers are killed and maimed, and the planet is engulfed by negative emotional energy. It is this energy on which many of the lower fourth dimensional reptilians either feed or use to manifest in this dimension. If you want undeniable proof that the Branch Davidians and their children were sacrificed at Waco, I strongly recommend you watch the video: *Waco: The Rules Of Engagement.*⁹ You will never believe an official statement again. The ritual names for the 'demons' are still the same today as those used in the ancient world and by later groups like the Templars. Confirmation of this comes from a stream of accounts by modern victims of Satanism. A friend of mine, the British therapist, Vera Diamond, has been working for nearly 20 years with people who have been subjected to Satanic and mind control abuse. She says:

> "Children say the word Satan is used more frequently than any other, but other demons include Baphomet and Behemoth. Molech (Moloch) seems to be one particularly associated with eating babies, and one called Choronzon. These do seem to be particularly involved with sacrificing babies." ¹⁰

Choronzon relates to Chronos, the Greek version of Nimrod. According to Greek legend, Chronos swallowed his children as fast as they were born because he feared they would overthrow him. Chronos was the most powerful of the Titans, the Greek name for the giants who resulted from the interbreeding of the reptilians with the human, 'daughters of men'. Greek myth symbolically referred to them as children of the union between heaven (extraterrestrials) and Earth (humans). Chronos was the father of Zeus who survived because his mother hid him from her child-killing husband. Zeus later waged a victorious war against his father and other Titans and then ruled as the King of Gods over a dynasty awash with child sacrifice. As you connect the different peoples across the generations, so you find the same themes of human sacrifice. The Cannanite-Hebrews were seriously into the sacrifice of humans and animals, much as their spin doctors have tried to deny it over the years. The Satanists among the 'Jewish' hierarchy today still perform the same rituals while the mass of the Jewish people worldwide have no idea that this is so. Stories throughout the centuries to the present day of the sacrifice of children by Jewish fanatics at the time of the Passover can be seen to have an historical basis when you realise the true meaning of the Passover. It had nothing to do with 'God' passing over the homes of Israelite children and killing only the first born Egyptians. This is more symbolism that only an initiate or a determined researcher would understand. Records from the 8th and 7th centuries BC, show that the Israelites burned their sons on sacrificial fires in the Valley of Gehinnon outside Jerusalem.¹¹ The infants were said to have been "passed over" or "passed through" the fire in sacrifice to Moloch-Baal. In the Book of Leviticus we find the line: "Thou shalt not let any of thy seed pass through the fire to Moloch". The prophet Jeremiah talks of the people: "burning their sons in the fire as burnt offerings unto Baal" and also in the Book of Jeremiah we are told that: "They have built the high places of Tophet, which is in the Valley of Hinnon, to burn their sons and daughters in the fire…" John Milton also wrote of Moloch in his *Paradise Lost*:

"First Moloch, horrid king, besmirched with blood,
Of human sacrifice, and parent's tears,
Though, for the noise of drums and timbrels loud,
Their children's cries unheard, that passed through fire,
To his grim idol."

The Old Testament abounds with stories of animal and human sacrifice. The same symbolism can be seen in a stream of ancient texts about the sacrifice of the first born or young children. The Jesus story includes this theme also, of course. At it's most extreme, the Jewish dogma is deeply sacrificial. Their temples were slaughterhouses with a constant supply of animals taken there for ritual murder and sacrifice. Look at the Jewish form of killing animals to this today. Meat is only considered 'kosher' if the animal has its throat cut and dies by being bled dry. The same with the 'halal' meat of the Muslims. Through the Brotherhood bloodlines the ancient rituals have been strictly maintained and the ruling Elite today are sacrificing children and drinking blood the same as they did in the ancient world. The Hindu faith and the information for its sacred books, the Vedas, were taken to the Indian subcontinent by the Aryans from the Caucasus Mountains, one of the centres for extraterrestrials/inner terrestrials and their offspring. It is therefore predictable that the Vedas contain the same instructions for sacrifice to the gods. The Vedas, written about 1,400 BC, list the names of the gods and the victim most suitable for each one. In the modern world, annual victims have been offered to the Mother Goddess Kali, the wife of the god, Shiva, and she was always believed to live off human flesh. A male child was offered every Friday evening at the temple of Shiva at Tanjor until the practice was stopped (officially) in the mid-nineteeth century. The Thugs, one of the ancient secret societies in the Brotherhood network, murdered their victims according to elaborate rituals dedicated to Kali, who is depicted wearing a garland of skulls.

Children or so-called 'young virgins' are used in these sacrificial rituals because the Satanists and their reptilian masters want to access the pure pre-pubescent energy for their own purposes. I have been told by Satanists, many of their victims, and by therapists working with victims, the same stories of 'regeneration rituals'. The ageing Satanist, sometimes a high ranking member of the Brotherhood, stands in the centre of a circle of babies or young children. As they are sacrificed the ritual allows the Satanist to absorb their life-essense, their life-force, and regenerate his or her body. The world's most famous Satanist, Aleister Crowley, who had connections to both Winston Churchill and the Nazis, advocated human sacrifice and admitted to sacrificing children. In his 1929 book, *Magick In Theory And Practice*, he explains the reasons for ritual death and why small boys are the best victims:

"It was the theory of the ancient magicians that any living being is a storehouse of energy varying in quantity according to the size and health of the animal, and in quality according to its mental and moral character. At the death of this animal this energy is liberated suddenly. For the highest spiritual working one must accordingly choose that victim which contains the greatest and purest force. A male child of perfect innocence and high intelligence is the most satisfactory and suitable victim."[12]

Crowley adds in a footnote that according to the records of the Satanist, Frater Perurabo, he performed just such a sacrifice 150 times every year between 1912 and 1928. Think about that. It means that this one man ritually sacrificed almost 2,500 young boys in that period alone. Do you still wonder what happens to many of the millions, yes millions, of children who go missing every year all over the world never to be heard of again? And that's without all of those bred for sacrifice that the public knows nothing about. We can begin to see that the estimates of ritual sacrifices every year are no exaggeration. Satanism at its core is about the manipulation and theft of another person's energy and consciousness. In olden times they called it "soul snatching". It may appear to be merely a sickening perversion, but those who truly understand the background to the rituals know that what really matters is the effect of the rituals, not so much the rituals themselves. They are the means to an end – stealing or manipulating energy. Sex is so common in Satanic ritual because at the moment of orgasm, the body explodes with energy which the Satanists and the reptiles can capture and absorb. Sexual activity inspired by love resonates to a much higher vibration and therefore cannot be accessed by the reptilians. Sex during a Satanic ritual or sacrifice, however, explodes the orgasmic energy at a very low frequency because of the intent involved and so the energy of Satanic sex resonates to the reptilian frequency. The astrological energies constantly generated by the movement of the planets and the cycles of the Sun and Moon are also employed to add to the power of the rituals. So there are particular Satanic days for their most important ceremonies. On these days unimaginable numbers of people, mostly children, are sacrificed. Some of the main dates are: Feb 1/2, Candlemas; March 21/22, spring equinox; April 30th/May 1st, Walpurgis Night/Beltane; June 21/22, summer solstice; July 31/August 1, Lammas – Great Sabbat festival; September 21/22, autumn equinox; October 31st/November 1st, Samhain/Halloween; December 21/22, winter solstice or Yule.

Let me emphasise again here that these dates and festivals are not Satanic in themselves. They are times in the annual planetary cycle when very powerful energies of various kinds are manifesting on the Earth and the rituals and ceremonies of both a positive and negative nature are performed on these dates. The cycle produces the energy and the Satanists simply harness that energy for their own purposes, just as the positive rituals do, like those performed by most modern Druids. Other dates for widespread Satanic ritual include every full Moon because the reflected energy of the Sun is at its most powerful on those occasions. Note also the significance to Satanists of May 1st, the day the Bavarian Illuminati was formed in 1776 and the day of celebration in the Brotherhood-created Communist and Socialist calendar.

The Key of Solomon is a book of occult magic which legend claims was written by 'King Solomon' himself. It includes the pentagram in its instructions of how to invoke demons and make sacrifices to demons. Such ancient works provide the foundations for the same rituals in each generation. The inner core of the Knights Templar was involved in black magic ritual and the Templars were accused of what today we call Satanism and of rejecting Christianity by denying Christ and spitting on the cross. They were said to worship a demon power called Baphomet, a black magic symbol, also known as the Goat of Mendes. Capricorn (the goat, also symbolised by the unicorn) is the sign of the initiate and it represents political power, while Leo (the Sun, the lion) represents royal power. Hence the lion is the King of the Jungle and is the main symbol on the flag of the British royal family. The planet Saturn rules Capricorn while the Sun rules Leo and Satanists and black magicians are very much focused on the Sun and Saturn in their rituals. The Saturn vibration has a much bigger impact on the Earth than is recognised. In astrology it is the planet of law and authority. Capricorn, the sign of authority, is also, according to astrologers, the astrological sign of England, that centre of global control. The name, Baphomet, is reckoned to derive from Greek words meaning baptism of wisdom or knowledge (initiation) and Dr Hugh Schonfield, one of the experts on the Dead Sea Scrolls, says that using the code of the Essenes, the word Baphomet can be translated to 'Sophia', the goddess of the Gnostics, and the Greek word for wisdom.[13] Sophia is another name for the female energy. Schonfield is sure there is a link between the Templars and the Essenes and so am I. He has demonstrated that the Templars used the same code, the Atbash Cipher, employed in some of the Dead Sea Scrolls.[14] Other accusations against the Templars were of killing children and teaching women how to abort.[15] It is true that most of these confessions were made under extreme torture by the Roman Church Satanists, the Inquisition. But not all of these reports were gleaned in this way and the themes are so strong, and the story so consistent, that it would be ridiculous just to dismiss them all. And one thing is quite provable. These very ceremonies involving the ritual murder of children, and the use of women called breeders to produce babies and aborted foetuses for sacrifice to a demon 'god', are most certainly performed today and this Satanic structure of abuse and ritual murder is controlled by the very secret society network the Templars helped to expand. The testimony of one Templar, Squin de Flexian, said they all had to swear never to leave the Order and to further its interests by any means, right or wrong. No crime committed for the honour or benefit of the Order was considered to be sinful. He also made allegations about sacrificing babies and aborting foetuses.[16]

It is the same with the inner circles of the Freemasons. Credo Mutwa, the Zulu shaman, told me that compared with the Freemason rituals he had seen in the United States and the United Kingdom, the voodoo and black magic of Africa was put in the shade. The secret password of Freemasonry is Tubal Cain, a descendant of the biblical Cain, who was an Anunnaki crossbreed. Tubal Cain's sister, Naamah,[17] is said to have been the one who brought human sacrifice and cannibalism into the world.[18] Tubal Cain is known as the father of witchcraft and sorcery and thus his name is a Freemasonic password.[19] The 'G' on the symbol of Freemasonry stands for Gnosticism (knowledge, knowing) and for generation, the fertility rites of the sex cults of ancient Baal and Ashtoreth.[20] No doubt it is also a symbol connected to generation and genetics, as in the reptilian bloodlines. You see the 'G' in the logo of the Gannett chain which has been buying up newspapers and television stations across the United States and publishes the national daily, *USA Today*.[21] The de Medici bloodline of the Black Nobility in Venice, who funded Christopher Columbus, included Catherine de Medici, the Queen of France, who was reported to have commissioned human sacrifice in a Black Mass in the 16th century. A young boy was sacrificed and the blood used in a communion designed to save her dying son, Philip.[22] Medici wore around her neck a talisman with the name of the Satanic demon, Asmodei.[23] Benjamin Franklin, a so-called pillar of the Christian Church and Founding Father of the United States, was a member of the Satanic Hellfire Club and the bodies of six children and four adults have been found under his former home in London dated to the time he lived there. Adolf Hitler and the Nazis were Satanists and so were their 'opponents' like Winston Churchill and Franklin Delano Roosevelt. The Rothschilds, formerly the infamous German occult family, the Bauers, apparently use the Canaanite Satanic rituals[24] while some of the bloodline families with long connections to the Celtic lands, like the St Clair-Sinclairs, prefer the Druid system.[25] It was the Satanic deity, Ashtoreth, which inspired the name, Astor, one of the bloodline families which has been heavily involved in Satanism.[26] The Astors have close connections to the British royal family and they were at the heart of the Profumo scandal in 1963 when the British Defence Minister, John Profumo, was forced to resign after lying to the House of Commons about his involvement with Christine Keeler, a call girl who was also having a sexual relationship with a Russian KGB agent. The Profumo-Keeler liaison was arranged by Stephen Ward, a sado-masochist and black magician, who lived in a house on the Astor estate at Clivedon in Berkshire. There was much more to this than was allowed to come out and if it ever does it will once again shine a light on some very dark practices and connect with the highest echelons of British society, including the Windsors. Prince Philip knew Stephen Ward and Lord Mountbatten was a guest at the infamous 'swimming party' at Cliveden which played a major role in Profumo's downfall.

What is called Satanism is the ruling hierarchy of the Brotherhood pyramid under the command of the reptilians. Like all the other parts of the network, it is strictly compartmentalised. The highest levels of the Satanic network lock into the highest levels of the Brotherhood, but the lower degrees are not allowed to know the true nature of the organisations they are involved in. Some of the levels of Satanism are known as the Sisters of Light, the Five Star Generals, Master Counsellors, Keeper of the Books, Keeper of the Seals, and there is one position called an Asmodeus.[27] One of the global centres of Satanism is the Castle of Darkness, the Chateau des Amerois or Castle of Kings, in Belgium, near the appropriately named village of Muno Bel. The castle is close to the French border and some 20 kilometres from Luxemburg. It is protected from view by thick forests and guards keep out the curious. In the grounds is a cathedral with a dome containing 1,000 lights.[28] When President George Bush talked of 1,000 points of light, he was speaking in code about this place of initiation for the highest initiates of the Satanic pyramid. In this Satanic cathedral is the throne of the high priestess of the upper hierarchy, a position known as the Queen Mother.[29] Every day, apparently, a child is sacrificed in the basement.[30]

Ceremonies are performed here to the Satanic 'goddess' known as Lilith, a demon in the Hebrew Cabala. In ancient Sumer the reptilian bloodline, as passed on through the female, was symbolised as a lily and the main reptilian gene carriers were given names like Lilith, Lili, Lilutu and Lillette. Elizabeth (El-lizard-birth) is a derivative of this. Another demon used by some 'Mothers' is called Bilair, Bilar, and Bilid, cabalistic names for the force others call Satan, etc.[31] It is from these lands in Belgium and northern France that the bloodline families came, including the Bruces, to take over Scotland all those centuries ago. Belgium, this little country between France and the Netherlands, is also the home of the European Union, NATO, and, I am told, a massive computer centre where databases on all the people of the world are being compiled. It is known apparently as 'the Beast' and there are a number of these around the world. An Elite mind control operation called the Janus Group is also based in the NATO headquarters. Nimrod was Eannus, the god with two faces, who was later known to the Romans as Janus. The reason that Belgium is a headquarters for Satanism and so many Brotherhood institutions is very simple. The Brotherhood created Belgium for just this reason in 1831 and they imposed upon it a reptilian 'royal' line, the House of Saxe-Coburg-Gotha, the bloodline of the British royal family and, through its branch in Prussia, the supporters of Adam Weishaupt, the founder of the Bavarian Illuminati.

The paedophile murder ring which came to light in Belgium in 1996 is but one part of the Satanic network operating from and in that country. It was organised by Marc Dutroux, who is connected to the Satanic Order of Abrasax, based in the village of Forchies-la-Marche near Charleroi in southern Belgium, not far from the Castle of Darkness. Abrasax is Abraxas, a fat-bellied demon from whom, it is likely, the magicians term, abracadabra, originated. Dutroux buried alive an accomplice, Bernard Weinstein, and among Weinstein's effects was a letter from the Abrasax group signed by someone describing himself as the Egyptian god, Anubis. It ordered him to provide 'presents' for the High Priestess of the Order and apparently gave specific details of the age and sex the victims must be. The British *Sunday Times* reported the accounts of witnesses describing Black Masses in which children were killed in front of audiences which included prominent members of Belgian society.[32] A Belgian newspaper reported that a former commissioner of the European Union was among a group of judges, senior politicians, lawyers, and policemen, who attended orgies at a Belgian chateau organised by Michel Nihoul, one of the accomplices of Marc Dutroux, the alleged leader of the paedophile ring. One investigator said it was "Like going back to the Middle Ages".[33] In fact there has not been an old, middle, and modern age with regard to these rituals. It is a seamless flow over thousands of years under the control of the same bloodlines. Human skulls were found at the sacrificial sites identified by witnesses, particularly at the sect's headquarters. The Satanic group behind the Belgian murders is said to interconnect with similar rings in Holland, Germany, and America.[34] In truth, it will be part of the global network which operates in all countries. Satanism is run like a transnational corporation.

Black magic rituals are going on all over the world and I have spoken with victims in country after country. In England I met a brave woman, then aged 40. The story she told me of her experiences mirrored those of so many others. She was born in Darlington in the 1950s, and soon after she was sold by her Satanic father to two other Satanists. She knew them only as Thomas and Helena. She was brought up in the most horrific circumstances at a children's home in Hull which was run by two child abusers. At night a torchlight was shone into their bedrooms and when it was held on a child for a minute or so, they knew it was their turn to go downstairs and be sexually abused. During holidays back in Darlington, from the age of just seven and eight, she met her father who linked her with the two Satanists, Thomas and Helena. She would be given drugs via orange juice and ice cream and be taken at night in a van to country churches in the Darlington area. The drugs were designed to make her easier to mind control and to prevent her from remembering what she saw. I will explain more about this in the next chapter. However, as is often the case when people enter their 30s and 40s, the victims can begin to have flashbacks of their ordeals. They experience them again like watching a movie screen. It is for this reason that so many are murdered before they reach that age, often for 'snuff' videos, which show in graphic detail a person being murdered. Others are subjected to the snatch back when they are abducted to undergo 'booster' mind-programming to keep the memories secret. Increasing numbers of people who survived their horrendous young lives, are now beginning to remember and they are telling the same basic tale. If you are one of them, please contact me if you have anything to add to what I outline here. An address is at the back of the book. Within days of speaking to me, my informant says she was grabbed off the street and bungled into a van by six Satanists. A syringe was held to her throat and she was warned to stop talking to "That dangerous prat, Icke" and to stop naming names. They threatened her life and those of her children if she continued. She was also told that if she didn't keep quiet, the family dog would be taken and "Posted back to you in pieces". Nice people.

In the ordeals at the country churches which she now remembers, my English informant and other children would be used in Satanic rituals involving sex, torture, and murder. The windows of the church were covered over with black drapes and the inside was laid out according to Satanic law with different colours used for different ceremonies depending on the time of year. Sometimes they would use the churches in secret, but don't underestimate how many people in the Christian clergy are also members of the Satanic network. The Satanists, she remembers, were dressed in robes and a number wore masks, including the face of a goat or Baphomet, the deity the Templars were accused of worshipping. In the UK, as in America, some of the best known names in the country are involved. She remembers vividly (God, the thought of it), being laid on her back on the floor of a church as a screaming boy, no more than six, was being held by the hair above her while a man, who she would later identify as a top politician in Northern Ireland, had anal sex with him. When it was over, a knife was produced to cut the boy's throat and the blood poured over her. "I remember this man's eyes," she told me. "The coldness of his eyes I will never forget." He prefers boys to girls, she said.

On more than one occasion, she says, she was brutally raped by a man who has been a major name in United Kingdom politics for decades. This man, she says, used to hold her naked body to him by using hooks inserted into her flesh at the hip. She was just a little girl when this was happening. She told me that this man was Edward Heath and his name comes up again and again in interviews with victims of Satanic abuse in Britain. Heath was the UK Prime Minister from 1970–74 and the Bilderberg Group member who signed the UK into the European Community, now Union. He has been one of the main architects of Britain's further integration into the United Fascist States of Europe. One of the many unconnected people who have identified Heath as a Satanist was the lady I mentioned early in the book who saw the 'lizard' figure at Burnham Beeches in Buckinghamshire, 25 minutes drive from the British Prime Minister's official country residence called Chequers. The game of chequers is played on a board of black and white squares – the floor plan of all Freemasonic temples. Burnham Beeches is not far from High Wycombe and the headquarters of the Hellfire Club of Benjamin Franklin and Sir Francis Dashwood. I'm sure Burnham Beeches would have been one of their haunts, too. This lady was the wife of the Head Keeper at Burnham Beeches and they lived on the land. She had been brought up by a Satanic family in Scotland and had been sexually and ritually abused as a child by the Scottish Brotherhood network. Her husband was also a Satanist which is why he was given the responsibility of looking after Burnham Beeches, an area of ancient groves and forests managed by the authorities in London and including an area called Egypt Wood. Late one night in the early 1970s during Heath's reign as Prime Minister, she was taking her dog for a walk when she saw some lights. Quietly she moved closer to see what was going on. To her horror she saw that it was a Satanic ritual and in the circle was the then Prime Minister, Edward Heath, and his Chancellor of the Exchequer, Anthony Barber. She says that as she watched him, Heath began to transform into a reptile and she said that what surprised her was that no-one in the circle seemed in the least surprised. "He eventually became a full-bodied Reptiloid, growing in size by some two foot." She said he was "slightly scaly" and "spoke fairly naturally, although it sounded like 'long distance' – if you can imagine the short 'time' lapses". I remember well meeting Heath on a television election programme in 1989 while I was a spokesman for the British Green Party and I have never seen such cold and unpleasant eyes in my life. I knew nothing of these subjects then, but the look of his eyes I have never forgotten.

Another famous paedophile and Satanist in Britain is Lord McAlpine, the former treasurer of Heath's Conservative Party, and executive of the McAlpine Construction empire. He also followed the late Jimmy Goldsmith as head of the Referendum Party in Britain which was created to hijack the groups opposing the European Union and lead them to glorious failure. McAlpine, who is heavily involved in a network of Brotherhood secret societies, including the Freemasons, has been publicly named as a paedophile by the investigative magazine, *Scallywag*.[35] He was accused of having oral sex with an underage boy in 1965 and was formerly cautioned by Strathclyde Police for sexual offences against a minor. McAlpine was also named by one of the former residents at the Bryn Alyn Children's Home in North Wales who said he was forced to have oral sex with him. The McAlpine family is one of the Elite bloodlines of Scotland, possibly connecting with the ancient Scottish king, Kenneth McAlpin. The McAlpine family has a long history of Satanism in its ranks, as does the Scottish Keswick family. Both are part of a web which operates across the world into the Far East and Australia. A close friend of the McAlpines is Willie Whitelaw, a chairman of the Conservative Party. He was also Deputy Prime Minister to Margaret Thatcher, who was 'minded' by Whitelaw, the McAlpines, and Sir Geoffrey Howe, during her years as Prime Minister. When she had outlived her usefulness to the Brotherhood, it was Howe who made the speech in the House of Commons which effectively ended her reign. Whitelaw was named as a leading Satanist by self-confessed Satanist, Derry Mainwaring-Knight, at Maidstone Crown Court in 1986. As usual, nothing was done about it.[36] Mainwaring-Knight lived near East Grinstead, one of the centres of Satanism in England. In Scotland, a foremost Satanic centre is Loch Ness, near Inverness, the home, according to the legend, of the famous reptile, the Loch Ness monster. So what could these legends really be symbolic of? Aleister Crowley, the best known Satanist of the 20th century, had a house at Loch Ness and it was to this area that he came to perform some of his most powerful black magic rituals. A rock formation near the loch called the Rock of Curses has been used by black magicians for hundreds of years and Crowley was particularly drawn to the energy emanating from a nearby mountain known as Mealfuorvonie.[37] There is much more to the legend of the Loch Ness Monster than meets the eye and the same is true of other unidentified creatures like the so-called Bigfoot. Some Native American shamans believe that the entity which manifests as the Bigfoot can also appear as an aquatic monster or a panther because it has the ability to shape-shift.[38]

Over and over I have been told by survivors of how they were abused or programmed at the stately homes of the aristocracy or in rooms under the British Museum and other official buildings in London. Names of Conservative government ministers keep recurring in survivor's accounts. Another paedophile is the former Leicester member of Parliament, Greville Janner, a vociferous campaigner for Jewish causes in Britain. A notorious location for paedophile activities is an apartment block called Dolphin Square in Pimlico, the biggest block of flats in Europe and the London residence of many members of Parliament. The building has been under surveillance by the British Customs after the discovery of pornographic material from Amsterdam. One resident was quoted as saying: "We often have underage boys wandering in the corridors totally lost, asking for the flat of a particular MP." Pimlico has been nicknamed 'Pimp-lico' because of the widespread use of boy prostitutes known as rent boys. The Dolphin Square resident, David Steel, the Scottish former leader of the Liberal Democrats, has actively supported campaigns for 'gay rights' by Ian Campbell Dunn, a planning officer at Edinburgh District Council. But Mr Campbell wants rather more than just 'gay rights'. He is a founding member of the Paedophile Information Exchange (PIE), which wants to legalise sex with children.[39] Should Mr Steel be supporting such a character? The former cabinet ministers, Michael Portillo and Peter Lilley, are apparently regular diners at the restaurant in Dolphin Square along with many famous political figures. I wonder what the attraction can be? Must be the food. Yes, definitely the food.

People think that ritual abuse and sacrifice, if it exists at all, is rare. Like hell it is. Human sacrifice and ritual abuse is rampant. Look at the Satanic child abuse and murder network exposed in Belgium which involves the police, judges, and top politicians. The same is coming to light in North Wales and other areas of the UK. The lack of interest by the media is stunning, if not surprising. Ted Gunderson, a man of 28 years experience with the FBI, told a mind control conference in the United States that after long and detailed research, he estimates there are 3.75 million practising Satanists in the US and between 50 and 60,000 human sacrifices a year. Therapists at the conference said that their clients had pointed to a massive Satanic grave site in open land outside Lancaster, California.[40] Another exists, apparently, at Matamoros, Mexico. The Satanic ritual network connects into the children's homes, care centres, and runaway hostels to ensure a constant supply of children. Please tell me what you know.

A short while before this book was sent to the printer, I was contacted by a friend in the United States who was deprogramming a mind controlled slave of the Brotherhood called Arizona Wilder. I will explain how this mind control is done in the next chapter. She had been mind controlled from childhood to be a so-called Mother Goddess, who conducts sacrificial rituals at the highest levels of the global Brotherhood. Arizona was one of only three women at that level in the world. She has performed rituals for the British royal family, as you will see in the chapter, The Goddess and the King, and this lady is so high in the Satanic hierarchy that even the Queen is, apparently, forbidden to speak to her during the ceremonies. She was genetically bred for this job and her mother is of French noble descent. Arizona told me that the reptilians do not appear to be that psychic, and I guess this has something to do with the lack of a fully formed emotional and spiritual level of being, and so they mind control and programme humans of particular bloodlines, like her, to perform the rituals and draw in the energies for them. She says she was personally programmed by Josef Mengele (she knows him as Green or Greenbaum), a shape-shifting reptilian, and the infamous Nazi mind controller and genetic manipulator, who escaped at the end of the war with the help of British and American Intelligence to continue his horrors in the United Kingdom, the United States, and South America. He once showed her a spider a foot wide which he had genetically developed and he introduced her to Adolf Hitler in the United States in the 1960s. She has described many top secret facilities in the United States which my friend has personally seen himself and every time she has been 100% accurate. She says that each of the ruling 13 families of the global Brotherhood have their own council of 13. The most powerful council in the United States is based in California and among the members are Robert Caldwell, his son Richard, Jim Christensen, Richard Hoehn, Richard Bradbury, Jim Efferson, Fred Danger and Frank Cohen. But the head of that council, and the highest-ranked member of the Illuminati (Brotherhood) that she knows, is a man code-named Pindar from the Alsace-Lorraine region of France. Pindar means 'Penis of the Dragon'. His name, Arizona says, is the Marquis de Libeaux. I have not yet established if this is his real name or another pseudonym – can you help? Libeaux relates to 'of the water' and is consistent with the ancient legends of reptilian gods coming from the water. She says that in the basement of his chateau in Alsace-Lorraine there is an opening into the subterranean world. Note the area – Lorraine, home to key reptilian bloodlines going back many centuries as I outlined earlier. This mind controlled high priestess/ Mother Goddess was impregnated by Pindar, she says, but her own mind began to reject the programming and she aborted the foetus and broke with the Brotherhood. As often happens, her programming began to break down when her programmer, Mengele, died in the late 1980s. Arizona says that Pindar, like all the reptilians when they shape-shift, has very powerful hypnotic eyes (the 'evil eye' of legend) and at sacrifices the victim's face is turned to Pindar at the moment of death for him to steal the person's soul or energy through this 'evil eye' magnetic process.

The following is information that has been supplied by Arizona: Pindar attends the major Satanic ceremonies in Europe and then flies to California for the rituals there. Beltane used to be celebrated in Trebuco Canyon in Orange County, California, but due to urban sprawl, the rites are now conducted in nearby Blackstar Canyon, which is closed to the public. Local streets are also cordoned off by members of the Orange County Sheriff's Department. The Samhain ritual is conducted at the Eastside Christian Church located at the junction of 7th Avenue and Temple in Longbeach. Outside the church is a logo of a white dove with a red goblet between its wings. This is Semiramis again and white is considered a demonic colour by these people, hence Pindar, the 'Marquis de Libeaux', travels in a white limousine. (A 'code-white' is a code understood by judges, police, the military, etc, and it means: look the other way or do not prosecute this person). Military guards carrying automatic weapons protect the church and inquisitive outsiders are ritually murdered and disposed of at the mortuary down the street. The Walpurgis ritual takes place at the west side of Catalina Island. The Coastguard vessel, Golden Eagle, takes sacrificial children who can't swim across to the site and they are thrown overboard. The bodies are recovered and placed in cages filled with starving sharks for disposal.

At outdoor rituals, Arizona says she wore a red robe and stood in the centre of a pentagram which was surrounded by a hexagram or Star of David. She was triggered into her 'Isis' program and conducted the Drawing Down of the Moon ceremony which, she says, made four snarling, hideous creatures materialise in the Satanists' circle. The sacrificial victims, who have been bred from birth for the role, are ritually killed by slashing the throat from left to right. This is the origin of the Freemasonic sign of pulling the flat hand across the throat from left to right, a movement which means "You're dead". The blood from the victims is collected and mixed with arsenic, which appears to be a necessary element for those of the human-reptilian bloodlines. This is poured into goblets and consumed by the Satanists, together with the liver and eyes. This is supposed to provide strength and greater psychic vision. Fat is scraped from the intestines and smeared over the bodies of the participants – like the fat of the 'messeh' in ancient Egypt. The corpse is then suspended from a tree and the Satanists stand naked to allow the dripping blood to fall on them. The Mother Goddess says that by this time the participants are in such a high state of excitement that they often shape-shift into reptilians and mostly manifest, she says, in a sort of off-white colour. They are also terrified, because at this point the Mother Goddess points to four of them and they are then ritually murdered. Clare Reeves, the President of Mothers Against Sexual Abuse in the US, told me that at least 12 ritually abused clients had reported that the participants shape-shifted into reptilians. Another ritual takes place in Orange County at Dana Cove Point in which a pregnant woman is drowned and her baby removed. The British royal family, Ronald and Nancy Reagan, Gerald Ford, George Bush, the two Bush Governor sons, Henry Kissinger, Newt Gingrich, Bill and Hillary Clinton, Rothschilds, Habsburgs, Bob Hope, Rupert Murdoch and a stream of other famous names have all attended sacrificial rituals at which this Mother Goddess has presided, Arizona says. She says that Hillary is the power that controls Bill Clinton because she is far higher up the hierarchy than him. He is mind controlled, she says, and Hillary is his handler. She also reports that she has seen reptilians, Greys, and reptile-human hybrids at many underground facilities, including the infamous Area 51 in Nevada. She says that astronaut Neil Armstrong took pictures on the Moon of translucent structures and an underground habitat. These pictures are, apparently, in a building in Oklahoma City. The Mother Goddess said that she had also conducted Satanic ceremonies in France involving Pope John Paul II. Another source within the mind control community reports that the Pope is also a mind contolled stooge and a contact with relatives in the Vatican told me that they were slowly poisoning the Pope to ensure that he dies in time for their chosen one to replace him at the right time. We should expect, he said, to see the Pope looking more and more frail and sick in the weeks and months ahead.

What the victims have told me would be almost unbelievable were it not coming from so many different, unconnected sources and were not the stories across the world not telling the same basic tale, even down to the details of the rituals and the mind programming techniques. The children, and the traumatised adults they become, have nowhere to turn. Their stories are so astonishing that few believe them and they are frightened of going to the police because they know that the Satanic network includes top police officers, judges, civil servants, media people, politicians, and many others who control our 'free' society. Questions like "Who are you going to tell?" and "Where are you going to run?" are used to break their spirit. Their sense of hopelessness makes them think there is nothing they can do to seek justice, so they give up and stop trying. The vast majority of Freemasons are not Satanists or child abusers, but there is a far greater ratio of them in secret societies like the Masons, than outside. How can you have confidence in justice therefore when, for instance, the Manor of St James's Freemasonry Lodge, No 9179, consists of the leading operational police officers from all the major units of London's Metropolitan Police, including the Anti-Terrorist Squad, Fraud Squad, and the Complaints Investigations Branch which is supposed to investigate allegations of police wrong-doing! The St James's Lodge further includes senior figures from the Home Office, judiciary, and the Directorate of Public Prosecutions, which decides if a person will or will not be prosecuted. The whole system of investigation, prosecution, and trial, or the suppression of them, can be achieved by members of this one lodge working together. What chance has a child got against that?

Also, as many of the victims have said, they themselves are drugged and programmed to take part in the ritual murder and torture of other children. This is videoed and played back to them when they are in a conscious state. They are so horrified at what they have done and so terrified of the consequences that they dare not speak to the authorities. Other techniques to prevent exposure include abusing children while wearing a Mickey Mouse face or a Devil's head. When little children say they were abused by Mickey Mouse or the Devil it makes them even less likely to be believed. One woman who contacted me said that her father sexually abused her while wearing a Devil's head and it was a long time before she realised that her father was responsible. The stories of the people I have talked to, and the accounts of others I have read, tell of events that are beyond comprehension or, at least, they would be if they were not actually happening. Drinking blood, eating the flesh of dead bodies, thousands of adults and children buried in deep graves, the murder of people on camera for the so-called 'snuff' videos, the story is just appalling. One mother told a television documentary in the *Dispatches* series on Channel Four in the UK, of how she was forced to place her new-born baby on a Satanic altar and push a knife through its heart. A Satanist then had sex with the dead body. This is happening in your country NOW!

Many of the victims are born into Satanic families and others are bred for sacrifice through the use of breeders: women kept in captivity to give birth to one child after another which are never formerly registered and so, according to official records, they don't exist. You can't murder someone who doesn't exist and so these children and foetuses are sacrificed without anyone outside the circle knowing the children have even been born. The Ku Klux Klan, the Aryan master race fanatics created by the Freemason Satanist, Albert Pike, are one of the endless groups who keep women under lock and key for this purpose.[41] These groups have their own midwives who supervise the births and they are also born in hospitals under the supervision of staff loyal to the Brotherhood and their Satanic ritual offshoots.[42] Other children from non-Satanic families are taken away at birth and the parents are told their child has died when in fact they are taken away to be sacrificed or to be used in the mind control projects I will discuss in the next chapter. Low income parents, and those addicted to drugs, are at the mercy of the Freemasons and Satanists operating among the social services hierarchy and judges. Their children are often taken away from them for Satanic ritual or mind control projects. So called 'crack' babies are apparently sought after for mind control operations, as are twins. I know of twins who were crack babies in Denver, Colorado, a major Satanic centre. They were first taken from their parents and given to foster parents. Later they were taken from the foster parents by Denver Social Services after the husband was murdered in very strange circumstances and they were given to a single woman who had turned up out of nowhere after the murder and offered to be a nanny to the children. The Satanic ring centred in Denver connects into Boulder, Colorado and this was where the child beauty queen, JonBenet Ramsey, was found murdered in her parents home in very mysterious and

unexplained circumstances in December 1996. The American coroner and
investigator, Dr Cyril Wecht, says that the evidence proves that her death happened
during sexual abuse by her parents, John and Patsy Ramsey.[43] JonBenet was murdered
on Christmas Eve and Josef Mengele created a sacrificial ritual for this date called
"The Last Bulb on the Christmas Tree". Mengele's pseudonym, Greenbaum, means
green tree and relates to the Cabalistic Tree of Life. A Brotherhood term for the Devil
is JonBet and the coincidence is so amazing that, given the other circumstances, I
cannot believe that this was not the true inspiration for her name.

A research project into ritual abuse at the University of Colorado at Boulder found
that all of those questioned had been subjected to intercourse or molestation; 97% saw
or took part in animal sacrifice; 97% forced to take part in sex with adults; 97%
experienced torture; 94% were sodomised; 88% were forced to watch or take part in
human sacrifice; 88% in cannibalism. A long, long list of child and other murders
across the world are the work of Satanic groups, including, I would strongly contend,
the still unexplained murder of 13-year-old Genette Tate near Exeter in Devon in 1978.
Her body has never been found. I have met with people who have been investigating
this case for many years and the evidence is overwhelming that it involved a Satanic
group which could well have included some leading personnel at the Devon and
Cornwall police headquarters, a short distance from where Genette was last seen
alive. Her father, John Tate, also has some significant questions to answer. A
manuscript exists of this evidence if there is a publisher out there who is interested in
exposing the case. When sceptics ask how such widespread Satanism, abuse and
murder can be covered up, they need to appreciate the sort of people who are
involved in these rings. David Berkowitz, the serial killer in New York known as the
Son of Sam, has written that he was part of a Satanic group which had orchestrated
the murders. In letters to a church minister, Berkowitz said:

"...this group contained a mixture of Satanic practices, including the teachings of
Aleister Crowley and Eliphas Levi (*another notorious Satanist*). It was (*and still is*) totally
blood orientated... The coven's doctrines are a blend of ancient Druidism, teachings of
the secret order of the Golden Dawn, black magick, and a host of other unlawful and
obnoxious practices...

"... Satanists (*genuine ones*) are peculiar people. They aren't ignorant peasants or
semi-literate natives. Rather, their ranks are filled with doctors, lawyers, businessmen,
and basically highly responsible citizens... They are not a careless group who are apt to
make mistakes. But they are secretive and bonded together by a common need and
desire to mete out havoc on society. It was Aleister Crowley who said: "I want
blasphemy, murder, rape, revolution, anything bad."[44]

Satanism is the creation of the reptilians, the 'fallen angels', and interestingly
they also had a son of Sam according to a one thousand-year-old account. The Arab
poet, Firdowsi, completed his legendary history of Iran in 1010 AD, a work called
the Shahnameh or Book of Kings. He writes about a king called Sam who married a

beautiful woman who gave birth to a baby of unearthly appearance. The description of the baby's features is exactly the same as the children born of the interbreeding between the Watchers and human women – very large, white skinned, and hair like snow. His name was Zal, a Nefilim child, a Watcher (reptilian) – human hybrid. And Zal was the son of Sam. In 1969, Charles Manson and his Satanic 'Family' murdered nine people, including the actress Sharon Tate. Manson operated in California in the Flower Power years when a group called the Process had a high profile in cities like San Francisco. The Process emerged in Britain and then established branches in California and New York. The group celebrates Adolf Hitler and worships a Trinity of Jehovah, Lucifer, and Satan. In the British occult magazine, *The Lamp Of Thoth*, a writer by the name of Soror H, said of Charles Manson: "(He) showed many of us what it is like to actually commit the crime we'd like to commit… Manson went astray where others like the Process succeeded. He got caught."[45] Another serial killer, Henry Lee Lucas, who is said to have murdered 360 people, including his mother, claimed he was a member of the Hand of Death Satanic group. He said that murder was part of the initiation and he admitted to drinking the blood of some of his victims. The Hand of Death, he said, was involved in drug running and the kidnapping of children for slavery and sacrifice. When they were killed, the group would drink their blood and eat part of their body, Lucas said. Mutilated bodies were found in Mexico and Arizona which appeared to support his story. Richard Ramirez, the serial killer known as the Knight Stalker, said he killed his thirteen victims in the name of Satan. Inverted pentagrams, the classic Satanic symbol, were found spray painted in the homes of several of his victims and he carved a pentagram on the thigh of an elderly woman.

The number of murders world-wide involving Satanic ritual is simply fantastic. While I was writing this book I heard from another researcher of the ritual murder of Alfred Kunz, a rebel Roman Catholic priest who performed exorcisms. He was found in March 1998 in his rectory at Madison, Wisconsin, hanging upside down with his throat cut from ear to ear. His head had then been cut off and his blood taken away. Such were the circumstances in the case that the FBI was called in to investigate. The assassinations of President Kennedy and Princess Diana were full of Satanic ritual, also, as I shall outline later. I hear the same themes of Satanic ritual, abuse and sacrifice in every country I visit and even on the Isle of Wight, the small island off the south coast of England where I have lived for many years, there is substantial Satanic activity. Britain's biggest selling Sunday tabloid, *The News Of The World*, published the revelations of a community worker on the Isle of Wight who exposed the nature and extent of the abuse there. She said that these Satanic sacrificers of children were pillars of the local community, owners of seaside hotels, business people, local government officers, and politicians. She described the breeding programmes on the island in which babies are bred for sacrifice and how it connected into the paedophile and drug smuggling rings, another common theme. Detective Chief Inspector Neil Kingman, who was heading the inquiry, said: " I have met the community worker several times and interviewed other people regarding this matter. I have no reason to doubt what I am being told."[46]

There have been many famous cases in which ritual abuse has been alleged, but these have been successfully covered up by the political and judicial authorities and a compliant, uninformed, and slanted media. In the United States, the McMartin case in Los Angeles which came to light in 1983 was a prime example. It involved allegations by 369 children at the McMartin Day Care Centre that they had been sexually abused. They told of animals being slaughtered and other Satanic rituals. They described how they were buried, locked in the dark, and taken to different locations to be abused. These included a grocery store, a cemetery, a church, and a crematorium. The children said they were forced to drink blood and urine and they saw the eyes of a baby ripped out and its body incinerated. Others said that a rabbit was killed in front of them to show what would happen if they told their parents. The case was under investigation for four years, on trial for two and a half years, involved 124 witnesses, 50,000 pages of transcript, and cost almost $23,000 a day. But in the end it fell apart and those responsible escaped with their freedom. Crucial to the children's stories was their description of a network of secret tunnels under the building through which they said they were taken to be abused. It was claimed at the trial that there was no evidence that these tunnels existed, but five months after the files were closed on the McMartin case and the official cover up completed, a team of trained investigators and excavators uncovered the tunnel system which connected to a vaulted room under the day care centre. They extended out to adjacent buildings where the children said they had been taken before they were driven to other locations. In 1991, an independent archaeologist also confirmed the existence of the tunnels and an alarm system inside the centre. In other words, the children had been telling the truth. In Britain there have been, among many others, cases in Orkney, Nottingham, Rochdale and Cleveland. Each time the social workers trying to expose Satanic abuse have been subjected to a blitz of condemnation by the mainstream media with the *Mail On Sunday* particularly vehement in its opposition. It went so far on one occasion as to describe the "spectre" of Satanism as "hysterical nonsense". Such remarks are so at odds with worldwide evidence that they can only be the work of an uninformed idiot (quite possible) or someone who wishes the truth to remain uncovered. As a result of such imbalanced coverage and, of course, the staggering nature of the children's evidence, most cases do not even come to trial and when they do very few lead to conviction. The public would rather believe the allegations are not true because they want to believe such horrors are not happening. Unfortunately they are, on a vast scale, and if you go into denial about it because you don't want to face the truth about your world, then you are helping to perpetuate this unspeakable treatment of children. As Caroline Lekiar of the National Association of Young People in Care, said:

> "I can understand people finding it difficult to believe, it's extraordinary, but yet, everything is showing that it is happening. Young kids are drawing pictures of the type of thing that don't come on TV. I've been dealing with this for the last two years, I've come across many cases of ritualistic abuse and a lot of it happens all over the place; people have really got to wake up." [47]

Satanic ritual abuse is a global network, another pyramid of interconnecting groups, with the high and mighty of society among their numbers, top politicians, government officials, bankers, business leaders, lawyers, judges, doctors, coroners, publishers, editors and journalists. All the people you need, in fact, to carry out and cover up your rituals and crimes against humanity. It is not that researchers see Satanists everywhere. The ratio of them in leading positions is very high because that's the way it is meant to be. The Satanic networks control the system and so they ensure that there is a far, far, higher ratio of Satanists in positions of power than there are in the general population. The higher you go up the pyramids, the more Satanists you find. Most of the non-Satanists are filtered out before they reach those levels. The result of all this for the children involved is beyond the imagination of anyone who has not experienced the level of trauma that they must suffer. The singer, Joan Baez, sings a song about recalling childhood abuse as the amnesiac barriers begin to fall, the mind control breaks down, and the memories come flashing back. The words capture the feelings of such people magnificently:

You don't have to play me backwards,
To get the meaning of my verse,
You don't have to die and go to hell,
To feel the Devil's curse.

Well I thought my life was a photograph,
On the family Christmas card.
Kids all dressed in buttons and bows,
And lined up in the yard.
Were the golden days of childhood,
So lyrical and warm?
Or did the picture start to fade,
On the day that I was born.

Let the night begin, there's a pop of skin,
And the sudden rush of scarlet,
There's a little boy riding on a goat's head,
And a little girl playing the harlot.
There's a sacrifice in an empty church,
Of sweet li'l baby Rose,
And a man in a mask from Mexico,
Is peeling off my clothes.
I've seen them light the candles,
I've heard them beat the drum,
And I've cried Mama, Mama, I'm cold as ice,
And I've got no place to run.

So I'm paying for protection,
Smoking out the truth,
Chasing recollections,
Nailing down the proof.

I'll stand before your altar,
And tell everything I know,
I've come to claim my childhood,
At the chapel of baby Rose.[48]

What an horrific experience this verbalises and many thousands of children will go through that same nightmare all over the world today and every day. Does anyone still believe that we should walk away and ignore it? That we should kid ourselves that it is not happening. Or is this get-off-your-arse time? A time to make a difference.

■ SOURCES

1   Nigel Davies, *Human Sacrifice, In History And Today* (William Morrow and Company, New York), p 46.

2   Ibid, p 21.

3   *Human Sacrifice, In History And Today*, p 22.

4   Ibid, pp 53, 56, 57.

5   Ibid, p 51.

6   Ibid, p 33.

7   *The Illuminati Formula*, p 46.

8   *The Curse Of Canaan*, p 67.

9   *Waco: The Rules Of Engagement* (Fifth Estate Productions, distributed by Somford Entertainment, Los Angeles, CA, USA).

10   Andrew Boyd, *Blasphemous Rumours* (Fount Paperbacks, an imprint of Harper Collins, London, 1991), p 142. This is a very balanced and first class investigation into the subject and I challenge anyone to read this and still deny that Satanic ritual abuse is a myth.

11   *Human Sacrifice*, p 64.

12   Aleister Crowley, *Magick Theory And Practice* (Dover, USA, 1929), pp 94–95.

13   *The Templar Revelation*, p 109.

14   *The Occult Conspiracy*, pp 39–40.

15   *The Temple And The Lodge*, p 53.

16   *The Hiram Key*, p 364.

17 *The Curse Of Canaan*, p 37.

18 Ibid.

19 Ibid.

20 Ibid.

21 Ibid, p 38.

22 *Blasphemous Rumours*, p 114.

23 Ibid.

24 *The Illuminati Formula*, p 46.

25 Ibid.

26 *The Top 13 Illuminati Bloodlines*.

27 Ibid, p 93.

28 *The Illuminati Formula*, p 213.

29 Ibid.

30 Ibid.

31 Ibid, p 214.

32 "Satanic Links to Belgian Murder Trial", *The Sunday Times*, December 29th 1996.

33 Ibid.

34 Ibid.

35 "Lord McAlpine and the Paedophile Ring", *Scallywag*, issue 22, 1994.

36 Peter Jones, *The Obedience Of Australia* (XPO-imprint, 26 Burlington Close, London, W9 3LZ, 1995), pp 10–11.

37 *Extraterrestrial Friends And Foes*, p 70.

38 Ibid, p 69.

39 "The Monster Man of PIE", *Scallywag*, issue 25, 1994.

40 *Contact* newspaper, April 4th 1995, p 23.

41 *The Illuminati Formula*, p 22.

42 Ibid.

43 *National Enquirer*, April 28th 1998, p 39, quoting a proposed book by Dr Wecht called *Who Killed JonBenet Ramsey*.

44 Quoted in *Blasphemous Rumours*, p 212.

45 Ibid, p 183.

46 *The News Of The World*, August 24th 1997, pp 30–31.

47 Quoted *Blasphemous Rumours*, p 30.

48 Written by Joan Baez, Wally Wilson, Kenny Greenberg and Karen O'Connor, published by Gabriel Earl Music/ Sony Cross Keys Publishing Company/Greenberg Music.

CHAPTER SIXTEEN

Where have all the children gone?

The Satanic networks are a vital part of the global mind control programmes designed to create a race of mindless zombies and an endless flow of mind controlled assassins, crazed gunmen, and agents provocateur. Human robots – mind controlled slaves – have been with us for thousands of years and it is an epidemic today. As Fritz Springmeier and Cisco Wheeler say in their detailed investigation into mind control:

> "The basic techniques were developed in German, Scottish, Italian, and English families and have been done for centuries. Some report that techniques go back to ancient Egypt and ancient Babylon to the ancient mystery religions. The Nazis are known to have studied ancient Egyptian texts in their mind control research. The records and secrets of the generational bloodlines are very well guarded secrets." [1]

Control of the human mind and emotions is the very foundation of the reptilian control of the human race. Control a person's mind and you control them. The external manipulation of the mind takes many forms and the question is not how many are mind controlled, but how few are not. Every time you allow a newspaper, news programme, or manipulating advertisement to affect your perceptions and decisions, you are being mind controlled. The emergence of today's vast network of mind control centres and operations can be traced back to the British Army's Directorate of Psychological Warfare commanded by Brigadier General John Rawlings Rees. This interlocked with the Tavistock Clinic which was founded in 1920 under the direct support of the British royal family through the Duke of Kent. Later came the Tavistock Institute of Human Relations in London and this is the centre of a global web which includes the Stanford Institute in the United States. The aim of these organisations is the control of humanity via the external manipulation of the mind. Rawlings Rees was a vehement racist and supporter of the eugenics 'master race' movement. He studied 'war neuroses' during World War I and he believed that by using the right conditions neurotic behaviour could be stimulated and controlled. He wrote in his book, *The Shaping Of Psychiatry By War*, published in 1945, that the Tavistock Group had demonstrated during the Second World War that there was a 'psychopathological tenth' of the population who were genetically stupid. The numbers of these people had to be controlled, he said, to protect civilised society and it was necessary to take steps, including the use of psychiatry, to prevent their increase in numbers – especially in the backward colonial countries which threatened the civilised world. This was the usual reptilian-Aryan bullshit and Henry Kissinger, David Rockefeller, and Adolf Hitler, could not have put it better. Rawlings Rees said there was another ten per cent of the population whose genetic superiority and psychological training made them suitable to occupy the seats of power (the reptilians and their crossbreeds). The other eighty per cent between these two extremes could, he suggested, be useful servants to the genetic élite if their neuroses could be controlled. Rawlings Rees wanted to see psychiatrists involved throughout society, in the home, at work, and in schools, and he arranged for the Tavistock group to train what he called the 'shock troops', the psychiatrists posing as 'advisors' to the business, military, political, and educational management. Their job was, and is, to shape the way people think in the educational, political and business sectors and therefore control the direction of the world. I was told by a member of the House of Lords in Britain that Dr David Owen, now Lord Owen (Bil, TC), the British Foreign Secretary in the 1970s, founder of the Social Democratic Party, and peace negotiator for the European Union in Bosnia, was trained at Tavistock, but I have not yet been able to confirm this or otherwise at the time of writing.

In 1947, Rawlings Rees took his 'vision' to the United Nations and formed the World Federation of Mental Health with Montegu Norman, the Governor of the Bank of England who had funded and manipulated Adolf Hitler and the Nazis to power. As usual, dozens of affiliated, and centrally controlled organisations with an identical agenda were formed around the world. In each country these groups targeted people for mind manipulation that ensured their unquestioning service to the Brotherhood Agenda. Many of these people became the leaders of the Third World countries which, on the surface, were winning their 'independence'. In truth they continued to be controlled by the same people as before. Running alongside this was the United Nations Social and Cultural Organisation under the leadership of another Brotherhood mind programmer, Julian Huxley. The late Dr Fred Wills, the Foreign Minister of Guyana, summed up the situation brilliantly when he said the United Nations was the world's largest, continuously-run, brainwashing programme for leaders of developing countries. The same applies to the leaders of the industrial countries too, who also have their minds played with before they are allowed to enter the positions of political and economic power. Rawlings Rees's protege, Eric Trist, was involved in a Tavistock project to 'restructure' the thinking of business management. This plan included breaking the power of the trades union movement and manipulating the thinking of top management. Among the corporations who hired Tavistock to do this were Shell, Unilever, the coal industry (then government owned), and a number of the leading financial institutions. Major corporations today use 'psychologists' and they employ 'facilitators' or 'group leaders' to run business meetings. What are they really there for? And who are they working for? This all fits into the Tavistock plan to have 'psychiatrists' at every level of society hiding behind other job descriptions. Tavistock was behind the drug culture of the 1960s and the hippie movement and it was they who controlled the purveyors of the 'tune in, drop out' philosophy. This was underpinned by the Brotherhood-CIA operation which made the drug LSD widely available. They are constantly in search of more powerful techniques to imprison the human race in complete servitude. Aldous Huxley, a Tavistock agent, and guru of the 60s 'revolution', revealed the agenda at a lecture to the California Medical School in San Francisco in 1961. He said:

> "There will be in the next generation or so a pharmacological method of making people love their servitude and producing dictatorship without tears so to speak. Producing a kind of painless concentration camp for entire societies so that people will in fact have their liberties taken away from them, but will rather enjoy it, because they will be distracted from any desire to rebel – by propaganda, or brainwashing, or brainwashing enhanced by pharmacological methods. And this seems to be the final revolution."

We are at that very point today. The work of John Rawlings Rees was continued by other Tavistock operatives such as Dr Kurt Lewin as Tavistock developed ever more sophisticated techniques for the individual and mass control of the human mind. These have increased the speed at which humanity has become unthinking and robotic. Tavistock became the centre of a global network as unlimited funds were made available through 'charity' trusts sponsored by the British royal family and from familiar sources like the Rockefellers, the Rothschilds, the Mellons, and the Morgans. Tavistock created 'terrorist' groups are used to create conflict and turmoil in countries where the Brotherhood want to change the government or justify the imposition of 'peace-keeping' troops. In the 1950s, Brigadier General Frank Kitson commanded a Tavistock project which used mind control and torture techniques on prisoners in British prisoner of war camps in Kenya. These robots were then released to penetrate groups opposing British control, destroy them from the inside, and kill their leaders. Others formed their own groups to fight the genuine ones and so Kenyan was fighting Kenyan. This is why the SAS are operating in Africa and South America today under the cover of the World Wide Fund for Nature and the 'security' organisations, as I shall document. This has happened in Algeria, Rwanda, Burundi, the Congo, the list seems endless. The same Brigadier General Frank Kitson who created such conflict and terror in Africa was sent to Northern Ireland in 1970 to launch the initial bombing and murder campaign which triggered the Northern Ireland conflict that still continues today. Such conflicts all over the world lead to demands that something must be done and that 'something' is always further centralisation of power. It is not surprising to learn, therefore, that Eric Trist launched the Tavistock operation in the 1980s designed to use its enormous international network to programme the collective psyche to accept a world government.

In 1991, the Tavistock journal, *Human Relations*, reported on the world government project. The collapse of the Soviet Union (orchestrated by the Brotherhood) had created great opportunities for world government and the end of the nation state, the report said. It proposed a reformation of the United Nations to hand over all operations to a network of hundreds of thousands of (centrally controlled) 'non-governmental organisations'. These would operate across national borders and not be subject to any control by elected governments. All this is a systematic plan to impose the will of the reptilians on the collective human mind and it has constantly gathered pace since the 1950s. After the Second World War the Brotherhood emphasis changed from control of territory to control of minds and finances. People will eventually rebel against occupation of their land, but it's very much more difficult to identify, and therefore resist, occupation of their minds and their financial choices. Winston Churchill told an audience at Harvard University on September 6th 1943, that to control what men think offered far better prizes than taking away other people's lands or provinces or grinding them down in exploitation. The empires of the future, he said, would be the empires of the mind. Lord Bertrand Russell said in his 1957 book, *The Impact Of Science Upon Society*, that when the techniques of mind control had been perfected, every government that was in charge of education for more than one generation would be able to control its subjects securely without any need for armies or policemen. That is what 'education' is doing to our children today.

Along with the British Psychological Warfare Department and the Tavistock operation, research also expanded rapidly under the fascists in Germany and Italy. Josef Mengele, 'the Angel of Death', conducted mind control experiments on thousands of twins under the supervision of Heinrich Himmler at the Kaiser Wilhelm Medical Institute in Berlin. Mengele was born into a rich Satanic reptilian bloodline. He was an expert in demonology and the Cabala and was at least a Grand Master in the Illuminati, though probably much higher.[2] As the camp 'doctor' at the Auchwitz Concentration Camp run by I. G. Farben, he was able to experiment on countless thousands of inmates. When the Allied armies were closing in on Germany in 1945 the British-United States Intelligence operation called Project Paperclip was launched to allow Mengele and the Elite Nazi leadership, 'scientists', 'doctors', and military personnel to escape. Mengele disappeared from Auchwitz in January 1945, and the public were led to believe he had escaped to South America. In fact, he travelled world-wide, working at both the Tavistock Institute in London and in the United States where he was known as Dr. Green or Greenbaum.[3] The official records in Germany detailing Mengele's mind control research were taken by the Americans at the end of the war and the millions of sheets of paper involved are still stored in the Suitland Annex in Washington DC where they are kept under strict security. Most of Mengele's research gleaned in the concentration camps is still classified.[4] Researcher Fritz Springmeier established the names of a number of people who had security clearance to access these files and every one was connected to the Brotherhood networks, including the Illuminati. Many other documents have been destroyed and in the bowels of the CIA headquarters at Langley, Virginia, just across the river from Washington DC, is a basement area known as the Pit where documents are shredded around the clock.[5]

Mind control survivors from this period recall Mengele's spotless uniform and shiny boots which he wore during programming sessions. They remember his thick

German accent, the space between his front teeth, and the way he jabbed with his thumb.[6] As in the concentration camps of Germany, he often had German shepherd dogs to frighten children in his programming sessions. Coordinating Project Paperclip and the subsequent mind control programmes in the United States were the Dulles brothers, cousins to the Rockefellers, both Satanists, reptilians, and Nazis to their core. John Foster Dulles became the US Secretary of State after the war while his brother Allen Dulles was appointed to head the new Central Intelligence Agency, the CIA. From this influx of Nazi mind-doctors into the United States came the now notorious and unspeakable mind control programmes known as MKUltra. MK stands for mind control; they used the German spelling of kontrolle in deference to the German Nazis who inspired the methods and techniques. It was headed, officially, by Ewen Cameron, an extremely sick individual, and a member of one of the Elite Scottish reptilian bloodlines. His favourite book as a child was *Frankenstein* which, he said, inspired him to follow a career in psychiatry. From his base in Montreal, Canada, he coordinated the infamous MKUltra mind control operation with funding from familiar names like the Rockefellers and he had regular meetings with Allen Dulles and the CIA. One of Cameron's institutions administered 60,000 electrical shocks to patients in one year alone: 1961. Cameron's code name was 'Dr White' and indeed colour was part of his research. He was trying to discover how to make brown eyes blue. Can it really be a coincidence that the country singer, Crystal Gayle, who is reported to be a mind controlled slave,[7] made a hit record called *Don't It Make Your Brown Eyes Blue*?

Many of the rituals and methods employed in the mind control projects are inspired by the ancient mystery schools. Admiral Stanfield Turner, the Director of the CIA, admitted publicly in 1977 that millions of dollars had been spent studying voodoo, witchcraft and psychics, and at the Senate hearing on August 3rd 1977, he said that the CIA had been mind controlling countless people without their consent or knowledge. MKUltra had involved at least 185 scientists, 80 US institutions, among them prisons, pharmaceutical companies, hospitals, and 44 medical colleges and universities. Some 700 drugs are used by the Babylonian Brotherhood's mad professors in their mind control projects to create their human robots. This is why so many drugs were found at the Jonestown Compound in Guyana in 1978 when 'cult' members were murdered in their hundreds. The People's Temple 'cult' was created by CIA operative, Jim Jones. It was not a new religion as portrayed in the media, it was a mind control experiment. See the chapter Cult or Con in ...*And The Truth Shall Set You Free*. Drugs have been used since ancient times to mind manipulate people and take them into altered states of consciousness. They can also suppress the will and allow what is called 'demonic possession'. The CIA-British Intelligence networks fund drug research (in other words the public do) to find more and more effective ways of suppressing consciousness and will. This includes vaccinations, food additives, and electromagnetic techniques. One of the centres involved in drug research for the CIA is the California Medical Facility at Vacaville where the work was done by Dr Arthur Nugent. Countless experiments have been carried out and continue to be so. They include the use of mind controlling drugs on servicemen at the Bethesda Naval Hospital in Maryland (since exposed in a television documentary). One of the experiments is in Haiti where the Vodoun cult, a CIA-front, has turned most of the people into little more than zombies.

Prozac is a drug that constantly appears in research into these matters and it is not confined to individual mind control projects, it is being issued like confetti by doctors who serve the profits and ambitions of the drug cartel instead of their patient's wellbeing. It is one of the world's most prescribed drugs for depression and, as I write, Eli Lilly is seeking approval to market a version of Prozac for children in peppermint and orange flavours. Already some 400,000 youngsters under 18 are being treated with Prozac in the United States alone and that is just the start. This is a mass mind control operation we are seeing here, creating a race of zombies like the ones in Haiti. Eli Lilly is closely connected to the Morgan and Rockefeller networks, US Intelligence, and George Bush. Other pharmaceutical companies involved in drug research for the mind control projects include: Sterling Drug (a spin-off from Hitler's I. G. Farben) which is connected to the bloodline family, the Krupps, the CIA's Tinker Foundation, and the Order of St John of Jerusalem; and Monsanto Chemical Company where the president Earle H. Harbison Jr is also president of the Mental Health Association and director of the infamous Bethesda General Hospital where slaves are programmed for a mind control operation called Project Monarch.[8] Monsanto is heavily involved with genetically manipulated food.

Trauma-based mind control

Project Monarch is one of the many offshoots of MKUltra, a programme which, despite official denials, is not only continuing today under other names, it has massively expanded. The foundation of these projects world-wide is a technique called trauma-based mind control and now we can see how the Satanic networks fit into this picture. The mind has a defence mechanism which compartmentalises the memory of extreme trauma. This is why people cannot remember serious road accidents. Their mind creates an amnesiac barrier around the event so they don't have to keep reliving such horrible memories. From ancient times this has been understood by the Brotherhood. In the concentration camps of Nazi Germany the methods of exploiting this phenomena for mind control were further perfected. Mengele and the Nazis realised that if you could systematically traumatise someone through torture, sexual abuse, and by sacrificing and torturing others as they watched, you could shatter a person's mind into a honeycomb of self-contained compartments or amnesiac barriers. Satanic rituals are widely used to do this. Once the mind's unity has been shattered, these various compartments, each unaware of the other's existence, can be programmed for various tasks or experiences. Using trigger words and hypnotic keys, sounds, or signals, these compartments can be pulled forward and pushed back like a mental filing cabinet. One self contained compartment or fragment of mind becomes the person's conscious level and it is then returned to the subconscious and another compartment accessed. This means that after the victim has performed a task they forget what they have done and who with. This condition has become known as Multiple Personality Disorder (MPD) or Dissociative Identity Disorder (DID). The latter is more accurate because the compartments are not 'personalities' as such, they are fragments of mind which have disassociated, become detached from, the rest of the consciousness. It is like moving a radio dial across the stations, the compartments, tuning into one and then another. Even this technique is primitive compared with the latest methods. I knew from my research that there is an obsession among Satanists and paedophiles with having anal sex with young girls, as well as boys, and the British therapist, Vera Diamond, told me that this is a way of creating multiples. Anal penetration is so painful to a child that it sends a surge of energy up the spine which explodes in the brain, causing further 'personality' splitting. It is called vaso-vagal shock. She showed me a painting by a female victim of this and it portrayed a surge of white energy rising from the bottom of the spine and exploding in all directions in her head. So even anal sex has an ulterior motive for those who understand its mental and emotional effect.

Most people are MPD or 'multiples' to an extent because we are all shutting out what we would rather not face, but we are talking here about an extreme and calculated version of it. Many soldiers become multiples when they witness unimaginable slaughter, as their mind walls off the memory and they have no recollection of what they saw. Traugott Konstantin Oesterreich, a professor at Tubingen University in Germany, wrote a classic study of Multiple Personality Disorder and 'demonic possession' in 1921 called *Possession, Demonical And Other*. This revealed that trauma-based mind control was being used in France, Germany and Belgium long before the dawn of the 20th century. Survivors and professionals have told of how the British used agents programmed through MPD in the First World War.[9] Although the trauma may be forgotten, subconsciously it is still affecting them and their lives, physically, mentally, and emotionally. Many people who are sexually abused and systematically traumatised as children appear mentally and physically unstable, especially if the programming has stopped and the compartment walls begin to dismantle. I have sat in on sessions with the British therapist, Vera Diamond, and seen people switch between vastly different 'personalities', one after the other, by the use of a single word or sentence. It is incredible to experience. One of her clients has to be attached to a plastic bag which collects her urine because her bladder has been destroyed by torture. Her medical records are so enormous it shocked a doctor who saw them. When I met her, this lady was just 30... 30... years of age. In the UK the psychologists, social workers, and police, glean their knowledge of Multiple Personality Disorder from the Tavistock group which claims to be the authority on treating the problem while secretly using it to programme people. Dr William Sargant, a psychiatrist at the Tavistock Institute, wrote in his 1957 book, *Battle For The Mind*:

"Various types of belief can be implanted in many people after brain function has been deliberately disturbed by accidentally or deliberately induced fear, anger or excitement. Of the results caused by such disturbances, the most common one is temporarily impaired judgement and heightened suggestibility. Its various group manifestations are sometimes classed under the heading of "herd instinct", and appear most spectacularly in wartime, during severe epidemics, and in all similar periods of common danger, which increase anxiety and so individual and mass suggestibility."

There you have another reason why the public are fed a constant diet of events which induce fear, anger or excitement. Once again, the knowledge of this is not new, it is just more widely used and focused today. People, or rather zombies, in a programmed state are used for many things. They are activated to carry out assassinations, as with the killers of John Lennon and Robert Kennedy. Sirhan Sirhan, the mind controlled puppet alleged to have murdered Robert Kennedy in 1968, was on a 'mind expansion' course with the Rosicrucians when he began to hear messages telling him to kill Kennedy. I detail the background to this in ...*And The Truth Shall Set You Free*. We can now see why so many assassinations are performed by people with the same mental profile – the so-called 'lone nutters'. They are neither alone nor, in most cases, insane if they were allowed to live in their natural state. They are programmed people, often since childhood. By this method, you can use these mind controlled robots to plant a terrorist bomb and then ensure they are in the right place at the right time to be accused and charged with the outrage. You can also program that person's mind while in custody to make sure that he even thinks he was involved. The infamous CIA mind controller called Dr Louis Jolyon 'Jolly' West, who features strongly in ...*And The Truth Shall Set You Free*, gave a 'mental examination' to Timothy McVeigh, the microchipped former US soldier who was convicted of the Oklahoma bombing. West was deeply involved in MKUltra and one of his keenest supporters was the then Governor of California, later President of the United States, Ronald Reagan.

We have seen a spate of 'lone nutters' in many countries who commit mass murder by going apparently crazy with guns. In the United Kingdom we have had horrendous examples of this in the little towns of Hungerford in Berkshire in 1987 and Dunblane in Scotland on March 13th 1996. A 'nutter' called Thomas Hamilton walked into a school in Dunblane and opened fire on little children in a gymnasium. He killed 16 five and six year olds and a teacher. The effect on the collective psyche of hundreds of millions of people across the world, especially of course, in the UK, was devastating. Shortly after that came the massacre in Port Arthur, a small town in Tasmania, Australia, when another lone gunman called Martin Bryant went 'crazy' on April 28th 1996 and killed 35 people. This was followed in England by a guy attacking children and their teachers with a machete at a school in Wolverhampton. In March 1998 came 'America's Dunblane' when two youngsters, Mitchell Johnson aged 13, and his cousin, 11-year-old Andrew Golden, opened fire on their school friends and teachers at the Westside Middle School in Jonesboro in Arkansas, just 130 miles from Bill Clinton's political base at Little Rock. 27 shots were fired killing four students and a teacher and wounding eleven others. Often reports emerge after these events that some of the killers were involved in Satanism. Similar incidents happened in Pearl, Mississippi, on October 1st 1997, and in December the same year at West Paducah, Kentucky, and Stamps, Arkansas.

Again, it was claimed hat those involved in Pearl had been taking part in Satanism. There have been many more since. These events have all the hallmarks of mind control operations. So what goes on here?

Look at the profiles of many of these people. Most have a background of being a bit strange, troubled or simple – "Not the full quid", as neighbours described the Port Arthur killer, Martin Bryant. This is perfect when you want them and their horrors to be dismissed as the work of a lone nutter. In Bryant's case, he had apparently just returned from a two week stay in the United States when he went berserk with his gun. People close to him said his character had changed after he came back from the US, although he had a long history of psychiatric problems and Bryant was a creation of the global mind control centre at Tavistock in London. He was 'examined' in 1983–84 by Tavistock's Dr Eric Cunningham Dax, who decided on his future 'treatment'. Dax was for decades a close associate of Dr John Rawlings Rees, the inspiration for the Tavistock brainwashing operation. It has been shown that terrorist groups like the IRA have what they call 'sleepers', people who lie low unused for years, even decades, until circumstances occur in which they and their cover can be exploited for a particular task. It is the same in this world of mind control. There are people programmed to live in the community with a certain character profile until the time comes when they can be used. They are known in the 'trade' as 'dead eyes'. They have no idea that they are being used in this way because they are not in control of their minds, their programmers are. There are so many unanswered questions, interestingly, about why the Dunblane killer, the Freemason Thomas Hamilton, was allowed to legally keep guns when his strange behaviour should have ensured his licence was refused. And why did the police in Port Arthur take an hour to respond when the scene of the massacre was close to the police station and they had been informed within minutes of Bryant's first shot? Also, Bryant, Hamilton, and so many other people who commit such outrages are reportedly taking Prozac. Side effects include nervousness, anxiety, suicidal tendencies, hypomania, and violent behaviour when the drug is withdrawn. Doctors are warned not to prescribe Prozac to anyone with a history of 'mania'. A number of people involved in mass shootings in the United States have been taking this drug. Traces of the active ingredient of Prozac were also found in the blood of Henri Paul, the driver of Princess Diana's Mercedes when it crashed in Paris in 1997.

So what is the motivation behind these gun massacres? The manipulation of the mind and emotions. Where did these mass murders take place? Not in the gangland areas of London, Glasgow, Los Angeles, or Sydney, but in quiet little communities where everyone felt perfectly safe. In the same way, the 'McVeigh' bomb and the school shootings did not happen in New York or Washington, but in Oklahoma. We would be advised not to underestimate the effect on the collective psyche in terms of fear and a desire for the authorities to 'protect' people from that fear. That means more cameras in the streets and more security guards and cameras in schools so that children are brought up to accept the culture of being 'protected' from danger by 'Big Brother' authority. A front page headline in, I think, the London *Daily Mail* encompassed the very reaction the manipulators wanted to stimulate. It said after the Australia killings: "Is nowhere in the world safe anymore?" When these things happen in quiet communities, it encourages even more powerfully the response of "My God, this could happen to me and my children – hey, we need protecting". A traumatised mind is far more susceptible to mind manipulation. The Brotherhood want to remove all guns from the general population in preparation for their final coup d'état. No-one wants to rid the world of weapons more than me, but we need to ask about the motivation behind the immense pressure for gun laws inspired by... Hungerford, Dunblane, Tasmania, Oklahoma, etc, etc. Problem-reaction-solution. Getting hold of illegal weapons is so easy that gun laws would not stop anyone who really wanted to kill. The gun used by Martin Bryant in Port Arthur was stolen and he had no licence. Gun laws would not have stopped that, but the reason such laws are being introduced all over the world is to prevent the population from defending themselves when the order goes out to round up those who are challenging the Agenda. In the UK the distraught parents who lost children in Dunblane were sickeningly and callously used to spearhead anti-gun legislation by the very people who orchestrated the murder of their loved ones. I don't think I would use a gun, but who knows what a person would do in certain circumstances? My instincts are that I don't see the point of using violence to oppose violence, but many people would and the Brotherhood know that. For this reason they want an unarmed population. Adolf Hitler introduced gun laws shortly before he began to transport people to his concentration camps. Similar camps, or 'holding facilities', have already been built in the United States by an organisation called FEMA, the Federal Emergency Management Agency, which was set up by Zbigniew Brzezinski, a shape-shifting reptilian, and the man who launched the Trilateral Commission with David Rockefeller. FEMA is headed by James Lee Witt and I would advise you to take a look at his eyes if you get the chance on television and ask yourself what they remind you of.

Mind controlled human robots are also used to pass messages between people outside the normal channels. These include unofficial communications between world leaders and between personnel within the Brotherhood-controlled illegal drugs network which involves presidents of the United States and many other world leaders and officials. People programmed through Multiple Personality Disorder apparently develop a photographic memory. The words of the communication are dictated under a form of hypnosis and then compartmentalised, often using a high voltage stun gun which lowers blood sugar levels and makes the person more open to suggestion. Later a trigger word, sentence, or action, activates that 'personality' compartment and the human robot repeats the message word for word like a recorded tape. I have no doubt that many world leaders are themselves under the influence of mind control by their handlers and I am convinced that the UK Prime Minister, Tony Blair, with his distant eyes and fixed smile, is under some sort of mental influence. People look at some of the people I name and say: "But he seems such a nice chap, he'd never do that". The point to remember is that the minds of these people, including many prime ministers and presidents, are compartmentalised and they can be switched from one mode to another. They are not one personality, but multiples of them and we need to appreciate this if we are going to follow the plot. Their closest friends won't realise that what they see is only one compartment of their mind. If they saw them switched to another compartment, they would not recognise them as the person they think they know. Mind controlled 'multiples' are also used to infiltrate organisations the Brotherhood wish to discredit and destroy. Once on the inside they are triggered to behave in ways that turn public opinion against the organisation.

Mind controlled robots, including very small children, provide bizarre sex for presidents, foreign leaders, politicians, and businessmen. Often this is done to encourage these leaders into the Brotherhood's way of thinking or to compromise and blackmail them into doing as they are told. When I say bizarre, I mean it and I don't find the information that follows easy to write or speak about. But it is so important that this veil is lifted, not least for those who are being subjected now, this minute, to some of this grotesque torture. For the most obvious of reasons, these human robots are rarely able to talk about what has happened to them. They are either in zombie mode and can't remember, or, when they are past their sell by date from the Brotherhood's perspective, they are murdered and sometimes their body parts used for black magic rituals attended by some very famous people. You think you know the personalities of people you see on the television? Please read on. Fortunately, one very brave woman who was mind controlled as a young child has spoken out after escaping from US government slavery. She was taken through long and painful deprogramming sessions lasting more than a year which dismantled compartments in her mind and allowed her to remember what happened to her – and who did it. She is Cathy O'Brien, an American of Irish decent, who together with Mark Phillips, has produced a self-published book about her experiences called *Trance Formation Of America*.[10] It is a stunning tale that she has to tell, but there have been millions more like her (still are) and that will continue to be the case until humanity wakes up to its responsibilities. Cathy describes in great detail the conversations she heard, the rooms and decor in the White House, the Pentagon, and top secret military establishments across the US. She can also describe physical details of the people involved which she could only know if she had seen them naked. There are a number of researchers who question some of the details in *Trance Formation Of America* and, as always, I have many questions myself. But the themes and many of the names in Cathy's book have come up again and again in the accounts of other recovering mind controlled slaves and in the research of myself and many others. Her story is a summary of what is happening all over the world so I will tell it at some length.

Cathleen (Cathy) Ann O'Brien was born in 1957 in Muskegon, Michigan. Her father Earl O'Brien is a paedophile and one of Cathy's first memories was being unable to breathe because his penis was in her mouth. Such trauma automatically triggers Multiple Personality Disorder without any need for programming because the child's own mind wishes to shut out the horror. Her father's friends were also allowed to abuse and rape the young Cathy and her brothers, just as her father and mother had been abused as children. Her mother was sexually abused by Cathy's grandfather, the leader of a Masonic Blue Lodge. Her mother's brother, Uncle Bob to Cathy, was a pilot in Airforce Intelligence who claimed that he worked for the Vatican. Uncle Bob was also a commercial pornographer and Cathy's father forced her and her older brother, Bill, to take part in pornographic films made for the local Michigan Mafia which was connected, she says, to the 'porn king' Gerald Ford, then a US representative. He would later be the vice-president of the United States under Richard Nixon and president when Nixon was ousted by Henry Kissinger and company via Watergate. Ford also served on the Warren Commission 'investigating' the assassination of President Kennedy and decided the official version was true even though it was impossible. While Cathy O'Brien was a little child at school, she says she was raped by Gerald Ford in the office of the Michigan State Senator, Guy VanderJagt, who also raped her. VanderJagt would become the chairman of the Republican Party National Congressional Committee which supported the child rapist and murderer, George Bush, the Queen of England's friend, in his successful campaign to become President of the United States.

Eventually, Cathy's father was caught sending child pornography through the post – a film of young Cathy having sex with a boxer dog. To avoid prosecution, Cathy was handed over by her father to the United States Government and the Defense Intelligence Agency. Her father was delighted with the deal because he was now immune from prosecution and could continue his pornography and paedophile activities while the authorities looked the other way. The agency was searching for sexually abused children with Multiple Personality Disorder who came from families with a history of intergenerational child abuse. They wanted the children for their studies into genetic mind control which operated under the title, Project Monarch, an offshoot of MKUltra. The name Monarch comes from the Monarch butterfly, more symbolism which relates in part to the butterfly net. The man who arrived at Cathy's house to give her father the ultimatum to "Hand over your daughter or be prosecuted" was… Gerald Ford. Cathy's father was sent to Harvard University near Boston to be instructed in how to prepare his daughter for the mad professors of the government agencies. Cathy says in her book:

"…in keeping with his government-provided instructions, my father began working me like the legendary Cinderella. I shovelled fireplace ashes, hauled and stacked firewood, raked leaves, shovelled snow, chopped ice, and swept – 'because', my father said, 'Your little hands fit so nicely around the rake, mop, shovel, and broom handles…' By this time my father's exploitation of me included prostitution to his friends, local mobsters, and Masons, relatives, Satanists, strangers, and police officers…

"…Government researchers involved in MKUltra Project Monarch knew about the photographic memory aspect of MPD/DID, of course, as well as other resultant 'super-human' characteristics. Visual acuity of an MPD/DID is 44 times greater than that of the average person. My developed unusually high pain threshold, plus compartmentalisation of memory, were "necessary" for military and covert operation applications. Additionally, my sexuality was primitively twisted from infancy. This programming was appealing and useful to perverse politicians who believed they could hide their actions deep within my memory compartments which clinicians refer to as personalities."[11]

All these methods of trauma, and others I will reveal, are not just gratuitous torture. For example, heavy exercise with little sleep causes the overproduction of endorphins in the brain and this makes the person start to robotically react to commands.[12] This is part of the training methods in the military, of course, which is nothing more than a school for mind control. The "Yes sir" mentally is pure mind control and subordination to the will of another. Soldiers are not encouraged to think and question, only to do as they are told. You want to be mind controlled? OK, simple – join the military. The sexual theme of the programming and abuse is also inspired by the manipulation of sexual energy, the creative force, and at the point of orgasm the mind psyche is wide open to access other higher or lower dimensions, depending on the state of being of those involved. These mind control programmers have high-tech equipment which stimulate those parts of the brain which trigger the orgasm and so open the mind of the victim to the lower 'demonic' dimensions, the reptilians. The programming techniques are highly sophisticated and often very subtle. One common Monarch technique is the 'double bind' in which you say two opposites in the same sentence to cause confusion: "Don't believe any of this, it's all true" is an example.[13] Slavery is not confined to history. Slavery is happening all over the world today, including, no, especially, in Britain, the United States, and other 'civilised' countries. Paedophiles make the news from time to time, but they are the tiniest tip of a massive network that goes right to the top (sorry, gutter) of 'free' societies. The truth about the abuse of boys at the Kincora Home in Northern Ireland was suppressed because one of the abusers was an agent of British Intelligence. It also involved at least one famous politician in Northern Ireland, but this fact has been covered up, not least by a now retired official of British Intelligence called Ian Cameron. Such child abuse networks provide the perfect vehicle to satisfy the sexual desires of those in control and for blackmailing those they wish to control. I want to know the names of those involved in whatever country you live. If you know something, please tell me. The information will be in the strictest confidence and if it can be substantiated I will make it public. If you hesitate just think about the children being abused today, now, this minute.

Cathy O'Brien says she was abused by Father James Thaylen when she sought comfort at a Roman Catholic Church called St Francis de Sales in Muskegon and another priest, a Father Don, helped Gerald Ford's friend, Guy VanderJagt, to confuse and abuse her in line with the 'requirements' of Project Monarch. Later she was sent to a Roman Catholic School, one of many used by the Brotherhood to safely house their mind controlled children under the strict regime designed to increase the depth of their Multiple Personality Disorder. Her school was Muskegon Catholic Central High School where she was raped by Father Vesbit many times, on one occasion during a Satanic ritual involving other mind controlled boys and girls in his private chapel. The Roman Catholic Church is the epitome of hypocrisy and deeply, deeply, sick. As this book has explained, it was the creation of the

Babylonian Brotherhood from the start, back at the time of the Roman Empire. The Roman Catholic Jesuit movement is an important vehicle for the manipulation of the global conspiracy. Like the Knights of Malta, who help to control the Vatican, the Jesuit hierarchy does not even believe in Christianity! That's just a front. The whole conspiracy is a lot of masks, mirrors and smokescreens. The Jesuits, the Knights of Malta, and the Roman Catholic hierarchy are part of the Babylonian Brotherhood. They were, and are, keen supporters of mind control outrages like Project Monarch and MKUltra. How appropriate, given that the Roman Catholic Church has survived by terrifying, brainwashing, and mind controlling its global congregation. Cathy says she was pressured and manipulated from a young age by the CIA's Roman Catholic branch into keeping secrets through a technique known as the Rite to Remain Silent. And there were so many secrets to keep locked away in her compartmentalised mind.

In the years that followed, she says she was under the control of the US 'Democrat', the senator for West Virginia, Robert C. Byrd, and her abuse by him and the government agencies expanded. Byrd is a 'constitutional' expert working to undermine and destroy the best parts of the American Constitution. She claims that Byrd controls a network of mind controlled slaves and loves nothing more than to whip them mercilessly until they are close to death. One of Byrd's associates, Senator Patrick Leahy of Vermont, would later torture Cathy by putting a needle in her eye while her daughter, Kelly, was forced to watch, she writes in her book.[14] Leahy was vice-chairman of the Senate Intelligence Committee and served on Byrd's Senate Appropriations Committee. Leahy and Byrd played out a public game of 'opposing' each other while actually working together to the same goals. The same masquerade goes on in the parliaments of the world every day. Byrd, a cocaine addict,[15] often bragged to 'safe' people of how he mind controlled President Jimmy Carter while he was Carter's 'confidant and advisor'. The hypnotic voice of Byrd became the 'voice of God' to a praying and meditating Carter who faithfully followed the 'guidance' he believed was divine.[16]

Cathy's torture and mind control was inflicted at many government establishments around the States, including the NASA Space and Rocket Centre at Huntsville, Alabama, where she and later her daughter, Kelly, were used for pornographic films. Yes – Man on the Moon, Space Shuttle – NASA does all this. Religions are used constantly to manipulate people and as a 'respectable' cover for torture and mind manipulation. One centre of Cathy's mind programming was Salt Lake City, Utah, the headquarters of the Mormon Church. Another establishment for mind controlling slaves is known as the Charm School at Youngstown, Ohio. This is a sex-slave 'school' where Cathy says she, Kelly and countless other women and children, were tortured and abused with electric shocks, sleep deprivation and sexual trauma. Cathy says an unnamed member of the Mellon banking family (more close friends of the Windsors) was the 'governor' of the Charm School. Other well known people involved were US Representative Jim Traficant and Dick Thornburgh, then Governor of Pennsylvania and later US Attorney General and Secretary for the United Nations, Cathy writes.[17] She, and so many others like her I have spoken with or read about, say that part of their torture programming took place at Disneyland in California and Disneyworld in Florida. The opening of the Disney park near Paris has given the opportunity for similar programming for mind-slaves in Europe. The Disney company is a major Brotherhood operation and its films and theme parks are perfect for creating the illusions that confuse the mind of the multiple. Satanic rituals go on here and trauma-based programming when the parks are closed, Cathy says. Children are targeted for kidnapping here and the ones they want get 'lost' in the crowds. One obvious example of a children's story full of mind-programming symbolism is the MGM epic, *The Wizard Of Oz*. The word 'Oz' is short for Osiris, another theme of the programming. Some slaves have the 'golden penis of Osiris' placed upon them.[18] The story of *The Wizard Of Oz* was published in 1900 by Frank Baum, a member of Madam Blavatsky's Theosophical Society, and it became a film in 1939. It is a mass of mystery school, Satanic and mind control symbolism and Fritz Springmeier and Cisco Wheeler include a superb analysis of the story in their book, *The Illuminati Formula Used To Create An Undetectable Total Mind Controlled Slave*. Other programming centres include Las Vegas, Nevada, and its surrounding area. The fantasy themes of the casinos in Vegas, like the MGM Grand, are used and one of the slave 'auction' sites is a remote spot 20 miles from the city.[19]

While still a child, Cathy says that she was raped, abused and tortured by some very famous people. She says that she was raped by Pierre Trudeau, the long time Prime Minister of Canada, who as a Jesuit, was working closely with the Vatican; she was raped again by Gerald Ford when he was actually President; raped by Ronald Reagan while he was President; and raped many times in the most brutal fashion by Dick Cheney, the White House Chief of Staff under Ford and the Defense Secretary of the United States under George Bush. Cathy is able to describe Cheney's office in the Pentagon in great detail. If you accept her often highly detailed evidence you can only conclude that Cheney, like Bush, has an immensely imbalanced mind capable of staggering violence and murder. Cathy says that Cheney told her on one occasion: "I could kill you – kill you – with my bare hands. You're not the first and you won't be the last".[20] These were the characters who launched the Gulf War to show that 'violence does not pay'! Cheney, Bush, and others have 'fun' playing something they call The Most Dangerous Game. It involves threatening government slaves like Cathy and other mind controlled children and adults with appalling consequences if they are caught. They are then allowed to 'escape' into a forest, usually in some top secret military area like Lampe, Missouri or Mount Shasta, California, which are surrounded by a high fence to prevent any escape. George Bush, the man who called for a "kinder, gentler America", Dick Cheney, and Bill Clinton often go after them with guns, Cathy says in her book and newspaper interviews. When they are caught, they are brutally raped, sometimes killed, she says. The Mount Shasta compound, where Bush and Cheney shared an office, is, according to Cathy: "The largest covert mind control slave camp of which I am aware".[21] There she saw an enormous fleet of unmarked black helicopters, which, as researchers have revealed, are part of the Brotherhood's private army which is being installed to instigate the coup d'état against dissidents when the moment is deemed right. These helicopters have often been reported near the scenes of 'alien' abductions and cattle mutilations. Part of the cover for these military and mind control operations at the Shasta compound, Cathy says, is the country music scene at Lake Shasta.

Cathy says she was forced to marry a mind controlled Satanist called Wayne Cox, a member of the Jack Greene country music band. Greene, a CIA operative, was also a Satanist, she says.[22] Cox's job was to further traumatise her to create more compartments which could be used to program new 'personalities', Cathy writes. One night, she says Cox took her with him to the ruins of the Union Railway Station in Nashville and, using a flashlight, found a homeless man asleep. He ordered Cathy to "Kiss the railroad bum goodbye" and proceeded to shoot him in the head. That was horrific enough, but then he produced a machete and chopped off the man's hands before putting them into a zipper bag.[23] As Cathy has stated at public meetings many times, Wayne Cox is a serial killer who invariably chops off the hands of his prey. This is a Satanic signature. In an interview published in the *Contact* newspaper, Cathy said:

> "By 1978, Wayne Cox, my first designated controller, was actively ritually and dismembering bums, children, and those who "wouldn't be missed" and blatantly distributing body parts from his Chatham, Louisiana, home base to key Satanic capitals of several states which included the "Little Rock-Missouri route."[24]

Government agencies know this, she says, but he is immune from prosecution because he works for them. Cox led Cathy to another spot on the Union Station site, the tower at the old railway depot, and waiting in the room for them, she says,were Jack Greene, members of his band and others, dressed in black robes. They were standing around a black leather altar, she claims. She describes the room as being draped in red velvet and lit by candles. Cathy was laid on the altar and subjected to rape and torture while the Satanists performed a black magic ritual that involved sex, blood, and cannibalism.[25] Years later when 'married' to another CIA asset, Alex Houston, she would be made pregnant and artificially aborted many times so the foetuses could be used for Satanic rituals, she says.

Bohemian Grove

There is a sexual playground for leading American and foreign politicians, mobsters, bankers, businessmen, top entertainers, etc, who are initiates of the Babylonian Brotherhood. It is called Bohemian Grove, 75 miles north of San Francisco in California, near the hamlet of Monte Rio alongside the Russian River in Sonoma County. I went to the area in 1997 to have a look around and when I told the hotel receptionist where I was going she warned me to be very careful because some people who had been to investigate had never been seen again. Here at Bohemian Grove, Cathy, and others I have interviewed, say they were forced to serve the perversions of their abusers. These include Satanic rituals, torture, child sacrifices, and blood drinking, which take place on the exclusive 2,700 acre estate in among the redwood trees. As Cathy says in her book: "Slaves of advancing age or with failed programming were ritually murdered at random in the wooded grounds of Bohemian Grove and I felt it was only a matter of time until it would be me".[26] She says the Grove has a number of rooms for different perversions including a Dark Room, a Leather Room, a Necrophilia Room, and one known as the Underground Lounge, spelt as 'U.N.derground' on the sign. I've seen a covertly taken picture of robed men at Bohemian Grove standing alongside a large fire worshipping a 40 foot stone owl (*see picture section*). The owl is the symbol of Moloch or Molech, an aspect of Nimrod/Baal. Moloch demands the sacrifice of children and it was to this deity that the children of the Babylonians, Hebrews, Canaanites, Phoenicians and Carthaginians, were sacrificially burned. This picture provided visual support for the claims over many years that Druid rituals were being performed at the Grove with people in red robes marching in procession chanting to the Great Owl, Moloch. The Romans called the owl by the same word that meant witch. The Greeks said the owl was sacred to Athene, the ancient Mesopotamian 'Eye Goddess', and her staring owl-like images have been found throughout the Middle East.[27] The owl was also the totem of Lilith, the symbol of the bloodline genes passed on through the female, and other versions of the triple goddess of the Moon. The owl has been symbolised as a witch in bird form and is associated with witches in the symbols of Halloween. The symbolism of being able to see in the dark and with a 360 degree range of vision are also appropriate for a Brotherhood deity. These world famous Brotherhood initiates at Bohemian Grove burn a Celtic wicker effigy at the start of their 'camp' to symbolise their 'religion'. The population of Britain has been manipulated into doing the same every November 5th when effigies of Guy Fawkes are burned to mark the day on which he tried to blow up Parliament.

A local community newspaper, *The Santa Rosa Sun*, reported in July 1993 about the Cult of Canaan and the legend of Moloch at Bohemian Grove, but police investigations into alleged murders on the site have predictably led nowhere. Regular attendees at Bohemian Grove are known as 'grovers' and among them are people like George Bush; Gerald Ford; Henry Kissinger; Dick Cheney; Alan Greenspan, the head of the Federal Reserve; Jack Kemp (Bob Dole's running mate at the 1996 US election); Alexander Haig, the former Defense Secretary; Casper Weinberger and George Shultz, former Secretaries of State; and a long list of the best known politicians, businessmen, media people, and entertainers in the world, let alone America. Steve Bechtel, the head of the world's biggest construction company, attended Bohemian Grove in the 1980s while his company enjoyed massive contracts thanks to the spending decisions of the World Bank and its president A. W. Clausen, another 'grover'. According to researchers, there is a waiting list of some 1,500 people anxious to pay the initiation fee of $2,500 and annual dues of $600. This is a 'summer camp' and Satanic centre for the Elite who run the planet and this is where many of the real decisions are made before they become public. I have a picture from 1957 of Ronald Reagan and Richard Nixon sitting at a table at Bohemian Grove listening to Dr Glenn Seaborg, who was involved in the discovery of plutonium and worked on the Manhattan Project which produced the bombs that were dropped on Japan. Doctor Edward Teller, the 'father of the H-bomb', was also a member. Both Reagan and Nixon, part of this Elite Satanic club more than 40 years ago, would go on to become presidents of the United States. In fact, every Republican president since Herbert Hoover in 1945 has been a member and most Democrats, including Bill Clinton.

It was in Sonoma County, not far from Bohemian Grove, that 12-year-old Polly Klaas was murdered, quite obviously by Satanists, in October 1993. She was kidnapped from her bed while her mother and sister slept in the next room. Her grandfather, Joe, had publicly endorsed a book called *Breaking The Circle Of Satanic Ritual Abuse* by the former Satanist, Daniel Ryder. It exposed the ties between Satanists and the mind control programmes MKUltra and Project Monarch. While a man was reluctantly charged with Polly's murder, the facts point conclusively to a retaliation by the Satanists against her grandfather. A woman called the FBI to say she had escaped from a coven in Sonoma County and that Polly might be killed as part of a five-day Satanic Halloween Festival. She said Polly might be found near the Pythian Road on Highway 12 which, coincidentally, is close to a 1,600 acre spread called the Beltane Ranch. The FBI ignored this warning and Polly's body was later found near the Pythian Road. She had been sexually assaulted and decapitated, but the authorities claimed she had been strangled. The man who kidnapped her, Richard Alan Davis, was not even charged with the murder by the Sonoma County District Attorney's office until they were forced to act by protests from police officers.

One of those who controlled Cathy O'Brien was Lt Colonel Michael Aquino of the US Army, a top man in the Defense Intelligence Agency's Psychological Warfare Division. I have named him in my last three books as the head of a Satanic Church known as the Temple of Set, an organisation inspired by the leader of Hitler's SS, Heinrich Himmler. When it was exposed that America's psychological warfare was being headed by a neo-Nazi from a Satanic Church, the official response was that a man's religion was his own business! But, as Cathy soon found out, people like Aquino and the rest of this disturbed and possessed bunch, are above the law, because their mentality controls the law right up to the President and beyond. Aquino's wife, who works with him, is called Lilith Sinclair. Lilith is a symbol of the reptilian bloodlines and the Sinclair/St Clair bloodline you know all about by now.[28] She founded the Lilith Grotto within Anton LaVey's Church of Satan and is a member of that Church's Council of Nine.[29] The term 'Council of Nine' is a recurring theme in the Satanism/Brotherhood structures. LaVey's Church of Satan is a good example of the way Satanism and the mind control operations interlink. The United States has become the home for a stream of Satanic organisations inspired by those in Europe, the Middle East and elsewhere. New York and California have long been major centres for Satanism and the Brotherhood. California was settled in the early 20th century by Haitians who practised voodoo and Satanists from Europe, South America and Cuba also headed for California and the San Bernandino Valley. Anton LaVey, student of Aleister Crowley, was the most famous of these and he founded the Church of Satan in 1966. LaVey's maternal grandmother came from Transylvannia, legendary home of the blood sucking 'vampire', and he loved horror movies. It was LaVey, it is claimed, who found Marilyn Monroe working in the strip clubs and used his contacts to make her a movie star. He has had connections with some of the biggest names in business, politics and entertainment, including President John F. Kennedy, Frank Sinatra, Sammy Davis Jr, Peter Lawford, and Jayne Mansfield. Sammy Davis was an early member of LaVey's Church of Satan and Jayne Mansfield was a high priestess. Michael Aquino of the US Psychological Warfare Department worked with LaVey before they had a disagreement and Aquino launched his breakaway, Temple of Set. This is now, apparently, based in Austin, Texas, the political base of George W. Bush, the son of the man himself.

Cathy conceived a child, Kelly, with her 'husband' Wayne Cox, and soon Kelly was being used in the same way as her mother. She says that Kelly was raped many times by George Bush and Dick Cheney. Bush's Satanism and paedophilia are common themes of my research. In his book, *The Franklin Cover Up: Child Abuse, Satanism, And Murder In Nebraska,* the Nebraska State Senator John W. DeCamp exposed a Satanic child abuse ring in Omaha, headed by the top Republican, Lawrence King.[30] It was King who sang the national anthem at the 1984 and 1988 Republican Conventions, but was later jailed for stealing some $40 million from the Franklin Credit Union. It was while investigating this scam that DeCamp uncovered the Satanic ring which involved local police chiefs and Harold Andersen the publisher of the local paper *The Omaha World-Herald.* Some of the paedophile 'parties' identified by DeCamp and his contacts were attended by… George Bush. Another Bush-related activity described by researchers was Operation Brownstone. A Brownstone building in Virginia, close to Washington DC, was used to compromise politicians during the Bush presidency by providing children for sex and filming what happened. Before he arrived for a presidential visit to Australia in December 1991, the publication *Inside News* asked the question: "Is George Bush the world's leading child abuser?". Bush's abuse of children is well known to anyone who has cared to look and you don't have to look far, either. Both Cathy and Kelly were forced to have sex with animals for videos made on the orders of President Ronald Reagan, Cathy says in her book. "Uncle Ron" liked nothing more than to watch these videos and they were known as "Uncle Ronnie's Bed-time Stories".[31] They were recorded and produced, Cathy says, by his pornographer, Michael Dante (also known as Michael Viti). She says that Dante had connections with the Mafia and the CIA (same thing at their top levels), and was a close associate of politicians like Guy VanderJagt, Gerald Ford, Dick Thornburgh, Jim Traficant, and Gary Ackerman.[32] It was Dante who installed the tiny hidden cameras which recorded the sexual activities of US and foreign politicians so they could be blackmailed into supporting the Brotherhood Agenda, Cathy recalls. How many 'leaders' today are following certain policies against the interests of the people because if they didn't, the evidence of their sexual exploits would be revealed. Cathy writes that Reagan's leading pornographer was a man called Larry Flynt of the pornography magazine, *Hustler*.[33] He was the subject of a film called *The People V Larry Flynt*. He too has CIA, Mafia and Vatican connections, she says.[34] Bill Clinton was compromised in this way, on one occasion, by his boss, oops, sorry, 'opponent', George Bush, Cathy told an American alternative newspaper. It happened at the Lampe, Missouri, mind control facility known as Swiss Villa. She says that Bush ordered her daughter, Kelly, to perform oral sex on Clinton while Clinton was doing the same with Cathy. She recalls the following exchange:

> "Clinton pushed his way out from under me and told Bush while he glanced around for the camera: "You didn't need to do that. I'm with you anyway. My position does not need to be compromised." Clinton was apparently referring to the blackmail tactics amongst the Order of the Rose elite. World leaders were always compromised through covertly filmed bizarre sexual activity as was my experience at the Bohemian Grove."[35] (*The Order of the Rose is another exclusive secret society*)

After this encounter, Bush and Clinton, discussed introducing Clinton's daughter, Chelsea, to the child abuse scene, Cathy says. Bush offered to "Open her up". Clinton said he would have to discuss it with Hillary.[36] Clinton and his vice-president, Al Gore, were quite a pairing. Two former Satanists from different groups have said that Gore is addicted to drinking blood.[37] This makes sense because Arizona Wilder, the Brotherhood Mother Goddess who escaped from their clutches, told me how she has seen Gore at sacrifice rituals when he shape-shifted into a reptilian. Many Satanic initiates have the same addiction to the adrenalchrome which is released in the body just before a person is sacrificed.[38] It is produced by the pineal gland during periods of terror. Cathy says that she and Kelly were raped by another Canadian Prime Minister, Brian Mulroney, who is addicted to sex with mind controlled slaves.[39] Mind controlled mothers and young daughters were, and are, regularly transported to Niagara Falls just over the Canadian border for Mulroney to rape them.[40] It was Mulroney in his period as Prime Minister who forced upon the Canadian people the North American Free Trade Agreement (NAFTA), which is set to become the Americas' version of the European Union. The agreement was manipulated into existence by his fellow rapist, George Bush, and later by Bill Clinton. Under the orders of President Reagan's personal attaché, Philip Habib, Cathy says, she was forced to have sex on several occasions with the Brotherhood stooge, King Fahd of Saudi Arabia. The Saudi royal family serve as puppet leaders while suppressing their people with a brutal religion which they themselves do not even begin to observe. American mind controlled slaves are also 'sold' to Saudi Arabia, Mexico, and other countries to help fund the covert operations of the New World Order.

Cathy was so powerfully mind controlled that she was 'promoted' to become what is known as a Presidential Model, a mind controlled slave who is detailed to operate with the top people in the White House and the Pentagon. She was used to pass messages between Reagan, Bush and their foreign associates such as the dictators, Baby Doc Duvalier of Haiti, President Miguel De La Madrid of Mexico and Manuel Noriega of Panama, a paid CIA operative working for the US government illegal drug trade. Cathy says she observed one party attended by Air Force officials and their wives, drug barons like the Pueto Rican, Jose Busto and the 'hero' (I feel ill) of the Iran-Contra drugs-for-arms scandal, Oliver North.

Upstairs were Noriega, Michael Aquino, and Senator Allen Simpson, the 'Republican' from Wyoming, she says.[41] While all this was going on, George Bush was having a "war on drugs" to "save the American children". Cocaine addict Bill Clinton would later do the same. Cathy says she met Clinton a few times and on one occasion in Arkansas, he was trying (successfully) to persuade a supporter, Bill Hall, to become involved in the drugs trade. Hall need not worry, Clinton said, because it was "Reagan's operation". Cathy says that Clinton told Hall in her then mind controlled presence:

> "Bottom line is, we've got control of the (*drugs*) industry, therefore we've got control of them (*suppliers and buyers*). You control the guy underneath you and uncle (*Uncle Sam, the United States Government*) has you covered. What have you got to lose? No risk. No-one's going to hang you out to dry. And whatever spills off the truck as it passes through (Clinton laughed here and snorted another nose-full of cocaine) you get to clean up." [42]

Later that night, Cathy says, she was taken by Bill Hall's wife to meet Hillary Clinton at the Hall's guest villa. There Mrs Clinton, another cocaine user,[43] performed oral sex on Cathy and then insisted it was done to her.[44] Both President Clinton and his first lady knew Cathy was a mind controlled slave and they know what is going on. So does Al Gore. They keep quiet because they are part of what is going on. Hillary Clinton is a sixth degree Illuminati witch and slave handler, according to some researchers.[45] Cathy acted as a robotic messenger for Clinton who was very adept at triggering her programming, as she has stated publicly many times. Clinton and Bush may seem to be opponents in 'different' political parties, but they are part of the same scam. Cathy O'Brien says she has confirmed from her own direct experience what researchers like myself and others have been suggesting for years: Bush was President during the 'Reagan years', President through his own 'official' period in the oval office, and pulled strings again during the 'Clinton' regime under orders from a higher authority. Cathy says she met Bush and Clinton together years before Clinton was even publicly considered a possible presidential candidate. She once observed them at Swiss Villa at Lampe, Missouri. The 'infirmary' on the site is home to a CIA near-death trauma centre, she says. Cathy, under mind control, had delivered a large amount of cocaine there in a motorhome when she saw the two future presidents:

> "...I noticed then Governor of Arkansas, Bill Clinton, at a corner table with Hillary talking to the then vice-president George Bush, and their two special forces 'toy soldiers' (*mind controlled*) who had transferred the cocaine to the infirmary building. My mind control owner, US Senator, Robert Byrd, told me that Bush and others had been grooming Bill Clinton for the presidency in the event that the American public became disillusioned with Republicans and believe that electing a Democrat would make a difference. Clinton obediently followed Bush's orders. Since the implementation of what Hitler termed 'New World Order', knew no party lines, the question should be raised as to the agenda of

Clinton's 1992 presidential campaign manager, James Carville, and his wife, Mary Matalin, who was Bush's campaign manager."[46]

Another Clinton-Bush connection is their love of hunting mind controlled men, women, and children, in The Most Dangerous Game. Cathy describes one of her experiences at Swiss Villa when Clinton and Bush went hunting with dogs for herself, her daughter, Kelly and two mind controlled 'toy soldiers', one of whom had Italian-looking features:

"Swiss Villa appeared deserted, except for Bill Clinton and George Bush who stood at the edge of the woods with their hunting dogs at the ready to embark on 'The Most Dangerous Game' of human hunting. (Clinton shared Bush's passion for traumatising and hunting humans)... Bush and Clinton were dressed alike in camouflage pants, army boots, and wind breakers. The two also shared the trademark of wearing a cap of cryptic meaning. This time, Bush's camouflage cap had an orange insignia which said 'Dear Hunter'. Clinton's blue cap read: 'Aim High' and had a picture of a rifle on it. Clinton appeared awkward with his hunting rifle, while Bush looked like an expert marksman with his black rifle with elaborate scope.

"'The rules of the game are simple' Bush began, triggering me by using the same words that always preceded a most dangerous game.

"Clinton interrupted: 'You run. We hunt.'

"Bush continued: 'This will be called "Hunt for a Virgin"' (Clinton chuckled) 'and she's it.' He pointed to Kelly who was still in my arms. 'I catch you, she's mine.'

"Clinton spoke up: 'You'll have plenty of time to play with the dogs because they'll have you pinned down while we...' (he slid a bullet in the chamber for emphasis) '...hunt down the bigger game.' Clinton glared at the 'toy soldier' with the waxy face. Toy soldier was a term I often heard referring to the mind-controlled robotic 'special forces' young men who operated under the New World Order.

"The two guys ran for the woods. Carrying Kelly I began running, too. Judging from the close proximity of the dogs barks, I had not gone far when they were turned lose. The five barking dogs caught me right away and surrounded me. Kelly screamed as one snapped at her leg and I automatically slapped at its face. I was convinced that the dogs were going to tear us up by the time Bush and Clinton walked into the clearing. They seemed to be engaged in a serious conversation until Bush looked up and smiled.

"'She's mine', he claimed (referring to Kelly). 'But then, she always has been. Let go.'

"As I walked passed Clinton, who was deep in thought, he mumbled 'I thought you'd be fucking a dog or something'. We walked the short way back in silence with

Clinton veering off to the right as Bush directed me toward the two helicopters. The door of the helicopter next to me slid open and Clinton pushed the Italian into the helicopter. 'I caught this one. He's going to ride jump seat.' Bush motioned for him to sit in the leather chair marked for death by the black rose while I rode in the actual jump seat.

"'Come here little one' Bush coaxed Kelly. 'You can sit on Uncle George's lap.' He lifted her onto his lap as Clinton got in front with the pilot who was started the engines. 'Over the lake, Jake', Bush told the pilot.

"Flying over Swiss Villa's deep remote lake, Bush set Kelly aside, stood up as far as he was able in the helicopter, and slid the door open. The powerful wind blew Bush's greasy strands from his face as he gestured for the man (the Italian) to stand up.

"'Free fall', Bush instructed. 'That's an order.'

"'Yes sir' he replied as he stepped out of the door fully clad in his camouflage uniform and military boots – with no parachute. I watched in horror as he fell to his death in the water below, splatter and submerge…" [47]

The United States might lose its freedom? My God. The United States has never been free. The mind controlled slaves are programmed to mind control others and there are now fantastic numbers of mind controlled children and adults at large. There are whole armies of them like the Delta Force, the 'toy soldiers', in the United States and other 'élite' (often psychopathic) groupings like the SAS and the Parachute Regiment in the United Kingdom. The name, Delta, symbolises the pyramid and also relates to the Nile Delta and the ancient Egyptians. 'Delta' programming creates killers, assassins. The training alone for these people is classic mind control, never mind all the individual stuff they experience. The children being prepared to join the Delta Force later in life are put through indescribable horrors to desensitise them from pain and death, both for themselves and others. One of the techniques to do this is to bond the child into a close relationship with another child and then to incinerate their friend while they are forced to watch. The Brotherhood know that to take over the world by open force eventually they must have a mind controlled army which would not be affected by what they do to their fellow countrymen and even their own families. Why in wars like Bosnia and in mass murders like those in Algeria do people report how sons have slaughtered their own families along with the rest of a village or community? Because they are mind controlled to do it, that's why. It is the same with the 'suicide bombers' and other 'kamikaze' operations. In the same way it is the mind controlled Elite, and their lower level 'gofers', who are in the positions of political, business, military, administrative, media, and religious power in the world. To an untrained eye, such programming is undetectable, but these people are following a programmed Agenda. At a deep level, they are automatons controlled by reptilians.

When the slaves outlive their usefulness or their programming begins to break down, they are murdered. The so-called Presidential Models like Cathy O'Brien are rarely allowed to live beyond their 30th year and when that came for Cathy in 1987/88, she was told it was her last year of life. Fortunately as her book explains, she and the then eight year old Kelly would be rescued from death by a businessman called Mark Phillips. He says he had considerable knowledge of advanced mind control techniques from his time working for the Ampex Corporation and the US Department of Defense as a civilian subcontractor. This gave him contact with the leading research scientists in this field and he had access to knowledge that is denied to the mainstream psychiatric profession, he writes in *Trance Formation Of America*. Psychiatrists, like doctors and scientists, are also mind-manipulated by the suppression of information which gives them a distorted picture of what is possible. Mark Phillips says he was apparently regarded as 'safe' because of his background and security clearance and he was approached by a man called Alex Houston for support with a business deal. Houston was now the 'handler' of Cathy and Kelly and he married Cathy at the instruction of her controller, Senator Robert C. Byrd, their book says.[48]

Alex Houston, a rapist, paedophile, and drug runner, according to Cathy, was an entertainer, a ventriloquist and stage hypnotist, who, she says, also had his mind and mouth worked by someone else – the US government's mind control network. She says it was his job to maintain her and Kelly in their programmed mode by following the instructions he was given, which included food and water deprivation and constant trauma. Houston used his travel to venues as a cover to transport Cathy and Kelly to their 'assignments' and Cathy says this introduced her to the truth about the United States country music industry and, indeed, the entertainment industry in general. Country music, she discovered, was used by the Brotherhood's US agencies to distribute massive amounts of drugs into American society and as a cover for its mind control projects. It was these agencies, she says, which paid for the promotion and hype that turned a singer called Boxcar Willie into a country music star. Some of this promotion, Cathy says, took the form of high-tech television commercials designed to have a hypnotic effect on the viewer. He became the leader, she writes, of the country music segment of the 'Freedom train' – the internationally recognised code name for the slave operations of Project Monarch. The name Boxcar Willie was not selected at random, it would seem. It makes a statement about the man and his role. Cathy names Boxcar Willie as a paedophile rapist of mind controlled women and children, including Kelly, who, she says, he raped regularly in three different mental institutions.[49] He is also heavily involved in the cocaine operations controlled by the government agencies, she says, and he was the man Bill Clinton's friend, Bill Hall, began to work with after Clinton persuaded him to become involved.[50] It was Boxcar Willie who inspired the moving of the country music 'capital' to Branson, Missouri, to be close to the CIA mind control and drug operation based at Lampe, Missouri, according to Cathy in her book.[51]

Many people in the entertainment industry are either connected with the conspiracy or mind controlled by it, she says. One of the latter was Marilyn Monroe, a lover of President John F. Kennedy. Both were to be murdered. The singer, Madonna, is a mind controlled slave according to Springmeier and Wheeler in their book on this subject. Springmeier says he was given a catalogue of the Vidimax occult porn video club based in New Jersey which included a video involving Madonna. It sells videos of people being murdered (snuff videos), cannibalism and sacrifices.[52] Springmeier and Wheeler say Madonna was a mind controlled slave given the name, Louise Chiccone, living in New York East Village when a film was made of her being raped and the rapist being taken away and sacrificed. Vidimax sell this video apparently for $19 to their members.[53] If, as they say, Madonna is a multiple, she will most likely have no recollection of this. Elvis Presley, a member of the Theosophical Society, has been named as a multiple slave by survivors and Cisco Wheeler, herself a recovering slave, says that her experiences led her to believe this about Elvis. His handler was his manager, 'Colonel' Tom Parker, she says.[54] When Elvis died (if he did), the Sun International Corporation released a Presley album called *Orion* with a winged sun-disc on the cover. This is an ancient Egyptian and Sumerian symbol used by the Order of the Oriental Temple and other Brotherhood groups. Barbara Streisand is a mind controlled asset of the Brotherhood, as revealed in detail by the recovered slave, Brice Taylor, in her book, *Thanks For The Memories*. Another mind controlled singer, according to Cathy, is Lorretta Lynn, a slave of the CIA. Her mental and emotional problems are caused by this, Cathy says. Lorretta's road manager Ken Riley is a paedophile and best friend to Cathy's handler, Alex Houston. Both were connected with US congressman, Gary Ackerman, the 'Democrat' from New York, who, Cathy reports, ran an elaborate drug operation through Long Island docks.[55] A mind controlled woman named by Mark Phillips is Seidina 'Dina' Reed, the daughter of actor-singer, Jerry Reed. Seidina had been used many times with Cathy in pornographic films, he says, under the control of her husband, the sadist, David Rorick, (also known as Dave Rowe). Rorick was trained in mind control by Alex Houston and Seidina's famous father Jerry Reed knew all about it, according to Mark Phillips. Seidina was a favourite sex slave of Prince Bandar bin Sultan, the Saudi Arabian ambassador to the US.[56] The singer and actor Kris Kristopherson, a drug-addicted alcoholic born into a CIA family, according to Phillips, is also involved as a seriously imbalanced controller and mind manipulator of slaves, Cathy recounts in her book and public statements.[57] She writes that she was tortured by him and Michael Aquino, using high voltage electric shocks.[58] Kristopherson, a Jesuit, is an associate of Senator Robert C. Byrd, Cathy's controller, she says. In that position, Byrd was, in mind control parlance, said to be 'married' to Cathy even though she was officially married to Alex Houston. Cathy says of Kristopherson in her book:

> "...Kristopherson nearly strangled me to death with his penis which further sexually aroused him, late in the Summer of 1987 during another incident related to Byrd."[59]

A world famous psychopath and drug runner for the government, Cathy writes, is the rock and roll legend, Jerry Lee Lewis, a friend of Elvis Presley. Cathy says she was threatened on many occasions with the words: "We'll sell you to Jerry Lee". Frank Sinatra and JFK's brother, Ted Kennedy, are reported by recovering slaves to have been particularly brutal, also. I spoke at a conference on mind control in the United States and met Brice Taylor who, like Cathy O'Brien, also became a Presidential Model. Her handler from the time she was a little girl in southern California was the comedian, Bob Hope, a member of Bohemian Grove. She had also worked extensively with Henry Kissinger, a highly skilled programmer, and Nelson Rockefeller, the four times Governor of New York. Rockefeller became vice-president of the United States when the paedophile, Gerald Ford, replaced Richard Nixon after Watergate. Brice claimed to have been forced to have sex with John F. Kennedy when she was only 12, although she said: "I was made up to look 16". Bob Hope is also named by Springmeier and Wheeler in their book as a slave handler and as a British Intelligence operative during the Second World War as he toured the world hosting concerts for the troops.[60] Hope and media mogul, Rupert Murdoch, were both awarded 'knighthoods' by the Roman Catholic Church in Los Angeles, California. They became Knights of the Order of St Gregory and while I was writing this book Hope was given an honorary knighthood by the Queen to elevate him to the same rank as Bush, Kissinger, and the other chosen few the Windsor's reward for services to the cause. Bob 'isn't he a hoot' Hope has been used to draw many top names in Hollywood into the net and one of his most famous films, *The Road To Mandalay*, was appropriately named because the most élite group at the Bohemian Grove is known as the Mandalay Camp. Hollywood and the entertainment industry is rife with both slaves and handlers.

Another famous figure named by Springmeier and Wheeler as a Satanist is the world's best known 'Christian' preacher, Billy Graham.[61] Springmeier and Wheeler have assembled a list of people who have seen Graham 'in action'. They also say he uses Project Monarch slaves for sex and he launders drug money through his evangelical operation. Graham is a Brotherhood stooge who carries messages between world leaders.[62] The witnesses say that Graham is a multiple who switches personalities, and the 'person' people see at the pulpit is only one compartment. There are others which are very different. 'Christianity' is a cover used by countless Satanists and programmers and Dr Loreda Fox says in her book, *The Spiritual And Clinical Dimensions of Multiple Personality Disorder*, that "Most survivors whom I have worked with had Satanist parents who were high in positions in churches; many were pastors".[63] Christianity was the creation of the Brotherhood and is still controlled by it. Billy Graham, a 33rd degree Freemason, is a close friend of George Bush and Henry Kissinger. He and Bush famously 'prayed' together after Bush had given the go ahead to kill countless men, women and children in the Gulf War. Another friend of Graham, Allan Dulles, was the Satanist Director of the CIA, who helped to fund Hitler. Dulles was one of the main architects after the war of MKUltra and Project Monarch. Billy Graham's first three Christian crusades were funded by William Randolph Hearst, the American newspaper tycoon and high degree Brotherhood initiate.[64] Other world tours have been funded by bloodline families like the Rockefellers, Whitneys, and Vanderbilts. The main people in the

Billy Graham Crusades and his Evangelical Association are Freemasons and they have included William M. Watson, President of the Occidental Petroleum Corporation of the Brotherhood frontman, Armand Hammer (Arm and Hammer). The Billy Graham television shows put messages on the screen carrying Monarch activation codes, Springmeier and Wheeler say.[65] When Billy Graham's family first went to the United States they were known as the Frank family and were related to Jakob Frank the leader of a branch of Satanism called Sabbatuanism, later, due to his leadership, Frankism.[66] The evidence that Springmeier and Wheeler present to support these claims about Graham is simply enormous and covers some 24 pages. A Presidential Model told me that Pope John Paul II is a programmed multiple and that certainly fits the picture.

Cathy O'Brien says that she and her daughter, Kelly, escaped from Project Monarch when Mark Phillips came on the scene. He says he worked with Alex Houston on a big business deal involving Hong Kong and China, but then he was told by a representative of the Chinese Ministry of Defence about Houston's background and his involvement with the CIA, drugs, money laundering, child prostitution, and slavery. Phillip's informant, who, he says, produced documentary proof, said that Houston was a "very bad man" and that his crimes were "of the White House". Mark Phillips writes in *Trance Formation Of America*:

> "My first response to this 'officer' was that Houston was too stupid and crooked to be connected with US 'Intelligence'. This comment was quickly countered with a gut-wrenching photograph of Houston. He was smiling a demonic grin while apparently having anal sex with a small, very young, frightened black boy. Later he was identified to me as Haitian."[67]

Phillips says he made contact with an old friend, now dead, who had been an Air Force general in the Intelligence Division and maintained close connections with the upper levels of US and foreign intelligence. He says the general told him about the CIA slave trade world-wide and that Cathy and Kelly had been subjected to trauma-based mind control. Mark Phillips recalls:

> "I was growing numb. The first words out of my dry mouth were: 'How would you spring these people out of it?'
>
> "He smiled and said: 'I wouldn't! What are you going to do with them if you get them out?' Before I could answer, he interrupted and said: 'Look. You're still the same, but nothing else is with Uncle (*the USA*). Now most of the CIA, FBI, and the Mob (*Mafia*) are the same and they're making moves on the military.'"[68]

Phillips says he was insistent that he wanted to attempt a rescue and he writes that his friend gave him the mind control codes (based on Christianity and God) that would activate Cathy to go with him. The full and detailed story is told in their book. Phillips says he took them to Alaska while leaving messages for the authorities that he had no intention of exposing the truth. He said he told them he would "…take them to Alaska and play like a voiceless chameleon". This he hoped would spare their lives at this stage, he says. Phillips told me that they have also been helped by many good people in Intelligence who want to root out this sickness. There is an internal 'war' unfolding within the Intelligence community, it would appear. In Alaska, Mark Phillips says he used his knowledge of mind control, with covert support from his contacts, to deprogram Cathy's compartmentalised mind. This immense task absorbed almost every spare waking moment month after month after month, he says. Cathy began to remember what had happened, she says, and what a story she now had to tell. Kelly's deprogramming proved even more difficult and she suffered from severe asthma caused by the constant trauma she has suffered. Attempts were made by the CIA mind controller, Dr Louis Jolyon West, and his associates, to take Kelly from Cathy and Mark. Eventually the authorities used the 'law' to ensure they had control of her once again. Kelly became a political prisoner under the custody of the State of Tennessee. This is a story constantly repeated. Brice Taylor and Arizona Wilder lost their children when they broke away. Brice's daughter is also called Kelly, a common illuminati name for such children. Her daughter was also sexually abused by Bush. The media and public were banned from court cases involving Kelly O'Brien and she was denied the right to an independent attorney, Cathy says. The court also banned the words 'president', 'politics', 'New World Order', 'mind control' and 'George Bush'.[69] All this was 'justified' by the interests of 'national security'. These restrictions were significantly eased after the publication of their book. The authorities refuse to deprogram Kelly from her Project Monarch-MKUltra mind control by invoking the National Security Act (amended by Reagan in 1984) which allows them the excuse of 'national security' whenever they want to put the lid on something. Whenever you see governments using the guise of 'national security' to deny justice and information, what they really mean is the security of their own criminal behaviour. Cathy and Mark say they have had their life threatened many times, but they have sent their information, with documented and sometimes audio tape support, to a catalogue of US politicians, government agencies, and pressure groups, including presidential candidate and Brotherhood yes man, Bob Dole. The silence has been deafening.

Cathy says she witnessed many conversations about the New World Order which support the themes that I and scores of others have written about, including the plans for a military coup of the United States. As Cathy's experiences confirm, the attempt to complete the takeover of the world is not a theory, it is REAL. It's happening now. Cathy says that she heard both Reagan and Bush insist that the only way to "world peace" is the "mind control of the masses". She reports that she was able to observe the planning of the New World Order project, Education 2000, while under the control of another of her and Kelly's programmers and sexual abusers, the reptilian Bill Bennett, a Jesuit-trained mind controller, who became US Education Secretary under Reagan-Bush.[70] She was then placed under the control of Bill Bennett's associate Lama Alexander, the former governor of Tennessee, with whom Cathy says she had been forced to take part in a Satanic ritual in an affluent area of Nashville.[71] Bill Bennett's brother, Bob, who is also alleged to have raped Kelly at the Bohemian Grove in 1986, later became legal counsel to Bill Clinton.[72] Another of Bill Bennett's roles was to head a 'war on drugs' for George Bush! Well at least Bennett could not be accused of a lack of experience in the subject. The Bennetts' were the ones who took her through one of her reptilian experiences I described earlier in the book. Cathy says she was used to compromise and provide 'favours' for key politicians to ensure support for Education 2000. She learned that this project, also known as America 2000 and Global 2000, is designed to increase children's 'learning' capacity while destroying their ability to critically think for themselves.[73] Our children are being mind controlled every day at school and most of the teachers don't even know they are doing it, because they have been conditioned by the same system. A friend who works in education research in the United Kingdom has had access to suppressed surveys which show that children are asking fewer and fewer questions about the 'facts' they are told in school – particularly after they move to the senior schools.

Cathy says she witnessed how the United Nations is just a vehicle for the manipulators. George Bush referred to the New World Order as his 'neighbourhood' and talked of how he simply told many other world leaders, like King Fahd of Saudi Arabia, what to do and say. No doubt the same applies to Saddam Hussein with whom Bush shared oil 'kick backs' totalling hundreds of millions of dollars (see *...And The Truth Shall Set You Free*). The US Secretary of State (formerly UN ambassador), Madeleine Albright, is a Brotherhood initiate. I call her the High Priestess of US politics. George Bush once described her in Cathy's presence as... "the reverend mother of all sisters (slaves)".[74] Albright knows about the US government mind controlled slaves and supports that policy. Yet there she was in front of the television cameras at the United Nations and as Secretary of State, lecturing other countries on human rights. Cathy recalls that Brian Mulroney, the Canadian Prime Minister and child rapist, talked about the plan for the New World Order while with Cathy and Reagan at the same White House cocktail party at which she met Albright. Cathy says she was subsequently taken to a White House bedroom with other slaves, including one controlled by the US Senator, Arlen Spector. Mulroney then arrived to rape them after activating their sex slave programming.[75] Cathy says she noticed that one of the slaves had a red rose tattooed on her left wrist and other people she met over the years, including Mulroney, wore the symbol of the red rose which indicates membership of the Order of the Rose, an Elite offshoot of the Rosicrucians. Other people connected to the Order of the Rose include Clinton, Bush, Byrd, Bennett and Trudeau. How fascinating, then, that the United Kingdom Labour Party should change its party symbol in the 1980s to a... red rose.

The handlers of slaves like Cathy carry with them a black or grey three-ring notebook – often these days a laptop computer – which lists the access keys and triggers.[76] Others memorise them. The data contains details of the methods of torture, the dates it happened, and the most important parts of the code are said to be written in 'Enochian' Hebrew (the 'magical' language of the Egyptian mystery schools), and Druidic symbols.[77] The scale of what is going on simply defies the imagination. I was told by a contact about thousands of caged children kept at the China Lake Naval Weapons Center in the California desert at Ridgecrest. This is in the same region as the mass grave for ritually murdered children at Lancaster, California, I mentioned earlier. Vast areas of land in this region between Los Angeles, the infamous San Bernandino Valley and Las Vegas, Nevada, are occupied by the United States Forces. It is also one of the greatest areas of Satanism on the planet. It includes the Edward's Airforce base, China Lake, and the town of Bakersfield. Springmeier and Wheeler write that other programming sites close to China Lake are Papa Ludo's Store and Tavern which has a secret underground programming centre, and Scotty's Castle in the appropriately named Death Valley.[78] The 'local' for the CIA personnel operating at China Lake is the Hideaway Tavern. Northwest of the airfield at China Lake the authorities have built a hexagram (Star of David – Seal of Solomon) on the ground, each section of which is a quarter of a mile long.[79] These lands run into the deserts of Nevada which are full of Brotherhood operations in and around their wholly-owned city of Las Vegas. I have driven through all these areas and it is one of blackest places you will ever experience.

Interestingly, the Springmeier-Wheeler research also documents the involvement of the China Lake Naval Weapons Center which I had also heard from other sources. They say that 'batches' of babies numbering one, two and three thousand, were kept at China Lake in cages piled to the ceiling of large hangers.[80] The cages, known as 'Woodpecker Grids' were electrified and the babies were tortured with powerful electric shocks.[81] A male survivor of Project Monarch tells of seeing the rows and rows of cages at China Lake and one of the programmers, he said, was dressed like a catholic priest.[82] He described how the electric current running through the cages made a humming sound and he said that children were sacrificed by people in black hooded robes in front of the children in the cages. This took place on a marble slab which served as an altar.[83] Charles Manson was a slave programmed at China Lake and his cult was based only 45 minutes drive away at the Myers and Barker ranches.[84] Josef Mengele (Dr Green or Greenbaum) and Ewen Cameron (Dr White) both worked at China Lake after the war. It was then called the Naval Ordinance Test Station or NOTS.

Survivors of China Lake recall flashing lights. The flashing creates disassociation, particularly with those who are programmed, and this is why the phenomenon of flashing lights was introduced into our culture. Discos and pop concerts are an obvious example. The operation at China Lake is closely connected with the California Institute of Technology at Pasedena.[85] Children are transported to China Lake by train, car and air. One of the main delivery routes into China Lake is by plane from the Santa Rosa airstrip near Bohemian Grove. The airstrip was built during World War Two as a training base. FEMA, the Federal Emergency Management Agency, has a radio station there.[86] FEMA is officially the government agency which responds to disasters like hurricanes and tornadoes. But in truth it is a major arm of the Brotherhood and it is building concentration camps in the

United States capable of holding thousands of people. This is no theory, video footage exists of some of these places. They have railway lines running into them in classic Nazi fashion. The tops of the barbed wire fences, which were formerly designed to keep people out, have now been changed to keep people in. The Santa Rosa strip is supposed to be closed, yet planes are leaving there every night and they do not put their lights on until they are hundreds of feet in the air.[87] They land at China Lake early in the morning. If you think the numbers of children claimed to be involved are an exaggeration, the truth is that this is only a fraction of the children in mind control projects and Satanic abuse rings in every country in the world. The children come through the breeding programmes, through adoption agencies (particularly, it seems, Catholic ones), some from kidnapping in the Third World, and from parents who sell their own children. They also come through the network of Social Services agencies. There are organisations whose job it is to find children of the right genetic background for these projects. The best known was the CIA/FBI group called the Finders and programmed children are also trained to procure other children. One case which came to light in February 1992 involved an American lawyer called Patrick Gagel, who exported three thousand children from the United States to Peru for 'adoption' and they were never seen or heard of again.[88] Gagel was arrested by Peruvian police, but then released after pressure from 'on high'.[89] This is another common theme in which the perpetrators of such abominations can operate outside the law. Don Ecker, the state director in Idaho for the UFO investigation network known as MUFON, wrote the following in the July-August 1989 edition of *UFO* magazine:

> "According to a recent report just received from Westchester County, New York, researchers have discovered that in a small area of the county, which has been the site of numerous UFO overflights and reported human abductions, over 3,000 missing children reports have surfaced. After extensive investigation by local police departments, these children have not yet been found at centers for young runaways or in red light districts. Researchers and law enforcement officials are baffled." [90]

The mind controlled Elite

The Brotherhood scientists realised that the ability to disassociate quickly is passed on from generation to generation through genetics. This is why the CIA targeted Cathy O'Brien. She was the daughter of parents who had themselves been sexually abused as children and therefore the parents ability to disassociate to cope with their childhood trauma would have been passed on to their children. This makes the children much more open to disassociation via trauma-based mind control. There is no greater example of this than the bloodline families themselves. They put their children through staggering traumas and abuse and this multigenerational genetic 'baton' has made these families particularly open to disassociation by mind control. They apparently put their children through a series of tests around the age of 18 months to determine which of them are most open to disassociation. They are then programmed through their childhood to think the way the Brotherhood wants them to think so they will take the Agenda forward into the next generation. It is the mind controlled manipulating the mind controlled. According to the experiences of Cisco Wheeler and many of the other victims and therapists involved in this subject, the child of the Elite families are conceived according to ancient rituals and their programming is agreed and set out largely before they are even born. One of these pre-birth rituals is called the Moon Child ceremony. Mothers who give birth to a so-called 'dark child' are called a 'Rosemary' – the rose of Mary. Roman Polanski, the husband of Sharon Tate, the actress murdered by Charles Manson's cult, made a film called *Rosemary's Baby*. Polanski's film was about a woman impregnated by a demon summoned by a Satanic cult. Over the centuries it became understood that if you torture a child in the womb the baby would disassociate or 'split' and so mothers are traumatised during pregnancy to traumatise the child. Needles are inserted into the womb to stab the baby. Many are induced prematurely because of the effect that has on them and it is also part of the selection process.

A child who shows the instinct and spirit for survival in a premature birth will normally enlist that same spirit during the trauma-programming which will often take them to near death. After birth, a programmer is assigned to them. This is normally a woman, although it can be male. The Brotherhood children are often assigned a programmer known in the hierarchy as a Grande Dame.[91] Children are 'bonded' to the programmers and taught to become dependent upon them. The idea is to manipulate the children to worship the programmer and see them as a god. The child is only allowed to develop a close relationship with the programmer and that relationship is based on adoration, dependency and obedience. They are taught total obedience to the programmer and later to the Agenda and the Brotherhood hierarchy. Once the process of crying has developed their lungs, they are taught not to cry through a series of punishments and rewards under the system known as behaviour modification. Already they are becoming robots. One foundation technique is to give them intense love and affection for the first 18 months of their lives and then suddenly withdraw it and treat them with extreme cruelty. This is a technique known as 'love bombing' and when the switch is made from love to cruelty the trauma this creates in the child is enormous. They will also be allowed to bond with a pet and then the pet is killed. The programmer the child loved so much is now the person the child fears with equal intensity. Springmeier and Cisco Wheeler, herself a victim of government programming, describe what follows:

"Everything imaginable can be used to overwhelm the caged little child's senses and create dissociation. Rotten foul odours of the child's excrement, of ammonia, and rotten food while it huddles in its cage will overwhelm the child's sense of smell. Being fed blood overwhelms the sense of taste. The chanting of the programmers dressed in Satanic garb, banging noises, rock music, and the electric hum, and ultrasonic stimulation overwhelms the child's sense of hearing. The child's natural developing sense of shapes is taken advantage of by spinning the child and making it feel like it is going to fall. The child will also be deprived of sleep and drugged…

"...The fourth stage is to strip the child of everything nice and lovely in the world. The child is caged and tormented by electric shock. The child's senses will be overloaded and they will become numb. Eyewitnesses have described these hundreds of numbered children as 'zombies'... In the fourth step, the child is starved, cold, and naked. When they finally see their beloved master or beloved adult caretaker appear after suffering from 42 to 72 hours, they are excited and they dissociate the pain of the previous hours of deprivation. Help appears to be on the scene. At that point the programmer/ beloved adult shows her/his most vicious side, and the child in order to deal with how this loving caretaker has not only rejected them, but is now hurting them, dissociates along the same lines of dissociation created by the trauma of the premature birth." [92]

How can the Brotherhood initiates be so inhuman? Because they are reptilians, or rather that group of reptilians on the lower fourth dimension and they do not have the emotions that we feel. This treatment is, in part, to ensure that any consciousness which incarnates into these bloodlines with the aim of removing their power, will find it almost impossible to manifest its true self. Those chosen for programming are usually very intelligent because people with low intelligence and creativity have been found to be almost impossible to program to the level required. Springmeier and Wheeler say that at the age of three the Elite Brotherhood children selected for later advancement into the hierarchy are taken before the Grand Druid Council and formal approval is given at a presentation by the Queen Mother of the Council. Interesting how George Bush told Cathy O'Brien that Madeleine Albright, the US Ambassador to the United Nations and Secretary of State, was the 'Reverend Mother of all slaves'. I stress again that this Grand Druid Council has nothing whatsoever to do with the many thousands of people who call themselves Druids today and they are not connected with these events in any way. We need to understand that the use of a name by the Brotherhood does not mean that everyone using that name is involved. Most of the Druids I have met in Britain are lovely people with love in their hearts and I have no desire to cast condemnation on them. Quite the opposite.

The most preferred candidates for programming are fittingly, like Cathy O'Brien, blond-haired and blue-eyed 'Caucasians' who are not physically defective in any way. The Brotherhood bloodlines are not only those which carry the names of the classic bloodline families. The Brotherhood also use 'breeders', women who give birth to their unofficial children. They use 'brooder' families where women bear Brotherhood children, or rear children from the time they are babies, who are connected to classic bloodline families, although there appears to be no relationship. Children are swapped, sent to foster parents (like Sir Francis Bacon), or mothers suddenly 'give birth' when no-one even knew they were pregnant, which, of course, they weren't. This allows Brotherhood bloodline members to be placed in the positions of power in politics, banking, business, the media and the military, without there being an outcry from the public that the same families are in all the positions of control.

Those who are not put through the birth trauma and programmed from the womb have to begin their 'preparation' before the age of six because this type of programming is more difficult after that. Some are still brought into the programme after that age, but this is rare. These children are put through even more gruesome torture to break down their developing minds. The programmers find out what phobias and fears the children have and use those to terrify them. This includes putting children in dark confined places with spiders and snakes. The children are told that if they 'play dead' the snakes and spiders won't bite them, so encouraging them to dissociate. Putting them in coffins emphasises that. They are forced to kill and eat other children and they are immersed in excrement, urine, and blood. Most of the slave children will have experienced all these things and more by the age of four or five.[93] One common sign of programming or childhood sexual abuse are eating disorders like bulimia. That is not to say that all bulimia is caused by that, of course not, but it is a regular occurrence in ritually abused and mind controlled people, as is attempted suicide and self mutilation. Finding it difficult to hold a stable relationship is another and so is a squint in the left eye. Cathy O'Brien says she was tortured by having a needle pushed into her eye. This eye trauma, and sometimes the insertion of a microchip behind the left eye, is quite common. Baron Guy de Rothschild has a drooping left eye. He is a major slave handler and programmer, but he would have been put through childhood trauma as part of his preparation for his role in the Brotherhood. The programmers create monsters and then those monsters create the next generation of monsters while the whole thing is controlled by the reptilians. The idea is to break the children's spirit so they will do exactly as they are told without question. That is precisely the aim and the methods of the British public school system and its like around the world, a system which, like the deeper mind-programming projects, are turning out the leaders and administrators who run the world to the Brotherhood reptilian Agenda.

The false memory scam

When Cathy O'Brien and thousands around the world began to recover their memories of abuse, the authorities retaliated with an organisation called the False Memory Syndrome Foundation (FMSF) which has sought to discredit their stories. It began in the United States in 1992, fronted by Pamela Freyd and her husband, Peter, a mathematician at the University of Pennsylvania, who have both been accused by their daughter, Jennifer, of abusing her as a child. Branches of the False Memory Syndrome Foundation have appeared in other countries, including the UK, and, as a result, many journalists have written deeply destructive articles dismissing the memories of mind control and ritual abuse victims as illusions. The FMSF claim that the victims of abuse are suffering from false memories and are not remembering what really happened. Of course this can happen, but the False Memory Syndrome Foundation is not satisfied with 'some'. It wants all of them to be dismissed in this way, which is utter nonsense. It has hounded responsible therapists, accusing them of putting the memories into their clients minds. Why the therapists would want to do that has not been explained, nor how those people who have never forgotten their childhood sexual and Satanic abuse could be suffering from a false memory. A FMSF 'scientific' adviser, Doctor Harold Merskey, testified in court that a woman claiming that her doctor sexually abused her as a child might be suffering from false memory syndrome, when the doctor had already been struck off for previous paedophile activities he had admitted. Merskey had not even examined the woman and said his conclusion came from observing her in the court!

One of the leaders of the FMSF, Doctor Ralph Underwager, was forced out when it was revealed publicly that he and his wife, Hollida Wakefield, had given an interview to a Dutch paedophile magazine called *Paedika* in 1993, in which he said that sex with children was "An acceptable expression of God's will for love". Three members of the Advisory Board of the False Memory Syndrome Foundation in the United States have been Doctor Martin Orne, a notorious CIA mind controller at the University of Pennsylvania; Doctor Louis Jolyon 'Jolly' West at the University of California, another infamous CIA mind controller (featured, like Orne, in ...*And The Truth Shall Set You Free*); and James Randi, a magician known as The Amazing Randi. Amazing indeed to hear a tape of him, as I have, propositioning teenage boys for sex and boasting about his 'nine inch willy'. Or maybe that tape and the transcript in my file is a false memory. Randi has also been used to discredit psychic powers and phenomena through a ludicrous organisation called the Committee for the Investigation of Claims of the Paranormal or CSICOP. This is headed by Paul Kurtz, the chairman of Prometheus Books, which publishes the works of James Randi and books about children's sexual encounters with adults. Kurtz is Professor emeritus of Philosophy at New York State University in Buffalo. Another member of CSICOP, Vern Bullough, the Professor at the Faculty of Natural and Social Science at the University of New York, is the 'Human Sexuality' Editor at Prometheus Books. He is also a board member of *Paedika*, the Dutch paedophile magazine which interviewed Ralph Underwager of the False Memory Syndrome Foundation. A number of people are board members of both FMSF and CSICOP. What a web we weave. Discrediting psychic phenomena, life after death, or the memories of childhood ritual abuse, its all the same to these guys. And what do both organisations have in common? They serve the Brotherhood Agenda by suppressing the exposure of the mind control and ritual abuse networks and the knowledge of the true nature of life. I am also staggered sometimes by the 'research' of some 'conspiracy writers' who dismiss the existence of Project Monarch and the highly detailed and documented work of people like Springmeier and Wheeler. If you read such authors in the light of the evidence presented here and elsewhere, one wonders if these 'conspiracy writers' are merely poor reseachers or part of the agenda to lead people away from the truth. One writer comes to mind immediately who turns out 'conspiracy' books full of old information with no original research and yet dismisses the detailed documentation and personal experience of Springmeier and Wheeler.

How easy it has been to keep people in ignorance by destroying the true records of the reptilian involvement in human history and by selling a version of life that is a perversion of the truth. It means that people are so divorced from reality that even when they are given the true, or truer, picture of the world, most people either laugh at the reptilian information or go into a state of complete denial over Satanism and mind control. "They wouldn't do that", I hear people say. Oh yes they would, and they do, and they are doing it to someone now. The reptilians can continue with the global dictatorship in all its grotesque forms because most people aren't bothered what is going on in the world and who is controlling their lives and those of their children. They are so pressured by debt and fear that they keep their heads down and their eyes closed; or they are more concerned at the price of beer, the latest 'scandal' on the television soaps, or how their soccer team is doing. Michael Aquino, the Satanist at the US government's Psychological Warfare Department, once told Cathy O'Brien: "95 per cent want to be led by the other five per cent and the 95 per cent do not want to know what is really going on in government". How sad that this is actually true. Anyone who still believes that the outcome of soccer matches or the price of beer is really important in the wider picture of life on this planet, might benefit from reading the following. It is an account in Cathy's own words of what happened to her child, Kelly, again and again:

> "Kelly became violently physically ill after her induction into George Bush's 'neighbourhood' and from every sexual encounter she had with him thereafter. She ran 104–6 degree temperatures, vomited and endured immobilising headaches for an average of three days (*as is consistent with high voltage trauma*). These were the only tell-tale evidences aside from the scaring burns left on her skin. Houston forbade me to call a doctor, and Kelly forbade me to comfort her, pitifully complaining that her head 'hurt too bad even to move'. And she did not move for hours on end. Kelly often complained of severe kidney pain and her rectum usually bled for a day or two after Bush sexually abused her. My own mind control victimisation rendered me unable to help or protect her. Seeing my child in such horrible condition drove my own wedge of insanity in deeper, perpetuating my total inability to affect her needs until our rescue by Mark Phillips in 1988.

> "Kelly's bleeding rectum was… one of (*the*)… physical indicators of George Bush's paedophile perversions. I have overheard him speak blatantly of his sexual abuse of her on many occasions. He used this and threats to her life to 'pull my strings' and control me. The psychological ramifications of being raped by a paedophile president are mind shattering enough, but reportedly Bush further reinforced his traumas to Kelly's mind with sophisticated NASA electronic and drug mind control devices. Bush also instilled the 'who ya gonna call?' and 'I'll be watching you' binds on Kelly, further reinforcing her sense of helplessness. The systematic tortures and traumas I endured as a child now seem trite in comparison to the brutal physical and psychological devastation that George Bush inflicted on my daughter."[94]

Come on gang, I know this chapter must have been terribly hard to read, but it's time to wake up. This has *GOT* to stop.

■ SOURCES

1   *The Illuminati Formula*, p 1.

2   Ibid, pp 371–372.

3   Ibid, p 355.

4   Ibid, p 2.

5   Ibid.

6   Ibid, p 11.

7   Ibid, p 355.

8   Ibid, p 56.

9   Ibid, p 1.

10 Cathy O'Brien and Mark Phillips, *Trance Formation Of America* (Reality Marketing, Las Vegas, USA, 1995). It is also available from Bridge of Love Publications in the UK and Europe. See back of this book.

11 Ibid, p 83.

12 *The Illuminati Formula*, p 40.

13 Ibid, p 102.

14 *Trance Formation Of America*, p 213.

15 *Contact* newspaper, the Phoenix Project, February 7th 1995, p 17.

16 Ibid, p 18.

17 *Trance Formation Of America*, p 115.

18 *The Illuminati Formula*, p 99.

19 Ibid, p 381.

20 *Trance Formation Of America,* p 100.

21 Ibid, p 194.

22 Ibid, p 101.

23 Ibid.

24 *Contact* newspaper, March 7th 1995, p 33.

25 *Trance Formation Of America*, p 101.

26 Ibid, p 170.

27 *The Women's Encyclopaedia Of Myths And Secrets*, pp 754, 755.

28 *The Illuminati Formula*, p 369.

29 Ibid.

30 John W. DeCamp, *The Franklin Cover Up: Child Abuse, Satanism And Murder In Nebraska* (AWT Inc., Lincoln, Nebraska, 1992).

31 *Trance Formation Of America*, p 127.

32 Ibid, p 128.

33 Ibid, p 111.

34 Ibid, p 162.

35 *Contact* newspaper, September 12th 1995, p 15.

36 Ibid.

37 *The Illuminati Formula*, p 378.

38 Ibid.

39 *Trance Formation Of America*, p 183.

40 Ibid, p 178.

41 *Trance Formation Of America*, p 150.

42 Ibid, p 155.

43 *Contact* newspaper, September 12th 1995.

44 *Trance Formation Of America*, p 155.

45 *The Illuminati Formula*, pp 375, 348.

46 *Contact* newspaper, September 12th 1995, p 12.

47 Ibid, p 13.

48 *Trance Formation Of America*, p 111.

49 Ibid, p 156.

50 Ibid.

51 *Contact* newspaper, March 7th 1995, pp 33–34.

52 *The Illuminati Formula*, p 352.

53 Ibid.

54 Ibid, p 355.

55 *Trance Formation Of America*, p 124.

56 Ibid, p 31.

57 Ibid, p 117.

58 Ibid, p 118.

59 Ibid, p 120.

60 *The Illuminati Formula*, p 353.

61 Ibid, pp 126–150

62 Ibid, pp 128, 132.

63 Dr Loreda Fox, *The Spiritual And Clinical Dimensions Of Multiple Personality Disorder* (Salida, Colorado), p 196.

64 *The Illuminati Formula*, p 133.

65 Ibid, p 138.

66 Ibid, p 143.

67 *Trance Formation Of America*, p 12.

68 Ibid, pp 13–14.

69 Ibid, p 223.

70   Ibid, p 179.

71   Ibid, p 172.

72   Ibid.

73   Ibid, p 175.

74   Ibid, p 176.

75   Ibid, p 177.

76   Ibid, p 4.

77   Ibid.

78   *The Illuminati Formula*, p 34.

79   Ibid.

80   Ibid, p 32.

81   Ibid.

82   Ibid, p 34.

83   Ibid.

84   Ibid.

85   Ibid, p 33.

86   Ibid.

87   Ibid.

88   Ibid.

89   Ibid.

90   *Extraterrestrial Friends And Foes*, p 74.

91   *The Illuminati Formula*, p 73.

92   Ibid, p 23.

93   Ibid, p 25.

94   *Trance Formation Of America*, p 158.

CHAPTER SEVENTEEN

The secret language

T he initiates of the secret society network have always had a code of
communication through certain phrases, words, funny handshakes and
symbols. There are also a series of Brotherhood 'signatures' which form their secret
language and these are all around us every day. They are obsessed with their rituals
and symbols because of their reptilian brain and I cannot overstress this point. It is a
means through which they can be tracked and read.

Their most used symbols are the lighted torch, the symbol of knowledge and
the Sun. When an initiate reaches a certain level in the pyramid they are said to be
'illuminated', more symbolism of the lighted torch. One of the recurring stories in
the ancient world is of a hero figure who takes fire (knowledge) from the 'gods'
and gives it to the people – the chosen few people, that is. The Watchers called
Azazel and Shemyaza were among those who gave advanced knowledge to
humans, according to the Book of Enoch. The most famous symbol of these
Watchers is the Greek god, Prometheus, who was said to have emerged from the
Caucasus Mountains. In many ways he was another 'Jesus' figure who died for the
people and it is not inconceivable that the story of Jesus was inspired, in part, by
the legend of Prometheus. At the Rockefeller Center in New York today is a gold
statue of Prometheus (gold, the solar metal of the gods) and he is holding the light,
the fire, in line with the legend (*see picture section*). To the Rockefellers this is not
just a statue, it is a symbol of the whole scam they are involved in. The Statue of
Liberty is another Brotherhood symbol highlighting the lighted torch. The Statue of
Liberty is actually the Statue of Liberties – the liberties perpetrated on the
American people by the Brotherhood. There she stands on her island in New York
Harbour holding her torch of 'freedom' and Americans believe she is the symbol of
their liberty in the Land of the Free. Nothing could be further from the truth. The
Statue of Liberty was given to New York by French Freemasons and her mirror
image stands on an island in the River Seine in Paris (*see picture section for this and
other symbols in this chapter*). These statues of liberty are representations of Queen
Semiramis and Isis et al, with the rays of the Sun around her head. The ancients
symbolised the Sun in this way. And they are not holding the torch of liberty, but
the torch of the illuminated ones, the reptilian-Aryan Elite. The Statue of Liberty
is a Brotherhood symbol which says: "We control this country and we are telling
you so, but you are too stupid to see it!" The torch is the most obvious
Brotherhood signature.

When the Brotherhood assassinated President Kennedy in 1963, they put a lighted torch, the eternal flame which has burned to this day, on his grave in the Arlington Cemetery. After the murder in Dallas the Freemasons erected an obelisk in Dealey Plaza a few yards from the spot where Kennedy was shot. At the top they placed a depiction of the lighted torch. When Diana, Princess of Wales, was murdered in the Pont de L'Alma Tunnel in Paris, the 'shrine' to her, where people left flowers, was a large gold symbol of the very 'eternal' flame held by the two Statues of Liberty, which just happened to be on top of the tunnel where her car crashed into the 13th pillar. Just a coincidence! On the island where she is said to be buried, they have placed yet another depiction of a lighted torch. The Brotherhood are telling us that they killed Kennedy and Diana, but unless you understand their symbolic language, you don't know. The lighted torch in the Olympic Games has the same meaning. I have to laugh when I see the different cities holding their breath to see which of them has been selected to hold the next Olympics. It was all decided years before, in line with what is most appropriate to the Brotherhood Agenda and its symbolism. You would have thought that the centenary Olympic Games would have been held in its original home of Greece, but instead it was given to Atlanta. Why the hell Atlanta, especially when the United States had only recently hosted the games in Los Angeles? One reason for this decision by the symbol-obsessed Brotherhood was the symbolism of the legendary, Atlanta, the goddess and huntress, who was said to be such a great athlete that no man could beat her. Everyone she defeated in a race had to suffer death and many were killed before one managed to trick her into losing a race by dropping golden apples to divert her attention. It was said that she and her bridegroom were turned into lions and pulled the chariot of the Great Mother of the Gods.[1] The Olympic Games in Atlanta also allowed multimillions to be spent on

Figure 28: *The All Seeing Eye on the dollar bill. Is it reptilian?*

roads and infrastructure in a city reported to be a major centre for the New World Order after the Millennium.

Another key Brotherhood symbol is the pyramid or the pyramid with the capstone missing. The street plan of Dealey Plaza where Kennedy was killed is shaped like a pyramid with the capstone missing and Dealey actually means 'Goddess Line' as in Dea (goddess) and ley (ley line). The pyramid with the capstone missing, or the pyramid and all seeing eye, is most famously depicted on the reverse of the Great Seal of the United States and the dollar bill. The all seeing eye is the eye of Horus, Lucifer, Satan, whatever name you want to use, and also relates to the so-called 'third eye', the chakra vortex in the centre of the forehead through which we connect with our psychic sight. According to Egyptian legend, Osiris

Figure 29: *The Pyramid and All Seeing Eye, the ancient Brotherhood symbol, on the dollar bill and the reverse of the Great Seal of the United States.*

was murdered by Set and Set was killed by Horus who lost an eye in the process, hence the Eye of Horus. For me it also symbolises the reptilians looking into this world from the lower fourth dimension and if you look at a magnification of the eye in *Figure 28* you will see that the skin texture even looks reptilian. The 33rd degree Freemason and Black Nobility president, Franklin Delano Roosevelt, had this symbol printed on the dollar bill from 1933. It was a symbol of secret societies in Europe long before anyone heard of the United States and it is awash with Freemasonic and secret society symbolism going back to the ancient world (*see Figure 29*). The number of states in America at the time of independence, 13, was no coincidence. Thirteen, the sacred twelve and one, is an ancient mystical number as we have seen throughout this book.

On the two sides of the Great Seal you find 13 stars above the head of the eagle. The motto E Pluribus Unum has 13 letters, as does Annuit Coeptis. The eagle holds 13 leaves with 13 berries in its right talon and 13 arrows in the left. There are 72 stones (another mystic number) on the pyramid arranged in 13 rows. The eagle evolved from the symbol of the phoenix, the sacred Sun bird of the ancient Egyptians and Phoenicians and the Native American version is the thunderbird. Manly P. Hall says that the original seal included the phoenix and it is known that one design for the Great Seal submitted by William Barton in 1782 included a phoenix sitting on a nest of flames.[2] The symbol of the Scottish Rite of Freemasonry is the double eagle with a head looking in both directions – the symbol of Nimrod.

This same symbol appears in at least two portraits of George Washington. The eagle is a widely used Brotherhood symbol and it can be found on the coats of arms of many countries, including Egypt, Libya and Iraq. It was a major symbol for the Nazis in Germany and it appears in the designs of pulpits and lecterns used by the Christian Church. Seals like the one used in the Great Seal of the United States can be traced back to at least 4,000 BC in Egypt, Babylon, Assyria and India. Our old friends, in other words. The first English Royal pendant seal was that of Edward the Confessor, who ruled between 1042 and 1066. This became a model for all future British and American seals.

The Latin words above and below the pyramid on the Great Seal/dollar bill announce the arrival of a new secular order. The New World Order is the insider name for the Brotherhood Agenda and George Bush used the term profusely when he was president. The date written in Latin on the bottom of the pyramid, 1776, is thought, understandably, to relate to the American Declaration of Independence in that year. But something else happened on May 1st (a date beloved by Satanists) in that same year of 1776. A very significant strand in the Brotherhood network was officially launched called the Bavarian Illuminati by the German professor, Adam Weishaupt. This was quite a year for the Brotherhood because also in 1776 the House of Rothschild was formerly founded and the Brotherhood-controlled economist from Scotland, Adam Smith, published his highly influential work, *The Wealth Of Nations*. Like I say, dates matter to these people because they represent energy flows and cycles. Weishaupt used his Illuminati to further infiltrate Freemasonry. Weishaupt was trained as a Jesuit, the Society of Jesus. The founder of the Jesuits, the Spaniard Ignatius Loyola, formed a secret society within this apparently 'Catholic' order and the initiates were called the Alumbrados, the 'enlightened', the 'illuminated'. Weishaupt created 13 degrees of initiation in his Illuminati (the same as the number of levels on the Great Seal pyramid) and the key personnel were to be found in the top nine degrees.

The obelisk and the dome are common sights in the monuments and buildings of the Brotherhood. The obelisk is an ancient phallic symbol of the male energy and solar energy and the dome represents the female or moon energy. Often they are placed together or close to each other. This is the symbolism of the Oval Office (the womb, female) in the White House which looks out on the Washington Monument, the vast stone obelisk (phallic, male). These symbols attract and generate the energy they represent: they are a physical thought form. The obelisk also symbolises the penis of the Egyptian Sun god, Osiris. According to legend, after Osiris had been sliced into pieces by his rival, Set, the Queen Isis found all the pieces except his willy. An obelisk claimed to come from Alexandria in Egypt stands in Central Park, New York, and its twin was erected in the 19th century, during the reign of Queen Victoria, on the former Templar lands alongside the River Thames not far from the Houses of Parliament. It is known as Cleopatra's Needle and originally stood in On (Heliopolis), the Egyptian City of the Sun, from at least 1500 BC, before it was moved to Alexandria (*see picture section*). A sphinx has been placed on either side at its London location. Another Egyptian obelisk which was built in Luxor 3,200 years ago now stands in the Place de Concorde in Paris, less than a minute's drive from the scene of Diana's crash.

On the other side of the crash scene is the Eiffel Tower, another gigantic obelisk in disguise. The Washington Monument in Washington DC is a colossal obelisk. The dome (from a Greek word meaning Place of the Gods) draws in and harnesses energy, as does the pyramid. So often you find that the great cathedrals are built around a massive dome because their builders and designers understood the power of geometry to focus energy in one spot. The vast golden dome on the 'Islamic' shrine on Temple Mount in Jerusalem, the dome of St Peter's at the Vatican in Rome, and the Church of Santa Maria which dominates the skyline of Florence, are obvious examples of this. Look around the major Brotherhood cities and you will find they have at least one major domed building. In the City of London you have St Paul's Cathedral designed by the initiate Sir Christopher Wren after the Great Fire of London had destroyed the original city. The mirror of St Paul's Cathedral is in Paris and known as the Pantheon. Look at the Congress building in Washington DC and you will find that it is another St Paul's (*see picture section*). In London's Leicester Square there is a dome-shaped skylight with concentric circles in the strangely named Notre-Dame de France built in 1865 on a site with Knights Templar associations and rebuilt in the late 1950s.[3] The building includes a stone slab from Chartres Cathedral and a mural of the crucifixion scene, full of occult symbolism and sacred geometry, by the French artist Jean Cocteau (1889–1963), a Grand Master of the Priory of Sion. His mural includes a black sun, a classic Brotherhood symbol, casting its rays into the sky, and a man with an eye drawn in the shape of a fish, which could well be symbolic of the Babylonian Nimrod. In Rome there is the dome at the Vatican, that ancient site of Mithra (Sun) worship, and alongside the dome you find obelisks in St. Peter's Square. In London, as I write, the Millennium *Dome* is being built next to the Greenwich zero longitude time-line which runs through the nearby Greenwich Observatory, which was also, incidentally, designed by Sir Christopher Wren. It is to this point in the world that all the watches, clocks, and time zones (therefore the collective human mind) are tuned and we view the universe from the same time-perspective. The measurement used in the Greenwich time-grid is solar time. On the other side of the River Thames, opposite the Millennium Dome, is the biggest building and obelisk in Europe, the Canary Wharf building. Again in the Brotherhood cities you will invariably find a skyscraper shaped like an obelisk because of the effect that has on the energy field and the harnessing of solar energy. Big Ben, the famous clock at the Houses of Parliament in Westminister is also an obelisk. The word ben is Cymric and Gaelic for mountain and in ancient Egypt 'Ben' related to the sacred ben ben stone on the top of the pillars in On, the city of the Sun. These pillars became symbolised by the obelisk and it was said to be the point where the gods descended to the Earth. The bennu bird – the inspiration for the Phoenix – sat on the ben ben stone, according to legend.[4] There is also another significance for the Millennium Dome and Canary Wharf which I will explain later.

The street plans of major cities are designed under the laws of sacred geometry in the same way that the great cathedrals, temples and stone circles were. As with the City of London after the Great Fire of 1666, the new city of Washington DC was designed according to these laws. Symbols, shapes and angles generate different energies and if you understand these principles you can vibrate the energy field of a place to the vibrational range you deem most suitable for what you wish to achieve there. Anyone living or working within that field will be affected by it. You can also focus solar and other astrological energies in that place.

I found Washington one of the most unpleasant energies I have ever encountered outside the Square Mile in the City of London. A French Freemason, Major Pierre Charles L'Enfant, was engaged to create the new Washington, and his work was based on plans officially prepared by leaders like Thomas Jefferson and George

Washington, although others with greater esoteric understanding would have been the real architects. Jefferson, however, had deep esoteric connections and when he died a code system which was very similar to ancient Rosicrucian secret manuscripts was found among his possessions by the Rosicrucian, Spencer Lewis.[5] Some researchers say Jefferson was a Grand Master of the Rosicrucians. He was an expert in astronomy and astrology, as was Benjamin Franklin who wrote a best-seller on the subject called *Poor Richard's Almanac*. L'Enfant had fought in the War of Independence and he, like Washington, was a member of the highly secretive and exclusive grouping called the Society of Cincinnati. It was officially a secret society for American and French officers in the War of Independence and it introduced hereditary membership which is passed on to the eldest son. Washington was its president for life. The diary entries of Washington and letters by Jefferson relating to L'Enfant and the street plan have 'disappeared'. L'Enfant was dismissed after a year, but the street plan continued. In 1909 his remains were exhumed and taken by military escort to Capitol Hill to lie 'in State' for just three hours. Thousands went to pay their respects and he was reburied at the Arlington National Cemetery. What goes on? The Arlington Cemetery was formerly the grounds of Vernon House the home of George Washington and the American Order of the Knights Templar hold their annual sunrise ceremonies in the amphitheatre there.[6]

Forty boundary posts were established a mile apart to mark the boundary of the ten square miles of Washington and in the centre was built the Congress building, Capitol Hill, named after the sacred place of the Roman secret societies called Capitoline Hill. It was no surprise, therefore, that the United States Secretary of State, Madeleine Albright, the high priestess of American politics, should make a pilgrimage to Capitoline Hill on her first official visit to Europe after her appointment. Capitol Hill is not a political building, it is a temple to the Satanic Brotherhood and underneath its 'St Paul's' dome is a crypt room. Beneath the floor of the crypt, marked by a pentagram star, is a vacant tomb. They say this was meant for George Washington, who decided to be buried elsewhere, but there is more to it than that. The bodies of Kennedy, Lincoln, McKinley, Garfield, Harding, Taft, Hoover, Wilson, Stevens, Dewey, Pershing, MacArthur, L'Enfant and two unknown soldiers have all been placed on the catafalque found in the tomb.[7] A catafalque for those, like me, who had never heard the word, is the structure on which the body is carried during a funeral procession or placed on for lying in state. The same format of a tomb under a dome is the 'tomb of St Peter' beneath the Basilica at the Vatican. The Congress building is a temple to a secret society which, under many names, originates in the ancient world. Within the Washington street plan, centred on Capitol Hill and the White House, are astrological symbols (which relate exactly to where certain constellations appear in the sky), hexagrams, Satanic pentagrams, squares, a Masonic compass, a 'Spear of Destiny', a skull and bones and scores of others. For more information and illustrations I strongly recommend an excellent book by Charles L. Westbrook Jr called *The Talisman Of The United States, Signature Of The Invisible Brotherhood*. Roads in Washington relate to the points where the Sun rises at the winter and summer solstice, just as the ancient mounds, temples and

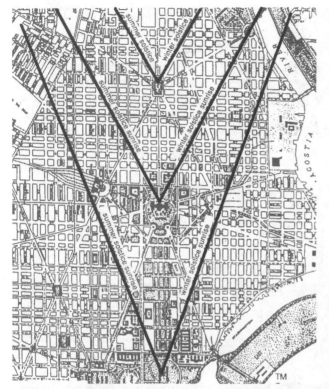

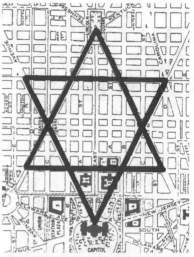

Figure 30: *The street plan of Washington DC, like all the major Brotherhood cities, is a mass of esoteric symbolism. The streets around the Congress Building are designed to mark the places the Sun rises and sets at the winter and summer solstice. There is also a hexagram or Star of David –* **Figure 31**.

stone circles like Stonehenge, were designed to do (*see* **Figure 30**). Other streets cross at precisely 33 degrees and still others mark the precession of the equinoxes, and there is a hexagram or Star of David (*see* **Figure 31**).

I described earlier how the Elite of America and further afield gather at the Bohemian Grove in Northern California and take part in ceremonies under a 40 foot stone owl. The owl is symbolic of Moloch or Molech, the ancient deity to which children were, and are, sacrificed. The Sumerian goddess, Lilith, known as the Lady of the Breasts, was also symbolised as an owl.[8] Lilith is symbolic of the bloodline. The Pagan religions knew her as the enchantress. In the picture section you will see the 'grovers' performing a ceremony at Bohemian Grove before the giant owl. How interesting that when I was looking at a map of Washington I found that the roads within the grounds of the Congress Building make the very clear symbol of... an owl! You also find that the owl is sitting on a pyramid. The pyramid and all seeing owl (*see* **Figure 32** *overleaf*). The collective word for owls is a parliament of owls, which is uncannily appropriate. The same owl symbol can be found hidden on the dollar bill if you know where to look and you have a very powerful magnifying glass. I also understand a new pedestrianisation scheme around Nelson's Column in Trafalgar Square, London, is going to look like an owl from above. There are at least three Satanic pentagrams in the Washington street plan. By 'Satanic', I mean pentagrams pointing downwards or with the lines made of different lengths to distort the shape. These reverses and

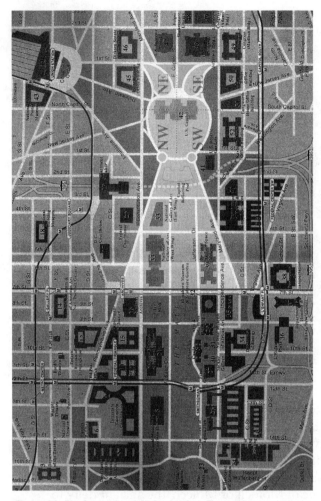

distortions of the pentagram are Satanic signatures in the same way that the Nazis reversed the swastika. One pentagram points down into Capitol Hill (*see Figure 33*), another into the White House (*see Figure 34*), and a third extends out from the giant obelisk called the Washington Monument and covers a large area of the inner city. At its centre is the sign for Aries, the ram or lamb. Similar Satanic pentagrams can be identified in the street plan of Rome, the old city of Jerusalem, the land around Rennes-le-Chateau, the pyramid site at Giza, and no doubt over London and other cities and sites. Across the Potomac River from Washington is the home of the United States military – the Pentagon Building which was aligned to the constellation of Taurus.[9] A pentagon, of course, is the centre of a pentagram. If you drive through the centre of the White House pentagram you come to a remarkable building at 1733 16th Street. Note the number: 1733. The number 17 recurs over and

Figure 32: *The Pyramid and All Seeing Owl. The roadways within the Congress grounds and the two main thoroughfares leading away create an owl sitting on a pyramid around the Congress Building. The owl is symbolic of Moloch, to whom children have been sacrificed for thousands of years.*

over in the story of Rennes-le-Chateau, and 33 is the official number of degrees in the Scottish Rite. This building has the feel of an Egyptian temple with two depictions of the Sphinx outside and a massive image of the rising Sun. A similar symbol was on the 'sun chair' of George Washington. This strange building is the Supreme Headquarters of the 33rd degree of the Scottish Rite of Freemasonry. The 33rd degree is known as the Revolutionary Degree and most heads of government are 33rd degree Freemasons even though they will be keen to deny this or keep it quiet. It is an honorary degree and they will have made an oath of loyalty to Freemasonry that overrides their oath to their nation. In the garden behind this building I saw through the hedge a bust of George Washington celebrating him as the first Freemason President of the United States. This building is home to the biggest collection of Freemason relics in the world (and that's only the members).

In the Smithsonian Museum, just down from the White House, there is a remarkable marble statue of George Washington which was once displayed at Capitol Hill. It was commissioned by Congress in the 19th century and sculptured in Florence, Italy, by Horatio Greenough. When the statue was unloaded at the Washington Navy Yard in 1840, people were horrified at what they saw. Washington was depicted sitting in a chair, naked to the waist, with a sheet laid across his nether regions. General Henry Wise, the Virginia statesman, remarked that: "The man does not live, and never did live, who saw Washington without his shirt".[10] So why portray him like that? And why was his right hand pointing up and his left hand pointing down? If you look again at *Figure 21* (*page 152*) you will understand. They

made the statue in the image of Baphomet of Mendes or Asmodeus, the Satanists' symbol of the 'Devil'. Asmodeus is said to have been the guardian of Solomon's Treasure and a portrayal of him was found among the possessions of Abbe Sauniere, the mysterious priest at Rennes-le-Chateau who placed a statue of Asmodeus at the entrance to his church. Asmodeus is named as the chief demon in the Hebrew Talmud. A painting of Washington by 'Caduceus'

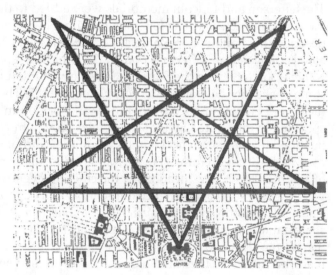

Figure 33: *The inverted and distorted pentagrams in the Washington streets, one points into Congress...*

...the other into the White House – **Figure 34**.

is a mass of esoteric symbolism and geometry. Two examples are that his hand is raised at the angle of the rising moon and his sword is at the angle of the Sun at the winter solstice.[11]

The Washington street design has been expanded over the years, but this has been done in keeping with a plan which appears to have been decided at the start. The same thing seems to have

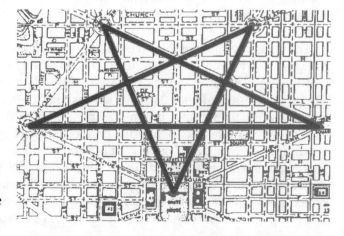

Figure 35: *The ancient sun, circle, and cross symbol and it is portrayed in...* **Figure 36:** *The Celtic Cross,* **Figure 37:** *The NATO logo and* **Figure 38:** *The cross and sun of the CIA badge.*

happened with some structures in the ancient world, most notably the site at Giza. The Jefferson and Lincoln memorials were added to the Washington street plan in the early 20th century. The Jefferson building, historians believe, is based on a design of the Pantheon in Rome. Like all of these key buildings, they are built alongside water or 'reflecting pools'. The building represents the Sun and the water is the Moon reflecting the Sun. The Washington monument, at 555 feet, the biggest stone obelisk in the world, was completed in 1885. The cornerstone had been laid by the Grand Freemasons Lodge of the District of Columbia. While travelling and speaking in the United States I saw a television item which said the authorities intended to build a memorial in the Mall, the heart of the street plan, to those who died in the Second World War. It would include at its centre, they said, a depiction of a lighted torch. The locations of the cities and centres of the Brotherhood relate to places where solar and other cosmic energy can be most powerfully harnessed. Charles L. Westbrook Jr, the author of *The Talisman Of The United States*, received some anonymous correspondence after his book was published. It consisted of a map of the USA and a piece of paper on which were written the words: "It's bigger than you think."[12] Lines drawn on the map revealed similar geometry to that in Washington, but on a much larger scale. Some of the points connecting the geometry, or highlighted by it, were Mount Vernon, Illinois, where George Washington is buried; Miami, which was dubbed the 'magic city' as early as 1820; and a place called Pike's Peak in Jefferson County, Colorado, just across the border from Arkansas. Pike's Peak, of course, is named after Albert Pike.

The ancient symbol of the circle and the cross I described a few chapters back, is still used today in the secret language. It is the one symbolising the Sun's progress through the 12 months and the 12 signs of the zodiac, the cross and circle with the Sun on the cross (*see Figure 35*). This has inspired the Celtic cross (*see Figure 36*), the logo of NATO, the world-army-in-waiting (*see Figure 37*), and the emblem of the CIA (*see Figure 38*). In the City of London financial district opposite St Paul's Cathedral, I also found the symbol in *Figure 39*. It is a zodiac circle with a black sun at the centre. This building was designed originally for the *Financial Times* newspaper and the face on the black sun is that of Winston Churchill. The black sun is more reverse symbolism which indicates the negative use of solar energy and the galactic sun around which the solar system orbits. The Nazis also spoke of the black sun. I feel the black horse symbol of that Brotherhood operation, Lloyds Bank, is a similar code. The white horse was a Phoenician Sun symbol. This same symbol of the circle and the cross was used by the Phoenicians and can be seen in their depictions of their goddess Barati, as it can on the shield in her British version, Britannia. The street plan of Paris, dominated by the Arc or 'arch' de Triomphe, is the same symbolism. The arch itself is a Brotherhood symbol. It is the meaning behind the name of the Royal Arch lodges in the York Rite of Freemasonry and relates in part to the key stone at the top which holds the arch together and gives it strength. The earliest record of such a lodge is in the annals of the city of Fredericksburg, Virginia, on December 22nd 1753. Fredericksburg was the location of the House of the Rising Sun, the Masonic meeting place where people like Benjamin Franklin, George Washington and other Founding Fathers used to gather. The arch symbolism of Freemasonry is also the inspiration for a vast concrete arch at St Louis, Missouri. The Arc de Triomphe is placed at the centre of a circle from which 12 roads go out across Paris. On the road circle around the Arc de Triomphe are 12 points on the road making a 12-pointed star. Again the sun at the centre of the circle broken up into 12 segments (*see picture section*). The main road going through this pattern is the famous Champs Elysees and when you follow this line you can see how planned it all is. When you stand underneath the Arc de Triomphe next to the 'eternal flame' of the unknown soldier, look in one direction, dead straight, and you see a big modern concrete arch in the distance. When you turn and look the other way, again dead straight, you look down the Champs Elysees to the 3,200 year old Egyptian obelisk in the Place de Concorde. Beyond that in the same direct line you find another arch, similar to the Arc de Triomphe, but much smaller, and that, in turn, is in direct line

with the big black glass pyramid built outside the Louvre Museum during the presidency of the 33rd degree Freemason, Francois Mitterrand. People were flabbergasted that anyone could build such an out-of-keeping structure alongside the beautiful architecture of the Louvre. The reason had nothing to do with architecture and everything to do with adding more power to the geometrical design of the city. A similar and vast black pyramid has been built with a massive Sphinx and an obelisk in that Brotherhood city, Las Vegas.

Figure 39: *The sun and zodiac circle at the entrance to a financial building in the City of London, near St Paul's Cathedral in the heart of the Brotherhood Spider's Web. The Black Sun represents the malevolent use of solar energy and the 'galactic Sun', and this one includes the face of Winston Churchill.*

Figure 40: *The Maltese Cross.* **Figure 41:** *The United Nations logo in Freemason blue with 33 sections within the circle in line with the 33 official degrees of the Scottish Rite of Freemasonry. The 'frame' is also directly from Freemasonry as you can see in* **Figure 42**.

The lion is seen so often in heraldry and flags because it is an ancient symbol of the Sun, as is the Sphinx most probably. The fish symbolises the sign of Pisces and also the legendary King of Babylon, Nimrod, who was depicted as a fish. The dove symbolises his partner, Queen Semiramis, and it is more reverse symbolism. While the dove means peace to most people, it symbolises death and destruction to the Brotherhood. This reversing allows them to use their symbols in the public eye in a way that no-one understands. Sinn Fein, the political wing of the Provisional IRA in Northern Ireland, has a dove as its symbol for this reason. It is this dove symbolism which gives us the fictitious name of Christopher Columbus who in fact used to sign his name Colon. The name Columbus was invented as yet more Brotherhood symbolism. The Romans used to worship a deity they called Venus Columba, Venus the Dove. Venus and dove are associated with Queen Semiramis in Babylon. The word dove in French today is still Colombre. Columba is also an 'Aphrodite' goddess which symbolises the negative, death and destruction, aspects of the female energy. Hence we have British Columbia, Columbia Pictures, Columbia University, Columbia Broadcasting (CBS), the Space Shuttle Columbia, and District of Columbia in which they placed Washington DC. You've only got to look at some of the names for places around Washington to see where their originators were coming from. The most obvious is Alexandria just over the border from the District of Columbia, in Virginia (the virgin – Isis, Semiramis). And, by the way, look at the logos of those Columbia organisations. Columbia Pictures has the lady holding the lighted torch, Columbia University has the lighted torch, and Columbia Broadcasting (CBS) has the eye, the all seeing eye. Doves can be seen standing on Maltese crosses on the sceptres held by the Queen of England in her ceremonies and there are Maltese crosses on the crown of the British monarch (*see picture section*). Sceptres and rods were symbols of power in ancient Egypt. The Maltese or splayed cross (*see* **Figure 40**) was found in caves in the former Phoenician lands of Cappadocia, now Turkey, dating back many thousands of years and it became the cross of the Knights Hospitaller of St John of Jerusalem (Knights of Malta), the Knights Templar, and the Nazis. If you look in the picture section at the Nazi soldier you will see that he has the whole set – the Maltese Cross, the reversed swastika, the skull and bones and the eagle! Three major symbols of the

Brotherhood are the lighted torch, the red rose and the dove. The symbols of the three main political parties in the United Kingdom which serve the structure headed by the Queen are the lighted torch (Conservatives), the red rose (Labour) and the dove (Liberal Democrats)! At the time of writing their three leaders are Tony Blair (Bilderberg Group), William Haig (Bilderberg Group), and Paddy Ashdown (Bilderberg Group). Just a coincidence, nothing to worry about.

The laurel leaves in the United Nations symbol are mirrored by the Freemasons (*see Figure 41*) and there are 33 sections in the circle. The logo is blue, a Freemasonic colour, as in the Blue Degrees of Freemasonry. The symbol of the European Union is also blue. The inspiration for the 'frame' around the UN logo can be easily seen in the Freemasons symbol in *Figure 42*. You find the black and white squares of the

Figure 43: *One square placed over another in any form means "we control everything". Appropriately we see that here in the badge of Sussex Police in England.*

Figure 44: *Chevron. You need to look at this as a three-dimensional, not a one-dimensional image. There are two boxes, symbolising one square on top of another. We control everything.*

Freemasons and the Templars (and endless other Brotherhood groups) on the uniform of British and American police forces (and many others), as well as on the floors of great cathedrals and the church at Rennes-le-Chateau. When American presidents put their hand on their breast while listening to the national anthem they are performing part of Freemasonic ritual. Americans who oppose the Freemasons do the same because they don't understand the symbolism. Another hand signal for the Brotherhood is to put your arm in the air with the two outer fingers pointing upwards and the two middle fingers held down by the thumb. This is the symbol of the Devil or Baphomet, the horns of Nimrod, and this is the sign that Bill Clinton made after his first inaugural speech as president in January, 1993. Baphomet is also symbolic of the Watcher-reptilian, Azazel, the 'goat'. The double square, one square on top of another in any form, is more secret society symbolism. In the secret language, one square by itself means control of what is right and just. From this we get phrases like "fair and square" and a "square deal". One square on top of another means control of all that is right and all that is wrong, all that is just and all that is unjust, all that is positive and all that is negative. In other words "we control everything". The double square, or eight pointed star, can be seen in the lobby at the heart of the British Parliament and a long list of world police forces surround their badge with the same symbol (*see Figure 43*). The chevron is another version of this (*see Figure 44*). You need to

Figure 45: *The double cross of the House of Lorraine which can be seen today in the logo of the Exxon Oil Company – **Figure 46**.*

look at this as symbolic of two three-dimensional boxes, one above the other, and not as one-dimensional 'ticks'. This is the logo of the Brotherhood oil company, Chevron, and the other oil and transnational corporations are a maze of symbols featuring the secret language of the force which controls the world. The double cross of the House of Lorraine is the origin of the phrase to 'double cross' someone, to manipulate them. This same symbol can be found in the Rockefeller-guided oil giant, Exxon (*see **Figures 45 and 46***). Texaco has the pentagram inside a circle with the T square of Freemasonry (*see **Figure 47***). The symbol of Atlantic Richfield Oil (ARCO) is a pyramid with the capstone missing looked at from above (*see **Figure 48***) and Amoco has the lighted torch (*see **Figure 49***). Look at the names of some of the Brotherhood's insurance companies: Sun Alliance, Sun Life, Britannic Assurance, Eagle Star. The Sun Alliance building in Piccadilly Circus, London, is decorated with two pillars, two flames, and a statue of Britannia (Barati) holding her circle and cross shield, the ancient Sun symbol! Note also the names given to space craft, military aircraft, and naval ships like Hermes, Nimrod, Atlantis, and Columbia. All symbolic to the Brotherhood.

The Fleur-de-lis is another ancient symbol which is widely used today, particularly by royalty, and you find it on the fences around many buildings. It can be found on one of the gates to the White House. It was used by the Merovingians in France and, apart from its connection to them, it symbolises the Babylonian god Nimrod, and Lilith, the name symbolising the reptilian bloodline. The red rose is another

Figure 47: *Texaco. The pentagram in the circle with the Tau cross, the T-square of Freemasonry.*

Figure 48: *Atlantic Richfield Oil and the pyramid with the capstone missing seen from above.*

Figure 49: *Amoco, now merged with British Petroleum. The lighted torch.*

Brotherhood signature and
the bell, as in the American
Liberty Bell, is symbolic of
Bel, Bil or Baal, the Aryan
Sun god of the ancient world.
The most obvious symbol of
the Brotherhood's intent is
the fasces, from which we get
the word, fascism. You can
see it at the bottom of a
United States 'liberty' symbol
and in the Congress Building
(*see **Figure 50***). It was a
symbol used widely in the
Roman Empire and it consists
of rods bound together
around an axe. This axe is the
origin of the term Axis
Powers for the fascist
countries in the Second
World War. The symbolism is
of people and countries

Figure 50: *Liberty? Then why the fascist symbols at the bottom which stand for anything but freedom.*

bound together under a common centralised dictatorship, the axe. That is a perfect
description of the European Union in which the nations of Europe are subordinate
to common laws decided and imposed by the unelected dictatorship in Brussels.
The European Union is truly a fascist state in accordance with the fascist symbol.

Another form of symbolism is known as reverse speech or word inversion. A
great deal more research is being done into this today and it is one of the mysteries
held by the Brotherhood since ancient time. Under this system, for instance, the car
hire company, Avis, becomes Siva, one of the gods in the Hindu triad or trinity. The
symbol of Siva is the penis and, like Neptune and Satan, Siva is usually pictured
with a trident.[13] Avis, which is owned by the Brotherhood's International Telephone
and Telegraph, have formerly registered the words 'Wizard' and 'Golden File' as
trademarks, as in 'The Wizard of Avis'. Sun and sex rite symbolism is constantly
used in advertising by the Brotherhood corporations. These words and symbols
communicate with the human subconscious and affect people without them
being aware of it.

But symbolism does not have to be negative. It is simply a form of
communication and it has also been used to keep the knowledge alive by those who
have a positive intent for humanity. Knowledge is neutral; it is the use of it that is
positive or negative. Tarot cards, the forerunner to our playing cards, were used to
pass on suppressed knowledge. Hence the reason why the church has so condemned
the tarot cards and dubbed them evil. In the centuries which followed the
elimination of the Cathars in France, the Tarot was circulated by travelling

entertainers and gypsies. Some researchers say the Tarot cards were introduced to Europe by the returning crusaders who had acquired them from mystical sects in the Middle East and that is certainly true to an extent. But what is often forgotten is the role played by the gypsies and why they have been persecuted so often, not least by Adolf Hitler. There is the legend, I believe based on truth, that priests from Alexandria saved whatever they could when the great esoteric library at Alexandria was burned by the Roman Church and they became wanderers, a people apart, with their own language and they symbolised their knowledge in the Tarot. When gypsies are first mentioned in English records at the time of Henry VIII, they are described as 'outlandish people, calling themselves Egyptians'.[14] The term, Tarot, is believed to be derived from two Egyptian words, Tar meaning road, and Ro meaning royal.[15] The royal road to wisdom if the knowledge is used properly and not malevolently. The Tarot consists of the Minor Arcana, four suits called swords (blade), cups (chalice), pentacles and sceptres, and the Major Arcana or 'Great Secrets', known as trumps. Among the trumps was the 'Joker' which has survived in modern playing cards. The Joker is the jester who used humour and clowning to pass on the message. The Joker also connects to the Trickster, a term you find in native American myth.

Today's playing cards are an abridged form of the Tarot. The colours black and red represent the two great divisions of the year, Winter and Summer, when the Sun is in the north or south. The four suits are the seasons. The 13 cards in each suit are the 13 lunar months of the year and the 52 cards in the deck are the 52 weeks of the year. If you count the joker as one point and the Jack, Queen, King, as 11,12 and 13, the sum value of the 52 cards is 365, the days of the year. There is astrological symbolism in there, too. The highly symbolic game of chess, the 'royal game', was played in China and India long before it arrived in Europe. A form of chess, more like draughts, was played by the Pharaohs in Egypt. The chess board consists of 64 black and white squares, symbolising the floor of the House of Mysteries. The black and white chess 'teams' symbolise the eternal battle between negative and positive, light and dark, among much else. The 64 squares on a chess board relate to the Chinese esoteric system known as the I Ching, which consists of 64 hexagrams. It is all the same knowledge hidden or presented in different ways. The singers and song writers known as the Troubadours of 12th and 13th century France sang the praises of their 'lady'. The name troubadour itself leads us back to North Africa because it comes from the Arab term 'tarab dour', meaning House of Delight, a remnant of the Muslim occupation of southern France. They hid their 'lady' behind the biblical Mary in order to stay alive, but the true meaning of their 'lady' was Isis. Later would come the stories of King Arthur and his search for the Holy Grail, stories that would clearly echo the themes of the Gospels, Mithra, Horus, etc., in their symbolism of the Sun, Isis and the astrological Round Table.

There you have just some of the symbolism which non-initiates, or those who have not taken the trouble to find out, simply cannot see. If you are new to this language of symbolism, I hope that now you will be able to read more easily the signs and signatures of the Brotherhood and therefore be more streetwise to their games and aims.

■ SOURCES

1   *The Woman's Encyclopaedia Of Myths And Secrets*, pp 73–73.

2   *The Secret Teachings Of All Ages*, p LXXXIX.

3   The Templar Revelation, pp 36–39.

4   My thanks to Ivan Fraser for this information.

5   Charles L. Westbrook Jr, *The Talisman Of The United States, Signature Of The Invisible Brotherhood*, p 48. To locate a copy, contact *The Talisman* newsletter, PO Box 54, Ayden, NC 28513, United States.

6   Ibid, p 50.

7   Ibid, p 12.

8   *The Woman's Encyclopaedia Of Myths And Secrets*, pp 754, 755.

9   *The Talisman Of The United States*, p 67.

10   Ibid, p 69.

11   Ibid, p 79.

12   Ibid, p 116.

13   *Secret And Suppressed*, p 90.

14   *The Secret Teachings Of All Ages*, p CXX1X.

15   Ibid.

CHAPTER EIGHTEEN

All the Queen's forces and all the Queen's men

In so many ways, the House of Windsor encapsulates almost every element of this story. They are of a Black Nobility bloodline who are knowingly working to the Brotherhood Agenda and when you look behind the façade what you find is very dark indeed. The Windsors are the highest profile reptilian family on the planet and they operate at the heart of the global manipulation. They are still 'gofers' of a kind and not at the very top of the pyramid, but they are close to those who are.

The very coronation of the British monarch reveals the true background to the Windsors and their predecessors. When the Queen was crowned Elizabeth II on June 2nd 1953, all the regalia of the ceremony, the crowns, sceptres, gowns, orb and bracelets, were taken from the Tower of London and kept overnight in the Jerusalem Chamber at Westminster Abbey. This chamber is where the scholars met to translate the King James 'authorised version' of the Bible under the overall supervision of Sir Francis Bacon and Robert Fludd, the Grand Master of the Priory of Sion.[1] The British Royal family still hold the copyright for this! The Jerusalem Chamber is panelled with cedar wood brought from the Lebanon because that was the wood said to be used to build Solomon's Temple. The tapestry in the chamber depicts the Judgement of Solomon. Westminster Abbey, the 'Christian cathedral', is in fact a Pagan temple. Even the floor is made of black and white squares like a Freemasonic temple.

At the start of the ceremony in 1953, the Queen sat on the Coronation Chair and under her bum was the Stone of Destiny which Edward I had stolen from Scone (pronounced 'scoon') Abbey in Scotland in 1246. The Stone was supposed to have been brought to Ireland from Israel via Egypt and is also known as Jacob's Pillar or Pillow. I think the basic theme of that is correct, but there is a great deal more to know about the detail and its true significance. The Archbishop of Canterbury turned to the north, south, east, and west (the four points of the Pagan cross) and the congregation shouted "God save the Queen". This was symbolic of the story in the Old Testament describing the crowning of 'Saul' as King of Israel when people shouted "God save the King".[2] This cry can be found eight times in the Old Testament when the Kings of Israel are crowned. The Queen sat in the Coronation Chair holding the Egyptian symbols, a sceptre and a rod. On the top of the sceptre is the Maltese Cross and on the rod is a dove. She also later holds an orb with a Maltese Cross on the top, the same as those used by the Dutch wing of the Black Nobility. Babylon is now London and Queen Elizabeth is seen by the Brotherhood as a symbolic successor to the legendary founder of Babylon, Queen Semiramis, who was symbolised as a 'dove'. The Queen was also anointed with oil at her Coronation, the ancient Aryan and reptile-Aryan tradition which goes back thousands of years. The word 'Christ' means the 'anointed one'. The oil at the Queen's coronation was the same mixture as that used in the ancient Middle East. It was carried in a gold vessel called the Ampulla made in the form of… a dove.[3] This is symbolic of the messeh fat used in Egypt by the Royal Court of the Dragon. The anointing at the Coronation is supposed to elevate the monarch to the rank of High Priest, in this case, appropriately, High Priestess of the Church of England as well as head of state. While this was happening, the Archbishop of Canterbury said:

> "As kings, priests, and prophets were anointed: and as Solomon was anointed by Zadok the priest and Nathan the prophet, so be thou anointed, blessed and consecrated Queen over the peoples, whom the Lord thy God hath given thee to rule and govern… "[4]

This is pure Brotherhood symbolism. The 'Lord thy God' means the 'gods' of the ancient world, the reptilian 'gods'. The crown used in the ceremony goes back to the time of Edward the Confessor. He was the King of England who built the original Westminster Abbey in 1065 and later the present one was begun by the Templar-controlled, Henry III. Edward died in 1066, the very year that William the Conqueror and his St Clair supporters invaded England and won the Battle of Hastings under instructions from the Black Nobility of Venice. The Coronation Crown is set with 12 jewels along with two depictions of the Maltese Cross which was one of the most prominent symbols of the Nazis. In the Levite-authored Exodus we hear of the Breastplate of Aaron which is set with 12 stones.[5] The same stones, in the same order, appear in the British crown.[6] The Archbishop placed his hands between the Queen's to pay homage to the new head of his Church and he kissed her right hand. Then he said:

> "The Lord Almighty… establish your throne in righteousness, that it may stand for evermore, like as the sun before him, and as a faithful witness in Heaven."[7]

This is almost a repeat of the words used in God's covenant with David in the Old Testament.[8] The 'Lord Almighty' was formerly El Shaddai or Ishkur, the son of Marduk, who is claimed to have been the son of the Anunnaki scientist, Enki, the guy who, according to the Sumerian Texts as translated by Zecharia Sitchin, was the one who created the human-Anunnaki hybrids with Ninkharsag. The Windsors are of a Brotherhood-Black Nobility bloodline and the Queen was crowned in a Brotherhood ceremony inside a Brotherhood temple. This will make sense of what you are about to read.

The Windsor blood

Elizabeth Alexandra Mary Windsor, or Queen Elizabeth II, is, like all the royal families of Europe, is the bloodline of that pivotal figure in the takeover of Britain, William III, Prince of Orange, the man who signed into existence the Bank of England. She is also blood related to earlier Black Nobility invaders of the British Isles, like William the Conqueror. She is an ancestor of Robert the Bruce, Kenneth MacAlpin, and the Kings of Scotland, and is related to the Irish Kings going back to the ancient coronation ceremonies at Tara. The Queen Mother, formerly Lady Elizabeth (El-lizard-birth) Bowes-Lyon, comes from a seriously Brotherhood-reptilian bloodline, a Scottish aristocratic family which connects with the Bruces, Stuarts, MacAlpin, and down through the Kings of Ireland.

Her father was Claude George Bowes-Lyon, the 14th Earl of Strathmore, and her mother was Nina Celia Cavendish-Bentinck. The wealth and power of many of these lines owes much, sometimes all, to William of Orange and those who controlled him. It was William who made a Bentinck the first Earl of Portland in recognition of services rendered and the second Bentinck/Duke of Portland married into the Cavendish fortune to become the Cavendish-Bentinks, the line of the Queen Mother's mother. This makes the Windsors blood relatives of the Cavendish family, the Dukes of Devonshire of Chatsworth House. The title Earl of Strathmore was given originally to the Queen Mother's ancestor, Patrick Lyon, in recognition of his support for William of Orange.[9] In short, the ancestors of the Windsors were fundamental in putting the Black Nobility's William of Orange on the British throne after which the Bank of England and the power of the City of London was firmly established. Queen Elizabeth (El-lizard-birth), through her Hanoverian ancestors, and others, carries the bloodline of the Black Nobility in Germany and all these strands, be they Irish, Scottish, German, Danish, Swedish, whatever, go back via the Black Nobility Venetians through to the Phoenicians, the Egyptians, to Sumer, and the reptilians. The bloodlines are incredible and Prince Charles can trace three thousand lines of decent alone from Edward III (1312–1377),[10] the monarch who formed the Brotherhood grouping the Order of the Garter. Nineteen presidents of the United States have also been related to Edward III[11] and therefore the line of Prince Charles. The Windsors even have a blood connection to that Brotherhood stooge, Mohammed, the official founder of Islam.[12]

William of Orange, William III, died in 1702. He and his wife, Mary, left no heirs and so Mary's sister, Anne, became queen. Anne was the last of the Stuart monarchs because although she had 17 children by her husband, George of Denmark, she survived them all. In 1714 the scene was set for the takeover of the British Crown by the German Black Nobility family, the Hanovers. They were closely connected with the House of Hesse which would become the launch pad for the House of Rothschild. The first Hanoverian king was George I. He couldn't even speak English and refused to learn. He began life as minor German nobility, a great grandson of the infamous James I, and ended it as King of Great Britain. This guy kept his wife, Sophia, in jail for 32 years for her alleged adultery with the Swede, Philip von Konigsmark, who was never seen again and was rumoured to be under the floorboards of George's Hanover Palace. George II became king in 1727 and died in 1760 while sitting on the toilet suffering from acute constipation. Yes he died of the shits – or rather the lack of them – and there can't be many monarchs you can say have literally died on the throne. His grandson became George III, whose reign spanned the American War of Independence and a massive expansion of British power. George IV and William IV followed before we come to Queen Victoria, who reigned as Queen of Britain and Queen-Empress of the Empire from 1837 to 1901. By this time the British (reptilian) Empire controlled 40 per cent of the Earth's land mass and more than a fifth of the population. It was the biggest empire the world had ever seen. Victoria married Prince Albert of the German Black Nobility House of Saxe-Coburg-Gotha and had nine children who married into the other royal families (family) of Europe. Victoria has an image of being very straight-laced, but like the Rothschilds, Winston Churchill, and other apparent pillars of the establishment, she was a frequent user of cocaine and heroin.[13] Drug parties were held at the royal summer residence at Balmoral in Scotland.[14] The first son of Victoria and Albert became Edward VII, a Grand Master of English Freemasonry, who reigned until 1910. It was now, during the First World War, that the name of the royal house was changed from the German Saxe-Coburg-Gotha to the House of Windsor. The German name, Battenberg, was also changed at the same time, 1917, to the anglicised, Mountbatten. The only reason for this sudden switch was public relations. The Germans and the British were slaughtering each other in the trenches of northern France at the time. In 1936 came Edward VIII who abdicated to marry an American divorcee, Wallis Simpson, and he was replaced by George VI, the father of Queen Elizabeth, and husband to Elizabeth Bowes-Lyon, the present Queen Mother. George died in 1952 and his eldest daughter was crowned Queen Elizabeth II at Westminster Abbey in 1953. By then she had married a fellow member of the Black Nobility, Prince Philip of Greece and Denmark, Baron Greenwich, Earl of Merioneth, Duke of Edinburgh. He was born in Corfu, the son of Prince Andrew of Greece and Princess Alice of Battenberg, the great granddaughter of Queen Victoria. Philip, a Battenberg, took the anglicised version of Mountbatten and, after his marriage to Elizabeth, the British Royal house became the House of Windsor-Mountbatten. Or rather it was Saxe-Coburg-Gotha-Battenberg. This arranged marriage was orchestrated by Lord Louis 'Dickie' Mountbatten, Prince Philip's uncle. Philip is extremely well represented by Black Nobility (reptilian) genes, one reason why he has found it so irritating to have to walk behind his wife according to royal protocol. The Queen is the great granddaughter of Queen Victoria and Philip is also related to Victoria through his mother. One thing to remember is that the royal 'families' of Europe are not families at all, they are one family, offshoots of the same bloodline operating to the same Agenda. Some will do this more enthusiastically than others, of course, but basically that's how it works. An example of this is the way Prince Philip's clan became the royal family of Greece. After British Intelligence had organised a coup against the 'Greek' King, Otto I (a German!), and removed him from the Greek throne in 1862, they selected Prince William, the nephew of the Danish king, to become King of Greece. I know all this sounds ludicrous, but to the Black Nobility this is like a multinational company filling its executive vacancies. Prince William of the Danes became King George I of Greece. (No, you didn't misread that.) William, sorry George, er, er, yes George, married a granddaughter of the Russian Tsar Nicholas I and Prince Philip is related to seven Tsars. He has massive bloodline connections into Germany and also Norway, Denmark, Sweden, and to most of the royal lines of Europe. One of his ancestors is Christian, Count of Oldenberg, who died in 1167, and, as I mentioned earlier, one of the two people who founded the European dynasties of the Black Nobility. Philip was in line for the Greek throne when, while he was still a child, another coup removed the Greek monarchy and the family headed for France where he began his education at a private school in Paris. In the years 1931 and 1932 Philip's four older sisters married into the German-Austrian aristocracy. Margarita married a grandson of Queen Victoria, the Czech-Austrian prince, Gottfried von Hohenlohe-Langenburg; Cecilia married a great grandson of Queen Victoria, Georg Donatus, Grand Duke of Hess-by-Rhine; Sophie's partner was Prince Christoph of Hesse; and Theodora married Berthold, the Margrave of Baden.

Berthold's father was Max von Baden, the German Chancellor during World War I. Max von Baden founded a school near Lake Constantine in Germany via his personal secretary, Kurt Hahn, who was trained at Oxford, the Brotherhood's premier training ground for new recruits. Hahn was head of the intelligence desk at the Berlin Foreign Ministry during the war and was Max von Baden's advisor at the Rothschild-controlled Versailles Peace Conference. It was to their fascist school in Schloss Salem that Prince Philip was sent to be 'educated'. At the time it was under the control of the Nazi Party and Hitler Youth, with Nazi 'race science' on the curriculum. It had quite an impact on Philip as we shall see. Kurt Hahn had left before Philip arrived, but he was not finished with the 'education' business. Hahn, a fascist to his core, went to Scotland and started the Gordonstoun Academy, the school where Prince Charles was sent to be indoctrinated. Hahn the fascist also became an advisor to the British Foreign Office. After four years at Hahn's German Nazi school, Philip was sent to Gordonstoun on November 16th 1937 as the approach to the Second World War gathered pace.[15] The British public school system, and its equivalent in the United States and elsewhere, is a vital part of the Brotherhood network. It is the recruiting and training ground designed to turn out either psychopaths or mentally and emotionally broken people who have learned to do exactly as they are told. You have only got to talk with some of those who have experienced it to know what a mind control operation it is. There are support groups to counsel people who have been mentally and emotionally scarred for life by what happened to them. It is legalised child abuse. In Britain, the children of the aristocracy and wealthy families (and others who know no better) are taken from home at the age of six and dumped at their first boarding or 'prep' school. 'Prep' means preparation to be indoctrinated. Already they are feeling unloved and frightened as their parents drive away, leaving them in a strange place among strange people. I repeat these kids are just six. Can you imagine the effect of that on a little child? From the formal, loveless life of prep school they go on to a public school. Eton and Harrow are the most famous and Prince William, the heir to the throne behind his father, Prince Charles, was sent to Eton. At these prep and public schools, the children either conform to the rules, regulations and thought control or they incur the wrath of the black gowns, the men in black. The 'fagging' system in which younger boys become slaves to the older ones has encouraged the desire to dominate and control others and introduced youngsters to the 'joys' of inflicting pain and torture on others. A friend of mine who was determined not to be broken by the endless beatings he received from both teachers and older boys, was forced to lie in ice-cold baths in an attempt to break his spirit. It is from these schools, and the Oxford and Cambridge Universities, that the often deeply imbalanced people emerge who enter the positions of financial, political, military and royal power. The psychopaths among them give the orders and those of broken spirit do as they are told without question, just as they have been trained to do. The lack of female company encourages homosexual activity and many of these people find it very difficult to relate to women. I'm not condemning homosexuality, by the way, everyone to their own as long as they don't force it on anyone else. I'm just explaining what happens, that's all. There are some strange goings on at such schools which are designed to affect the minds of the children involved. Sexual abuse is definitely part of that. Tony Blair, the Brotherhood chosen one who became British Prime Minister on May 1st 1997, attended the public school called Fettes College in Edinburgh, Scotland, where one of his close friends was the school chaplain, the Very Reverend Ronald Selby Wright, a senior figure in the Church of Scotland. Selby Wright was later revealed to be a persistent paedophile abusing boys at Fettes and elsewhere.[16] Blair, who is close to the Windsors, went on to Oxford University and became a barrister at the ancient Inns of Court at Temple Bar in London. The public school system is horrific and schools such as Gordonstoun and Schloss Salem, which Philip attended, are at the extreme end even of that.

Prince Philip's family were supporters of the Nazi Party and by 1935 Prince Christoph, the husband of his sister Sophie, was a colonel in the SS on Himmler's personal staff and head of the Forschungsamt, an Elite intelligence operation controlled by Hermann Goering. The Forschungsamt gathered intelligence on Jews and others the Nazis wished to destroy, worked with the Gestapo, and also spied on members of the Nazi Party itself. It was they who carried out the famous Night of the Long Knives when Hitler removed his key opponents. Christoph and Sophie named their eldest child, Karl Adolf, after Adolf Hitler and Prince Philip would be involved in his education. Christoph's brother, Philip of Hesse, was related to the King of Italy and he was the official liaison between the fascists of Italy and Germany. At the same time, the British King, Edward VIII, was also a Nazi supporter and Philip maintained communications with him after his forced abdication in 1936. The official reason for this was Edward's relationship with the American divorcee, Wallis Simpson. After just 325 days Edward went into exile to the Rothschild mansion in Austria and later settled in Paris. Edward's Paris home was bought by Mohamed Al Fayed in the 1990s and Diana and Dodi Fayed visited the house on the day they died. One of Edward's biggest supporters was the fascist paedophile and Satanist Lord Louis Mountbatten, uncle of Prince Philip and Philip's route into the British Royal Family. Mountbatten was a great grandson of Queen Victoria and Prince Albert and was born at Windsor Castle in 1900. While Mountbatten (Battenberg) was apparently fighting on the British side during the war, he was maintaining communications with his, and the Windsors', German clan via his sister Louise, the Crown Princess of Sweden and wife of King Gustav. Louise was Prince Philip's aunt. At the end of the war, in June 1945, the British king, George VI, the father of Queen Elizabeth and husband of the Queen Mother, sent the former MI5 officer, Anthony Blunt, to the Kronberg Castle of Philip's sister Sophie, and her Nazi husband Prince Christoph of Hesse, to recover correspondence between the British Royal family and their Nazi relatives.[17] Blunt was the 'Surveyor of the Queen's Pictures' and a world expert in the paintings of Poussin, the initiate who painted pictures called *The Shepherds Of Arcadia* which very much related to the mysteries of Rennes-le-Chateau. Blunt was exposed as a member of a 'KGB' unit inside British Intelligence along with Burgess, Maclean and Philby. The fifth man, who was never named, was Lord Victor Rothschild (see *...And The Truth Shall Set You Free*). In fact it was a Brotherhood unit and not, ultimately, answerable to the KGB. When Blunt was finally collared in the 1980s, Queen Elizabeth apparently demanded that he was not questioned on his clandestine mission to Kronberg Castle.[18] Lord Mountbatten, this arch manipulator for the Black Nobility, held key positions at vital moments in history. He was Supreme Commander in south east Asia during the Second World War (where Prince Philip also served); he was the last Viceroy of India and the Governor-general during the British withdrawal; and he was First Sea Lord, the pinnacle of the British Navy, at the time of the British invasion of Suez in 1958. Mountbatten was killed by an IRA bomb in Ireland in 1979, but as these terrorist groups subcontract 'hits' between each other the true origin of the assassination cannot be stated with certainty.

The Windsor wealth

The Windsors are wealthy beyond description. The Queen's title of the 'richest woman in the world' hardly tells the story and no wonder Prince Philip calls the Windsors 'the family firm'. They have inherited the accumulated wealth of the Queen's Black Nobility ancestors in land, homes, art treasures and jewels. Some of them the Queen owns and others are officially owned by the 'state', which, as a result, she can pass on untaxed to each generation of her family. Ownership by the state means ownership by the Black Nobility which controls the state. This is just some of the Windsor booty:

The Queen has more than 300 residences, including castles or palaces like Buckingham Palace, Windsor Castle, Kensington Palace (where Diana lived), St James Palace, (the London base of Prince Charles), Holyrood House in Edinburgh, Balmoral Castle in Scotland and Sandringham in Norfolk where Diana first met Prince Charles. She owns the Duchy of Lancaster with around

40,000 acres of land, mostly agricultural, but including prime development sites of enormous value. Parliament passed a bill in 1988 to allow her to develop and sell some of this land around the Strand in London. Like much of her wealth, the contents of the Duchy of Lancaster was stolen, in this case from Simon de Montfort junior by the son of Henry III after de Montfort's efforts to establish a strong parliament were defeated in 1265. If you look at the records you will probably find that the de Montforts stole it from someone else. The Windsors own another Duchy, that of Cornwall, administered by Prince Charles. This is another 44,000 acres which also includes plots in the most expensive parts of London. The Queen has inherited or purchased the world's biggest private collection of jewels. The Koh-i-noor Diamond, then the world's largest, was presented to Queen Victoria after the East India Company had defeated the Maharajah of the Punjab in 1851. The Cullinen Diamond was a peace offering to British royalty after the Boer War in South Africa which was engineered by Cecil Rhodes, Alfred Milner, the Rothschilds and the Round Table. Other gifts have come from Arab oil sheikhs and various heads of state. More than 7,000 paintings and 20,000 drawings by old masters are owned by the Royal Collection Trust which the Queen controls. She privately owns a vast collection of other works and all this will be passed down the Windsor line when she dies, unless the nation wakes up and brings an end to the monarchy.

No-one knows what the Windsors really own because it is forbidden for Parliament even to discuss the fact that the Queen keeps her private wealth a secret.[19] Such secrecy is vital to prevent outrage by her 'subjects' and to allow her to use her privilege for insider trading, a practice which is illegal. Insider trading is to be in a position to hear privileged information which could be used to make a financial killing and then to use that knowledge to do just that. The Queen, with her colossal portfolio of global investments, is in the perfect position to make unlimited profits. She is constantly kept informed, via meetings with prime ministers, ministers, officials, British Intelligence and other sources, of the secret happenings in the world. She knows through these channels and others, where the best and worst investments are going to be and through her secret network she can ensure that the most effective financial use is made of that information. It was exposed in 1977 that the Bank of England, the creation of the Black Nobility, had established a company called the Bank of England Nominees Ltd (BOEN), to hide the Queen's investments.[20] The Windsor line has had a particularly profitable relationship with the City of London since the reign of Edward VII, the son of Queen Victoria. Edward's leading financial advisor was Ernest Cassel, the Black Nobility banker. Cassel's daughter and heiress, Edwina, would marry Lord Louis Mountbatten, the foremost influence on both Prince Philip and Prince Charles. Edward VII, a leading Freemason, was also close to the Rothschilds, the Sassoons (an offshoot of the Rothschild bloodline), and the American Payseur-Rothschild clones, Morgan and Harriman. Other financial names with long royal associations are Barings and Morgan Grenfell. The private financial advisor to George VI, the father of Queen

Elizabeth, was Sir Edward Peacock of Barings Bank and the Bank of England. The King awarded Peacock a Grand Cross of the Royal Victorian Order, so the advice was obviously very profitable. George VI also made Lord Cromer his Lord Chamberlain, the highest rank in the Royal Household. Cromer was at one time managing director of Barings.

Researchers like Philip Beresford, the author of *The Book Of The British Rich*, say that Queen Elizabeth invests in the major corporations like Rio Tinto (formerly Rio Tinto Zinc or RTZ), Royal Dutch Shell, ICI and General Electric. This makes sense because these are all pillars of the Black Nobility. The Queen appears to have substantial investments in Rio Tinto, the biggest mining company in the world. It was established in 1873 by Hugh Matheson of the global drug running operation called Jardine Matheson. Rio Tinto was in at the start of North Sea oil and, along with Texaco, was using the refineries of BP in which the Queen is also believed to have major investments. The Queen would have made enormous profits at each point in the operation and she would have had insider knowledge of the North Sea potential. Perhaps the most blatant conflict of interest to be identified was Rio Tinto's involvement in a cartel formed in 1971 to fix the price of uranium. A federal grand jury and the 1976 US Senate Foreign Relations Committee, chaired by Frank Church, exposed the sting. It also included a company called Mary Kathleen Uranium of Australia. This company had been secretly encouraging the Aborigines to occupy uranium lands in Australia to take them out of production and so raise the price on the world market.[21] The manufactured shortage of uranium had a serious effect on the American Westinghouse company who sought to take legal action against Rio Tinto for price rigging. An American court ordered that Rio Tinto officials answer questions, but this was quashed by the British Law Lords (Black Nobility and their clones). The Australian government passed legislation to the same effect. This was after the Australian Prime Minister, Gough Whitlam, had been dismissed from office by the Queen's Governor General of Australia, Sir John Kerr. Whitlam was pursuing a policy of buying out the mining and raw material cartels, like Rio Tinto and Anglo-American, to stop them raping Australia's resource base, while giving nothing in return. The Queen, with enormous investments in both companies, removed Whitlam by using some of her wide range of 'Prerogative Powers' which she can instigate when necessary. The Queen has no power these days? Sure. Part of the scam is to encourage people to believe that she has no power while giving her amazing powers should the need arise for emergency action by the Brotherhood. Sir John Kerr, a former high level operative for British Intelligence, an arm of the Black Nobility, was made a member of the Privy Council and the Royal Victorian Order for his loyal and most profitable service to the Queen's portfolio. He was later murdered, however, when there was a danger of the truth coming out about the removal of Gough Whitlam.[22]

The Queen has massive investments in America and many of these relate to the founding of the Virginia Company under James I and Sir Francis Bacon which carved up those lands from the very start. The British Crown still owns America (possibly on behalf of the Vatican) and, with the London-based Brotherhood, the

Queen enjoys an amazing income from the raw materials and other profits generated by the United States (the Virginia Company). In 1966 two US congressmen described in the congressional record how the Queen owned one of the world's largest plantations in Scott, Mississippi, close to the Arkansas border, called the Delta and Pine Land Company. It was worth even at that time some $44.5 million and yet it paid its hundreds of black labourers a pittance. Note the name, too. Delta (the triangle or pyramid) is a major symbol which is why the Elite US Military unit is called Delta Force. The pornography collection in the Library of Congress is known as the Delta Collection and the Delta, or Triad, is featured in the logos of hundreds of American businesses, including Delta Airlines. Not by coincidence Delta is also the symbol of Royal Arch Freemasonry. This is where the name of the Chinese organised crime operation, the Triads (triangle), comes from and the Elite grouping called the Trilateral Commission. When Adnan Khashoggi, the notorious global arms dealer, opened an American branch of his operation he called it Triad America. Khashoggi, a relative of the Fayeds, is an associate of George Bush, who is a close friend of Queen Elizabeth and Prince Philip. From 1968 the Queen's Delta and Pine company attracted US government subsidies of $1.5 million. Senator McIntyre said in Congress on April 16th 1970 that the government had "Paid the Queen $120,000 for not planting cotton on farmland she owns in Mississippi".[23] The New Yorker Magazine also reported that the Queen is the biggest owner of slum property in New York City and her holdings include the theatre district, 42nd Street.[24] It is reckoned that between 3,000 and 5,000 families own and control the world economy, but the number of people at the core of that control is far, far fewer: a relative handful. The Windsors are definitely among or very close to that inner circle Elite. This Brotherhood cartel controls every aspect of the global economic network, the banks, insurance companies, raw materials, transportation, factories, finished products, major retail groups (and by market rigging all the rest), the stock and material markets, governments, media, intelligence agencies and so on. This is coordinated through the secret societies and one of their most important vehicles is the City of London-House of Windsor operation called the Club of the Isles. It was named after King Edward VII, Queen Victoria's son, who was the first to carry the title Prince of the Isles. The title is held today by Prince Charles. Edward was heavily involved with Black Nobility barons of the Square Mile London financial district and helped them to engineer the Crimean War, the Russia-Japan War, the preparations for the First World War and the Opium Wars with China. Through the central organisation of the Club of the Isles comes the fantastic web of interlocking directorships which hold apparently 'independent' companies in a network of common control and common agenda. Some of this web include:

The Bank of England; Anglo-American Corp of South Africa; Rio Tinto; Minorco Minerals and Resources Corp; De Beers Consolidated Mines and De Beers Centenary AG; N. M. Rothchild Bank; Barclays Bank; Lloyds Bank; Lloyds Insurance Market; Midland Bank; National Westminster Bank; Barings Bank;

Schroders Bank; Standard Chartered Bank; Hambros Bank; S. G. Warburg; Toronto Dominion Bank; Johnson Matthey; Klienwort Benson Group; Lazard Brothers; Lonrho; J. P. Morgan and Co; Morgan Grenfell Group; British Petroleum; Shell and Royal Dutch Petroleum; Cadbury-Schweppes; BAT Industries; Assicurazioni Generali SpA, (Venice) Italy; Courtaulds; General Electric; Cazeenove and Co; Grand Metropolitan; Hanson plc; HSBS Holdings (Hong Kong and Shanghai Bank); Imperial Chemical Industries; Inchscape plc; Inco Ltd; ING Group; Jardine Matheson; Peninsular and Oriental Steam Navigation Co (P & O); Pilkington Glass; Reuters Holdings; Glaxo Wellcome; SmithKline Beecham; Unilever and Unilever NV; Vickers plc;

And that is just a few of them! Each of these corporations have staggering lists of subsidiaries going on for page after page. Lonrho alone at the time of writing has 640 subsidiares.These London-based operations connect with those in other developed and developing countries giving the Black Nobility-Windsor cartels control over world banking and mineral, energy and food production. One of the Black Nobility companies in the United States is Archer Daniels Midland, headed by the Bilderberger, Dwayne Andreas, one of the main financial backers of the deeply corrupt US politician, Bob Dole, who so meekly 'opposed' the Brotherhood choice, Bill Clinton, in the 1996 presidential election. The Black Nobility has made the City of London the world financial centre since its arrival en masse with William of Orange. Today this centre is home to over a quarter of the world's foreign exchange turnover and the London Stock Exchange lists more foreign companies than any other. Ninety per cent of cross-exchange trading in Europe is handled by the City and it is the world's biggest issuer of Eurobonds. The leading commodity futures markets in Europe are based here, as are the London Metal Exchange, the International Financial Petroleum Exchange and the London Commodity Exchange. I understand from contacts in America that it is through organisations like the London Metal Exchange that profits from the Virginia Company (United States of America) are channelled back to London. The City is the centre for international marine, aviation, and commercial insurance and reinsurance. The City dominates world fund management for foreign institutions and governments and all these City operations have Freemasons in prominent positions.[25] More than 500 foreign banks have offices in the City and in 1993 UK-based banks accounted for 16% of lending worldwide, an astonishing figure for these small islands. The interlocking directorships between these banks and businesses are simply breathtaking. I can only give you a selection of them here, but they will give you a feel for what is going on:

- **Sir Peter Ingram Walters:** deputy chairman since 1992 of HSBC Holdings (the Hong and Shanghai Bank, a heart centre of global drug money laundering); BP director (1973-90); BP Chemicals chairman (1976-81); Lloyds Register of Shipping (1976-90); National Westminster Bank director (1981-89); Midland Bank director (1991-94); Blue Circle Industries chairman (1990-); London Business School governor (1981-91); National Institute of Economic and Social Affairs governor (1981-90); SmithKline Beecham director (1989-); Thorn EMI director (1989), deputy chairman (1990-).

- **Sir Martin Wakefield Jacomb:** Practised at the Bar, Inner Temple 1955-68; Bank of England director (1986-95); Hudson's Bay Company director (1971-86); Barclays de Zoete Wedd chairman (1986-91); Barclays Bank deputy chairman (1985-); Telegraph Newspapers director (1986-); Commercial Union Assurance director (1988-); Rio Tinto director (1991-); British Council chairman (1992-).

- **Sir John Chippendale Keswick:** Bank of England director (1993-); Hambros Bank chairman (1986-); Charter Consolidated director; De Beers director (1994-); Edinburgh Investment Trust director; Queen's Body Guard for Scotland; Royal Company of Archers.

- **Sir Christopher Anthony Hogg:** Bank of England director (1992-); Courtaulds chairman (1980-94); Reuters Holdings chairman (1985-); SmithKline Beecham director (1993-); International Council of J. P. Morgan (1988-); Ford Foundation trustee (1987-)

- **Sir George Adrian Hayhurst Cadbury:** Bank of England director (1970-94); Cadbury Schweppes chairman, deputy chairman, and managing director (1969-89); IBM director (1975-); served on the Panel on Takeovers and Mergers (1990-); Committee on Aspects of Corporate Governance chairman (1991-).

- **Lord Howe of Aberavon (Geoffrey Howe):** Glaxo Wellcome director (1991-); Queen's Privy Council and Chancellor of the Exchequer (1979-83); Secretary of State for Foreign and Commonwealth Affairs (1983-89); deputy prime minister (1989-90); Sun Alliance and Insurance Group director (1974-79); BICC director (1991-); Framlington Russian Investment Fund (1994); International Council of J. P. Morgan.

- **Lord William Rees-Mogg:** General Electric director (1981-); Times Newspaper editor (1967-81); Times Newspapers director (1968-81); Sidgwick and Jackson chairman (1985-88); British Arts Council chairman (1982-88); American Trading Company chairman (1992-); International Business Communications plc chairman (1993-); J. Rothschild Investment Management director (1987-); St James's Place Capital director (1991-); Broadcasting Standards Council chairman (1988-93); Telegraph Newspapers director.

And finally, how about this for a Brotherhood CV?

- **Lord Armstrong of Illminster:** British Treasury civil servant (1950-64); assistant secretary of the Treasury (1967-68); private secretary to the Chancellor of the Exchequer (1954-55 and 1968); principal private secretary to Prime Minister

Edward Heath (1970-75); permanent under-secretary of state (1977-79); Cabinet
Secretary (1979-87); head of the Home Civil Service (1981-87); Rhodes Trust (1975);
Inchcape director (1988-); N. M. Rothschild director (1988-); Rio Tinto director
(1988-); Shell director (1988-); Royal Opera, Covent Garden director (1988-).[26]

Imagine the power you have to control events when you control all these
companies and the governments making decisions affecting those companies. Add
to that the control of the media via organisations like the BBC, the Reuters news
agency, Hollinger Inc.,Thomson, News Corporation, Pearson, Reed Elsevier, *The
Washington Post*, *New York Times*, NBC, CBS, ABC, etc, etc... and you control the
world. More than that, the people don't know this is happening and therefore you
can continue indefinitely without challenge or exposure.

One of the banks close to the Queen is Hambros plc, a Black Nobility stronghold
based in Tower Hill, London. Joseph Hambro was a banker to the kings of
Denmark, Norway, and Sweden, and did much business with the Rothschilds. His
son, Carl Joachim Hambro, moved from Copenhagen to London in 1839 and four
years later Parliament passed legislation to make Hambros a 'British' bank. Like the
Rothschilds, the Hambros family made much of their fortune funding wars and,
again like the Rothschilds, they became heavily involved in British Intelligence. J. H.
'Jack' Hambro, the head of the firm from 1933, ran the United Kingdom Corp, the
economic warfare operation of British Intelligence during the First World War. His
son, Sir Charles Hambro, was director of the élite Special Operations Executive
during the Second World War while Victor Rothschild was also manipulating
events within the British Intelligence network. It was the Special Operations
Executive (SOE) which formed the company now known as Hollinger Inc., the
media giant headed by Conrad Black, the son of the SOE agent who helped to set it
up. Sir Charles Hambro's son, Lord Hambro, now heads the firm. His CV includes
Guardian Royal Exchange Insurance (chairman); the Peninsular and Oriental Steam
Navigation Company, the drug running operation during the Opium wars, now
known as P & O (director); San Paolo Bank Holdings (director); and the
Conservative Party (senior treasurer). Also on the Hambros Board are Sir
Chippendale Keswick of the infamous drug running family who is also connected
with De Beers, Anglo-American and the Bank of England among many others;
Hambros director, Lord Kingsdowne, has a CV including Glaxo Wellcome, the Bank
of England, National Westminster Bank, Redland plc, Foreign and Colonial
Investment Trust, National Economic Investment Council, and the Ditchley
Foundation, a Brotherhood circle which interlocks with others like the Bilderberg
Group. Also among the Hambro directors are Lord Halifax and John Clay, a director
of the Guardian Media Group which claims to be 'anti-establishment' while being
part of the web. In the 1970s, a Hambros director was Lord Carrington, close
associate of Henry Kissinger and chairman of the Bilderberg Group from 1991. It
was during the 1970s that Hambros had a significant stake in a bank called the
Banco Privata which was involved in the P2 Freemasonry scandal and was
connected to the bank at the centre of the scandal, Ambrosiano Bank. The

coordinator of this fraud was Michael Sindona, the main shareholder in Banco Privata and another of his holding companies, La Centrale Finanzaria, had Jocelyn Hambro and Evelyn de Rothschild on the board. The Sindona financial network was funding P2 and bleeding the Vatican Bank of enormous sums. In turn, P2 was funding and organising terrorism in Italy including the bomb which killed 85 people at Bologna railway station. Exposure of P2 was followed by the murder, in accordance with Freemasonic ritual, of the head of the Ambrosiano Bank, Roberto Calvi under Blackfriars Bridge in London alongside the financial district. I bet the Hambro clan were so relieved that he wasn't able to talk. Sindona later said that Freemasons from South America had carried out the killing. Each part of the network sub-contracts its assassinations to another branch to make the truth harder to establish. The Hambros operation, like all the others, stinks so high it would take the world's supply of deodorant to suppress the stench. But save your most powerful air freshener for the Queen and the House of Windsor. They are connected with all the titled criminals who are ripping off the planet and causing death, destruction and misery all over the world. And get this: if you are British you are paying them to do it! The Windsors are knowingly part of this web and their public face is a mere façade to hide the cesspit from which they operate behind the scenes. This control cascades out of London to the rest of the world where the Elite bloodlines rule on behalf of the reptilian Agenda.

The Windsor power

The British Royal family have always been close to Freemasonry and their own orders like the Knights of the Garter, the Order of the Thistle, and the Royal Victorian Order interlock with the Freemasonic networks. So, of course, does the Order of St John of Jerusalem (Knights of Malta). The expansion of Freemasonry in England in the 18th century coincided with the arrival of the German Hanoverian dynasty. The current Grand Master of the English Grand Lodge in Great Queen (Semiramis/Isis) Street in London is the Queen's cousin, the Duke of Kent. Prince Philip was initiated into the Navy Lodge number 2612 on December 5th 1952.[27] His father in law, George VI, the Queen's father and husband of the Queen Mother, was an ardent Mason,[28] as was Edward VII and most other monarchs since the emergence of Freemasonry. The Queen is 'Grand Patroness' of Freemasonry. She is served by the 390 members of the so-called Privy Council which connects with its equivalent in other Commonwealth countries. It is legally above Parliament because of its prerogative powers. Its members, who are appointed for life, include Prince Philip, Prince Charles, the Archbishop of Canterbury, and the Prime Minister. Nine official meetings are held each year and the government ministers stand to attention while the Queen is told of the government measures they are asking the Queen to approve. This Privy Council of inner-circle politicians, courtiers and public servants have to bow to the Queen and shake her hand before standing in line and they are sworn to conduct their business in the utmost secrecy.[29]

Another of the Windsor-Black Nobility vehicles for global manipulation is the Crown Agents. This organisation was formed in 1833 as 'Crown Agents for the

Colonies' to run the day-to-day administration in the Empire and serve as private bankers to government officials, colonial authorities and heads of state. It also supplied a vast range of goods, including arms. Given the methods and background of the British Empire, it would certainly have been involved in the drugs market. The Crown Agents has a long history of involvement with organised crime and operates covert arms shipments into Africa which are used to cause the genocidal wars.[30] This was, and is, a Crown Agency working for the monarch and yet had its entire debt guaranteed by the British government. In the 1970s it was bailed out by a Bank of England rescue costing hundreds of millions of pounds. For many years it managed the personal wealth of the Sultan of Brunei, the friend of the Queen and a funder of many private projects for Prince Philip, Prince Charles and George Bush. The Sultan is also a financial backer of unofficial British and American Intelligence operations[31] and a man who has funded the operation of Mohamed Al Fayed, father of Dodi. The Crown Agents were 'privatised' in 1996 with the name Crown Agents for Overseas Government and Administrations Ltd. 'Privatisation' is Brotherhood-speak for the transfer of power from Black Nobility via government agency to Black Nobility via direct ownership. The new Crown Agents acts as a holding company for a long list of companies and ventures and it continues as before as a vital cog in the network throughout the world. It's chairman, David H. Probert, is the former director of the British weapons manufacturer, Birmingham Small Arms Ltd, and a director is F. Cassell (that name again), a Companion of the Bath (a Queen-awarded title), and former executive director of the International Monetary Fund and the World Bank for Great Britain. The Crown Agents Foundation, which holds the share capital in trust, is headed by Sir David Rowe-Ham, Knight Grand Cross of the British Empire. This trust includes Barclays Bank, Standard and Chartered Bank, Unilever, Tate and Lyle, Securicor (a global operator of 'security services'), British Telecom, the Prince of Wales Business Leaders Forum (headed by Prince Charles), and the Aga Khan Foundation. The same old crowd. The Crown Agents manages the customs services for Mozambique and, through a company called Europe SA, is in charge of all economic construction procurement for Bosnia... yes, Bosnia. It is also involved in a joint venture with a Monaco-based company, ES-KO, to provide all the food for United Nations peacekeeping forces in Angola and Bosnia.[32] So the more wars and conflict, the more money the Crown Agents has the potential to make.

An important part of the Windsor-Black Nobility-City of London web are the so-called 'City Livery Companies'. These allege to represent the various groups of merchants like the gun makers, stationers and newspaper makers, the goldsmiths, and such like. In fact they are secret societies fundamental to the control of the City institutions and much further afield. In the 1350s, in the wake of the plague known as the Black Death, government of the City was passed from the ward councils to the City Livery Companies. The Templars were still very active behind the scenes and the power appeared to be concentrated in the Masons Guild. This network interlocks with its offshoots around the world. In 1979, the year that Margaret Thatcher became British Prime Minister, the Honourable Company of Freemen of the City of London of North America began to hold meetings in New York and

Toronto, and on October 21st 1991 the Association of Liverymen of the City of London in Hong Kong was founded and all their members appeared to be architects (Freemasons).[33] The late author, Peter Jones, researched some of the Livery Companies in the 1990s for his book, *The Obedience Of Australia*, which exposed the manipulation which led to the removal by the Queen of Australian Prime Minister, Gough Whitlam. These are some of the names he found within these 'Companies':

- **Engineers:** Duke of Edinburgh.
- **Airline Pilots and Navigators:** Duke of Edinburgh, Prince Andrew.
- **Butchers:** Queen Mother, Lord Vestey (of the meat family and the Lord Prior of the Order of St John of Jerusalem).
- **Merchant Taylors:** Queen Mother, Lord Whitelaw (alleged Satanist and former deputy prime minister to Margaret Thatcher), Lord Hailsham.
- **Glovers:** Margaret Thatcher, Sir John Fieldhouse (the Admiral of the Fleet), both at the forefront of the 1982 Falklands War.
- **Poulterers:** Margaret Thatcher, Duchess of Devonshire (Chatsworth House).
- **Fishmongers:** Duke of Devonshire, Duchess of Devonshire, C. E. A. Hambro (Hambros Bank, Taylor Woodrow, P & O), Lord Inchcape (Inchcape plc, P & O, Her Majesty's Lieutenant of London).
- **Goldsmiths:** J. H. Hambro.
- **Grocers:** Edward Heath (Satanist and former British Prime Minister, Bilderberg Group and architect of Britain's entry into the European Community).
- **Salters:** Duke of Kent (Grand Master of English Freemasonry), Lord Armstrong (the man with the long list of government and business appointments I mentioned earlier).
- **Clothworkers:** Sir Peter Gadsden (a Grand Master at the United Grand Lodge), Lord Carrington (Bilderberg Group chairman, President of the Royal Institute of International Affairs and major Brotherhood operative).

Another name that appears in many of these Livery Companies is McAlpine, the construction family, with the Satanist tendencies. These groups link into the Freemason networks. There are more Freemasons per square foot in the Square Mile of the City of London financial centre than anywhere else on Planet Earth. The Bank of England has its own Freemasonry Lodge (Lodge No 263), so do other banks like Lloyds (Black Horse of Lombard Street Lodge, No 4155), and there is the élite Guildhall Lodge, based at the Mansion House since 1905. The Mansion House is the official residence of the Lord (Freemason) Mayor of London and more than 60 Mayors have been Masters of the Lodge.[34] Look at that Lloyd's symbol, the Black Horse (Black Sun) of Lombard Street Lodge. Lombardy was a financial fiefdom of the Black Nobility Venetian/Phoenicians.

The Windors are part of this reptilian network of financial and political manipulators, Satanists and ritual child killers. Knowingly so. The network has among its number, via its countless secret societies, the leading judges, policemen, politicians, business people, top civil servants, media owners and editors. Under these kings and generals of the network come the corporals and the foot soldiers who have no idea of the scale of the Agenda they are involved in. If the Brotherhood want someone framed, prosecuted, or murdered, it happens. If they want one of their people protected from prosecution, it happens. If they want a controversial proposal like a new road, a building or law change to be approved, they make sure one of their guys is appointed to head the official 'inquiry' to make the decision they want. This network selects the prime ministers through their manipulation of all political parties and appoints the leading government officials. The Black Nobility networks do the same in other countries, including, no, especially, in the United States. See *...And the Truth Shall Set You Free* for details of this.

The Windsor friends

You can tell a lot about the attitudes and motivations of people by the company they choose to keep and those they choose to 'honour'. It is rare for the Queen to give knighthoods to people outside the Commonwealth and those she has chosen for such 'Honorary Knighthoods' read like a business meeting of Brotherhood operatives. The titles are dubbed 'honorary' because the American Constitution forbids the acceptance of titles from the monarch of a foreign state without the permission of Congress. So few of these honours are given because, as a British government official put it: "One must not debase the currency".[35] I wonder if you think the following names debase the currency: Henry Kissinger, the Satanist, ritual child killer and mass murderer, was made Knight Commander of the Order of St. Michael and St George at a ceremony at Windsor Castle. This is normally awarded to top British diplomats and that is very appropriate because Kissinger has always served the Black Nobility of London. This included the time when, as US Secretary of State and National Security Advisor, he manipulated the Watergate affair to remove Richard Nixon and replace him with the rapist and child abuser, Gerald Ford, and his vice-president, Nelson Rockefeller (See *...And The Truth Shall Set You Free*). Kissinger 'gofer' Brent Scowcroft, an executive of Kissinger Associates and top advisor to George Bush, was made an Honorary Knight of the British Empire by the Queen. So was Casper Weinberger, another Bush clone, who was involved in the Iran-Contra drugs-for-arms scandal. George Bush himself, the paedophile, ritual child killer, mass murderer and Satanist, is a very close friend of the Windsors. The Queen made him an Honorary Knight Grand Cross of the Order of the Bath, as she did with that Brotherhood script-reader and rapist of mind controlled slaves, Ronald Reagan, himself a product of mind control. This is the highest award it is possible for her to give to someone outside the Commonwealth. The Order of the Bath sounds a silly title unless you understand the symbolism. The resurrection bath of alchemy symbolises rebirth and purification or absolution. Baths are given to Masonic 'Knights of the Bath' before they perform horrendous deeds, hence 'blood baths'.[36] George Bush and the Queen get on so well because they are both of European 'royal' and aristocratic-reptilian blood. They are both shape-shifters. George and his wife, Barbara Pierce Bush (of Merrill, Lynch, Fenner, and Smith), are descended from the same Pierce family of England as the

American President, Franklin Pierce. The Pierce family is, in fact, the powerful Percy aristocratic family of England which changed its name to Pierce and some of them emigrated to America when their involvement became known in the failed gunpowder plot which attempted to blow up Parliament. One of the Percy homes where the plan was hatched was called Syon House.[37] Other Bush relatives include the Grosvenor families of England and America and the Taft family of Ohio. The English Grosvenors are the Dukes of Westminster who own the prime properties in the City of London, the financial headquarters of the Black Nobility. The Grosvenors of America founded the National Geographic which is notorious for removing the archaeological treasures of the world, especially those with religious significance, and relocating them at the Smithsonian Institute in Washington DC. The Institute is controlled by the Grosvenor's cousins, the Smithsons, who are also descended from the Percys.[38] The ancestry of George Bush can also be traced to England's King Alfred the Great and to Charlemagne, the celebrated monarch who served the Brotherhood Agenda in France in the eighth and ninth centuries. The same genealogical line can be traced to 32 other Presidents of the United States, who are therefore all related to Bush.[39] The Queen was most grateful to Bush and her other friends who manipulated and 'won' the Gulf War. The military commander, Stormin' Norman Schwarzkopf, who has lied through his teeth about the cause of Gulf War Syndrome, and Colin (Colon) Powell, the Brotherhood's chairman of the Joint Chiefs of Staff, were both awarded by her most gracious majesty, fawn, fawn, the title of Honorary Knight of the British Empire. Douglas Fairbanks, the actor and tool of the British and US military, was aide-de-camp to the Satanist and fascist, Lord Mountbatten, and was rewarded with a stream of chivalric honours, including Knight of the British Empire.

Another name that stands out is Paul Mellon, a very close friend of the Queen. She made him an Honorary Knight of the British Empire. The Dutch wing of the Black Nobility, through Prince Philip's buddy, the SS officer, Prince Bernhard, made Mellon a Knight of the Order of Orange Nassau. The title is in honour of William of Orange and the secret society, the Orange Order. Paul Mellon is a central figure in the London-based control of the United States by another incredible network of families, including the Rockefellers, Harrimans, Bushes, Kennedys and Morgans, which is based in New York, Virginia (Washington) and Boston. Thus it is known as the Eastern Establishment. The Mellon family association with the Windsors goes back a long time. Paul's mother was an heiress to the Guiness fortune and his father, Andrew Mellon, became a confidant of the Windsors when he was US Ambassador to London (the 'Court of St James's') in 1932 and 33. He was followed by another Brotherhood crook, Joseph Kennedy, the father of JFK. Mellon was three times US Secretary of the Treasury under Presidents Harding, Coolidge, and Hoover, representing Black Nobility interests. It was he who financed the creation of the aluminium cartel known as ALCOA to control the price and supply of aluminium, in the same way the Brotherhood have done with oil, gold, diamonds, drugs, ad infinitum. It was Mellon and ALCOA which introduced the policy of putting fluoride into drinking water to make money from a by-product of the aluminium industry which at the time they were struggling to dispose of. It has nothing to do with saving teeth. Fluoride was actually used as a rat poison for 40 years and it is an intellect suppressant. See *The Robots' Rebellion* for that story. Andrew Mellon financed the creation of Gulf Oil which worked closely with British Petroleum (formerly Anglo-Persian). One of their operations was the coup against the Iranian Prime Minister, Dr Mohammed Mossadegh, in 1953. Mossedagh wanted to stop the exploitation of his country, but the Anglo-American Elite conspired against him and imposed on the Iranian people the vicious, murderous regime of the Shah of Iran. One of the people involved in the coup was Norman Schwarzkopf senior, the father of the Gulf War commander so honoured by the Queen. This story is told at length in ...*And The Truth Shall Set You Free*. Andrew Mellon was also behind the Dawes and Young Plans which financed the Nazi war machine and caused the economic collapse in Germany that brought Adolf Hitler to power. His son, Paul Mellon, was brought up in England, but returned to the United States to attend Yale University, home of the Skull and Bones Society. He turned down membership of that, but instead joined the Scroll and Key, another Brotherhood operation. After Yale, it was back to England to study at Cambridge University where so many British Intelligence operatives are spotted and recruited. His father and mother divorced and he settled with her in Virginia, some 40 miles from Washington DC, where you find names for counties like Loudoun and Orange. This area had long been occupied by the US representatives of the Black Nobility like the Harrimans. The Queen and Prince Philip have often visited Paul Mellon at his Rokeby Estate in Virginia and both Prince Charles and Princess Anne have been there.[40] Prince Philip went to Mellon to fund the World Wildlife Fund. Buckingham Palace told *Executive Intelligence Review* investigator, Scott Thompson:

"I am commanded by The Queen to thank you for your letter... concerning Mr. Paul Mellon. The Queen has known Mr. Mellon for many years and visited his estate at Upperville, Virginia, probably for the first time in the 1950s." [41]

The Queen was following in the footsteps of her uncle, the ill-fated Nazi supporter Edward VIII, the Duke of Windsor, who abdicated in 1936 to marry Wallis Simpson. Paul Mellon's sister, Ailsa, was part of the Duke's intimate circle of friends in Virginia. Wallis Simpson, formerly Wallis Warfield, attended the exclusive Foxcroft School in this area. Another of the Queen's close friends, and the Mellons', is William Farish III. The Queen keeps some of her breeding mares at his Lane's End Farm, near Versailles, Kentucky, and she has been a regular visitor. Paul Mellon often flies in by private jet to join them. William Farish III is a close associate of the Queen's close friend, George Bush. Farish came to prominence when he was the keeper of Bush's 'blind trust', the system in which presidents are not supposed to know where their money is invested while in office. Unlike the Queen! But, of course, it's all a sham and Bush made a fortune for his own investments while in office, as does the Queen. I can see why the Queen and Prince Philip enjoy the company of Farish. His grandfather, William Farish senior, was the president of the

Rockefellers' Standard Oil of New Jersey during the Second World War when it was supplying oil and technological know-how to the Nazis and their chemical giant I. G. Farben which operated the slave camp at Auchwitz. Indeed Standard Oil and I. G. Farben were basically the same company. ...*And The Truth Shall Set You Free* will give you the background to all this. Wherever you look, the Windsors can't seem to avoid Nazis, Nazi sympathisers and supporters.

The Windsor genocide

The numerous Anglo-Dutch alliances and intrigues are, in truth, nothing to do with the British and Dutch people. If we are going to stop being duped, we have to stop screaming "It's the British", "It's the Dutch", "It's the Americans", "It's the Germans", "Its the French", "It's the whites", "It's the blacks", "It's the Jews", or even "It's the reptilians". It is not all these peoples that are involved, it is certain bloodlines and factions within them. Blaming one race, nation or belief system is precisely what the Brotherhood want us to do, because if people are divided amongst themselves they will become disunited, quarrelsome or even become warring factions. Divide and rule. Manipulation comes from a network of bloodlines and their 'gofers' who work through all these countries and groups while keeping the population in ignorance. The close cooperation between 'Britain' and the 'Netherlands' means the British and Dutch wings of the Black Nobility. This is definitely the case with Prince Philip, the consort of the Queen of England, and Prince Bernhard, the consort of Queen Juliana of the Netherlands until she stepped down for her daughter, Beatrix. Philip and Bernhard are from the same reptilian bloodline and both have a Nazi view of life and people. Philip and his family are steeped in Nazi connections and Bernhard was a member of Himmler's murderous SS. He was born a German in 1912, the cousin-in-law of Princess Victoria of Hohenzollern, the sister of Kaiser Wilhelm. He was recruited into Nazi Intelligence at the University of Berlin in 1934 and worked for the SS operation within I. G. Farben, the chemical giant which had such close connections with the Rockefeller/Farish Standard Oil and British companies like ICI. Bernhard's background caused a scandal in the Netherlands when he married Queen Juliana of the infamous House of Orange, to become the Netherlands equivalent of his bosom buddy, Prince Philip. Bernhard helped to found the Bilderberg Group which officially met for the first time in 1954, and in 1961 he co-founded, with Philip, the World Wildlife Fund (now the World Wide Fund For Nature), funded in part by the Mellons.

Lets get one thing straight here. The World Wide Fund For Nature (WWF) was not created to save endangered species. Its record on that front is quite appalling as a suppressed report by the Oxford professor John Phillipson revealed in 1989.[42] A few months before Philip launched the WWF, he was with the Queen on a royal tour of India. This included a tiger shoot in which a tiger was lured into range by tethered goats to be shot dead by Philip the 'conservationist'.[43] This later caused worldwide outrage when the story and a photograph of Philip standing over the tiger found its way into the newspapers. On the same tour, this time in Kathmandu,

Philip was in a shooting party with Alec Douglas Hume (Lord Home), the
Conservative Prime Minister, Bilderberg Group chairman and bloodline of the
Scottish Brotherhood families. Ian MacPhail, the WWF's first international appeals
director, told a British television crew how a mother elephant and her calf came into
range. Philip shot the mother and her calf ran off in terror. MacPhail said he helped
to cover up the incident because the WWF was about to be launched and he
believed the Fund would benefit wildlife conservation. He later thought differently:

> "…with a heavy heart I have to report that I was wrong. The rhino, the elephant and the
> panda missed the boat, and the new Noah's Ark sailed on without them."[44]

It has always mystified the public to see the contradiction between Philip, the
founder and driving force behind the WWF, and Philip the killer of animals and
birds for the sheer enjoyment of it. The same with WWF 'conservationist' Prince
Charles riding with the hounds to tear a fox to pieces. But there is no contradiction,
that's the point. Philip, like Bernard, doesn't give a stuff about animal welfare. The
WWF was created for very different reasons. It is a vehicle for controlling wildlife
parks in Africa and elsewhere in which terrorist groups and mercenaries can gather,
train, and cross borders to bring genocide to places like Rwanda and Burundi. The
WWF coordinates and funds the systematic slaughter of people and animals and
has made a fortune from the illegal trade in ivory it was supposed to be trying to
stop. Much of this is being paid for by donations from the public who think they are
supporting wildlife and collected by fund-raisers in the towns and cities who
believe the same. The best contribution you can make to the protection of wildlife is
to stop funding the WWF in my view. Sir Peter Scott, the celebrated conservationist,
was another founder of the WWF and in 1972 he commissioned a report by a big
game hunter, Ian Parker, into the illegal trade in elephant tusks and rhino horn.
Parker produced evidence that the family of the Kenyan President, Jomo Kenyatta,
was at the centre of this trade. He also named Kenya's most prominent
'conservationists' as the poachers. Within hours of handing his report to Scott,
Parker was arrested by Kenyan Special Branch, beaten for three days, and told if he
did not shut up his wife would be killed.[45] Parker's report was never published by
Scott and at around the same time Prince Bernhard, as WWF International
President, awarded Kenyatta the 'Order of the Golden Ark' for saving the rhino![46]

I need do no more than list some of the names in the WWF's 1001 Club to show
where this organisation is really coming from. This is an exclusive group, formed by
Prince Bernhard in 1971, to raise money for the WWF's 'activities'. The members,
recruited by invitation only as with all the Brotherhood secret societies, give a large
annual donation. Here is a flavour of the membership of the 1001 Club over the years:

Conrad Black: agent for British Intelligence and head of the Hollinger media
empire which was originally formed by his father, George, a British Intelligence
operative. Black is a member of the steering committee of the Bilderberg Group;
Prince Johannes von Thurn und Taxis (deceased): one of the most prominent

Venetian families of the Black Nobility and the Holy Roman Empire. Close associate of the Rothschilds. His father, Max, founded Hitler's Allgemeine SS which had its headquarters at the family's Regensburg Castle in Bavaria, home of the Bavarian Illuminati; **Tibor Rosenbaum** (deceased): Mossad logistics operative and head of the Geneva-based Banque du Credit International (BCI), the forerunner to the notorious BCCI which was dubbed the Bank of Crooks and Criminals. *Life* magazine exposed Rosenbaum's bank as a money launderer for the Meyer Lansky US-based organised crime network and Rosenbaum was also a backer of Permindex, the assassination unit of British Intelligence which was at the centre of the assassination of John F. Kennedy (see *...And the Truth Shall Set You Free*); **Major Louis Mortimer Bloomfield** (deceased): British Intelligence agent who fronted the Permindex operation; **Robert Vesco**: sponsored by the Swiss branch of the Rothschilds and part of the American connection to the Medellin drug cartel in Colombia. Last heard of on the run, possibly in Cuba; **Henry Keswick**, chairman of Jardine Matheson, one of the biggest drug running operations on the planet. His brother, John Keswick, a backer of the WWF, is chairman of Hambros Bank and a director of the Bank of England; **Sir Francis de Guingand**, former head of British Military Intelligence, now living in South Africa; **Sir Kenneth Kleinwort**: a member of the banking family behind Kleinwort Benson; **King Juan Carlos of Spain**: Black Nobility and founder and president of honour of WWF-Spain; **Prince Henrik**: President of WWF-Denmark; **Dr Luc Hoffman**: vice-president of WWF International and director of the Swiss pharmaceutical company Hoffman-LaRoche; **John H. Loudon**: chairman of Shell Oil until 1976 and chief executive of Royal Dutch Shell. Given knighthoods by both the British and Dutch royal families and Bernhard's successor in 1977 as International President of WWF.[47]

Yes, sounds like a bunch of conservationists, doesn't it? Martin Palmer, an advisor to Philip on environmental matters, said the WWF was a "missionary organisation".[48] It is, too. The first wave of missionaries began the destruction of Africa and South and Central America, and now the latest wave, in the guise of operations like the WWF, are seeking to finish the job. The environment is being used as a central plank in the Brotherhood Agenda and I speak as someone who saw the movement from within when I was a national spokesman for the British Green Party in the late 1980s. To those who condemn environmentalists as 'eco-fascists' I can tell you that, like all the organisations used by the Brotherhood, including the Freemasons, the vast majority would be horrified at the thought of playing a part in the Agenda I am exposing. Most of them are decent people, incredibly naive and sometimes incredibly arrogant, but certainly not fascists. Once again it is the manipulating core who *are* fascists that we have to identify and we won't do that by screaming abuse at everyone who talks about conservation. The same is true of the so-called New Age movement which is being manipulated beyond belief. One of the New Age heroes is the Dalai Lama, yet another world figure who is not what he seems to be. Nancy Nash, the former director of the

WWF, was transferred to become the Dalai Lama's minder and controller. In ...*And The Truth Shall Set You Free*, I detail the manipulation of the global environmental movement through organisations like the Club of Rome and individuals like the Canadian oil millionaire (and the rest), Maurice Strong. Not surprisingly, Strong has been a member of the WWF 1001 Club and so has Alexander King, the co-founder of the Club of Rome in 1968 with Aurelio Peccei, the Fiat executive and number two to Giovanni Agnelli, one of the foremost members of the Black Nobility and an inner circle member of the Bilderberg Group. Strong is also close to the Dalai Lama and an advisor to Kofi Annan, Secretary-general of the United Nations.

The environment is being used in many ways to further the Agenda through problem-reaction-solution. If you are looking to impose global 'solutions' you need global 'problems' and the environment is perfect for that. It allows you to pass international laws and create centralised, global organisations to police them. It allows you to move native peoples from their ancient lands to create wildlife parks and 'conservation' areas all over the world, particularly Africa and the Americas, which then come under your centralised control. It gives you footholds in strategic areas from which you can launch 'freedom fighters' to start civil wars. The advantages are endless. Transnational agreements like the Biodiversity Treaty are handing control of large tracts of land in the United States and elsewhere to United Nations control.[49] The situation is the same as in Africa where the parks are administered by outside agencies over which the people have no control. The 'Global Biodiversity Strategy' was launched by the International Union for Conservation of Nature (IUCN) the Swiss-based organisation formed by Sir Julian Huxley in 1948 with a constitution written by the British Foreign Office. This sits at the centre of a network connecting 68 countries, 103 government agencies and 640 non-government organisations. It worked with others like the Rockefeller-funded World Resources Institute in the United States headed by Lester Brown (CFR), and its strategy was presented at the 1992 Rio Earth Summit by... Maurice Strong, the Windsor-Black Nobility leg-man, who with his wife, is also seeking to play the same scam with the New Age Movement. One of his vehicles for this is the Dalai Lama.

The Club of Rome was formed by the Brotherhood at the Rockefeller estate in Italy in 1968 to launch the environmental movement on the world. All the major global environmental reports saying there is an environmental crisis and something must be done, have been funded and fronted by the very people who are dismantling the planet's ecology and killing the wildlife. Maurice Strong is a major voice in the Club of Rome. Canada is still a Commonwealth country and it acts as a massive centre for Windsor-Black Nobility operations. This is why so many Canadians, including Strong, Conrad Black, the Bronfman gangster family, and prime ministers like Pierre Trudeau and Brian Mulroney, are involved in the game. Strong is also part of the Rockefeller organisation, leading representatives of the Windsor-Black Nobility in the United States. Strong served with the Rockefeller Foundation which shares a common leadership with all the other 'independent' foundations in the United States like Ford and Carnegie. His main role in the past 20 years, however, has been to front the manipulation of the environmental movement. Who was the first head of the United Nations Environment Agency? Maurice Strong. Who was the head of the 1992 Earth Summit in Brazil? Maurice Strong. Who compiled the highly influential environmental report called *Our Common Future*, better known as the Bruntland Report? Maurice Strong's Canadian associate, Jim MacNeil, an 'advisor' to the Rio Summit. Who compiled the document called *Global 2000, Report To The President*, during the Carter administration in America? Cyrus Vance (CFR, TC, Bil) and other Brotherhood personnel. Strong is a member of the infamous Aspen Institute in Colorado formed by the Bilderberger Robert O. Anderson of Atlantic Richfield Oil (ARCO). His company has a pyramid with a missing capstone as its logo. Anderson was a funder of the environmental group, Friends of the Earth, which, at the highest level, interlocks with others like Greenpeace, WWF, the Sierra Club, Survival International, Earth First, World Resources Institute, the Zoological Society of London, Royal Geographical Society, Nature Conservancy, the Flora and Fauna Preservation Society, the United Nations Education, Scientific and Cultural Organisation (UNESCO), and many, many others. These provide another web of national and international agencies through which to organise covert operations which often have no connection to 'conservation'.

The assault on Africa and other developing countries by Prince Philip and his WWF is part of an ongoing operation. The Royal Geographical Society, which was founded in 1830 and given a royal charter in 1859, sponsored the expeditions into Africa of Doctor David Livingstone and Sir Richard Burton which helped to open up the continent to exploitation and takeover by the European Black Nobility. When the European invasion of Africa began it was also achieved through organisations chartered by the British Crown, including the British South Africa Company of Cecil Rhodes, the British East Africa Company and the Royal Niger Company. The operation was a mirror of what happened in America with the Virginia Company. One of the leading lights in the Royal Geographical Society in the last century was Francis Galton, founder of the eugenics (master race) movement which continues today under the heading of 'population control'. This is a favourite theme of Prince Philip and his American paedophile and Satanist friend George Bush (see *...And The Truth Shall Set You Free*). The Zoological Society of London was founded in 1826 by Sir Stamford Raffles, the Brotherhood's Viceroy of India and founder of Singapore. Prince Philip is a former president of this organisation and it connects with the Zoological Society of New York and Frankfurt, two other major Brotherhood centres. The boards of these two organisations and the WWF are virtually the same.

The Sierra Club was founded in 1892 by John Muir with funding from the American bloodline family, the Harrimans, who also funded Galton's eugenics movement. It was the leaders of the Sierra Club in Canada who started Greenpeace in 1971 and David Ross Brower, former executive director of the Sierra Club, was the founder of Friends of the Earth in 1969. Ross Brower moved to England in 1970 with funding from Rothschild interests, the billionaire financier and Rothschild cousin James Goldsmith, and the zoo owner John Aspinall, who, with Goldsmith, was a close friend of Lord Lucan, the missing earl still wanted for the murder of the family nanny. Friends of the Earth reached its peak of prominence in Britain under the directorship of Jonathan Porritt, the son of the former British governor-general of New Zealand, and later an advisor to Prince Charles. The founder of FOE in France, Brice LaLonde, was a partner in a Rockefeller law firm and became environment minister to the French president, the high level Freemason and friend of the Rothschilds, Francois Mitterrand, under whose reign the black glass pyramid was erected alongside the Louvre Museum. As with Prince Philip, people were surprised when the late Sir James Goldsmith became a 'born again' environmentalist after a lifetime of financial manipulation and 'investment' which served both the Brotherhood Agenda and devastated the environment. Again, there are no contradictions when you understand the plan they are working to. Goldsmith, formerly Goldschmidt, had a German-English father and a French mother. His father, Frank, was a friend of Winston Churchill and became a Conservative MP. The Goldschmidts had joined forces with other Rothschild cousins, the Bischoffsheims, to form a banking partnership which financed the North in the American Civil War.[50] Goldsmith's family were part of the Black Nobility financial web in Europe and there is no doubting the source of Goldsmith's 'inspiration' when he suddenly sold all his stocks just before the enormous stock-market crash of 1987. He further served the Brotherhood by launching the Referendum Party in Britain to hijack the anti-European Union opposition and lead it to failure. It also split the Conservative vote in key constituencies which helped the Brotherhood choice, Tony Blair, to become Prime Minister. Part of this strategy involved the former Conservative Party Treasurer, the Satanist and paedophile, Lord McAlpine, making a very public transfer to Goldsmith's party and he later became its leader. Goldsmith's elder brother Edward, 'Teddy', founded *The Ecologist* magazine and has connections with the WWF. According to published reports, Teddy and James Goldsmith have long had close ties with the Wall Street banker, John Train, the brother of Russell Train, the president of WWF USA. Russell Train is also the top trustee of the African Wildlife Foundation, and intimate of Prince Philip and George Bush. John Train comes from a bloodline family and his grandfather was a founder of the J. P. Morgan banking group. He married into the Venetian Cini family and his, now divorced, wife was the daughter of Vittorio Cini who played a major role in the fascist movement in Italy in the 1930s. Train has deep ties with the intelligence community and is a 'gofer' for both Bush and the Windsors.[51]

The environmental network is just part of the web through which Prince Philip and his WWF genocide operations can work and I stress most emphatically that most of those who work for and support the WWF are genuine people who have no idea of the Agenda they are unwittingly serving. The Crown companies which stole Africa from its people in the 19th century spawned many of their modern day equivalents who continue what people like Cecil Rhodes began. The Lonrho (London-Rhodesia) company, headed most famously by the late Tiny Rowland, was a subsidiary of Rhodes' British South Africa Company and has been responsible for much of the genocide and war in Africa which has kept the people divided and ruled. At the time of writing, Lonrho has 640 subsidiaries in 48 countries. It is the biggest food producer in Africa, the biggest distributor of motor vehicles, and the biggest producer of textiles. It even produces 90% of British, sorry, Her Majesty's, postage stamps.[52] Tiny Rowland was little more than a figurehead to take the blame for what the Queen and the Windsors were orchestrating on behalf of the Black Nobility. The real power behind the upgrading and expansion of Lonrho was Harley Drayton, the personal financial manager to the British Crown, and Angus Ogilvy, the husband of Princess Alexandra, the Queen's first cousin.[53] Contacts in Canada tell me that Ogilvy is very active there too, in the Windsor operations. Princess Alexandra is the head of WWF-UK.[54] Other exploiters of the great African continent today include Rio Tinto, Anglo-American, Minorco, De Beers, Barclays, Shell, N. M. Rothschild, Imperial Chemical Industries (ICI), and Unilever, all, or most of whom, are reported to enjoy substantial investments by the Queen. Incidentally, Lord Melchett, the grandson of the founder of ICI, a pillar of the world chemical cartel, became head of Greenpeace, United Kingdom. The three biggest mining companies in the world, Anglo-American, Rio Tinto, and Minorco, are in truth the same operation. Minorco is the international holding company for the Oppenheimer empire, the family which have monopolised the world diamond market with the Rothschilds through De Beers, the company established by Cecil Rhodes in 1880. Twenty directors of Minorco are also directors of Anglo-American, which is also full of De Beers personnel.

The destruction of Africa can be described in three distinct phases. First the invasion and overt control of the continent by the Black Nobility branches of Europe, the British, Dutch, Belgians, Germans, Portuguese and French. Then came the transition from colonial rule by physical occupation to rule by financial occupation via corrupt presidents and prime ministers imposed by the Brotherhood. Anyone seeking power who will not play the game is removed by assassination, scandal or coup. The faces change, but the masters stay the same. Rhodesia became Zimbabwe under the manipulation of Britain's Margaret Thatcher (Bil) and Lord Carrington (RIIA, TC, Bil, Comm 300), but all that happened was that the white dictatorship of Ian Smith was replaced by the dictatorship of Robert Mugabe. The lives of the people of Africa have not changed because the same people are still in control. Only now its more difficult to spot them because they work behind the scenes. The third phase of this African operation is to turn the continent into a bloodbath which will destroy all coherent society and justify the imposition of rule by NATO and United Nations 'peacekeepers'. The environment is being used as an excuse to steal more and more land and the debt crisis is being 'solved' by the banks of the Brotherhood offering to forgive 'debt' in return for the rights to the mineral resources – forever.

The mass murder in places like Algeria, Rwanda and Burundi is not spontaneous, it has been organised in great detail, just as the conflict and genocide in the former Yugoslavia, Afghanistan, Cambodia, Laos, Sri Lanka, etc, have been. In *...And The Truth Shall Set You Free*, I reveal the background to many of these conflicts. The International Red Cross (red cross, the Templar/Phoenician symbol) have been caught supplying arms to the Tamil Rebels in Sri Lanka and the Zapatista rebels in Mexico.[55] The Red Cross, as I document in …*And The Truth*, is a front for the Brotherhood, although its genuine employees and volunteers have no knowledge of this. You don't need an intelligence test to know why Elizabeth Dole, the wife of Bob Dole, is head of the Red Cross in America. Other apparently genuine organisations like Oxfam and Amnesty International are also used for Brotherhood manipulation. Afghan Aid UK was a vehicle through which the Mujahideen terrorists were organised and deployed to trigger the war in Afghanistan.[56] It was headed by Viscount Cranborne (Robert Cecil). The Cecil family are one of the oldest Black Nobility bloodlines in Britain and were most active in the time of Cecil Rhodes. Robert Cecil's great-great-grandfather was the Third Marquess of Salisbury, the prime minister who helped to manipulate the outbreak of the First World War. Another intelligence operative involved in the creation of the Afghanistan war was Lord Bethell, the Lord in Waiting to the Queen, who ran Radio Free Kabul.[57] The Windsor-Black Nobility covert operations create the 'terrorist' groups and 'freedom fighters' then light the fuse and watch hundreds of thousands of people, sometimes millions, be slaughtered. They can rely on their media barons like Black, Murdoch, Turner and Packer to sell the public a smokescreen story through 'journalists' who mostly haven't got a clue what is happening.

Game reserves and national parks already account for more than eight per cent of the land in sub-Saharan Africa and in Tanzania it is 40%.[58] Under some of these lands are fantastic reserves of mineral resources and in some cases untapped reserves of uranium. The 'parks' are often in strategic areas across borders and those who administrate them can keep out anyone they choose. Who administrates them? Agencies like Prince Philip's WWF and other Brotherhood organisations such as the International Union for the Conservation of Nature, the UN Food and Agriculture Organisation, and the UN Development Programme. They employ military and intelligence personnel to do this and as such they are subverting the sovereignty of the African nations. Two horrifying examples are Operation Stronghold and Operation Lock. Stronghold was supposed to be supporting the Zimbabwe Department of National Parks and Wildlife Management to save 700 black rhinos in the Zambezi Valley, but it emerged that the Chief Game Ranger Glen Tatham and his staff were simply killing 'poachers' without warning. Official figures show that between July 1984 and September 1991, 145 'poachers' were killed, most of them from a helicopter funded by Prince Philip's WWF and manned by WWF contract employees.[59] But when you look at the figures more closely, you find that the overwhelming majority of those killed were unarmed! Why no prosecutions then? Because when the story first came to light a bill was rushed through the Zimbabwe Parliament called the Protection of Wildlife (Indemnity) Act which gave the game wardens immunity from prosecution.[60] The WWF was now able to kill whoever it liked whenever it liked in the reserves. In Operation Lock, the WWF deployed an élite squad of SAS men to 'neutralise' the cartels smuggling wildlife and wildlife 'products'. It turned out that these SAS guys had started to deal themselves in the illegal sale of ivory and rhino horn.[61] People on the ground in

Africa have long known that the main killers of wildlife in the parks are those, often employed by the WWF, who are supposed to be protecting them.

The Operation Lock scandal erupted in late 1989 and early 1990 and it should also be noted that, as with Operation Stronghold, the arrival of the SAS coincided with a rapid rise in the number of dead 'poachers'. This is not surprising given that the training of 'élite' squads such as the SAS, the Parachute Regiment, the Green Berets, the Delta Force, and such like, is designed to turn out fully qualified psychopaths. The organisation of the WWF's Operation Lock was headed by Colonel David Stirling, the founder of the SAS during World War Two. He formed a company for the operation which he named KAS Enterprises, a name inspired by his membership of the Capricorn Africa Society (CAS), which in the words of the governor of Kenya Sir Philip Kerr, was created to 'preserve apartheid in a sugar coating'.[62] The treasurer of Capricorn Africa Society, Mervyn Cowrie, was the man behind the Kenyan park system along with Elspeth Huxley. She married into the family of Julian Huxley, the inspiration behind the International Union for the Conservation of Nature, the architects of 'biodiversity', and an organisation with a constitution written by the British Foreign Office. The interconnecting web is incredible. The Queen and Prince Philip knew exactly what Stirling's SAS assault team were going to do in Operation Lock. Stirling is extremely close to the Windsors and played a significant role in the Queen's Coronation ceremony under the title of the 'Golden Stick'.[63] As a Scottish aristocrat, Stirling was particularly close to the Queen Mother, another Black Nobility Scottish bloodline who is certainly not the person she appears to be in her public charade as the nation's 'grandma'. Stirling, along with all members of the SAS, MI5, MI6 and so on, swears his oath of loyalty to the monarch, not the state. You can't even take your seat as a British MP unless you make the same pledge even though you have been elected by the people. Stirling admitted he had been in close contact with the British Defence and Foreign Ministries, two other links in the Windsor-Brotherhood chain. Stirling's operational officer in KAS and Operation Lock was Lt Colonel Ian Crooke, one of the hooded men on the balcony when his SAS team stormed the Iranian Embassy in London in May 1980, while millions watched on live television.[64] People like this were employed by Prince Philip and his WWF to protect wildlife in Africa? No, no, they were there as part of the Windsor-Black Nobility operation to turn Africa into a devastated blood bath. The wildlife parks are used as safe havens for the Brotherhood-Windsor-sponsored terrorists responsible for so much genocide in Africa. Nearly 20 per cent of Rwanda is covered by these reserves. The 1990 invasion of Rwanda by the 'Rwanda Patriotic Front' (RPF) came via the Gorilla Park and Akagera Park in Uganda on the Rwanda-Zaire border, and the Volcans Park in Rwanda.

The RPF (a British-controlled terrorist force) were also based in parts of the Virunga Park in Zaire.[65] A few months before these events, a 'gorilla protection programme' had begun in the Virunga, Gorilla and Volcan Parks. This programme was administered by... the WWF. In 1994 the 'Rwanda Patriotic Front' invaded Rwanda via the Akagera Park to trigger a conflict which has so far killed well in excess of a million people. I understand the violence began shortly after a 'diplomatic mission' to Rwanda by Henry Kissinger and Lord Carrington and it followed the sale of weapons to Rwanda by the Israeli government, then headed by Yitzhak Rabin. In truth this invasion was not by the 'Rwanda Patriotic Front' (RPF) at all. Almost every member of that group was a soldier in the 'National Resistance Army' (NRA) of Uganda's President Museveni. The leaders of both the RFP and the NRA are the same! The Rwanda Patriotic Front's David Tinyefuza was the Ugandan Minister for Defence, whilst Paul Kagame the Rwanda Defence Minister under the RPF was head of Intelligence and Counter-Intelligence in the Ugandan army, and the RPF's Chris Bunyenyezi is the former commander of the Ugandan army's murderous 306th Brigade.[66] The same crowd under Museveni were involved in the attempted coup in Burundi in 1993 in which President Melchior Ndadaye was murdered and an estimated 100,000 people lost their lives.[67] Another aspect of this policy in Africa, and Central and South America, is to reduce the population of what Henry Kissinger calls the "useless eaters". The genocide in Africa is being coordinated to a large extent out of Uganda which has long been controlled by the Windsor-Black Nobility cartels of banking, business and intelligence agencies. The British Minister of Overseas Development at the time was Margaret Thatcher's favourite, Lynda Chalker, who had a number of meetings with Museveni and his officials. South Africa with the end of Nelson Mandela's presidency is going to be a major target for those who are working to turn black against black to justify the intervention of the white peace keepers. We have seen only the start of the problems in the African continent: it is time for the people there to open their eyes.

Exactly the same operation is being played out in the Americas and Australia where the same names and techniques are there to see. In South and Central America, Brotherhood-controlled governments are 'privatising' their mineral and mining companies and handing them to the Black Nobility-Windsor cartels, particularly Rio Tinto, Anglo-American, Barrick Gold and Newmont Mining. Barrick Gold, based in Toronto, was formed in 1981 by Adnan Khashoggi, the Saudi financier and global arms trader and the uncle of Dodi Fayed. Peter Munk, formerly with the British royal household, became chairman of Barrick which appeared from nowhere to be the second biggest gold producer in the world.[68] One reason for this was the active involvement of the George Bush-Harriman networks. Khashoggi was a backer of President Bush's Iran-Contra drug-for-arms operation (see ...*And The Truth Shall Set You Free*). Newmont Mining is based in Denver, Colorado, a highly significant, and growing, Brotherhood centre. It appears to be an American company, but is once again controlled from London. It has been owned by the Hanson group who sold it to James Goldsmith. He sold 14% to George Soros, one of the Brotherhood's most active and identifiable financial manipulators, especially on behalf of the Rothschilds. Other shareholders in Newmont are Lord Jacob Rothschild, the Fidelity Mutual Fund, and Boston-based drug syndicates.[69] Alongside the assault on South America by the mineral corporations has come the takeover of the continent's banking system by the City of London cartel, led by HSBS (Hong Kong and Shanghai Bank which owns Midland Bank) and their interlocking American and Canadian counterparts like Citibank, the Bank of Montreal, and the Bank of Nova Scotia or Scotiabank.[70]

The Queen is Commander-in-Chief of all armed forces in the United Kingdom and the countries of the Commonwealth. The British army is deployed in many strategic parts of the world either directly or via the NATO and UN peacekeeping operations. British military 'advisors' are at work in some 30 countries. Every week the Queen is briefed by the Joint Intelligence Committee on all secret operations. (I wonder if she briefs them on hers?) The Windsor-Black Nobility has its own private armies, too. Among these are the Corps of Commissionaires and Defence Systems Ltd. The Corps of Commissionaires was formed, like Crown Agents, under royal sponsorship in 1859 when the British Empire was at the peak of its powers. The idea, so they said, was to find employment for soldiers coming home from the Crimean War and a number were deployed as armed and uninformed security guards at the Black Nobility buildings in the City of London. Branches followed in Australia, South and East Africa, New Zealand and Canada. Another network had been created to post British military personnel and their families to strategic centres. After the election of Margaret Thatcher in 1979, the Corps of Comissionaires was reorganised and a new division was established to provide 'specialist security functions'. More members of the military and paramilitary élite were employed and the Queen, the Patron of the Corps of Commissionaires, hosted a reception at Buckingham Palace in 1986 to celebrate the expansion. The Corp's Board of Governors in every country were full of the loyal friends of the Queen and Prince Philip. These included Major General David Alexander, Companion of the Bath and former Equerry and Treasurer to Philip, and Air Marshall Sir Thomas Kennedy, Knight Grand Cross of the Bath, Commander of the British Empire, the former Commander-in-Chief of the Royal Airforce in Germany. He was Aide-de-camp to the Queen between 1983 and 86. The Corps of Commissionaires is a Windsor operation through and through. It won't be a shock to learn, therefore, that the Corps is an umbrella organisation for hired killers. Some of the companies in its network are Sandline Ltd, Executive Outcomes and Defence Systems Ltd. Like the Corps of Commissionaires these are London-based and employ from the Special Air Services (SAS) and the military and police forces in the United Kingdom and the Commonwealth. The Corps have a permanent office in Papua New Guinea and the government there was voted from office in 1994 for negotiating a contract with Sandline International to use its mercenaries to put down a local insurgency. Sandline, in turn, subcontracted to Defence Systems Ltd (DSL), which has private and government contracts in more than 40 countries. It is employed by almost all the City of London cartels, the Club of the Isles, and has branches in Washington, Jacksonville, Hong Kong, Singapore, Bogata, Lima, Maputo, Kinshasa, Luanda, Port Moresby, Moscow, Kazakhstan, Jersey and Sarajevo.[71] Sandline was behind the coup in Sierra Leone which removed a legitimately elected government shortly after they cancelled a $20 million a year contract with the company.[72] This also triggered the inquiry into illegal arms sales to Sierra Leone by British suppliers through the Sandline network. A debt of some $16 million owed to Sandline by Sierra Leone before the coup, was paid by turning over diamond concessions to Executive

Outcomes' London underwriters Branch Energy.[73] This firm is owned by Tony Buckingham of Sandline International and yet another former member of the SAS.[74] He had pulled the same diamonds-for-mercenaries 'arrangement' on Angola and he floated these concessions on the Vancouver stock-market as a company called Diamond Works.[75] Another business partner of Tony Buckingham is David Steel, the former leader of the British Liberal Party and Anti-Apartheid Movement, and a member of the Queen's Privy Council.[76] Steel's Heritage Oil and Gas shares London offices with Branch Energy.[77]

In Sarajevo and the former Yugoslavia it has been working in conjunction with the Queen's agency, the Crown Agents. Defence Systems Ltd has substantial contracts with the United Nations, the World Bank, BP, Royal Dutch Shell, S. G. Warburg, Credit Suisse, Robert Fleming, Kleinwort Benson, British Airways, Cadbury Schweppes, Jardine Matheson, Rothmans, the Rothschilds, Exxon, Mobil, Amoco, Texaco, Chevron, Brown and Root, General Motors, Coca Cola, and Bechell.[78] A directory of the Black Nobility if ever I saw one. Defence Systems Ltd was established in 1981, again the early years of the Thatcher regime, and its rise was meteoric thanks to its supporters and patrons. At one point in 1980 it was a wholly-owned subsidiary of Hambros Bank.[79] The first managing director of DSL was Alestair Morrison, Order of the British Empire, the former number two in the 22nd regiment of the SAS. The first chairman was Major General Viscount Gilbert Monckton of Brenchley, Companion of the Bath, Order of the British Empire, and former chief of staff of the British Army of the Rhine. His father was in Winston Churchill's cabinet and chairman of Midland Bank, and his son was editor of *The Daily Telegraph* (Hollinger) Sunday Magazine and advisor to Margaret Thatcher. Philip Warner of the shipping company P & O was another founding director of Defence Systems and a later chief executive was Richard N. Bethell, another former SAS officer. His father, Lord Nicholas Bethell, was an agent with British Intelligence (MI6) and Lord-in-Waiting to the Queen. He was involved in the manipulation of the war in Afghanistan through the 1980s and the terrorist organisations which have come from that. Defence Systems interlocks with a similar company, Control Risks, a very important part of the network founded in 1974 to serve Lloyds of London.[80] The managing director of Control Risks is Major Arish Turle, former SAS, and among its directors is General Sir John Stanier, former Commander in Chief of UK land forces and Aide-de-Camp-General to the Queen. Lord Soames, the senior Tory politician and son-in-law to Winston Churchill, is another Control Risks director. Soames was 'advisor' to Prince Charles at the time that Princess Diana gave her outspoken interview with the BBC programme *Panorama*. Soames, (nicknamed 'fatty'), questioned her mental state. I've got a feeling she was rather more mentally stable than Soames, somehow. In that *Panorama* interview Diana spoke in a way that no insider ever has about the Windsors. According to Stephen Dorrill in his book, *The Secret Conspiracy, Inside The Secret Service In The 90s*, Control Risks is the most important of the private secret services operated by the Queen's Privy Council.[81]

Defence Systems was bought by the American company Armor Holdings for $26 million. Armor is a front company for the George Bush circle and the idea was to give Defence Systems an 'American' owner to allow expansion into the United States security market. Body Armor and Equipment Inc. was a small family-owned company until it went bankrupt in 1992 and was reorganised as Armor Holdings by the introduction of Wall Street investors and Windsor associates. One director, Richard C. Bartlett, is chairman and trustee of the Nature Conservancy of Texas which was founded by the British Privy Council in 1946. One of the companies using Defence Systems in South America is British Petroleum who employ Control Risks. BP is one of the most unpleasant business operations on the planet and a front for the British Foreign Office, British Intelligence and The Crown. British Petroleum is a jewel of the Brotherhood and the Windsor cartels and so it is only understandable that they would use the Brotherhood-Windsor 'security' network. The BP chairman, Sir David Simon, was invited to join the government of golden boy Tony Blair after he became Prime Minister on May 1st 1997. Simon is also director of the Bank of England, Grand Metropolitan, Rio Tinto, Alliance AG, and a member of the International Advisory Council of the Deutche Bank.[82] His role in the government is for 'European affairs' and this is Blair-speak for ensuring that Britain becomes a member of the European single currency and central bank and therefore loses all power to govern itself. Simon was replaced as head of BP by Peter D. Sutherland (Bil), a notorious Brotherhood front man. Another company I should mention with regard to the manipulation of Africa and the Americas is Transparency International which is a member of the Crown Agents Foundation and has the managing director of the Crown Agents on its own board. Transparency International is used to destabilise governments under the guise of exposing corruption.[83]

These interconnecting 'security' companies operating world-wide are the private army of the Windsors and the Black Nobility based in the City of London. Want some trouble in Africa to advance your Agenda. No problem. Where do you fancy, Rwanda? Algeria? The Congo? How about South America? Where do you fancy? Bolivia? Peru? These are part of the network being developed for a planned global coup some time in the not too distant future. Confirmation that the Royal Family are close to the intelligence agencies and operate outside the 'democratic' process came in an interview given by Colonel David Stirling, the founder of the SAS, who worked for Prince Philip's World Wide Fund for Nature in African covert operations. Before he died, he told the authors of the book *Who Killed Diana?*,[84] that in late 1974 or early 1975 he attended a dinner at a royal palace hosted by a senior member of the monarchy. Prince Philip I would guess. Prince Charles' uncle, Lord Mountbatten, was also there along with ten representatives of British Intelligence including the heads of MI5 and MI6. They were there in an unofficial capacity and Stirling pointed out that all military officers swore allegiance to the Queen and regarded her as the ultimate authority, more important than elected governments. The meeting was called to discuss the state of the country and the need for intervention in political affairs. The use of force was on the agenda, he said. Stirling told the meeting of his involvement in an operation to create a coup d'état in Libya and at the time he was the leader of an organisation called GB75 which was designed to take over public services in times of crisis. John Mitchell, the chairman of the shipping company Cunard, also confirmed that he had been approached to take part in a coup because they wanted his ships. One of the orchestrators was Sir Basil Smallpiece, financial advisor to the Queen. Mitchell said:

> "They asked me to take part in a coup. They said it would involve the army. They implied it had the highest backing... I went out of there in a state of shock."[85]

Yet people still believe that the idea of secret groups manipulating from the shadows is the nonsensical invention of the paranoid. In fact the evidence for this, and the Windsors' involvement, is overwhelming. Do we really believe that this Windsor-Intelligence agency network which was planning an armed coup in Britain, would not conspire to kill Diana, Princess of Wales, when she threatened their power? Come on. What I have outlined in this chapter is a mere fraction of what there is to tell about the Windsors, the Black Nobility, fascist, reptilian family which operate from Buckingham Palace, London, on behalf of the global network of the reptilian-Brotherhood. The Windsors have been responsible, through their global networks, for the deaths of untold millions. As the Brotherhood-controlled police won't be knocking on the door of Buckingham Palace, it is the people who, in my view, need to impose so much pressure on the Windsors and the establishment that they have to abdicate. Then we can begin to dismantle their source of power, the enormous structure headquartered in the City of London.

The Windsors in their present mode must know the game is up and they may be planning to abdicate and move to the United States. It may even be part of the Brotherhood Agenda for them to abdicate soon, who knows? To the reptilians, the Agenda is far more important than any individual or family line, even theirs.

■ SOURCES

1   Thomas Foster, *Britain's Royal Throne* (Acadia Press, Victoria, Australia, 1986), p 2.

2   Samuel 10:24.

3   *Britain's Royal Throne*, p 6.

4   Ibid, p 8.

5   Exodus 28:1-21.

6   *Britain's Royal Throne*, p 12.

7   Ibid, p 14.

8   Psalm 89: 35-37.

9   *The Curse Of Canaan*, p 85.

10 *In The Blood*, p 62.

11 Gary Boyd Roberts, *Ancestors Of The American Presidents*, New England Historic Genealogical Society.

12 Ibid.

13 *The Top 13 Illuminati Bloodlines*, p 99.

14 Ibid.

15 The information about Philip's Nazi connections is available through many sources, but this and a catalogue of other information about the Windsors can be found in a series of articles pulled together in a document called "The True Story Behind the Fall of the House of Windsor". It was published in September 1997 by Executive Intelligence Review (EIR) in the United States. I do not agree with all the conclusions reached by the EIR, especially the way it defends Bill Clinton when he is also part of the web. But the EIR does some outstanding research. Their Windsor report is expensive, but well worth it if you want to know more. Their address is Executive Intelligence Review, PO Box 17390, Washington DC 20041–0390. Through the rest of this chapter I will source this document with the name of the writer and the title of the article, followed by (EIR).

16 "Blair's School Mentor Was Sex Abuser", *The Sunday Times*, May 25th 1997.

17 Scott Thompson, "The Nazi Roots of the House of Windsor" (EIR), p 70.

18 Ibid, 71.

19 Scott Thomson, "The Ultimate Insider Trader is the Queen" (EIR), p 73.

20 Ibid.

21 Ibid, p 74.

22 For the full story on this see the Peter Jones book, *The Obedience Of Australia*, published by XPO-imprint, 26 Burlington Close, London, in 1995.

23 "The Ultimate Insider Trader is the Queen", p 74.

24 Ibid.

25 Stephen Knight, *The Brotherhood* (Granada Books, London, 1985), p 223.

26 Anthony K. Wikrent, "The Anglo-Dutch Corporate Empire" (EIR), pp 113–132.

27 *The Brotherhood*, p 211.

28 Ibid.

29 *The Mail On Sunday*, August 12th 1998, p 9.

30 Dean Andromidas, "Crown Agents: the Queen's Managers" (EIR), pp 141–142.

31 Ibid, p 141–142.

32 Ibid, p 141.

33 *The Obedience Of Australia*, p 55.

34 *The Brotherhood*, p 217.

35 Scott Thompson, "The Queen's Honorary Knights in America" (EIR), p 81.

36 James Shelby Downard, "Sorcery, Sex, Assassination and the Science of Symbolism", an article in the book, *Secret And Suppressed*, edited by Jim Keith (Feral House, PO Box 3466, Portland, Oregon 97208, 1993), p 65.

37 Brian Downing Quig, "Who Dismantled Our Constitution", *Grapevine* magazine, January 2nd 1995.

38 Ibid.

39 This information comes from an American who has spent decades researching the genealogy of the big names in America. He operates under the pseudonym, John Gaunt.

40 Scott Thompson, "Sir Paul Mellon, Lord of Loudoun", (EIR), p 79.

41 Ibid.

42 Allen Douglas, "The Oligarchs' Real Game Is Killing Animals and Killing People" (EIR), p 32.

43 Ibid, p 31.

44 Ibid.

45 Ibid, p 32.

46 Ibid.

47 Scott Thompson, "The 1001 Club: a Nature Trust" (EIR), p 15.

48 Mark Burdman, "Martin Palmer, Prince Philip's Guru" (EIR), p 91. He was quoting from Palmer's book, *Dancing To Armageddon*.

49 "Globalized Grizzlies", *The New American* magazine, August 18th 1997.

50 *The Times*, July 21st 1997, p 23.

51 "Prince Philip's Friends Ran 'Get LaRouche' Plot" (EIR), p 17.

52 *The Anglo-Dutch Corporate Empire*, pp 125–126

53 Ibid.

54 Ibid.

55 Joseph Brewda, "The Invisible Empire of the NGOs" (EIR) p 91.

56 Ibid, pp 89–90.

57 Ibid, p 90.

58 Linda de Hoyos, "World Wide Fund For Nature Commits Genocide in Africa" (EIR), p 24.

59 "The Oligarchs' Real Game is Killing Animals and Killing People" (EIR), p 34.

60 Ibid.

61 Ibid, p 35.

62 Ibid, p 34.

63 Ibid, pp 35–36.

64 Ibid, p 36.

65 Linda de Hoyos, "The British Royal Family's Policy at Work: Mass Death in Rwanda" (EIR), p 38.

66 Ibid.

67 Ibid.

68 Richard Freeman and Cynthia Rush, "British Cartels Break Up Brazil's CVRD, Target Continents Raw Materials" (EIR), p 192.

69 Ibid, p 193.

70 Dennis Small, "British Banks Establish Death Grip Over Ibero-America" (EIR), p 187.

71 Roger Moore, "Executive Outcomes vs the Nation State" (EIR), p 147.

72 Ibid.

73 Ibid.

74 Ibid.

75 Ibid.

76 Ibid.

77 Ibid.

78 Dean Andromidas, "Defence Systems Ltd: A Crown Jewel" (EIR), p 148.

79 Ibid, p 149.

80 Ibid.

81 Quoted by Javier Alamario, "British Run Private Armies in Colombia" (EIR), p 199.

82 "The Anglo-Dutch Corporate Empire" (EIR), p 113.

83 "Directors, Councillors, of Crown Agents" (EIR), p 143.

84 Peter Hounam and Derek McAdam in *Who Killed Diana?* (Vision Books, London, 1998).

85 Ibid, p 124.

CHAPTER NINETEEN

The Goddess and the King

Agencies under the control of this spider's web of interconnecting families and interests were responsible for the murder of Diana, Princess of Wales. Of that I have no doubt. But please don't take my word for this. Look at the evidence and judge for yourself.

Many people dismiss the idea that Diana was assassinated because it would be impossible to kill her in a public situation and then cover up the evidence. After all, there would need to be coordination between so many different agencies. Well that's precisely what happened in the United States with the assassination of President John Fitzgerald Kennedy in 1963 and that was even more difficult to cover up. It wasn't staged as an accident which immediately creates the diversion of was it an accident or was it murder? The Kennedy assassination was quite clearly murder. He literally had his brains blown out in front of hundreds of onlookers and it was captured on film by one of them, Abraham Zapruder. In ...*And The Truth Shall Set You Free*, I feature the Kennedy killing in detail and you will see that the same people who supported or arranged the assassination were also appointed to the commission of the Chief 'Justice' and 33rd degree Freemason, Earl Warren, to investigate what happened! Among the Warren Commission 'team' were Allen Dulles, the head of the CIA sacked by Kennedy, and the paedophile, rapist, Bohemian Grove member and pornographer Gerald Ford, who would later become President of the United States after Richard Nixon was removed by Watergate. When Representative Hale Boggs, the only Catholic on the Commission, began to question its findings, he died in a plane crash. How convenient.

Jim Garrison, the New Orleans District Attorney, is the only man to charge anyone with Kennedy's murder. This was the CIA operative and former wartime friend of Winston Churchill called Clay Shaw. Garrison failed to win a conviction against the guilty-as-hell Shaw because many of the key witnesses were murdered before the trial. Garrison was astonished at the way apparently unconnected agencies, including the Dallas police, the FBI, the press, and the Washington establishment, could work so obviously as one unit to carry out the assassination and then cover it up. This was possible because of the networks I have been exposing in this book which have their operatives, 'gofers' and yes men, in all the agencies representing all sides and shades of opinion. Getting on for 40 years after the murder of President Kennedy in a public street on a public occasion we are no nearer to anyone being convicted. As usual the 'culprit' was identified immediately by those who were really responsible and he was eliminated so he couldn't contradict the official 'tale'. For Lee Harvey Oswald in Dealey Plaza, Dallas in 1963, read Henri Paul in the Pont de L'Alma Tunnel, Paris in 1997. Once the scapegoat has been sacrificed, no other story is entertained by the authorities and public interest wanes with the weeks, months and years. It's an old and well tried technique. A President is killed in a public assassination; Lee Harvey Oswald, the scapegoat or 'patsy', is murdered in public a few days later; and those who orchestrated their demise go to their graves unexposed and unconvicted. The Princess of Wales could not be murdered in a staged accident and the whole thing covered up? You've got to be kidding.

As I've described the background to the Kennedy assassination in a previous book, I won't repeat it all again here, but there are elements to that story that need to be highlighted and added to. Diana's family, the Spencers, are of an Elite bloodline and so are the Kennedys, who come from the Kennedy clan of ancient Ireland and later Scotland. They are descendants of the Irish king, Brian Boru, also known as Brian Caeneddi, which later became O'Kennedy. They were the Lords of Ormond in what is now called north Tipperary.[1] From around 1600 a Scottish branch of the Kennedys can be identified and this intermarried with the Irish line.[2] The Scottish Kennedys became a powerful strand of the aristocratic bloodlines of Scotland and married into Scottish royalty. One notable Kennedy was Archibald Kennedy, the 15th Earl of Cassillis, better known as the Marquess of Ailsa. He lived from 1872 to 1943 and held many leading positions in the Grand Lodge of Scottish Freemasonry including Grand Principle.[3] He was a member of the key Holyrood House Lodge no 44 in Edinburgh which has close ties with the British royal family.[4] In the 18th century, a Matthew Kennedy from Ireland went to Paris to work with his good friend, the Illuminati frontman called Saint Germain, who presided over the Illuminati Lodge at Ermenonville near Paris.[5] The lodge took part in blood rituals on an altar made from human bones.[6] This Kennedy produced a work called *A Chronological, Genealogical and Historical Dissertation of the Royal Family of the Stuarts who connect into the Merovingian line established in France*. The JFK wing is related to the Fitzpatricks, a powerful Irish family with a coat of arms which includes the classic Brotherhood symbols of three fleur-de-lis, a dragon, and a lion.[7] It seems likely that the Fitzpatricks go back to France and the Holy Grail story.

The family of JFK's wife, Jackie Bouvier Kennedy (later Onassis), are related to the Auchinclosses, one of the major Elite Scottish bloodlines, via the marriage of Jackie's sister into the Auchincloss clan. Other Auchincloss bloodlines have manifested as names like Bundy, Grosvenor, Vanderbilt, Winthrop and Rockefeller.[8] Hugh D. Auchincloss Sr married Emma Brewster Jennings, the daughter of Oliver B. Jennings, who co-founded Standard Oil with John D. Rockefeller. James Shelby Downard describes Jackie Kennedy-Onassis, Caroline (Lee) Bouvier, and the writer, Gore Vidal, as the 'stepchildren' of Hugh D. Auchincloss.[9] Vidal has described John and Jackie Kennedy as the "Sun God and Goddess".[10] The Bouvier bloodline has been traced back to Grenoble, France, where it is first mentioned in 1410 and Jackie's great-great-grandfather, Eustache Bouvier, fought in a French regiment under the command of George Washington.[11] It was noted earlier that the Kennedys also married into the Dukes of Devonshire family at Chatsworth House, one of the leading Brotherhood families in England. The marriage of John Kennedy to Jackie Bouvier was another arranged marriage by the Eastern Establishment, the American bloodlines who run the United States according to the Agenda decided in the British Isles and France. Both bloodlines connect with the key centres of London and Paris. The fact that their marriage and presidency was known as 'Camelot' with its King Arthur and Mars connotations, is thoroughly appropriate because the King Arthur symbolism is used by the Brotherhood as part of their secret language. The Kennedy family have been closely involved with drugs, organised crime, the British monarchy, and the mind controlled slave operations like Project Monarch. This adds credibility to the claims by a recovered mind controlled slave I met who said she was taken to have sex with John F. Kennedy at the age of eleven – "Although they made me up to look about 16".

The Kennedy presidency was certainly not the way it was portrayed at the time. Kennedy had a stream of sexual partners and three of them, Marilyn Monroe, Jayne Mansfield and Zsa Zsa Gabor, were also girlfriends of Anton LaVey, head of the Church of Satan. Jayne Mansfield was a high priestess. Other long term relationships included two with members of Elite Scottish bloodlines, Lady Jean Campbell daughter of the Duke of Argyll, and Kay-Kay Hannon Auchincloss[12] of the family to which his wife was related. Behind JFK's rise to fame was his father, Joseph Kennedy, a member of the Brotherhood's Pilgrim Society. He was a crook with close connections to the Mafia and other organised crime. His fortune was assured when Winston Churchill awarded him the franchise to import British liquor into the United States. Joseph Kennedy was an associate of the Rothschilds and the Bronfmans, another 'Jewish' crime family in Canada which owns the liquor giant, Seagrams. Among Joseph Kennedy's contacts in Britain when he was US Ambassador to the Court of St James's in London were the Astors and the Rothschild bloodline offshoot, the Sassoons. Another intimate friend was Sir John Wheeler-Bennett, a leading executive of the Royal Institute of International Affairs. Joseph Kennedy's wife, Rose, came from the Black Nobility Fitzgerald family. The Fitzgeralds were one of the mighty Black Nobility clans of Italy which supported William the Conqueror's conquest of England in 1066. This established Black Nobility rule of the British Isles via ancient families like the St. Clairs/Sinclairs. So the 'F' in JFK was a Black Nobility family going back thousands of years. Rose's father and JFK's grandfather was John F. (Honey Fitz) Fitzgerald, the vote-rigging mayor of Boston. The Fitzgeralds lived in Hanover Street near the former site of the Green Dragon Tavern in Boston, home to the St Andrews Lodge which was heavily involved in the manipulation of the American War of Independence and orchestrated the Boston Tea Party.[13]

Joseph Kennedy was a member of the Order of St John, the British version of the Knights of Malta, and the Bouvier family was intermarried with the Radziwills who established the Knights of St John/Knights of Malta in Poland in 1610 and also helped to establish the order in the United States.[14] The Kennedys support the

Knights of Malta hospice movement in the United States via the Kennedy Institute for the Study of Human Reproduction and Bioethics at the Jesuit-controlled Georgetown University. The hospice movement, while presented with a compassionate face, is a front to gather support for euthanasia. Most people involved with the hospice movement are compassionate, it is the motivation of those who are manipulating it that I am talking about. Once euthanasia is accepted in law, it opens the floodgates for the legalised murder of what Kissinger calls the "useless eaters". As has been well documented in the countless biographies of JFK, he endured a loveless childhood under the iron rule of his father Joe and mother, Rose. He wasn't even told that his brother Teddy had been born and it was only when he came home from boarding school that he realised he had a new brother. There were no hugs, no show of affection, and the Kennedy children were not allowed to show pain. His upbringing has all the classic signs of the mind control techniques the Elite use on their own children. Prince Charles went through exactly the same upbringing under his aggressive and deeply unpleasant father, Prince Philip. JFK was groomed from an early age to take high office for the Brotherhood and he was supported by all the classic names like the Rothschilds, Tafts, Russells, Rockefellers, and media barons like Henry Luce, the head of Time-Life, and Randolph Hearst, the most powerful newspaper tycoon in the United States. When Kennedy ran for political office, the Boston American newspaper, owned by Hearst, refused to accept the paid advertisements of his opponent.[15]

But when JFK and his brother, Bobby, became President and Attorney General of the United States after their defeat of Richard Nixon in 1960, it seems that they began to pursue policies and people that were far from conducive to the introduction of their paymasters agenda. This included withdrawal from the Vietnam War, the introduction of some interest-free money, an assault on organised crime (in public at least) and, as Kennedy put it, a pledge to break up the CIA "Into a thousand pieces". It doesn't matter who you are, if you don't do as you are told, you are removed in the most appropriate way, bloodline or not. The Agenda is far greater than any individual or family. I can't help thinking, however, that there was more to the assassination than this and it has the feel of a long planned sacrificial murder, in accordance with the Brotherhood's ancient ritual laws. The location of the assassination, Dallas, Texas is close to the 33rd parallel of the 33rd degree of latitude. The top level of the Scottish Rite of Freemasonry is the 32nd degree and the 33rd degree is only for those who have contributed significantly to the Great Work, the takeover of Planet Earth. Dealey Plaza is a mass of esoteric symbolism and is officially named after a 33rd degree Freemason called George Bannerman Dealey, an early executive of the Dallas Morning News. Dealey means 'goddess line'. Ley can also mean rule or law in Spanish, so translating as 'goddess-rule'. Either is perfect symbolism for the Brotherhood, especially the latter. Dealey Plaza, the site of the first Freemason temple in Dallas, is shaped like a pyramid with the capstone missing (*see **Figure 51** overleaf*). The top is truncated by a railway bridge. The main pyramid is cut into two more by Main Street which runs directly through the centre. It is, in fact, three pyramids, two inside the one:

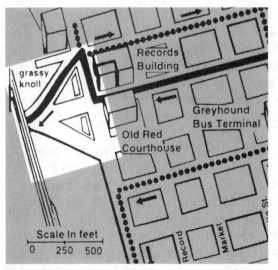

Figure 51: *The pyramid with the capstone missing. This is Dealey Plaza where John F. Kennedy was assassinated.*

the trinity or triad. Two energies interacting produce a third. If anyone thinks this is mere coincidence they should do a little research into the background of the Brotherhood secret societies at the top levels and see the staggering obsession they have with their symbols and rituals. Kennedy was killed near the so-called grassy knoll on the right of the pyramid and Lee Harvey Oswald was murdered while under police 'guard' in an underground car park at the bottom of the pyramid on Houston Street. Only a few yards separate the two points. The old Court House nearby which looks into Dealey Plaza is decorated with gargoyles. On top of the Court House is the symbol of the ancient Order of the Dragon or the Snake. Dealey Plaza, to the secret societies, is a Sun temple.

Kennedy was assassinated in an outdoor temple of the Sun by initiates of the Brotherhood network including the Knights Templar, the Knights of Malta, the Order of St John of Jerusalem, the Rosicrucians and the Freemasons. As James Shelby Downard writes: " Masonry does not believe in murdering a man in just any old way and in the JFK assassination it went to incredible lengths and took great risks in order to make this heinous act correspond to the ancient fertility oblation of the Killing of The King".[16] Kennedy was shot just after noon when the Sun was "most high". In ancient times it was said that when the Sun was "most high", he was doing his father's work in the temple (more symbolism used in the Jesus story). Kennedy was shot in the back, the head, and the throat, and they are the same wounds suffered by the mythical Hiram Abiff according to Freemasonic legend and initiation. Bill Cooper, a former operative with US Naval Intelligence, believes that the mythical Freemason hero, Hiram Abiff, is really a symbol for Jacques de Molay, the Grand Master of the Knights Templar when they were purged in France in 1307. De Molay was burnt to death on the Ile de la Cite, the original Paris, in the shadow of Notre Dame Cathedral, which the Templar's had built on a former site of worship to the goddess Diana. His death was ordered by the Roman Church Inquisition with support from King Phillipe the Fair, who could well have been under the control of the Priory of Sion. Cooper says that the assassination of JFK was the revenge of the Knights Templar against the Church, the state and the people. Kennedy is the only Roman Catholic President of the United States, the same Church of Rome which killed Jacques de Molay. On Dealey Plaza today, standing near the points where Kennedy and Oswald were murdered, is the obelisk erected by the Freemasons after the murders. The obelisk is symbolic of the penis of

Osiris in Egyptian legend and the one in Dealey Plaza has the flame or lighted torch at the top (*see picture section*). The eternal flame on the Kennedy grave in Arlington Cemetery is there for the same reason. The flame or lighted torch is the most obvious Brotherhood signature and on Kennedy's grave the flame is within a circle, the ancient symbol of the Sun. Kennedy was also laid in state in the centre of a circle under the dome on Capitol Hill. There are 14 stones on the obelisk in Dealey Plaza, the number of pieces into which Osiris was cut by Set, according to Egyptian myth. The one part that his sister-wife, Isis, could not find was his penis, represented by the obelisk itself. She replaced the penis of Osiris with one she made herself and this became the symbol of the Brotherhood. The Dealey Plaza obelisk was built for, and dedicated to, a Freemasonic lodge of the Scottish Rite. They have found stone phalluses in cathedrals and churches hidden inside altars and when the investigation team of New Orleans District Attorney, Jim Garrison, searched the home of Clay Shaw they found penises.

In this book I've exposed the secret language at its basic level, but the depth to which it goes is astonishing. The science of numbers and names is one of these deeper levels of communication and symbolism which only an advanced initiate or focused researcher would fully understand. Numbers and names are, once again, vibrational frequencies and the amazing synchronicity of these is due, I feel, to the law of what I call vibrational attraction. Many of the number-name 'coincidences' will be consciously made to happen, but others are simply due to the energy field, the consciousness, of the person or people attracting to themselves vibrational fields which synchronise with the energy they are generating. This is how we create our own reality. Our inner self, our vibrating consciousness field, attracts other 'fields' – people, places, ways of life, experiences – which sync with the energy we are generating. It's a vibrational attraction between like energy fields. Therefore, our outer physical experience is merely a reflection of what is happening inside. What we vibrationally project with our attitudes and emotions, we attract back to us in people, places, ways of life and experiences which vibrate to the frequency we are projecting or broadcasting. So when we change what is happening within us, we change our physical experience because one is a reflection of the other. It is this 'magnetic' attraction of like vibration to like vibration that leads to people living in streets of a certain name or having relationships with those of a certain name, etc., because everything has its own vibrational code, including sounds, numbers, words, colours and names. In ritual magic the correct sounds, words, incantations, and colours, are all used to manifest a desired energy field or vibratory field. Sound is especially important and this is why the Phoenicians were concerned more with the sound of their words than their spelling. Mantras, the constant repeating of the same phrase or sound, are part of this same knowledge. And, like all knowledge, they can be used for good or ill. The training of Japanese Samurai warriors included instruction in producing the fighting cry, "Kiai". This sound is supposed to cause a lowering of blood pressure and partial paralysis in the hearer. Thus we have a 'blood-chilling' cry. Low frequency sounds of three to five cycles a second can kill you. The American researcher, James Shelby Downard, has written of this science of sounds, numbers and names in relation to the Kennedy assassination. The writer, Robert Anton Wilson, says in his book *The Cosmic Trigger*, that Downard's theory is "The most absurd, the most incredible, the most ridiculous Illuminati theory of them all". This makes me even more certain that Downard must definitely be on to something. My own research supports this, too.

Kennedy was killed on November 22nd 1963. This date was the anniversary of the order or papal bull by Pope Clement V for the Knights Templar to be subjected to torture by the Dominican Inquisition. It was issued on November 22nd 1307. November is also the 11th month and if you add that to 22, again you have 33. John and Jackie Kennedy left Fort Worth on the morning of November 22nd 1963 and the plane came to a stop at gate 28 at Love Field Airport in Dallas. The number 28 is assigned the name 'Beale' in Solomonic cabalistic numerology. Beale is a word which derives in this way: Bel (El), Baal, Be al, Beal, Beale. These all relate to Sun gods. The 28th degree of the Knights Templar is the 'King of the Sun degree'. JFK was born at 83 Beal Street, Brookline, Massachusetts, on May 29th 1917. The 'protection' of the President on this fatal trip to Dallas was organised by the New Orleans CIA station which was housed in a Masonic temple building. Dallas is just ten miles south of the 33rd degree of latitude and the founding lodge of the Scottish Rite of Freemasonry was in Charleston, exactly on the 33rd degree. The first atom bomb was exploded at the 'Trinity' Site on the 33rd degree of latitude. The Kennedy motorcade travelled down Elm Street once home to the Blue Front Tavern, the meeting place for Freemasons, and at 12.22 pm it arrived in Dealey Plaza. Elm Street was known as 'Bloody' Elm Street because it was the scene of countless gun fights, stabbings and other acts of violence. The national offices of Texaco Oil are on Elm Street. Close to Dealey Plaza is the Trinity River which used to flood the Plaza for many years until the introduction of flood defences. Into this open air temple of the ancient Brotherhood came Jackie Kennedy, representing the goddess, the Queen of Love and Beauty and her scapegoat Sun King, John F. Kennedy. He was the sacrifice in the ancient ritual of the Killing of the Sun King: the 'Ceannaideach' which is Gaelic for Wounded Head. Kennedy, of course, was shot in the head. I have it from a very good source that Kennedy didn't die until the following spring. My source claims that the 'Kennedy' who appeared in the post mortem photographs was J. D. Tippet, the police officer and Kennedy look-alike who was supposed to have been shot by Oswald with a gun that wasn't working!

When JFK was 22, a sculpture was made of him as a winged angel and it was presented to the Vatican where it was used as part of a panel in which the angel hovers over St Therese as she writes in a book.[17] After the assassination, Kennedy's body was code-named 'Angel' and the same name was used for the plane, Air Force 1, which flew his coffin back to Washington.[18] Both Kennedy and Oswald were buried in places related to 'Arlington'. Kennedy at the Arlington National Cemetery near Washington DC and Oswald at the Rosehill Cemetery, near Arlington, Texas. Arlington is a word related to Freemasonic sorcery and pertains to necrophilia, a morbid attraction to corpses. Oswald is Os or Oz, the Egyptian Sun god Osiris as in the Wizard of Oz. If you are looking at the synchronicity in the science of names and numbers, look at the astonishing coincidences between the assassinations of JFK and Abraham Lincoln, who was also killed by the Brotherhood. Lincoln was elected to Congress in 1846 and Kennedy was elected to Congress in 1946. Lincoln was elected president in 1860 and Kennedy was elected president in 1960. Lincoln's assassin, John Wilkes Booth, was born in 1839 and Lee Harvey Oswald, the alleged assassin of Kennedy, was born in 1939. Their successors were both called Johnson. Andrew Johnson, who succeeded Lincoln, was born in 1808 and Lyndon Johnson, who succeeded Kennedy, was born in 1908. Lincoln's secretary was called Kennedy and Kennedy's secretary was called Lincoln. Both presidents were murdered on a Friday in the presence of their wives and both were shot in the head.

Kennedy's vice-president, Lyndon Baines Johnson, had prior knowledge of the assassination and when he became president he immediately reversed all the policies on Vietnam, interest-free money, and the CIA which Kennedy was implementing. The Brotherhood Mother Goddess, Arizona Wilder, says she saw the shape-shifting Johnson at sacrifice rituals. Johnson's middle name, Baines, comes from the related Scottish clans of Bain, Bayne, Beathy, Binnie, Beath and Beth. Freemasons from these clans claim the same ancestor.[19] The term, Mac, means 'son of' and so the son of Bain becomes MacBain and the interconnected clan, Beth, becomes MacBeth, the Scottish king made world famous by the writings of 'William Shakespeare'. Bain in French means bath and this is an origin of the Order of the Bath title awarded by the British monarch. Purification or absolution baths are given to the Masonic 'Knights of the Bath' before they cause murder and mayhem on the Brotherhood's behalf. After her husband's death, Jackie Kennedy journeyed to the island of Delos in the Aegean Sea which is considered by legend to be the birthplace of the goddess Diana and Apollo the Greek Sun god. Diana (the Moon) and Apollo (the Sun) are often brought together in Brotherhood symbolism. Delos is also known as the Island of the Dead because another version of the goddess Diana, known as Hecate, is said to be the patroness of the 'infernal arts'. Jackie went on to the Temple of Apollo at Delphi in Greece and in the ruins of a Greek theatre on that site she performed an ancient rite known as the Greeting of the Sun. She performed this, according to James Shelby Downard, "With the expertise of an Aleister Crowley".[20] Another stop on her tour was the island of Santorina with its reputation for vampires. The origin of the vampire stories are the blood drinking and blood sucking rituals of the Brotherhood and their 'energy sucking' rituals, also. The vampire stories put the truth before our eyes in a way that we think is only fiction. This is something the Brotherhood loves to do via its biggest vehicle for communication, Hollywood, a name which comes from the holly bush, the holly (holy) wood of the Druid magicians. Hollywood is called a place of magic. Exactly what it is. It's playing with our minds, manipulating illusions.

There are so many similarities between the Kennedy assassination, the ritual killing of a Sun King, and that of Diana, Princess of Wales, in what I am convinced to have been a ritual murder of the Moon goddess known to the ancients as Diana. It was planned that Kennedy would die on that spot at that time long before he became president and so, I believe, Diana was groomed for at least many years to die in Paris at that spot at that time, also. It is quite possible that this was planned from their childhood, even birth. I know how extreme that sounds, but when you study the Brotherhood in depth you realise very quickly that they are not formulating their plans weeks or months in advance, but literally centuries. From the lower fourth dimension they have a very different perspective of time in this dimension than we do. In the concluding chapters I will look in more detail at this and how and why such ritual assassinations are performed with such an eye to detail. Planning the murder of the Roman Catholic John Kennedy, the Sun King, to mark the anniversary of the Roman Church's Inquisition against the Knights Templar (or some other ritual) could quite obviously have been agreed decades in advance and the scapegoat decided and groomed for office. In the same way, Diana's birth to the bloodline family the Spencers in 1961 could have led to her being chosen as a symbol of the goddess Diana who would be led to a ritual death in an ancient sacred place of Diana worship and sacrifice, the Pont de L'Alma tunnel in Paris. I think there is an excellent chance that this is what happened. Just as Kennedy was manoeuvred into the presidency in 1960 for his ritual murder in 1963, so Diana was manoeuvred and manipulated into a marriage with Prince Charles and, finally, into the Pont de L'Alma tunnel. People say that to arrange the murder of Diana would have involved enormous planning and a great deal of time. Yes, that's probably right. But they had plenty of time.

Diana Frances Spencer was born at Park House on the Queen's Sandringham estate in Norfolk on July 1st 1961, the third and youngest daughter of Viscount Althorp, later the 8th Earl Spencer, and his first wife Frances Roche. Her parents separated when she was six and divorced in 1969, and her mother married the wallpaper tycoon Peter Shand-Kidd. Diana had a younger brother, Charles, the present Earl Spencer, and two sisters, Jane and Sarah. Another son was born before Diana, but he died and she believed that her parents would much rather she been a boy, a son and heir. Diana said that her childhood was very unhappy and she was to crave all her short life for the love and warmth denied her as a child. Living at Sandringham she knew the Queen from the time she was a little girl and she used to play with the royal children. It is said that Charles first saw Diana when she was still in her pram. She remembered, with less than affection, being shunted over to the Queen's residence during the holidays year after year to watch the film *Chitty Chitty Bang Bang*. The choice of movie is interesting because it was written by Ian Fleming, the intelligence agent, friend of Aleister Crowley and author of the James Bond novels. The movie features a king and queen who hate children. They employ a child catcher to lure children, abduct them, and put them in a cage. They are then taken to the castle and locked in a dungeon. It is all symbolism for what is actually happening and there is no way that the Windsors played this for Diana so often by accident. Certainly Diana was already picking up the Windsor 'vibes' at Sandringham. She told Andrew Morton in his book, *Diana: Her True Story*: "The atmosphere was always very strange when we went there and I used to kick and fight anyone who tried to make us go".[21] So the Windsors were well aware of Diana from the moment she was born. When she was 13, Diana moved from Norfolk to live at Althorp in Northamptonshire, the Spencer family's ancestral home, after her father inherited the title of Earl Spencer. Diana was particularly devastated when her father married Raine, the daughter of the novelist Barbara Cartland. Diana had a deep loathing for her. She said in *Diana: Her True Story* that in September 1989 she had unleashed her years of frustration on Raine: "I told her what I thought about her, and I've never known such anger in me. I remember really going for her gullet". I said "If you only knew how much we all hated you for what you've done, you've ruined the house (Althorp), you spend all daddy's money, and for what?" The empathy that Diana had with people in emotional distress came from her own emotional scars which she carried all her life.

The Spencers are an Elite bloodline family. They are cousins of the Spencer-Churchills and related to the Marlborough family at Blenheim Palace in Oxfordshire, where Winston Churchill was born. Other forebears included the Duke of Marlborough, Sir Robert Walpole, and the Spencer family inherited a considerable fortune from Sarah, Duchess of Marlborough. They also married into the Cavendish family, the Dukes of Devonshire at Chatsworth House, and that offshoot became known as Spencer-Cavendish. Diana shared common ancestors with Prince Charles in the 3rd Duke of Devonshire and, most significantly, King James I, the first Stuart king of England and Scotland and sponsor of Francis Bacon. It was King James who played a highly influential role in the expansion of the Brotherhood, the formation of the Virginia Company which still controls the United States, and the creation of the King James version of the Bible. Diana was also descended through several lines from the Stuart kings, Charles II and James II, which connected her, as with James I, to the Merovingian bloodline in France. Charles II had so many children out of wedlock that goodness knows where some of their bloodlines are today. One thing's for sure, the Brotherhood will know. As Elite families go, the Spencers are an important bloodline and Diana was related to countless aristocratic lines, including the Earls of Lucan. Further afield the Spencers have blood ties with many leading American families and they are distantly related to the Rockefellers. They have a long history of serving the monarch and the tradition continued with Diana's father. He was equerry to King George VI (who was married to the Queen Mother) and to Queen Elizabeth. Diana's sister, Jane, is married to Sir Robert Fellowes, the Queen's Private Secretary at the time of Diana's death. Both of Diana's grandmothers, the Countess Spencer and Ruth Lady Fermoy, were inner circle members of the Queen Mother's court, as were four of her great aunts. The Spencers and the Queen Mother were very close and it was Lady Fermoy and the Queen Mother who manipulated Diana into her marriage with Prince Charles. This could be most significant when you hear about the true nature of the Queen Mother.

The countdown to the marriage began when Diana met Prince Charles at Althorp while he was having a relationship with her sister Sarah, in 1977. Diana was 16, but it was three years later that the Windsors really made their move on her. With the Queen Mother and Lady Fermoy manipulating behind the scenes, she was invited to a dance at Buckingham Palace to celebrate Charles' 30th birthday. Then, in July 1980, a friend of Charles, Philip de Pass, asked her to stay with them while the Prince was there. In Diana's own words, Charles was all over her and "He leapt on me practically".[22] He asked her to travel with him to Buckingham Palace the next day and an invitation followed to join the Windsors in the September at Balmoral, their residence in Scotland. Eventually Charles asked her to marry him and she accepted. "I love you so much" Diana said to him. "Whatever love is" Charles replied.[23] That is such a telling statement about the Windsors and the way they bring up their children. They don't understand love because they give and receive so little. Imagine being a young child and having to line up with everyone else to shake your mother's hand when she returned from an overseas visit. That is how the Queen and Prince Philip treated Charles. Diana was a kindergarten nanny when the story of the relationship broke in the media and her life in the public eye and the constant spotlight had begun. So had her nightmare with the Windsors. Looking back, Diana could see that Charles had never been genuine in his affection for her. She realised even before the wedding that he was having a relationship with his real love, Camilla Parker-Bowles, and this continued and grew during their marriage. Charles and Camilla communicated using the code 'Gladys and Fred'. Camilla, like the Windsors, is close to the Rothschilds and on the first anniversary of Diana's death, she was on the Ionian island of Corfu enjoying the hospitality of Lord Jacob Rothschild.[24] He has also spent £16 million leasing and restoring the Spencer's 18th century mansion overlooking Green Park in London, close to Buckingham Palace.[25]

The Windsors wanted Diana to produce heirs with Spencer genes and that was all she was to them: an incubator. A week after her engagement to Charles, her bulimia began. This is an eating disorder in which you make yourself sick every time you eat food. Diana was throwing up three or four times a day and became desperately thin. As I mentioned in an earlier chapter, many victims of childhood sexual and Satanic abuse suffer from bulimia later in life. She said that the bulimia was 'triggered' when Charles put his hand on her waist and said "Oh, a bit chubby here, aren't we?" Bulimia is a disease of the emotions, as most diseases are, and Diana was in emotional turmoil even before the wedding. She described the attitude of Charles like this:

"He'd found the virgin, the sacrificial lamb, and in a way he was obsessed with me. But it was hot and cold, hot and cold. You never knew what mood it was going to be, up and down, up and down... He was in awe of his mama, intimidated by his father, and I was always the third person in the room."[26]

She met her sisters and told them she couldn't go through with the marriage, especially with Camilla still on the scene, but they said she had no choice because "Your face is on the tea towels and you're too late to chicken out". Before the wedding, Diana stayed at Clarence House, the London residence of the Queen Mother. When she had arrived no-one was there to welcome her, she said, it was like going to a hotel. Diana and Charles were married in St Paul's Cathedral on July 29th 1981. That morning at Clarence House she said she felt calm, deathly calm: "I felt I was a lamb to the slaughter. I knew it, and I couldn't do anything about it".[27] What prophetic words those would prove to be. They spent the first night of their honeymoon at the Mountbatten family estate at Broadlands in Hampshire before sailing around the Greek islands in the royal yacht Britannia (Barati). The bulimia got worse and she considered suicide, such was the scale of her unhappiness. "My husband made me feel so inadequate in every possible way that each time I came up for air he pushed me down again. I hated myself so much". One of Diana's royal duties in 1982 was to represent the Queen at the funeral of Princess Grace of Monaco, another victim of Brotherhood murder when the brakes on her car failed. Princess Grace, formerly the actress Grace Kelly, ran the Monaco branch of the Order of the Solar Temple with Jean Louis Marsan, the close friend of her husband, Prince Rainier. The Windsors got what they wanted when Prince William was conceived. Diana was told that the birth had to be induced to fit in with Charles' polo playing programme and the blond-haired, blue-eyed William was born on June 21st 1982, the summer solstice. Now first of all, what kind of father and husband insists that his wife and son be given needless drugs to suit his polo diary? And secondly, does anyone believe that was really the reason? The Windsors are obsessed with astrology and the esoteric arts to such an extent that the psychic-astrologer mother of an Irish friend of mine could predict with uncanny accuracy the colours the Queen and Queen Mother would be wearing every day. She was correct again and again because she knew the colours connected to each day according to esoteric law. A family so steeped in Satanism, the esoteric mysteries, and the Sun cult, induce the heir to ensure he is born on the summer solstice, when the Sun is at the peak of its power, and that's just a coincidence? No way. He was christened William (after the Black Nobility William the Conqueror) Arthur (after the Sun God symbol, King Arthur) Philip (after the Duke of Edinburgh) Louis (after Louis Mountbatten). William's first serious girlfriend, according to the British press, was Emma Parker-Bowles, the niece of his father's lover, Camilla. Prince Harry was born in September 1984 and Diana's usefulness to the Windsors was over. "Then suddenly as Harry was born it just went bang, our marriage, the whole thing went down the drain", she told Andrew Morton.[28] Diana and Charles separated in 1992 and divorced on August 28th 1996. Almost exactly a year later she was dead.

Diana lived in apartments at Kensington Palace or 'KP' as she called it. Prince Michael of Kent, the Grand Master of English Freemasonry, has his home there, also. The Brotherhood-Windsor machine attempted to destroy Diana's credibility and public esteem. A tape of an intimate telephone conversation between her and the car dealer, James Gilbey, was released through the media in 1992. On the tape Diana said that Charles was a real torture. She told Gilbey: "I'll go out and conquer the world, do my bit in the way I know how and leave him behind".

But despite, perhaps because of, the efforts to discredit her, Diana's popularity continued and grew. Her unique combination of a big heart, a global public profile, and an intense desire to settle a score with the Windsors, threatened the very survival of royalty. Her natural compassion and empathy with people were putting the emotionless Windsors in the shade and exposing them as out of date and irrelevant. The naive, shy 19-year-old, who was enticed into the Windsor web, was now a woman who was realising her true power and was prepared to use it. She took the issue of landmines from obscurity to the front pages across the world and she had the platform to do that with any subject she chose. To the Windsors and the Brotherhood, this lady was dangerous with a capital D. She also knew many intimate secrets of the Windsors and the establishment. She knew where the bodies were buried as they say, and she had shown in her famous interview with the BBC current affairs programme, *Panorama*, in November 1995, that she was prepared to reveal some of them. That interview, in which she talked of her unhappy relationship with the royal family in very forthright terms, did immense harm to the Windsors and they must have wondered what on earth she would do next. In my travels around the world I met a man who had a call from Diana in March 1997, a few months before she died. He was amazed when she said it was the Princess of Wales and he didn't believe her at first, especially when she said that she was calling from a 'supermarket phone' in England. But Diana and this man had a mutual friend, and a close confidant of Diana told me that she often rang people from public phones, particularly from a department store in Kensingston, when she wanted to be certain the conversation would not be tapped. Diana admired this man for his wisdom and knowledge. She said she had something to reveal that would shake the world and she wanted his advice on how best to do it. He will not reveal what she told him, but when I said that I knew she was aware of the Windsors' connection to global drugs trafficking, he said: "Oh no, it was much worse than that". You might get an idea of what it could have been later in this chapter. Diana knew far more than people realise, as we shall also see. But that was only one level of the plot to kill Diana. At the highest level of the black magicians who control the Brotherhood networks, I have no doubt that her death had long been planned according to their ancient and deeply sick ritual. These two levels, the practical need to remove her (lower initiates) and the need for a ritual killing of the 'goddess Diana' (highest initiates) would run side by side, exactly as they did with President Kennedy.

The final sequence of events which led to her death involves, at almost every turn, a man called Mohamed Al Fayed, the Egyptian 'owner' of Harrods, the top people's store in Knightsbridge, London, and the father of Dodi Fayed who died in the crash with Diana. Al Fayed also owns the Ritz Hotel in Paris. This is the guy who bleats on and on about the need for "truth" and "justice" over the death of Diana and yet he would not recognise truth if it bit him on the bum. You can always tell when Mohamed Al Fayed is lying – his lips are moving. He fought a long, public, and vicious battle for control of Harrods and the House of Fraser with Tiny Rowland, the head of another Brotherhood front, Lonrho, the London-Rhodesia company, which has been responsible for so much manipulation of Africa and Africans. At one stage there was a Department of Trade and Industry inquiry into the Harrods takeover and it concluded: "The lies of Mohamed Fayed and his success in 'gagging' the press created a new fact: that lies were the truth and the truth was a lie".[29] This would be a suitable epitaph for what *Private Eye*, the British satirical magazine and others, have dubbed: The phony pharaoh. The report also revealed that Al Fayed had lied about his family background. He had claimed to come from a wealthy Egyptian family and it was this money, he said, that he was using to buy Harrods. In fact he comes from a far from rich family and he didn't have any such money of his own. He was born on January 27th 1929 in Alexandria, the son of a school inspector. He sold Coca-Cola in the streets and later knocked on doors selling Singer sewing machines. It was an introduction to Adnan Khashoggi, now the world's most famous arms broker, which changed his life. Khashoggi was the son of the personal physician to the King of Saudi Arabia and the Khashoggis employed 'Al' Fayed (then Mohamed Abdel Moneim Fayed) in their business ventures. He later fell out with the Khashoggi family, apparently, and proceeded to lie his way through a stream of business deals which made him a lot of money from setting up deals for others and taking a commission. The construction company, Costain, was one of his main sources of income in the early days, but he made nothing like as much money as he claimed to be worth. See Tom Bower's book, *Fayed, The Unathorised Biography*, for the detailed background.[30] Al Fayed's involvement with the Haiti dictator, Papa Doc, led to interest in his activities by the CIA. One CIA report on him remarked that: "He strikes one as being friendly and evil at the same time".[31]

While he became wealthy by the standards of the rest of the population, he did not have nearly enough of his own money to buy Harrods and he used the wealth of the Sultan of Brunei, one of the richest men in the world. It was the Sultan who provided the money for Harrods and Al Fayed also acted for him in the purchase of the prestigious London hotels, the Savoy and the Dorchester. Al Fayed may act the big tycoon, but in the biggest game he is a 'gofer' who takes orders and does as he's told. This is fascinating because we are led to believe that Mohamed Al Fayed and the Queen are on different sides and oppose each other over what happened to Diana. Funny, then, that Mohamed Al Fayed is subordinate to the Sultan of Brunei and the Queen of England is a friend of the Sultan of Brunei. She went to stay with him between September 16th and 20th in 1998.[32] What is going on here? Al Fayed's most prominent sycophantic media poodle is the *Daily Mirror* which has acted as his personal newsletter. The *Mirror* made strenuous efforts to secure an interview with me in June 1998, despite my initial reluctance. But when I made my thoughts about Al Fayed known to the reporter, the article was dropped by the Editor, Piers Morgan, who personally conducts the *Mirror* interviews with Al Fayed.

Doing as you are told by the very rich and powerful and using highly unscrupulous business methods, has proved extremely profitable for Al Fayed. He owns a fleet of bullet proof Mercedes, a £3.5 million Sikorski helicopter, a £13 million Gulfstream Jet, a £15 million yacht, The Jonikal, castles and 50,000 acres in Scotland, and expensive homes in Gstaad, New York, Dubai, Geneva, Gerona, London, Surrey and Los Angeles, all fully staffed and equipped.[33] Balnagown, his Scottish castle, is close to Loch Ness. As long as he does as he is told and is useful to the Brotherhood his wealth will continue. If he doesn't – gone. They will hang him out to dry. Another source of income for the Fayeds, again interconnected with the Sultan of Brunei, is arms dealing. Al Fayed's former brother-in-law and Dodi's uncle, Adnan Khashoggi, the infamous Saudi arms dealer and fixer, has arranged weapons sales, legal and illegal, worth multibillions of dollars. Many of the discussions for such deals take place at the Ritz Hotel in Paris owned by Mohamed Al Fayed (or the Sultan?). This is one reason why Al Fayed has the Ritz bugged to eavesdrop on his VIP guests. In fact, he has everything bugged, as we'll see. He is deeply involved in brokering arms sales and Dodi was often an unofficial broker for arms-for-oil deals between the Gulf states and America.[34] Adnan Khashoggi is a close associate of George Bush and bankrolled part of Bush's 'Iran-Contra' arms-for-drugs operation in the 1980s. George Bush, in turn, is a bosom buddy of the Queen and Prince Philip. Al Fayed is involved in many underground deals and plots involving events, people, and subjects that he is desperate to ensure remain secret. Certainly not a man to trust under any circumstances, in my view. I should emphasise, too, that the Islamic élite, like the Sultan of Brunei, are significant players in the Brotherhood pyramid and the Grand Lodge at Cairo is one of the most powerful secret society centres in the world. This is hardly surprising given the Brotherhood's obsession with ancient Egypt and it's ritual and symbols. The reptilian bloodlines may be predominantly Aryan, but they are far from exclusively so. They work through streams within all races, the Arabs and the 'Jews' most certainly among them. One of the predominant secret societies in the Arab world is the Order of the Mystic Shrine or the 'Shriners'. They are connected to the Knights Templar, and the York and Scottish Rites of Freemasonry. Among their members in the United States have been President Franklin Delano Roosevelt and his successor President Harry S. Trueman. There is also a Prince Hall Shrine for black members of the Brotherhood, including that self-styled spokesman for the black community in the United States, Jesse Jackson.

Al Fayed has served the interests of the Brotherhood and the establishment in a number of ways while presenting an anti-establishment public profile. For instance it was he who exposed the two Conservative MPs, Neil Hamilton and Tim Smith, who were taking money to ask certain questions in the House of Commons. This is quite illegal. Al Fayed knew that this was true because he was the one giving them the money! This story did enormous harm to the Conservative Government and did much to help the Brotherhood chosen one, Tony Blair, to a landslide victory for the Labour Party at the following General Election. Al Fayed has also escaped prosecution so far for a growing number of allegations from young female members of staff at Harrods that he sexually assaulted them. His obsession with sex is legendary. One girl, 17-year-old Samantha-Jane Ramsay, said that when she complained to her supervisor that she had been groped by Al Fayed, the supervisor sighed: "Another one". Al Fayed sacked her for making the complaint, as he does all those who speak out against his sexual molestation and style of business 'management'. John Monks the general secretary of the Trades Union Congress, said that at Harrods there was "A regime of fear and terror". When Samantha-Jane took her complaint to the local Marylebone Police Station, she said that the officer told her: "You're not the first to come to us. We have files inches high on Mr Al Fayed, but no proof. It would be your word against his".[35] A file inches high of different girls making the same complaint about the same man would, I suggest, constitute rather more than "No proof". But Al Fayed, the man we are told the establishment would love to crush, survives untouched. So this is just some of the background to the liar, double-dealer, sexual molester, Satanist and Sultan of Brunei frontman, who had complete control of Diana's security in the days and hours leading up to her death. I wouldn't trust him with the security of my cat. Indeed, as Tom Bower has documented, Al Fayed has ordered his hit men to shoot a cat he didn't like.

Al Fayed had become close to the Spencer family through Diana's father, Earl 'Johnny' Spencer, and stepmother Raine. He helped 'Johnny' through financial difficulties and said he considered the Earl to be a brother.[36] He had given Raine, whom Diana couldn't stand, a place on the Harrods board. Al Fayed sponsored prestigious royal events like the Royal Windsor Horse Show and polo competitions, but he especially backed the causes and charities supported by Diana. Bob Loftus, the head of security at Harrods between 1987 and 1996, told the British Channel Four programme, *Dispatches*, in June 1998, that he was ordered to tell Al Fayed immediately if Diana came into the store. Al Fayed would then go to the department where she was shopping and 'accidentally' meet her. Every Christmas a green Harrods van would call at Diana's home, Kensington Palace, with gifts for her and the boys from 'Uncle Mohamed'. When you look at the evidence, he made it his business to court the friendship of the Princess of Wales in every way possible. On June 3rd 1997, he invited her to join him for a Summer holiday at his beach-side villa in San Tropez in the south of France. On June 11th he got the breakthrough he had been working so hard for: she accepted. The following day he completed the purchase of a £15 million yacht, The Jonikal, through his Bermudan company Mohafa Shipping, and it was on this boat that Dodi and Diana's romance was soon to blossom.

On July 11th Diana arrived in San Tropez with her sons, William and Harry, to stay in an eight-bedroomed luxury apartment on the ten acre Al Fayed estate on the exclusive Le Parc development. At this time, Dodi Fayed was still at his apartment in Paris with his fiancée Kelly Fisher, the American model. The 41-year-old Dodi was a 'gofer' for his father and lived on his father's wealth, although he had enjoyed some success in the movie industry at one time as the hands-off producer of the hit British film *Chariots Of Fire*, again thanks to his father's money. He had a playboy reputation and was a very big spender, once famously running up a $100,000 bill in two months on his Amex card. He was dominated by his father and even in his film operation every decision had to be approved by Al Fayed. Dodi did whatever his father told him to do. He had been engaged to Kelly Fisher for eight months and she was expecting to spend her holiday on The Jonikal. But on the evening of July 14th, Dodi took a phone call from his father who ordered him to go immediately to San Tropez to be with Diana. Kelly Fisher described what happened next in an interview with the *Dispatches* programme:

" (*Dodi*) said he was going to London and he'd be back and then we were going to San Tropez. That evening he didn't call me and I finally got him on his portable phone. I said 'Dodi where are you?' and he said he was in London. I said 'OK, I'll call you right back at your apartment'. He said 'No, no, don't call me back.' So I said 'Dodi where are you?' and he admitted he was in the South of France. His father had asked him to come down and not bring me, I know now."

Two days later Dodi sent a private plane to fly Kelly to San Tropez. But while he stayed with Diana, Kelly was kept aboard another Fayed boat. "I'm sitting here stuck" she said. "So he had me in my little boat cage and he was, I know now, seducing Diana." On July 31st, Diana returned to San Tropez for a second holiday with Dodi, this time alone. Kelly Fisher was back in Los Angeles preparing for her wedding to Dodi which she said was due to take place on August 9th. But two days before that, the story broke in the world media of the romance between Dodi and Diana. Kelly heard from a friend who saw a picture in the paper. She recalls:

"I started calling him in London because at this time I was expecting his arrival in a day. I called his private line, but there was no answer. So then I called the secretary and asked to speak to him and she wouldn't put me on. So Mohamed got on and in so many horrible words told me to never call back again. I said 'He's my fiancee, what are you talking about?' He hung up on me and I called back and the secretary said don't ever call here again, your calls are no longer to be put through. It was so horrible."[37]

Ironically, Diana used to have Kensington Palace swept for listening devices and now she was in the clutches of a man for whom bugging was an obsession. The Al Fayed villa in San Tropez was bugged, as were all Fayed properties. Everything Diana said could be heard. Bob Loftus, the former Head of Security at Harrods, said that the bugging there was "A very extensive operation" and was also always under the direction of Al Fayed.[38] Henry Porter, the London Editor of the magazine *Vanity Fair*, had spent two years investigating Al Fayed and he said they came across his almost obsessive use of eavesdropping devices to tape telephone calls, bug rooms, and film people. Through mutual friends, Porter warned Diana about Al Fayed's background and activities "Because we thought this was quite dangerous for her for obvious reasons".[39] But Diana apparently felt she could handle it and although she knew Al Fayed could "Sometimes be a rogue", he was no threat to her, she thought. He is rather more than a rogue and rather more often than 'sometimes'. She apparently told friends: "I know he's naughty, but that's all". The *Dispatches* programme said they had written evidence that Al Fayed bugged the Ritz Hotel and given his background and the deals that are hatched at the Ritz, it would be staggering if he did not. Kelly Fisher said that the whole time she was in Fayed property she just assumed everything was bugged. It was known, she said, and Dodi had told her everywhere was bugged. She went on: "As a matter of fact, when I confronted him about Diana, he said: 'I can't talk to you on the phone'. He said 'I'll talk to you in LA'. I knew what that meant". Diana was under the 'protection' of the Al Fayed security machine and even her most private conversations were being monitored.

Diana went with Dodi to Al Fayed's Elizabethan-style mansion called Barrow Green Court at Oxted in Surrey, formerly owned by the Satanist Lord McAlpine. Throughout the house Al Fayed had placed statues of semi-naked Greek goddesses. On August 21st, despite Henry Porter's warning, Diana returned again to San Tropez for another holiday with Dodi. Al Fayed was milking the situation, briefing journalists and photographers and enlisting the advice of publicist Max Clifford.[40] The Al Fayed machine was leaking the couple's whereabouts to ensure maximum publicity. Al Fayed complained after the crash that photographers and journalists would not leave the Princess alone, a statement which, in the circumstances, beggars belief. The Diana-Dodi romance was now in full swing and Al Fayed was urging his son to intensify the relationship.[41] And what Al Fayed said, Dodi did. Nothing was left to chance. Diana's favourite music, the theme from *The English Patient*, was played over and over as the couple cruised on The Jonikal. Diana and Dodi had much in common. Both had been born into wealthy families and their fathers were distant figures. Both had experienced the breakdown of their parents' marriages as their mothers left home. They even attended finishing schools close to each other in Switzerland. But we should not rule out the possibility of mind manipulation techniques being used on both parties. I have met a number of former mind controlled slaves who were programmed to fall madly in love with someone they normally would not even like and there are endless examples of 'love spells' concocted by black magicians to cause someone to fall madly in love with them. My scientist friend, Brian Desborough, tells me that the feeling of being in love is dependent upon the brain producing phenylethylamine. This is a chemical which also diminishes the ability to discriminate effectively, hence the term 'love is blind'. Production of this chemical is sustained by the release of endorphins, a naturally occurring chemical linked to memory, learning, pain suppression, sex drive and hormone regulation. If these chemicals could be stimulated in both parties they would fall instantly in love.

I think there is a very good chance that something like this happened as the sting was set up for both of them. There was talk of engagement in the air, but it is impossible to say how imminent that was, because reports conflict. I have great doubts about that myself. Diana and Dodi left the South of France from Olbia Airport at 1.30pm on August 30th bound for Paris on Al Fayed's Gulfstream jet. They apparently intended to stay one night at Dodi's apartment, which looks out on the Arc de Triomphe, before going on to London where Diana was due to meet her sons. It was to be her last full day alive. The plane touched down at Le Bourget Airport in Paris at 3.20pm and they were met by 20 or so celebrity photographers known as the paparazzi (from an Italian word meaning 'buzzing insects'). A Mercedes was waiting for the party and a green Range Rover was to follow on behind. This is normal security procedure and the very minimum you would expect to protect someone so globally famous. With Diana and Dodi in the Mercedes was Dodi's bodyguard, Trevor Rees-Jones, the 29-year-old former member of the élite British military regiment, the Paras or Parachute Regiment. Along with the SAS, the Paras are the most highly trained (and therefore mind controlled) regiment in the British forces. In the Range Rover were the driver, Henri Paul, the acting Head of Security at the Ritz, and another bodyguard, Kes Wingfield. They drove from the airport to the Villa Windsor on the Bois de Boulogne, the former home of the Duke and Duchess of Windsor. The Duke and Duchess lived there after the duke, as King Edward VIII, abdicated the British throne when the government and establishment would not accept his marriage to the America divorcee, Wallis Simpson. They then moved to Paris as the Duke and Duchess of Windsor. Their house is now owned by Mohamed Al Fayed and it is said that he was going to give it to Dodi and Diana as a wedding present. This talk of a wedding, however, is unsubstantiated, much as Al Fayed has sought to promote it. His publicity machine led the public to believe the couple had spent time at Villa Windsor discussing decor, but the bodyguard Kes Wingfield said that they only stayed there for "Around ten minutes".[42] From here they were driven to the Ritz Hotel where they arrived at 4.20pm.

The Ritz is in the Place Vendome and all around that square at first floor level are symbols of the Sun and the cross, very much like the symbols used by the ancients to symbolise the 'journey' of the Sun through the year which I featured earlier in the book. This was the symbol of King Louis XIV, who was known as the 'Sun King'. At his palace at Versailles in the 17th century he decorated rooms in honour of Apollo, the Sun god, and Diana, the goddess of the Moon. There was also a statue of the goddess Diana at Versailles. In the centre of the Vendome Square is an immense pillar with a statue of Napoleon on the top and it mirrors the famous Nelson's Column in Trafalgar Square, London. At this stage Diana still had the same level of security that she'd had since the airport, but this could have been increased considerably if support from the French High Protection Police Security Service (SPHP) had been requested. It is there to protect VIPs visiting the city, but a request for their services must be made. It wasn't. All Diana's security was provided by Al Fayed's people from start to finish. If they had enlisted the protection of the French police, Diana would still be alive. When a celebrity like Madonna visits Paris, the French Police have one car in front of hers and another behind, together with two motorcycle riders front and back of the motorcade. The cars are driven by trained drivers and they carry armed security men. According to reports, the SPHP made three, possibly four, offers to protect Diana, but each one was refused by Dodi. Was he, himself, under instruction to reject these offers from someone to whom he could not say no? An officer of the SPHP told Dodi: "If you will not use our car, we recommend that two police cars accompany you on your excursions around the city."[43] This advice, too, was ignored.

Diana and Dodi went straight to the $6,000 a night 18th century Imperial Suite at the Ritz. From there, Diana rang her friend, the *Daily Mail* journalist Richard Kay. She told him she intended to retire from public life in November and he said that he had never heard her so happy. The couple booked a table at the Chez Benoit restaurant for 8.45pm and they intended to spend the night at Dodi's apartment. At 6.30pm Dodi went across the Place Vendome to a jewellers, Repossi, to buy a

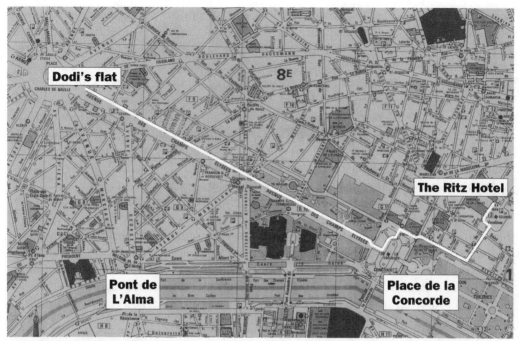

Figure 52: *The journey to Dodi's apartment in the early evening of August 30th. A straightforward journey with no need to go through the Pont de L'Alma tunnel.*

diamond ring for Diana which was later delivered to the Ritz. A little after 7 pm, the couple were driven in the Mercedes along the Champs Elysées to Dodi's apartment on Rue Arsene-Houssaye close to the Arc de Triomphe. Here they unpacked and prepared for dinner. Again the back up Range Rover was there and so was another car carrying bodyguards for added protection. Why was this level of security thought necessary in the early evening, but not in the early hours of the morning at the time of the crash? Dodi's apartment is known as the 'Etoile flat' after the Place de L'Etoile, the 'Sun or star circle' road around the Arc de Triomphe. The route they took to the apartment was out of the Place Vendome onto the Rue de Rivoli, and half way around the Place de la Concorde they turned right onto the Champs Elysées and drove straight up that famous avenue to Dodi's apartment (*see* **Figure** 52). Remember that route, it is crucially important. As they arrived at the apartment at 7.15pm, bodyguards were seen to rush from their car to hold back six paparazzi. Diana and Dodi became concerned about eating at the unprotected Chez Benoit restaurant and decided to head back to the Ritz to eat. They took the same route back, down the Champs Elysées and around the Place de la Concorde. The couple, with bodyguards Wingfield and Rees-Jones, walked into the Ritz, captured by the now famous video pictures, at 9.47pm. As the paparazzi gather in numbers outside, amid rumours of an engagement announcement, Diana has already started the last three hours of her life. Who was feeding the rumours and the whereabouts of Diana during the day to create the paparazzi stampede that dominated Diana and Dodi's movements and decisions that night? I think I can guess, somehow. Al Fayed. And who were some of these 'paparazzi' making life uncomfortable for Diana, thus changing the plans for the evening? The Ritz security video also identified a number of people who had been outside among the onlookers for most of the day and were still there on the edge of the crowd.[44]

Now the plot seriously thickens. After speaking on the phone with his father at his estate in Oxted, Surrey, Dodi Fayed announced a quite ludicrous plan. To avoid the paparazzi, the Mercedes which had been transporting them all day together with the back up Range Rover were to be taken around the front of the hotel and used as a decoy for the paparazzi. At the same time another Mercedes would be brought around to the back entrance of the hotel to whisk the couple away to the apartment on the Champs Elysées. Henri Paul, the 41-year-old acting head of security at the Ritz, was called on his mobile phone by Dodi and told to report back to the hotel. He went off duty at 7pm and by the time he returned it was 10pm. No-one has established where Paul was in those three hours. Dodi said that his father, Mohamed Al Fayed, had personally authorised that Henri Paul should drive the Mercedes. For me, that is Dodi-speak for "My father told me this is how it is going to be". Henri Paul was not a qualified chauffeur and had no hire car permit. L. Fletcher Prouty, a former colonel in the US Airforce who worked closely with the intelligence agencies, once said:

> "No-one has to direct an assassination – it happens. The active role is played secretly by permitting it to happen. This is the greatest single clue. Who has the power to call off or reduce the usual security precautions?"[45]

Absolutely right. If we apply Prouty's rule to Diana and ask who had the power – and used that power – to reduce the usual security precautions for her that night, we have a rather interesting answer: Mohamed Al Fayed. Given these circumstances he must answer the obvious question: Why was this security reduced? When President Kennedy was assassinated, there were no bodyguards standing on his car while four were standing on the one immediately behind (*see picture section*). He was also in an open-topped car at a dangerous time in a dangerous city. When Martin Luther King was shot dead at the Lorraine Motel in Memphis, Tennessee, on April 4th, 1968, the black police officer in charge of security for King was sent home against his will hours before the shooting. The only two black firemen at the station next to the motel were sent to other stations just for that day. The scapegoat for this assassination was a guy called James Earl Ray. Not even King's family believed he was responsible. So much so that they attended his funeral a few years ago. When Bobby Kennedy was murdered after making a speech at the Ambassadors Hotel in Los Angeles on June 4th 1968, again the security arrangements were tampered with. The plan was for Kennedy to walk off the stage and through the crowd to the exit. But immediately after the speech, Kennedy's 'aides', especially Frank Mankiewicz, insisted that it was safer for him to go out through the hotel kitchen. When he walked into the kitchen he was met by the mind controlled Sirhan Sirhan with a gun in his hand. It is far more likely that

Bobby Kennedy was actually shot by members of his 'security' team, particularly Thane Eugene Caesar, the 'security guard' who was employed at the last minute and had endless connections into far right groups and the intelligence community. But with Sirhan Sirhan at the scene with a gun, they had a mind controlled scapegoat to take the rap and that was all they needed. Sirhan Sirhan had been on a 'mind expansion' course with the Rosicrucians in the weeks before he was implicated in Kennedy's death (see *…And The Truth Shall Set You Free*). Frank Mankiewicz, who guided Kennedy to the kitchen, was a former public relations man for the Mossad-front in America, the Anti Defamation League. He turned up later as head of publicity for the Oliver Stone film, *JFK*, which claimed to be an exposé of the assassination of President Kennedy. It wasn't. When the Israeli Prime Minister, Zitzhak Rabin, was shot dead by an assassin in Tel Aviv in 1995, an extraordinary video taken by an onlooker showed how Rabin's security detail stepped back in unison to leave the assassin alone and free to kill his target. You can see the pattern. And what happened in the crucial last minutes of Diana's life? They withdrew her security on the orders of Mohamed Al Fayed via his son. That is a fact. All day she had travelled in the same Mercedes with the Range Rover as a back up vehicle. Now she would transfer to another Mercedes with no back up support whatsoever. This was an extraordinary decision for a man obsessed with his own security. Bob Loftus, the former Head of Security at Harrods, said:

> "Compared with the protection that Al Fayed affords himself, which is very professional, of a very high standard, that which was afforded to the mother of the future King of England was a Mickey Mouse operation."[46]

He added that "Al Fayed was absolutely paranoid about his personal protection". Just for him to walk around his own store, there would be three or four plain clothes members of his personal protection team who travelled with him all the time, plus another four uniformed security who would act almost as 'outriders' to create two rings of security around him. That's in his own store! But is it paranoia, or the knowledge of the seedy, cesspit, world of arms dealers and Brotherhood fixers of many kinds, in which Al Fayed constantly operates? People who think nothing of the mass murder of children, let alone the assassination of a wealthy 'yes' man like him. Dodi Fayed was obsessed with his security for the same reason. A lot of this security was also inspired by the size of Al Fayed's ego, to be fair. Mostly he recruited his body guards from the SAS and the Parachute Regiment and used the Brotherhood operation, Control Risks, to make recommendations. Tom Bower tells in his book about Al Fayed of how armed guards at the Oxted estate hide behind bushes wearing full combat uniform and blacked out faces. Whenever Al Fayed travelled in his Mercedes there was always a back up Range Rover carrying emergency medical equipment and security staff, but now he withdrew that protection from Diana. More than that, a new car was introduced for her, another Mercedes was sent to the rear entrance of the Ritz, supplied by a car hire company called Etoile Limousines, the same name as Dodi's flat. Etoile Limousines is based at the Ritz and depends for its entire income on contracts with the hotel and its guests. In other words, it is controlled completely by Mohamed Al Fayed and whoever controls him. The new Mercedes was an S-280, lighter in weight than the 600 series they had used all day and without the dark tinted windows. Other cars were available, but this one was chosen instead. A director of Etoile, Niels Siegel, told the inquiry into Diana's death that he delivered the car to the rear entrance of the Ritz, but the *Dispatches* programme showed that this is a lie. It was delivered by a driver called Frederic Lucard and he can be seen doing so on the security video. Lucard said he found it very strange that Etoile would allow Henri Paul, a man not qualified as a chauffeur, to drive one of their cars. So why did they do it? Because Mohamed Al Fayed told them to, that's why. Brian Dodd, the former Head of Security for Al Fayed in the 1980s, gave his assessment of the situation to *Dispatches*:

> "It's a new car that's come into the system. They wouldn't have had time to check that car out. It should have been checked out. There could have been a bomb on the car, for instance. It was a most stupid plan. It shouldn't even have been considered. The back up vehicle is there, not just to avert the paparazzi, but for instance, a motor cyclist with a pillion rider to pull up and shoot, or put a magnetised bomb on top of the car. That's why the back up car is there – to stop any of that. Why they never had a back up car, God only knows. (*I think I can offer a good guess without the need for Divine inspiration.*)

> "I had probably six or eight men I would consider professional bodyguards who I would have had on that job and Trevor Rees-Jones and Kes Wingfield, after what I have seen happened, would not have been in Paris that night."

The Mercedes with Henry Paul at the wheel sped off from the rear entrance of the Ritz at 12.20am with Paul telling the paparazzi not to bother following because they would never catch him. Diana and Dodi were in the back seat and in the front was Trevor Rees-Jones, the former 'Para' with the reputation for being 'fearless'. Rees-Jones says he disagreed with the change of plan. He was not wearing a seat belt which is normal practice because body guards need to be free to react quickly. The car was driven at speed down the Rue Cambon and turned right down the Rue de Rivoli into the Place de la Concorde where it stopped briefly at the lights. The paparazzi photographer, Romuald Rat, on the back of a motor cycle, drew up alongside them here, but he says that Henri Paul jumped the lights on red and headed onto the dual carriageway alongside the River Seine called the Cours la Reine. The car plunged down into one tunnel, came back to the surface, and almost immediately went down into the very short tunnel at the Pont de L'Alma. Here it went out of control and struck the *13th* pillar in the centre of the tunnel which is lined with concrete pillars unprotected by crash barriers. Henri Paul and Dodi Fayed died immediately. According to the autopsy report Diana was clinically dead within 20 minutes and this was long before she arrived at hospital. Trevor Rees-Jones survived the crash because he was wearing a seat belt and Diana and Dodi were not. This could be highly significant. Rees-Jones was not wearing a belt when they left the Ritz in accordance with normal practice for body guards, and when Romuald Rat took a photograph at the lights at the Place de la Concorde, Rees-Jones still did not have a seat belt on. But little more than a minute later when the car struck the pillar, he was wearing a seat belt. Why? If he donned the belt because for some reason he sensed danger, why did he not scream at Diana and Dodi to put their seat belts on? After all it only takes a second and the whole reason he was in the car was to protect them. Rees-Jones has some serious questions to answer here and he is giving no answers. Some bodyguards do put a seat belt on when the car is on a fast road, but Rees-Jones is not saying this. He says he doesn't know why he strapped himself in. And if they were going to Dodi's flat, they would have been on the fast road for about a minute. All he says is that he remembers they were followed by two cars, one of them white, and a motorcycle, which is in keeping with the smokescreen story. But one simple fact about the crash has been missed by all the newspaper articles, magazine features, television documentaries and discussions I have seen, and by all but a few researchers. Everyone is agreed that the couple were being driven back to Dodi's flat near the Arc de Triomphe when the crash happened. Well there is one glaring problem with that:

The Pont de L'Alma tunnel is not on the way to Dodi's flat.
It takes you away from that area.

I have been to Paris and walked the route the car took that night, in fact I have walked extensively around that whole area, and the route to Dodi's apartment is the same as the one they took earlier that night. You go to the Place de la Concorde and, half way around, you turn right into the Champs Elysées and drive straight up to Dodi's flat on the right near the Arc de Triomphe (*see **Figure 53** overleaf*). At that time of night it would take only a few minutes. But Henri Paul did not do that. He drove past the turning for the Champs Elysées, jumped the lights on red and sped down the duel carriageway to the Pont de L'Alma. This took them AWAY from Dodi's flat. I have heard it said that Paul was going a long way round to avoid the photographers and traffic, but the photographers would have been waiting at the flat anyway by the time they got there. What is most important to stress here is that Henri Paul's route was not the direct one to Dodi's apartment, but it did ensure that it took them through the Pont de L'Alma Tunnel, the significance of which is fantastic, as you will soon appreciate. Interestingly, it was after Paul went past the turning to Les Champs Elysees and headed towards the Pont de L'Alma that Rees-Jones put his seat belt on. He says he can't remember why, but I can help him there. There can only be two reasons for this. Either he knew what was coming or he realised when Henri Paul screamed off from the lights that something was seriously wrong and he put the seat belt on to protect himself. But again if that is the case, why did he not tell Dodi and Diana to do the same? And if Rees-Jones had realised a potential danger, why had Dodi and Diana not seen it and taken the appropriate action to protect themselves? I'm sorry if that upsets Rees-Jones' family, but given the circumstances these are questions that need to be asked.

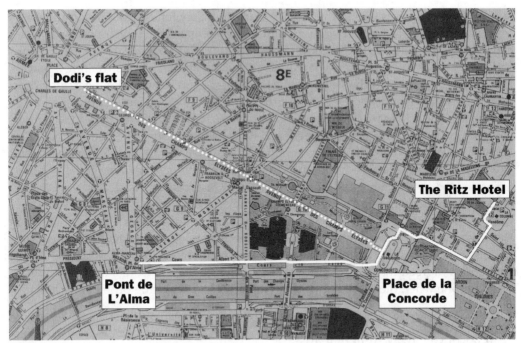

Figure 53: *The change of route which cost Diana her life. Instead of going directly to Dodi's apartment, Henri Paul sped off in another direction away from their destination. It is said that he was taking the long way round to avoid the paparazzi, but what an amazing 'coincidence' that this took the car into the Pont de L'Alma tunnel, one of the Babylonian Brotherhood's most sacred sites for the goddess Diana!*

Once the deed was done; the scapegoat was produced. The methods are so predictable, but they keep working so why change them? The Lee Harvey Oswald, Sirhan Sirhan and James Earl Ray of the Diana assassination was the driver, Henri Paul. Once the paparazzi card had been played and focused public and media attention in the days after the crash, it was announced that Paul was three to four times over the French drink driving limit and that his blood contained traces of anti-depressant drugs, including Fluoxetine, the active ingredient of the infamous Prozac. "The cause of the crash was simple," we were told. "The driver was drunk." Tampering with blood samples or creating alcohol in the blood is child's play and so is the insertion of tiny 'balloons' which release alcohol into the blood stream in stages. There was certainly no sign before he drove away from the Ritz that he was intoxicated to the extent, according to his blood tests, that he must have drunk the equivalent of eight Scotches on an empty stomach. A behavioural psychologist on the Independent Television documentary, *Diana – Secrets Of The Crash*, could find no evidence that he was drunk after studying the Ritz videos of him that night, but there could be an explanation for this which I will come to shortly. Only two days earlier, Paul had undergone a rigorous medical for the renewal of his pilot's licence and there was no sign of the alcohol abuse the post-crash propaganda claimed. Quite the opposite. And there was another strange anomaly revealed by the ITV documentary in 1998. The Haemoglobin in Henri Paul's blood was found to contain

20.7% carbon monoxide and this would have been at a much higher level earlier because the carbon monoxide content halves every four to five hours once exposure to it has stopped. Haemoglobin carries the oxygen. Debbie Davis of the Carbon Monoxide Support Group said that with these levels in his blood, Henri Paul would not have known his left hand from his right, because of the reduced oxygen reaching the brain. Dr Alastair Hay, an expert on carbon monoxide poisoning, agreed and could not explain why Paul showed no signs of the considerable symptoms that should have been evident:

> "I find it difficult to rationalise everything. A blood-carbon monoxide level of 20% and (*a high blood-alcohol level*) suggests this would be someone with a much slower reaction time, certainly be someone who would be slowed up in the way he did things, would probably also be somebody who was in some pain, but none of those things appear to be evident from the pictures that we see of him. It is a bit of an enigma."[47]

There is a lot more to know about Henri Paul. His best friend, Claude Garrec, told the ITV documentary that Paul had contacts within the French and foreign intelligence services and maintained them throughout his time at the Ritz. This is no surprise because the intelligence agencies recruit the security men at the top hotels and the Ritz, with its VIP clientele and reputation for espionage and arms dealing, would have been a prime target. Paul certainly had unexplained sources of income. He earned about £20-25,000 a year at the Ritz and yet he was a keen pilot with 605 hours of flying time at about £300 an hour. He had a string of bank accounts. There were two in a bank outside Paris and three accounts, plus a safe deposit box, at the Banque Nationale de Paris near the Ritz. He had three accounts at the nearby branch of Barclays and one current and four deposit accounts at the Caisse D'Epargne de Paris. In the eight months before the crash, sums of £4,000 were paid into an account here on five separate occasions. In total he had £122,000 (1.2 million francs) and no-one knows where it came from. Then there is the question of where Paul was in the three hours between 7pm when he went off duty and 10pm when Dodi called him on his mobile phone and told him to return to the Ritz. His whereabouts in this period are a mystery. A very significant one.

To understand how the Brotherhood operates requires immensely detailed research over a vast array of interconnecting subjects. Everything from ancient history, to Satanic symbolism and ritual, the Earth's magnetic grid, the power of the Sun, the banking system, and mind control. The journalists who have produced the articles and documentaries about the crash came to the subject cold and they can never uncover the truth because they don't understand what they are dealing with. Their vision of possibility is limited by their indoctrinated view of reality. They can't see, for instance, that there are organisations within organisations which means that one force can work through apparently unconnected agencies like British and French Intelligence, the Paris police and medical services, and the inquiry investigating the cause of the crash. I mean, you don't have to search far for evidence of that. Look at the Kennedy assassination for one. It is this lack of research of the big picture that leads reporters like Martyn Gregory on the *Dispatches* programme to state categorically that "there is not a shred of credible evidence to support the conspiracy theory" and that the suggestion of Prince Philip's involvement was "ludicrous". I wonder after reading the evidence so far – and there is a great deal more to come – which you think is more ludicrous: the idea of a plot to kill Diana or Martyn Gregory's statement? It was an unfortunate comment in a programme that produced some good information about Al Fayed. Then there was the 'investigation' into the crash by John Stalker, the former deputy chief constable of Greater Manchester, in the *News Of The World* newspaper, in which he dismissed all idea that Diana was murdered. Ironically, Stalker claimed, quite rightly, that he was the victim of a conspiracy to remove him from the police force after he identified a policy by the Northern Ireland police, the RUC, to shoot people they believed were terrorists and ask the questions later. This was the so-called shoot-to-kill policy. Pushing aside every suggestion of a conspiracy to kill Diana, Stalker asked: "Why would the French want to cover up the murder of an English woman?"[48] The naivety of that statement is so breathtaking, I need a glass of water. At the same time, Stalker did ask some pertinent questions about the crash and its aftermath: "Why was the Fayed security around the princess reduced to one wholly inadequate man with no back up? Why did the police not appeal for help from the public? Why was there no post mortem-autopsy on Dodi Fayed's body?" Answers: because of the very conspiracy you dismiss, Mr Stalker.

One of the most important subjects to research if we are to understand how Diana was killed, is the power and potential of mind control. I'll give some examples. In the 1980s the best part of 30 scientists working in top secret projects, mostly computer programmers, died in very strange and unexplained circumstances. Marconi was the major company involved, but there were others like Plessey and British Aerospace. In 1986, Vimal Dajibhai, who was working for Marconi Underwater Systems, drove from London to Bristol, a city with which he had no connection, and threw himself off the famous suspension bridge there. A few months before, Arshad Sharif, a computer programmer with Marconi Defence Systems, also drove from London to Bristol and hanged himself. Why Bristol? It is a former Knights Templar port and its name has evolved from Barati, the Phoenician goddess. It just so happens that an élite unit of British Intelligence called the Committee of 26 is based there and they use the runway at the British Aerospace complex to fly British and foreign agents in and out of the country. I was called once, from what sounded like a plane, by a guy claiming to represent the CIA. He said he was flying into the British Aerospace runway to sort me out. "The Company (CIA) are not happy," he said. Oh, I thought, I am sorry, I do hope they cheer up soon. I drove over to meet him just to check it out, but he didn't show. He was probably a guy who needed help, or perhaps they were seeing how I would react to threats. Either way, they got the airport right. In that period in the 1980s, not only in Bristol, there were strange deaths galore of people at the cutting edge of development in the 'defence' industries.

What possesses a man to get into his car, drive more than two hours to the Bristol Suspension Bridge, and jump off? This may seem a long way from the Diana assassination, but it's not. I'm talking about mind control. A CIA scientist told me that he was put through forms of mind control to stop him recalling his knowledge once a project was completed. I'll give you an example of mind control in a situation very similar to the one in Paris. David Sands was a highly skilled scientist working in a very sensitive area of defence, but at 37 he was talking about leaving the industry and changing his lifestyle. He was happily married with two small children, a son aged six and a three year old daughter. Sands and his wife had just returned from an enjoyable holiday in Venice when he died in mysterious circumstances. Although they are not so mysterious if you understand mind control. He worked for Easams who, in turn, were operating contracts for the Ministry of Defence. It appears that while Sands and his wife were in Venice, the company was visited by members of the élite British police unit, the Special Branch. Then, on Saturday, March 28th 1987, David Sands told his wife he was going out to refuel the car, but he didn't return for six hours. No-one has any idea where he was, but I think I do. His wife, Anna, called the police and constable John Hiscock was at the house when Sands returned at 10.20pm. Asked the obvious question: "Where have you been?", he said that he had been driving and thinking. His wife said that it was out of character for him to be away for so long and she didn't think he realised how long he had been out. He seemed confused, but happy, she said. Two days later, on Monday, March 30th, he climbed into his excellently maintained Austin Maestro and began his regular journey from his home in Itchen Abbas, near Winchester, to Easams at Camberley in Surrey. His wife said there was nothing unusual about his demeanour or behaviour and driving conditions were good. But about 30 minutes into the journey when David Sands was driving along the A33 at Popham, near Basingstoke, he suddenly did a U-turn across the duel carriageway and headed at high speed in the opposite direction to his destination. Turning onto a slip road at about 80 miles an hour, Sands then drove his car straight into a disused cafe building killing himself in an explosion of flame. There were no skid marks. He had not even tried to stop.[49] It is so clear that during the time he was missing, his mind was being programmed and all it took was a trigger word, sign, sound or action, and the programming was activated. At that point he would have switched from his normal self to a man focused only on driving into the cafe building and blowing himself away. The subconscious programming overpowers the conscious mind and robot replaces human.

That, I am convinced, is what also happened to Henri Paul in Paris. Sands went missing for six hours before he drove into the café. Paul went missing for three hours before he drove into the 13th pillar in the Pont de L'Alma tunnel. This is what I suggest happened in Paris. The Brotherhood networks were working through many people and agencies to ensure that Diana was in Paris that night because, at its foundation, the plan was to perform a specific Satanic ritual and the timing, circumstances and the place of death had to be arranged in intricate detail. Diana was under Al Fayed's security web for much of the time leading up to the crash and all of the time in those last few days. Her conversations were heard and monitored throughout by the Al Fayed bugging system. During his missing hours, Henri Paul, the asset of French and British Intelligence, was being programmed for his role, or perhaps the final touches were being put to programming already installed. Diana's ritual death was arranged from the very top of the Brotherhood and, by comparison, people like Al Fayed are small and powerless nonentities, pawns in the game they probably do not fully understand. The Mercedes which was brought to the rear entrance of the Ritz had been stolen some weeks earlier – before the Diana-Dodi relationship began – and when it was recovered it underwent extensive repairs. It had been standing outside the exclusive Taillevent restaurant when the driver's door was flung open and the chauffeur pulled out by three Arabic-speaking men with hand guns. The vehicle was missing for two weeks and when it was found the wheels were missing, the door ripped off, and the electronic system and equipment controlling the braking system had gone. Al Fayed, as we have seen, controlled the company, Etoile Limousines, which supplied the vehicle. No wonder the French authorities turned down the offer by experts from Mercedes to examine the car after the crash.

When Henri Paul came back on duty that night he seemed his normal self to most observers. The programming was deep within his psyche still waiting to be activated. He may well have had a couple of alcoholic drinks in the Ritz bar, but his intake and demeanour did not correspond with the later medical report. Claims that he was an alcoholic also do not match with the examination of his liver. But if, as I suggest, Henri Paul was a mind controlled 'multiple' he could have been drunk in one compartment of his mind and not in another. I have heard from recovering 'multiples' who have experienced this. Someone close to Paul that night, his handler, was switching his compartments. In this way he could have had a considerable level of alcohol in his blood while, in some compartments, he would have been unaffected by it. The same with the carbon monoxide. Just before or just after the Mercedes pulled away from the Ritz, Henri Paul was given the trigger which activated the programming. It could have been a sound, a sign, a colour or more likely a word or sentence. With Paul's subconscious programming now overwhelming his conscious mind, he sped away to the Place de la Concorde and down the dual carriageway to the Pont de L'Alma. Rees-Jones put his seat belt on, but apparently did not alert Diana and Dodi to the danger. Thus they stay unbelted. As Paul entered the Pont d L'Alma tunnel at an estimated 80 miles an hour (some reports say slower), he braked fiercely, scraped the right hand wall of the tunnel, and then aimed the car at the 13th pillar. It is the 13th pillar that gives it away. The Brotherhood throughout history has had such an obsession with the number 13 that to believe this was a coincidence is taking chance to the level of fantasy. There must be 30 pillars in that tunnel and the car hit the 13th because it was meant to. Diana had an aversion to the number 13 and she would not allow a 13th lot in her dress auction at Christies the June before she died. If, as some witnesses have suggested, the crash was caused by the Mercedes hitting a white Fiat Uno or by a motorcyclist flashing a powerful light into Paul's eyes from a motor cycle, there is no way he could be sure of hitting the 13th pillar. But a person with a deeply programmed subconscious would be able to put the car right on the button, even at speed.

Mark Phillips is the man who helped to deprogramme Cathy O'Brien when she was a mind controlled slave of the CIA. He has worked in these fields for much of his adult life and after I reached my conclusions about the events in Paris, I rang him to ask if it would be possible to mind control Henri Paul to pick out that pillar at speed. Mark was in no doubt: "Yes, Yes" he said "More than yes, absolutely yes". He pointed out that the subconscious worked much faster than the conscious mind and to the subconscious 80 miles an hour would actually be quite slow compared with its ability to think and react. If the speed was considerably slower as some reports suggest, it would have been even easier. "There are many techniques they could have used to programme his mind during those three hours he was missing", Mark said. The number of ways they could have caused the crash, another vehicle, an explosive device, stun weapons, etc, etc, would fill a book and any of them is possible on the face of it. But not if they wanted to be sure of hitting the 13th pillar, which they did. To do that, they needed a driver with a programmed subconscious.

I think the stories about the mysterious Fiat Uno and the motorcyclist with the flashing light are diversions to lead researchers away from the simple truth. So much time and effort has been wasted on the Fiat in particular, fueled by Al Fayed's own investigation team. Whenever such assassinations are staged, there are always a stream of false 'clues' and 'leads' which divert attention. The Kennedy assassination was full of them. Another possibility for the cause of the crash is external control of the car. Randulph Fiennes, famous for his polar expeditions, was an officer in the Royal Scots Greys and attached to the élite SAS. He wrote a book about a secret group of assassins called the Clinic and how they murdered people while making it look like an accident. The death of Major Michael Marman is particularly relevant to what could have happened in Paris. He was driving a Citroen 2CV along the A303 near Stonehenge in November 1986 when a BMW coming the other way careered across the carriageway and killed him instantly. Fiennes says that the BMW had been tampered with and the braking system was operated by remote control which could override the normal system via compressed air from a tiny scuba diving cylinder hidden in the engine compartment. The remote control equipment was operated from a Volvo which followed the BMW, Fiennes reported. The BMW was driven by Sir Peter Horsley, a retired Air Marshall, who survived the crash. Fiennes says that the Clinic knew that Horsley would be travelling along that road at the same time as their target. In his autobiography, *Sounds From Another Room*, Horsley says that he was accelerating to about 60 miles an hour when the car began to react strangely. He saw a grey Volvo closing up quickly behind him and as he was about to wave it past, his BMW spun sharply to the left, the brakes screeching, and then sharply to the right and back again. This is remarkably similar to what happened to the Mercedes before it struck the 13th pillar. Horsley was by now desperately trying to maintain control and he went on:

"Out of the corner of my eye I saw the grey Volvo accelerating past me at high speed. My car had now developed a mind of its own as it swung broadside and skidded down the road. With a lurch it hit the central reservation, mounted the grass verge separating the two lanes of the highway and crossed over into the opposite carriageway. I had just time to see a small car approaching from the opposite direction. I hit it sideways on with tremendous force. In a split-second the driver's horror-stricken face was visible and I heard his hoarse scream."[50]

It is possible that Diana's Mercedes was externally controlled in this way, because it is clear that the steering on Horsley's BMW was also remotely controlled. Certainly a highly skilled operator could direct the Mercedes into the 13th pillar. Support for the contention that no other car was directly involved in Diana's crash comes from Eric Petel who claims to have seen the crash. Petel says that he was riding his motorcycle towards the entrance to the tunnel when he was overtaken by the Mercedes. No other vehicle was nearby. He said:

"I saw a car in my rear-view mirrors flashing its headlamps. I moved across to let it by and it raced past even though I was doing about 70 miles per hour. An instant later I heard a deafening noise and saw the accident. The car was spinning in the road... I stopped. There were no other cars or bikes around at all and I could see all the way through the tunnel. The roof of the Mercedes was totally smashed in. The right hand rear door was partly open and I looked in and saw a woman. She seemed to have been thrown forward from the back seat and had her head between the front seats."[51]

Petel said blood was flowing from her right ear and as he brushed her hair from her face and placed her head on the arm rest, he realised it was Princess Diana. Her eyelashes were fluttering, but she had not opened her eyes at this stage, he said. Petel estimates he was at the scene for about a minute before climbing back on his bike to ring the police. He told them that Diana had been in an accident, but they laughed and told him to stop wasting their time. In despair at this, he rode to the police station in Avenue Mozart. His lawyer, Antoine Deguines, says that Petel was kept waiting for 25 minutes and taken into a backroom where he was handcuffed. For reporting an 'accident'? When eventually freed, he was told to follow a police car to another police station where he gave a statement which he signed without reading. "I was outraged" he said "They didn't seem to care about the crash." He heard nothing from the authorities for months before he enlisted help from a lawyer to tell his story to the official inquiry.

Whenever an assassination occurs in a public place, two things happen. The person named as responsible is a 'patsy' or 'scapegoat', most often these days under mind control, and diversions galore are created to lead investigators away from the truth of what happened. The first method allows you to make an immediate arrest, or expose the person to blame, and no further investigations are necessary because everyone knows who was responsible. We have seen this technique with Lee Harvey Oswald, Sirhan Sirhan, Timothy McVeigh, and now Henri Paul. It is endless. The second method, the diversion, ensures that the crucial hours and days after the event are wasted as people chase a mass of false stories and 'leads'. This was a technique used in Paris with the paparazzi, the flashing lights from motorcycles and later the Fiat Uno. Also when people are fed a constant barrage of conflicting reports and theories they become confused and a confused mind switches off and loses interest. So first they tell you the paparazzi were to blame, then they were not. Then they tell you the car speedometer was found stuck at 120 miles an hour, then they say it was found on zero.

I thought it strange how many American witnesses to the crash were quickly located. The Pont and Place de L'Alma were not, before Diana's death, a popular tourist area. There is nothing there except a restaurant or two, a tunnel, and a maze of crossing roads. And yet at 12.25 in the morning, several American tourists say they witnessed what happened. The number of witnesses in general was unusual anyway, given the late hour and the fact that Paris empties at that time of year as vast numbers of Parisians take their annual holiday to the French coastal resorts. I can understand that some people in the few cars travelling along the road at the time may have seen the crash and its immediate aftermath, but I know from visiting the spot myself, that the main pedestrian routes have virtually no view of the tunnel at all. The police failed to control the crash scene according to normal police procedure and so much evidence was lost immediately. They failed to question important witnesses and leaked some information while maintaining unshakable secrecy over other areas of the investigation.[52] It all stinks.

Today there is an added challenge for would-be assassins and assassination plots with the 'traffic' cameras that are located all over cities. Smile, you're on TV. It would be impossible to keep secret the methods and personnel used to kill Diana if the whole thing was being videoed. But when you are the Brotherhood with connections at the highest levels in politics, police and intelligence agencies, the traffic cameras present no such problem. You simply switch them off! There are 17 traffic cameras on the route between the Ritz and the Pont de L'Alma, including those inside the tunnel itself. If they had been working that night there would be no mystery, because you could play back the whole event on your television set. One camera looks down on the entrance to the tunnel and would have recorded any Fiat Uno or men on motorbikes with flashing lights. But that camera, like all the others, was switched off at the crucial moment. Never before in Paris had the whole system malfunctioned at the same time and the police refuse to explain what happened. The system runs on an independent power supply and it is controlled by the police and, ultimately, by the French Intelligence agencies, because the cameras are there to monitor far more than just traffic problems. At the same time as the camera system failed all the police communication frequencies in central Paris also went off. Simon Reagan in his excellent book, *Who Killed Diana?*, quotes a contact called André who, like many people, loves to listen in to police radio messages. André was sitting on a bench near the Eiffel Tower, a few minutes walk from the Pont de L'Alma, on the night Diana died. He was, as usual, using a receiver to monitor the police communications. But suddenly, at 12.20am, all the lines went down. There was a radio blackout. It lasted for 20 minutes and then, André said, the signal came back and there was a mass of radio traffic as people all wanted to talk at once. "I have never… come across such chaotic radio traffic", he said. "It was extraordinary." When the lines went down Diana was leaving the Ritz on her last journey alive. By the time they came back she was lying in the tunnel under the complete control of the emergency team and according to the autopsy report within a few minutes of clinical death. And there is not a shred of credible evidence for a conspiracy, is there, eh? My God, it's in our face. But within ten days of the crash, the French police had produced a 350 page preliminary report which assumed it was an accident and they did not consider any other possibility.

Now, talking of that 'emergency team' brings me to another vital point. As a contact on the fringes of British Intelligence told me, causing the crash is easy for the powers involved, but you cannot be sure of killing your target. Therefore you have your people controlling the medical team because, although your target hasn't died, there is now a credible reason for them to die. There has been a crash. The medical team's job (or those in charge, anyway) is to make sure that the target does not survive, no matter what condition they may be in to start with. Even those who dismiss the idea that Diana was murdered have questioned the astonishing delay in getting her to hospital when, according to the official medical reports, she was suffering from an injury that required urgent surgery. The doctors say that the pulmonary vein had been ruptured near the heart and this was filling her lungs with blood. Diana was lying in the tunnel bleeding to death, if that is correct. The only way her life was going to be saved with such an injury was through immediate surgery. So why was it more than an hour and a half before she arrived at the hospital? Within a minute of impact, Doctor Frederic Mailliez with an American 'friend' Mark Butt, drove into the tunnel from the opposite direction. A private investigator I know has made extensive inquiries into Mailliez and Butt and, while these investigations continue, his findings strongly suggest there is more to both of them than we are being told. The crash happened at 12.25am and by 12.26, Doctor Mailliez said he had seen the crushed Mercedes, stopped his car, turned on warning lights, run across to the Mercedes to establish there were two people dead and two alive and had rung the emergency services. This man must be a seriously quick worker. He is one of 160 Parisian doctors who are on constant call for emergencies in hospitals and private homes as part of a French insurance system, SOS Medecins. He had treated accident victims many times when he was a member of SAMU, the French emergency ambulance service. And yet a doctor on constant call for emergencies says that all he had in his car to help Diana was an oxygen cylinder and mask! Mailliez was in control of Diana and her condition for the crucial 15 to 20 minutes before his former employers, the SAMU emergency team, arrived to take over. He claims that Diana did not say anything to him, but this contradicts his comment to the London *Times* that "She kept saying how much she hurt as I put a resuscitation mask over her mouth". Trevor Rees-Jones, the bodyguard, also says he had flashbacks of hearing a female voice calling out in the back of the car: "First it's a groan. Then Dodi's name was called… And that can only be Princess Diana's voice" he told the *Daily Mirror*.[53] How reliable that statement is, however, is open to debate. What does seem to be clear is that Diana was conscious or at least semi-conscious when Mailliez arrived. He told the CNN chat show host, Larry King, that:

"She looked pretty fine. At the beginning… from the outside, you know, she looked pretty fine. But inside, you know, the internal injury was already starting… It's really funny. That's the only part, where she was sitting, that's the only part which was still intact." Mailliez on one hand told a French medical magazine that: "I thought her life could be saved" and yet said another time that "It was hopeless. There was nothing we could do to save her." He also told King that although Diana is the most photographed woman in the world, and the paparazzi were taking shots of her while he was with her in the tunnel, he had no idea that she was Princess Diana until he saw the news reports the following morning. Excuse me? The pigs are airborne again. When the emergency team arrived, Malliez says he left the scene because there was nothing more he could do.

The official explanation for the incredible delay in taking Diana to hospital is that she was trapped in the wreckage. This is a lie, lie, lie. One of the ambulance crew told the French newspaper, *La Parisien*, that when he arrived Diana was lying with most of her body out of the car with her legs resting on the rear seat. "She was agitated, semi knocked out, but conscious… she was groaning and struggling feebly. She murmured 'Oh my God' several times." *The Scotsman* newspaper, in an investigation published on September 11th 1997, established that Diana was removed from the car shortly after the fire brigade arrived and the excuse of her being 'trapped' does not stand up. Another official excuse for the delay is that the emergency doctors had to give her a blood transfusion. This is another lie, lie, lie. SAMU teams do not carry blood transfusion equipment because they would not know the victim's blood type. When the ambulance did leave the tunnel, the driver was ordered to go no faster than 25 miles an hour and some reports say it took as long as 40 minutes to cover the 3.7 miles (6km) to the La Pitie-Salpetriere. Four other hospitals quite capable of treating Diana were closer to the scene and the ambulance stopped twice on the way for 'delicate interventions', one of them within sight of the hospital. Diana arrived at La Pitie-Salpetriere about 2.10am, an hour and 45 minutes after the crash happened. By any medical criteria whatsoever this delay was utterly ludicrous, unless it was meant to happen. It doesn't take a genius to see why, despite such apparent incompetence, there has been no inquiry into the medical response that night. Waiting at the hospital were a surgical team headed by Professor Bruno Riou, the duty surgeon who, we are told, first heard about the crash while doing his rounds. Is it only me that finds it strange that a renowned surgeon is 'doing his rounds' in the early hours of the morning? Waiting with him when Diana arrived were Professor Pierre Coriat, the head of anaesthetics, Professor Alain Pavie, a chest and heart specialist, and Professor Pierre Benazet, another experienced surgeon. They had been in telephone communication with the emergency team in the tunnel throughout. We are told they opened Diana's chest cavity, repaired the vein, and 'battled to save her' for an hour and a half before admitting defeat. I find this remarkable, also, because the autopsy report apparently shows that Diana was clinically dead at 12.45am while still lying in the tunnel. She would therefore have been clinically dead for an hour and 25 minutes before she even arrived at the hospital and for three hours before the professors walked out of the operating theatre to announce that she had died. Having the body examined at a location you control is vital in such assassinations. President Kennedy's body was flown immediately out of Dallas to the Brotherhood-front, the Bethesda Naval Center near Washington DC, for the post mortem. Here the president's brain went missing (or his look-alike's did) and, as the US Assassination Records Review Board revealed, the autopsy notes and the first draft of the post mortem were burned.

So who was behind Diana's assassination? It is important to stress that those who gave the order and those who did the deed would be very different. We are looking at a Brotherhood here, a spider's web, and while the order will have come from the spider or spiders in the centre, it will have been mostly carried out by the flies. It is highly unlikely that it would have been done directly by British Intelligence because that would be too obvious. Intelligence agencies subcontract the assassinations of their own citizens to put them at arms length from the incident and to allow them to 'plausibly deny' that they were responsible. For instance, there is considerable evidence that President Kennedy was shot by members of an élite rifle team within a renegade unit of French Intelligence called the OAS, or at least that they were involved in the plot. Olof Palme, the Bilderberger Prime Minister of Sweden, was murdered in Stockholm in 1986 on the orders of, among others, George Bush. But the killing was carried out by members of BOSS, the South African Intelligence agency (see ...*And The Truth Shall Set You Free*). The British Foreign Office has its own assassination squad called Group 13 (that number again) and British Intelligence has a long and sick history of political and economic assassinations. British Intelligence consists of MI5 (Military Intelligence 5) which is responsible officially for domestic security, and MI6 which deals with overseas matters. MI5 announced in 1988 that they do not assassinate people. No, they get others to do it for them. This pathetic denial was prompted by the revelations of the former MI5 agent, David Shayler, that MI6 had organised a plot to assassinate Libya's Colonel Gaddafi. The attempt had failed because the bomb was put under the wrong car. Shayler was head of the 'Libyan Desk' at MI5 and was in the perfect position to know. Robin Cook, the Foreign Secretary, who is so far out of his depth he needs a frogman's suit, said that he had been assured that no such event took place. Oh, that's OK then. The attorney-general banned David Shayler from appearing on the ITV programme, *Diana – Secrets of the Crash*, and later Shayler was arrested and jailed in Paris awaiting extradition to London. Why do that if what he is saying is such nonsense? Because, of course, he's right. By the way, the oath of allegiance by British Intelligence officers is not to the government, but to the monarch. It is the same with Members of Parliament and the military. Ultimately the Queen is their boss under the law, although, in truth, their boss is whoever controls the Queen because even she is not at the top of the pile.

The type of organisation most likely to have been involved in Diana's death, at the operational level is typified by the Pinay Circle or 'Le Cercle' which has a number of British establishment figures in its ranks. Le Cercle is an offshoot of the even more élite Safari Club, which was set up by Count Alexander de Maranches, the Director during the 1970s of the French Service for External Documentation and Espionage. It was the Safari Club which arranged for the alliance between a French

Intelligence front-company called Group Bull and the computer giant Honeywell which is, you will be surprised to know, the world's biggest manufacturer of landmines. This alliance supplied landmines to both sides in the Bosnian conflict. The Safari Club began as a consortium of the secret police of the Shah of Iran called SAVAK, Saddam Hussein in Iraq, Anwar Sadat of Egypt and Saudi Arabian Intelligence. It has been involved in countless coups in Africa to further its goals and is heavily involved in arms trading and supply. Out of the Safari Club came the Pinay Circle or Le Cercle, named after the French Prime Minister, Antoine Pinay, who attended the first Bilderberg Meeting in Oosterbeek, Holland, in May 1954. Others involved with Le Cercle included the Habsburg family. To give you an idea of its make up and range of influence, the Le Cercle membership has included Nicholas Elliot, a department head at MI6; William Colby, a former director of the CIA; Colonel Botta of Swiss Military Intelligence; Stefano Della Chiaie, a leading member of the Italian Secret Service; Giullo Andreotti, the former Italian Prime Minister from the notorious P2 Freemasonry Lodge and the man who gave the Mafia official protection; Silva Munoz, a former minister for the fascist, Franco, in Spain and a member of the Elite secret society, Opus Dei; Franz Josef Strauss, the German defence minister; and Monsignor Brunello, an agent to the Vatican. In America, one of the Le Cercle fronts is the CIA-backed Heritage Foundation in Washington. Look at the potential for such an organisation to be the coordinating force between countless different agencies and countries all to achieve a common aim. The Safari Club-Le Cercle network provides the Arab-British-French connection necessary to arrange for Diana to be in Paris at the right time, the security for her to be withdrawn, the assassination to be carried out, and those involved to get away with it. What was that John Stalker said? "Why would the French want to cover up the murder of a British woman?" It is also interesting that Simon Regan in his book, *Who Killed Diana?*, says that it was Le Cercle which destablised the Gough Whitlam government in Australia in 1975. The Queen was certainly involved in that, too. As I explained earlier, it was her Governor of Australia, John Kerr, who removed Whitlam in the end. If the Windsors and Le Cercle worked together to bring down an elected Australian Government, why could they not have worked together to eliminate Diana?

Paris, with its immense Brotherhood associations going back centuries, has long been a favourite location for their murders and plots. Amschel Rothschild from the English branch of the family, was murdered there in his hotel room in 1996 in what some claim to have been part of one of the inter-Brotherhood wars which have littered their history. For an organisation like Le Cercle, or its many mirrors in London, it would have been easy to place its people in the right places. Mohamed Al Fayed's security operation is awash with former members of élite British military and police units who know the consequences of saying "No" to the Brotherhood, even if they don't wish to be involved. In the same way, these spider structures ensure that their people control the inquiries into their assassinations, as they did most famously with Kennedy. Even Mohamed Al Fayed's personal investigation into Diana's death was headed by Pierre Ottavoili, a former chief of the Criminal Brigade, the criminal investigation department of French Police. This is the same organisation which is also responsible for the official investigation. Al Fayed's chief lawyer in Paris is a former French Justice Minister, and in overall charge in London is John Macnamara, his head of security and a former Chief Superintendent at the headquarters of London's Metropolitan Police, Scotland Yard. In the Spring of 1998, Macnamara was part of a 'sting' operation involving the FBI, CIA and possibly, the Israeli (Rothschild) Intelligence Agency Mossad, to arrest a former CIA agent Oswald Le Winter, a 67-year-old American born in Austria. Le Winter contacted Al Fayed claiming to have documents for sale proving the involvement of MI6 and the CIA in Diana's murder. He was asking $10 million and after a meeting with Macnamara he was given an advance of $15,000. A further meeting was arranged in Vienna, Austria, for the key documents and the rest of the money to be handed over. In the meantime, however, Al Fayed called a friend in the FBI, who contacted the CIA. Le Winter was followed, spied on, and lured to the Ambassador Hotel in Vienna on Wednesday April 22nd, where with support from the Austrian police a combination of FBI, CIA and possibly Mossad agents pounced on him. All this for an alleged hoaxer? The story would have remained secret, but for Peter Grolig, an Austrian journalist on the *Kurier* newspaper. He reported what happened and established that when Le Winter's hotel room was searched, four documents, two of them in code, were found and appeared to be genuine CIA documents. The CIA have since admitted tapping Diana's phone calls in, and to, America and passing the contents to British Intelligence. Le Winter was arrested and held in custody. Grolig's story forced Al Fayed to admit that it was true. So was Le Winter trapped by such an array of international security personnel because he was selling a hoax to Al Fayed or because he was selling the truth? Another intelligence insider also insists the crash was not an accident. Richard Tomlinson, a former agent of Britain's MI6, gave evidence to the French inquiry into Diana's death. In 1997 Tomlinson served a six month jail sentence under the Official Secrets Act for trying to sell his memoirs. In August 1998 he was arrested again, at gun point, in Paris at the request of the British Government who were concerned at his association in that city with the MI5 whistle-blower, David Shayler, who was also arrested and jailed in Paris.[54] Tomlinson apparently told Herve Stephan, the judge in charge of the 'inquiry', that Diana was murdered. According to a report on the BBC's news service, Ceefax, on August 28th 1998, he told the judge that Henri Paul was an asset of British Intelligence and so was "One of the bodyguards". Which one was not named. Meanwhile Herve Stephan, a Brotherhood placeman, is doing all he can to hold the line that it was an accident.

The most important question to ask when you are trying to identify those responsible for a crime is: "Who benefits?" As the Roman writer, Seneca, said: "He who most benefits from a crime is the one most likely to have committed it". Well the Windsors benefited magnificently. No longer is Diana there to continue her inevitable destruction of the Monarchy's credibility and public esteem with her actions and her knowledge of their secrets. No longer is she there to bring her influence on the upbringing and attitudes of the future king, Prince William and his brother Prince Harry. The Windsors now have complete control of them, to mould them into their image. They couldn't do that before because Diana's influence was too strong and I hope the memory of that will encourage the princes to withstand the indoctrination. The way is now paved for Charles' marriage to Camilla Parker-Bowles without the complication of Diana and, of course, his royal duty to produce Windsor heirs with Spencer genes, although as we shall see, William might not be his child. Understandably, it has been suggested that Diana was killed because of her campaign against landmines. This is not true, not directly anyway. The landmine manufacturers have done very nicely from her campaign, because they make far more money from clearing mines than they do making them. A mine costs about £30 to produce, but at least £3,000 to clear. Clearing all the mines around the world is estimated at £330 billion. No, the landmine manufacturers like Honeywell were not against Diana's campaign, they loved it for their own reasons. But what she showed very clearly was the power she had to take an issue from the shadows and hurl it into the public arena. The question could well have been: "What will she do next?". And what was it that Diana had to reveal, as she told my contact, that would "Shake the world"? Henry Kissinger, one of the greatest Brotherhood manipulators of the 20th century, met Diana a number of times and sickeningly attended her funeral. He said in an interview after her death that: "She was politically and diplomatically uncontrollable". That is Kissinger-speak for "That's one reason she was killed". From the perspective of the operational level of the Brotherhood pyramid, as with Kennedy, there were many reasons why they wanted her dead. But, as I keep emphasising, that is only one level. At the top are the Elite black magic adepts, the reptilian full bloods and crossbreeds. At the highest level of the Brotherhood, Diana's death, like Kennedy's, was a ritual killing. It was long planned for the effect it would have on the people and the magnetic field of the Earth, and to symbolise the introduction of the New World Order. Don't underestimate the fantastic power of ritual and symbolism in affecting the human psyche and the planet's magnetic field. These people are not obsessed with it for no reason.

The Brotherhood and Satanic symbolism surrounding Diana's death is endless and to understand the background to her ritual murder we must, once again, go back a very long time. Diana was one of the greatest goddesses of the ancient world and she represented the female energy also known as Barati, Britannia, Isis, Artemis, Aphrodite, all these different names for the same energy. If you go back far enough, they symbolise the same entity, also, Ninkharsag. Diana was known as a Moon goddess. One tribe of Elite bloodlines who worshipped the goddess Diana were called the Sicambrian Franks who can be traced from Troy (that name again), through Asia Minor, now Turkey, the Caucasus Mountains (again) and up into Europe. They lived at one time in an area west of the River Danube and settled in Germania, named by the Romans after the Scythian 'genuine ones' with their centre in Cologne. They also invaded parts of Roman-occupied Gaul, the land which is now Belgium and northern France, from where the 'noble' families of Scotland were to come. It is from these Sicambrian Franks that we get the name France. At the time of King Meroveus, who was named Guardian of the Franks in 448, this people became known as the Merovingians and Princess Diana, through the Stuart bloodline, was related to them. Many seem to believe that the Merovingians are descended from the bloodline of Jesus, but how they can be genetically descended from a myth defeats me. This is a diversion to mislead. They are, however, an Elite bloodline that goes back to the Aryan race in the ancient Middle and Near East and eventually goes off planet. The Merovingians were the sorcerer kings who were noted for their esoteric knowledge and magical powers which they inherited from the underground bloodline streams of secret groups and initiations. Francio, the founder of the Franks, claimed to be a descendant of Noah and his ancestors once resided in ancient Troy of wooden horse fame. The French city of Troyes, where the Templars were officially formed, was named by the Sicambrian Franks after their former home. The Iliad says that Troy was founded by Dardanus, the son of the Greek god Zeus, who was depicted as both an eagle and a serpent. Zeus was born in Arcadia in Sparta, it is said, and the Spartans migrated into France. These are the bloodlines we are talking about here, not those of 'Jesus'.

The city of Paris was established by the Sicambrian Franks in the 6th century after they became known as the Merovingians. It was named after Prince Paris, the son of King Priam of Troy. It was the relationship between Prince Paris and Helen of Sparta which supposedly caused the Trojan War in which the Trojan Horse (infiltration) assured victory for the Spartans. Both the Trojans and the Spartans were branches of the same Aryan peoples and within them were the reptilian bloodlines. Paris in those days was confined to an island in the River Seine which is now known as the Ile de la Cite or Isle of the City. The Notre Dame Cathedral, built by the Templars on a site of former Diana worship, stands on the Ile de la Cite today and this is where the Templar Grand Master, Jacques de Molay, was roasted to death. The Merovingians established the city of Paris on a major vortex point which is why the Notre Dame Cathedral is built on that spot. Meroveus, the founder of the Merovingian dynasty, followed the goddess cult of Diana and this is not surprising because the epicentre for Diana worship was at the famous temple at Ephesus in Asia Minor, not far from the alleged site of Troy. The temple is named as one of the Seven Wonders of the Ancient World. Diana was known as Queen of Heaven, just like Semiramis. Outside the original Paris – and now very much inside the modern city – the Merovingians established an underground chamber for the worship of the goddess Diana and for the blood rituals and human sacrifices to her. This site dates back at least to 500–750 AD and it was here that kings in dispute over property would settle the issue in combat. According to legend, anyone killed there goes straight to Heaven and sits at the right hand of God. Now get this: The location today of this underground sacrificial site for the goddess Diana is… the Pont de L'Alma tunnel!

The word pont relates to Pontifex, a Roman high priest, and it means passage or bridge. Alma comes from Al-Mah, a Middle Eastern name for, wait for it… the Moon goddess. So the Pont de L'Alma translates as 'Bridge of the Moon Goddess' and the adjoining Place de L'Alma is the 'Place of the Moon Goddess'. And the Moon goddess is Diana. It can also translate as 'Bridge of the Soul' and a 'Maiden' of the goddess Diana was called an Al-mah! This is why Henri Paul was programmed to drive past the turning to Dodi Fayed's flat and head for the Pont de L'Alma tunnel.

This is why the emergency team kept her in the tunnel for so long instead of rushing her to hospital where her life would have been saved. She wasn't meant to be saved and they only moved her when she was clinically dead, as the autopsy report confirmed. According to Brotherhood Satanic ritual, Diana had to die in that underground chamber on the ancient sacrificial site and it had to happen at night under the Moon in the goddess month of August, ruled according to legend by the Roman version of Isis, Diana, etc: Juno Augusta. The Satanists in the emergency team simply ensured that Diana would not leave the tunnel (sacrificial chamber) alive. We are told she bled to death and, if this is correct, it was precisely in accordance with their blood rites and sacrificial rites. But was the bleeding caused in the way we are told, or by some other chemical means? We now know that Diana was clinically dead about 12.45 am, yet she was taken to the La Pitie Salpetriere Hospital and kept in the operating theatre for an hour and a half while the medical team, Professor Bruno Riou, Professor Pierre Coriat, Professor Alain Pavie and Professor Jean Pierre Benazat, cut open her chest and "battled to save her". Save a woman who had already been clinically dead for an hour and fifteen minutes when she arrived at the hospital? When they had finished, the French Minister of the Interior, Jean-Pierre Chevenement, decreed, according to his senior advisor, Sami Mani, that there would be strictly no admittance to the room in which her body was laid out.[55] Chevenement was one of several 'VIPs' who rushed to the tunnel and observed the medical operation at this former sacrificial site.[56] The Brotherhood Mother Goddess, Arizona Wilder, said that Guy de Rothschild had talked about Diana's death in early 1998 when he tried to reprogramme her at a house in Sherman Oaks, Los Angeles. Rothschild was using a pseudonym, Dr Barrington. He said that he was in the tunnel that night to "Steal Diana's soul" through the 'evil eye' hypnotic gaze the reptiles use at the point of death. I explained this earlier in relation to Pindar. A contact in Denmark told me that during her last year of medical studies at the Copenhagen University in 1983 she realised that severely mentally ill patients were being used for experiments by being inseminated with genetically tampered semen. The pregnancy, she said, was very painful and often unsuccessful. Sometimes the patient died and the foetus was dissected in secrecy. She went on: "The doctors conducting these experiments were professors, heads of departments, PhDs, the most outstanding in their field. They had a kind of Brotherhood... many of them were psychic and monkeyed with black magic. Incredible amounts of money were flowing to them." A story that could be repeated thousands of times all over the world.

Another name for the goddess Diana is Hecate. One of the ancient 'triads' or 'trinities' was that of Diana, Luna and Hecate who were said to be three aspects of the same female energy. It was called Diana on Earth, Luna in Heaven, and Hecate in Hell. Hecate is one of the premier deities of Satanism and she is a version of Aphrodite and Venus, different names for the same energy. After her husband's death, Jackie Kennedy travelled to the Greek island of Delos in the south west Aegean Sea, the legendary birthplace of Diana and Apollo and the considered domain of Hecate, the goddess of the 'infernal arts'. Delos is known for this reason as the Island of the Dead. Hecate was portayed as both the virgin and the whore and crossroads are the sacred places of Diana-Hecate. It is at crossroads that the witches and the Grand Masters and sorcerers of Freemasonry perform their rituals. Crossroads are symbolic of the vortex points created where ley lines cross. In ritual sex magic, the wearing of clothes of the opposite sex and the performance of bi-sexual acts are called 'Crossroad Rites'. The women involved were called 'dikes'. Crossroads are also places of human and animal sacrifice and Hecate is known as a 'sex and death goddess' and the goddess of witchcraft and sorcery. At the Pont de L'Alma, right at the spot where Diana died, the road that goes through the tunnel is crossed on the surface by another road which leads onto the Pont de L'Alma Bridge. In fact this spot is a maze of crossroads. And Diana died in the early morning of August 31st. Hecate's Day in the Satanic calendar is August 13th, but under the Satanic law of reverse symbolism and reverse numbers, Hecate's day of sacrifice is... August 31st!!

So just look at the symbolism of this. Diana, named after the ancient Moon goddess, was driven from the Ritz and through the Place de la Concorde where she passed the 3,200 year-old Egyptian obelisk brought to Paris from Luxor with it's tip or pyramid coloured bright gold symbolising the penis of Osiris. It was at this very point, a minute from where Diana died, that Queen Marie Antoinette was beheaded at the guillotine during the Brotherhood-engineered French Revolution, another symbolic blood sacrifice of the female energy. Diana was then driven at speed to the Pont de L'Alma tunnel, the Bridge or Place of the Moon Goddess, where the car struck the 13th pillar, the symbolism for which is simply enormous for obvious reasons and for others I'll come to later. Now she was left to die on the very site of an ancient underground sacrificial chamber to the goddess Diana and bled to death according to Satanic ritual. She also died at a crossroads with one road under the ground, the other above; and the crossroads is the sacred place for the Satanic deity, Hecate, another aspect of the 'Diana' energy. And it all happened on Hecate's day for sacrifice, August 31st. Does anyone doubt that this was a ritual murder? And I've not even nearly finished with the symbolism surrounding her death. Remember what David Berkowitz, the Satanist serial killer in New York known as the Son of Sam, wrote about those involved in the Satanic network:

> "...Satanists (*genuine ones*) are peculiar people. They aren't ignorant peasants or semi-literate natives. Rather, their ranks are filled with doctors, lawyers, businessmen, and basically highly responsible citizens... They are not a careless group who are apt to make mistakes. But they are secretive and bonded together by a common need and desire to mete out havoc on society. It was Aleister Crowley who said: 'I want blasphemy, murder, rape, revolution, anything bad'."[57]

It is worth emphasising again here the Satanists' relationship with female energy. The challenge we all face is to balance male and female energies and so enjoy the best aspects of them and not the extremes. The Satanists, however, seek to express only the extremes, thus creating disharmony and conflict. They use the malevolent, highly negative expressions of the female energy (covert manipulation behind the scenes) to create the events and circumstances which the extremes of the male energy (macho men, soldiers, terrorism) can play out in the public arena. Because of this it appears that the world is controlled and dominated by male energy – it's a 'man's world', but in truth it is not a world dominated by the male, it is a world dominated by extremes of male and female. I am not talking men and women here, I mean male and female energy which can be expressed by both men or women. For instance, the Brotherhood manipulators like Henry Kissinger never see a gun fired in anger. They are not out there physically fighting (male energy) in the wars they engineer. They are manipulating events from the shadows and behind our backs, a trait of the negative female energy and symbolised by the story of the Trojan Horse. The female energy is also the creative force and you can create negatively or positively. The Brotherhood are highly malevolent, but very creative. For this reason, in esoteric law and symbolism, the female energy (Diana, Semiramis, Isis, Barati, Britannia) is given different names for its different expressions. The Egyptians portrayed Isis in white in her positive mode and in black to symbolise her negative aspect. In the same way we have the symbolism of Diana (positive female) and Hecate (negative female). They are simply different symbolic names for different manifestations of the female energy. The Satanists of the Brotherhood work with the Hecate energy and that is why they worship this deity. They are actually worshipping the extreme negative female energy and it is for this reason that in Satanism the high priestess is considered as important as the priest, if not more so. At that Elite centre for Satanism in Belgium, the Castle of Darkness I mentioned in an earlier chapter, the top position in the hierarchy is not known as the king, but the Queen Mother. So in the Pont de L'Alma Tunnel the positive female energy (love, compassion, intuition), symbolised by Diana, was eliminated by the negative female energy (manipulation, ritual death), symbolised by Hecate and the crossroads.

   The death of Dodi Fayed was also crucial to the Satanic symbolism. Given the circumstances of his death, it is quite a coincidence that his real name, Emad El Din, is Arabic for 'Pillar of Faith'. Dodi was a nickname he was given as a toddler by his family. This, too, is interesting. It is very close to Dido and in fact 'Dido' was the nickname he gave to Diana. Dido in Greek mythology was the legendary founder and queen of Carthage (an Aryan people connected to the Phoenicians) and she was the daughter of Belus, king of the Phoenician city of Tyre. When Dido's husband was killed by her brother, Pygmalion, she fled with her followers to North Africa where she purchased Carthage from the native ruler, Larbus. He later threatened Dido with war unless she married him, but instead she killed herself. But the most likely symbols for Dodi Fayed's death can be found in his birthplace, Egypt. The Brotherhood are obsessed with the symbolism in ancient Egypt of the Osiris-Horus-Isis trinity (Nimrod-Tammuz-Semiramis) which is expressed in Christianity as father, son, and holy ghost. Among many things, it symbolises the male and female energies coming together to create a third force, new life. To the Egyptians, and therefore the Brotherhood, the son of God was Horus. He was born to Isis after her husband, Osiris, had been murdered by Set. She gathered together 14 parts of his mutilated body, but she could not find the penis. So she created a penis and impregnated herself to conceive Horus, the Sun God – Sun King, Horus was Osiris reborn. In Paris, part of this ritual was played out again. The car passed the golden-tipped Egyptian obelisk, the penis of Osiris, in the Place de la Concorde, and inside the vehicle were Diana (another name for Isis) and the Egyptian, Dodi Fayed, representing Osiris. I have heard from many sources that Diana was pregnant. Her foetus symbolised Horus, the Sun King. In ancient Egypt, they said that Osiris had to die before Horus could come in. This will sound amazing to most people, but if you study the unbelievable obsession these people have with ritual and symbolism it makes perfect sense. Diana may not even have realized she was pregnant. It could have been the foetus they were removing on the operating table in Paris while they "battled to save her" for hours after she was clinically dead. I have heard suggestions that the cells from the foetus are being used to clone babies from this genetic mix. These will be 'Sun gods' according to Brotherhood ritual. The cloning of humans has been possible for a long time, as the cloning of sheep at the Roslyn Institute near Rosslyn Chapel in Scotland has clearly shown. The Brotherhood's secret science is always far in advance of anything allowed into the public domain and because of this the public find it impossible to believe what the Brotherhood can do with drugs and technology. So it is with their mind control techniques and I am sure that both Diana and Dodi had been under the influence of mind manipulation over many weeks to ensure the ritual happened as required. For goodness sake, a stage hypnotist can take over the mind of someone from the audience. Just think what is possible for those mind manipulators at the global cutting edge.

The Pont de L'Alma is one of the most sacred places in the world to the Brotherhood and, as with the street plans in all their key cities, they made sure the site was full of appropriate symbolism: the bridge, the underground chamber, the crossroads and the name. Since my own spiritual awakening in 1990 I have been guided by my subconscious intuition to many Earth power centres. Often I have not been aware of this at the time and only with hindsight have I seen how, on a non-conscious level, I had been drawn to a major vortex point on the magnetic grid system and often to those of particular importance to the Brotherhood. In 1994 I was on holiday with my family near the Normandy coast in France and we decided to visit Paris. It was a long drive, but we had never seen the city before. We drove to Versailles outside Paris and took the train from there to the station at the Eiffel Tower. It was a hot, humid, and sweaty day, and the area was packed with people and heavy with traffic. This combination was so unpleasant that we decided not to stay very long before taking the train back to Versailles, but first we went for a short walk. We crossed the River Seine by a footbridge near the Eiffel Tower and walked a hundred yards or so alongside the river bank on the far side before finding a seat to rest. After sitting there for about ten minutes we walked over the nearby road bridge and back to the railway station to leave the city. We were in the place for little more than an hour and that is all I had experienced of Paris until I went back to research Diana's death for this book.

When I returned to Paris I had quite a shock because I found that seat again where we rested in 1994. It is on top of the Pont de L'Alma tunnel very close to the 13th pillar where the car crashed! Also, near that seat above the mouth of the tunnel is a large depiction of a lighted torch (*see picture section*). This, of course, is the most obvious Brotherhood signature of them all and after President Kennedy's ritual killing, the Freemasons erected an obelisk in Dealey Plaza with a lighted torch at the top. Another flame was placed on his grave. The one on the Pont de L'Alma Tunnel stands on a black pentagram and there isn't a more powerful Satanic symbol than that. It is supposed to be a 'Flame of Liberty' (a copy of the flame held by the Statue of Liberty) to commemorate those who died in the Second World War, but it's location has, predictably, ensured that it has become a shrine to Diana. One newspaper report said that the French authorities were considering a permanent memorial to Diana at the Pont de L'Alma – a continuation of the 13th pillar above the ground! I can't think of anything more sick or more symbolic than that. The last I heard they planned to open a vegetable garden to commemorate her death and they were going to pull down a building to make way for it. The garden is an area of Paris that Diana is never known to have visited and she had no recorded passion for growing vegetables. So what goes on? Well, first I bet you'll find that the vegetable garden will be on another ancient site of some kind, and most importantly such an inadequate and bizarre memorial will ensure that the flame above the tunnel will now remain the public shrine to Diana.

The Flame of Liberty was placed on the tunnel entrance in 1987 and I am certain the assassination of Diana at that spot was planned well before then. It is quite conceivable, given the Brotherhood's long term planning and meticulous attention to ritual and symbolic detail, that it was planned for decades. Definitely before the sacrificial lamb was hooked into the Windsor web to marry Charles. It was Brotherhood symbolism which decided the location of their wedding at St Paul's Cathedral. St Paul's, with its vast dome, was designed by Sir Christopher Wren, the high Brotherhood initiate. It's design is mirrored by both the Congress Building in Washington DC and by the Pantheon in Paris. Brutus, the Trojan who became first king of the Britons in about 1,103BC, was the man who founded 'New Troy', known today as London. He was another who worshipped the goddess Diana and he is reported to have erected a temple to her on what is now called Ludgate Hill on the site of a former stone circle.[58] This is in the heart of the City of London financial district, that centre of Brotherhood control, and today on this site of Diana worship you will find… St Paul's Cathedral. In Paris, the Notre Dame (Our Lady) Cathedral is on an ancient site of Diana worship and the ambulance carrying the princess's body passed Notre Dame during that bizarre journey to hospital. So Diana was married on an ancient sacred site to the goddess Diana and she died on the site of an ancient sacrificial chamber of the goddess Diana. She was also hunted and used by the Windsors to produce heirs and Diana was the ancient goddess of hunting, fertility and childbirth.

When Prince Charles and Diana's sisters went to Paris to escort her body back to London, the coffin was draped in the royal standard, the flag of the Windsors which is covered with the Sun symbol, the lion. Not the flag of the country, you'll note, but the flag of the Windsors. Another strange coincidence happened at the Hammersmith Mortuary in London. As her coffin arrived, the one carrying Dodi was leaving and they apparently crossed at the entrance. What are the statistical chances of that when both made such very different journeys from Paris? Dodi, we were told, had to be buried within 24 hours of his death according to Muslim religious law and there was a mad rush by his father to meet the deadline. There was no autopsy on his body, a quick external examination was considered enough.

At this point, Diana's brother, Charles, Earl Spencer, then 33, came on the scene after flying back from his home in Cape Town, South Africa. When Earl Spencer, the Queen's god-son, made his maiden speech in the House of Lords in 1993, he chose a rather strange subject, *Satanism On The Spencer's Althorp Estate In Northamptonshire*. He acknowledged that it was going on, but he said he was doing all he could to eradicate it. What a remarkable topic to introduce in your first speech in the Houses of Parliament. The Brotherhood Mother Goddess, Arizona Wilder, reports seeing Earl Spencer and his father at some of the sacrificial rituals she conducted. It was Earl Spencer who announced that, despite her wishes, Diana's body would not be interred in the family tomb at the local village church at Great Brington near the estate. Earl Spencer said he wanted to avoid swamping the village with sightseers and he had decided that Diana would be buried on a man-made island in the centre of a lake on the Althorp Estate. The lake is called The Oval and when looked at from above, the island looks like a dot within a circle, a symbol of the Sun. The flame in a circle is on Kennedy's grave. Also on the island, Spencer has placed the Brotherhood symbol of a burning flame and at one stage, Mohamed Al Fayed said he was going to put an 'eternal flame' to Diana and Dodi on the roof of Harrods to mark the first anniversary of their deaths in August 1998.[59]

Islands are very much part of the legends of the goddess Diana and she was supposed to have been born on the island of Delos in the Aegean Sea. It is also known as the Island of the Dead after Hecate, the patroness of the 'infernal arts', the negative aspect of the Diana goddess energy. Diana is another name for Brito-Martis, the goddess of Crete which was colonised and developed by the Phoenicians who created the Minoan civilisation. Brito-Martis was actually a Phoenician goddess, according to Greek and Roman legend. She was the divine 'daughter' of Phoinix (correctly spelt) the King of Phoenicia, and was armed, like Diana, with weapons for the chase. Legend says that Brito-Martis (Diana) sailed from Phoenicia to Argos in Southern Greece and onto Crete where she was pursued by her unwelcome admirer, Minos. She escaped by retreating to the sea and sailed to Aegina, an island in the Aegean where stands the temple of Artemis or Diana. Islands and Diana are very much connected in the legends. Earl Spencer put Diana's grave among trees on the island and this is classic symbolism because the ancients used to worship the goddess Diana in the tree groves and this was said to be her most sacred place. Sir James Frazer describes in his book, *The Golden Bough*, the Diana rite known as the King of the Wood at Lake Nemi (again a lake is a big part of Diana legend). The Lady of the Lake is also Brotherhood symbolism. Frazer says that on the northern shore of Lake Nemi, under the cliffs on which the modern village of Nemi, near Aricia, is perched, was the sacred grove and sanctuary of Diana Nemorensis, or Diana of the Wood, the goddess of hunting. Lake Nemi is the most celebrated shrine to the goddess Diana and here, says

Frazer, there grew a tree around which the figure of a priest would be seen with a sword. A candidate for the priesthood in the cult of Diana could only succeed by killing the present incumbent and he would only keep the job until someone in turn killed him. The post carried the title of king – King of the Wood – and a long line of priest-kings who served Diana met a violent end. So the goddess Diana is associated with islands and a lake and was worshipped among the trees. And Earl Spencer puts his sister's grave among the trees on an island in a lake.

Then there is the strange tale of the black swans. In June 1998, Earl Spencer gave an interview for BBC Television in which he told of a dream he claimed to have had between the crash in Paris and Diana's funeral. In the dream, he said, he had been told to put four black swans on the lake around the island. When he called his estate manager the next morning and asked him where he would find four black swans, the manager is supposed to have said: "You've heard then?". "Heard what?", Spencer claims to have asked. "We've been offered four black swans", the estate manager replied. Maybe this is true, but, in my view, this story has more to do with flying pigs than flying swans. Black swans are profound occult symbols used in rituals and were the seal of the infamous Satanist, Catherine de Medici, who, Arizona Wilder says, was a previous incarnation of the Queen Mother. They appear most obviously in the ballet, *Swan Lake*, when the black swan, symbolising the negative female energy, kills the white swan, symbolising the positive. In other words, Hecate kills Diana. What better symbolism can you have of *Swan Lake* than black swans on a lake, as at Althorp? A swan is a derogatory term in Druidism. Project Monarch slaves who rebel are told that they will be "Turned into swans" and Diana, of course, rebelled against the Windsors. The number of swans also fits here. Monarch programming includes a term called The Four Gates of Heaven and four could also symbolise the four phases of the Moon. Earl Spencer has established a 'temple' to Diana at the side of the lake. A number of the stately homes of the British aristocracy have temples or areas featuring the goddess Diana, among them Blenheim Palace home of the Marlboroughs and Chatsworth House, headquarters of the Cavendish's, the Dukes of Devonshire, and both families are related to the Spencers. Diana was carried in a lead-lined coffin and lead is the metal associated in ritual magic with Saturn, possibly from where we get the name Satan. The colour associated with Saturn and Satanism is black. Diana was also led to her death across the two key Brotherhood days of Saturn-day and Sun-day. The 15th-century Italian philosopher-doctor from Florence, Marsilio Ficino, produced talismans for protection and the one for Saturn was engraved on pure lead. It was said to protect the wearer against death by assassination and ambush and protected women in childbirth. On Diana's lead coffin during the funeral were lilies, the flower of Lilith, another version of Hecate and a symbol of the bloodline. The lilies were chosen by Earl Spencer, Diana's brother. The lily was also sacred to Astarte, another Diana deity, and it was used to symbolise the impregnation of the virgin Mary. The 'blessed virgin' Juno, ruler of August, was said to have conceived her saviour-son, Mars, on a magic lily. The lily is symbolic of the reptilian bloodlines. In the year 656, the 10th Council of Toledo officially made the day of Juno's legendary conception of Mars into the

Christian Festival of the Mother of God, or Lady Day, insisting that it commemorated Mary's miraculous conception of Jesus with the aid of a lily.[60] In France the people knew Lady Day as Notre Dame de Mars. The symbolism of the lily with the pregnant goddess giving birth to the saviour-god (as in Isis and Horus) is fascinating, given the stories that Diana was pregnant at the time of her death and the way I have connected this to the legend of Osiris, Isis and Horus.

There have also been questions about whether Diana is even buried on the island. In the Summer of 1998, the *Star* magazine in the United States quoted an unnamed "senior source" at Buckingham Palace as saying she was secretly cremated and according to a report in the *Los Angeles Times* some people in the village of Great Brington also don't believe she is buried on the island. I know these reports are true from my own sources. One resident quoted by the *LA Times* said that the night her coffin was taken to Althorp for burial, the village had been 'invaded' by the army, police and special forces units, and all the villagers were hustled into their homes. She said that the crematorium at the church was working late into the night. Betty Andrews, the former cook and housekeeper at Althorp, is quoted by *Star* magazine as saying: "There's a strange feeling amongst the villagers that we may not be hearing the complete picture".

While researching this book I was introduced to Christine Fitzgerald, a brilliant and gifted healer, who was a close friend and confidant of Diana for nine years. Because of Christine's understanding of the esoteric, Diana was able to talk to her about matters she would not dare to share with anyone else for fear of being dubbed crazy. It is clear that Diana knew about the true nature of the royal family's genetic history and the reptilian control. Her nicknames for the Windsors were "the lizards" and "the reptiles" and she used to say in all seriousness: "They're not human". There is a very good reason for Diana using this description of the Windsors. As her deprogramming continued, Arizona Wilder remembered clearly a ritual she attended at Clarence House, the Queen Mother's home near to Buckingham Palace, in which Diana was shown who the Windsors really are. It took place in the first seven days of July 1981, just before Diana and Charles were married on the 29th. This period is the last seven days of the cycle of the Oak Tree, according to esoteric law, and the ritual was called The Awakening of the Bride. This is a ritual for all females of the 13 bloodlines who are going to be in publicly high positions and marry reptilians to produce the new generation of rulers. Arizona says that the Queen Mother, the Queen, Prince Philip, Lady Fermoy, Diana's father Earl Spencer, Prince Charles and Camilla Parker-Bowles were all present when Diana was brought into the room. She was wearing a white gown and a drug had been administered by Lady Fermoy. Diana was told that she should consider her union with Prince Charles as only a means to produce heirs and nothing else. Camilla Parker-Bowles was his consort, not her. Arizona says that Prince Philip and the Queen Mother then shape-shifted into reptiles to show Diana who they really were. 'Diana was terrified, but quiet', she said. Diana was told that if she ever revealed the truth about them, she would be killed. (Remember the guy I mentioned who had a call from Diana in the March before she died asking for his advice on how to reveal information about the royals that would 'shake the world'?) The Queen Mother told Diana at the ritual that "all ears" would be listening to everything she said and "all eyes" would forever be watching her. This is the classic 'nowhere to run' bind imposed on all mind controlled slaves. Does anyone believe, therefore, that they would allow Diana into the clutches of Mohamed Al Fayed if he was not under their control? The ritual also involved the use of a golden penis (Osiris symbolism) which was used on Diana to signify the 'opening of the womb'. Arizona says it was of reptilian shape and size and had needle-like protrusions designed to superficially puncture the walls of the vagina and cause bleeding. Diana was told that after this ritual, she would never be "honoured" again by attending their rituals and she was not to ask questions about them. Now do people understand why Diana suffered from bulimia and serious emotional problems from the time she married Charles?

Diana told Christine Fitzgerald that the Queen Mother was the power behind the Windsors, along with Prince Philip. But Philip was subordinate in the hierarchy to the Queen Mother, Diana said. The Queen Mother is connected to a long list of Brotherhood groups and societies and she is the head of the Inner Temple, the élite and highly secret society for the upper levels of the legal profession on the 'former' Knights Templar land at Temple Bar in London. It was the Queen Mother and her close friend, Diana's grandmother, Ruth Lady Fermoy, who manipulated Diana into the marriage with Prince Charles. This is why Diana was given quarters at the Queen Mother's home, Clarence House, in the weeks before the wedding and she left from there to marry Charles at St Paul's Cathedral. "Diana used to tell me that the Queen Mother was evil", Christine Fitzgerald said, "She actually used that word, evil. She said she hated the Queen Mother and the Queen Mother hated her." Most people in Britain will be astonished to read this because the Queen Mother's propaganda has turned her into the nation's favourite grandmother. "Oh yes, the Queen Mum, such a lovely, gentle, kind old lady." But this woman is not what she is claimed to be. I can't emphasise that enough. During her time at Clarence House before the wedding, Diana says herself that she was being given drugs like the anti-depressant, Valium, to treat her bulimia. And what else were they giving her? "They drugged her", Christine said "I'm sure of it, they had her doped from the start." Christine had many conversations with Diana and she opened her heart about her nightmare life with the Windsors. But Christine's contacts through her work have given her access to other sources with inside knowledge of the British Royal Family, too. This was the first time she had talked publicly about her experiences with Diana and what she knows of the reptilian agenda. She told me:

"The Queen Mother... now that's a serious piece of wizardry. The Queen Mother is a lot older than people think. To be honest, the Royal Family hasn't died for a long time, they have just metamorphosised. It's sort of cloning, but in a different way. They take pieces of flesh and rebuild the body from one little bit. Because it's lizard, because it's cold-blooded, it's much easier for them to do Frankenstein shit than it is for us. The different bodies are just different electrical vibrations and they have got that secret, they've got the secret of the micro-currents, it's so micro, so specific, these radio waves that actually create the bodies. These are the energies I work with when I'm healing. They know the vibration of life and because they are cold-blooded, they are reptiles, they have no wish to make the Earth the perfect harmony it could be, or to heal the Earth from the damage that's been done. The Earth's been attacked for zeons by different extraterrestrials. It's been like a football for so long. This place was a bus stop for many different aliens. All these aliens, they could cope with everything, including the noxious gases. They're landing all the time and coming up from the bowels of the Earth. They looked like reptiles originally, but they look like us when they get out now through the electrical vibration, that life key I talked about. They can manifest how they want to. All the real knowledge has been taken out and shredded and put back in another way. The Queen Mother is "Chief Toad" of this part of Europe and they have people like her in each continent. Most people, the hangers on, don't know, you know, about the reptiles. They are just in awe of these people because they are so powerful.

"Balmoral is a very, very nasty place. That's somewhere they want to dig underground. They will find reptile fossils, it goes back that far. Don't think of people like the Queen Mother and Queen Victoria, as different people. Think of them as the same person which after a while has had to replace their coat. When the flesh dies, that energy, while it's dying, will be immediately up someone else's jacksy (*backside*). It's very vampire, worse than vampire. They are not going to come to you with hooked teeth and suck you're blood. Fear is their food, they can actually take fear and manifest it into a tangible thing. The key is the vibrational current. At that vibrational current, they can manifest anything from anything. Its like a holographic image. We are all minerals and water vibrating. This is all an illusion we are living in. That's the secret. You know when the monarchy's fallen, it's not the end of it. They will manifest in another form. The reptiles have never been defeated and this is the closest they have come to it. The reason they are so threatened today is because the Earth is in such trouble and the mental power of people is returning. This is their most frightening time, but this is not going to kill them. There are long centuries before it's over yet. The difference this time is that it'll be more difficult for them and they are going to have to settle for less and the Earth people are going to get more. But even though these reptilian ones are fuckers, they are sad, pathetic beasts really, while humanity is galloping towards light. They're just pathetic lumps of nastiness who aren't going to win. I can't talk about this everywhere because they would just go 'Christine, get a white coat, put it on backwards, get out'. But I want an end to the bullshit."

I was astonished to hear someone else talking about these subjects, which I knew from my own research to be true. She was not aware when she told me this of my own research into reptilians. Christine Fitzgerald, thanks to her insider contacts and her knowledge of metaphysics, had been able to grasp the biggest secret: that reptiles on another dimension are controlling the world by working through physical bodies which look human. And also that the Windsors are one of these reptilian bloodlines. Christine also knew about the reptile Satanic rituals, the sexual rites and the widespread sacrifice of children. She said it is the pure essence of the pre-pubescent the reptiles want. "If you looked at where all the castles are built and where there are a lot of street children in the Third World, they're galloping it at the moment. They're pulling the kids in en masse now." She said the reptiles want the children's life essence because they can't continue to manifest without that pure energy. "The contaminated essence of us adults is not worth anything to them", she said. "All the rituals, the knives, and sodomy, its that easy for these people to snatch a piece of your soul." Christine also spoke about the sex rituals and orgies involving the Windsors. The very word orgy comes from the Greek, orgia, meaning 'secret worship' and relates to the sexual rites of the ancient mystery religions. Christine said:

"There used to be an elect circle who took part in ritual orgies at Buckingham Palace. This was told to me by one of the participants. They were all couples. The lights used to go out at a certain time and they all swapped round and did their things. You know about the butler ringing the bell at six o'clock in the morning so that everyone goes back to their bed? These people are nasty pieces of work, sweetheart, these people are nasty. Nothing you can think of can ever be as nasty as they really are. Diana used to say that if the world knew what they were really like, they wouldn't want them, but I knew that. My chin was on the couch now, hearing about all these orgies at the palace. Just the laugh that these serious people who are going on like butter wouldn't melt up their jacksy and they are carrying on like that. But the sex thing is a big part of their rituals because it's kundalini energy, see, which is the core, our generator. The orgies stopped because one of the couples died and they had an odd number and they didn't want to bring in anyone else. So even that was ritual. Everything about them is ritual... all that heraldry, all that pomp and ceremony. Negative energy gets drawn to negative energy."

Many of the Queen's Ladies in Waiting have told Christine Fitzgerald about Prince Philip and his affairs. "The royal family has got lots of black babies all over the world", she says. The recovered mind-slave Brice Taylor tells in her book, *Thanks For The Memories,* how she was forced to have sex with Philip and Charles. It is not without reason that the former British Intelligence officer, Peter Wright, said in his controversial book, *Spycatcher*, that "The palace had enjoyed several centuries of scandal burying." Christine said that another controversial book, *The Royals*, by the American author Kitty Kelly was true, but "She's left out a lot of stuff, she's been quite kind". She's not kidding as you will soon appreciate. Christine told me about other members of the royal clan including Prince Philip's uncle, Lord Mountbatten, another Satanist. She said: "Lord Mountbatten was a big shit, too. It was him who fucked up Charles and got him on the nasty road." So this is the family which hooked an unsuspecting 19-year-old and used her, in Diana's words, as a "brood mare" to produce Windsor heirs with Spencer genes. But it was more than that. Much more.

Only a few weeks before this book went to press, and months after Christine gave me her information in England, I was contacted by a friend in the United States who was deprogramming a very high level mind controlled slave from Project Monarch. He believes her to be the highest ranked woman in the Satanic hierarchy in the United States and she was one of only three Mother Goddesses in the world. This is Arizona Wilder, formerly Jennifer Greene. At the time my friend and Arizona had no idea what Christine Fitzgerald had said. Arizona had been programmed and trained since childhood to become a Mother Goddess who conducted Satanic rituals at the highest levels of the Brotherhood all over the world. She described to my friend the inside of many secret and underground facilities that he has personally seen. What she described was accurate every time. He also checked her story with other contacts and the truth of her memories was continually confirmed. What she told my friend, and later told me on audio and video tape, supports the information supplied by other slaves and by Christine Fitzgerald about the Windsors and their true nature. Arizona said that she officiated at Satanic rituals at Glamis Castle in Tayside, Scotland, the childhood home of the Queen Mother, who still owns the property, and also at Balmoral, the Queen's Scottish residence. The Brotherhood obsession with Scotland, she said, was because there are many entrances there into the inner-Earth where the physical reptilians live. Glamis Castle is built on the site of an 11th century royal hunting lodge and the present building dates from around 1687. It is mentioned in the 'Shakespeare' story of *Macbeth*. Arizona said that the Queen, Prince Philip, Prince Charles and Princess Anne are present at the rituals and so is Charles' girlfriend, Camilla Parker-Bowles. Doesn't it all now start to make sense?

She said that during the sacrificial rituals the Queen wears a cloak of gold fabric inlaid with rubies and black onyx. The Queen and Charles have their own ritual goblets, inlaid with precious stones signifying their Illuminati-Brotherhood rank. The Mother Goddess says that the Queen makes cruel remarks about lesser initiates, but is afraid of the man code-named 'Pindar' (the Marquis de Libeaux) who is higher than her in the Satanic hierarchy. This also supports a claim made to me by another recovered slave who said she had seen the Queen physically beaten by someone above her in Satanic rank. Pindar, apparently, bears a resemblance to Prince Charles and Arizona says that Pindar is Charles' real father. She said that the sacrificial victims used in the rituals at Glamis Castle are mostly under five years of age and the ceremonies are guarded by members of Scotland's Black Watch. She also confirmed that Lord Mountbatten was a paedophile and that the Windsors are reptilians in human form. Her interview with me was taped, as were the ones with Christine Fitzgerald, and copies are now at various addresses. The video interview with Arizona is available and details are at the back of the book. I stress that this Mother Goddess had no idea what Christine Fitzgerald had told me and yet their statements match again and again. Arizona says that Diana definitely knew that the Windsors were shape-shifting reptilians and Diana's comments to Christine Fitzgerald support this. Apparently, reptilians have been seen to shape-shift during sleep. Here is a summary of just some of what Arizona said about the royal family:

- **The Queen Mother:** She's cold, cold, cold, a nasty person. None of her cohorts even trusted her. They have named an altar (mind control programme) after her. They call it the Black Queen. I have seen her sacrifice people. I remember her pushing a knife into someone's rectum the night that two boys were sacrificed. One was 13 and the other 18. You need to forget that the Queen Mother appears to be a frail old woman. When she shape-shifts into a reptilian she becomes very tall and strong. Some of them are so strong they can rip out a heart and they all grow by several feet when they shape-shift." (*Exactly what the lady who saw Edward Heath said, among many others.*)

- **The Queen:** "I have seen her sacrifice people and eat their flesh and drink their blood. One time she got so excited with blood lust that she didn't cut the victim's throat from left to right in the normal ritual, she just went crazy, stabbing and ripping at the flesh after she'd shape-shifted into a reptilian. When she shape-shifts she has a long reptile face, almost like a beak, and she's an off-white colour. The Queen Mother looks basically the same, but there are differences. (*This description fits many depictions of the gods and 'bird gods' of ancient Egypt and elsewhere.*) She also has like bumps on her head and her eyes are very frightening. She's very aggressive."

- **Prince Charles:** "I've seen him shape-shift into a reptilian and do all the things the Queen does. I have seen him sacrifice children. There is a lot of rivalry between them for who gets to eat what part of the body and who gets to absorb the victim's last breath and steal their soul. I have also seen Andrew participate and I have seen Prince Philip and Charles' sister (*Anne*) at the rituals, but they didn't participate when I was there. When Andrew shape-shifts, he looks more like one of the lizards. The royals are some of the worst, OK, as far as enjoying the killing, enjoying the sacrifice, and eating the flesh, they're some of the worst of all of them. They don't care who sees them at the rituals, they are what they are, they show it outright. They don't care if you see it. Who are you going to tell, who is going to believe you? They feel that it is their birth-right and they love it. They love it."

Given the evidence I have presented in this chapter about the background to Diana's murder, I was not surprised to hear this Mother Goddess recall the following about Mohamed Al Fayed:

"I saw Mohammed Al Fayed at a ritual at the Mothers of Darkness castle in Belgium in the 1980s. The Queen and the Queen Mother were also there. The Queen Mother was talking to him and he was looking around as if he didn't believe this sort of thing went on. It was on December 24th at the ritual of the old king and the new king. They didn't let him in to see the worst of it. It was kind of like, 'let's introduce him into this'. But he would have seen a baby being born and introduced as the new king and the sacrifice of an old man. The Queen Mother was there, the Queen, Pindar, Rothschilds, a lot of people I don't know and a guy named Tony Blair. He was being groomed because my understanding of it was that people are picked out and groomed for certain positions. And to be considered for those positions you have to accept the reality and the necessity and the sovereignty of the Illuminati, and that the reptilians run the show. Tony Blair's attitude was like 'I belong here'. Dodi Fayed's father seemed bothered by it, but not Tony Blair. I remember seeing him talking to the royals about something. I have seen Blair, Al Fayed and the Royal Family at rituals at Balmoral as well."

Once you know this astonishing background, the why, who and how of Diana's murder become crystal clear. They were all in it together and still are. Diana's murder had been planned for a long time, probably from birth, and it was in the 1980s, around the time Al Fayed was at the Mother of Darkness castle with the royal family and Tony Blair, that the flaming torch symbol was placed on top of the Pont de L'Alma tunnel. Arizona said that Diana was a product of the multiple personality disorder programme, which she said would have started before she was five. She said Diana was also three months pregnant when she died. Diana would probably not have known this, she said, because the techniques the Brotherhood use often mean that the women continue to menstruate for some months before they are officially confirmed to be pregnant. Arizona said that when she, herself, was artificially impregnated in a mind controlled state with Pindar's sperm, she menstruated for three months before she was told by a doctor that she was more than three months pregnant. It could have been Pindar's child and not Dodi Fayed's, Arizona suggested. "That is a really powerful sacrifice" she said, "to sacrifice a pregnant woman". If Diana was, as appears highly likely, a product of the mind control programme, those who plotted her murder could have ensured all that they required to play out their ritual to perfection. She would have accepted the invitation from Al Fayed at the right time, fallen for Dodi Fayed, agreed to go to Paris for the night and so on. She could also have been, like Arizona, impregnated artificially and have no recollection of it. Arizona says that she knows that Diana was impregnated with Pindar's sperm in this way to conceive her son William, the blond-haired, blue-eyed baby born on the summer solstice. And she is in no doubt that Diana was a 'multiple'. As she said:

> "The things that she did with her eyes, like the eye rolling, is very, very common in multiples. Sometimes she'd be very shy and then suddenly she's blossoming and she's really social. These are the different altars (*programmes*) coming out, someone's shy, someone's not shy, someone's angry, someone's not angry. Then there was the weight gain and the weight loss. The bulimia and the cutting herself are all signs of a multiple. Some are told that if you feel bad about yourself or you remember something, cut yourself. To me it was real obvious with Diana. Someone with this stuff just doesn't announce to the world that something's wrong, They spend their lives trying to hide it. 'I was out grocery shopping', or 'I was out clothes shopping', 'I was taking a walk', whatever, but you weren't."

The recovered mind-slave Brice Taylor confirms that Diana was a 'multiple' in her book, *Thanks For The Memories*, and she says that William and Harry are also. I think Dodi was another, thus making it child's play to make he and Diana 'fall in love'. The symbolism of Osiris, Isis and Horus, in the Pont de L'Alma tunnel that night was also confirmed by Arizona. "Diana was Isis, Dodi Fayed was Osiris, and the child was Horus. I don't think it symbolised the birth of a child so much as the birth of an age – the Age of Horus which begins by the year 2,000. This means the New World Order, the Age of Horus, the terrible child." She said that the foetus would have been divided among certain high ranking leaders of the Brotherhood/Illuminati and consumed in ritual. She said that from her long experience of the rituals, she was sure that parts of Diana's body would have been consumed also. Again I ask, is her body even on the island at Althorp Park? It makes you wonder what Tony Blair and the Royals were doing when they came together at Balmoral immediately after Diana's death. Another part of the ritual was that Diana was blond-haired and blue-eyed. Cathy O'Brien is the same, so is Arizona although she had dyed her hair to break that spell when I met her. She said that even when the Elite sacrifice cats they are blond-haired and blue-eyed. There is something about that genetic structure which is fundamental to them and this is the blood they need to survive in this dimension. At least most of the Monarch slaves have blond hair and blue eyes. "There were no blue eyes on this planet until the extraterrestrials came", Arizona said.

Diana told Christine Fitzgerald in 1989 that they were going to kill her: "It sounded outlandish at the time", Christine said, "because she had the boys and they were little and I thought, no, they need her to bring the boys up." But there were to be many indications that Diana was indeed in danger from the Windsors and the Brotherhood in general. In the late 1980s with her marriage nothing more than a public show, Diana was having a relationship with her personal detective, Barry Mannakee, but he died in a motorcycle 'accident' in 1988. By 1990, with the Gulf War threatening, Diana was having a relationship with Captain James Hewitt. One day, about this time, she went rushing into Christine's healing centre in London in a terrible state. Christine remembers:

> "She was crying hysterically and I said 'What's the matter?' You know it was dog's died stuff, bottom lip out, full sob. She came galloping through the door. I gave her rescue remedy, clutched her, hugged her, calmed her down, and said now tell me what's going on. 'I can't believe it, I can't believe it, they killed him, they killed him' she sobbed. I said: 'Who did they kill?' She told me about her affair with the detective (*Barry Mannakee*) and how he was decapitated on a motorbike and how she thought it was a terrible accident. But now she knows the Royal Family killed him because Prince Charles' senior detective had just told her that if she didn't cool it with Hewitt, the same would happen to him. He told her she should not think that she was indispensable, either."

Officially, Barry Mannakee died in a 'road crash'. How dangerous the roads seem to be if the royals don't like you. Christine said that Diana was very much in love with Mannakee and she had visited his grave regularly. Diana had, apparently, been unaware of his death at the time until she was being driven with Prince Charles to the airport to fly to the Cannes Film Festival. He waited until she was about to get out of the car in front of waiting photographers and he said: "Oh, by the way, I got word from the Protection Unit yesterday that poor Barry Mannakee was killed. Some sort of motorcycle accident. Terrible shame, isn't it?" Diana burst into tears, but Charles said sarcastically: "Let's go darling, your press awaits you."[61] I would emphasise again that the confirmation that Mannakee was murdered, and the personal threat to Diana, came from Prince Charles' senior detective, according to the Princess. Would he be making statements and threats to her like that without the approval of Prince Charles? Of course not. In 1998 in the Independent Television documentary, *Diana – Secrets Of The Crash*, James Hewitt said that he too had been warned to stop seeing Diana or the consequences would not be pleasant. He said:

> "The telephone calls were anonymous, but left me in no doubt that they knew what the situation was. They were threatening. They said it was not conducive to my health to continue the relationship."

He said that other warnings came from Diana's personal police protection officers, the Royal Household, and a member of the Royal Family, whom he would not name:

> "The (*member of the Royal Family*) said your relationship is known about. It is not supported, we cannot be responsible for your safety and security, and suggest that you curtail it forthwith."

James Hewitt was further quoted in the London *Times* about these threats and his comments supported completely the story Diana had told Christine Fitzgerald. Hewitt said that his clearest warning came when he was told that he would suffer the same fate as Barry Mannakee.[62] Does anyone still believe that the Windsors and their networks were not involved in the murder of Princess Diana? Or that they had prior knowledge and played an active role in the decision to assassinate the mother of William and Harry? According to reports in the United States, Susan Barrantes, the mother of Sarah 'Fergie' Ferguson, had been telling friends that she thought Diana had been murdered in the weeks before she was decapitated in a mysterious car crash in Argentina on September 19th 1998.[63] Confidential mail for Diana was delivered to Christine Fitzgerald and this included packages from a former member of the élite SAS who was concerned for Diana's safety. He was warning her of what was going on behind her back." Half of MI6 were on Diana's side too you know", Christine said. One day a client, who had involvement with the security agencies, saw some of these packages being delivered. Christine described what followed:

> "She said I'm really worried for you, you don't know what you're getting involved in here. Diana's basically mad, she'll drop you in it, she will hang you out to dry, you'll end up dead, your kids will end up dead, your cats, your business will be ruined. I couldn't believe how she was carrying on. She was so full of hate. Diana came in the next day and I gave her the mail. I said not everyone who bows to you has your best interests at heart. I told her what happened and she went purple with rage. When she died, everybody came in and said 'They bumped her off didn't they?' But that client was the only one who was outraged at the suggestion. I was checked out by MI6, my phones were tapped, my house was burgled, the royal family kept a big check on me while I was dealing with Diana."

Christine and her contacts have no doubt about what happened in Paris: "She was bumped off, she was left to die at the roadside. Those responsible were above the élite of the army", she said. "It was not the 'secret squirrels' (British Intelligence)", she understands, "it was above that". She said that "Mohamed Al Fayed 'in his tortured little sense' wants to be part of the reptilian power because 'he likes all that'." Christine believes that Diana's romance with Dodi was engineered. She said:

> "Diana fell in love quite easily and he's a master of the smile. She was unfortunate in her love affairs because she rescued others in her own distress. So the men she went for were all emotional cripples because she was a healer, too. Most people who went with Diana used her and I think Dodi did also. He would have used her for his ego, the contacts, and his dad. The Royal Family killed her for her light energy, especially when she was pregnant. I don't believe she was as badly injured as they say. If they checked her body they would see that the scar the surgeons made starts at her pubis and goes right up to her throat. They've even taken her thymus gland, the way we make interstellar communication. I know from the best sources that she was pregnant and they took the baby. Pieces of that foetus will have been delivered everywhere. They can make babies from the cells. Parts of her body will have been used in their rituals as well. Diana was always having Kensington Palace swept for bugs, but they had Dodi bugged and they knew exactly what was going on. This was not the first time she thought she was pregnant and this nearly happened before, but she wasn't pregnant. That was with Hewitt."

Christine Fitzgerald shared the most intimate details of Diana's life and knew her in ways, and at levels, that very few others did. The incredible revelations of the Windsors' treatment of Diana over so many years, the threats made to her by Prince Charles' personal detective, the ritual sacrifices and the confirmation that they were responsible for the murder of Barry Mannakee, cannot be allowed to pass by. There must be a campaign to press the Windsors to face these matters and for Al Fayed, Trevor Rees-Jones, Earl Spencer, and the others I have named, to answer the questions that have to be addressed. Power must be stripped from the Windsors, their royal dynasty dismantled, and their crimes against humanity publicly exposed. More than that, however, those in the political, security, and medical professions, who are also involved, must be equally exposed. The Royal Family, Earl Spencer, and the British Prime Minister, Tony Blair, have all dismissed claims that Diana was murdered and called for such suggestions to cease 'for the sake of the boys'. The questions must not be allowed to be ignored or another Brotherhood assassination will have been achieved while those responsible go free. Earl Spencer went to the extent of issuing a statement on behalf of the Spencer family in February 1998 in which he asked: "Is there any good in all this speculation? I ask that because there is clearly a lot of harm in it. All we, her family, ask is that Diana's memory be respected, and that sensational speculation be left out of the public arena, where it undermines our aims to come to terms with her loss". When you see the evidence presented in this chapter while people like Earl Spencer and Tony Blair say there is no evidence of a conspiracy, what does that make you think? If Diana had been your sister would you not be determined to find out what happened? If you were Prime Minister when such a famous and much loved Princess had been killed, would you not insist that the truth be established? So why don't they? Diana's relationship with her brother was less than harmonious to say the least. When you know the background, Earl Spencer's famous speech at her funeral can be seen as a diatribe of hypocrisy. So was his bitter condemnation of the media, in a statement after her death outside his home in Cape Town, a statement which, like Al Fayed's, fueled the belief that the paparazzi were to blame for the crash. Christine Fitzgerald said of him:

> "Charles Spencer is a shit, major shit. He's quite a spiteful little shit, too. When Diana was going through the trauma and really needed a new home, he said to her: 'You're not bringing your shit down to me and mine.' He wouldn't even give her one of the houses. He's not a powerful man at all. He knows he's sniffing around something dangerous and powerful and so he's attracted to it. Satanism goes on on the Spencer estate. Diana knew about it."

Diana had a profound affect on millions of people as we saw after her death and they did not know the half of what she had to suffer after the Windsors sank their fangs. In many ways Diana was a mirror of Marilyn Monroe, used by the establishment and then cast aside and murdered. Marilyn had affairs with President Kennedy and, it seems, his brother, Bobby, and when she became dangerous and surplus to requirements she was killed because of what she knew. In another of those remarkable examples of synchronicity there are many 'coincidences' that connect her life and Diana's. They were both born on the first of the month and died at the age of 36 in August. They both married on the 29th of the month to men twelve years older. Marilyn called herself the Queen of Diamonds and Diana the Queen of Hearts. And both were the subject of the Elton John song, *Candle In The Wind*, which he sang at Diana's funeral. Since Christine Fitzgerald first spoke to me the threat to destroy her business has been implemented. Suddenly the phone stopped ringing and when I met her again she was seeing as many clients in a week as she had been in a day. This is unexplainable when you consider she is one of Britain's most gifted and effective healers working in the centre of London. Unexplainable, that is, unless you know the story. But she told me she is determined the truth shall be known, whatever the authorities seek to do to her: "I don't want a war, I just want an end to the bullshit", as she puts it. Looking back on Diana's life and their conversations together, she says:

> "Poor cow, she was in a house where no-one gave a damn and it's a terrible state of affairs. She was all alone in a nest of vipers. I used to just patch her up. She just found me and just came to me. I made her wait for a fortnight until I checked it out. They used to say that I was giving her anger therapy. I didn't. I used to just listen to her, take it all in, and think Jesus Christ! But I didn't think they would kill her. I can't believe that this

information is so close to home and yet they are still managing to keep it at bay. My room is the truth room and its a real place of safety and I don't judge anyone on their shit, and that's why I haven't spoken about any of this in the past. She was as screwed up as anyone, you know, and if you are going to tell the truth, you have to tell the whole truth. She wasn't crazy, she was mentally and physically abused, I feel, from a little girl. Her father was a nasty piece of work and her stepmother (*Raine*), too.

"The Royal Family were very afraid. She would have taken the public away from them, she would have taken the world from them gradually. They recognised her worth and fed off her in a psychic vampire way for a long time. All she wanted was to get married and have children you know, bless her little heart. She wanted to live out what she had never had. The world would have come to rights with Diana because, as fucked up as she was, she was a light being and wherever she went she manifested love. It was amazing. The sad thing was that she didn't know she was doing that and she needed proof of her worth and she was looking in the wrong quarters for that. But when she tried to break away, we went out and did normal things. She did kung fu with my husband for five years. She wanted to be normal, to link arms and walk down the street. She knew where her heart lay. She really and truly did amazing things."

Diana said she could not believe how cold the Windsors were and the public had a graphic example of this in the days after her death. They stayed out of sight at Balmoral in Scotland while the people mourned Diana in their tens of millions with an unprecedented explosion of grief. Only pressure from the public through the media forced the Queen, kicking and screaming, to make a cold, emotionless and pathetic 'tribute' to Diana on television the night before the funeral. Cold is a word constantly used about the Queen, Philip, and Charles, and that's the mental and emotional profile of the Brotherhood and its networks. Bill Cooper said that the initiates that he met in his work for US Naval Intelligence had "No conscience, no morals, no regrets, no feelings, no emotion". This is precisely the same character profile as the Windsors and, according to all the people I have met who have encountered them, the character profile of the reptilians of the lower fourth dimension. There is a reason for that, of course.

The people have been hoodwinked for thousands of years. Hoodwinked about their history, hoodwinked about who they really are and the true nature of life. Hoodwinked about the true background and Agenda of those they have allowed to rule them. How apt, therefore, that this word should also derive from Freemasonry. Dr. Albert MacKey, the 33rd degree Freemason and foremost Freemason historian of the 19th century, defined the term 'hoodwinked' in his Encyclopaedia of Freemasonry as: A symbol of secrecy, silence and darkness, in which the mysteries of our art should be preserved from the unhallowed gaze of the profane.

The human race has indeed been hoodwinked.

■ SOURCES

1   *The Top 13 Illuminati Bloodlines*, p 89.

2   Ibid, p 90.

3   Ibid.

4   Ibid.

5   Ibid.

6   Ibid, p 91–2.

7   Ibid, p 89.

8   Ibid.

9   *Secret And Suppressed*, p 66.

10   Ibid.

11   Ibid, p 68.

12   *The Top 13 Illuminati Bloodlines*, p 94.

13   *Secret And Suppressed*, p 80.

14   *The Top 13 Illuminati Bloodlines*, p 99.

15   Ibid, p 102.

16   *Secret And Suppressed*, pp 19, 65, 85.

17   Ibid, p 66.

18   Ibid.

19   Ibid, p 65

20   Ibid, p 69.

21   Andrew Morton, *Diana, Her True Story* (Michael O'Mara Books, London, 1992, republished as *Diana: Her True Story In Her Own Words*, 1997).

22   Ibid.

23   Ibid.

24   The London *Daily Mail*, Thursday, August 27th 1998.

25   Ibid.

26   *Diana: Her True Story*.

27   Ibid.

28   Ibid.

29   *Private Eye* magazine, No 956, Friday, August 7th 1998, p 5.

30   Tom Bower, *Fayed, The Unauthorised Biography* (Macmillan, London, 1998).

31   Ibid, p 22.

32   The London *Daily Mail*, Friday, June 26th 1998.

33   Simon Reagan, *Who Killed Diana?* (a *Scallywag* publication, Amsterdam, 1998), p 57.

34   Ibid, p 62.

35 *The News Of The World*, Sunday, January 18th 1998, pp 18, 19.

36 Peter Hounam and Derek McAdam, *Who Killed Diana?*, p 17.

37 *Dispatches*, Channel Four, June 1998.

38 Ibid.

39 Ibid.

40 *Fayed, The Unauthorised Biography*, p 425.

41 Ibid, p 420.

42 Ibid, p 421.

43 Peter Hounam and Derek McAdam, *Who Killed Diana?*, p 64.

44 Ibid, pp 73, 74.

45 Jim Marrs, *Crossfire: The Plot That Killed Kennedy* (Carrol and Graf Publishers, New York, 1989), p 382.

46 *Dispatches*.

47 *Diana – Secrets Of The Crash*, ITV, 1998.

48 "Diana, the Unsolved Mystery", *News Of The World* News Special, January 18th 1998.

49 The information about David Sands death comes from the Tony Collins book, *Open Verdict*, an account of 25 mysterious deaths in the defence industry (Sphere Books, London, 1990).

50 Sir Peter Horsley, *Sounds From Another Room* (Leo Cooper, England, 1997). The story is also told by Peter Hounam and Derek McAdam in *Who Killed Diana?*, pp 126–133.

51 Peter Hounam and Derek McAdam, *Who Killed Diana?* (Vision Paperbacks, London, 1999), pp 175–177.

52 *The News Of The World*, News Special, January 18th 1998.

53 *Daily Mirror*, Monday, March 2nd 1998, p 2.

54 London *Daily Mail*, August 29th 1998, pp 1, 2.

55 *Dispatches*.

56 Peter Hounam and Derek McAdam, *Who Killed Diana?*, p 145.

57 Quoted in *Blasphemous Rumours*, p 212.

58 *The Phoenician Origin Of Britons*, p 64.

59 "Fayed's rooftop flame of love for Dodi and Diana", London *Daily Express*, Friday, July 24th 1998, p 3.

60 *The Women's Encyclopaedia Of Myths And Secrets*, p 543.

61 Kitty Kelly, *The Royals* (Warner Books, New York, 1997), p 347

62 *The Times*, Wednesday, June 3rd 1998.

63 "Fergie's Mom Was Murdered", *The Globe*, October 6th 1988.

CHAPTER TWENTY

Casting the spell

The Brotherhood's obsession with ritual and symbolism is not the bizarre behaviour it might at first seem to be. They are casting a spell on the human mind and emotions. This has been going on for thousands of years and it is so important to understand this if we are going to break free from reptilian control – as we are.

Everything that exists is an energy field, a unique vibrational pattern of energy created by thought and emotion. All that exists is the same energy, but these infinite patterns create infinite forms, just as water can manifest as liquid, clouds, steam and ice. They look and feel very different, but they are still water in different forms. Some energy patterns manifest as the human body, others the human mind, still others the birds, trees, insects, water, sky and air. At the level of pure energy everything is connected to everything else. There is no us and them, only we and ultimately 'I'. Potentially we have the ability to access all other energy and, as energy and consciousness are the same, the ability to access all consciousness, the infinite mind we call 'God'. This 'God' is not apart from us, it *is* us and we are it. We are an aspect of the infinite mind – as are the reptilians and all that exists – and therefore we have the potential to tap into all of the infinite mind because, at our highest expression, that is what we all are. Everything. We are like droplets in an infinite ocean, individual to an extent, but together we make the whole, the sum total of droplets. Without the droplets there can be no ocean. The question, however, is this: How much of this ocean are we connecting with? If it is a tiny fraction you will live in a cocoon, an egg shell as I call it, delinked from your infinite potential for knowledge, love, understanding and wisdom (*see Figure 54*). You will live a predictable life dominated by worry and fear and believe that you are ordinary and powerless to control your own destiny. If you open your mind and open your heart and break out of that cocoon you connect with more and more of infinity and, in doing so, you understand that you are more than a physical body experiencing one meaningless lifetime. You are infinite consciousness experiencing this world as part of your eternal journey of evolution through experience (*see Figure 55*). You are everything and you have the potential to know everything and do everything.

Now which one of those two states of being is more easy to control? Of course the answer is obvious and this explains so much about the world we have seen throughout known human history. This is why the knowledge of who we really are has been systematically destroyed in the public arena. Humans who understand

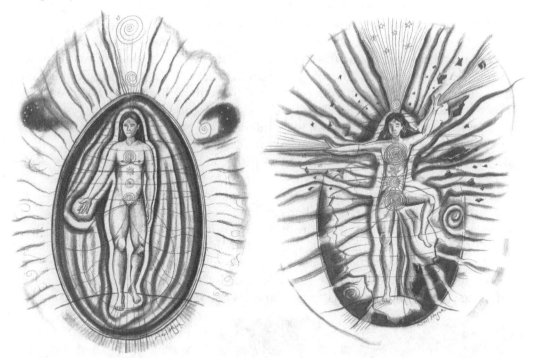

Figure 54: *Imprisonment.*   **Figure 55:** *Freedom.*

their true nature, power and worth would be impossible to manipulate in the ways we have seen. Only by delinking humanity from this knowledge has it been possible to orchestrate the reptilian-Brotherhood Agenda over thousands of years. The creation of religion and official 'science' has been fundamental to that and, as we have seen, the same secret society streams were responsible for establishing both. The individualisation of the concept of 'God' into a man, a physical form, has suppressed the understanding that everything is God. So much so that to say you are God is to invite enormous ridicule or condemnation, as I know myself when I spoke very publicly of such things in Britain in the early 1990s. It has become a blasphemy to say what you are, what we *all* are. For those who will not buy a religion, we have this-world-is-all-there is science which denies the very existence of the infinity and eternal nature of life. The Brotherhood plan has been to so programme and manipulate humanity's perception of itself and Creation that we disconnect from our multidimensional infinity and operate on a tiny fraction of our potential. But the reptilians are also an expression of the Infinite and they are offering us an experience that we can use to evolve, just as those challenging the reptilian control are offering them an experience. Humans are learning what happens when they give their power away and this reptilian group are about to learn the consequences of abusing power. It is a game in the end, a game called evolution, learning to master our mind and emotions. What I have been describing in this book is an evolutionary experience for all parties concerned. We all make decisions and choices and face the consequences of them. Those consequences are what we are experiencing now. If we make new choices, we will create different consequences. We are in control of our destiny, and people are waking up to that.

The reptilians manipulate from the lower fourth dimension, the so-called lower astral frequency range. To control this planet they have to keep the mass of humanity at or below that level and disconnect them from anything higher (*see Figure 56*). When this is understood, what has happened in the world and is still happening, again makes perfect sense. Crucial to maintaining the human psyche in disconnected ignorance is the manipulation of low vibrational emotion, fear, guilt, resentment, dislike of self and condemnation of others which, in the end, are all expressions of fear. These are the very emotions which resonate to the frequency range of the lower fourth dimension and once we succumb to domination by these emotions we succumb to the control of the reptilian consciousness. Notice that I said domination. Feeling these emotions as part of the life experience is fine. This is important in our evolution to greater understanding and wisdom. It is when these emotions control you that the whole focus of your psyche becomes plugged into the lower fourth dimension to such an extent that the reptilian consciousness can connect and infiltrate your thought patterns. So the Brotherhood use horrific Satanic rituals and sacrifice to synchronise their initiates with the reptilian wavelengths. They also seek to stimulate the character traits of our R-complex, the reptilian part of our brain, which manifest as aggression, ritualism, a desire for hierarchical structure, and so on.

What I am suggesting here about the nature of life is not some theory. It can be proved. Scientists and researchers in the United States have shown that the emotion of fear resonates a low vibrational pattern, a long wavelength, while the emotion we call love resonates a high vibrational pattern, a short wavelength. This is extremely significant for this reason, as the author, researcher and archaeologist Gregg Braden shows in his video, *Awakening To Zero Point*,[1] the genetic material of the human body is

Figure 56: *The reptilians have imprisoned so much of human consciousness within the lower fourth dimensional prison of fear, guilt, and frustration. Only by opening our hearts and minds can we escape and reconnect with our infinite self. Love is the answer.*

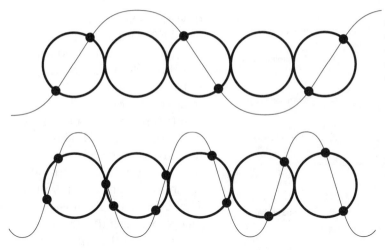

Figure 57: *Fear is a long, slow wavelength and activates very few of our DNA 'antennas' which connect us with the Cosmos.*

Figure 58: *Love is a short, fast wavelength which activates many more antennas and reconnects us with all that is.*

a highly sophisticated transmitter and receiver of frequencies. Experiments have shown that when you place a piece of DNA, the body's genetic blueprint, in a tube of electrons, the electrons form themselves together in the pattern of the DNA. When you remove the DNA, the electrons still hold the same pattern. In other words, the DNA is constantly affecting the energy around us. Our state of being affects the world second by second. When you change your attitudes and state of being you change the whole because you are part of the whole, indeed you *are* the whole. Still feeling ordinary and powerless? We have within us a series of micro-antenna called amino acids which interact with the DNA and, according to Braden, there are 64 potential human genetic codes or antenna to transmit and receive frequencies. In short, a potential 64 antenna to connect us with higher frequencies and higher dimensions of ourselves. But, he says, only 20 are activated while 44 remain 'switched off'. This means that our ability to connect with our full power, wisdom and potential is massively undermined. No doubt the fact that we use only a fraction of our brain's potential is a consequence of this also. Research by the Institute of HeartMath and others in the United States has further shown that these 'antenna' on the DNA are activated or closed down by the wavelengths of emotion which constantly pass through the DNA. The emotion of fear (from which all negative emotion derives) is a long, slow wavelength and so can only trigger a few of our potential antennas (*see Figure 57*). But love (from which all positive emotion derives) is a fast, short wavelength and so sparks into action far more of these antennas (*see Figure 58*). Thus when we are under the spell of fear we delink ourselves from our true connection to infinity and live our lives within a small droplet of consciousness, the egg shell. When we express the emotion of love we reconnect with our multidimensional self and our potential becomes infinite because we become infinite. We reconnect with the ocean, with 'God'.

There is another way of putting this. Our consciousness is a series of interconnecting energy fields. We have our intellect, emotions, spirit and so on, all resonating to different frequencies, but interpenetrating each other through a series

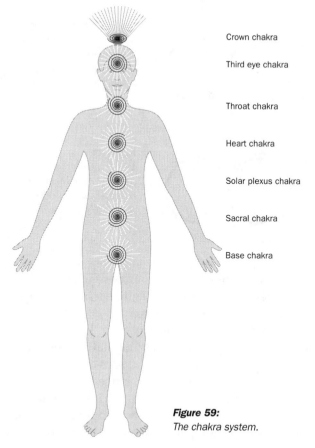

Crown chakra

Third eye chakra

Throat chakra

Heart chakra

Solar plexus chakra

Sacral chakra

Base chakra

Figure 59:
The chakra system.

of vortices known as chakras, a Sanskrit word meaning 'wheels of light'. As I mentioned earlier, it is through these chakra vortices that emotional imbalances are passed to the mental level and, if it continues, to the physical level. This is how stress causes illness and why we stop thinking straight when we are emotionally upset. The seven main chakras are placed between the bottom of the spine and the top of the head as in *Figure 59*. The lower three connect us to the Earth and the top three connect us to the spirit, the 'ocean'. In an ideal state, a human being is the connection between the physical and the spiritual: Heaven and Earth. The balance point in the chakra system is the heart chakra from which we express the emotion of love or hatred, the highest and lowest expressions of this chakra's frequency range. This is the origin behind the symbolism of the heart and love. Today love is associated with the physical heart, but it is really the spiritual heart, the heart chakra, that was the inspiration for this symbolism. When you are expressing love in its true and purest sense, unconditional, non-judgemental love, as we call it, that heart chakra opens like a flower and spins very quickly with enormous power. Flower power! This resonates your whole lower consciousness to the frequency of pure love and, in doing so, reconnects you with your higher dimensions which resonate to that love frequency. I don't care who you are or what you have done, your soul is pure love. I don't care if you are a reptilian on another dimension, the Queen of England, George Bush, Henry Kissinger, whoever, your soul is pure love. What has happened, however, is that their lower consciousness has become delinked from that highest level of themselves and once that happens the lower consciousness can do some unbelievably horrendous things. But how can they reconnect with their true self – pure love – while they are resonating such hatred? They can't. As with all of us, the only way to reconnect with pure love is to express and live pure love. To do that, of course, they must give up their desire to control and dominate because while they continue with that Agenda they will stay isolated from their infinite selves.

Instead, they have sought to manipulate humanity into an even lower range of consciousness. The reptilians and other lower fourth dimensional entities are in a consciousness prison themselves and they want humanity to live in a smaller one. Interestingly, the Dutch surrealist painter, M. C. Escher, depicts reptiles trapped in a prison of time and space as you can see in *Figure 60*. That is the situation, I feel, and until they change they will remain in jail, unable to evolve into infinity. Their aim is to keep us in there with them. The reptilian method for achieving this over these thousands of years has been, not surprisingly in the wake of this evidence, through the emotion of fear. The constant wars, conflicts, terrorist outrages, financial worries and the countless other negative events engineered by the Brotherhood have been designed overwhelmingly to maintain humanity in a state of fear, therefore limited and disconnected from its true self. The encouragement of hatred, resentment, revenge, and condemnation (all manifestations of fear) have not only added to this, they have ensured the conditions for further conflict and fear. Still more fear, in unimaginable amounts, has been stimulated by religion. The fear of God (fear of self) and the fear of death and 'his' judgement. It is the same with 'science' and the fear of dying and going to oblivion. Humanity is consumed and overwhelmed by fear and

its multifaceted expressions and that's why we are delinked from who we are. The Babylonian Brotherhood has made sure we have remained ignorant of this by controlling what is taught in schools and universities, the institutions of 'science' and, therefore, what the media considers possible and credible in its arrogant and pathetic dismissal of anything which challenges the 'norm'. Humanity spends its life watching a movie screen believing it to be reality while the world as it really is remains hidden from view. Journalists are not reporting what is going on in the world, they are reporting the story line in the movie. I call CNN the movie channel. There is an added bonus for the manipulators of fear. Whenever anyone is in fear

Figure 60: *The reptilians symbolically trapped in time and space. They are imprisoned on the lower Fourth Dimension by their own attitudes and until they open their hearts they cannot escape. The reptilians need love more than anyone.*

they give their power away to anyone they believe will protect them. The technique I call problem-reaction-solution is the manipulation of fear. It is fear, and its offshoots like resentment, which stimulates the calls for "Something must be done" after wars and other outrages which then leads to the Brotherhood frontmen offering their solutions.

What we are talking about here is mass mind and emotional control. If you take the definition of mind control to be manipulating a person's mind so they think and act in ways that you want, how many people on Planet Earth today are not mind controlled? The deaths of President Kennedy and Princess Diana were part of this. Whatever people say about the true character of JFK, the perception was that he represented a new hope for the future. Whether he did or not doesn't matter. People thought he did and so that is what he represented to them. As many Americans have told me over the years, something died in the American psyche when he was murdered. Call it hope, innocence, whatever you like. Something deep in the spirit of America died with him. The underlying feeling was that the good die young and evil always seems to win. It was the same with Diana, the lady associated, quite rightly in this case, with the genuine expression of love. When she died that wave of emotion which followed was not so much for her, the human being, it was for her, the symbol of love. The mass outpouring of grief was, if you look below the surface, the grief that something else had died with her. Love had died. Goodness had died. The good die young and evil always wins. These are just two global examples of the mass psyche being manipulated into a sense of powerlessness and despair by the mind doctors of the Brotherhood at places like the Tavistock network in London. People in a state of fear, powerlessness and despair eventually switch off and become the sheep they are encouraged to be, drifting through their lives in numb subservience.

But the manipulation of the human mind and emotions, and the disconnection from the infinite ocean, goes much, much, deeper than this. Remember that while the reptilians of the lower fourth dimension are spiritually and emotionally unplugged, they are very mentally sharp and come from a high level of intellectual knowledge. This knowledge has been hoarded in the Brotherhood secret society network since the ancient world while being sucked out of the public domain by the destruction of native cultures, the horrors of the Inquisition, and the burning of great esoteric libraries like the one in Alexandria. Balance = harmony. Imbalance = disharmony. If you want disharmony you need imbalance. It is a simple fact and this has played a fundamental part in the Brotherhood's techniques. The balanced female energy is the energy of intuition and reconnection. This is where the idea of a 'woman's intuition' comes from. A female body is far more likely to manifest female energy in abundance and so most of the oracles, channellers and psychics in the ancient and modern world have tended to be women. But they don't have to be. Men are just as capable of accessing their female polarity and using this creative force to connect with higher, intuitive levels of themselves. But such a reconnection is not what the Brotherhood has wanted to see. They want humanity to stay in the consciousness prison. So they have done all they can to suppress the use of the balanced female energy. They used religion to make women servile to men with no opportunity to express themselves in their full glory. At the same time they suppressed the female polarity in the male by creating the blueprint for what a man should be. Macho and aggressive is what we call a 'real' man (a lost and frightened little boy, in truth). These 'real' men were and are so delinked from their female energy that their intuition and connection with their higher selves is all but extinguished. Meanwhile the Brotherhood initiates have been using the negative frequencies of the female energy (Hecate) to connect with their reptilian masters on the lower fourth dimension and to manipulate the world secretly from behind the movie screen. The suppression and perversion of sexual energy, the creative force, is another fundamental means of limiting human potential to manifest their infinite power for creativity and self-determination.

Interconnected with the manipulation of the female energy is the manipulation of time. This is another aspect of the symbolism in the Pont de L'Alma Tunnel. The Brotherhood has tuned the human consciousness into a false perspective of time and in doing so they have disconnected humanity from the rest of creation which operates on a different version of time. Thus humanity is living its life out of sync with the universe. No wonder there's so much imbalance. In truth there is no time. Everything just is and past, present and future are happening at once. It is only our perception of time that make events appear to be happening in a linear time line. But even in linear time, we have been unplugged from the natural flow. Nature is tuned to Moon time, the 28-day 13 cycles of the Moon. The woman's menstrual cycle is tuned to the Moon and, appropriately, it is the Moon which takes the male solar energy and reflects it back at the Earth in a female form. The Satanists have their rituals and sacrifices every month under the full Moon when that female energy is at the peak of its power. They take this energy and manifest its negative polarity: Hecate. The more negative female (intuitive) energy they can focus, the more powerful their connection with the 'demons' they seek to access and communicate with on other dimensions. This is why they programme sensitive psychics like Arizona Wilder to conduct their rituals. The native peoples of the world who still live by Moon time are far more in tune with nature because they are operating on the same time-energy flow as nature. They are in sync with it. But in 1572 Pope Gregory announced that a new calendar was to be introduced, the Gregorian Calendar, and it was implemented in October 1582. It was another Brotherhood scam and the Gregorian Calendar became the fixed standard time for the planet. This means that the human mind is tuned to this manufactured flow of 'time' when we look at a clock, a watch, or plan the future with a diary. And where is the centre of this time system, the zero point from which all the world's people tune their timepieces? Why, it's only Greenwich in London, across the River Thames from the City of London financial district, the Brotherhood's operational heartland! And what was the inspiration for the Gregorian Calendar? The one used in... Babylon. The ancient Greek name for the Watchers or sons of the gods who interbred with the daughters of men was Grigori.[2] It is the calendar of the Grigori, the reptilians.

It was the reptile-Brotherhood priests of Babylon who played the same game with time all those thousands of years ago. The Gregorian Calendar is a farce. It is the time equivalent of throwing all your clothes in a wardrobe and leaning against the door to stop it flinging open. The clothes may just about fit in the space if you push them in hard enough, but what a mess. Here we have a 12 month year of 60 minute hours and 24 hour days with the months so ill-fitting that some are 30 days, others 31, another 28, or 29 every four years. Yes, fits like a glove. But a sensible measurement of time was not the motivation. Disconnecting human consciousness from Moon time was the idea and the Gregorian Calendar removed the 13th Moon. There should be 13 Moon-cycle months of 28 days, but instead we have 12 months and 12 Moon cycles. The Brotherhood hierarchy still operate their calendars to Moon time – another reason for their obsession with 13. Crashing the car of Diana (the Moon Goddess) into the 13th pillar was also symbolic of this removal of the 13th Moon from the human perception of time. And when you disconnect people from the natural flow of time, you are disconnecting them from all that operates in that flow of time. Thus the Western (and increasingly global) 'civilisation' has lost its rapport with the natural world and is out of sync with its environment.

The Millennium is a manufactured point in time. The moment at which the Millennium is crossed to the year 2000 only exists because of the Gregorian Calendar, but as the human psyche is tuned to that, the Brotherhood is again planning to manipulate time across the Millennium. As the Millennium approached, the tallest building in Europe was built across the River Thames from the Greenwich Observatory in London, the zero point of so-called Greenwich Mean Time. This building, named Canary Wharf, was built by a consortium of Brotherhood business interests and it is an enormous glass obelisk. Later the British Government decided to spend the best part of a billion, yes a billion, pounds to build a vast dome, the Millennium Dome, which will be the focus of official celebration at the time of the Millennium. This dome is beside the River Thames and on the opposite side, close to the global zero time line, is the Canary Wharf obelisk (*see picture section*). The obelisk and the dome are both premier Brotherhood geometric symbols which draw in solar and cosmic energy. The man in charge of the Millennium Dome project was Peter Mandelson, the man dubbed 'the Prince of Darkness' who was forced to resign after revelations about his personal finances. It was Mandelson who was the Labour Party's chief spin doctor when they introduced the red rose as the party symbol.

I am sure that in some way the Brotherhood plan to 'flick' time at this zero point at Greenwich to further scramble human consciousness and stimulate still more imbalance and conflict. The symbol for the Millennium Dome is a naked, long-legged woman reaching for the Sun as dawn breaks over the Greenwich Meridian. It has been dubbed 'New Britannia' and is said to represent 'female icons from prehistory to the present day'. Icons or one icon, Queen Semiramis, under different names? The artist was paid £90,000 from the National Lottery fund for his efforts. Playing with time is a major Brotherhood weapon against human consciousness. I am sure there were also originally 13 astrological signs too, and that the 13th was represented by the spider. This sign, I feel, was one which encompassed all the others – weaving together their various energies and I always see it as located in the centre of the astrological circle. Interestingly at Bohemian Grove their Shakespearean (Francis Bacon) motto is: "Weaving spiders come not here".

All is consciousness in different manifestations and we are interacting with other vibrating energy fields every moment of our lives. We often feel this when we meet someone and feel their 'vibes' or we go to a house and either feel uncomfortable or immediately at home. It is the energy of the person or place that we are feeling. As we are living within the energy fields of the Earth we are constantly affected by their vibrational state. The reptilian-Brotherhood know this and here you have another reason for their symbolism and ritual on such an apparently obsessional scale. Everything resonates at a frequency and symbols are very powerful examples of this. A symbol is a physical representation of a thought. What that symbol means to you is the energy it will resonate. An obelisk symbolises male sexual energy, the phallus, and so that is the energy it generates and attracts. The dome represents the womb, the female, and that is the energy it generates and attracts. The same with a pentagram, a lighted torch, whatever. If they are placed in particularly powerful vortex points and crossover points on the Earth's magnetic grids, they will affect the vibrational state of the global energy field even more efficiently. So it is with the geometrical street plans and the geometrical placement of certain buildings in relation to each other. The assassination of President Kennedy in a powerful vortex point like Dealey Plaza, and the human thought energy of horror, grief and fear focused on there, will have had a massive effect on the vibrational resonance of the Earth energy. The same, even more so, with the death of Diana on that Moon-energy site in Paris. This is all part of the spell cast by the reptilians on the human mind and emotions to delink us from our true and infinite power. Also the more negative emotion we can be manipulated to feel by these and other events, the more we generate our own fear into the Earth fields and the downward spiral goes on.

There is another point here which is highly relevant to the next section. Research has shown that there is a pulse, an electrical signal, which is generated from the centre of the Milky Way Galaxy to our Sun (and other suns) and from there to the Earth. This pulse is then picked up by the human heart, passed onto the brain, and goes out from there to the cells of the body. When that pulse, that resonance, is passed through that sequence intact and unbroken the human being is at one with the cosmos. Every cell is connected to, and in harmony with, the cosmic pulse. What gets in the way, however, is low vibrational emotion and imbalance which breaks the circuit and, once again, disconnects us from the Earth and the wider universe. The heart-brain connection has been broken in most people by the separation of the head and the heart, the intellect and the intuition, the physical and the spiritual. The reason the reptilian-Brotherhood is pressing forward with its Agenda so quickly today is that it knows it has a colossal challenge on its hands. Creation is governed by energy cycles. At one level we see them with the Earth seasons, spring, summer, autumn and winter. But there are much bigger cycles, too, and these have been recorded in numbers and symbols by the ancients like the Sumerians, Egyptians, Hindus, Chinese, the Maya of Central America and the Native Americans like the Hopi of Arizona. These measure the cycles of solar, lunar and other cosmic energies which transform the Earth's energy fields and so transform life on this planet. We are now in the midst of perhaps the greatest of these transformative cycles, one which happens, it is estimated, only once every 26,000 years, and the Maya calendar predicts that the critical changeover point is December 12th 2012. This is the real focal point of the transformation, not the manufactured Millennium. These consciousness cycles are like doorways or gateways which open for those who are ready to move through into a much higher state of consciousness. I see it as a sort of cuckoo clock in which, at certain key moments in time (or rather cycles), the door or gateway opens. When these gateways are missed, the cycle begins again until another gateway opens. But what we are facing now, it would seem, is not so much a gateway as a vast chasm of opportunity for a global transformation that will defy all current belief. Religious and mystery school texts have been openly or symbolically predicting this for thousands of years. Now the physical, spiritual and, increasingly, scientific evidence is there to confirm that the so-called 'Great Shift of the Ages' is upon us.

A series of events, described by Gregg Braden in *Awakening To Zero Point*, have confirmed that the times they are a changing. In 1991 a new frequency was identified resonating from the centre of the spiral of our Milky Way Galaxy and in 1994 the Ulysses Probe was sent to investigate changes on the Sun. From the mid-1980s there was a terrific increase in solar flares and X-ray bursts, and Ulysses discovered that the Sun's magnetic field was rapidly decreasing. The readings at the north and south poles and at the equator were much lower than expected. Also, while the Sun is cooling, the planets of the solar system, especially the outer ones, are heating up. This suggests that the source of planetary heat comes from within, although this may be stimulated by magnetic and electrical changes in the Sun. At the same time these changes were happening on the Sun, a storm on Jupiter, first documented by the Chinese 3,000 years ago, showed sudden changes also. A vast spiral within this Jupiter storm began to spin in the other direction. The shock waves and other phenomena caused by the collision of the comet Shoemaker-Levy into Jupiter in 1994 have also affected the wider solar system, including the Earth. What is clear is that the changes in the Sun's magnetic field have been mirrored here.

The Earth is a giant magnet with different levels rotating to create a magnetic field. The faster the Earth rotates, the more powerful and dense the magnetic field. Two thousand years ago this magnetic field reached the peak of its intensity in the current cycle and it has been falling ever since as the planet has rotated slower and slower, Braden says. The field is now 50% less powerful than it was 1,500 years ago and the speed of this fall is increasing very quickly. There is no need to panic because this is all part of a natural cycle, a longer and infinitely more powerful version of the annual seasons. Alongside this comes the news that the Earth's resonant frequency, it's heart beat if you like, is increasing rapidly. This frequency, called the Base Resonant Frequency or Schumann Cavity Resonance, was identified in 1899. Between then and the mid-1980s, it maintained a constant pulse of around 7.8 Hertz or 7 cycles per second. But from 1986-87 it apparently began to quicken. By the end of 1995 it had reached 8.6 according to some estimates and the last I heard it was said to be above ten and still rising. Gregg Braden believes that by the Maya transformation year of 2012, the Earth's resonance could be 13 cycles per second while her magnetic field could be at or near zero. He calls this Zero Point when the Earth's magnetic field will all but disappear because the planet's rotation will have stopped. This doesn't mean there will be no gravity because that is created by other phenomena, not the spin of the planet. Something like this seems to have happened at least 14 times in the last 4.5 million years. The last is estimated to have been about 11-13,000 years ago, a window of time which corresponds with many estimates of the end of Atlantis and the beginning of the recovery from that great cataclysm after about 10,500 BC. 13,000 years ago would have been the halfway point in the Great Cycle of 26,000 years which is ending now, another time of great change. I am not saying the Earth is going to stop rotating, but I certainly would not dismiss the possibility.

It could be, however, that there was a magnetic pole shift more recently, about 3,500-600 years ago from examination of the ice in Greenland and the polar regions. Every time the Earth has experienced the rapid fall in the magnetic field that we are seeing now, it has led to a pole shift when magnetic north and south change places. People like Braden estimate that the Earth will stop rotating for some days before it begins to spin in the opposite direction. As you can see when the flow of electricity through an iron bar is reversed, the poles reverse. As the planet spins in the other direction, the flow of electricity will reverse and so, therefore, must the poles. If the planet stopped rotating, one side of the Earth would be in constant sunshine and the other in darkness in this period and that is what the ancients said happened thousands of years ago. The Peruvians talked about the 'long night' of three days and in the Bible there is reference to daytime lasting 20 hours, the longest day. The Hopi Tribe record how the Sun rose twice in one day. First it rose in the west and set in the east and then later it rose in the east and set in the west – the cycle ever since. Other ancient accounts say the Sun used to rise in the west and set in the east, another indication that the Earth used to spin the other way. Back in the early 1990s when I was just waking up to these things, I was given some channelled information by a psychic which said: "The world is changing and the north will become south and the east, west. So it has been commanded since the beginning of time."[3] Spot on, it would seem. Brian Desborough, the scientist-researcher in California, also told me that some major geophysical events are happening which are subject to a media blackout. He confirms that the Earth's geomagnetic field is dropping at an exponential rate and will soon reach zero. He believes, as I do, that we are, to say the least, in for a very bumpy ride geologically. The US Geological Service says that the Earth's magnetic field drops to zero every 500,000 years, then slowly rebuilds, and that these are periods of cataclysmic Earth changes, earthquakes and volcanoes, because of the temporary halt in the planet's rotation. I think it happens more often than that. According to Brian's contacts, the Sun's magnetic field has already dropped to zero and it appears to have reached a higher level of conversion of hydrogen to helium. He says that solar flares are being emitted above and below the Sun's equator at a latitude of 19.5 degrees. This is the point where energy is exchanged between rotating spheres and it is at this latitude on the Earth that the pyramids are located. The energy being received from the Sun at these latitudes must now be phenomenal.

We have followed the connection between changes in the resonance from the centre of the galaxy, to changes in the Sun, to changes in the Earth. It goes on from there to the human heart, then the brain and to every cell in the body. The more you open your heart the more powerful this flow and the quicker you will synchronise with the rising vibrations and transform into a higher state of consciousness. If you close your heart and close your mind, you will be resisting these changes and more and more of your energy will be spent fighting the very energies that will transform your life and set you free. Also, your body will get increasingly out of sync with the energy around you and the consequences, mentally, emotionally and physically will be obvious. You can stand in this fast flowing river trying to hold it back, or you can relax, lie on the air bed and flow with it. It is your choice and whatever happens you live forever. If we allow ourselves to be infused by this high frequency light, our bodies will repair themselves and we will not age. We will live in physical bodies indefinitely if we wish to and our mental and psychic powers will know no bounds, no limitations. If it is also correct that we are entering a massive electrical field called a Photon Belt we are going to experience some amazing things. The ancients knew of these great cycles of change and all the ancient calendars of the Egyptians, Maya, Tibetans, Chinese and others end in the period we are living through now. That Egyptian calendar dates back some 39,000 years and the Mayan one perhaps 18,000. The Maya said that there would be a transition period between the old world and the new as one version of time was replaced by another. They called this period 'No Time' and they said this would begin in July 1982 and lead to the shift on December 12th 2012. The effect of all this on humanity is easy to see. I have visited more than 20 countries in the last few years and there is an awakening unfolding in all of them. Not yet the majority by any means, but the numbers are gathering by the day as this spiritual alarm clock awakens people from their slumber. It is the quickening vibration of the Earth, and indeed the galaxy in general, which is giving the impression that time is passing faster and faster. This is an illusion because there is no time, in truth, but it feels that way because the frequency is getting faster. I remember I was given a channelled communication through a psychic in the early 1990s which said that the day was coming when time would seem to be moving so quickly it would be frightening. That moment is near. It's nothing to worry about, just a natural cycle, but it will present many challenges and therefore infinite opportunities.

The universe, like the whole of the physical world, is a hologram – beams of light colliding to create the appearance of three-dimensional form. It is like throwing stones into a pond and watching the waves collide and create patterns. Two scientists in the United States, Terrance and Dennis McKenna, suggest that the universe is a hologram of 64 waves or time scales and this is why we have the 64 hexagrams of the I-Ching, 64 keys of the Tree of Life, and the 64 codons of the DNA. Their computer analysis suggests that all 64 of these waves are going to peak together in 2012. This is going to make the next few years a period of staggering change. The McKennas' say that the speed of change has gone on doubling in a

Year	Jan	Feb	Mar	Apr	May	Jun	Jul	Aug	Sep	Oct	Nov	Dec
1997	019	022	027	030	034	040	044	050	054	060	066	071
1998	077	082*	088	093	099	103	109	113	119	123	128	131
1999	136	139	142	146	148	151	153	154	156	157	158	159
2000	160	160	160	160	159	158	157	156	155	154	152	150
2001	148	146	142	140	137	134	131	128	124	121	118	114
2002	111	107	103	100	097	093	089	086	082	079	076	072
2003	069	066	062	060	057	053	051	048	046	043	041	039
2004	036	034	032	030	028	027	024	023	021	020	109	017
2005	016	014	013	012	012	011	010	009	009	008	***	***

Figure 61: *The dramatic increase in solar flares which will be bombarding the Earth across the Millennium years. These figures are the numbers of major flares in each month.*

smaller and smaller time frame, manifesting as the leaps in technological development in this century. Projecting forward they say that this will continue to the transformation year of 2012 when in a period of 384 days there will be more transformations of consciousness than in all the previous cycles put together. After this there will be a six day cycle in which events will move even faster and in the last 135 minutes there will be eighteen further enormous leaps in human consciousness, culminating in the last .0075 of a second when another 13 will occur. I don't think we'll be watching *The Price Is Right* while this is happening somehow. "I say dear, I think I've just gone though a number of life-changing transformations while that last advert was on. Cup of tea?"

As I write these words the cycle of solar flares is increasing rapidly and heading for maximum power and effect between 1999 and 2002 (*see* **Figure 61**). This is not *the* transformation, but it is part of the gathering cycle. A good source of information on these subjects is the *Solar Web Site*.[4] It is significant that the solar cult of the reptilian-humans should create a measurement of time which synchronised their year 2,000 with the maximum burst of solar flares in this cycle (cycle 23 as it is known). These solar storms of highly charged energy are likely to increase thunderstorm activity, weather changes, incredible auroral displays in the sky and, possibly, cause widespread power cuts and satellite malfunctions. The underground bases and cities built by the Elite in this century are in preparation for the monumental changes that are going to occur between now and 2012. The Telstar 401 satellite was destroyed by, apparently, higher than normal electron densities and they were nothing compared with what is to come. In March 1989 the electrical grid in Quebec, Canada collapsed within two minutes amid a similar storm of solar energy and, again, far greater storms are now expected. The maximum years for major geomagnetic storms is projected to peak between 1999 and 2002; severe storms should peak between 1999 and 2005; and the year for the maximum number of minor storm days is predicted to be 2005 as solar cycle 23 goes into decline.[5] The biggest solar flares of this solar cycle are reckoned to be 10,000 times more powerful than those observed in the mid-1990s.[6]

The Brotherhood have technology to mess with the weather and they use it, no doubt about that. But the phenomena I have described in this chapter are the real reason for the dramatic changes in global weather patterns which are becoming more extreme by the month. We have seen nothing yet. As I said, amid great public ridicule in Britain in the early 1990s, enormous changes in climate patterns and extremes of weather are likely in this period, along with geological effects as the Earth restructures herself and prepares her body for the shift in the same way that humans are having to do. We and the Earth are being challenged to synchronise our consciousness and its physical expression with the rapidly accelerating frequencies now bathing the planet. The Brotherhood are seeking desperately to hide these facts by blaming the weather changes on the 'Greenhouse Effect' or 'El Nino'. They know that once people realise that something very different is happening the dominoes will fall and the game will be up. It was the Brotherhood who created the New Age Movement to divert the awakening. The term *New Age* is the name of a Freemasonic magazine. A mind controlled slave of the American Government, now recovering, confirmed to me that the New Age was launched covertly by Henry Kissinger and others while she was under his control in the 1970s. Whenever I have made these points, New Agers have dismissed the idea because, they say, the Brotherhood would not want the people to encompass a different view of life. No, not in an ideal world they wouldn't, but this is not an ideal world for them because the energy changes are waking people up. The Brotherhood knew this was coming and what its affect would be. They couldn't jump in a spacecraft and fiddle with the Sun or go into the centre of the galaxy to switch off the new vibration. Their only alternative was to hijack the awakening consciousness and lead it into another cul-de-sac, another rules-and-regulations-religion, where it would be no threat to the Brotherhood Agenda. This they have done with the New Age Movement. There are some very sensible and aware people within the New Age doing some great work, but so many others are in denial of what is going on in the world. They are being misled by other dimensional entities, Brotherhood transmissions on the psychic frequencies and channelled communications from the lower fourth dimension. They sit around their candles or wait for an extraterrestrial 'Ashtar Command' to come and whisk them off the planet in a spaceship. Ashtar is a Brotherhood concoction and a play on words with ancient deities like Ashteroth and Ishtar, another name for Queen Semiramis. Much of the New Age mentality will not even talk about the Brotherhood manipulation because 'it's negative'. Yes it is and it will stay that way until we acknowledge it and change it. Running away or hovering near the ceiling won't make a difference. So much of the New Age is not spirituality as change, but spirituality as escapism. It is suppressing and diverting the awakening, not advancing it.

We are clearly being prepared for revelations about the reptilians, because the highly charged, higher frequency energies will increase dramatically the number of people who see the reptilians of the lower fourth dimension. Arizona Wilder told me that the number of sacrificial rituals has increased massively since the 1980s because the reptilians need more and more human blood and energy to hold their human form. They need the microchipped control in place before they are seen openly as reptiles as the vibrational changes advance. The changes are taking away the reptilians' vibrational cover and the truth has to come out. In preparation for this there is a very long list of movies and television programmes for adults and children about reptile humanoids, friendly and otherwise. I have mentioned *The Arrival* and *V: The Final Battle*, but there are many more. In *Stargate*, the story of time-travelling to an ancient Egypt controlled by extraterrestrials, the possible reptile nature of the 'alien' is revealed when his skin is ripped away at the end. *Stargate: SG-1* continues the theme of reptilians occupying human form; *Enemy Mine* and *Dreamscape*, both starring Dennis Quaid, feature reptile humanoids; *Theodore Rex* is about a seven foot tall upright-walking dinosaur; *Babylon 5*, the television series, includes the reptile humanoids called the Narns and the same theme can be seen in *Star Trek*; *Star Trek, The Next Generation*; *Space Precinct*; *Seaquest DSV*; *Outer Limits*, and elsewhere. Steven Speilberg's *Jurassic Park* and *Lost World* bring dinosaurs back to life and his video animation for children, *We're Back*, features two-legged speaking dinosaurs. In one scene a T-Rex is taken into a spaceship, endowed with intelligence and taken forward in time to the present day. Children's movies and television series are awash with reptilian imagery. *Mario Brothers* is based on the idea that the dinosaurs were not wiped out by the meteorite and in fact the impact created a parallel dimension where the dinosaurs continued to live and thrive and evolved into intelligent humanoids. The film's heroes go into an underground passage where they fall into that other dimension and battle with humanoid dinosaurs to prevent the invasion of this dimension. *Dinotopia* and *Dinotopia: The World Beneath*, the children's books by James Gurney, are stories of an inner-earth world in which intelligent reptilians and dinosaurs living under the ground with humans. *Land Of The Lost* features a family who travel back in time to a dinosaur-dominated land where they are attacked by a race of reptile humanoids called the Sleestak. In one episode, a reptilian humanoid studies humans who radiate 'emotional heat' – the human emotional energy on which the reptilians thrive. The children's series, *Barney*, is about a friendly reptilian and *Mutant Ninja Turtles* are amphibian-reptilian fighters of crime and injustice. *Dinosaurs* in the early 1990s was a children's television programme about a loveable family of dinosaurs, interestingly called the Sinclair family! One of them is called Earl! Cartoons like *Dinosaucers*; *Mutant League*; *G. I. Joe* and *Dino Power House* also include intelligent reptile beings.[7] A coincidence? Of course not.

For a long time the reptilian-Brotherhood has been preparing to stop humanity making the consciousness shift. The pyramid hierarchical nature of their structure has allowed them to instigate the same plan through countless different institutions and agencies. First they have attacked us at the physical level with drugs, food additives and fluoride in the water. The ancient methods of healing (known today as alternative or complementary) are under constant assault from the medical establishment which is awash with Freemasons and under the control of the Brotherhood pharmaceutical cartel. The Rockefeller empire alone now owns more than 60% of the pharmaceutical industry in the United States. These, and the other wings of the global pharmaceutical cartel, fund the 'research' into new treatments and, of course, these 'treatments' always turn out to be drugs. There is an excellent book documenting this called *The Medical Mafia* by a Canadian doctor, Guylaine Lanctot, which is available through Bridge of Love Publications. The pharmaceutical cartel interlocks with the major global 'food' producers like Nestle, Kellogg, Proctor and Gamble and the rest. Through this network the Brotherhood can orchestrate a concerted attack on the human body and its mental processes through the drugs, vaccines and food additives. Genetically-engineered animals and food is part of this, also. When one of the British scientists involved in the development of genetically-engineered food publicly questioned its safety, he was immediately sacked. So much for living in a country with freedom of expression. Fluoride in the water is a mind suppressant and so are sweeteners like aspartame which you find today in almost all the soft drinks. These additives are designed to make it more difficult for the brain and the cells to tune into the new frequencies. Workers in the food factories have no idea what they are doing as they just follow orders. The decisions are being taken at a much higher level. It is the same with vaccinations, one of the biggest medical scams of them all. The doctors (most of them) and the nurses have no idea of the damage they are doing to a child's body, mind and immune system, when they administer vaccinations. But those who orchestrate the vaccination programmes certainly do. The Brotherhood have also created a highly complex network of technology to capture the human collective consciousness and delink it from the rest of its multidimensional self. This starts out in space with the 'Star Wars' technology which is part of a vast electromagnetic web on and around the Earth. It includes: Extremely Low Frequency (ELF) transmitters which are broadcasting their signals all over the world; microwave transmissions which include direct attacks on those the Brotherhood wish to kill or discredit through mind manipulation; the mobile phone networks which do enormous mental and physical damage and allow the owner to be tracked even when the phone is switched off; emissions from televisions, microwave ovens and other technology; and, of course, the microchip. The main reason for the campaign for a microchipped population is to suppress the awakening and disconnect us from the pulses that are setting us free. A CIA scientist told me that microchipping the population will give the Brotherhood control of a person's thoughts, emotions and physical health.

A contact in the financial world, who accepts the reptilian connection from his own experience, gave me some interesting background to the modern energy systems. He had worked with a number of free energy inventors and he realised that free energy technology worked in a 'clockwise' direction and so was in harmony with the spin of the chakras. But most conventional electrical technology was 'anticlockwise', therefore in conflict with the chakras. He believed that this was helping to close down the chakra system and delink humanity from other levels of consciousness. This is one reason why the reptilian-Brotherhood have suppressed, often through murder, the development of free energy technology. The average wiring system in the home works at 60 cycles per second which is very detrimental

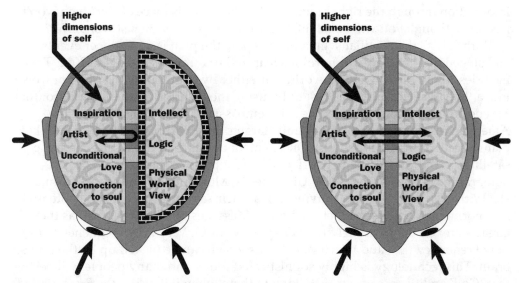

Figure 62: *The Brotherhood system seeks to imprison the human psyche in the left brain, the 'rational' intellect which only believes what it can see, touch, hear or smell. The 'education' system and the media are structured for this and most teachers, lecturers, scientists and journalists are left brain prisoners themselves.*

Figure 63: *When we open our hearts and minds we activate the right brain, the intuition and inspiration which connects with the cosmos.*

to the body and affects brain wave activity. Brian Desborough told me how people develop back ailments and other problems if their bed is pushed against a wall which carries internal wiring. Their complaints often clear up if they move the bed a few feet from the wall. We live in a pulsating ocean of electromagnetism generated by 'modern' technology and this is constantly affecting human physical, emotional and mental health. The human mind, body and emotions are under an incredible assault in the countdown to the Great Shift because the Brotherhood are desperate to ensure that humanity as a whole does not make the consciousness leap that will take us beyond the reptilian frequencies.

The Brotherhood have also structured the 'education' system and the media to lock people in what I call the left brain prison. The left brain is the area which deals with the physical world view, 'rational' thought and all that can be seen, touched, heard and smelled (*see Figure 62*). The right brain is our intuition and our connection with higher dimensions. This is where you find the artist and creativity, inspired by our uniqueness of thought and expression (*see Figure 63*). The education system and its offshoots, like the media and science, are designed to speak to the left brain and to switch off right brain thinking. This is why spending on the arts in schools is being cut back all over the world and rigid, left brain programmes imposed. 'Education' fills the left brain with information, much of which is untrue and inaccurate, and it demands that this is stored and then regurgitated on the exam paper. If you do this like a robot you pass. If, however, you filter the information through the right brain and say "Hey, this is piece of shit", you won't pass even though you will be telling the truth. Isn't education just wonderful?

With fear as the reptilians' greatest weapon, the plan is to engineer events, real and staged, that will create enormous fear in the countdown years to 2012. This includes a plan to start a third world war either by stimulating the Muslim world into a 'holy war' against the West or by using the Chinese to cause global conflict. Maybe both. The bombs placed near US embassies in Africa in 1998 and the American response of bombing Islamic targets is all part of this. One of their key plans is called Project Bluebeam. One element of this is to use laser-generating satellites in the 'Star Wars' network in different parts of the world to project holographic images in the sky of UFOs, Jesus, Mohammed, Buddha, Khrishna, etc. With each belief system convinced that their saviour has come, the potential for enormous religious conflict is obvious. Messages will be broadcast (as they already are) on the Extremely Low Frequency (ELF), Very Low Frequency (VLF), Low Frequency (LF) and microwave bands which can be picked up by the human brain. This technology is highly sophisticated today and many people will believe that 'God' and their 'saviour' is talking to them when it is really the Brotherhood manipulators. Much 'channelled' information comes from this source already. Project Bluebeam also involves the manifestation of 'supernatural' phenomena of many kinds to terrify the population and amid the terror and conflict, also via holographic image in the sky, the Brotherhood 'saviour' will come. It must be emphasised also, as we consider Project Bluebeam, that the crop circle phenomena does not have to be extraterrestrial or 'supernatural', as most investigators believe. It could be, but it doesn't have to be. In the period before the complex crop patterns first appeared in the 1980s the technology was developed which could create them. This was a high frequency gamma-ray beam device which was developed for the military. Some of the main characteristics of the genuine crop circles (many have been hoaxed) are: the stalks bend at the lowest node and do not break; the cell structure changes; the crop pattern emits microwave energy; dead animals inside are carbonised; a high frequency sound or clicking noise is heard when the pattern is first formed; plasma lights are sometimes seen. Every one of these effects would be caused by the gamma-ray beam device. The scientist and researcher Brian Desborough says:

> "The high frequency gamma-ray beam would cause the moisture in the nodes to boil, swelling and softening the nodal cells and causing the straw to bend in the direction swept by the beam. Such beams are capable of creating extremely fine detail; the high frequency sound which is emitted from newly-formed crop circles strongly suggests that the beam systems employed in this duplicitous act incorporate Mossbaur technology. The soil within the circle would emit radiation and any creature unfortunate enough to be irradiated by the beam would be carbonised... Prior to commencing a crop circle, the gamma-ray beam would require adjustment for focus and power setting. This could account for the one or more small circular depressions usually to be found adjacent to the crop circle."

Some people will ask why, if they are made by the authorities, such an effort would have been made to discredit them with hoaxers to the point where the media now ignore them. It's a very good question, but the fact remains that human technology can make them and we should know that. Incidentally, Desborough suggests that flight TWA 800, the jumbo jet which exploded shortly after take-off from New York, was struck by a Mossbaur beam weapon. The autopsy on the victims revealed that their blood had gelled in their veins and their brains had 'turned to mush'. This is what the weapon would produce, and at the time the aircraft was flying near the Brookhaven Naval Research Station where this very weapon was developed.

The UFO scam

The main ambition for Project Bluebeam is to convince the people that the Earth is being invaded by extraterrestrials. It is vital we do not buy this crap. The extraterrestrials are not invading, they've been here for thousands of years and they look, on the surface, like you and me. In 1938 the actor Orson Welles claimed to be broadcasting live from the site of an 'alien' landing in New Jersey. He wasn't, he was using actors and special effects to broadcast from a radio studio. The programme, a broadcast of the 'novel' *War Of The Worlds* by H. G. Wells, caused terror and panic in the place the invading Martians were said to be. One guy committed suicide and there were traffic jams of people trying to get away because they thought the Martians had come. Welles said it was just a play and people had misunderstood. This was in fact an experiment to see how people would react to such a situation and they used a story written by H. G. Wells, a Brotherhood clone who advocated the reptilian Agenda, including mass mind control. Think about it. If you wanted an excuse to globally centralise all government, finance, military, police and other institutions, you would need a threat to the planet as a whole. What better way than to kid the people they are being invaded from space? You would have a global problem, a global demand that "Something must be done" and an opportunity to offer a global solution: a world government and army to meet this 'threat'. That is the plan we are now being prepared for.

Back in the 1960s during the Kennedy administration, it is claimed that a group of 15 experts in their various fields were brought together to produce a report into ways of controlling the population and centralising power without the use of wars. It became known as the Report from Iron Mountain, an underground facility in New York State, where they held their first and last meetings. One of the members leaked the contents to a friend who leaked it more widely, it is said. I detail the report in ...*And The Truth Shall Set You Free*. It is claimed to be a hoax, but if it was, it was an inspired one. Two of the recommendations it made to centralise power were: a threat to the global environment and a threat from an extraterrestrial invasion. The report was completed in 1966, the story goes, and in 1968 came the Club of Rome, the Brotherhood-front I talked about earlier, which created the environmental movement. The environmental recommendation in the Report from

Iron Mountain clearly happened. Now they are playing the extraterrestrial card. For decades the idea of extraterrestrials was dismissed and laughed at by the media, but suddenly, now the time is right, they are taking it more and more seriously. UFO 'research' in the United States has been funded by Laurance Rockefeller and this has included a panel of nine scientists led by the Stanford physicist Peter Sturrock. He told American television that they had found 'compelling physical evidence' that something is going on that they do not understand. Now, I wonder what that can be? And look at the stream of fear-based extraterrestrial television programmes and movies like *Independence Day* (made by 20th Century Fox owned by Rupert Murdoch), *Alien Resurrection* (made by 20th Century Fox owned by Rupert Murdoch) and *X-Files* (made by Fox Television owned by Rupert Murdoch). And, I should add, Rupert Murdoch is owned by the Brotherhood.

Underpinning these messages are the countless reports of UFOs being seen and the experiences of large numbers of people who claim to have been abducted by extraterrestrials. I am not saying this does not happen at all, but some things we can say. The 'abductees' invariably recall one, some or all of the following: missing time, clicking or buzzing sounds, sexual feelings and a sulphurous odour. Brian Desborough points out that these are all typical of contact with intense electromagnetic fields and are caused by neurochemical changes in the brain as he explains in detail. As long ago as 1930, Professor Cazamalli discovered that hallucinations could be induced by electromagnetic frequencies of 500 Megahertz. These phenomena can even be stimulated by areas of geopathic stress in the Earth and by overhead power lines, both of which produce electromagnetic fields and they can certainly be produced by the electromagnetic technology used by the Brotherhood in their mind control projects. The effect and potential of electromagnetic fields to take people into altered states of consciousness and to trigger many 'supernatural' phenomena is enormous. Unless we understand this, extraterrestrial explanations can be given for very terrestrial events. This applies to plasma balls and lights in the sky which are commonly caused by electromagnetic projections from the Earth. The modern explosion of UFO sightings did not begin until after the Second World War, by which time the Germans for one had developed forms of 'flying saucers'. Project Paperclip was the British Intelligence-American Intelligence operation to spring the top Nazi scientists, engineers, geneticists and mind manipulators from Germany and take them to North or South America. This would have transferred this 'UFO' knowledge across the Atlantic and it was soon after this that the flying saucers were reported in increasing numbers in the United States. The famous Roswell incident happened in 1947. Cattle mutilations have been blamed on extraterrestrials because, it is said, there is no human technology that could dissect the cattle and drain their blood in this way. But Brian Desborough points out that this is not true. A portable laser of the type necessary was developed by the US Airforce Phillips Laboratory for use by special forces personnel and it was after this that the cattle mutilations began. Some of the first ones happened near the chemical warfare laboratory at Dulce in New Mexico and Desborough suggests that the cattle are being abducted as part of this research.

This would explain why many of them are daubed with luminous paint which can only be seen at night. These cattle can be winched aboard a craft, their body parts removed, and returned to a different area of the field, so leaving no footprints and creating a great 'mystery'. Many uninformed (or otherwise) UFO researchers say that craft like the one at Roswell must be extraterrestrial because they are made of a material with a non-crystalline structure which cannot be produced on Earth or cut with human tools. Not true again. Desborough says that the process of producing such metals is called splat cooling. "Molten metal is deposited on a cryogenically-cooled surface (which) results in a non-crystalline product. Similarly, when metal is compressed at temperatures approaching absolute zero, the metal attains a room temperature hardness of a diamond."[8]

The UFO 'research' community is alive with Brotherhood disinformants and intelligence gatherers. A number of the main 'whistle-blowers' and UFO authors are members of an intelligence unit known as the Aviary because their code names are all birds. It makes you wonder how 'former' intelligence operatives are allowed to talk freely about secret projects when to do so should mean severe action against them and the loss of all pension rights for violation of their oath of secrecy. Then there's the technology known as EDOM (Electronic Dissolution of Memory) which is used on former intelligence operatives to extinguish knowledge the authorities do not want revealed. Other Aviary members or operatives include many of the hypnotists who 'help' the 'abductees' to recall their 'memories' of 'alien' abduction. Some of the 'star' contactees have connections to secret projects. George Adamski was involved with scientists at the Point Loma Naval Electronics Laboratory and a similar operation in Pasadena, when he announced his extraterrestrial contacts to the world. The microchips which are claimed to have been implanted in abductees by extraterrestrials are, in fact, very much of the Earth. They were developed by a consortium of engineers from Motorola, General Electric, IBM and the Boston Medical Center. One example is the IBM 2020 chip used in the Project Monarch mind control programme. These are also implanted in their unsuspecting patients by doctors and dentists under contract to the intelligence agencies. More and more books are now being published about evil aliens who are invading the planet and so where is all this leading? I'll let Henry Kissinger answer that one in a passage from a speech at the 1992 Bilderberg meeting at Evian-Les-Bains, in France. It was written down, it seems, by a Swiss delegate. Kissinger said:

"Today, America would be outraged if UN troops entered Los Angeles to restore order; tomorrow they will be grateful. This is especially true if they were told that there were an outside threat from beyond, whether real or promulgated, that threatened our very existence. It is then that all peoples of the world will plead with world leaders to deliver them from this evil.

"The one thing every man fears is the unknown. When presented with this scenario, individual rights will be willingly relinquished for the guarantee of their well being granted to them by their world government."

That's the reason for the UFO scam. Problem-reaction-solution. The extra-terrestrials are not invading they are already here and they are the ones, operating through physical bodies, who will offer to 'save' us! The UFO investigator and lecturer Norio Hayakawa says this plan is called 'Project Panic' and that high technology equipment will be used to create an optical illusion of a UFO invasion. This will give governments and the United Nations the excuse to call a global state of emergency and all those emergency powers and executive orders will be implemented. The Y2K computer 'virus', which is predicted to bring chaos across the Millennium, is another manipulated 'problem' with this in mind. As I detailed earlier, the executive orders passed this century by Presidents of the United States without Congressional debate or approval will allow the Government to take over transport, energy, your home and all media. These executive orders allow the Government to tell you where you will live and to put you to work in any way they want. Your children can be taken away from you, anything goes when those orders are enforced by a manufactured 'emergency'. You will find that similar powers are available to all governments in these circumstances. Other aspects of the Brotherhood Agenda, across the 'Millennium' and the years to 2012, include: a global financial collapse to introduce the one-world electronic currency; conflicts and terrorism galore; and a whole range of other events to terrify and dispirit the human population into unquestioning servitude.

But it doesn't have to be like this. You are not an 'ordinary', 'powerless' human being. You are an aspect of eternal consciousness, a genius waiting to happen. All you need to do is open your heart, open your mind, reconnect with that genius and grasp your infinite power to create your own destiny. That is our challenge in this incredible time of opportunity and we are going to see freedom return to this planet for the first time in so, so long.

■ SOURCES

1   Gregg Braden, *Awakening To Zero Point* (Laura Lee Productions, 1996).

2   *From The Ashes Of Angels*, p 18.

3   David Icke, *The Truth Vibrations* (Gateway Books, Wellow, Bath, England, first published by Aquarian Books in 1991).

4   http://solar.uleth.ca/solar/

5   "Solar Cycle Status Report", taken from the Solar Website, July 4th 1997.

6   Ibid.

7   John Rhodes, the Reptoid website.

8   Brian Desborough, "An Overview of UFO Contact and Abduction Phenomena", information paper for author, 1998.

CHAPTER TWENTY-ONE

Breaking the spell

What I am about to outline is the information the Brotherhood most want to suppress. It is the knowledge that you are in control of your destiny and no-one else is. You always have been and always will be.

Reading this book you may find that strange. After all, have I not detailed how the Brotherhood have controlled the world for thousands of years? Yes, but how have they done that? By manipulating the way humanity thinks and feels. How we think and feel creates our physical experience and if we allow an outside force to manipulate our mind and emotions, we will allow them to control our physical experience, our destiny. But we can change that in an instant if we take back control of our thinking and emotions. Creating our own reality and deciding our own destiny is, at its heart, a very simple process. It can be summed up by "What we give out is what we get back". It works like this...

Our mind and emotions resonate wavelengths of various frequencies depending on how we are thinking and feeling. This applies not only to our conscious self, but also our subconscious, that cauldron of suppressed thoughts, attitudes and emotions that we would rather not deal with. You can resonate the vibration of anger from that level without actually feeling the emotion consciously at the time. For instance, an adult who is holding on to suppressed anger about their childhood, will still be broadcasting that frequency, even though they might not be consciously aware of being angry. This will draw to them, by the law of vibrational attraction, other people who are consciously and subconsciously angry. I know, I've been there. In the words of a song I heard in the United States: "When you hold anger, guess what comes to you? A lot of very angry people do." Our mental and emotional 'vibes' of all kinds are broadcast as a series of wave patterns and these draw towards us similar wave patterns in the form of people, places, ways of life and experiences. What we give out, we attract to us. Within this cocktail of vibrations are our conscious thoughts and feelings and the astrological patterns we take on at birth and/or, some say, conception. When we are born we absorb the energy pattern in the Earth's field at the time and in the place we enter this world. This pattern depends on where the planets are in their cycles and, therefore, which of their energies are most effecting the Earth. Every second the energy field is changing and so when and where we are born matters enormously to the energy field we inherit. We choose where and when we are born to take on the energy pattern most appropriate for our lifeplan. Look at the endless evidence of how people in certain professions tend to be born in the same period of the year. The Babylonian Brotherhood, particularly through Christianity and 'science', has sought to condemn astrology as either evil or ridiculous to encourage people to dismiss it. Once again, Christians have done excellent work for the Brotherhood in this regard, most of them without any idea of the Agenda they were advancing.

This cocktail of interacting vibrations draws towards us a reflection of itself. When we think we are a victim and we are not in control of our lives, we will synchronise with the energies (people, experiences) which resonate to that frequency. We will therefore create a victimised, powerless physical experience. When we believe that the best things in life happen to others, they do, because we are not connecting with the energies that will manifest the best things in life. When you believe you will never have enough money, you won't. Money is an energy and if you are going to attract that energy, you need to make a vibrational connection with it. Thinking that you will never attract money, consciously or subconsciously, ensures that you will be out of sync with that energy and you stay poor. The Brotherhood know this and they have created an energy flow which attracts money to them. Fear of something is always guaranteed to attract what you fear. The energy of fear attracts like energy and so what you fear becomes what you physically experience. Fear of being without money becomes the circumstances in which you are without money. Fear of being alone, rejected or attacked all become that physical experience unless you deal with the source of the energy which manifests these things – YOU. So its no good blaming anyone else for your life. You have either created it by your own thoughts and feelings or the Brotherhood has done so because you have allowed your thoughts and feelings to be manipulated by religion, the media, politics, doctors, teachers and all the rest. Whichever it is, the one responsible for your life is… YOU. No getting away from it, I'm afraid, you are stuck with it. But then, this news is just wonderful. It means that if you created the present reality that you don't like, you can just as easily create a new reality that you do like. You are in control. You have all the answers. You are the centre of your own universe and you can make it whatever you choose. You are simply incredible. Feel it, live it and your world will be transformed.

My book, *I Am Me, I Am Free*, is all about this need to restore our mental and emotional powers because unless we do so we can never be free. But we need to do more than that. We need to set ourselves free, yes, but just as importantly we need to set each other free. We have been manipulated by the Brotherhood into our personal prisons and the prisoners have been further manipulated into policing each other. Humanity is both the sheep and the sheep dog. The Brotherhood set the religious, political, medical and scientific 'norms' by controlling those professions and, therefore, the norms promoted by the mesmerised media. Most people then live their lives within these norms and allow them to programme their sense of possibility, potential and who or what they are. This is the eggshell and if people want to concede their uniqueness and infinite power in this way, fine, go ahead. Couldn't care less. But what happens is that those who live in these prisons are not satisfied with that. They insist that everyone else does the same. It's not enough for them to believe in a religion, they also seek to impose that belief on everyone else or condemn them if they do not accept that religion's view of life. There would be no religious wars if we respected each others' right to believe whatever we choose, so long as we don't impose it on anyone else. I don't have a problem with people taking part in Satanic ritual if everyone involved is making that choice while in complete control of their own thinking processes. People want to sacrifice each other and all involved have made a free choice? Go ahead, but please, someone clear up the mess. Eventually they will learn from the experience and evolve to a higher level of understanding. If George Bush, Henry Kissinger, the Windsors and the rest of the gang want to start a self-contained community and run it as a fascist state with everyone willingly taking part, please feel free. They'll have no challenge from me. I'm interested when these things are imposed on people through secrecy and manipulation or by physical, mental or pharmaceutical force. Surely we can summon the maturity to think for ourselves and allow others to do the same? Is that really too much to ask? If it is, we are in serious trouble.

The only way the few can control the world is if the masses help them to do it: and we do. I have spoken to audiences about freedom and had wild applause, but do we understand what the word means? "Yes, freedom, that's what we want!" Oh really? Then why do many of these same people who wildly applaud the concept of freedom, insist that those who are not Christians are lesser human beings or the Devil incarnate? Why do they insist (the Muslims, Hindus and 'Jews', as well) that their children are brought up from birth to believe what they believe, at the expense of other views and information? The times I have been asked at meetings in America if I am a Christian, as if I become more credible and believable if I am. The very need to ask that question is confirmation that the questioner is in mental servitude to a belief system of Brotherhood creation. And that's the point. We are imprisoned by what we are manipulated to *believe*. The power of belief to entrap a mind is incredible. The Brotherhood do not care what you believe as long as you believe something to the exclusion of other possibilities. I am quite happy to change my views on any or all the information in this book if that is where new information leads me. I am not attached to it because I am only seeking the truth, whatever it is. If it is something different to what I think now, fine. So be it. Rigid beliefs defend themselves from all comers because the belief becomes the person's sense of self, their sense of security, and so they would rather cling on to the belief than face the mental and emotional challenge of letting it go. But we are now facing a time of the most phenomenal change in which all beliefs are going to crumble. You can write the future on a blank piece of paper far easier than one that is full of old data. You can plant new flowers on an empty piece of garden far easier than one still consumed by weeds. It is time to clear our minds of belief and be open to all possibility. Only then can we be free to tap into infinity.

What I have detailed in this book is one level of the picture, the one which most directly affects people in human bodies today. But there are other levels to consider also. It is important to realise that two conflicting statements can both be equally true depending on the level from which you observe the same situation. An example is to say on one hand that this world is imperfect and on the other that everything that happens on the Earth is perfection. How can both be true? Well they are. From the perspective of everyday life, the world is not perfect. We have wars, hunger, disease, unhappiness and pain of all kinds. That's true. But from the perspective of the evolution of humanity everything is perfect. That's equally true. The only way we can evolve is by learning from experience and that means experiencing the consequences of our thoughts and actions. If there were no unpleasant consequences for our actions, how could we possibly learn and evolve to higher levels of understanding? It would be like a child daubing paint all over the walls of your house or throwing stones through your windows. If the child did not face the consequences and see that such behaviour is deeply upsetting for the home owner, what would happen? The child would go on daubing paint over other houses and smashing more windows. Humanity has given its mind away all these thousands of years and if we are to regain that power to consciously control our own destiny, we have to be kicked in the backside by facing the consequences until, at last, the penny drops and the light goes on. So we have the wars and conflicts and manipulations of all kinds. I don't hate these reptilians. I want to love them because that is what they need so desperately. Their behaviour can only come from a lack of self-love because only by loving yourself for what you are, can you begin to truly love others for what they are. So I love you Queen of England, Queen Mother, Prince Charles, Prince Philip, Pindar, Henry Kissinger, George Bush, Edward Heath and all the rest. If these people would only love themselves this nightmare (and their nightmare) would be over. Until they do, their heart connection to their infinite soul (pure love) will remain closed and they will continue to manifest these same attitudes and this behaviour. I would also stress again, before I finish, that when I talk of reptilians I am talking only of those who are seeking to manipulate humanity, not the species as a whole. Many of the reptilian species are trying to help us break the spell and even the manipulating reptilians are possessed by a fifth dimensional force. In the end we're all One, anyway.

I know that many people who are aware of the Brotherhood and its Agenda feel the only way to respond is by stockpiling weapons and preparing for an armed defence of their liberties. I can't think of a response more certain to bring about the very fascist state they say they want to avoid. The idea of meeting violence with violence is so obviously contradictory and so utterly devoid of the faintest spark of intelligence, that one wonders how few brain cells must be activated to conjure such a thought. When you meet violence with violence what do you get every time? Twice the violence. Yes, that's going to make an enormous contribution to peace. Also, when anyone uses violence against the system, it gives the Brotherhood a public excuse to use its high-tech weaponry to blow away the opposition in the name of the rule of 'law'. I think we need to be just a touch more subtle than stockpiling weapons, somehow. I have met some of the more extreme Christian patriots in the United States and as I said to one: "I don't know which I dislike more, the world controlled by the Brotherhood, or the one you want to replace it with". This particular guy talked about freedom and the need to defend it with armed resistance while claiming that black people were genetically inferior to whites and that the Native Americans were only "looking after" the lands of America "until we (the whites) arrived". He would have got on so well with his hero, the Founding Father Thomas Jefferson. But here we see the theme again. People like this chap will, I'm sure, end up in armed conflict with the Brotherhood forces at some point. Indeed it is inevitable unless he changes his attitudes, because what will happen is that the two same states of being under different names (the Brotherhood and the extreme Christian Patriots) will attract each other into their lives to play out their drama of mutual violence. They both believe in the use of violence and so they are both in the same frequency range. They may call themselves by different names, but they are not opposites, they are oppo-sames. The confrontation has to happen for them to evolve and learn that violence solves nothing. Never has, never will. When you hear the Christian Patriots describe their alternative to the Brotherhood Agenda they say they want to have "One nation under God". OK, but who's version of God? The Christian God? The Muslim God? The Hindu God? The God as visualised by Ethel in New York or Bill in Los Angeles? No, they mean, of course, the Christian God, the vision of God that they believe in. They don't actually want to replace the Brotherhood Agenda with freedom, but with their own version of dictatorship. Again, because both want to impose their will on others and suppress other lifestyles and beliefs, they are bound to attract each other because they are operating within the same frequency range. What is true of the extreme Christians is equally true of the extreme Muslims, Hindus, Jews and other religions. To an extent the same was true of the Native Americans when the white Europeans came. The Native American culture contains some tremendous wisdom and has a far greater understanding of the connection of all things. But let's not go overboard here as so many in the New Age Movement often do with their starry-eyed vision of Native America. Before the whites came scores of Native American tribes used to war with each other simply because they were in different tribes. There was much slaughter and conflict. Such a macho, war-paint mentality will attract into its life another energy that equally thinks that violence is justified. Whenever you have two groups who think violence is an option they are a vibrational confrontation waiting to happen.

Fortunately many Christians, Muslims, Hindus, Jews and Native Americans are not extreme and there is an alternative to violence. We can either learn from the hardest and most painful of experience or we can use our intelligence and our love to observe this situation and change our state of being without a gun being fired. Then these confrontations will be avoided because there will no vibrational attraction between the Brotherhood and those who wish to scupper their Agenda. We can do it without confrontation. The reptilian vibrational connection to humanity is through the emotion of fear. They are themselves consumed by fear which is why they behave as they do. If they can manipulate humanity into a state of fear, as they have, they make the vibrational connection which allows them to control the human psyche. They are also playing at home, you might say, because they are experts on the emotion of fear. This reptilian group are the very expression of it. If we seek to stop the reptilian-Brotherhood with a confrontation on their home

SOUL

Figure 64: When people are conditioned to close down their consciousness they delink from their eternal soul and all the love, wisdom, knowledge and inspiration waiting to be tapped. It is not that we need to seek enlightenment – we are enlightened. We just need to remove the barriers of fear which disconnect us from our own enlightenment outside the 'egg shell'.

ground of fear by using hatred, aggression and violence, then forget it. The game is already over. But if we meet this challenge from a frequency range the Brotherhood cannot even conceive of – love – we will transform the world and the reptilian control will be no more. There are many reasons for this. Firstly, when we open our hearts to love, the heart chakra spins with tremendous speed and power, whipping up the frequency of our incarnate consciousness to the highest vibrational expression of life, pure love. As our soul is pure love, we reconnect with the awesome power of our multidimensional self (*see Figure 64*). The eggshell explodes.

The fast, short, wavelength of love also activates the 'antenna' in our DNA which reconnects us with the cosmos and an open heart chakra tunes into the cosmic pulse from the Earth, the Sun and the centre of the Galaxy, and transmits that changing drumbeat to our brain and every cell in our bodies. This will dramatically transform our minds, emotions and physical form as they synchronise with the quickening vibrations at this time of unbelievable change and evolution. The subsequent leap in our personal frequencies will lift us out of the vibrational pit of fear and onto levels far beyond the lower fourth dimension. The reptilian control will be over because they will be on a different radio station, if you like, and they will have to face the consequences of their own actions on their road to enlightenment. The choice is ours, fear or love, prison or freedom.

If the reptilians did not exist we would have to invent them because their current state of being represents something that human consciousness had to experience. If that was not so, the reptilians would be manipulating someone else. We would not have attracted them. They have given us a gift in our eternal evolution, a gift of experiencing the consequences of fear and of conceding our infinite power to another force, be it a parent, boss, peer pressure, or, ultimately, the reptilian-Brotherhood. The evolutionary process is about love, not punishment. It does not punish us for our actions, it gives us the consequences of them, which is very different. Without that we cannot evolve. We are loved along this journey by consciousness levels (other aspects of self) which seek to help us to become more loving and more enlightened, to be masters of ourselves. Our choice is how much of this experience we need before we learn and move on. Are we going to change now or do we require more wars, hunger, and suffering, before the light bulb flashes? Are we going to walk through the fast-approaching gateway to a whole new state of being? Or are we going to stay where we are and face another cycle of incarnation and reincarnation until another opportunity comes? The reptilian group I have highlighted are deeply imbalanced because they are disconnected from those levels of self which resonate to the rhythm of love. But they are still part of everything that exists, they are still you and me, an aspect of the glorious whole we call God. So if we hate them, we hate ourselves. If we are violent to them, we are violent to ourselves. And it would be all so self defeating. I say: forgive them for they know not what they do. By forgive and by love, I don't mean to walk away and let them get on with it. They are seeking to impose their will and therefore there is a legitimate cause for a challenge to that. But if this Brotherhood control is caused by giving our minds, power and responsibility away, and by insisting that others do the same, it is *ourselves* we need to address, not only the behaviour of the reptilians. If we take back our power and set ourselves and each other free from imposition of thought, belief and lifestyle, it doesn't matter what the Brotherhood do. Control from the centre will be impossible because you cannot centralise control of diversity, only uniformity. Three things will transform life on Earth and remove the reptilian control of the human psyche:

1   We let go of our fear of what other people think of us and we express our uniqueness of view and lifestyle, even (no, especially) if it differs from the 'norm'. At this point we cease to be a sheep following the flock.

2   We allow everyone else to do the same without fear of being ridiculed or condemned for the crime of being different. When we do this we cease to be the sheep dog for the rest of the flock, pressuring them to conform to what we believe is right.

3   No-one seeks to impose what they believe on anyone else, so always respecting free will and free choice.

There is no way the Brotherhood Agenda can survive such changes in attitude. People ask me what they should do in response to my information, but I never answer that question. The only person who knows what is best for you, *is* you. The trick is to clear the channel to your higher dimensions so you can connect with the highest level of your wisdom, love and inspiration to guide you to do what is most appropriate for you. We don't need to sit around in smoke filled rooms or start new political parties. We need to remove the egg shell of low vibrational emotion – fear – and the law of vibrational attraction will connect us with all the people and organisations we need to transform the planet. When we get ourselves right, the world must come right because we are the world and the world is us. What we call society is the sum total of human thinking and feeling. It is a reflection of our attitudes. When we change them, we change society. We are only a change of mind away from real freedom, the freedom to express our God-given uniqueness and celebrate the diversity of gifts, perceptions and inspiration that exist within the collective human psyche. The creative force is within us all and desperate to express itself. It is the suppression of this energy which leads to so much pent-up frustration and therefore violence and depression. Imagine you are a gifted artist or dancer, but peer pressure, parent pressure and the demands of the system insist that you work in a bank or sit next to a factory machine all day. Or you want to express your creativity and make a contribution to the world, but the Brotherhood manipulation of the financial system means that you can't find a job. That all-powerful creative force within you cannot be suppressed, so it comes out in an imbalanced way, impregnated with the vibration of anger, despair or frustration, and so we have violence and the demand for drugs and alcohol to shut off the emotional pain. If we respected the value of all creativity and sought ways of allowing it to be expressed, these things would not happen on the scale that they do. Instead we demand that such creativity must 'pay for itself' or contribute to the economy – the Brotherhood's economy. We know the price of everything and the value of nothing. If, however, we could open our hearts to a greater vision of possibility, we would unleash the creative force in everyone and allow it to express its uniqueness. What a world of incredible diversity and inspiration we would then experience. A world guided by the flow of the creative force and not by the profit demands of the Brotherhood bankers.

I talked at the start of the book about thinking the unthinkable. The information here has challenged you to do that. To consider the evidence that reptilians on another dimension of existence have manipulated humanity for thousands of years. To consider that far from being ordinary and powerless, you are extraordinary and all powerful. Both are unthinkable for most people given the current level of conditioning. But they are not un*feel*able. There is such a difference. You think with your intellect and that is so vulnerable to programming through the eyes and ears by the daily diet of lies, suppression and misrepresentation in the media and by all those Brotherhood clones to which it offers a platform. But when we *feel*, we are tapping into our heart centre, our intuition, that connection with the cosmos. How often has what you think and what you instinctively feel been in conflict? What transformed my life more than anything was the moment I decided to follow my intuition whenever it was at odds with my intellect. Every time I have done this, my intuition has turned out to be correct. It can be challenging and painful sometimes because your intuition, which is unbounded by the need to follow 'norms', often stands out against convention. But it will always lead you to do what is best for you and your eternal journey of evolution through experience. For most people when they instinctively feel to do something, the chatterbox mind begins to list all the reasons why they should not do it. "You can't do that, what will the neighbours say, or your family, the people at work, and the guys down the bar?"… "You can't do that, you've got a mortgage, a car, a family, and the life insurance policies to pay for."… "You can't, you can't, you can't." But you can, you can, you CAN. There is nothing wrong with the intellect. It keeps you grounded, stores and processes this-world information, and it has an important part to play. It is when it becomes our controlling force and sole decision-maker that we find ourselves in the prison of the mind. The intellect is there to make physical the guidance and inspiration of the intuition, not to dictate the odds. Don't work for your mind, make your mind work for you.

So it's not what you think about the information in this book that matters, it is what you *feel* about it. Some of the content will challenge your intellect to breaking point, but your intuition will have no such problem. To that level of you, it either feels right, or it doesn't. If it doesn't, walk away. I am not trying to 'convert' anyone to a belief. I could not care less what you think or feel about me and my work. But I care passionately about your right to hear what is currently being denied to you. How you react to it is none of my business, let alone my concern. You are, however, going to see unfolding before your eyes in your every day experience, the Agenda I have described. You will never watch a news bulletin, read a paper, or hear a political or economic announcement, in the same way again. You will also see the weather changes advancing and staggering geological events as the transformation of the Earth's energy fields continues apace. You will feel the gathering vibrations in your heart and your mind. Your rapidly changing perception of life and yourself will open you to unimaginable possibility and potential. Thinking the unthinkable will become a way of life for those who grasp this opportunity to reconnect with all that exists. There are many who will consider this book negative, but they have misunderstood what is happening here. This information is rising to the surface after thousands of years at the same time that more and more people are waking up to who they really are. The same vibrational changes are responsible for both. There is a healing going on and for the healing to start the cause of the disease has to be addressed. The rising frequency is bringing to the surface all that has remained hidden, collectively and individually, to allow the healing to begin. This is why people who have opened up to the changing cosmic rhythm have found that all hell breaks loose in their lives at first. Relationships break up, jobs are lost, family and people they considered friends walk away. There are many different experiences that people have. With me it was massive public ridicule because I never do anything by halves. You can think you have made a monumental mistake at the time, but quite the opposite is happening. We create our own reality and control our own destiny and the way we do that is overwhelmingly through our intent. So often people have said to me that nothing ever happens in their lives and nothing ever seems to work. But when I ask them what they really want to do they reply: "I don't know, really." Well if that is their state of being, their physical experience will reflect "I don't know really", and nothing of significance will happen. If, instead, you focus your intent on a specific goal, what you need to do to achieve it will always come towards you as one vibrational pattern attracts reflections of itself in people, experiences and opportunities. This is where the journey ends for most people. When they are faced with what they need to do to achieve their goal, they suddenly think that perhaps it wasn't such a good idea after all! And that's the question. You say you want something? OK, but how badly? Just a little bit? Fine, then don't waste your time. With every fibre of your being? Well, go for it because the world is yours.

I have seen countless people say they want to transform themselves and their lives and tune into the new vibration. But when the challenges have come, which are necessary to make that happen, they want out immediately and go back to life as before. Yet these challenges set us free. The reason we face personal and emotional mayhem when we start this journey is because of the need to clean out our emotional cesspit of suppressed and unprocessed emotional debris that we have pushed deep into our subconscious because we don't want to deal with it. If we don't clear the emotional gunge of this and other physical lifetimes, we can't reconnect with our multidimensional self. We can't be free of the reptilian manipulation and control from the lower fourth dimension. So when we say we intend to transform, that intent draws to us the people and experiences necessary to bring that suppressed emotion to the surface where we can see it and deal with it. The same is happening collectively as the information presented in this book comes into the light of public attention, so we can see it, address it and heal it. Much of the New Age is in denial of this collective cesspit because it doesn't want to face its own personal cesspit. It would rather sit around a candle and kid itself it is enlightened while, in fact, it is an emotional wreck with a crystal in its hand. The information in this book is part of the healing of Planet Earth and the human consciousness as the veil lifts on all that has remained hidden and denied.

Hey, this is a wonderful time we're living through here. We are tuning to the cosmic dance, the wind of change, the rhythm of reconnection with all that is, has been, or ever will be. You have come to make a difference, for yourself and for the world. You have the opportunity to do that now, now, now. Grasp it and let's end this nonsense. A few can only control billions because the billions let it happen. We don't have to. And we can change it just by being ourselves, allowing other people to be themselves, and enjoying the gift of life. This is not a time to fear and it's not a time to hide. It is a time to sing and a time to dance.

Take your partners, please. Let's go!

BIBLIOGRAPHY

Alder, *The Battle Of The Trees* (Freedom House, Crete, Greece, 1995).

Allen, D. S. and Delair J. B., *When the Earth Nearly Died* (Gateway Books, Wellow, Bath, England, 1995).

Andrews, George C., *Extraterrestrial Friends And Foes* (IllumiNet Press, Lilburn, GA, USA, 1993).

Andrews, George C., *Extraterrestrials Among Us* (Llewellyn Publications, St. Paul, Minnesota 55164-0383, USA, 1993).

Andrews, Richard, and Schellenberger, Paul, *The Tomb Of God* (Little Brown and Company, London, 1996.)

Baigent, Michael, Leigh, Richard, and Lincoln, Henry, *Holy Blood, Holy Grail* (Corgi Books, London, 1982).

Baigent, Michael, and Leigh, Richard, *The Temple And The Lodge* (Arcade Publishing, New York, 1989).

Berlitz, Charles, *Atlantis, The Eighth Continent* (Fawcett Books, New York, 1984).

Bernard, Dr Raymond, *The Hollow Earth, The Greatest Discovery In History* (Carol Paperback, New York, 1991).

Boyd, Andrew, *Blasphemous Rumours* (Fount Paperbacks, an imprint of Harper Collins, London, 1991).

Bramley, William, *Gods Of Eden* (Avon Books, New York).

Brennan, J. H., *Occult Reich* (Futura, London, 1974).

Bromberger, Merry and Serge, *Jean Monnet And The United States Of Europe* (Coward-McCann Publishers, New York, 1969).

Bryant, Alice, and Seebach, Linda, *Healing Shattered Reality: Understand Contactee Trauma* (Wild Flower Press, Tigard, Oregon, 1991).

Bullock, Alan, *Hitler, A Study In Tyranny* (Pelican Books, London, 1960).

Chaitkin, Anton, *Treason In America*, 2nd edition (New Benjamin Franklin House, New York, 1984).

Christopher, Alex, *Pandora's Box Volumes I* and *2* (available from Pandora's Box, 2663 Valleydale Road, Suite 126, Birmingham, Alabama 35224).

Churchward, Albert, *Of Religion* (first published 1924 and now available from Health Research, Mokelumne Hills, CA 95245).

Coleman, John, *Conspirators Hierarchy* (Joseph Holding Company, Nevada, USA, 1995).

Collins, Andrew, *From The Ashes Of Angels, The Forbidden Legacy Of A Fallen Race* (Signet Books, London, 1997).

Collins, Piper, Michael, *Final Judgement, The Missing Link In The JFK Assassination* (The Wolfe Press, Washington DC, 1995.

Collins, Tony, *Open Verdict*, an account of 25 mysterious deaths in the defence industry (Sphere Books, London, 1990).

Cooper, William, *Behold A Pale Horse* (Light Technology Publishing, PO Box 1495, Sedona, Arizona, USA, 1991).

Crowley, Aleister, *Magick In Theory And Practice* (Dover, USA, 1929).

Daniel, John, *Scarlet And The Beast, Volume III, English Freemasonry, Banks, And The Drug Trade* (JKI Publishing, Tyler, TX, USA, 1995).

Davies, Nigel, *Human Sacrifice, In History And Today* (William Morrow and Company, New York).

Deane, Rev. John Bathhurst, *The Worship of the Serpent* (J.G. and F. Rivington, London, 1833).

Doane, T. W., *Bible Myths, And Their Parallels In Other Religions* (Health Research, PO Box 850, Pomeroy, WA, USA 99347, first published 1882).

Drosnin, Michael, *The Bible Code* (Weidenfeld and Nicolson, London, 1997).

Editors of *Executive Intelligence Review*, Dope Inc. (Executive Intelligence Review, Washington DC, 1992).

Findlay, Arthur, *The Curse Of Ignorance, A History Of Mankind* (Headquarters Publishing Company, London, first published 1947), Volumes I and II.

Foster, Thomas, *Britain's Royal Throne* (Acadia Press, Victoria, Australia, 1986).

Fox, Dr Loreda, *The Spiritual And Clinical Dimensions Of Multiple Personality Disorder* (Salida, Colorado).

Gardner, Laurance, *Bloodline Of The Holy Grail* (Element Books, Shaftesbury, Dorset, 1996).

Goldberg, Hirsch M.,*The Jewish Connection* (Stein and Day, New York, 1976).

Hall, Manly P., *America's Assignment With Destiny, The Adepts In The Western Tradition* (Philosophical Research Society, Los Angeles, 1979), part five.

Hall, Manly P., *The Secret Teachings Of All Ages* (The Philosophical Research Society, Los Angeles, California, the Diamond Jubilee Edition, 1988).

Hancox, Joy, *The Byrom Collection* (Jonathan Cape, London, 1992).

Hesemann, Michael, *The Cosmic Connection* (Gateway Books, Wellow, Avon, England, 1993).

Higgins, Geoffrey, *Anacalypsis* (first published 1836, republished in 1972 by Health Research, PO Box 850, Pomeroy, WA, USA 99347), Volume I.

Hitching, Francis, *The World Atlas Of Mysteries* (Pan Books, London, 1981).

Hoagland, Richard, *Monuments On Mars* (North Atlantic Books, California, USA, 1996).

Horn, Dr Arthur David, *Humanity's Extraterrestrial Origins, ET Influences On Humankind's Biological And Cultural Evolution* (A and L Horn, PO Box 1632, Mount Shasta, California, 96067, 1994).

Horowitz, Dr Leonard G., *Emerging Viruses* (Tetrahedron Inc., Rockport, MA, USA, 1996).

Horsley, Sir Peter, *Sounds From Another Room* (Leo Cooper, England, 1997).

Hounam, Peter, and McAdam, Derek, *Who Killed Diana?* (Vision Books, London, 1998).

Howard, Michael, *The Occult Conspiracy* (Destiny Books, Rochester, Vermont, 1989).

Jones, Peter, *The Obedience Of Australia* (XPO-imprint, 26 Burlington Close, London, W9 3LZ, 1995).

Jones, Steve, *In The Blood* (Harper Collins, London, 1966).

Knight and Lomas, Christopher and Robert, *The Hiram Key* (Arrow Books, London, 1997).

King, Francis, *Satan And Swastika* (Mayflower Books, London, 1976).

Keith, Jim, *Casebook On Alternative 3* (IllumiNet Press, Lilburn, USA, 1994).

Keith, Jim, *Secret And Suppressed* (Feral House, PO Box 3466, Portland, Oregon 97208, 1993).

Knight, Stephen, *The Brotherhood* (Granada Books, London, 1985).

Koestler, Arthur, *The Thirteenth Tribe – The Khazar Empire And Its Heritage* (Hutchinson, London, 1976).

Leedom, Tim C., (editor), *The Book Your Church Doesn't Want You To Read* (Kendall/Hunt Publishing, Iowa, USA, 1993. Available from the Truth Seeker Company, PO Box 2872, San Diego, California 92112).

Lilenthal, Alfred M., *What Price Israel?* (Henry Regnery, Chicago, 1953).

Maclellan, Alec, *The Lost World Of Agharti, The Mystery Of Vril Power* (Souvenir Press, 43 Great Russell Street, London, WC1B 3PA, 1982).

Marrs, Jim, *Crossfire: The Plot That Killed Kennedy* (Carrol and Graf Publishers, New York, 1989).

Morton, Andrew, *Diana, Her True Story* (Michael O'Mara Books, London, 1992, republished as *Diana, Her True Story, In Her Own Words*, 1997).

Mullins, Euctace, *The Curse Of Canaan* (Revelation Books, PO Box 11105, Staunton, VA, 1987).

Mullins, Euctace, *The World Order, Our Secret Rulers* (Ezra Pound Institute of Civilisation, Staunton, VA, 24401, USA, 1992).

Nichols, Preston B, and Moon, Peter, *Pyramids Of Montauk* (Sky Books, New York, 1995).

O'Brien, Cathy, and Phillips, Mark, *Trance Formation Of America* (Reality Marketing Inc., Las Vegas, Nevada, USA, 1995).

O'Brien, Christian, with O'Brien, Joy, *The Genius Of The Few – The Story Of Those Who Founded The Garden Of Eden* (Turnstone Press, Wellingborough, England, 1985).

O'Toole, Fintan, *Brand Leader, An investigation Of Tony O'Reilly* (Granta).

Perloff, James, *The Shadows Of Power: The Council On Foreign Relations And The American Decline*.

Picknett, Lynn, and Prince, Clive, *The Templar Revelation* (Bantam Press, London, 1997).

Pohl, Frederick J., *Prince Henry Sinclair. His Expedition To The New World In 1398* (Nimbus Publishing, Halifax, Novia Scotia, originally published 1967).

Quinn, Bob, *Atlantean, Ireland's North African And Maritime Heritage* (Quartet Books, London, 1986).

Ramsey, A. H. M., *The Nameless War* (Omni Publications, London, 1952).

Ravenscroft, Trevor, *The Spear Of Destiny* (Samuel Weiser, Inc., Maine, USA, 1982).

Raymond, Capt. E., *Missing Links Discovered In Assyrian Tablets* (Artisan Sales, Thousand Oaks, California, 1985).

Reagan, Simon, *Who Killed Diana?* (a *Scallywag* publication, Amsterdam, 1998).

Reuchlin, Abelard, *The True Authorship of the New Testament* (The Abelard Reuchlin Foundation, PO Box 5652, Kent, WA, USA, 1979).

Staniland, Wake C., *Serpent Worship And Other Essays* (Banton Press, Largs, 1990).

Schweitzer, Albert, *The Quest For The Historical Jesus* (Macmillan Publishing, New York, 1968).

Shahak, Israel, *Jewish History, Jewish Religion* (Pluto Press, London, 1994).

Sitchin, Zecharia, *The 12th Planet, Stairway To Heaven, The Lost Realms, When Time Began, The Wars Of Gods And Men, Genesis Revisited* (Avon Books, New York).

Sklar, Holly, (editor), *Trilateralism, The Trilateral Commission And The Elite Planning For World Management* (South End Press, Boston, USA, 1980).

Smith, Homer, *Man And His Gods* (Grossetts University Library, New York, 1956).

Smith, Morton, *The Secret Gospel* (Victor Gollancz, London, 1974).

Springmeier, Fritz, and Wheeler, Cisco, *The Illuminati Formula To Create An Undetectable Total Mind Controlled Slave* (Springmeier, SE Clackamas Road, Clackamas, Oregon, 97015, 1996).

Springmeier, Fritz, *The Top 13 Illuminati Bloodlines* (Springmeier, SE Clackamas Road, Clackamas, Oregon, 97015, 1995).

Stitch, Rodney, *Defrauding America* (Diablo Western Press, Alamo, California, 1994).

Sutton, Anthony C., *Wall Street And The Rise Of Hitler* (Heritage Publications, Melbourne, Australia).

Tarpley, Webster Griffin, and Chaitkin, Anton, *George Bush, The Unauthorised Biography* (Executive Intelligence Review, Washington DC 1992).

Taylor, Ian T., *In The Minds Of Men, Darwin And The New World Order* (TFE Publishing, Toronto, Canada, 1984).

Thompson, Hunter S., *Fear And Loathing In Las Vegas* (Vintage Books, New York, 1998, first published in 1971).

Thomson, Arthur Dynott, *On Mankind, Their Origin And Destiny* (Kessinger Publishing, PO Box 160, Kila, MT 59920, USA, first published 1872).

Valerian, Valdamar, *Matrix II* (Arcturus Book Service, USA, 1990).

Van Helsing, Jan, *Secret Societies And Their Power In The 20th Century* (Ewertverlag, Gran Canaria, Spain, 1995).

Vermes, Geza, *The Dead Sea Scrolls In English* (Penguin Books, Harmondsworth, 1990).

Waddell, L. A., *The Phoenician Origin Of Britons, Scots And Anglo Saxons* (The Christian Book Club of America, Hawthorne, California, first published 1924).

Walker, Barbara G., *The Woman's Encyclopaedia Of Myths And Secrets* (Harper Collins, San Francisco, 1983).

Westbrook, Charles L., *The Talisman Of The United States, Signature Of The Invisible Brotherhood* (to locate a copy, contact the *Talisman* newsletter, PO Box 54, Ayden, NC 28513, United States).

Wood, David, and Campbell, Ian, *Geneset* (Bellevue Books, Sunbury on Thames, England, 1994).

Zim, Herbert S., and Baker, Robert H., *Stars, A Golden Guide* (Golden Press, New York, 1985).

INDEX

Please note: *a lot of information was added to this book at the last minute which affected the page numbers, and therefore some of the index references may be slightly out.*

INDEX OF ILLUSTRATIONS

Copyright

As a small publishing operation, created solely to publish material that no-one else will touch, we do not have the people or resources of a major publishing company. In fact, David Icke has compiled all the information and illustrations between and during speaking tours around the world. This, and the urgent need to put this astonishing information before the public, has made it impossible for him to locate the copyright for every picture in the book. To do so would have delayed publication for far too long at a time when, for all our sakes, people need to know what is going on. Not least for the children.

Therefore, if you feel the copyright of any picture belongs to you, please contact us at the addresses or phone numbers listed and we can agree the appropriate fee. Or you may wish, in the light of the content, to contribute the use of your picture to the cause of human freedom. Either way, thanks for your understanding.

Can you help?

It is vital that *The Biggest Secret* is circulated as quickly and as widely as possible. There is a 35% discount for anyone buying ten or more copies in one order directly from Bridge of Love Publications Ltd in the UK.

To order *The Biggest Secret* contact:

UK   **Bridge of Love Publications**
                          PO Box 43
                          Ryde
                          Isle of Wight
                          PO33 2YL
                          England

USA   **Bookworld**
                          1933 Whitfield Park Loop
                          Sarasota
                          Florida 34243
                          USA

Order number   **1-800-444-2524**

Website   **www.davidicke.com**

Can you help?

Can you also help to circulate Bridge of Love books and videos, spread the word and earn an income?

All Bridge of Love publications are available at a 35% discount if you purchase ten or more of any title or combination of titles.

Contact Bridge of Love UK for details:

Bridge of Love Publications
PO Box 43
Ryde
Isle of Wight
PO33 2YL

Other work by David Icke

*Books, videos, and cassettes by David Icke are available from **Bridge of Love Publications**...*

The Freedom Road $59.95   £35.00

The new double video by David Icke. A six hour, profusely illustrated presentation on three video cassettes. He begins in the ancient world and ends with the transformation of Planet Earth in the countdown to 2012. Mysteries galore are unveiled as Icke pulls together his incredible wealth of information across countless subjects and shows how they all seamlessly connect. What *has* happened? What *is* happening? What *will* happen? All are revealed in this eye opening, heart opening, mind opening video package.

...And The Truth Shall Set You Free $21.95   £12.95

Icke exposes an astonishing web of interconnected manipulation which reveals that very few people control the daily direction of our lives. A highly acclaimed book, constantly updated. A classic in its field.

I Am Me, I Am Free $19.95   £10.50

Icke's book of solutions. With humour and powerful insight, he shines a light on the mental and emotional prisons we build for ourselves... prisons which disconnect us from our true and infinite potential to control our own destiny. A getaway car for the human psyche. A censored sticker is available for the faint hearted!

Lifting The Veil $10.00   £6.95

Another new book by David Icke, compiled from interviews with an American journalist. An excellent summary of Icke's work and perfect for those new to these subjects. *This title is available from the TruthSeeker Company in the USA.*

Turning Of The Tide – video $19.95   £6.95

A 2-hour presentation, funny and informative, and the best way to introduce your family and friends to Icke's unique style and information.
(Also available as a double audio cassette)

Speaking Out – video $24.95   £15.00

A 2-hour video interview with David Icke.

David Icke's books published by Gateway: *The Robots' Rebellion, Truth Vibrations,* and *Heal The World*, are also available through Bridge of Love.

USA order number: 1-800-444-2524

Other books available from Bridge of Love...

The Medical Mafia

The superb expose of the medical system by Canadian doctor, Guylaine Lanctot, who also shows how and why 'alternative' methods are far more effective. Highly recommended.

Trance Formation Of America

The staggering story of Cathy O'Brien, the mind controlled slave of the US Government for some 25 years. Read this one sitting down. A stream of the world's most famous political names are revealed as they really are.
Written by Cathy O'Brien and Mark Phillips.

What If Everything You Knew About AIDS Was Wrong?

HIV does NOT cause Aids, as Christine Maggiore's outstanding book confirms. Concisely written and devastating to the Aids scam and the Aids industry.

The Last Waltz

Jacqueline Maria Longstaff encompasses the work of David Icke into her own spiritual vision. Funny and very thought provoking. She describes the book as "the enlightened consciousness embracing the collective shadow".

For a catalogue of all Bridge of Love books, tapes and videos, please send a self addressed stamped envelope to:

Bridge of Love publications
PO Box 43
Ryde
Isle of Wight
PO33 2YL
England
Tel/fax: 01983 566002
email: dicke75150@aol.com

Bridge of Love publications USA
1825 Shiloh Valley Drive,
Wildwood
M.O. 63005
USA
Tel: 314 458 7824
Fax: 314 458 7823
email: bridgelove@aol.com

How to contact us...

For North American inquiries contact:

Bridge of Love Publications USA
1825 Shiloh Valley Drive
Wildwood
M.O. 63005
USA
Tel: **314 458 7824**
Fax: **314 458 7823**
email: **bridgelove@aol.com**

For details of direct ordering contact the David Icke website address below.

The Biggest Secret, ...And The Truth Shall Set You Free and *I Am Me I Am Free* are also available in North America from:

Bookworld
1933 Whitfield Park Loop
Sarasota
Florida 34243
Order phone number: **1-800-444-2524**

Lifting The Veil can be purchased in North America from the Truth Seeker company. To order from Truth Seeker ring: 1-800-321-9054.

David Icke conferences and presentations

If you would like David Icke to speak at your conference or public meeting, contact Royal Adams in the United States on 602 657 6992 or fax: 602 657 6994. For British and European inquires, contact Bridge of Love on 01983 566002.

David Icke on the internet

The Bridge of Love website is: **www.davidicke.com** – details of all David's books, tapes, videos and speaking appearances around the world are listed here.

The e-mail address for Bridge of Love USA is: **bridgelove@aol.com** and in the UK is: **dicke75150@aol.com**

Can you help?

If you have any information you think will help David Icke in his research, please write to (in the UK and the rest of the world outside North America):

Bridge of Love
PO Box 43
Ryde
Isle of Wight
PO33 2YL
England

or

e-mail: **dicke75150@aol.com** *if outside North America* or
e-mail: **bridgelove@aol.com** *if within North America.*

Please source the information wherever you can and it will be held in the strictest confidence.

The Truth Campaign

For a quarterly update on what is really happening in the world read *The Truth Campaign*, the magazine that tells it like it is.

It covers the whole range of subjects from alternative health to the global conspiracy, UFOs, the truth about religion, mind control and much more. The magazine can be sent to you anywhere in the world. Perhaps you could distribute the magazine in your area or country?

For details of how to subscribe please send a stamped, self-addressed envelope to:

Ivan Fraser
The Truth Campaign
49 Trevor Terrace
North Shields
Tyne and Wear
NE30 2DF
England